Standard Oil Company (Indiana)

Oil Pioneer of the Middle West

By PAUL H. GIDDENS

The Birth of the Oil Industry, 1938

The Beginnings of the Petroleum Industry:
Sources and Bibliography, 1941

Pennsylvania Petroleum 1750–1872:
A Documentary History, 1947

Early Days of Oil, 1948

ENTRANCE TO THE GENERAL OFFICE, 910 SOUTH MICHIGAN, CHICAGO, ILLINOIS

STANDARD OIL COMPANY
(INDIANA)

Oil Pioneer of the Middle West

by

PAUL H. GIDDENS

APPLETON-CENTURY-CROFTS, INC.
New York

Preface

THIS IS A HISTORY OF THE STANDARD OIL COMPANY (INDIANA) FROM its beginning to the end of 1951. It is an account of the company's growth, operations, policies, and practices—all phases of its business. It is a story of one of America's great industrial enterprises.

Organized in 1889 by the Standard Oil Trust, Standard of Indiana has played a leading role not only in the development of the petroleum industry but in the industrial and agricultural growth of the Middle West. Favored by being early established in the Middle West, which offered the greatest potential oil market in the world, the company has had a phenomenal growth.

Standard began by building at Whiting, Indiana, the first large oil refinery in the West and one of the largest in the country. At Whiting the company pioneered in using Frasch's copper oxide process for the first time on a large commercial scale to eliminate sulphur from crude oil, provided a market for Ohio-Indiana crude which had been regarded as useless owing to its sulphur content, and helped to lessen the possibility of an oil shortage in this country. For a brief time the company's principal function was to supply kerosene, lubricants, greases, and other petroleum products to various Standard marketing companies.

In 1892 Standard of Indiana commenced to acquire different marketing companies and laid the foundations for a vast retail marketing organization in the Middle West. Through its establishment of direct marketing facilities—main stations, bulk plants, and tank-wagon deliveries—all over the Middle West, kerosene, gasoline, greases, and lubricants were made easily available for consumers. The company's pioneer move in extending tank-wagon deliveries to the farmers of the Upper Mississippi Valley brought petroleum products still closer to the consumers. By making high-quality petroleum products readily available at low cost to every farm and hamlet, Standard led the way in expanding the market for these products. When the automobile came into use, Standard's executives, foreseeing the great need by motorists for gasoline and

v

motor oil, inaugurated a policy of building and operating company-owned service stations everywhere in the region. This pioneer development greatly facilitated the expansion of the automobile market and made gasoline and other petroleum products convenient for motorists.

After the dissolution of the Standard Oil Company (New Jersey) by the Supreme Court in 1911, Standard of Indiana, as well as thirty-two other companies owned by the holding company, became free, separate, and independent. Standard of Indiana was left with three large refineries and an extensive marketing organization but without any crude supply or pipeline system of its own. For several years it continued to be a refining and marketing company. It made no effort to acquire crude oil production or build pipelines. Crude oil for the company's refineries was obtained through purchase arrangements with the Prairie Oil & Gas Company and other producers, and Prairie continued to transport the crude to Standard's refineries.

Owing to the rapid commercial development of the automobile, the establishment of service stations, and the enormous demand for gasoline and other petroleum products, a severe crude oil shortage developed, especially after 1916. Standard of Indiana found it increasingly difficult to purchase large quantities of crude necessary for its refining and marketing operations. Fortunately for Standard—and the country—its executives had foreseen as early as 1909 the possibility of a gasoline shortage and had started its chemists to work on the problem of getting a greater yield of gasoline from crude oil. After extensive research and a large expenditure of money, its chemists developed the first practical process for producing gasoline by cracking the heavy oil into gasoline through the use of high temperature and pressure. Through the Burton process, as the new process came to be known, a barrel of crude oil yielded twice as much gasoline as under the ordinary distillation process. The use of the Burton process on a large commercial scale not only resulted in an increased supply of gasoline but awakened the petroleum industry to the commercial possibilities of bringing about chemical changes in crude oil and created a greater interest in research within the petroleum industry. With the initial advantage it possessed in developing the Burton process, Standard became a leader in research in the petroleum industry. Its research has resulted through the years in improving the quality and yield of all important petroleum

products and developing all kinds of new products for consumers.

In 1917 the company began to purchase proven crude oil properties in order to insure its growth and development. The acquisition of a stock interest in the Midwest Refining Company in
Wyoming in 1920–21, the purchase of a 50 per cent interest, later
a 100 per cent interest, in the Sinclair Pipe Line Company and
Sinclair Crude Oil Purchasing Company, and the acquisition of
the extensive oil properties of Pan American Petroleum & Transport Company in Mexico, Venezuela, and the United States constituted major steps in the development of a crude oil supply and
a pipeline system. Although the company continued to purchase
proven crude-oil producing properties, it began about 1932 initiating through its subsidiary, the Stanolind Oil and Gas Company,
an active program of exploring, wildcatting, and development
rather than emphasizing the purchase of proven producing properties. A long-run objective was the development of a domestic
crude oil production equal to at least 50 per cent of the company's
refinery runs, which the company has achieved.

In the years since 1889, Standard of Indiana has grown and developed into a great integrated oil company, one which engages in
all phases of the oil business—exploring, producing, refining, marketing, and transporting. At the end of 1951, where this narrative
stops, Standard with its subsidiaries was the second largest oil
company in assets and the fourth largest industrial concern in the
United States. It produced 3.9 per cent of the total domestic production of crude oil and natural gas liquids. Standard's chief
producing subsidiary, the Stanolind Oil and Gas Company, one of
the leading crude oil and gas producers of the country, operated
through twelve states stretching from Montana to Mississippi and
produced 3.5 per cent of the nation's total supply of crude oil. The
twelve refineries of Standard and its subsidiaries processed 8 per
cent of the total domestic refinery input. Through the Service Pipe
Line Company (formerly the Sinclair Pipe Line Company and the
Stanolind Pipe Line Company), Standard's pipeline system handles
more traffic than any other pipeline system in the world. Besides
the crude oil pipelines of Service, the parent company owned 1,596
miles of products pipelines. Standard was the largest marketer of
petroleum products in the fifteen North Central states. In addition,
through three subsidiaries—the American Oil Company, Pan-Am
Southern, and the Utah Oil Refining Company—Standard of In-

diana marketed in twenty-six additional states and the District of Columbia and was one of the largest marketers of petroleum products in the United States.

The striking growth of Standard of Indiana was due to a large extent to the expanding economy of the nation and especially the Middle West. In 1889, when Standard of Indiana was organized, the Middle West was a new and growing region. Great areas of land were yet to be settled. The westward movement of population and industry was rapidly increasing. More railroads were to be built. Ten states were to be carved out of the great West. As the Middle West grew to economic maturity after 1889, Standard also grew. In turn, Standard contributed directly and immeasurably to the growth of the region because it was the first large oil company to build large refineries and establish an extensive marketing organization in the region. It was the first to make petroleum products easily available for consumers, large and small, rural and urban. Out of Standard's refineries and through its marketing organizations flowed hundreds of petroleum products which reduced the amount of human toil, helped to revolutionize transportation and farming methods, facilitated the growth of industry, and made life more comfortable and pleasant. It led the way in expanding the use of petroleum products in the Upper Mississippi Valley.

In 1947 the author was invited by the officers of Standard to write a history of the company. In order that the work might be done as objectively and impartially as possible, the company made a research grant to Allegheny College, with which I was then associated, to defray the expenses of this project. Furthermore, the officers agreed that all company records would be opened to the author, that no restrictions would be imposed upon what he might write, and that they would co-operate to the fullest extent. From the beginning of this work to the end, the officers of the company have fulfilled those obligations. Whatever faults or shortcomings this book may have in any respect are the sole responsibility of the author.

It is not possible to list the names of all persons who gave freely and generously of their time in assisting the author in his research. However, as this work comes to a conclusion, he recalls with pleasure the contribution, large and small, each one made. For the courtesies extended and the co-operation given by these people during the course of his investigation, the author is most appreciative.

I am particularly indebted to Edward G. Seubert, William M. Burton, Amos Ball, J. W. Curry, Roy J. Barnett, and John F. Cullen, all of whom are now deceased, and to Robert E. Humphreys, Allan Jackson, Louis L. Stephens, Seth C. Drake, Edward J. Bullock, Herbert G. Naylor, Leon C. Welch, John D. Clark, F. O. Prior, O. E. Bransky, C. F. Hatmaker, Harvey Cochran, F. L. Cochran, F. M. Rogers, Frank V. Martinek, Joseph Nevotti, T. A. Dines, A. E. Johnson, Harold D. Roberts, A. N. Johnson, E. S. Holt, L. J. Wise, M. J. Greenwood, D. J. Smith, James A. Carroll, Jr., J. E. Whitely, E. T. Storey, B. F. Warren, H. E. Cotton, E. J. Sullivan, J. H. Arbuckle, J. M. McCord, J. H. Ross, Mark Raleigh, W. R. Wallace, Frank Gainer, Albert L. Hopkins, H. M. Gage, H. C. Bretschneider, and Thomas M. Debevoise for the time they gave in enlightening me about various aspects of the company's history. L. E. Harmon, Secretary, S. K. Botsford, Assistant Secretary, and M. A. McNulty, Comptroller, have been most helpful in answering a multitude of questions. I am grateful to Thomas J. Mullaney for preparing the charts, Donald A. Gilling for drawing the sketches of the vapor-brush still and the "sweetening" still, and William P. Tucker, Director of the Library and Professor of Political Science, Macalester College, for compiling the index.

I wish to thank Allan Jackson, Robert E. Humphreys, Albert L. Hopkins, and John D. Rockefeller, Jr., for the privilege of using some of their personal papers and records. I also wish to thank the John G. Crerar Library, the Newberry Library, the Chicago Public Library, the University of Chicago Library, and the library of *The Chicago Daily Tribune* for the use of their facilities and resources. The assistance given by the Kansas State Historical Society and the South Dakota State Historical Society is gratefully acknowledged.

For his sympathetic aid at the inception of this project, I want to thank Stanley Pargellis, Librarian, Newberry Library, Chicago.

I desire especially to express my deep appreciation and sincere thanks to Robert E. Wilson, Chairman of the Board of Standard, A. W. Peake, President until May 3, 1955, and Conger Reynolds, Director, Department of Public Relations, for their active personal interest and assistance.

For granting me a leave of absence for two and a half years from

my regular academic duties, I am grateful to the late President
J. R. Schultz, former President Louis T. Benezet, and the Board
of Trustees of Allegheny College.

Finally, I want to acknowledge with profound thanks the excellent work done by Martha-Belle Bowers and Max Rosenberg,
my research assistants for a year and a half. They did a superb job.

PAUL H. GIDDENS

Hamline University
St. Paul, Minnesota

Contents

Illustrations

xiii

Charts

Standard Oil Company (Indiana)

Oil Pioneer of the Middle West

CHAPTER I

The First Large Oil Refinery
in the Middle West

FOR MORE THAN A QUARTER OF A CENTURY AFTER THE COMPLETION
of Drake's famous oil well in 1859 nearly all of the petroleum
produced in the United States came from western Pennsylvania.
During the first five years of the history of the petroleum industry
most of the drilling operations were along Oil Creek between
Titusville and Oil City, a distance of about sixteen miles. In 1865
oilmen discovered that they could get oil in the hilly region away
from Oil Creek, so they moved to Pithole, then to Shamburg,
Pleasantville, and Tidioute. As the excitement and production in
these places declined, the more daring drillers moved down the
Allegheny River below Oil City into Clarion, Armstrong, and
Butler counties. Between 1870 and 1875 the Lower Region, as
this area was called, completely overshadowed all other fields.

Beginning in 1875 energetic "wildcatters" started drilling in
every direction around Bradford, and they were amply rewarded.
By 1881 the Bradford field had been thoroughly defined and production reached its peak—80,838 barrels per day.[1] It was the
greatest oil-producing area in the world. It furnished nearly 83 per
cent of the world's demand for petroleum. With thousands of
producing wells, Pennsylvania reached its zenith in 1882 when
the state produced 30,053,509 barrels.[2] Thereafter, except for one
year, there was a gradual decline in Pennsylvania's annual production, but the state continued to be the leading producer
until 1895.

Owing to the decline in production and a steady increase in the
consumption of petroleum, few were confident of the future of
the petroleum industry. Many predicted that the Oil Region
would be drained and completely exhausted in a comparatively
few years. In an address before the American Institute of Mining

1. *The Derrick's Hand-Book of Petroleum*, II, 162-170.
2. *Mineral Resources of the United States*, 1900, 542.

Engineers in Pittsburgh in February, 1886, Professor J. P. Lesley, State Geologist of Pennsylvania, said: "I take this opportunity to express my opinion in the strongest terms, that the amazing exhibition of oil which has characterized the last twenty, and will probably characterize the next ten or twenty years, is nevertheless, not only geologically but historically, a temporary and vanishing phenomenon—one which young men will live to see come to its natural end." [3] Because of his uneasiness over the situation, John D. Archbold of the Standard Oil Trust sold some of his oil stock at seventy-five to eighty cents on the dollar. [4]

While oil springs and seepages were locally known to exist in Texas, Oklahoma, Kentucky, Kansas, California, and other places in the West and some oil wells had been drilled, the production in these states in 1885 was negligible. No one foresaw the development of a vast source of crude oil in the Mid-Continent area or the Southwest. In fact, many oilmen scoffed at the idea of securing any great quantity of oil west of the Mississippi River. In discussing the matter with one of his associates, John D. Archbold said that he "would undertake to drink all the oil that was ever produced in that section." [5]

Fortunately, a new and adequate supply of crude oil was discovered in the spring of 1885 near the town of Lima, Ohio. Within a few weeks there was the same mad rush to Lima as had taken place so many times in western Pennsylvania. In 1886 the Lima field produced more than 1,000,000 barrels. By 1888 its production exceeded 10,000,000 barrels. In 1891 the Indiana field, just across the Ohio line, was opened, adding more oil to the already large production. Four years later Ohio produced 19,545,233 barrels, which surpassed that of Pennsylvania, and it became the leading oil-producing state. [6] Together the Lima-Indiana fields produced more than 25,000,000 barrels of oil in 1896.

The Lima-Indiana field proved to be a keen disappointment. While its crude was richer in products that ran to benzine and naphtha than any other oil, it was, unlike Pennsylvania crude, "sour." If you got a drop on you, you smelled like a rotten egg. That coming from the north and central part of the Ohio field

3. John F. Carll, *Seventh Report on the Oil and Gas Fields of Western Pennsylvania for 1887-1888*, 24.
4. *Transcript of Record, Defendants' Testimony, United States of America, Petitioner, v. Standard Oil Company of New Jersey Et Al., Defendants*, XVII, 3250.
5. *Ibid.*, XVI, 3251.
6. *Mineral Resources of the United States*, 1900, 542.

contained ½ to 1 per cent sulphur by weight, which was several times the amount found in typical Pennsylvania crude. Several of the early refineries built at Lima experimented with the oil, but they could not make acceptable kerosene. It would not burn in common lamps without smoking and giving off an offensive odor. No matter how well Lima crude was refined, the ordinary refining process and treatment with sulphuric acid and alkalis, used successfully for so many years, would not remove most of the sulphur. Many are the stories about refiners who sent Lima kerosene to market only to have it returned—charges collect. Petroleum exporters refused to handle it. Without any market for "pole cat" oil, as it was called, the price of Lima crude dropped from 40 cents per barrel in 1886 to 23 cents in 1887 and to 15 cents in 1888 and 1889. For the first time in its history the petroleum industry found itself at a standstill. Some refining process had to be found that would eliminate most of the sulphur. Otherwise, Lima crude was useless.

In the face of strenuous opposition from most of his fellow associates, who held up their hands in holy horror, John D. Rockefeller, the head of the Standard Oil Trust, insisted that they should build pipelines and tanks, buy crude, and store large quantities of Lima crude. His associates opposed the buying of Lima oil at any price. After an unusually heated argument, Rockefeller threatened to invest two or three million dollars personally to get the oil.[7]

Taking a chance that some way might be found to refine Lima crude successfully, Rockefeller's associates finally agreed to use the Trust's funds for what was regarded as an exceedingly hazardous investment. In 1885 they organized the Solar Refining Company which began the construction of a small experimental refinery at Lima. At the same time the National Transit Company, one of the companies owned by the Trust, organized the Buckeye Pipe Line to purchase some previously constructed gathering pipelines and build others. The Trust organized the Ohio Oil Company in 1887 to buy and lease producing lands. This was a radical departure from Standard's previous policy. Until this time, it had not engaged in the production of oil except in a small way. Simultaneously with these events, Standard bought enormous quantities of crude oil and put it in storage. Even though there was no

7. Allan Nevins, *John D. Rockefeller*, I, 680; *Transcript of Record, Defendants' Testimony, United States of America, Petitioner, v. Standard Oil Company of New Jersey Et Al., Defendants*, XVII, 3423.

market, Standard purchased all the Lima crude offered by producers. It was their only buyer. By 1888 it held over ten million barrels in storage.

With millions of barrels of crude oil in storage, Standard made a frontal attack upon the problem by first trying to sell fuel oil made from Lima crude. Under the direction of Major Charles W. Owston, general manager of the Fuel Oil Department of the Buckeye Pipe Line, an "Oil Fuel Brigade," composed of a large force of experts, was sent all over the country in the spring of 1887 to introduce "the fuel of the future," convert coal furnaces to oil burners, and instruct people in their use.[8] Through these agents, Standard gave away thousands of barrels of oil as samples, and many furnaces were converted at company expense to burn oil. An enormous amount of time, labor, and money were spent in this activity.

The "Apostles of Oil Fuel" rendered valiant service. Their efforts were especially successful in the West among the prairie dwellers and in industrial centers. In Chicago, despite opposition from insurance companies, oil became tremendously popular as a fuel in homes, hotels, iron and steel works, brick factories, and all sorts of mills. Chicago consumed more oil fuel than any other city in the country. Milwaukee was the next largest consumer. One of the agents reported that in Minneapolis "they grab for oil fuel." The demand far exceeded the supply, and the agents had more difficulty in delivering oil than in finding customers. To overcome the scarcity of tank cars and high freight rates, the Standard Oil Trust began building early in 1888 an eight-inch pipeline from Lima to Chicago.[9] Terminal facilities to receive the oil were located on Lake Michigan at the foot of 100th Street. The station was called Fleming Park. Later, it became a part of Calumet Park. By September, 1889, the pipeline was delivering about 10,000 barrels of fuel oil per day. In addition, 5,000 barrels per day were being delivered to Chicago from Lima by rail.

In the meantime, Standard Oil officials made desperate efforts to find a method by which Lima crude could be successfully refined. Until this time professionally trained chemists had not played any part in the development of the petroleum industry

8. *Bradford Era,* August 24, 1887, November 5, 22, 1887, January 21, 1888, May 14, 1888, January 26, 1891; *Trusts,* House Report No. 3112, 50th Cong., 1st Sess., 305-306; *The Chicago Tribune,* September 23, 1889.

9. *Trusts,* House Report No. 3112, 50th Cong., 1st Sess., 283-284, 305-306.

because oilmen had little confidence in them. However, Standard sent samples of Lima crude to Professor Edward W. Morley, a chemistry professor at Western Reserve University, to see if he could extract the sulphur and make a satisfactory illuminant. He suggested heating the oil under pressure, but that proved impractical and nothing came from his examination.

Despite the negative results, Standard officials still had an open mind about chemists. They turned to Herman Frasch, who had gained some knowledge of chemistry as a pharmacist in Germany.[10] After his arrival in America, Frasch had charge of the laboratory at the Philadelphia College of Pharmacy. Becoming more interested in industrial chemistry than pharmacy, he set up his own laboratory in 1874, and began making investigations which resulted in some of the most important achievements in industrial chemistry. By 1876 he had developed a process for refining paraffin wax, which the Standard Oil Company of Ohio purchased. The company was so well pleased with his first invention that it induced him to move to Cleveland and make petroleum his specialty.

Frasch was an exceedingly able man, but his vigorous and aggressive, rip and roar manner made him a most disagreeable person to work with. However, he devoted himself diligently to a study of petroleum and made many improvements in the refining process. Between 1876 and 1887 Frasch obtained five patents relating to oil refining and one for an improved lamp.

Following the discovery of petroleum in 1868 near Petrolia, Ontario, the Canadian government, refiners, and producers made every effort to discover a method by which the objectionable sulphur could be removed from Canadian crude, but practically nothing was accomplished. Challenged by the thought that he might find a satisfactory refining process for Canadian crude, Frasch, upon the expiration of his contract with Standard in 1885, moved to Canada. There he started a small refinery and went into the oil business for himself. Within a short time he discovered a process for eliminating sulphur from "skunk bearing oils," and on February 21, 1887, he applied for a patent. The essence of his process was to distill crude oil in the presence of copper oxide,

10. The significant achievements of Frasch, as related by C. F. Chandler in his presentation of the Perkin Medal to Frasch in 1912, and Frasch's address of acceptance are to be found in *The Journal of Industrial and Engineering Chemistry*, IV, No. 2 (February, 1912), 132-136.

which reacted with the sulphur, formed sulphide of copper, and left the oil odorless and sweet.

Once Frasch had discovered the copper-oxide process, he returned to Cleveland and talked with Frank Rockefeller about using the process on Lima crude. There was doubt and hesitancy. "Vell," declared the "wild Dutchman," as Frasch was called, "I can demonstrate it, by God." After a thorough investigation, Standard in May, 1888, bought Frasch's plant at London, Ontario, and his patents, employed him on a salary basis, brought him back to Cleveland, and set him to work at the Kinsman Street refinery to perfect his process and make possible its use on a large commercial scale.

To assist Frasch, Standard employed William M. Burton, a young twenty-four-year-old Ph.D. in chemistry just out of Johns Hopkins University. Burton had always lived in Cleveland. The Burton home was located near John D. Rockefeller's in Forest Hills. Burton's father was a physician. His mother had been a schoolteacher who had at one time taught Laura Rockefeller. Young Burton had attended Western Reserve University and studied chemistry under Professor Morley. Fascinated by his study of Ira Remsen's textbook on organic chemistry, he decided to go to Johns Hopkins University for graduate study under Remsen and become a teacher. No other university had such an eminent chemist or so fine a chemistry department.

In 1887, while at home on a visit, Burton became interested in petroleum because his uncle, a Cleveland refiner, was interested in the Lima field and, like others, wanted to eliminate the sulphur. Upon Burton's return to Hopkins, his uncle sent him five gallons of Lima crude with which to experiment, much to the disgust of the other graduate students in the laboratory, who called it "skunk juice." [11] Remsen was not particularly interested in petroleum but provided Burton with laboratory facilities to conduct his experimentation. Many experiments and tests were made, and finally Burton found that copper oxide would eliminate the sulphur from Lima crude. He applied for a patent on the process but soon learned that Frasch had already been granted one.[12]

During the winter of 1888–89, while Burton was in Cleveland on vacation, he was undecided as to what he would do when he

11. *Transcript of Record, Defendants' Testimony, United States of America, Petitioner, v. Standard Oil Company of New Jersey Et Al., Defendants,* XVI, 2632.
12. Interview with William M. Burton, August 2, 1948.

finished his graduate work in the spring. Acting upon his father's suggestion, he secured an introduction to Frank Rockefeller.[13] "What do you want to do?" Rockefeller asked. "I want to do something with chemistry in petroleum," replied Burton. "Report tomorrow morning!" said Rockefeller. Burton explained that he could not do that because he wanted to finish his graduate work. "Come back when you get your degree," Rockefeller told him, "and I'll hold a job for you." To have a chemist go into industrial work was contrary to tradition at Hopkins, and Remsen was not very enthusiastic over Burton's prospective job. Should Burton go into industrial work, however, Remsen felt that his thorough training in a pure science was the best foundation.

Upon securing his doctorate, Burton returned to Cleveland in June, 1889, and started to work for the Standard Oil Company of Ohio. He was one of the first professionally trained chemists to enter the petroleum industry. After working on the problem of leaky kerosene cans for a few weeks, Burton was transferred to the Kinsman Street refinery, where he was associated with Frasch and Clarence I. Robinson, the latter a chemist from Cornell University.[14] Within a short time, Robinson was assigned to the Solar refinery at Lima.

When Burton started to work, Frasch had already filed nine additional applications for patents relating to the copper-oxide process, and he was experimenting with a cheesebox still. A vapor-brush still was in the process of being built. During the next few months Frasch and Burton experimented with every conceivable idea relative to eliminating the offensive-smelling sulphur from Lima crude. After experimenting with a great many different methods, they always came back to the inevitable conclusion that the copper-oxide process was the only one that would make a satisfactory illuminant from Lima oil. To overcome the difficulty of converting the sulphide back to the oxide so it could be reused, they found that the McDougal roasting furnace, on which the patent had expired, could be satisfactorily employed. This made Frasch's process an inexpensive method for recovering copper oxide. To remove copper sulphide from the oil after the distillation had been

13. *Ibid.*

14. For an account of Burton's work with Frasch see *Transcript of Record, Defendants' Testimony, United States of America, Petitioner, v. Standard Oil Company of New Jersey Et Al., Defendants,* XVI, 2632-2635; William M. Burton, "Dr. Burton Reminisces About Early Days," *Stanolind Record,* VIII, No. 6 (April, 1927), 21; William M. Burton to Giddens, November 7, 25, 1949.

completed, they devised a filter press. By the fall of 1889 Frasch had filed an application for a patent on a roasting oven to recover copper oxide and one on a vapor-brush still in which to use it.

Although Frasch's process was not fully perfected and Standard's manufacturing officials were not sure that it would work successfully on a large commercial scale, they decided to use the process in the Solar refinery at Lima.[15] They also decided to build one of the largest refineries in the country near Chicago, install the Frasch process, and use Lima crude as the source of supply. This decision, according to John D. Archbold, was based upon the hope "that we would be able to refine it, and failing to refine it and failing to be able to make illuminating oil, we expected to take off the light portions from the crude and market the products in a divided way, as fuel and naphtha." [16] If the results proved successful, Standard had patents, through assignment by Frasch, which would give it a tremendous advantage over all competitors and provide millions of dollars in profit from refining Lima crude oil.

The decision to build a new refinery in the Chicago area was due to the rapid growth of the West and the vast potential market for kerosene and lubricants which it offered. Between 1880 and 1890 the population of the North Central states had increased 28 per cent and that of the Western states 71 per cent. They were the fastest-growing areas in the country.[17] The population of Chicago had increased 119 per cent, Des Moines 123 per cent, Kansas City 138 per cent, St. Paul 221 per cent, Minneapolis 251 per cent, Omaha 360 per cent, Sioux City 413 per cent, and Duluth 851 per cent. Out of 161 cities in the United States in 1890 with a population of 25,000 or over, thirty-nine were located in the North Central states.[18]

To tap this rich agricultural and industrial market, the Standard Oil Company of Ohio had started to develop its own retail distributing system in the West through the purchase of various independent marketing firms and the organization of new ones. In

15. *Transcript of Record, Defendants' Testimony, United States of America, Petitioner, v. Standard Oil Company of New Jersey Et Al., Defendants,* XVI, 2632-2636, 2641, 2654, XVII, 3425.
16. *Ibid.,* XVII, 3425.
17. In the North Central states between 1880 and 1890 the population of Indiana increased 10.8 per cent, Ohio 14.8, Iowa 17.7, Missouri 23.6, Illinois 24.3, Michigan 27.9, Wisconsin 28.2, Kansas 43.3, Minnesota, 66.7, Nebraska, 134.1 and the Dakotas 278.4. *Twelfth Census of the United States,* I, Part I, xxiv.
18. *Ibid.,* lxix-lxx.

1878 Alexander McDonald & Company of Cincinnati and Standard of Ohio organized the Consolidated Tank Line Company. The latter acquired the business of Alexander McDonald & Company and extended its retail trade through southern Ohio, Indiana, Illinois, and to various states beyond the Mississippi River. In the same year Standard of Ohio purchased an interest in the Waters-Pierce Oil Company of St. Louis and rapidly expanded its marketing activities in the Southwest. In addition, Standard of Ohio established its own marketing stations in northern Ohio, Indiana, Illinois, Wisconsin, Michigan, the Rocky Mountain states, and California.

After the organization of the Standard Oil Trust in 1879, which was formed to clarify the legal status of various companies under the control of the Standard Oil Company of Ohio, special attention was given to the expansion of direct marketing activities in the West. In 1883 the Trust purchased the business of P. C. Hanford, one of the largest independent oil dealers in Chicago, who marketed through northern Illinois and Wisconsin. The P. C. Hanford Oil Company was then organized, with the Trust holding 2,550 shares and Hanford 2,450, to take over the property and operate the business. It also leased the bulk plants of the Standard of Ohio in Englewood, Chicago, Milwaukee, and Rock Springs, Wisconsin. A year later the Continental Oil Company was formed. To it was transferred the distributing stations of the Standard of Ohio in Colorado, Montana, Utah, Wyoming, and New Mexico. In 1885 the Trust organized the Standard Oil Company of Iowa, which became its marketing organization on the Pacific Coast.[19]

Organized in 1886, the Standard Oil Company of Kentucky acquired the marketing properties of Chess, Carley & Company of Louisville, Kentucky. This firm had a large oil trade in the South and Southwest. In the same year the Standard Oil Company of Minnesota was formed to absorb the marketing facilities of Bartles & Richardson in Minnesota, Wisconsin, and the Dakotas. Between 1887 and 1890 the Trust purchased the Globe Oil Company and the Chester Oil Company in Minnesota, the West Michigan Oil Company, and the Des Moines Oil Tank Line, all oil marketing organizations. In the spring of 1890 the Trust bought the minority stock interest of the P. C. Hanford Oil Company and transferred the property to a new company, the Standard Oil Company of Illinois. As the marketing organization developed, each Standard

19. Until the organization of the Standard Oil Company of California in 1906.

company was assigned a definite geographical area in which to operate exclusively, and that company was held responsible for sales in its territory.

With the rapid growth of Standard's western trade, all of its kerosene and lubricants had to be shipped either from the Cleveland refinery or those farther east. In order to save on freight charges, keep prices down, and get closer to consumers, there was a need for a refinery in the West. Chicago, with railroad trunk lines fanning out to the South, the Southwest, West, and the Far West and cheap water transportation available on the Great Lakes, seemed to be the logical site. It had become the greatest distributing center in the country next to New York City. Moreover, with a pipeline already laid from Lima, Chicago afforded the greatest market for fuel oil in case good illuminating oil could not be manufactured from Lima crude.

Standard originally planned to build the refinery on its seventy-five-acre tract in Fleming Park in South Chicago, which was the terminal of the pipeline from Lima and where it had tanks, loading racks, and from which it distributed fuel oil.[20] Opposition by the local residents to locating a refinery in the area on account of the odor from Lima crude and the fire hazard, the lack of sufficient land in Fleming Park and the poor prospect of securing more, and a desire to get away from high taxes in Chicago, where there was a tendency to soak big corporations, led Standard officials to look for a different site. After a thorough investigation of various locations, the officials finally decided to locate the new refinery in a desolate spot on the sand dunes along the southern shore of Lake Michigan about two miles east of the Illinois-Indiana line and seventeen miles from the center of Chicago at a place called Whiting, Indiana.

Surrounded by marshy lands, sand dunes, and wilderness, Whiting was a most uninviting spot. However, the site was wisely chosen, for here the refinery would be out of the way, and it would not annoy or endanger anyone, yet it was so near to Chicago as to be practically a part of the city. Here there was plenty of cheap land and an inexhaustible supply of water so necessary in refining. Three railroad trunk lines—the Lake Shore & Michigan Southern, the Baltimore & Ohio, and the Pittsburgh, Ft. Wayne & Chicago— and one belt line, the Chicago & Calumet Terminal Railroad,

20. Interview with William M. Burton, August 2, 1948.

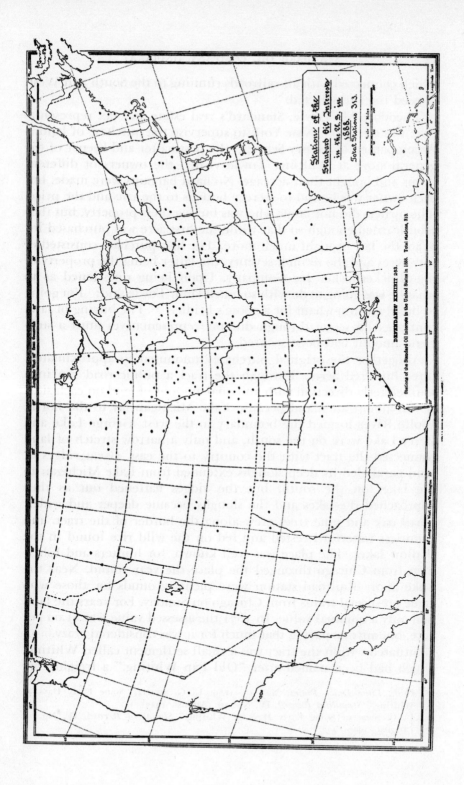

Stations of the Standard Oil Interests in the U.S. in 1888. Total Stations 313.

Scale of Miles

DEFENDANTS EXHIBIT 263.

Stations of the Standard Oil Interests in the United States in 1888. Total stations, 313.

which connected with all railroads running to the South and West, crossed the site selected.

Theodore M. Towle, Standard's real estate and tax representative, was sent from New York to supervise the purchase of land.[21] Accompanied by Henry Schrage, the postmaster and keeper of the general store at Whiting, Towle visited the owners of different farms and bought their acreage. No hard bargains were made, but each owner was bound to secrecy both as to the sale and the price. The owners did not know who was buying their property, but they soon learned enough so that while the first acre was purchased for $150, the last brought much more. The first purchase consisted of fifty acres and the second, seventy, the latter being the property of the Knickerbocker Ice Company. Upon being questioned as to what he was going to do with so much land, Towle said: "I'm going to build a whim-wham for a goose's bridle." [22] The buying of land continued in secret through dummy representatives until a sufficient amount had been secured.

Altogether the original purchases amounted to approximately three hundred acres. Through the tract a public road ran in a southeasterly direction with an equal amount of land on each side. It was almost an island because Lake Michigan lay to the north, Wolfe River formed the boundary to the west, George Lake and Berry Lake were on the south, and only a narrow stretch of land connected the tract with the country to the east. Great ridges of sand paralleled by deep sloughs extended from Lake Michigan to the lakes on the south, but the ridges flattened out as they approached the lakes and the sloughs became deeper and wider. Small oak and pine trees grew along the border of the tract, and countless waterfowl rested and fed on the wild rice found in the shallow lakes. The place was well known, for hunters and fishermen from Chicago thronged the place the year round. Near the Lake Shore Railroad station were picnic grounds for those who came on special trains from Chicago on Sunday. For years the land had only a nominal value. In 1871 the assessed value was $1.00 per acre, but anyone paying that much for it was considered crazy.

Situated within the tract was a small settlement called Whiting, which had been named after "Old Pap Whiting," a freight con-

21. *Ibid.*; *Lima Daily Times*, May 17, 1889; U. G. Swartz, "Some Early Days at Whiting," *Stanolind Record*, IV, No. 10 (August, 1923), 14.

22. U. G. Swartz, "Some Early Days at Whiting," *Stanolind Record*, IV, No. 10 (August, 1923), 14.

W. H. TILFORD. PRESIDENT 1889–1890, 1892–1904

JAMES A. MOFFETT, PRESIDENT 1890–1892, 1904–1911

PURCHASING DEPARTMENT, 5 WABASH AVENUE, CHICAGO, IN 1904

From left to right, an office boy, a salesman, Silas Wright, Purchasing Agent, Fred Bosworth, A. E. MacMeekin, and James Chadwick

FARMHOUSE USED AS AN OFFICE AND BURTON'S LABORATORY, WHITING REFINERY, 1890

The "experimental house" is in the rear

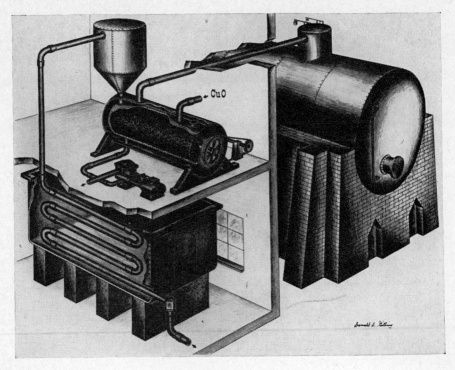

A VAPOR-BRUSH STILL

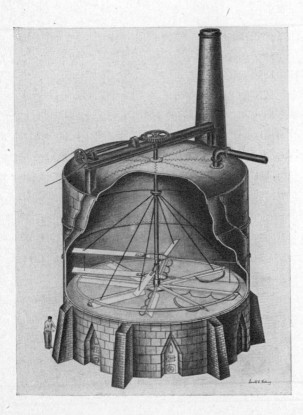

A "SWEETENING" STILL

ductor on the Lake Shore Railroad. Whiting was a colorful character who was known to every crew on the line. One day "Old Pap Whiting" had a heavy train which was trying to make a siding in order to clear the main line for a fast passenger train. On a bad bit of track his train was wrecked and left the track clear as if he had pulled his train onto a siding. From that day forward the spot was always known to railroad men as "Pap Whiting's Siding." [23] In 1871 a post office was established for the settlement. The "s" in Whiting's was dropped, and the place officially became known as Whiting.

The settlement was composed of about fifty families, mostly Germans, who hunted, trapped, fished, supplied boats, meals, and lodging to fishermen and hunters, carried on a little farming, and worked as section men on the railroad. Chicago provided a market for their fish, game, and berries. They lived a peaceful and contented life. With only trails through the soft sand, long stretches of lakes and sloughs on the south, and no bridges, it was difficult for the settlers at Whiting to keep in touch with the outside world. In 1889 the village had a school, three railroad stations, and Henry Schrage's general store in which was located the post office. [24]

The construction of the new refinery at Whiting was entrusted to three experienced Standard refinery men—W. M. Irish of Olean, New York, James A. Moffett, manager of the Pratt Works in Brooklyn, and W. P. Cowan, superintendent of the Cleveland plant. In February, 1889, they called on William Curtis, master mechanic at the Cleveland refinery, showed him some sketches of the land at Whiting and penciled drawings of the proposed plant, and arranged with him to make the blueprints. [25] To maintain the utmost secrecy, Curtis made the drawings in his own home. Plans for the first units of construction called for building eighty crude stills, each with a capacity of six hundred barrels, steam stills, agitators, pump houses, and other equipment necessary for a first-class refinery. It was estimated that the new plant would cost $5,000,000. [26]

As soon as the plans were completed, Cowan, who was forty-three

23. On the origin of Whiting's name see the *Whiting Democrat*, August 2, 1894; *Whiting Sun*, December 3, 1898; *The Chicago Tribune*, March 4, 1900.
24. U. G. Swartz, "Some Early Days of Whiting Refinery," *Stanolind Record*, IV, No. 9 (July, 1923), 11-14; *Whiting Sun*, October 26, 1907.
25. U. G. Swartz, "Some Early Days at Whiting, Part Two," *Stanolind Record*, IV, No. 10 (August, 1923), 13.
26. *The Chicago Tribune*, September 22, 1889.

years old, was placed in charge of construction and sent to Whiting. Cowan had been with the Standard of Ohio since 1875, rising from the position of paymaster to superintendent of the Cleveland works. Ambrose M. McGregor, while superintendent of Standard's plants in Cleveland, had boarded with Cowan's widowed mother. He had taken an interest in Cowan, and strong ties of friendship developed between the two men. McGregor later made "Billy" Cowan his assistant at Cleveland. When it came time to build the refinery at Whiting, McGregor requested that Cowan be placed in charge because he was the best available construction man. Although slow, phlegmatic, and dilatory, Cowan was sure and correct in his decisions and commanded the respect of everyone. Honest and dependable, this quiet, genial, and corpulent man assumed his new assignment and calmly directed the work in the way he wished it to go.

Curtis accompanied Cowan to Chicago and established a purchasing department at 52 Pacific Avenue in the Commerce Building opposite the Board of Trade.[27] Opened late in April, 1889, the office was placed in charge of Alexander Marshall. Curtis then became master mechanic at Whiting. Without any purchasing organization and with the sources of supply in Chicago to a large extent unfamiliar to him, Marshall was confronted with immense problems because of the urgent demand for steel, machinery, and building materials of all kinds. He quickly proceeded to create an organization. Among those employed were W. S. Newell and Silas Wright. Newell served as a general utility man. If a long list of miscellaneous hardware was needed, Newell scurried about, picking it up here and there, and saw that it got on the train to Whiting. If special valves or fittings were required, he jumped into a cab, went over to the Crane Company and got them. Wright, the telegraph operator, transmitted messages over a private line between the purchasing office and Whiting; he also served as bookkeeper and stenographer.

Experienced construction men from other Standard refineries soon began to arrive to supervise the work of the brick masons, carpenters, painters, blacksmiths, pipe fitters, tinners, common laborers, and others. They were called the "satchel and trunk men" by the local inhabitants. To house and feed these men the

27. For a history of the Purchasing Department see A. E. MacMeekin, "Spending Fifty Millions a Year in All Parts of the World," *Stanolind Record*, X, No. 3 (January, 1929), 3-5.

company built a "bunkhouse," a rough frame building. One part served as an office with a drafting room above, another served as the dining hall with bedrooms on the second floor, and a third part served as the commissary. For many months Cowan occupied one of the bedrooms. Nightly he held conferences with his foremen, going over the day's work and laying out the next day's schedule. Within a short time, this small but well-organized force had orders for materials and equipment flowing to the Purchasing Department.

Construction work with company forces began on May 5, 1889, when laborers under the direction of W. A. Barstow were put to work clearing brush and trees. Others erected temporary shops on the north side of the Pennsylvania Railroad tracks. A large number of teams were hired from the Knickerbocker Ice Company for excavating and hauling. In addition, the company bought many teams. The great ridges of sand were scraped down into the low places, and north of the Pennsylvania Railroad tracks a level field was made, but it was several years before the area was completely filled in. Excavating for buildings and leveling was difficult because the soft sand was almost fluid. Wagons had to have great wide steel tires, and trails about the plant were covered with straw or hay to keep the wheels out of deep ruts in the sand. Once the grading and drainage was done and certain areas were available, carloads of lumber, brick, cement, iron and steel pipes, and gravel began to arrive, and the building of storage tanks, an acid works, a steam powerhouse, crude stills, steam stills, tar stills, condensers, agitators, pump houses, a paraffin works, a waterworks system, and a sewage system soon got under way.

Cowan, as superintendent, had to be everywhere in order to supervise the construction work. Being short and fat and finding the sand difficult to walk in, he rode a beautiful bay Indian pony. One of the memorable sights recounted by old-timers is of seeing "Bessie" with "Billy" Cowan on her back, galloping here and there about the plant. Cowan made a great pet of "Bessie," and she would come anywhere at his call.

With the beginning of construction, the rate of pay for different classes of workers had to be established.[28] There were no previously established rates to serve as a standard, for there were no plants of even moderate size in the vicinity except one in Hammond and

28. U. G. Swartz, "Some Early Days of Whiting, Part Four," *Stanolind Record*, IV, No. 12 (October, 1923), 13.

another in East Chicago. The company, therefore, followed a policy of paying as high a wage as those in the vicinity and a little more. The current rate for common laborers was 12½ cents per hour but Standard paid 15. Pipe fitters got 22½, bricklayers 45, and others in proportion. Clerks on the open payroll received 15 to 20 cents an hour. All worked ten hours per day.

Within a short time the place swarmed with workmen. They came by the hundreds from every direction as the demand for construction workers increased. The coming of Standard to Whiting was like bringing in an army. The majority of the men were native Americans and Irish transferred from other Standard refineries and especially from Cleveland. A large force of boilermakers was brought from Buffalo. They built the tanks and agitators north of the tracks which soon became known as the "Buffalo Side." The south side was known as the "Cleveland Side." Cowan heartily disliked making these distinctions and frowned upon the practice, but it was attractive to the men. One might have expected to find many tough and bad characters among the construction workers, but Cowan's policy was to get rid of them just as soon as they appeared. Preference was given to married men of orderly habits.

Every morning those looking for work thronged the main gate. Foremen would take their pick. Hundreds were turned away, but they returned morning after morning, hoping to succeed in landing a job. Common laborers formed the majority of the force. They were largely foreigners of non-English-speaking races. Immigrants were employed because there were very few laborers in the locality, and refinery officials were forced to use those who appeared at the main gate. In addition to being available, these laborers could be employed without the company incurring any heavy transportation cost. Each morning the Lake Shore & Michigan Southern ran a special train, called the "Hobo," of ten or twelve cars carrying those who lived in Chicago to Whiting. In front of "Matt's Place," a favorite saloon, the cars ground to a stop and the workmen poured forth into the refinery. In the evening the "Hobo" returned them to Chicago.

Saloons, boardinghouses, and dwellings sprang up rapidly at both the east and west entrances to the plant.[29] At the west entrance, most of the saloons were along Front Street, but within a short time 119th Street was dotted with buildings, and it became

29. U. G. Swartz, "Some Early Days at Whiting," *Stanolind Record*, IV, No. 10 (August, 1923), 14, 16.

the main business center of Whiting. It was here that the first retail stores opened their doors. On the corner of 119th and Front Streets was located the general store, where Henry Schrage not only distributed the mail but sold groceries, shoes, shirts, and other necessities.

Along the road running through the tract and on land not included in the original purchase a little town—Oklahoma—began to develop. Dance halls, gin mills, and gambling joints made it a rough place.

The growing demand for houses led the company to lay out a town site, "The Village," as it was called, and build houses for supervisory employees. As fast as they were completed, they were assigned to department heads, foremen, stillmen, and others with families who required homes on the spot. Rentals were based on a small per cent of the cost. In order to make Whiting a decent and tolerable place in which to live, agreements were made with adjoining property owners that no saloons would be built near the houses, and for many years this was the most desirable part of town. Even though not a restricted area, the south side of Whiting rapidly developed. Those unable to get a company house either rented or built homes here. If "tough joints" appeared, they were quickly suppressed.

Thus far all of the planning for the building of the Whiting refinery and the beginning of the construction work had been under the supervision of the Standard Oil Trust. This novel form of industrial organization had been created in 1879 by the Standard Oil Company of Ohio for the purpose of clarifying the ownership of various companies and properties it had acquired. According to the trust agreement of that year, the stock and other interests of the different subsidiary companies were transferred to three Trustees—men in Rockefeller's Cleveland office. They were to administer these interests for the benefit of the stockholders of the Standard of Ohio. To further unify and centralize the management of these companies, a new trust agreement was made in 1882 whereby the stockholders of Standard of Ohio and the three Trustees agreed to set up a Board of Directors for the Standard Oil Trust, nine men in all, and place in their hands all of the properties owned or controlled by the Standard of Ohio, including its own stock. Every stockholder was to receive for each share in Standard of Ohio twenty trust certificates representing his share in the whole. Profits from the different companies were to be sent so the Trustees and trust certificate holders would receive dividends at such times and in such amounts as the Trustees decided. Legally, the Standard Oil Trust did not exist. It had no name and no charter. Actually, however, it was one great company which the Trustees managed.

On June 18, 1889, the Trustees proceeded to organize and incorporate a Standard Oil Company in the State of Indiana and place the construction of the Whiting refinery and its operations under the new company's jurisdiction.[30] The object of the corporation, as stated in the Certificate of Incorporation, was to "manufacture products of Crude Petroleum, to transport and sell the same, to manufacture barrels and packages for containing said products, to erect the necessary buildings and manufacture the necessary machinery and to do all business found to be necessary or convenient in carrying on the business specified." The company was organized for a term of fifty years with a capital stock of $500,000 furnished by the Trust. Five Directors—W. P. Cowan, Frank Q. Barstow, Ambrose M. McGregor, George H. Vilas, and W. H. Tilford—were named to manage the company. Each Director held one share of stock and the Trust 4,995.

On August 29, 1889, at a brief meeting of the Directors held at 26 Broadway, New York City, Tilford was chosen President, Cowan Vice-President, and Vilas Secretary-Treasurer.[31] The President's salary was fixed at $7,000 per year and the Vice-President's at $7,500. Tilford was the nominal head, who resided in New York. He had entered the oil business about 1869 and was originally associated with the firm of Bostwick and Tilford.[32] In 1878 he joined Standard, became one of the Trustees in 1887, and in 1889 served as a Director of the Standard Oil Company of Kentucky and Vice-President of the Standard Oil Company of Iowa. Cowan was actually in charge of the affairs of Standard of Indiana in Chicago and Whiting. He was authorized to sign checks on the company's account, endorse checks and drafts for the company's credit, and sign drafts on the company's customers for the collection of accounts.

30. Minutes of the Board of Directors' and Stockholders' Meetings, 1889–1912, 1-4; *Transcript of Record, Defendants' Testimony, United States of America, Petitioner, v. Standard Oil Company of New Jersey Et Al., Defendants*, XVII, 3281, 3475, 3479.
31. Minutes of the Board of Directors' and Stockholders' Meetings, 1889–1912, 5.
32. *Transcript of Record, Petitioner's Testimony, United States of America, Petitioner, v. Standard Oil Company of New Jersey Et Al., Defendants*, I, 99-184.

From the inception of the idea that a refinery should be built at Whiting, Standard's policy of secrecy prevailed. Even after Cowan had arrived at Whiting and construction was under way, everything was done in his name. Incoming shipments arrived in his name; pay checks were signed as if paid by him personally; and all other matters were similarly handled. It was not until about October that the use of his name was discontinued and Standard's was substituted. Despite the secrecy, reports began to appear in the Chicago papers in May to the effect that Standard would build a refinery in Chicago. Within six days after construction had started at Whiting, a dispatch from Cleveland appeared in *The Chicago Tribune* saying that the largest refinery in the world would be built at Whiting.[33]

One might suppose that such a great enterprise was too conspicuous to be kept from public attention, but to Standard all things seemed possible. When an inquiring reporter visited the purchasing office on Pacific Avenue in September he did not find any ostentatious display of the name of the corporation on the door. The door carried no lettering of any kind. The reporter talked with Alexander Marshall and found him to be a typical servant of the Standard Oil Company. "The number of things which he does not know and regarding which he has not formed the slightest opinion," declared the reporter, "would satisfy ten lawyer Forrests. The one lone fact in the situation which Mr. Marshall had grasped was that he was in the office of the Standard Oil Company of Indiana. As to what was being done at Whiting he was entirely ignorant. They might be erecting a $5,000,000 oil refinery or they might be putting up a pork packing establishment. He didn't think it was a pork packing establishment, but he wasn't sure. He never heard of anything of the intentions of the company. In fact, his understanding of what the company was doing was extremely foggy. He could not even offer an opinion whether or not the Standard Oil Company was the same as the popularly known Standard Oil Trust. He didn't know whether Lima oil could be refined. He had no definite opinion of the Clan-na-Gaels, and he had forgotten where he was on the night of May 4." [34]

The same reporter interviewed Cowan with no better results. "After a period of careful reflection," the reporter wrote, "Cowan frankly admitted yesterday that an oil refinery was being built.

33. *The Chicago Tribune*, May 11, 12, 1889.
34. *Ibid.*, September 22, 1889.

To a series of questions about how extensive the refinery would be, whether or not they would refine Lima or Pennsylvania oil, and others Cowan did not know." "Then," inquired the reporter, "you are putting several million dollars into a refinery plant here and you haven't decided yet what you are going to refine nor where you are going to get it from?" "Well, yes," replied Cowan, "that's about it." To assist in maintaining secrecy, a close hemlock fence, eight feet high, was built around the plant. Watchmen guarded all gates and no one was allowed to enter without a pass; and few passes were issued. Newspaper men were barred but every now and then one slipped by the guards only to be ingloriously bounced out by company detectives who roamed about the plant.[35]

Before fall, great changes had been made in the surroundings. The grounds at the refinery were covered with huge piles of lumber, pipe, brick, gravel, boiler iron, and all sorts of construction materials. Two sidetracks had been laid into the plant by the Lake Shore Railroad on the "Buffalo Side" and one on the "Cleveland Side" by the Chicago & Calumet Terminal Railroad. Loaded cars were run onto these sidetracks and then Standard's own locomotives moved them to unloading points. Eight hundred men were hammering rivets through great plates of boiler iron to make huge tanks fifty feet across and many feet high. Fifty tanks were either completed or well under way; they extended for half a mile down the tracks east from the station. "The din of an ordinary boiler shop would be but a Schubert serenade," wrote one eyewitness, "compared to the Wagnerian racket these 800 hammers are making." [36] About $2,500 a day was being paid out in wages. In the big boiler shop many men were rolling and punching the plates from which more tanks were to be made. Big pipes to convey oil and water were being run in every direction. Refining stills were in all stages, dozens of them nearly completed, and an army of bricklayers worked on others. About a half mile north of Whiting, on the lake shore, the pipes of the National Transit Company were discharging Lima crude into storage tanks. Construction work suffered little interruption during the winter of 1889–90 because it was mild.

To supply water, workmen began sinking in January, 1890, a

35. A reporter for the *Lima Daily Times* managed to elude the guards and roam about the refinery for a couple of hours before he was discovered; his observations are reported in the issue of October 16, 1890.
36. *The Chicago Tribune*, September 22, 1889.

shaft five feet in diameter to a depth of seventy-five feet. When an inquiring reporter asked Cowan about this, he replied that the company had not decided what it was going to do with it after it was finished. "You see," said Cowan, "we just thought we'd put a pipe in and find out what is down there." [37] At the bottom of the shaft they tunneled under Lake Michigan for nearly one-half mile, where a connection was made with a crib on the bottom of the lake. On the shore end of the tunnel, pumps were attached to pump water to all parts of the refinery. Great foresight was exercised in making this tunnel, for it had the capacity to supply not only the immediate need but all increased demands of the plant and the town of Whiting for many years. An immense sewage system was also started, one adequate for present and future needs. Once the sewers were completed, they drained off the surface water, and within a few years great stretches of slough and parts of Berry Lake went dry.

By the spring of 1890 many storage tanks and stills had been built, and a copper-oxide restoring plant was under construction. In order to have a sufficient supply of crude for the refinery, a second pipeline from Lima to Chicago was built alongside the first.[38] Also, in order to be in a position to ship oil throughout the West to the greatest advantage, the Wisconsin Central Railroad, a Standard interest, gained control over the Chicago & Calumet Terminal Railroad.[39] The latter had its eastern terminal on Standard's property at Whiting. It ran to East Chicago, Hammond, Dolton, Riverdale, Blue Island, and La Grange and connected with almost two dozen trunk lines serving the Southwest and West. By acquiring control of the railroad, Standard could deliver freight directly to each railroad, avoid paying high tolls for switching, and have the exclusive use of the tracks for the handling of its own cars. Since it ran just outside of the Chicago city limits, it was all the more valuable because Standard was not hampered by city ordinances regarding the storage and transportation of oil within the city.

With the approach of summer W. S. Rheem, Beaumont Parks, F. W. Weller, and other manufacturing men from Oil City, Titusville, Cleveland, and Buffalo, began arriving in Whiting. While waiting for the refinery to start operations, they went to work

37. Ibid.
38. Ibid., June 13, 1890.
39. Ibid., June 7, 1890.

supervising various kinds of construction work, serving as sub-foremen, timekeepers, and doing whatever needed to be done. Among others who arrived was William M. Burton.[40] A short time before, Frank Rockefeller had asked Burton in Cleveland: "How would you like to go to Whiting?" Burton replied: "Fine." Any move to get away from Frasch was agreeable with him. So, with a salary of $1,200 a year, Burton was told to report to Cowan, for a chemist was needed at Whiting. There was no thought or desire of any research on petroleum being done. Burton was to do routine work. "I remember," said Burton, "landing in Whiting on a very hot day in June and the general appearance of the situation was anything but attractive. Sand burrs, sand fleas, scrub oaks, etc., predominated, but on all sides one could hear the busy hum of construction work." [41] Burton reported at once to Cowan, who informed him that they were not yet ready to begin manufacturing operations, and they had little for him to do. Burton expressed a willingness to do anything to which he might be assigned. Thinking that chemists carried their tools with them, like carpenters or plumbers, Cowan asked, "Have you your 'kit' with you?" Burton said he had nothing; he had been told that Cowan would provide a laboratory, facilities, and supplies. Cowan took Burton to the old Wuestenfeldt farmhouse and said he might use the second floor as a laboratory. Burton cleaned out the two bedrooms, and it was here that one of the first chemical laboratories in the petroleum industry was established.

Without any apparatus or material with which to work, Burton purchased from E. H. Sargent & Company, a Chicago drug and chemical supplier, several hundred dollars' worth of equipment—a combustion furnace, a Becker balance, all kinds of beakers, test tubes, burettes—and standard chemical supplies.[42] No limit was placed upon his purchases, for the Rockefeller policy was to buy whatever was needed to do the best work. It took a month or more before Burton was ready to do any laboratory work. As soon as his "kit" was ready, Burton spent several weeks making analyses of paints and other building materials to see if the company was getting what had been ordered. Although Cowan thought there

40. Interview with William M. Burton, August 2, 1948.
41. William M. Burton, "Dr. Burton Reminisces About Early Days," *Stanolind Record*, VIII, No. 6 (April, 1927), 21-22.
42. Interview with William M. Burton, August 2, 1948.

was little to do, Burton found plenty to occupy his time during the summer.

In employing a professionally trained chemist and establishing a laboratory in connection with its refinery, the company set a precedent. Even though the laboratory at Whiting was small and seemed negligible, it represented a significant development in the petroleum industry, one that was destined to be of utmost importance in the history of the company. Recognizing the value of scientists at an early date was to give Standard a tremendous advantage over all other oil companies and make it an outstanding leader in research.

Since more than a year had passed and construction work at Whiting had proceeded too slowly, a change in leadership was decided upon. At a special meeting of the Directors of the company in New York on July 1, 1890, Tilford resigned as President and Vilas as a Director. James A. Moffett was elected a Director and made President.[43]

Later in the month, on July 22, the first annual meeting of the stockholders was held at Whiting. Cowan reported on the operations of the company for the year ending June 30, the bylaws were read and adopted, and Directors were elected to serve until March, the date of the regular annual meeting.[44] In accordance with the new bylaws the Directors met on July 29 and elected Moffett President, Cowan Vice-President, and L. D. Clarke Secretary-Treasurer.[45] They also designated the members of the Manufacturing Committee of the Standard Oil Trust in New York as the company's Manufacturing Committee. This committee devoted its attention to the supervision of refining in all plants of the Trust; it formulated policies for all operations; it watched manufacturing costs and expenditures; it received and studied reports from the different companies; and it gave advice and counsel. All officers and agents of Standard of Indiana were instructed to carry out whatever measures the committee proposed unless contrary notice was given by the company's Board of Directors.

Moffett was an experienced manufacturing man. He had started in the oil business in 1869 in West Virginia and had been trained under J. N. Camden in Parkersburg and later under Charles Pratt and H. H. Rogers in New York. With a keen, analytical mind,

43. Minutes of the Board of Directors' and Stockholders' Meetings, 1889–1912, 6.
44. *Ibid.*, 8.
45. *Ibid.*, 15.

Moffett could quickly get to the core of any problem. His memory was remarkable. He could read or write an important letter and remember it long afterwards. Outstanding was the fact that he was a driver, a vigorous and dynamic executive whose walk and personal bearing indicated a man of supreme confidence and assurance. He knew what should be done, told subordinates to do it, and it had better be done. In spite of his seeming harshness, Moffett inspired a staunch loyalty among employees because they felt that they were working for someone worth-while. When something went wrong, Moffett would explode, wave his arms, shout, and swear fluently—and with ease. "Moffett," according to one who knew him, "was the thundercloud with its blinding shafts of lightning, its deep bellows of thunder, the rushing, roaring wind, the driving hurricane." [46] Once the storm had passed, he was gracious, repentant, and the episode was forgotten. Like as not he would remark: "I didn't mean all that." One day he told Burton: "Bill, a man doesn't have to rant and rave like I do to get things done. He can just be positive."

Although Cowan had been relegated to second in command, and it hurt, he and Moffett worked together in a long association. Under their leadership were developed many young men who later achieved prominent places not only in Standard of Indiana but in other Standard Oil companies. The daily association with Moffett and Cowan stimulated everyone to greater achievement. They were stirring examples of men in higher places reaching down to those in subordinate positions and helping them climb the ladder of success.

Upon his elevation to the presidency, Moffett came to Whiting, took charge of all operations and infused new life into the construction work. At Moffett's suggestion, Burton converted an old cowshed in the rear of the Wuestenfeldt farmhouse into a laboratory for large-scale experiments and built two 100-gallon stills, one for crude and one for copper oxide distillation, a small steam still, and a sulphuric acid agitator.[47] This installation constituted the "first research department" of the company. To assist Burton, although they were not trained chemists, Frank B. Lewis made sulphur determinations and A. C. Stover and Pat Hickey, experi-

46. Interview with William M. Burton, August 2, 1948; U. G. Swartz, "Some Early Days of Whiting, Part Three," Stanolind Record, IV, No. 11 (September, 1923), 9-13.
47. William M. Burton, "Dr. Burton Reminisces About Early Days," Stanolind Record, VIII, No. 6 (April, 1927), 21-22.

enced stillmen from Parkersburg, West Virginia, worked in the "experimental house" on methods of getting larger yields of kerosene from Lima crude.

Much displeased over the fact that only a few copper-oxide stills approached completion and wanting kerosene to sell as soon as possible, Moffett conceived the idea that some Lima crude could be refined by the lead-oxide method, and the product could be mixed with kerosene produced by the copper-oxide process. The latter required far more apparatus, and it was considerably more complicated than the lead-oxide process. To strengthen his position, Moffett referred the question to the Manufacturing Committee in New York, and it sent several representatives to Whiting to confer. Burton and some of his associates protested vigorously against the plan, but they were overruled and preparations were made to use the lead-oxide method to supplement the copper-oxide process.[48]

By the end of the summer, the gigantic task of building the refinery was nearing completion. The construction of vapor-brush stills, steam stills, the acid works, millhouse, and agitators had proceeded far enough to begin manufacturing operations. On September 2, 1890, without any fanfare or excitement, the first six-hundred-barrel, vapor-brush still was charged with Lima crude under the direction of George P. France, superintendent.[49] At the same time, various departments—Barreling, Switching, Lubricating Oil, and others—were organized to handle the finished products. Because of his excellent sales experience and knowledge of lubricants, H. S. Morton of the Consolidated Tank Line Company was employed as manager of the Lubricating Oil Sales Department to direct the manufacture and distribution of lubricants, greases, wax, and candles. On Thanksgiving Day, 1890, the first shipment of kerosene was made from Whiting. Since he had done so well in billing out the first shipments, Edgar Bogardus, freight agent for the Lake Shore & Michigan Southern at Whiting, was employed by the company and placed in charge of the Freight and Order Department.

The process used in refining Lima crude was identical with the ordinary refining process except for the treatment of the oil with

48. Interview with William M. Burton, August 2, 1948; William M. Burton to Giddens, November 9, 1949.
49. U. G. Swartz, "Some Early Days of Whiting, Part Three," *Stanolind Record*, IV, No. 11 (September, 1923), 13.

copper oxide, a black powder.[50] The first forty vapor-brush or "sweetening" stills built at Whiting were of the horizontal shell type, about eight feet in diameter and thirty feet long. Each had a capacity of 600 barrels. There were ten of these in a row, and each row was called a battery. A stillman had charge of two batteries. Once a still had been charged with crude, a fire was started. There was one fireman for every three stills. When the temperature became sufficiently high, the crude oil began to vaporize and the "sour" vapors passed to a cylinder which held a mixture of pulverized copper oxide and a little "sour" oil agitated by an immense revolving wire brush.[51] The vapors lost their sulphur content as they passed through the cylinder to the condenser. The condenser box had an immense coil of pipes submerged in running water in which the vapors were condensed and cooled. The oil then flowed to the receiving tanks. There was a receiving house for each battery. The stillman went from receiving house to receiving house, where the oil ran into small compartments, watching and testing the gravity of the oil. He issued orders to the firemen to slacken or increase the fire as the case might require. While stillmen, firemen, and others were busy with their work, messenger boys, since there was no telephone system within the plant, carried messages from the refinery to the main office and samples of oil to the laboratory, where they were constantly checked for their flash point, color, and other factors. First to vaporize, condense, and run into the receiving house was naphtha, then benzine and gasoline—the lighter oils. After the gravity reached a certain point, a heavier fraction—kerosene—began to appear, and the stream was "cut" into a different tank. This fraction was run into the agitators, treated with sulphuric acid, washed with water, and treated with caustic soda. After being treated in the steam stills, the finished product was stored to await shipment to market.

In running Lima crude through the vapor-brush stills, it gave off a very poisonous vapor containing hydrogen sulphide, and one or two breaths of it proved fatal. During the first years of refining operations several men lost their lives from inhaling it. Even horses, caught in the draft of vapor from the agitators, were prostrated. Danger lurked everywhere—in the pump house, on top of

50. *The Chicago Tribune,* June 21, 1896.
51. U. G. Swartz, "Some Early Days of Whiting, Part Three," *Stanolind Record,* IV, No. 11 (September, 1923), 11-12; William M. Burton to Giddens, November 7, 1949, December 1, 1949.

the storage tanks, and in other places. After the danger became generally known and proper precautions were taken, accidents ceased.

"Sour" oil in storage tanks was dangerous in still another way. The hydrogen sulphide in the vapor space formed sulphide of iron on the inside of the storage tanks, and it sometimes ignited spontaneously. If a tank had the right mixture of air and vapor, an explosion would blow off the top of the tank, set fire to the oil, and sometimes menace the plant. This danger was greatly reduced, however, by lowering the contents of the storage tanks every six months and scraping off the iron sulphide.[52] Since the corrosion gradually ate away the metal, the tanks were filled with water after they were cleaned. If they held water, which was heavier than oil, they were used for another six months.

When about 55 per cent of the crude oil had been distilled off, the still was shut down, and the resulting tar was pumped out for use as fuel oil or pumped to the paraffin works for making lubricating oils, greases, and wax. The copper oxide in the brush cylinder was hauled to the dump where the oil was burned out.[53] Smoke from burning oil became such a nuisance that it led to the removal of the inhabitants at Berry Lake to more desirable locations. The resulting copper sulphide was then hauled to the millhouse where it was put through a McDougal furnace and prepared for use again. In the meantime, the still was pumped out, cleaned, and made ready for another charge of crude. The vapor-brush still was more or less successful but the process required heavy, cumbersome machinery; it was an expensive method; and it involved many repairs.

The millhouse was like an ordinary flour mill, except that it had roasting furnaces.[54] The copper sulphide was first roasted at a high heat in the McDougal furnace until the accumulated sulphur was burned out, then it was pulled out of the furnaces by scrapers onto the floor in the middle of the millhouse. After it had cooled, it was put into a crusher, thoroughly pulverized, and then fed into the millstones where it was ground and, afterwards, sifted like flour. From the millhouse the restored copper oxide was hauled

52. William M. Burton to Giddens, November 25, 1949.
53. *Ibid.*, December 1, 1949.
54. U. G. Swartz, "Some Early Days of Whiting, Part Three," *Stanolind Record*, IV, No. 11 (September, 1923), 11-12.

in carts to the stills, drawn to the top of the stills in buckets, and poured into the cylinders.

The noxious sulphur dioxide produced in roasting the copper sulphide and the fine floating dust made the millhouse an inferno. It was the dirtiest and most unhealthy work about the refinery. No one coveted the job of working there. The work was done mostly by foreigners. Workmen had to wear respirators, and most men could stand only a few days of it. If they stayed too long, the fumes ate the skin off their faces, turned their hair green, and made their eyes bloodshot. One of the greatest curiosities about the refinery was an old white horse that hauled the copper sulphide to the dump. Its white hair had turned green. On certain days, when the wind blew from the right direction, the fumes were very disagreeable for people living in Whiting. Eventually, the mill-house was remodeled so that the compound was cooled in a water-jacketed cooler and fed through dust-tight pipes from one part of the mill to another.

In the fall of 1890, the Whiting refinery had a charging capacity of about 10,000 barrels of crude oil per day.[55] At first a barrel of crude yielded about 30 per cent kerosene, but later, the yield ran as high as 45 per cent. By January, 1891, there were forty vapor-brush stills in operation, and a mighty stream of kerosene, the principal product, was flowing to market. Whiting did not seem to be a very large refinery, but forty stills would refine approximately 2,500,000 barrels of crude per year, which was then about one-tenth of the total production of the United States.

After experimenting more than three years and spending several hundred thousand dollars to discover and perfect a method of utilizing Lima crude, Standard had finally licked the problem. Many risks had been taken by Standard in its history for the general good of the business because its officials believed in the ultimate success of those ventures. However, John D. Archbold, Vice-President of the Standard Oil Company of New Jersey, stated in 1908, "The most striking single instance of the farsightedness of those interested in the Standard Oil business in taking risks which they deemed justified by the importance of the object aimed at, is afforded by the history of their dealings with Lima crude and the construction of the refineries at Lima, Ohio, and Whiting,

55. *Transcript of Record, Defendants' Testimony, United States of America, Petitioner, v. Standard Oil Company of New Jersey Et Al., Defendants*, XVI, 2635-2636.

Indiana." [56] Frasch's process had opened the way by which Lima oil could be successfully refined. Once considered almost useless, Lima oil now became exceedingly valuable and eliminated the possible shortage of oil that had threatened the country in 1886.

With the consumption of oil increasing and a successful method available for refining, the price of Lima crude steadily rose from 30 cents a barrel in 1890 until it reached $1.14 in 1903. This meant millions of dollars per year added to the income of the farmers and oil producers of Ohio and Indiana. For Standard, success in devising a method to refine Lima crude meant that the millions of dollars it had invested in the oil business were no longer jeopardized by the lack of a crude supply. Frasch's process enhanced the value of Standard's oil-producing properties in Ohio and Indiana and the millions of barrels of Lima crude held in storage. It provided the opportunity to make huge profits from refining Lima crude at Whiting. "Standard has enjoyed some big rake-offs in the Pennsylvania fields in the past," declared one observer, "but this rake-off on Ohio oil is the greatest of them all. The Whiting refinery alone will bring millions into the over-flowing Standard coffers. . . . When it gets down to work in earnest it will force all independent refiners out of business and break the oil market into bits. I tell you this Ohio oil is great stuff, and it is the most powerful club the Standard ever held or ever will hold on the oil trade of the country." [57]

56. *Brief for Defendants on the Facts, United States of America, Petitioner, v. Standard Oil Company (New Jersey) Et Al., Defendants*, I, 88.
57. *Lima Daily Times*, October 16, 1890.

CHAPTER II

Early Manufacturing and
Marketing Operations

ALTHOUGH MANUFACTURING OPERATIONS BEGAN AT WHITING IN 1890, the refinery was incomplete and construction work continued for several years. When the second group of forty vapor-brush stills was about half completed, a better method for treating crude oil with copper oxide was discovered. Orders were issued to stop all work on vapor-brush stills and build "sweetening" stills similar to the cheesebox stills which had long been used in the Pennsylvania oil field.[1] These were cylindrical iron tanks with dome-shaped tops and flat steel bottoms resting upon brick foundations. They were enclosed with brick in which were firing places connected to a central flue. Before starting a run, pulverized copper oxide was poured into these stills from the top. To mix the copper oxide and the "sour" oil and, at the same time, keep the former from settling on the bottom, a mechanical stirring apparatus was used, which constantly turned, dragging chains around and around. This method kept the mixture agitated while the oxide reacted with some of the sulphur compounds and the vapors rose and passed to the condenser.

About thirty of these cheesebox stills were ultimately constructed. The unfinished vapor-brush stills were never completed, and the materials were gradually used for other purposes. Those completed and in use were gradually abandoned. The expense involved in making this major change was enormous, but it resulted in a simpler and less expensive process. Except for mechanical improvements, there were no fundamental changes in the refining process at Whiting until about 1906.

Between 1891 and 1894 a can factory, wax works, paraffin compounding house, roundhouse, tank car shops, barrel house, sweating ovens, candle works, and additional tar and cheesebox stills

1. William M. Burton to Giddens, November 7, 25, 1949, December 1, 25, 1949.

were built. As the work of the chemical staff increased, the laboratory became inadequate, and Burton urged the building of a new one. In the fall of 1895, while on a trip to Germany, Burton visited several chemical laboratories and got ideas, many of which were incorporated in the plans for the new laboratory. Built at a cost of ten to fifteen thousand dollars, the two-story, modern brick building was the finest structure in the refinery. The first floor served as the refinery office with the laboratory on the second.[2] This new laboratory was a part of the main laboratory until 1946. In the laboratory there were three rooms, one for making sulphur determinations, one for general work, and another for a library. Though the library was small, it had a full set of Rudolph Fresenius' *Analytical Chemistry* of thirty to forty volumes and various scientific journals. A new "experimental house" was also built in the rear of the laboratory building. In 1896 John Compton was sent from the Standard refinery at Cleveland to build a grease works, which was completed within a year, and to direct its operations.[3]

Manufacturing operations at Whiting were under the general supervision of the Manufacturing Committee of the Standard Oil Trust at 26 Broadway in New York.[4] To it the company executives made regular and detailed reports. A private telegraph wire between New York, Chicago, and Whiting enabled Trust officials to keep in close touch with local affairs. Frequently, Ambrose M. McGregor, Chairman of the Manufacturing Committee, visited the plant, and the Chicago officials went to New York. From time to time McGregor made "suggestions" and those at Whiting knew what was meant when he made a "suggestion." Moffett was not the type of man, however, to permit much interference in the operation of Whiting, for he was an experienced manufacturing executive and a forceful man. All auditing of the books of the company was done under the direction of the general auditor in New York. Moreover, every capital expenditure over $5,000 had to be approved in New York.[5] When requests were made for approving an appropriation, the usual question was: How soon can you pay for this out of operating savings? If it could be done within two years, it was generally approved. Apart from close supervision over

2. Interview with William M. Burton, August 2, 1948; *Whiting Democrat,* March 6, 1896.
3. Interview with William M. Burton, August 2, 1948.
4. Nevins, *John D. Rockefeller,* I, 675.
5. Interview with William M. Burton, August 2, 1948.

finances and auditing, Moffett and Cowan exercised considerable discretion in the management of Whiting.

In the spring of 1891 several changes were made in the Chicago organization. The office of Secretary-Treasurer was separated, and George W. Stahl became Treasurer. "Uncle George," as Stahl was familiarly called, was a brother-in-law of John D. Archbold. Somewhat short and stubby in stature, "Uncle George" had a bald head and was always seen with a cigar in his mouth. His presence and bearing inspired confidence in the soundness of the company. Although genial, smiling, and with a flair for telling stories, Stahl never forgot that he was the man who held the purse strings of the company. The Directors also designated the Domestic Trade Committee, the Case and Can Committee, the Cooperage Committee, and the Lubrication Committee of the Standard Oil Trust in New York as committees of Standard of Indiana. To accommodate a larger manufacturing and sales organization than could be maintained in Whiting, the company opened offices in Chicago at 5 S. Wabash Avenue which became the executive headquarters.[6] Into these quarters Moffett, Cowan, Stahl, the Purchasing Department, the auditors, and the traffic manager moved in April, 1891. As Moffett and Cowan became more and more involved in the general administration of the business in Chicago, they visited Whiting less and less. Consequently, the superintendent of the refinery became an increasingly important executive.

Realizing the importance and necessity for having a scientifically trained man in the refinery, Moffett took Burton out of the laboratory and made him assistant superintendent under France in 1893. The appointment was very agreeable to Burton, for he had become tired of laboratory work. The routine work he was charged with did not challenge his interest.[7] He was glad to get out and see how things went around the plant. As assistant superintendent Burton worked at everything, but he still continued to do whatever chemical work was necessary. In the fall of 1895 the superintendent, George P. France, left Whiting to become general manager of the Bayonne refinery, and Burton became his successor. The promotion of a chemist to an important executive position was a pioneer development which marked the beginning of a policy that has been observed from that day to the present. After Burton

6. A. E. MacMeekin, "Spending Fifty Millions a Year in All Parts of the World," *Stanolind Record*, X, No. 3 (January, 1929), 3-5.
7. Interview with William M. Burton, August 2, 1948.

became superintendent, he did little or no laboratory work. Dr. George W. Gray, a Ph.D. in chemistry from Johns Hopkins, succeeded Burton as head of the laboratory. Moffett's regular visits to Whiting grew more infrequent after Burton became superintendent, but Cowan's continued until 1903 when Burton was transferred to Chicago as general manager of manufacturing.

The Whiting refinery, like most refineries, ran continuously night and day, seven days a week, manufacturing gasoline, kerosene, wax, lubricating oil, greases, fuel oil, and coke. Beginning in 1891 the crude run to stills amounted to 5,127,736 barrels per year, or a daily average of 14,049.[8]

Refined oil, or kerosene, was the most important product made until 1910, and for it there was a tremendous demand. During the 1890's Whiting annually produced about three million barrels.[9] There were several grades.[10] Water white, or Perfection Oil, with a flash point of 150° F., was the first grade and the most popular brand. Prime white, or standard white, with a flash point of 112° F., was the second and the cheaper grade. Prime white was not as well refined as Perfection Oil and was chiefly used in the export trade. It had a slightly yellowish tinge, more sulphur, and a less favorable "floc" test. It contained more wax and other foreign substances which caused it to congeal in winter and prevent a free flow of oil through the wick. Perfection Oil burned better and left less wick char and discoloration of the chimney. Its cost was so low that the difference between the two grades was about ¼ or ½ of a cent per gallon. Perfection Oil sold for 4½ to 5 cents per gallon in tank cars and prime white for 4¼ to 4½ cents.

Diamond Headlight kerosene with a flash point of 175° F. was a special brand made for railroad locomotives. It sold for about 6 cents per gallon. Palacine and Elaine, two very high-grade brands of water-white kerosene, made from Pennsylvania crude by Warden & Oxnard of Philadelphia, were shipped to Whiting in bulk, canned or barreled with labels showing the name of the eastern manufacturer, and distributed in Standard's territory.[11] These oils were handled by the company for many years. Without any sulphur or offensive odor, these brands appealed to a very high-class trade.

8. A summary statement showing the crude run and products yields for the Whiting refinery from 1890 to 1912 furnished by Max G. Paulus, Vice-President in charge of Manufacturing, Standard Oil Company (Indiana), January 13, 1950.
9. *Ibid.*
10. William M. Burton to Giddens, December 18, 1949.
11. *Ibid.*

Since it was not to the best interest of the company to buy and distribute these brands, it developed at Whiting a special brand called Eocene. It was made by heavy acid treating of western crude to meet the competition of Pennsylvania oils. Eocene was the best brand of kerosene made at Whiting, and it sold for a fancy price. In time, the company eliminated some of these grades of kerosene and concentrated solely upon the manufacture and sale of Perfection Oil.[12]

The production of fuel oil ranked second in volume during the nineties with two to four million barrels annually produced. However, after 1898 the volume fell off appreciably. Naphtha, or gasoline, ranked third in volume. About a million barrels per year were manufactured. Some of the crude oil yielded as much as 20 per cent of this explosive and inflammable by-product for which there was little demand. At first it was manufactured as "Deodorized Stove Gasoline." Later, it was called "Special Red Crown" and finally "Red Crown." The "Red Crown" brand name, it is believed, originally belonged to W. H. Doan, a Cleveland refiner, whose oil business had been purchased by the Rockefeller organization.[13]

Lubricating oils were fourth in volume but showed a marked increase during the nineties. Formulae for making both greases and lubricating oils were brought from Cleveland and the already well-known Standard brands—Renown Engine Oil, Atlantic Red Engine Oil, Zone Paraffin Engine Oil, and Capitol Cylinder Oil— were made at Whiting. For quite a while Mica Axle Grease, already a famous Standard brand, was the only grease made at Whiting. The company made large purchases of lubricating oil from the Vacuum Oil Company, another Standard unit, which made a wide variety of excellent lubricants, and these were reshipped from Whiting under Vacuum's brand names. It was difficult to make high-quality lubricants from Lima crude. After John Compton arrived at Whiting in 1896, much experimenting was done.[14] Compton was an indefatigable experimenter. He secured samples of competitors' greases from the field, had them analyzed by company chemists, and within a short time he was making greases to meet competitors' products. He was the first man to make petrola-

12. Interview with Edward J. Bullock, July 20, 1948.
13. Company Encyclopedia: Manufacturing—Gasoline, Motor and Aviation, 3; Interview with William M. Burton, August 2, 1948.
14. Interview with William M. Burton, August 2, 1948.

tum from western crude. In time, the company had all sorts of regular and special brands to meet various price situations and the particular needs of large buyers.

The Galena-Signal Oil Company of Franklin, Pennsylvania, a Standard Oil unit, specialized in the manufacture and sale of oils for railroads. Other Standard refineries did not manufacture these oils until after 1911. While Galena-Signal made a superior oil for use in railroad signals, lanterns, and lamps, it could not profitably supply the demand at distant points in the Middle West and the Far West because of competition. Hence, Standard of Indiana made and sold an oil for this purpose under the brand name Mineral Seal.[15] Later it developed and manufactured another famous oil—Fortnite Longtime Burning Oil—that would burn in switch lights without attendance or service for at least two weeks. It was a superior product which saved the railroads so much in terms of service that they were willing to pay the higher cost involved in order to use it at points far distant from Chicago.

The volume of wax produced was relatively small. With the completion of the candle factory in 1893, paraffin was chiefly used in making candles.[16] At first plain paraffin wax candles were made. Later, paraffin was mixed with stearic acid to make more rigid candles, and these were sold mostly for mining purposes under the brand name Granite. The aerated, or snowflake candles, were first made in 1898. One-pound cakes of pure refined wax were made in 1896 by pouring melted wax into individual pans and allowing it to cool. After the wax solidified, it was removed, wrapped in blue paper, and shipped in twenty-, forty-, and one-hundred-pound cases. It was, and still is, largely used in sealing jars in home canning. In 1904 the product was named Parowax, and the first molding machines were purchased to mold quarter-pound cakes and imprint the word Parowax on the end of each cake.

In the early days at Whiting vast quantities of wooden barrels were required for shipping all classes of petroleum products. Kerosene was shipped in blue-painted barrels, gasoline in red barrels with paper labels and a Red Crown printed thereon glued to the end. At first, the labels were lithographed in the print shop at the Cleveland refinery and sent to Whiting. Gasoline was shipped in the same type of barrel as kerosene but invariably new

15. Memorandum written by Allan Jackson to Giddens during the summer of 1948.
16. Company Encyclopedia: Manufacturing—History of the Whiting Plant, Heavy Oils Department, Candles, 20.

barrels were used for gasoline. They needed to be well seasoned and tightly coopered. To minimize leakage, they were usually sized inside with glue. While a barrel for crude oil held 42 gallons, those used for shipping refined products usually held from 50 to 52 gallons and, in some instances though rarely, as much as 55. Staves, heads, and hoops were purchased and the barrels were assembled at the refinery, which required a large force of coopers.

In the early nineties a considerable quantity of illuminating oil was shipped in "box tank cars," an ordinary boxcar with two square tanks inside, one in each end of the car and each capable of holding 2,500 gallons. They were used chiefly to ship oil to the Far West.[17] To avoid the return of an empty car, the cars brought back bullion and valuable ores from western mines. When this style of tank car became obsolete, the tanks were removed and used for storing refined oil at many points within the company's sales territory.

During the summer of 1895 Standard began using two tank barges, owned and operated by the Standard Oil Company of New York, for the purpose of distributing products on the Great Lakes. The first barge, "S. O. Co. #75," towed by a whaleback steamer, arrived late in June, 1895, at South Chicago.[18] Made of steel, the barge was somewhat smaller than the regular "pig" barges and differed little in appearance. It had a small boiler and engine for steering and handling sails and three masts carrying 1,000 yards of canvas, but at no time did it move under its own power. One hundred and eighty feet long, with a beam of thirty-three feet, and a hold seventeen feet deep, the barge had eight tanks, each with a capacity of 1,000 barrels of oil. A cofferdam, containing a wall of water two feet thick, separated the engine room from the tanks and kept gas and heat from getting to the tanks from the engine room.

Held at South Chicago for nearly a month until a pier at Whiting could be completed, the "S. O. Co. #75" moved to the loading pier at Whiting on July 20th. Its shining black sides and gleaming masts created a flurry of excitement as, towed by a tug, it moved past the town and docked at the pier opposite the refinery. Immense

17. Company Encyclopedia: Marketing, I, Methods of Distribution, Distribution in Tank Cars, 25.
18. *The Chicago Tribune*, April 9, 28, 1895, June 29, 1895, July 12, 16, 25, 1895; *Whiting Democrat*, July 4, 25, 1895; "From the Log of a Tanker Fleet," *Stanolind Record*, XIII, No. 8 (June, 1932), 1-16.

rubber lines were connected, the big pumps were started, and the oil flowed into its tanks. Since the new pier was not completed and the barge was tied up in about eleven feet of water, it could not carry more than half a load. Towed by the steamer *Havana*, the barge left for the company's water terminal at Superior, Wisconsin, on July 24th. This pioneering event marked the beginning of transporting oil in bulk on Lake Michigan. Another new barge, the "S. O. Co. #76," arrived at South Chicago on July 26th and was put into service.[19]

Considering the vast quantity of oil daily processed and stored at Whiting, it is strange that fires and explosions were not more common. Occasionally they did occur, but they were not serious.[20] Though it was generally necessary to allow a tank to burn out, the fire was always kept under control and did not spread. Several factors accounted for the limited number of fires. Profiting from the experience of other refineries, Whiting was built to avoid the spread of fires. With plenty of available land, Whiting pioneered in building storage tanks five hundred feet apart and having a fire bank around each tank great enough to hold its entire capacity in case of fire and explosion.[21] Moreover, there were four fire departments in the refinery, each having its own part of the works to guard and each fully equipped for immediate service. Taking proper precautionary measures was still another factor. Though fires burned under the stills, they were kept closely confined. The stillmen were generally old, reliable hands who had worked for the Standard organization for many years, and they were cautious in handling oil. Nothing but electricity was used for lighting. Watchmen patrolled the plant, keeping close watch against workmen smoking. In all of these things lay security.

When the refinery began operating in 1890 most of the same laborers who had been employed on the construction work remained to operate the different departments. As refinery operations expanded more laborers were added, and by 1896 between 2,500 and 3,000 persons were employed. The hiring of employees was largely done by departmental heads or their representatives.[22]

19. *The Chicago Tribune,* July 27, 30, 1895, August 1, 1895.
20. Between 1892 and 1896 there were three minor fires and explosions. For accounts of these fires see *The Chicago Tribune,* May 25, 1892, November 19, 1895, February 23, 1896.
21. Interview with William M. Burton, August 2, 1948.
22. Company Encyclopedia: Personnel—Labor Relations, Employment Bureau at Whiting, 1-6.

A majority of the new employees were selected from among those who congregated each morning at various entrances to the refinery. Oftentimes the head of a department might know some of those waiting because they had been previously employed or else they lived in the community. On the other hand, there were many strangers who sought work for the first time. Sometimes the men were interviewed, but usually it was just announced that so many boilermakers or other types of workers were needed. Men who could do the job stepped forward, were asked a few questions, hired, and told to step inside the gate. When hired, they were placed in charge of a foreman who directed them to the job. Firing was done by the foremen for whatever reason they thought sufficient. However, any man who felt he had been unjustly treated could present his complaint to his department head or even to officials at the main office. No time clock was used in the refinery, except possibly in the candle factory, even as late as 1928. A timekeeper made the rounds every day to check the time for each man with the foreman and sign up any new men found at work.

The steady demand for laborers brought an increasing number of foreign-born people—Poles, Slovaks, Croatians, Magyars, Swedes, English, Turks, Welsh, Italians, Bohemians, Lithuanians, Ruthenians, and Jews—to Whiting.[23] Nearly every nationality could be found in the community. The company found European immigrants very desirable workmen; they were physically strong and often possessed good mechanical ability. Others were valued because they would do the most disagreeable work about a refinery willingly and without objection. Next to Americans, the Slovaks constituted the greatest number of employees. Very few of the foreign-born, except the Poles, had any previous refinery experience; they had been largely farm laborers. Americans, Germans, Irishmen, Swedes, Norwegians, Finns, Canadians, Danes, and some Slovaks, Magyars, Croatians, Ruthenians, and Poles constituted the bulk of the skilled and semiskilled laborers. They served as boilermakers, firemen, helpers, lead burners, mechanics, pumpmen, stillmen, switchers, and treaters. Unskilled Croats, Slovaks, and Poles cleaned the stills, which was a hot, dirty, and undesirable job. Germans, Poles, Slovaks, and Irish, in the order named,

23. An exceptionally thorough and enlightening study on the employment of European immigrants at Whiting is to be found in a report of the U. S. Immigration Commission published on June 15, 1910, on *Immigrants in Industries*, XVI, Part 20, 745-806. See Senate Document No. 633, 61st Cong., 2nd Sess.

showed a marked tendency to advance themselves from the lowest grades of work and enter the skilled occupations. A number of Germans, Irish, and Slovaks, owing to their ability, rose to be foremen. Among other people from southern and eastern Europe, there was little or no tendency for the men to work up to foremen's positions; they were slow in learning English.

The only place where women were employed was in the candle factory. About thirty-five German, Irish, Polish, Slovak, and American girls worked here sorting and packing candles in small pasteboard boxes. Irish and American girls proved most efficient for this work.

The company policy was to work mixed gangs in all departments in order to reduce clannishness and, in the opinion of the officials, secure better work. Consequently, all nationalities associated freely while at work, but outside the plant and in nonworking hours there was little association between the Americans and the immigrants or between the various nationality groups.

In employing labor the company made no discrimination against immigrants because they were immigrants. Preference was given, however, to English-speaking laborers. Such a policy reduced the operating costs of certain departments; it tended to eliminate an important contributory cause of accidents; and it enabled the company to maintain a higher standard of efficiency among employees through easily effected discipline. Inability to speak English proved a disadvantage, but personal efficiency in several occupations at the refinery was little affected by the immigrants' lack of English.

Payday came every two weeks.[24] For the first two years the paymaster used a light wagon with the top enclosed with screen wire to distribute the pay in cash during working hours. The paymaster and the head timekeeper drove from group to group about the plant and by the company cottages, issuing the pay. In 1891 a small office with pay windows on each side was built near the main office. The pay was brought from Chicago every payday morning, and the cash was placed in each man's envelope. Great care was taken to protect the pay by having armed watchmen always on duty. The danger involved, however, led eventually to paying with checks. On payday the noon hour was only twenty-five minutes, and the whistle for quitting work in the afternoon blew an hour earlier than on other days. Long lines quickly formed at each pay window.

24. Payday at the refinery is vividly described by U. G. Swartz in his article, "Some Early Days of Whiting," *Stanolind Record*, IV, No. 12 (October, 1923), 13-16.

A few wives often waited near the pay house to get a share in the earnings before their husbands visited the saloon.

Quitting an hour early on payday made the little town of Whiting a lively place. Almost all the buildings on the west side of Front Street, extending from the Pennsylvania Railroad tracks to 119th Street, were saloons. In front of each were four or five steps running the entire width of each building. Perched on these steps, with their dinner pails between their knees, the men proceeded to quench their thirst and celebrate. Rollicking songs and careless laughs resounded everywhere. Various signs on the buildings in foreign languages appealed to the workmen "to take another in memory of loved absent ones." And how they loved the absent ones! No one was forgotten.

For those who kept the stores in Whiting, payday was also a happy occasion. It meant the settlement of bills for food and supplies for the previous two weeks because no one bought or sold for cash. Patrons were urged to buy on time, and there was great rivalry among firms to extend credit for any article in the store.

Payday always created a rush at the money-order window at the post office until late hours in the evening, for many of the foreigners regularly sent money to relatives in the old country. Often several hundred dollars were sent in a day. At one time the Whiting post office had a record for doing the second largest foreign money-order business in the state.

Intoxication while at work was not tolerated. If an employee reported for work under the influence of liquor, he was not allowed to enter the plant. If the offense were repeated, the offender was fired. This policy was rigidly enforced irrespective of position or race.

Working conditions at Whiting were a little better than those which prevailed in industry and the company had the reputation of being a good one to work for. The ten-hour day prevailed for common labor and mechanics; stillmen worked a twelve-hour stretch.[25] There were no company stores; an employee traded wherever he desired. The general sanitary conditions in the refinery were good. Work was regular and little affected by industrial disturbances.

During the panic of 1893 the rate of pay for common laborers at South Chicago and vicinity fell to 10 cents per hour. Men thronged the streets and wanted work at any price, but at Whiting, every

25. William M. Burton to Giddens, December 25, 1949.

possible man was employed who could be used, and none were paid less than the regular rate of 15 cents an hour.[26] Whiting had the distinction of being almost the only town in the area in which wages did not fall during the panic. Wages were always kept at least up to those in the surrounding industries, and the company followed a policy of paying about 5 per cent more than other industries in the vicinity. The editor of the *Whiting Democrat* summed up the experience of the Whiting community by proudly writing in 1895: "The tendency of wages at Whiting has always been upward. Common laborers, boilermakers, engineers, coal shovelers, mill men, all have, as classes, enjoyed a raise in wages, as have, also many individuals in particular lines, while wages have never been lowered in Whiting." [27]

The company furnished free medical treatment for all employees injured at work through no negligence of their own. Seriously injured employees were sent to a Chicago hospital and cared for until completely recovered. There was no limit to the length of time an employee might receive free medical care, and full wages were paid during his confinement. The only special liability to accident or disease to which employees of the refinery were exposed was that of "lead colic," which often affected men working in the sealing department in connection with lead burning. When fully developed, the disease forced an employee to stop work, and in many cases the sufferer was permanently prevented from returning to lead-burning work.

Bricklayers, carpenters, boilermakers, stationary firemen, and nearly all of the employees in the mechanical department belonged to unions but, in general, the company did not recognize unions, did not bargain collectively, and avoided, if possible, making any formal contract with labor organizations.[28] Whenever any grievance arose, the workmen were told to select a committee, come to the main office, and discuss the matter. Owing to the good pay and working conditions, a large foreign labor group not far removed from the poverty of Europe, the desire to work for a stable company, and the fact that unions were not very strong, labor difficulties were relatively few. There were only three strikes prior to 1899 and they were of a minor character.[29] In handling strikes the

26. *Whiting Democrat*, July 18, 1895.
27. *Ibid.*
28. Interview with William M. Burton, August 2, 1948.
29. *The Chicago Tribune*, June 5, 9, 1893, July 11, 1894, September 5, 6, 8, 1895; *Whiting Sun*, December 31, 1898.

policy of the company was to stand firm and, if necessary, use strike-breakers and court injunctions.

Those who first came to live and work in Whiting found it a lonely and barren place. There were few trees, no grass, sidewalks, telephones, street lights, parks, or city government. Great piles of sand greeted the eye everywhere. Few towns presented a more desolate appearance. Homesickness was prevalent among all, especially the women. Within a short time, however, institutions of a more settled society began to appear, and life became more pleasant.[30] Dances were held in unfinished houses and storerooms. "Billy" Myers played the violin, and frequently "Doc" Burton accompanied him on the guitar. Churches, lodges, and clubs were organized. The Lakeside Pleasure Club, composed of about twenty married couples and a few unmarried men and women, afforded its members an opportunity to play cards and dance.

To make life more bearable, some of the young men at the refinery met at night for a social gathering at the main office. As a result of the good fellowship that grew out of these meetings, they organized the Owls Club in 1893. Through the succeeding years the Owls Club took an active leadership in social and sporting events and helped to make Whiting a better place in which to live. Of the forty-one charter members, many later rose to high positions of responsibility in the company and in the oil industry.

Various sports provided pleasure and a diversion. Though the streets were rough, bicyclists rode on a summer night over a continuous course from Oliver Street through Center Street to Berry Lake, a distance of one to two miles. Baseball was tremendously popular. Organized in the spring of 1891, the "Whiting Greys" played the best teams in Chicago. Baseball teams were organized within the refinery and games between the "Crude Stills," "Sweetening Stills," "Pumpers," and other groups were popular. In the spring of 1894 the Whiting Athletic Association was organized under the leadership of W. S. Rheem for the purpose of promoting baseball and other sports, and it became an active recreational organization in the community for many years to come.

Established by U. G. Swartz, the *Whiting Democrat* began publication in May, 1894. It actively supported the movement to incorporate Whiting as a town. After a legal battle lasting about three

30. On the character of Whiting and its early social and political development see U. G. Swartz's account, "Some Early Days of Whiting," *Stanolind Record*, V, No. 1 (November, 1923), 24-30, No. 2 (December, 1923), 22-27.

years, Whiting, with a population of about 4,000, was incorporated as a city in 1903. By that time, Whiting had lost some of its frontier appearance. Cement walks were beginning to be built; the streets were cindered; shade trees, shrubs, and flowers had been planted; and other civic improvements had been made.

By 1897 practically all of the plant construction work at Whiting had been completed. There was little change in the size of the refinery from then until 1911.[31] With a plant investment exceeding $6,000,000, not counting the value of the land, Whiting was one of the largest and most complete refineries in the country. It processed more than ten million barrels of crude oil per year, or a daily average of 27,967. The Standard Oil organization had many refineries in the East, but most of them were small concerns compared with Whiting. The chief function of the Whiting refinery was to manufacture and supply petroleum products in carload lots to industrial plants, jobbers, and various marketing units of the Trust in the West—the Continental Oil Company, Waters-Pierce, Standard of Kentucky, Illinois, Minnesota, and Iowa. It did not have any retail direct marketing organization of its own.

As a result of a decision of the Supreme Court of Ohio on March 2, 1892, prohibiting the Standard Oil Company of Ohio from maintaining the trust agreement of 1879, Rockefeller and his associates liquidated the Trust, restored the twenty companies in the combination to a separate and independent legal position, and made a realignment of functions among the different companies.[32] The liquidation of the Trust affected Standard of Indiana in three respects. In the first place, the exchange of trust certificates for stock in the company increased the number of stockholders. As of October 8, 1893, there were now twenty-two stockholders. The Trust was still the largest owner with 4,907 whole shares; John D. Rockefeller held 2,641 shares, Charles W. Harkness 659, the estate of Charles Pratt 514, and H. M. Flagler 359.

In the second place, there was a change in the organization of the company.[33] Moffett resigned as President and W. H. Tilford became President and the nominal head in New York. Moffett was elected First Vice-President and Cowan Second Vice-President. They were the actual operating executives in Chicago. The mem-

---

31. One of the earliest and best descriptions of the Whiting refinery appears in *The Chicago Tribune,* June 21, 1896.
32. Nevins, *John D. Rockefeller,* II, Chapter XXXIII.
33. Minutes of the Board of Directors' and Stockholders' Meetings, 1889–1912, 25.

bership of the Board was increased from five to nine; John D. Rockefeller, Frank Rockefeller, Henry M. Flagler, and John D. Archbold were the new Directors. The various Trust committees—Manufacturing, Domestic Trade, Lubricating, and others—designated by the Board on March 26, 1891, to act for the company were discontinued. To represent the company in New York, Silas H. Paine was appointed Sales Agent for Lubricating Oils in the West and E. T. Bedford Sales Agent for Lubricating Oils in the East and for export. Theodore M. Towle was made Tax Agent.

The chief effect of the reorganization upon Standard of Indiana was to expand its functions to include retail marketing. On March 16, 1892, the capitalization of the company was increased from $500,000 to $1,000,000 and divided into $100 shares, effective April 2nd. With the increased capital stock, the Directors purchased the property of the Standard Oil Company of Illinois, formerly that of the P. C. Hanford Oil Company, and that of the Standard Oil Company of Minnesota. At the same time, the company purchased the property of the Chester Oil Company of Minnesota.[34] These purchases, effective as of January 1, 1892, provided retail marketing facilities—main stations, bulk plants, tank wagons and equipment—in Minnesota, the Chicago area, northern Illinois, and northeastern Wisconsin.

The sales territory of the company was greatly enlarged in 1896 when it acquired the marketing properties of the Standard of Kentucky in Iowa, Nebraska, Missouri, and Kansas, which formerly belonged to the Consolidated Tank Line. In 1899 the marketing stations of the Standard of Ohio in Detroit, South Bend, Grand Rapids, and Marquette were sold to Standard of Indiana. All of these acquisitions provided Standard of Indiana with the nucleus of a retail marketing organization and with men of long marketing experience like S. S. Gano, Stephen N. Hurd, Seth C. Drake, E. J. Bullock, B. T. Thompson, and T. J. Thompson, all of whom later became prominent executives in the company.

By 1901 the company was marketing through its own organization in eleven states of the Upper Mississippi Valley—Kansas, Nebraska, Iowa, North and South Dakota, Minnesota, Wisconsin, Michigan, Illinois, Indiana, and the northern portion of Missouri. With the establishment of direct marketing facilities, sales to jobbers gradually diminished because they were unnecessary.

34. *Ibid.*, 21.

MAIN OFFICE, WHITING REFINERY

Built in 1896, the first floor served as the refinery office and the second
as Burton's laboratory

OFFICE EMPLOYEES, WHITING REFINERY, IN THE 1890's

Dr. William M. Burton is the sixth from the left, top row

HOME OFFICE SALES FORCE, 5 WABASH AVENUE, CHICAGO, IN 1898

Thirty-six men and two girls comprised the Home Office sales force of the Sales
Department in 1898

WHEN STANDARD PRODUCTS WERE SOLD IN BARRELS, THESE OMAHA
COOPERS HELD KEY JOBS

STANDARD BULK PLANT, PETOSKEY, MICHIGAN, 1907

STANDARD AGENT, CHARLES AUSTIN, AND TANK WAGON, 1904

STANDARD AGENT, C. E. LUCAS, DELIVERING KEROSENE AND GREASES IN 1908

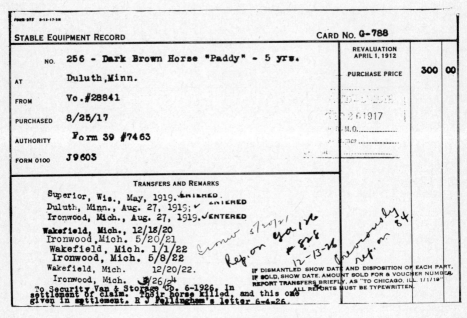

STABLE EQUIPMENT RECORD

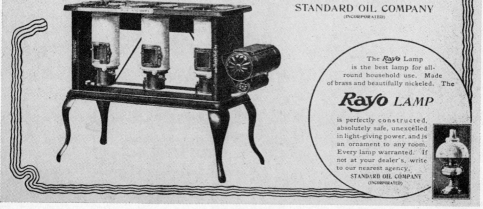

The
NEW
PERFECTION
Wick Blue Flame Oil
COOK STOVE

You could not have a more convenient and efficient stove in your kitchen than the New Perfection Wick Blue Flame Oil Cook Stove—the oil stove of new principle and design.

The New Perfection has advantages over all other kinds of stoves regardless of fuel. It proves the economy and efficiency of oil as a fuel and, unlike other oil stoves, is not limited in its usefulness.

The New Perfection will toast, roast, bake, broil, fry as well as any coal, wood or gas range, and with less expense of fuel and less trouble to the cook.

Best of all, you have any exact degree of heat at your instant control with the turn of the wrist.

Particularly for summer use is the New Perfection the ideal cook stove, because the heat it generates is a clean, blue, concentrated flame, which is confined to the burner by the enameled chimney and not thrown off to make an unbearable temperature in the kitchen.

Made in three sizes, with one, two, and three burners. Every stove fully warranted. See it at your dealer's, or write our nearest agency for descriptive circular.

STANDARD OIL COMPANY
(INCORPORATED)

The *Rayo* Lamp is the best lamp for all-round household use. Made of brass and beautifully nickeled. The

Rayo LAMP

is perfectly constructed, absolutely safe, unexcelled in light-giving power, and is an ornament to any room. Every lamp warranted. If not at your dealer's, write to our nearest agency.
STANDARD OIL COMPANY
(INCORPORATED)

The Saturday Evening Post, May 18, 1907. Reproduced through the courtesy of *The Saturday Evening Post*

ADVERTISEMENT OF PERFECTION COOK STOVES AND RAYO LAMPS

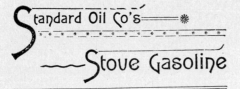

To organize a sales department and direct its marketing activities, the company appointed L. J. Drake General Manager of Sales. Drake was an experienced sales executive who had been in the oil business for twenty years, first with his own company in Keokuk, Iowa, and then with the Consolidated Tank Line Company and the Standard of Kentucky.[35] Drake was an excellent organizer and salesman. He knew how to get along with people and get the maximum amount of work done. On the job early and late, without any thought of long hours, this large and determined-looking man set an inspiring example for hard work. Always aggressive and forceful, Drake's attitude was that Standard ought to have all the business, yet he never asked an employee to do a dishonest thing and, on the contrary, he reprimanded anyone on his staff who suggested any shady or illegal practice that might bring some advantage. If a competitor cut prices, Drake matched it. No business was to be lost on account of a competitor's price cut. Rarely did he lose his temper, but if he did, he broke down and cried instead of exploding like Moffett. Drake was not the kind of executive who sat in a swivel chair in the General Office in Chicago and issued orders. He spent more than half of his time in the field keeping in close touch with conditions and his sales force. Among the sales employees Drake developed a loyalty and devotion to the company's business that was both amazing and infectious. So far as they were concerned, Drake was next to God.

To be his secretary, Drake employed a young man, twenty years old, by the name of Allan Jackson, who had just finished a short course in stenography at Dixon, Illinois. A Chicago employment agency referred Jackson to Drake but advised him to put on a clean shirt before he went for an interview. Drake immediately hired him at a salary of $50 per month. Since Drake spent so much time in the field, Jackson answered the correspondence and cared for other matters that came to Drake's desk. When in doubt over what should be done, Jackson sought the advice of Cowan or Moffett. In time, Jackson gradually became familiar with the business procedures, and prepared all kinds of reports for the New York office. Drake and Jackson were the only two people in the office of the General Manager of Sales in Chicago in 1896, but the work in this office quickly increased owing to the rapid construction of bulk

35. *Transcript of Record, Petitioner's Testimony, United States of America, Petitioner, v. Standard Oil Company of New Jersey, Et Al., Defendants,* III, 1139. Also, *Defendants' Testimony,* XIII, 1067.

stations and the inauguration of tank-wagon deliveries to retail dealers. Others were soon added to the staff.

Drake personally directed the sale of kerosene, for that was the most important part of the business. H. S. Morton had come to Chicago prior to Drake's arrival and had established a lubricating oil sales department with his own sales organization in the field. Until his retirement, except for a few years spent in New York, Morton directed the Lubricating Oil Sales Department controlling prices and policy, but the bulk of the sales were made through Drake's organization. In October, 1896, Drake brought B. T. Thompson to Chicago from Kansas City, where he had been with the Standard of Kentucky in charge of lubricating oil and specialties sales, and made him assistant to Morton. W. H. Leonard, also in Chicago before Drake's arrival, continued in charge of fuel oil sales.

Through the various marketing companies acquired by Standard of Indiana, main distributing stations had already been established in 1889 at Aurora, Chicago, Elgin, Joliet, Rockford, La Crosse, and Milwaukee, in 1891 at Kankakee, in 1892 at Mankato, St. Paul, and Winnipeg, Canada. As the company expanded its marketing business after 1892 new main stations were established, and by 1899 there were twenty-four.[36] They were carefully located with a view to the volume of business to be handled and their advantage as a shipping point. Every station had many storage tanks, each with a capacity of five to ten thousand barrels. Usually a thirty to sixty day supply was kept on hand. For barreling kerosene and gasoline and storing a large stock of petroleum products, oil stoves, lamps, heaters, and lanterns, each station had a large warehouse. In addition, there was a cooperage shop for assembling new barrels and repairing old ones. Main stations served as a collection point for empty barrels constantly being shipped in from the field. Some were repaired, cleaned, and refilled with kerosene or gasoline; others were returned to the refinery for refilling. Each main station functioned as a complete unit in the management of the business in its area, but certain accounting reports had to be made to Chicago.

Within the jurisdiction of the main station were many substations, better known as tank stations or bulk plants, in charge of an

36. Company Encyclopedia: Marketing, I, Historical Statement, 5; *Transcript of Record, Defendants' Testimony, United States of America, Petitioner, v. Standard Oil Company of New Jersey, Et Al., Defendants*, XIII, 1077 ff.

agent who made deliveries to dealers. When Drake became general manager of sales in 1896 the company, through previously acquired marketing companies, had 481 bulk plants within its sales territory.[37] Tank-wagon deliveries of kerosene and other petroleum products from the bulk plants to retail dealers was in its infancy in the Middle West, and most of the grocers, who were the principal dealers, still received their kerosene in barrels which were stored in a shanty or shed behind the store. With a vast and rich potential industrial and agricultural market to be reached, Drake began covering the Middle West with bulk plants and extending the tank-wagon delivery system in order to bring oil products within easy reach of everyone. He laid the foundation for one of the greatest marketing systems ever seen in this country.

In 1897 sixteen new bulk plants were built, in 1898 one hundred and eighty-seven, in 1899 twenty-seven, in 1900 eleven, and in 1901 forty-seven, or a total of 288 in five years.[38] What Drake and his sales organization did was a pioneering effort of tremendous magnitude. With the extension of the tank-wagon delivery system, grocers and other dealers were induced to buy storage tanks holding 250 to 500 gallons with pumps, which provided a more convenient and cleaner method for dispensing kerosene and gasoline.

The cost of erecting bulk stations varied.[39] In cities like Chicago or Kansas City, where more equipment was required, the expense amounted to $150,000 to $200,000. The company not only needed plenty of warehouse space but room for more horses and wagons, land was more expensive, and the buildings had to conform to stricter fire requirements. Other stations cost five to six thousand dollars; the smaller ones two thousand.

The policy of the company was to establish bulk plants so close together that its entire marketing area was covered. In general, the rule was to locate bulk plants about twelve miles apart, a distance that could be covered by team in a day's time.[40] At each bulk plant there was a four-hundred-barrel tank for kerosene and one for gasoline. The size, of course, varied a little according to the volume of business to be done. As in the case of a main station, a thirty to sixty day supply was kept on hand. Each bulk plant had a ware-

37. Company Encyclopedia: Marketing, I, Historical Statement, 5.
38. Company Encyclopedia: Marketing, I, Stations in Operation from 1896 to 1940.
39. *Transcript of Record, Petitioner's Testimony, United States of America, Petitioner, v. Standard Oil Company of New Jersey, Et Al., Defendants,* III, 1143.
40. *Ibid.,* 1142.

house for storing greases and lubricants, housing for tank wagons, and stables for the horses.

In the early days the storage tanks were located at about ground level, which made it difficult to unload a railway car and load tank wagons, for only a portion of the oil could be unloaded by gravity; the rest had to be pumped out by hand. Later, when storage tanks were elevated from the ground and a pumping system was installed, the tank wagons could be loaded by gravity.

It was natural when the tank-wagon delivery system was first established in any community for the local drayman to become the agent for Standard. He had the horses and the time between his duties as drayman to make tank-wagon deliveries. The company furnished the wagon, the agent the horses. Standard laid out the route and paid the agent a commission, except in the smaller communities, where the driver worked for about $60 a month.[41] In time, if business was good, he gave up draying and devoted full time to making tank-wagon deliveries. Some tank-wagon drivers made as much as eight or nine thousand dollars a year, depending upon their industry and initiative. They made so much money that about 1907 or 1908 the company began to hire its own drivers, pay them a salary, and carry on the tank wagon business itself, or else it reduced the amount of the commission.[42] Some tank-wagon drivers accepted a reduction in the commission or became salaried employees, but much of the incentive was lost. Other agents did neither; they resigned and became agents for a competitor. Such a policy on Standard's part helped to build up some of the most severe competition that it later encountered.

The first tank wagons were pretty crude affairs; they were coffin-shaped boxes lined with metal with faucets at the rear.[43] These were shipped to the field, loaded onto dray wagons, filled with kerosene and gasoline, and used to make deliveries. Within a short time a new type of tank wagon appeared, which was used for years. It became a most familiar sight on the streets of midwestern towns. Old-timers proudly speak of the beauty of these new wagons. The tank, with a capacity of 450 gallons, had compartments for gasoline and two grades of kerosene. The body was painted green with the company name in gold letters on the sides. The wheels and run-

41. Interview with Edward J. Bullock, July 20, 1948.
42. *Ibid.*
43. Company Encyclopedia: Marketing, I, Historical Statement, 5.

ning gear were red. No change took place in the character of this tank wagon until the coming of the motor tank truck.

Salesmen were assigned to supervise a certain number of bulk plants and stimulate sales within the jurisdiction of the main station. Often in the early days, where there was no bulk plant a salesman would take orders from farmers, grocers, hardware dealers, and others. He would then have a carload of fifty to sixty barrels of kerosene shipped to that point, store them in a barn or shed, and employ the local draymen to make the delivery. Salesmen also purchased all usable empty barrels in the various towns. Those in which a competitor's oil had been shipped were also purchased inasmuch as all barrels, when recoopered, were repainted.

Standard paid about $1.10 for first-class kerosene and gasoline barrels. Second-class barrels brought 10 to 20 cents less depending upon the schedule of deductions for broken staves, heads, and missing hoops. Barrels that had contained lubricating oil were only worth about 85 to 90 cents because they required more cleaning. Barrels that contained black oil were worth still less. Empty whiskey barrels, while very similar to petroleum barrels, were not purchased because the inside contained char which was detrimental to petroleum products. As the business expanded, the number of barrels in service increased and, at times, at such points as Kansas City or Fargo, there were as many as 10,000 empty wooden barrels piled tier upon tier. However, these piles could be quickly reduced when winter approached and more kerosene was used or when spring and summer approached and there was a greater demand for oil on the farms.

Exercising supreme authority over all company business within the area served by a main station was a manager. He had a multitude of duties to perform. At a time when the bulk plant and tank-wagon delivery system was being rapidly expanded, he spent a great deal of his time locating sites and securing from town and city councils ordinances which would give the company the right to locate a bulk plant in a community and guarantee that no change would be made in the conditions for at least twenty years. This was particularly difficult because of the prejudice against storing gasoline at the bulk plant.[44] Salesmanship and diplomacy were not enough. Usually a manager had to demonstrate to the city or town council the safety with which these local bulk plants

44. Interview with Allan Jackson, July 13, 1948; Company Encyclopedia: Marketing, I, Historical Statement, 7.

could be operated. Equipped with two two-gallon cans and a thimble, a manager would put a thimbleful of gasoline in one can, shake it, and then apply a match. A sizable explosion occurred. Then the manager would light a match to the second canful of gasoline. Much to the amazement of everyone, it did not explode; it simply burned slowly. Thus the manager demonstrated that full tanks of gasoline would not explode. By agreeing to keep Standard's tanks reasonably full, the manager usually succeeded in getting permission to store gasoline.

Another duty of the manager was to take inventory regularly of the storage. Allowances naturally had to be made for stock losses due to natural shrinkage, but there were sometimes instances where an employee was dishonest and attempted to make a personal gain. To avoid this as much as possible the manager insisted upon tank-wagon drivers' making out a delivery ticket at the time of delivery since tank-wagon deliveries were cash sales. Some agents did this religiously, others were often negligent and careless.

The manager also purchased horses, when needed, for the tank wagons in his area. An alert manager spent a considerable time with his salesmen on the road visiting dealers and keeping in touch with local conditions. Daily sales reports from the salesmen were made to him. Usually he scrutinized every voucher for expenses incurred before forwarding it to Chicago for payment. On the all-important matter of prices the Chicago office indicated what it thought the price should be and uniformity of prices was maintained, if possible, but the early managers had discretionary power to make variations up or down to meet price cuts and local competitive conditions.[45] Most all of these duties were performed by the manager personally but, as business expanded, he became by about 1911 more and more an office man and an advisor to the sales force in his field.

Sales efforts were largely devoted to selling kerosene—Perfection Oil. It was the chief product in the refining process and sold for about 7 cents per gallon. However, it was not easy to sell kerosene manufactured at Whiting. The first shipments brought loud complaints from far and wide because of the odor. Indignant customers insisted upon returning it. The finished kerosene, which had been produced by blending kerosene from the copper-oxide process and

45. Interview with Amos Ball, August 17, 1948.

the lead-oxide process, smelled good, but when put in storage it
went "sour." [46] When Moffett discovered this fact, the lead-oxide
process was discontinued in December, 1890, and only the copper-
oxide process was thereafter used. Even so, the kerosene was still
heavy and smelly. It did not burn well in lamps, stoves, heaters,
and lanterns. Competitors effectively advertised and sold "extra
choice Pennsylvania" kerosene, and people much preferred it, even
at a higher price, to the kerosene made from Lima oil.

In order to sell kerosene made at Whiting, the company waged
a real battle. Special emphasis was placed upon calling it "western
oil," and salesmen appealed to the people of the Middle West to
burn the oil of a home industry. To offset competition from Penn-
sylvania-made kerosene, Standard agents widely distributed two
small pamphlets, one called "Plain Facts—Ohio vs Pennsylvania
Oil" and the other "Points on Lamps," in which the "true" facts
were set forth for dealers and customers. Personal calls were made
on dealers, and form letters were sent out answering complaints
and urging the buying of Perfection Oil rather than Pennsylvania
kerosene.[47]

A more realistic approach to the problem involved a company
operation of great magnitude. Standard had lanterns, cookstoves,
lamps, and heaters especially manufactured to burn "western
oil." [48] It furnished the designs and specifications, and even loaned
the capital to various manufacturers to make them. Perfection
cookstoves and heaters in different sizes and models, glass-door
ovens, griddles, and other cooking utensils were manufactured by
the Cleveland Foundry Company of Cleveland, Ohio.[49] At the
same time, Standard had the Bradley-Hubbard Company of Meri-
den, Connecticut, make several different designs of Rayo kerosene
lamps and lanterns which would satisfactorily burn Perfection Oil.
In order to get the best results Standard also had a special type of
chimney and cotton wicks manufactured. All of these products
were the best that could be obtained.

46. William M. Burton to Giddens, November 7, 1949.
47. For samples of correspondence, see letters of Robert Gunton, Standard Manager
    at Evansville, Indiana, to C. P. Kluger, April 22, 1899, A. W. Brand, February
    17, 1900, A. F. Kline, January 31, 1900, and W. C. Fisher, April 3, 1901. Robert
    Gunton File.
48. Memorandum written by Allan Jackson to Giddens during the summer of 1948.
49. Memorandum written by R. F. McConnell, Vice-President in charge of Sales,
    to Giddens, August 23, 1948; C. H. Foulds, Vice-President, Perfection Stove
    Company, Cleveland, to Giddens, January 31, 1950.

Once everything was in readiness, these products were put on the market through regular Standard dealers. Scores of trained salesmen—men and women—were sent through the Middle West to introduce them and demonstrate the superiority of Perfection Oil.[50] They were sent especially to county fairs and country stores where they ran tests in such a manner as to make Lima oil burn as well as Pennsylvania kerosene.[51]

The sale of Perfection cookstoves and heaters and Rayo lamps and lanterns was a great success both from the point of view of the company and customers. They filled a real need in the agricultural sections where coal had to be imported, and there was no electricity or gas. They provided a source of heat and light for millions of people. For the manufacturers of these products it meant an enormous amount of business. For Standard the sale of stoves, heaters, lamps, and lanterns was only a means to an end. Since kerosene stoves, lamps, lanterns, and heaters were used the year round, their sale effectively increased the consumption of kerosene. These demonstrations in the field continued for many years, and Standard of Indiana continued to market lamps, lanterns, heaters, and stoves until about 1918.

Gasoline was a by-product for which there was little demand. One hundred and fifty gallons of gasoline was a good day's business for one of the largest bulk plants in Chicago, and it could be purchased for 4½ cents per gallon about 1890. Prior to about 1897 gasoline had either been dumped by refiners as a useless product or else sold in relatively small quantities for cleaning purposes and for the thinning of paints and varnishes. It was principally used for lighting stores. Some villages, towns, and cities used gasoline street lamps. In their outlying areas some larger cities used gasoline street lamps rather than incur the expense of extending the gas mains.

With more gasoline on hand than the company could sell, Drake started an intensive campaign about 1897 to sell gasoline cookstoves throughout the plains region which would, in turn, stimulate the sale of gasoline.[52] It took years of educational work, however, by Standard of Indiana to get gasoline cookstoves gener-

50. Interview with Amos Ball, August 17, 1948.
51. Interview with Edward J. Bullock, July 20, 1948.
52. Transcript of Record, Defendants' Testimony, United States of America, Petitioner, v. Standard Oil Company of New Jersey, Et Al., Defendants, XVII, 3524-3540.

ally accepted by the public, for the general opinion was that only a reckless fool would use a gasoline stove. The company purchased "Quick Meal" gasoline cookstoves from an outside manufacturer to market through its dealers, inaugurated an advertising campaign, and sent about two hundred agents through the Middle West to show people how to use them. The agents also urged the purchase of gasoline stationary engines for grain elevators and general farm use. Hundreds of thousands of dollars were spent by the company in this promotional work—and it was effective. With gasoline much cheaper than coal, the demand became very large in 1899, and the price rose to about 7 cents per gallon. On several occasions in subsequent years the demand almost outran the supply, and no further promotional efforts were made after about 1907.

While the main effort of the sales force was devoted to selling Perfection Oil and "Deodorized Stove Gasoline," the sale of lubricating oils, greases, paraffin, and candles was pressed to the limit.[53] They were of considerable importance in the growth of the company, for they brought good prices and were manufactured from fractions of crude which would have otherwise gone into fuel oil. Lubricating oils and greases ranked next in importance to kerosene and gasoline sales during the nineties. Since animal and vegetable oils were still being used for lubrication purposes when the company started in business, it sent a large force of experts throughout the Middle West to demonstrate the use of lubricants made from petroleum and stimulate sales among farmers and industrialists. Capitol Cylinder Oil sold for 34 cents per gallon, Eldorado Castor for 15½, Eldorado Engine Oil for 14½, and Amber Engine Oil for 10. Salesmen found competition even keener than in the case of kerosene, for Pennsylvania lubricants were widely distributed and advertised, and they were excellent products. However, Atlantic Red Engine Oil, Zone Paraffin Engine Oil, Capitol Cylinder Oil, Renown Engine Oil, Eldorado Engine Oil, and Harvester Oil, Standard's leading brands of machine oil, and Mica Axle Grease had large sales. On products like Continental Hoof Ointment and Boston Coach Oil, lubricants for special purposes, the volume was not large. When the regular brands of lubricants and greases did not meet the need of a particularly large con-

53. The figures for the volume and dollar sales from 1892 to 1918 by the Sales Department only were furnished by M. A. McNulty, Comptroller, Standard Oil Company (Indiana), on May 11, 1950.

sumer or competitive situations, Standard developed new oils according to specifications.

The volume of wax and paraffin sold was limited, but its use in canning, chewing gum, and candles brought good prices. The company did a large business in the sale of candles to Roman Catholic churches. Made from low-melting-point wax, Miner's Sunshine was sold in large quantities to mine operators for use in the lamps on the caps of miners. Linseed oil and turpentine were purchased, not manufactured, and distributed by Standard until about 1905 when the sale of these products was discontinued.[54] While Mineral Seal and Fortnite Longtime Burning Oil were sold, sales were not large because the Galena-Signal Oil Company specialized in railroad products.

From the beginning of operations at Whiting, it was necessary to find an outlet for the heavy fuel oil. While some was used under the stills in the refinery, there was at all times a surplus. The quantity sold varied from time to time, depending upon the price of coal and oil. Efforts were made to find large consumers and make long-term contracts which would justify consumers' installing the necessary oil-burning equipment. When preparations were being made for the World Columbian Exposition at Chicago, fair officials asked for bids in the spring of 1892 for 60,000 tons of coal or 180,000 barrels of fuel oil. Standard was the only company to bid on furnishing fuel oil; it bid $130,500.[55] The lowest bid to furnish coal was $142,800. Over the protest of the coal companies, the Exposition officials finally awarded the contract to Standard.

During the first decade of its history the company had nearly all of the petroleum product market to itself. It sold about 88 per cent of the business in kerosene and naphtha.[56] National Oil, Paragon, Scofield, Shurmer & Teagle, along with some smaller companies whose source of supply was in the East, were the chief competitors. Competition was fitfully growing, but it was by no means a threat to the young giant—Standard of Indiana.

Many factors accounted for the company's dominance of the market. It was the first and the only large refining and marketing company in the Middle West for many years. Strategically located, it had the advantage of being nearer to its customers than any other oil company, and freight costs were less. Through the rapid

54. Interview with Amos Ball, August 17, 1948.
55. *The Chicago Tribune,* March 20, 22, 24, 1948.
56. Company Encyclopedia: Marketing, I, Historical Statement, 10.

expansion of its bulk station and tank-wagon delivery system, the company was the first to put kerosene and other petroleum products within easy reach of the people in the Middle West. Its products were of a uniform quality. Last, but not the least, was the aggressiveness of the sales force under Drake's direction in getting the business. Salesmen and agents not only pushed sales but kept themselves fully informed as to the competitors' business in every community and reported to whom they sold and how much. Customers of competitors were then written or visited, and an effort was made to get them to buy Standard's products.

In some of the larger places, Standard set up subsidiary companies, cut the price, and drove out competitors. In 1900 there were about 300 retail wagons peddling oil from door to door in Chicago. To gain control of this business and keep dealers selling Standard products ignorant of the fact, Standard put about 60 retail wagons on the streets under the name "The Electric Light, Oil & Gasoline Delivery." [57] Later, it scratched this name from the wagons and sold without having any name on them. By 1910 all but about 60 of the 300 retail peddlers had been forced out of existence, and Standard was in control.

One of the most important instances of where Standard willfully destroyed a competitor, and probably the first instance of where Standard was convicted and had to pay damages for such depredations, arose in connection with the Crystal Oil Company of Des Moines, Iowa.[58] In 1893 Crystal began retailing kerosene from tank wagons in Des Moines. Within five years its business covered the entire city, requiring from five to eight wagons, and it sold from 2,000 to 2,500 gallons per month. Its only competitors were druggists and grocers who handled Standard products. In the fall of 1898 Crystal and Standard, which had supplied Crystal with all of its oil for five years, had difficulty over Crystal's demand for a ½ cent more margin. Failing to secure this, Crystal began buying some oil from the Paragon Refining Company which had opened a wholesale plant in Des Moines. Crystal was informed that it must buy all of its oil or none from Standard. Crystal's refusal led to a complete severance of business relations.

57. *National Petroleum News,* II, No. 2 (April, 1910), 7.
58. *National Petroleum News,* II, No. 4 (June, 1910), 3, 7; II, No. 5 (July, 1910), 32-33; IV, No. 9 (November, 1912), 15; XXVIII, No. 43 (October 21, 1936), 56. For the court decisions in *Dunshee v. Standard Oil Company, Et Al.,* see 126 N. W. 342-345, 132 N. W. 371-376, and 146 N. W. 830-836.

Standard, through Milton Storer, manager, John D. Stewart, city salesman, and Lee Edgington, in charge of the retail department, secretly employed seven drivers to act as dummies for Standard, supplied them with horses, tank wagons, kerosene, and entered the retail business in competition with Crystal. Every effort was made to conceal the fact that the wagons, horses, and oil were the property of Standard. Crystal had regularly established routes for its tank wagons and supplied its customers with green cards which were displayed in the window when oil was wanted. During the first month of its retail business, Standard's drivers canvassed the houses with the green cards, represented themselves as independents, offered to sell kerosene for 1 to 3 cents a gallon less than Crystal, and secured the business.

After several months of "war," Crystal was driven out of business. Crystal's property, worth about $17,000, was sold for $2,100 in 1899 to C. L. Nourse, who, in turn, turned the business over to Standard. The day after the sale the price of kerosene in Des Moines went up 3 to 5 cents a gallon. Standard continued retailing for a month or two thereafter, then abandoned the practice, and resumed its wholesale business.

In April, 1900, Frank S. Dunshee, an attorney, a stockholder, and an assignee of Crystal's claim for damages against Standard, filed suit against the Standard Oil Company of New Jersey, Storer, Stewart, and Edgington in the Polk County District Court, Des Moines, to recover $15,000 actual damages and $35,000 punitive damages, alleging that through unfair and unlawful competition Standard had destroyed Crystal's business. Dunshee's view, unique for the time, held that the courts must not look so much at the methods but at the intent of those methods as disclosed by the results. In support of this view there were few court decisions awarding damages to victims of unjust marketing practices. Standard of New Jersey filed a demurrer, which was sustained on March 14, 1901, but no judgment was entered nor was any further pleading filed. Dunshee continued to gather evidence on the legal question involved, and on July 24, 1907, he filed an amended petition. A motion to dismiss the petition was overruled and the case went to trial in 1908. Three of the leading law firms in Des Moines and Colonel Robert W. Stewart of Chicago represented Standard.

The trial lasted several days and resembled, in some respects, a comic opera. Near the end of the trial, Milton Storer, the last witness in the case, testified that he was an employee of Standard of

Indiana, not of Standard of New Jersey, and that the suit was against the latter, which did not do business in Iowa. Counsel for the New Jersey company then pleaded that he did not have authority to appear for Standard of Indiana. Dunshee moved the court to change the name of the defendant to Standard of Indiana, which the court allowed, and it ruled that all evidence in the case was against Standard of Indiana. Counsel for Standard of New Jersey protested violently against such a ruling inasmuch as Standard of Indiana did not have any counsel present.

While all this was taking place, a lawyer appeared in court with a telegram in his hand. He said that Standard of Indiana had heard it was involved in some kind of a dispute and wanted him to investigate. Although this lawyer had been in court a dozen times during the trial, he professed ignorance of the case and demanded a postponement. The court held that his actions were a mere pretense and that trial would continue without delay. The climax came when the eminent counsel for the New Jersey company, who had previously declared he could not represent Standard of Indiana, made the closing argument to the jury for the latter company.

The judge instructed the jurors that the display of a card by Crystal's customers was, in reality, an order upon it for oil and if the order was interfered with by Standard so that Crystal lost business, such interference was willfully and maliciously done, and it was an unlawful act. The jury found Standard of Indiana and its agents guilty, and that they had gone beyond the bounds of legitimate competition. Damages of $7,000 were awarded.

Standard of Indiana appealed to the Supreme Court of Iowa, but on May 16, 1910, the high court upheld the District Court's decision. In a rehearing the Supreme Court reversed the District Court and remanded the case for a new trial because the jury in awarding damages had failed to indicate how much was actual and exemplary, and the interest. Upon a retrial the jury found the company guilty but not its agents and assessed damages of $6,120 plus interest at 6 per cent for the past ten years. Standard appealed the decision assigning many errors, but the Iowa Supreme Court in the spring of 1914 sustained the trial court on all points and the long, hard-fought case finally came to an end.

Profits from Lima crude refined at Whiting during the 1890's were large.[59] For the first eight years, from 1892 to 1899, the net

59. Company Encyclopedia: Condensed Profit and Loss By Years, 1892–1921.

earnings of the company varied from a low of $605,781 in 1896
to a high of $4,195,751 in 1899, and there were deficits in 1893 and
1894.[60] Beginning in 1894, the company paid its first cash dividend
of $26.83 per share, and it has not missed paying at least one cash
dividend in any year since that time. Cash dividends between 1894
and 1899 fluctuated from $20 to $60 per share. Following a conservative policy, the company retained a very large percentage of
its net earnings in the business. The amount between 1892 and
1899 varied from 34.03 to 100 per cent; it was 56.33 per cent or
above in six of these years. There was a marked growth in assets
during the decade. The assets on January 1, 1890, amounted to
$1,271,654.62 with liabilities of $771,654.62, making a net worth
of $500,000.[61] By 1900 the assets amounted to $15,154,408.16 with
liabilities of $5,004,831.05, making the net worth $10,109,577.11.
Yet the company had a capitalization of only $1,000,000.

60. Statement of Net Earnings, Dividends, Etc., for the Years 1892 Through 1929.
    Furnished by Robert E. Wilson, Chairman, Standard Oil Company (Indiana),
    September 30, 1949.
61. Figures on the increase of assets are from the balance sheet of the company
    for 1890 and 1900.

CHAPTER III

A Decade of Expansion

ROCKEFELLER AND HIS ASSOCIATES WERE NEVER RECONCILED TO THE dissolution of the Standard Oil Trust in 1892. Their hold upon the organization proved to be too insecure. It depended upon the continued ownership of a majority of the stock in twenty companies, including Standard of Indiana, held by a very small group willing to act as a unit. Furthermore, the management arrangement did not fall into any recognized form of legal organization, and it might be subject to legal attack. By the beginning of 1899, therefore, Rockefeller and his associates had decided to alter the form of the loose organization.[1] The member companies could sell out to a single corporation or they could use a new business device known as the holding company. Standard officials studied and pondered the problem.

The holding company offered definite advantages over any other form of industrial organization. It was simpler and less expensive for one central corporation to acquire stock control in the other companies than to buy their property and fuse them. It could be done gradually without publicity and without arousing public antagonism. It required no action on the part of the stockholders of the companies involved, and it did not affect the position of the bondholders. Moreover, the outstanding stock of any controlled company could later be purchased gradually, if necessary. Therefore, in June, 1899, the charter of the Standard Oil Company of New Jersey was amended to make it a holding company. Its capital was increased from $10,000,000 to $110,000,000 with 1,000,000 shares of common stock and 100,000 of preferred stock. John D. Rockefeller was elected President of the new company and John D. Archbold Vice-President and the actual operating executive.

The Directors on June 19th authorized the officers to exchange Jersey stock for that of the twenty companies. This was done at the rate of one share of Jersey common stock for a designated frac-

1. Nevins, *John D. Rockefeller*, II, 353-356.

tional share in each of the other companies.[2] The fractional share in every case was the same as that to which the holder of a Trust certificate became entitled on the distribution of stock by the Trustees in 1892. The total amount of common stock of the Jersey company to be issued was 972,500 shares, an amount exactly equal to the number of Trust certificates outstanding in 1892. Under this arrangement one share of Jersey common stock was issued for 10,000/972,500 of a share in Standard of Indiana. The same method of exchange was followed in the case of the other nineteen companies. Through the exchange of stock the Jersey company acquired 9,971 and 182,500/972,500 shares of Standard of Indiana stock in 1899; by 1904 it held 9,990 and 892,500/972,500 shares.[3] When the reorganization had been completed, Standard of New Jersey was one of the richest and most powerful corporations in the world.

As a result of the reorganization, some important changes in the personnel of Standard of Indiana were made. "Uncle George" Stahl became both Secretary and Treasurer of the company. In 1901 James A. Moffett, the First Vice-President and operating head, was elected a Director of the Jersey company and left Chicago for New York, but he continued to hold his position with Standard of Indiana. Cowan, the Second Vice-President, was left in actual charge in Chicago. Moffett had not been in New York long before he sent for Drake, who became sales agent for refined oil for domestic trade for the parent company in 1902. P. C. Crenshaw, who had been assistant general manager, succeeded Drake as general manager of sales in Chicago. He was a hard worker, intelligent, progressive, able, affable, and well liked by the employees, except for some of the managers who resented his appointment because he was younger and less experienced. Brought in to assist Crenshaw as assistant general manager was Harry T. Snell, manager at South Bend. Dr. Burton was transferred from Whiting to Chicago late in 1903 to be general manager of manufacturing, leaving W. E. Warwick as superintendent and Beaumont Parks as assistant superintendent at Whiting. In 1904 the practice of having a first vice-president and a second vice-president was discontinued. Moffett became President and Cowan Vice-

2. *Transcript of Record, Petitioner's Testimony, United States of America, Petitioner, v. Standard Oil Company of New Jersey, Et Al., Defendants,* I, 83-84.
3. *Transcript of Record, Petitioner's Exhibits, United States of America, Petitioner, v. Standard Oil Company of New Jersey, Et Al., Defendants,* VII, 4, 52.

President. In the same year, H. S. Morton was transferred to the
Jersey company to be sales agent for lubricating products in the
West and B. T. Thompson succeeded him. E. J. Bullock was transferred from Milwaukee to become Thompson's assistant. These
were the major executive changes in the company between 1900
and 1911. Under the guidance of these leaders, Standard of Indiana made remarkable progress in the decade after 1900.

Between 1897 and 1912 there was not much change either in
the size or character of the Whiting refinery; the total amount of
new money invested in the plant during these years fell short of
a million dollars. However, it was the largest refinery west of the
Atlantic seaboard and one of the greatest refining and distributing
centers for oil in the world. The Bayonne refinery of the Jersey
company was the largest, the Philadelphia works of the Atlantic
Refining was second, and Whiting was third.[4] The amount of
crude run at Whiting each year after 1900 was usually more than
8,000,000 barrels but less than 9,000,000. The average daily runs
varied from 21,000 to 26,000 barrels.[5] In 1910 and 1911 the amount
of crude annually processed jumped to more than 10,000,000 barrels or a daily average of about 28,000.

To provide additional room for plant expansion at Whiting,
over $90,000 were invested in land, the principal acquisition being
a strip about a mile long and two or three blocks wide located in
the heart of the refinery area which the company had not originally
purchased.[6] Along the road that ran through this tract was the
little town of Oklahoma which had a population of about eight
hundred people. In order to secure this property the company
bought a tract of land in 1903 on the west edge of Whiting through
Charles Davidson, a Whiting real estate dealer.[7] It then offered to
give the various property owners in Oklahoma an equal amount
of land in the new tract, move them free of charge to their new
homes, and give them a good price for their old property. Some
readily accepted the proposition but a few resisted, so they were
left to sweat it out for a while. Among the last to agree was Harry

4. *Transcript of Record, Defendants' Exhibits, United States of America, Petitioner, v. Standard Oil Company of New Jersey, Et Al., Defendants*, XIX, 267.
For an excellent description of Whiting and the refinery, see *The Chicago
Tribune*, June 3, 1906.
5. A summary statement showing crude run and products yields for the Whiting
refinery from 1890 to 1912 furnished by Max G. Paulus, Vice-President in
charge of Manufacturing, Standard Oil Company (Indiana), January 13, 1950.
6. *The Chicago Tribune*, March 18, 1903.
7. Interview with William M. Burton, August 2. 1948.

Gordon, a saloonkeeper, who finally agreed to sell for $4,000. Dr. Burton and Davidson presented Gordon with a check for $4,000 and the papers to sign, but his wife refused because there was no cash. She did not know what a check was. Burton, therefore, sent Davidson to the bank where he got $4,000 in one-dollar bills. When Mrs. Gordon saw the cash, she signed.

Within the strip was an old cemetery, Whiting's first burial ground, owned by Henry Schrage. No interments had been made in the cemetery for several years. The company made a deal with Schrage to buy the land, but the corpses had to be removed to a cemetery in Hammond at company expense. The company's action aroused considerable indignation among the citizens because many of the early settlers had been buried here, but the threatened storm quickly subsided.[8] Schrage's records showed about seven hundred interments.[9] The company contracted with a local undertaker to move the dead at $3 per body, but when he came to do the work, the undertaker found over eleven hundred bodies.

In order to help make Whiting a better place in which to live, the company in January, 1900, deeded to the public school of Whiting a lot, 100 x 150 feet, for $1 and an adjoining lot of about the same size for $1,260 on which to erect a new schoolhouse.[10] When the schoolhouse was completed, it was named for Ambrose M. McGregor, who had been Chairman of the Manufacturing Committee for the Trust. Again, in 1904 or 1905 the company sold a tract of land and leased another to the city for school purposes. The following year the company gave a piece of land to the Public Library Board of Whiting on the condition that within two years from the date of conveyance a public library should be erected and maintained for all time to come.[11]

One of the most progressive steps taken by the company was the adoption in 1903 of a pension system for its employees. The plan was a noncontributory type, similar to those of the railroads. Effective January 1, 1903, the plan provided that any officer or employee who had given twenty-five years of continuous and satisfactory service to the company and had attained the age of sixty-five might be retired at the discretion of the Directors and receive

8. *The Chicago Tribune*, March 18, 19, 1903.
9. William M. Burton to Giddens, December 6, 1949.
10. Minutes of the Board of Directors' and Stockholders' Meetings, 1889–1912, 64, 124.
11. *Ibid.*, 123.

an allowance of 25 per cent of his or her average pay for the ten years preceding retirement.[12] Any officer or employee between the ages of sixty and sixty-four who had twenty years of continuous service might retire at his request, if the Directors approved, or be retired by the Directors and placed on the annuity roll with a pension equal to 50 per cent of his or her average earnings for the ten years preceding retirement; after the age of sixty-five the rate was reduced to 25 per cent. All annuities were to be paid quarterly and terminate upon the death of the annuitant. The Directors reserved the right at any time to abolish or modify the annuity system.

The action of the company in adopting a pension plan was a pioneer move among industrial concerns of the United States. There were only ten industrial firms in the United States prior to 1902 that had any pension system. Except for two, all of them were railroads. In 1903 ten other industrial firms inaugurated a pension plan. Three of them were oil companies—the Atlantic Refining Company, the Standard Oil Company of New York, and Standard of Indiana.[13] The latter was, therefore, one of the first twenty industrial concerns in the United States to have a pension plan, and it shares the honor with the Atlantic Refining and Standard of New York of being the first oil company to have a pension plan. The early adoption of such a plan proved to be an exceedingly important factor in the maintenance of stable labor relations in later years. The plan was liberalized in January, 1910, in two respects: The time of service was reduced from twenty-five to twenty years, and for the first year after retirement an annuity of 50 per cent of the average pay for the ten years preceding retirement was to be paid, then 25 per cent thereafter.[14]

In spite of the pension plan and a policy of paying wages as high as or a little higher than firms in the neighborhood, there were some labor disturbances. The most serious strike occurred in the summer and fall of 1906. Caulkers at Whiting had been receiving 35 cents an hour and riveters 33⅓ cents. They wanted an increase to 40 and 37½ cents respectively.[15] When the company denied the request, every member of the union went on strike early in July,

12. *Ibid.*, 90.
13. *Industrial Pensions in the United States*, 141-157.
14. Minutes of the Board of Directors' and Stockholders' Meetings, 1889-1912, 198-199.
15. *The Whiting Call*, July 7, 1906.

1906, and work came to a standstill in the boiler shop. The strike occurred at a moment when heavy repairs were needed on the tar stills but, in order to overcome the effects of the strike, the foreman of the tar stills devised a plan for bolting on patches with asbestos gaskets. The strike put a number of cheesebox stills out of operation, but the other stills were put on a faster schedule and refining operations were not seriously interrupted.

Early in September the stationary firemen asked for a "living wage." They had been receiving 22½ cents an hour and wanted 25 cents.[16] Officials at Whiting countered with the argument that nearby steel plants were only paying 15 cents. The company not only refused to meet the demand but discharged seven officers of the union who had presented the demand. The company was generally more intelligent in the handling of its labor problems than to discharge employees who seemed to be getting agitated. In this instance, however, officials misjudged the situation and made a tactical error. The men were really more dissatisfied than it was thought and discharging the leaders provoked a strike. At noon on September 20th about one hundred and fifty men walked out. With the firemen out, the refinery switched to burning oil in the boilers and stills. Officials, such as Burton, even took turns at firing

In the afternoon one hundred and fifty still cleaners also walked out. They were led by a "tough guy" who threatened to kill any man who worked.[17] Selecting one of the workers, plant officials took him into court where he swore that he was afraid of his life. The court ordered the "tough" to appear, and it put him under a peace bond of $500. Unable to post the bond, the "tough" was sent to jail. Others walked out in the sympathetic strike until over seven hundred men were idle. There were fears on the part of some of the strikers that they might be evicted from their company houses in order to make room for strikebreakers, but Dr. Burton denied that anyone would be asked to vacate unless the strike went on indefinitely. Almost every department in the plant was at a standstill because of the walkout or a lack of materials.

When strikebreakers were imported on the 24th, several hundred strikers besieged the plant.[18] To prohibit picketing and interference with the nonunion men going to work, the company immediately secured an injunction against the officers of the sta-

16. *The Chicago Tribune*, September 23, 1906.
17. William M. Burton to Giddens, December 25, 1949.
18. *The Chicago Tribune*, September 25, 1906.

tionary firemen's union, and thirty deputy sheriffs were sent to prevent further disorder. The next day Dr. Burton met with a committee of the union and agreed to reinstate the officers who had been discharged, recognize the union, and discuss their wage demand.[19] Upon the advice of union officers, the strikers voted to return to work. Left unsettled was the strike of the boilermakers who had been out since early in July. This strike did not end until early in November, when a 5 and 10 per cent raise in wages of all employees was made.[20]

Referring to the wage increases, the editor of the *Whiting Sun* asserted: "Whatever criticism may be offered the Standard by others, there will be none from the employees of the company, nor from the business men of Whiting, who have indirectly benefitted by the steady wages and liberal wages of the men." [21] Further comment upon the situation was made by Will Payne who, after visiting Whiting during the strike, wrote in *The Saturday Evening Post* that the company "has always, I believe, paid the fair going wage; sometimes, when the air appeared to be getting disturbed, it has paid a little over the going wage—always, you understand, just exactly as much as seemed necessary to get the best results. Thus, probably, it has had less trouble from labor unions than any other so large employer." [22] When the panic of 1907 hit the country in the spring and increased with severity during the summer and fall, it did not affect the workers at Whiting in any serious way. The company promptly met the regular payroll by paying in gold.[23] The psychological effect of such a move was beyond calculation in contributing to good labor relations.

The second notable advance in the period from 1900 to 1911 was the expansion of Standard's refining facilities through the building of two new refineries, one at Sugar Creek, Missouri, and the other at Wood River, Illinois. This was due to the rapidly increasing demand for petroleum products, the decline of the older oil fields in Pennsylvania, West Virginia, and Ohio toward the turn of the century, the opening of new and prolific sources of crude oil in Texas, Louisiana, Kansas, and Oklahoma, and a desire to get closer to the consumers of oil.

19. *Ibid.*, September 26, 1906; *The Whiting Call*, September 27, 1906.
20. *The Chicago Tribune*, November 10, 1906.
21. *Whiting Sun*, December 28, 1907.
22. Will Payne, "Cities Made to Order," *The Saturday Evening Post*, November 3, 1906, 3-4.
23. *Whiting Sun*, November 9, 1907.

Beginning about 1900 Kansas and Oklahoma were showing signs of becoming great producing areas. The first commercial crude oil production in Kansas was obtained in 1892 when W. A. Mills, a Pennsylvanian, drilled the Norman Well at Neodesha.[24] Other wells were drilled, but Mills was forced to suspend operations because of a lack of funds. J. M. Guffey and John H. Galey of Pittsburgh bought Mills' interest, secured more oil leases and, even though they had no immediate prospect for a market, drilling operations were widely and rapidly expanded. Unable to dispose of their oil, they sold their properties in 1895 to the Forest Oil Company, a producing subsidiary of Standard of New Jersey. Rising crude prices stimulated exploration, and drilling and oil field discoveries in southeastern Kansas in the next few years came in quick succession. In order to refine crude, the Standard Oil Company of Kansas, organized in 1892, constructed a small refinery at Neodesha in 1897 with a capacity of five hundred barrels a day, and for three years it was the only refinery in Kansas.

To own and operate producing properties and to buy, sell, and transport oil through pipelines, the Prairie Oil & Gas Company, a subsidiary of the Standard of New Jersey, was organized in December, 1900.[25] The short pipelines laid by the predecessors of Prairie were extended, and in 1903 a six-inch pipeline was laid to connect Neodesha with new pools at Chanute and Humboldt. This marked the beginning of a trunk pipeline system which was in time destined to become the largest in the country. Prairie purchased all oil offered by the producers, paid for it promptly, and the feelings toward Prairie were most cordial. Encouraged by Prairie and its need for crude, the hunt for oil in Kansas continued. Everyone went mad over oil stocks and leases. Soon there were over four hundred oil-producing companies. Kansas production increased from 930,000 barrels in 1903 to 4,251,000 in 1904. The supply far exceeded the facilities for transporting and refining.

To aggravate the situation of the Kansas producers, the first real oil boom in what is now Oklahoma began in 1901 with the

24. For oil developments in Kansas, see Carl Coke Rister, *Oil! Titan of the Southwest*, Chapter III; F. A. Parsons, "What, in Oil, Is the Matter with Kansas?" *National Petroleum News*, II, No. 10 (December, 1910), 3, II, No. 11 (January, 1911), 7; J. A. White, "The Story of Oil in Kansas," *Stanolind Record*, VI, No. 12 (October, 1925), 16-18.

25. J. L. Dwyer, "Prairie Aided Mid-Continent Growth," *The Oil and Gas Journal*, October 7, 1926, C-77.

drilling of a well in the Indian Territory at Red Fork.[26] A further impetus to developments in the Indian Territory came with the striking of the first flowing well near Bartlesville in 1903 and the opening of Cleveland in 1904. As a result, Oklahoma's production increased from 139,000 barrels in 1903 to 1,367,000 in 1904. To provide an outlet for this oil, Prairie built a pipeline from Red Fork to its storage farm at Humboldt and one from Cleveland which joined this line.

Prairie frantically built scores of storage tanks at Neodesha, Humboldt, Caney, and other places. The capacity of the little refinery at Neodesha was increased to 2,500 barrels a day, but this was not nearly enough to refine all of the oil offered for sale. By January, 1905, Prairie was storing over 25,000 barrels of crude per day, and within a short time it had over 8,000,000 barrels in storage. Until February, 1905, it purchased approximately all of the oil produced in Kansas. In the meantime, little refineries were constructed, and by the end of 1907 sixteen refineries were in operation in Kansas with a combined capacity of 6,650 barrels per day.[27]

Although oil developments in Kansas and Oklahoma were significant and important, they were dwarfed by those taking place in Texas. The drilling of the wild and unprecedented "Lucas" gusher at Spindletop on January 10, 1901, rocked the world. With oil spouting at the astounding rate of 75,000 barrels a day, the roar of this gusher could be heard around the world. In 1901 Texas produced 4,394,000 barrels of crude. By 1905 it was producing 28,136,000.[28]

As a result of the opening of Spindletop, hundreds of oil companies were organized to produce, refine, and market petroleum. Among those which grew and developed into major oil companies and powerful competitors of Standard of Indiana were Gulf and The Texas Company. With oceans of cheap oil available, Gulf and The Texas Company expanded their refineries at Port Arthur as rapidly as possible. Gulf soon had a refinery with a capacity almost as large as Standard's at Whiting. Although organized in 1889 in Ohio, the Sun Oil Company early came into the field at Spindletop, began to buy oil, send it to Port Arthur through the

26. Rister, *Oil! Titan of the Southwest*, Chapters II, VII.
27. Report of L. W. Keplinger, Commissioner of the Supreme Court, filed June 11, 1912. See *Eighteenth Biennial Report of the Attorney General of Kansas, 1911–12*, 80.
28. Rister, *Oil! Titan of the Southwest*, Chapter V.

pipelines of other companies, and ship it by tanker to Philadelphia.

As the executives of the Standard organization at 26 Broadway, New York, closely watched the declining production of the older fields and the sensational developments in the Southwest, they decided upon two courses of action. First, in order to provide refining facilities for Oklahoma and Kansas oil, they would build a new refinery near the Mid-Continent field and get closer to their consumers. Secondly, they would build a pipeline from the Mid-Continent field to supply Whiting, which depended solely upon the declining Lima field for its crude supply. Such a line would also connect with the National Transit line at Chicago and serve, if necessary, the parent company's eastern refineries.

Standard officials decided to locate the new refinery near Kansas City, Missouri. It was a metropolitan area fairly close to the new producing areas. It was a large and growing city. It was a great railroad center with many trunk lines spreading over a rich and populous agricultural area to the West and Southwest. By shipping oil to market from Kansas City rather than from Whiting, the company could reduce freight costs. Furthermore, the Missouri River afforded an abundance of water. Once the location had been selected, the planning, construction, and operation of the refinery were assigned to the Standard of Indiana.

In the fall of 1903 Cowan and Burton tramped the suburban hills around Kansas City in search of enough ground above flood level on which to erect a refinery.[29] They finally selected a site three miles north of Independence and about ten miles east of Kansas City where a break in the bluffs afforded a frontage of about 2,000 feet on the Missouri River. It stood well above the high-water mark of the big flood of 1903 and had possibilities for railroad connections with both the Santa Fe and the Kansas City Southern. Various tracts of the land were purchased through Brent & Crittenden, a Kansas City real estate firm, and deeded to the Fidelity Trust Company of Kansas City which, in turn, transferred them to Standard of Indiana. The original site consisted of a triangular piece of one hundred and twenty acres having high hills on two sides and the Santa Fe Railroad and the Missouri River on the other with a small stream, called Sugar Creek, run-

29. G. W. Thompson, "Pioneering at Sugar Creek," *Stanolind Record*, I, No. 3 (December, 1919), 19-20; Company Encyclopedia: Manufacturing—G. H. Moffett to O. E. Bransky, August 10, 1938; *Whiting Sun*, March 19, 1904.

ning in a haphazard way through it into the Missouri. A little over $30,000 was invested in land.

In March, 1904, J. E. Evans arrived from Whiting as superintendent in charge of construction. With him came others from Whiting—W. B. Jennings, Frank Gainer, W. A. King, W. P. Stenhouse, Robert C. Wetmore—all office men. C. A. Zimmerman, P. A. Scholl, James Burton, W. A. Eaton, and Thomas Duggan came as foremen for various construction gangs. Meanwhile, the shops at Whiting were turning out all kinds of materials for the Sugar Creek refinery, and carloads of iron and other materials were loaded and shipped daily.[30]

Construction began on a few level acres paralleling the Santa Fe tracks.[31] It seemed as if most of the buildings and stills were floated into place, for it rained for seventy-six days out of the first ninety. Despite rain and mud, the construction work progressed with astonishing speed and by fall the plant neared completion. G. H. Moffett came from Whiting to take charge as the operating superintendent. To supply the refinery with crude, Prairie Oil & Gas built an eight-inch pipeline from Humboldt to Sugar Creek. In October, 1904, thirty stills were put into operation. The cost of the plant, excluding the land, approximated $1,149,000. With the completion of the refinery, it began supplying, instead of Whiting, the trade in Kansas, Nebraska, western Missouri, Iowa, and parts of Oklahoma, Colorado, and Wyoming. By 1906 the refinery had a daily capacity of about 12,000 barrels, or 3,011,980 barrels per year.

In order to take care of the rapidly increasing production in the Mid-Continent field and insure an adequate supply of crude for Whiting and its eastern refineries, executives of the parent company decided in 1904 that Prairie should build an eight-inch pipeline from Kansas City to Griffith, Indiana, just south of Whiting, where it would connect with the pipeline running to the East.[32] Built at a cost of about $16,000,000, the line was completed in June, 1905, and oil was started on its way toward Whiting.

The extension of the pipeline had several important effects upon Whiting. As the production of Lima crude declined, the Kansas and Oklahoma wells insured the refinery of an adequate

30. *Whiting Sun*, May 14, 1904.
31. R. C. Harris, "Building a Refinery in the Hills," *Stanolind Record*, II, No. 5 (March, 1921), 19-21.
32. *Whiting Sun*, April 30, 1904, August 20, 1904; *The Chicago Tribune*, August 15, 1904, November 10, 1904, May 2°. 1905, June 27, 1905.

supply of crude. In the second place, crude oil from the Mid-Continent was sweet, not sour like Lima, so they stopped using Lima crude at Whiting about 1906 and discontinued the use of the old cheesebox stills and the copper-oxide process. The old cheesebox stills were either dismantled or converted to other purposes. Consumers were greatly prejudiced against kerosene and gasoline manufactured from Kansas and Oklahoma crude during the early days because of its low gravity. In order to convince consumers that specific gravity had nothing to do with the burning qualities or safety of the oil, Standard of Indiana sent experts into the sales field to make demonstrations and practical tests. As a result of these efforts and the growing demand for oil, the company gradually overcame consumer resistance. Thirdly, in the fall of 1906, a tower was placed on one of the crude stills at Whiting, and tests were made to determine the possibility of running Kansas crude down to coke. This proving successful, other tower crude stills were built at Whiting, and by 1909 forty-two had been completed.[33] These were a great improvement over any other stills in that several cuts, with improved fractionation, could be made at the same time. From start to 50° gravity was stove distillate, 50° to 40° first distillate, 40° to 34° gas oil, 34° to 27° paraffin distillate, 27° to 24° heavy paraffin distillate, 24° to 17° slop, and 17° to off, wax tailings.

Simultaneously with the rise of the Mid-Continent field, a new and large source of crude oil developed in southern Illinois near the Indiana line. Although oil had been produced in this area as early as 1889, intensive developments did not begin until 1904 with the discovery of oil in large quantities at Casey in Clark County. Drilling operations soon extended over many of the southeastern counties.[34] In 1906 Illinois produced 4,397,000 barrels and in 1907, 24,282,000 barrels. From 1907 to 1914 inclusive, Illinois ranked third among the crude-oil producing states. As in Kansas and Oklahoma, the large production in Illinois led to the organization of many oil companies. One of these, which grew and became a competitor of Standard of Indiana, was the Indian Refining Company. With its largest refinery located at Lawrenceville, Indian Refining rapidly extended its bulk plant system to Cairo, St. Paul, and New Orleans and supplied them by barge.

33. Company Encyclopedia: Manufacturing, History of the Whiting Plant, Light Oils, 3-4.
34. Ralph Arnold and William J. Kemnitzer, *Petroleum in the United States and Possessions*, 294.

Developments in Illinois led Standard officials in New York to study the advisability of establishing a refinery somewhere in the St. Louis area. Such a refinery could serve a highly concentrated industrialized area, also a great agricultural area, in which not only Standard of Indiana marketed but also the Standard of Kentucky, Waters-Pierce, and Republic Oil. A saving could be made on shipping refined oil to market, and coal from nearby mines could be secured cheaply.[35] There was an abundant supply of water, and excellent railroad transportation facilities were available. Oil might even be transported on river barges.

Early in the fall of 1906 three "strangers"—Dr. Burton, W. P. Cowan, and J. E. Evans—were seen walking over the peaceful Mississippi bottom lands below Alton, Illinois, where Lewis and Clark had camped the winter before they started on their famous journey. Little did the farmers know that these Standard officials were there to choose a refinery site.[36] Wood River Valley, located between the bluffs and the Mississippi River and through which Wood River flowed, seemed ideal for the purpose. Except for a few scattered farmhouses and some railroad tracks, the valley was empty. Four railroads and one electric line ran through Wood River Valley in a north and south direction about a half mile from the Mississippi. Though the soil produced fine crops, it was not very valuable land. Agents immediately began purchasing land on both sides of the railroad tracks at prices ranging from $200 to $500 an acre. The original investment in land ran better than $93,000. That purchased on the west side of the tracks gave the company a frontage of 5,700 feet on the Mississippi. A much larger tract on the east side of the tracks was purchased for the refinery site.

Construction started in April, 1907, under the direction of J. E. Evans, who had built the Sugar Creek refinery. R. B. Roach was chief engineer, W. P. Stenhouse was chief clerk assisted by F. J. Gainer; and W. A. Eaton was labor superintendent. A temporary bunkhouse was built, and a large camp established to house employees. Most of the employees, however, came from Alton to

35. William M. Burton to Giddens, December 6, 1949; Harry F. Glair, General Manager, Manufacturing Department, Standard Oil Company (Indiana), to Giddens, December 6, 1949.
36. On the early history of Wood River and the construction of the refinery, see "Brief Review of the Growth of Wood River Refinery," *Stanolind Record*, I, No. 1 (October, 1919), 30-31; Loyal D. Palmer, "History of Wood River Refinery," *Stanolind Record*, VI, No. 6 (April, 1925), 1-13; "Wood River Grew With Standard," *Standard Torch*, II, No. 1 (January, 1949), 3-4.

work and for a short time the company provided free transportation. The first time-book used by F. J. Gainer showed among other
names that of Harry F. Glair, a surveyor, later a Director of Standard of Indiana, with a salary of $65 a month. Common labor
worked ten hours for 17½ cents per hour. Foremen received 25
cents. Hiring was simple. "Pop" Eaton would come to the main
gate, point his finger at one of the men gathered there, and he
was hired. Firing was just as simple.

A country road passed through the refinery site. In order to
eliminate this, the company built a road around the north and
east sides of the tract. For many years the new road was the main
street in the village of Wood River. Right across the street from
the refinery site, A. E. Benbow owned a tract of land on which
a lawless frontier town with saloons and disorderly houses developed. Benbow City, as it was called, became one of the wickedest
and wettest cities in Illinois; at one time it had eighty-seven inhabitants and twenty-three saloons.[37] In spite of Standard's opposition, Benbow incorporated his town in 1908, built a city hall
and jail, and established a post office. From the beginning, Standard made repeated efforts to buy the land and clean out the town
but without success until 1916.

As the work on the refinery approached completion late in
1907, numerous employees were transferred from Whiting to assist in the operation of the plant. Originally a telegraph operator
for the New York Central Railroad at Whiting, E. M. Clark was
early employed by Standard as a shipping clerk. Within a short
time, he was promoted to other duties and proved so successful
that he was selected to be the manager at Wood River. S. A. Beach
was appointed superintendent. On January 7, 1908, the first stills
were charged with Illinois crude. They created so much curiosity
among many of the workmen, who had never seen a still in operation, that they gathered around the stills at noon or when off duty
to see how kerosene was made. When completed, the refinery,
excluding the land, represented an investment of about $2,500,000,
and it had a capacity of about 6,000 barrels per day.

The expansion of Standard's manufacturing facilities was a direct
result of a tremendous increase in its marketing activities in the
Middle West. The Sales Department's volume of sales increased
from 21,356,062 pounds in 1897 to 203,003,822 in 1911 and the

37. *The Chicago Tribune*, November 28, 1916; "Lawless Benbow City Spelled
    Trouble," *Standard Torch*, II, No. 1 (January, 1949), 8.

dollar value from $11,166,494 to $36,539,245.49.[38] The extension of the company's marketing territory and the steady increase in the number of bulk plants built, which brought the company closer to consumers, was one of the factors responsible for this amazing growth.

Between 1900 and 1906 the number of bulk plants of Standard of Indiana increased from 722 to 1,059, which was nearly a third of all the 3,573 Standard bulk stations throughout the country.[39] The company was marketing in 13,693 towns and cities, and it was doing one-third of the total merchandising business of all Standard Oil companies. It eclipsed all other Standard Oil companies in the distribution of oil through bulk stations and the tank-wagon delivery system.

In 1906 the marketing territory of Standard of Indiana was considerably enlarged through the purchase of some of the marketing properties of the Standard of Kentucky in southern Indiana and Illinois. Two months later it acquired the marketing properties of the Republic Oil Company of New York in Illinois, Iowa, Michigan, Indiana, Nebraska, and at Sedalia and St. Joseph, Missouri. In June, owing to an antimonopoly campaign which developed in Nebraska, the Standard of Nebraska was quickly organized and all of the marketing facilities of Standard of Indiana in that state were transferred to the Nebraska company. The net result of these transactions plus the construction program of Standard of Indiana was to increase the number of bulk stations in 1907 to 1,115. Between 1907 and 1912, 292 new bulk plants were built, bringing the total to 1,407.

The company's revolutionary move in extending the tank-wagon delivery system to the farmers of the Upper Mississippi Valley was another factor responsible for the enormous increase in business. It had pioneered in establishing tank-wagon deliveries for dealers in the Middle West. The extension of tank-wagon deliveries to farmers was another step in the evolution of its marketing system, which was designed to increase the volume of business, get nearer customers, and keep the price of oil low. No exact date can be set for the inauguration of tank-wagon deliveries to

38. Figures for the Sales Department only. Furnished by M. A. McNulty, Comptroller, Standard Oil Company (Indiana), on May 11, 1950.
39. Company Encyclopedia: Marketing, I, Stations in Operation from 1896 to 1940; *Transcript of Record, Defendants' Exhibits, United States of America, Petitioner, v. Standard Oil Company of New Jersey, Et Al., Defendants,* Defendants' Exhibit No. 264.

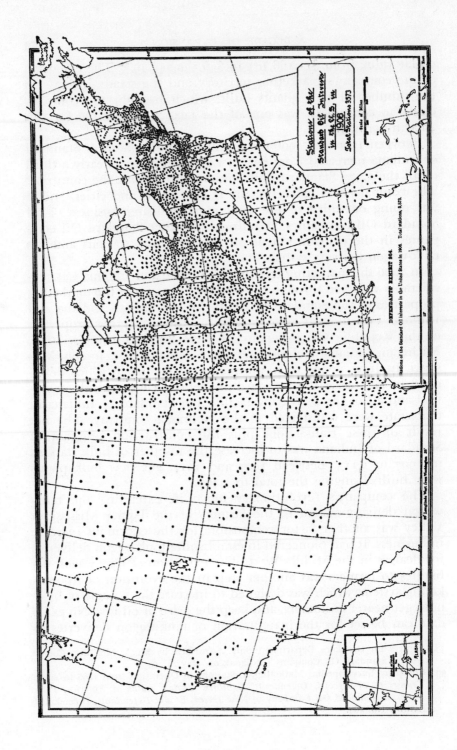

Stations of the
Standard Oil Industry
in the U. S. in
1906
Total Stations 3573

Scale of Miles

DEFENDANTS' EXHIBIT 264

Stations of the Standard Oil interests in the United States in 1906. Total stations 3,573.

Longitude West from Greenwich

Longitude West from Washington

ALASKA

farmers. It developed in different ways and at different times in various parts of the marketing territory and apparently without any formal action by the Board of Directors. Some deliveries were made in the nineties where the roads were good and large farm customers lived fairly close to bulk plants. Generally speaking, however, the inauguration of rural tank-wagon deliveries did not begin until sometime between 1905 and 1910.[40]

The origin and development of tank-wagon deliveries to farmers can be illustrated by what happened in the Mankato Division in Minnesota. One day about 1910 Allan Jackson, manager at Mankato, was in a store at Hanska when a farmer came in with an empty five-gallon can to get kerosene.[41] The dealer filled the can and charged the farmer 15 cents a gallon. Surprised at the price, the farmer asked why it was so much more than previously. The dealer said: "Well, John D. has given another million to the University of Chicago." The dealer was paying 7 or 8 cents a gallon, making 100 per cent profit, and blaming Standard for high prices. Aroused and indignant, Jackson pondered the situation and wondered why the company did not deliver oil directly to farmers and eliminate the middlemen. As an experiment, Jackson sent one of his tank-wagon drivers from Medalia to Hanska by one route, then had him return via another route, calling on the farmers along the way. On the next trip the tank-wagon driver went still another route selling oil to farmers at the dealer's price where fifty gallons or more were purchased. The plan worked so successfully that Jackson developed a systematic plan of delivery to farmers in each township of that area.

Upon learning of these activities by Jackson and by a few other managers who had been doing the same thing, the General Office urged other managers to adopt the practice, for it was quickly recognized that here was a rich and undeveloped market. The extension of the system, however, depended to a large extent upon the development of good roads and, in many parts of the Middle West, it was not until after 1915 that farm deliveries on a large scale were possible. In time, however, the whole marketing territory was completely covered with a network of rural tank-wagon routes. Since it was a long time before competitors followed the

40. Company Encyclopedia: Marketing, I, Historical Statement, 5-9; Methods of Distribution—By Tank Wagon to Farmers, 57-58.
41. Interview with Allan Jackson, July 13, 1948.

practice, it gave Standard of Indiana an initial advantage in one of the greatest potential markets of the world.

Apart from the rural free delivery of mail by the government, there has been no more impressive example of free delivery service than the company's inauguration of tank-wagon deliveries to farmers. Today there is scarcely a farmer in the Middle West who is not on a regular or occasional route of some Standard tank-wagon driver. No farm customer is too remote from a bulk station to receive this free service.

In the early days a tank-wagon driver left home at 5 A.M., fed and harnessed the team at the company bulk plant, hitched onto the tank wagon, and started out over the dirt roads calling on farmers and making deliveries of Red Crown gasoline, Perfection Oil, Mica Axle Grease, Capitol Cylinder Oil, and other petroleum products. No day was too cold or hot or wet to interfere with the delivery of oil. As long as the roads were open and horses could pull, tank-wagon drivers delivered the oil. In inclement weather four, six, or eight horses were hitched to the wagon. At night a driver might find himself miles from home and his horses exhausted. If so, he would lodge overnight with some farmer and continue along his route the next day. Sometimes he was away from home for several days. For over a half century, people in the Middle West have been passing on to posterity stories of how Standard tank-wagon drivers, traveling through rain, sand, mud, and blizzards, met some emergency and delivered the oil.

The popularity of the tank-wagon driver was enhanced by the fact that he brought to the isolated farmers the latest news from town, market reports, and bits of information picked up along the route. Frequently, he was called upon to aid the farmer's wife in killing a chicken or to tighten the sewing machine belt or to change an automobile tire. Hours of labor never seemed to matter much to tank-wagon drivers. There were no definite working hours or overtime pay. There was a certain amount of work to do. Everyone worked until it was done. Upon the tireless efforts of this vast army of men, the reputation of Standard for courteous, prompt, efficient, and dependable service was built and firmly established in the Middle West.

When Standard began selling direct to farmers at the same price as to dealers, it created considerable lasting animosity on the part of dealers toward Standard. The company lost many good dealer accounts to competitors who were not selling direct to consumers.

GEORGE THOMPSON DRAMATIZES HIS RECOLLECTION OF STANDARD AND
THE PANIC OF 1907

SUGAR CREEK REFINERY IN THE EARLY DAYS

CONSTRUCTION CREW FROM THE WHITING REFINERY UNDER WHOSE
DIRECTION THE SUGAR CREEK REFINERY WAS BUILT

STANDARD'S FIRST FILLING STATION ERECTED IN MINNEAPOLIS
AT 10TH STREET AND HARMON PLACE IN 1910 OR 1911

STANDARD FILLING STATION IN PITTSBURG, KANSAS, IN 1911 OR 1912

STANDARD FILLING STATION, CARRINGTON, NORTH DAKOTA, 1916

STANDARD FILLING STATION, 2ND AVENUE, MINNEAPOLIS

In any event, the volume gained by selling direct to farmers more than offset the losses and, in time, dealers were forced to recognize the soundness of the company position in giving farmers discounts on quantity purchases. As important as the farm trade was in the growth of the company, it is amazing to note in passing that no accounting records for the different classes of trade were separately kept until 1936, and the company never knew the amount of oil products purchased by farmers or any other class of the trade.

A third factor playing a major role in the expansion of the company's business was the development of the internal combustion engine and its application to automobiles and tractors. In 1879 George B. Selden of Rochester, New York, applied for a patent for a gasoline motor like that used as a stationary engine, to drive a road vehicle. It was not until 1892, however, that the first "horse-less carriage," designed and made by Charles F. Duryea of Chicopee, Massachusetts, appeared in the United States.[42] It was such a curiosity that Barnum & Bailey featured it in their circus. Henry Ford, a Detroit mechanic, who was soon destined to provide the country with cheap automobile transportation, completed his first car in 1893. Elwood Haynes, R. E. Olds, Alexander Winton, and Charles P. King followed closely in developing "gasoline buggies." By September, 1895, the Patent Office was deluged with over five hundred patents for automobiles and parts. No less than three hundred types of cars were contemplated.[43]

No gasoline-propelled automobiles were made for sale in the United States until about 1896 although steam and electric cars were already on the market. At the end of the nineteenth century, it was a question as to whether steam, electric, or gasoline-propelled automobiles would become the most important. The gasoline-powered automobile required a fuel that evaporated at a comparatively low temperature, had a high heat value, burned without leaving any objectionable residues, did not possess any objectionable odor, was low-priced, and could be produced in large quantities. Benzol, toluol, and alcohol were fairly well suited, but their cost and limited availability rendered them largely unsatisfactory. With plenty of gasoline available and selling for about 7 cents a gallon, the "gasoline buggy" soon completely eclipsed steam and electric cars.

Once the gasoline motorcar was launched, it had a phenomenal

42. David L. Cohn, *Combustion on Wheels*, Chapter II.
43. *Ibid.*, 28.

growth. The total number of automobiles registered jumped from four in 1895 to 8,000 in 1900. More cars were made every succeeding year, and there was a corresponding increase in sales. In 1903 the Ford Motor Company was incorporated. Six years later Henry Ford standardized his Model T and announced: "I will make a motor car for the multitude." Nearly 19,000 Fords were sold the first year and, as the number increased, the price was reduced. By 1910 the total number of cars registered in the country exceeded 450,000. In 1913 there were 1,260,000, an increase of more than one hundred and fifty times the number in 1900.

When the first automobiles came into use there were no agencies for servicing them. General merchants and hardware dealers had been the chief outlets for petroleum products, and they were naturally the first to provide automobile owners with gasoline, greases, and lubricating oils. To fill an automobile tank with gasoline, the merchant or hardware dealer took a gallon or five-gallon can to a small shed back of his store, filled it from a barrel, carried it the full length of the store to the street, and poured the gasoline into the customer's car through a chamois-lined funnel in order to catch the water. This was a cumbersome method, and many automobile owners bought a tin tank of their own so they could store gasoline in or near a shed or barn where their car was stored. Standard, on an order from the dealer, filled these tanks and the dealer billed the customer. This was a current practice from about 1909 until 1911 when the company began to sell direct to automobile customers, but it was careful not to admit to the dealer any change in policy. This dual arrangement continued until about 1914.[44]

As the automobile owner had occasion to frequent machine shops for repairs more often than the hardware store, the alert machine-shop owner saw an opportunity to make additional profit by selling gasoline. He provided air and water and installed a hand pump on the edge of the sidewalk in front of his shop so that automobile gasoline tanks could be conveniently filled. Grocers and hardware dealers also put in curb pumps. Lubrication service was unknown. A car owner gave the grease cups a turn or two every fifty or hundred miles and squirted a few drops of oil on various moving parts.

The margin of profit obtained by many dealers on early gasoline sales was large, for in many localities there was no competition.

44. Memorandum written by Allan Jackson to Giddens during the summer of 1948.

They figured that if a man was financially able to own a car, he could afford to pay a good price for gasoline. In some instances, therefore, prices were all out of reason. Efforts were made by different Standard managers to get dealers to reduce their prices with some success, but there were always those who resisted.[45]

Some automobile owners drove to Standard's bulk plant, if there was one in town, at a time when they knew the agent would be there and, either for the account of the dealer or by direct purchase, they were supplied as an accommodation. They usually purchased five or ten gallons of gasoline, which was a nuisance because it interfered with the ordinary routine of the agent.

As more and more car owners drove to Standard bulk plants for their gasoline, they insisted that inasmuch as they had saved Standard the cost of delivery from the tank wagon to the dealer, they should be able to buy as cheaply as the dealer. Since sales to individual dealers were not large, there was some merit to the appeal. Where it seemed advisable, managers permitted certain important customers to buy at the wholesale price. Gradually, it became more or less of a general policy.

To avoid interfering with the work of the agents at bulk plants and to provide better service for the auto owner, Standard, where business warranted it, rented a small store building in town where lubricants could be stored and a gasoline pump could be installed on the edge of the sidewalk. The first store of this kind was opened at Rockford, Illinois, about 1914.[46] So accustomed was the automobile owner by this time to getting his gasoline at the dealer's price that the price established for the delivery of gasoline from the store was the same. Thus the first step was taken in eliminating the middlemen and selling direct to consumers as in the case of tank-wagon deliveries to the agricultural trade. Automobile owners swarmed to the store, and it was not uncommon to see a line of automobiles two or three blocks long waiting to get gasoline.

The increase in the number of automobiles created a demand for better service and led to the establishment of service stations. Just where and when the first service station was started and who started it is difficult to state because it depends upon the definition of a service station. In 1910 or 1911 Standard of Indiana moved an old galvanized-iron pump house from its 8th Ward bulk plant

45. *Ibid.*
46. *Ibid.*

in Minneapolis to 10th Street and Harmon Place in an alley and opened its first filling station. Automobiles would drive into the alley, and attendants would bring out the gasoline in buckets and fill the tanks. Late in 1911 or early in 1912 Standard erected a small collapsible metal building on West Third Street in Pittsburg, Kansas, and installed a rotary pump. When an automobile stopped at the curb, the gasoline was pumped into a one- or five-gallon bucket and poured into the car with the use of a funnel.[47]

The idea of a service station, where a motorist might drive in and have his gasoline tank conveniently filled, seems to have originated about 1907 with several companies. The Standard Oil Company of California claims that it established the world's first service station in the country at Seattle, Washington, in 1907.[48] In the same year the Automobile Gasoline Company opened a drive-in station in St. Louis, and the Oriental Oil Company opened a filling station in Dallas, Texas.[49] Later, in 1911, Oriental opened a drive-in station. Standard of Ohio claims it erected the first drive-in station in Columbus, Ohio, in 1910.[50] Gulf lays claim to the opening of the world's first drive-in service station at Pittsburgh in 1913.[51]

Simultaneously with the evolution of the automobile, there was an increasing use of gasoline engines for boats, at grain elevators, and especially on the farms to pump water, run washing machines, churns, cider presses, and hay balers, and to saw wood. Both the McCormick and Deering companies placed motor-driven mowing machines on exhibition in 1900. Built in 1889, a Burger tractor, with the engine mounted on the chassis of a steam engine, operated in 1890 in South Dakota.[52] The J. I. Case Company built its first tractor in 1892, but it did no further work on gasoline tractors until 1910. A group of farmers living near Sterling, Kansas, brought out the Sterling tractor in 1893, but no sales were

47. For data on the Minneapolis station, see H. G. Moshier to Conger Reynolds, September 5, 1952, and Robert Siebert to Giddens, December 2, 1952; for data on the Pittburgh station, see H. F. Fikes to J. W. Wilson, February 13, 1939; F. W. Brinkerhoff to Giddens, February 13, 1951; H. E. Purdy to Conger Reynolds, October 10, 1952.
48. *The Oil and Gas Journal*, July 12, 1947, 37.
49. *National Petroleum News*, September 18, 1929, 40; March 4, 1936, 70.
50. *Ibid.*, December 25, 1929.
51. *The Pittsburgh Press*, April 9, 1951.
52. On tractor history, see "Farm Power and the Post-War Tractor," an address by L. B. Sperry, Manager of Engineering, Farm Tractor Division, International Harvester Company, before the Chicago Section of the Society of Automotive Engineers, February 8, 1944.

made. Otto built a tractor, as well as an automobile, in 1894, and fourteen of these were sold by 1896. In 1899 S. S. Morton and the Ohio Manufacturing Company entered the tractor field. Hart-Parr, the real founders of successful gasoline tractors, came into the field in 1901 with their first tractor. In 1903 they built fifteen. Experimental work on gasoline tractors was started in 1905 by the International Harvester Company and in the same year it and the Ohio Manufacturing Company began to build tractors. Many companies were manufacturing tractors after 1905, but even so, in 1910 only four thousand tractors were manufactured in the United States. However, the possibilities of tractors for farm use were beginning to be appreciated.

The growing use of gasoline engines and automobiles had a revolutionary effect not only upon marketing methods but upon the character of the oil products manufactured and sold. Although the sale of kerosene by Standard of Indiana steadily increased from 74,713,492 gallons in 1897 to 138,555,173 in 1911, the growth in gasoline sales was astounding.[53] They increased from 31,510,633 gallons to 156,936,096—more than five times that of 1897. In 1910 the manufacture and sale of gasoline surpassed kerosene for the first time, indicating that the "Gasoline Age" had arrived. The development of the internal-combustion engine and its adaptation to many purposes had made gasoline the dominant factor in the petroleum industry.

Sales of lubricating oil jumped from 7,445,258 gallons in 1899 to 34,431,593 in 1911. To meet the requirements of the automobile, Standard began to manufacture at Whiting in 1908 a special brand of motor oil, which would withstand the heat developed by motors and not solidify but remain fluid though quite viscous in winter weather as low as zero, whereas other oils had only a 25° to 30°F. cold test.[54] Within a short time, Polarine, as it was called, became the most widely known motor oil and was used all over the Middle West. It sold by the barrel at 51¼ cents per gallon. Five gallons cost 54¼ cents per gallon.

Road oil and asphalt for use in road building became increasingly important.[55] In driving over the dirt streets of villages, towns,

53. Figures for the Sales Department only. Furnished by M. A. McNulty, Comptroller, Standard Oil Company (Indiana), on May 11, 1950.
54. Company Encyclopedia: Manufacturing—Motor Oils and Aviation Engine Oils, 1-2.
55. *The Oil and Gas Journal*, X, No. 10 (August 17, 1911), 10, X, No. 29 (December 28, 1911), 1.

and cities of the United States, motorists stirred up great clouds of dust. It was most annoying to storekeepers and housewives. To lay the dust, road oil was sprinkled on the streets of some towns in California about 1907, and it was most effective. Standard of Indiana quickly began to experiment and developed a road oil at Whiting, which was put on the market in 1909.[56] Generally speaking, engineers did not become interested in the scientific use of road oil until about 1912. When they did, they found that by first properly draining, smoothing, and shaping the road, road oil would not only keep down the dust but bind the road, giving it a waterproof surface and protection from rapid wear. Sales of road oil and other asphaltic products continued to increase until Standard of Indiana became the largest marketer of asphalt in the world.

In shipping more gasoline, wooden barrels would not stand up well under the stress of being loaded and unloaded, so about 1905 the company started making and using a barrel of sheet steel for shipping products to bulk stations.[57] Since these rusted and leaked, the substitution of galvanized sheets proved more satisfactory.[58] About 1900 the Pressed Steel Tank Company of Milwaukee patented and began making a pressed-steel barrel which could stand heavy usage.[59] It was practically indestructible through usage, and it became very popular. Adopted by the company, the pressed-steel barrel was used at first for shipping naphtha and gasoline and later for refined and lubricating oil.

It was not long before railroad safety regulations required the use of steel barrels for all shipments of gasoline, which resulted in a greater demand than the manufacturers of the patented barrel could supply. Consequently, all agents and salesmen of Standard expedited as much as possible the emptying and returning of these barrels for refilling. At one time, every salesman made a note on his daily sales report of the number of wooden barrels purchased and the number of steel barrels returned. Each steel barrel was serially numbered and stamped "Property of the Standard Oil Company." With thousands of barrels, costing $7 or $8 each, scattered through many states, some centralized control was necessary.

56. Arthur Shearer, "Introducing the Bulkiest Department of the Company," *Stanolind Record*, XI, No. 3 (January, 1930), 1-6.
57. Company Encyclopedia: Manufacturing—History of Whiting Plant, Barreling Department; Marketing, I, Methods of Distribution, Distribution in Barrels, 42-44.
58. William M. Burton to Giddens, December 18, 1949.
59. Memorandum written by Allan Jackson to Giddens during the summer of 1948.

For many years F. M. Bradshaw, head of the Barrel Department at 5 S. Wabash Avenue, Chicago, had an ingenious but simple and efficient system whereby his office knew the location at all times of every numbered steel barrel.[60] Through a follow-up system, barrels were not allowed to linger long in one place. They were kept moving in order to make as many round trips as possible in the course of a year. Stamping the company name on each barrel and the numbering of each one kept them out of the hands of competitors who were not financially able to invest in a stock of steel barrels or who could not get immediate delivery.

As steel barrels came into more general use, Standard abandoned about 1915 its policy of retaining the ownership of the barrels and sold them to customers or made an allowance for their return. However, wooden barrels continued in use for many years because steel barrels were costly, and consumers were unwilling to pay a deposit of $10. As new bulk stations were built so that Standard could deliver by tank wagon to almost every foot of its marketing territory, the use of barrels gradually declined, but many thousands of them continued to be used and the investment therein constituted no small item.

Standard of Indiana continued to have between 1900 and 1911 about 88 per cent of the gasoline and kerosene business in its territory. In explaining this situation W. N. Davis of the Keystone Oil Company of Kansas City. a competitor of Standard, pointed out, "The facilities of the Standard Oil Company are such that few independents could raise the money to successfully compete against them. In all towns from 1,500 inhabitants up they have got tank stations established, and they furnish oil in bulk while the independents would be forced to ship in barrels. Another advantage is by shipping in tank cars they save about 30 per cent on freight rates. Then their system of dealing in tank wagons is such that the trade do not want to buy in barrels when they can possibly buy in bulk, and in order to compete with Standard it would require vast sums of money. And, further, to compete successfully you could not localize yourself. You would have to spread over the same territory, and do business in the same manner, and it is a well known fact that no combination of independents could raise that amount of capital. Lubricating oil is handled differently—it is handled in packages, and is sold directly to the consumer." [61]

60. *Ibid.*
61. 116 S. W. 927.

Despite Standard's advantages, the competitive situation was beginning to change. Kansas and Oklahoma refiners, with a flood of oil to market at almost any price, were becoming serious competitors in the Middle West. Setting up an iron-barrel station— just a shack or an old building—in a town, a jobber of Kansas or Oklahoma oil would start distributing and cutting prices. Even though consumers were not satisfied with these competitive products because of the irregularity of supply and their poor quality, the activities of these jobbers, according to Amos Ball, formerly Vice-President in charge of Sales for Standard, "scared the daylights out of us," and a battle began to hold the market.[62] More salesmen were added to solicit business and salesmen's meetings were held in the field where every phase of the business was discussed. To meet a local competitor's cut price, Standard's agent, after consultation with the manager, would match the price or go below. Unable to compete with the quality of Standard's products, its service or efficient operation, and without adequate financial resources, a competitor could not hold out very long and many were inevitably eliminated.

Standard's practice of lowering prices in one locality but not in others, in order to eliminate a competitor, gave rise to a demand by competitive oil companies and jobbers in the early years of the twentieth century for the passage of what were known as antidiscrimination laws. Iowa was among the earliest to pass such legislation about 1904; Kansas followed in 1905, and Nebraska and Minnesota in 1907. By 1909 thirteen states, all of them in the Upper Mississippi Valley, had some kind of an antidiscrimination law.[63] These laws required a company to maintain uniform prices throughout a state, making due allowance for differences, if any, in grade, quality, and freight charges to different points. In the debate over the passage of these laws, considerable doubt had been expressed about their constitutionality. When the Supreme Court of Nebraska in 1908 upheld the Nebraska law, many oilmen were jubilant, for it was the first time such a suit had been brought and the law upheld in every particular. It was with confidence, therefore, that over one thousand refiners and jobbers, members of the Independent Petroleum Marketers Association and the National Petroleum Association, joined together late in 1909 to launch a

62. Interview with Amos Ball, August 17, 1948.
63. *National Petroleum News*, I, No. 1 (February, 1909), 10. The Minnesota law was upheld by the State Supreme Court on May 20, 1910. See 126 N. W. 528.

nationwide campaign for antidiscrimination laws in all states.[64]

As a result of the enactment of such laws, Standard managers no longer had the flexibility they formerly had in adjusting prices to meet local competition. Except to meet local competition, they could not lower the price in one place without lowering it over the entire state. If there was a difference in price between various localities in a state, managers had to be exceedingly careful and make sure that they could justify the price. Standard was a large organization and its operations could be easily watched by law enforcement officials. On the other hand, competitors were small and numerous. Many were local companies that operated in only one or two places; hence the law did not affect them. Some of the larger competitors had no scruples in violating the law and cutting prices locally; it was more difficult and less popular for law enforcement officials to watch them as closely as a large outfit like Standard. Consequently, the law and its biased enforcement penalized Standard and favored the growth and development of competitors.

Since Standard had the bulk of the kerosene and gasoline business, there was little or no need for it to advertise. However, it was probably the growth of competition that led the company to make its first advertising expenditures in 1905. The amounts annually spent from 1905 to 1910 were small, varying from approximately $13,000 to $28,000. In 1910 advertising expenditures amounted to $162,640.05 and in 1911 to $210,078.25.[65]

The tremendous expansion of Standard's business and its general prosperity from 1900 through 1911 was reflected in large earnings. Net earnings mounted steadily each year, jumping from $4,981,571 in 1900 to $10,715,712, the highest, in 1910.[66] Net earnings per share ranged from a low of $498.21 to a high of $1,071.68 in 1910. The percentage of net earnings retained in the business varied between a low of 1.63 per cent and a high of 57.21 per cent. There were four years when the percentage was less than 4, six years in which it was less than 20, and four years in which it was 40 or above. The earnings plowed back into the business

64. *National Petroleum News*, I, No. 9 (November, 1909), 3, I, No. 10 (December, 1909), 10.
65. Company Encyclopedia: Marketing, I, Comparison of Advertising Expenditures With Sales of Petroleum Products 1907 to 1940 inclusive.
66. Statement of Net Earnings, Dividends, Etc., for the Years 1892 through 1929. Furnished by Robert E. Wilson, Chairman, Standard Oil Company (Indiana), September 30, 1949.

through the years without increasing the number of shares naturally made the investment per share many times its $100 par value.
The cash dividends paid on a $100 share were unprecedented.
They ranged from $175 per share in 1900 to a high of $1,400 in
1908. Between 1901 and 1911 the cash dividend per share was
never less than $300 and, in most years, it amounted to consider-
ably more.

CHAPTER IV

Governmental Attacks Upon Standard

DURING THE LAST HALF OF THE NINETEENTH CENTURY THE MOST striking feature of the industrial development in the United States was the growth of manufactures and the trend toward the formation of great industrial combinations. The first great trust to appear was the Standard Oil Trust. It set an example which was followed in the organization of the American Cotton Oil Trust in 1884, the National Linseed Oil Trust in 1885, the Distillers' and Cattle Feeders' Trust in 1887, the American Tobacco Company in 1890, and others.

As the number of giant corporations, trusts, and holding companies grew, the Grangers, Greenbackers, Populists, antimonopoly parties, and labor groups demanded regulative and restrictive action by the government. Numerous state and federal investigations of the Standard Oil Trust were launched after 1879 in which its officers, as well as its enemies, were given ample opportunity to testify about its policies and practices. In 1881 Henry D. Lloyd began his attack on the Standard Oil Trust in "The Story of a Great Monopoly" published in the *Atlantic Monthly,* which drew national attention to the subject. That issue went through seven printings. An increasing amount of periodical literature appeared stressing the evils of large-scale industries, dishonest practices, unfair privileges, the ruthless exploitation of natural resources, the growth of huge fortunes, and the concentration of wealth. Public agitation over the power, size, and practices of Big Business finally led to the passage by Congress of the Sherman Anti-Trust Act in 1890, which proved ineffective and disappointing in its immediate effect.

Between 1891 and 1897 the number of large industrial and business corporations that came into existence was small, but from 1898 to 1904 combinations in the form of holding companies increased at a remarkable rate. In 1900 there were 185 industrial combinations with a total capitalization of $3,000,000,000; in 1904 there were 318 representing a total capitalization of more than $7,000,000,000. The increase in the number of trusts, the rapid consolidation of the railroads, and the continuing abuses of Big Business revived the attacks upon large corporations on a more widespread scale than ever before. Public conferences were held by citizens' groups to discuss and demand more effective control.

A younger generation of state and national political leaders— Theodore Roosevelt, W. J. Bryan, Robert M. La Follette, Tom Johnson, and others—demanded liberal reforms. One of the most powerful influences in arousing the public to the evils of Big Business and in paving the way for reform was a group of fearless journalists, popularly known as "muckrakers." They wrote for the popular magazines—McClure's, Collier's, Everybody's, and Cosmopolitan—between 1901 and 1908, exposing American business methods and practices. Lincoln Steffens revealed the corruption in municipal politics. Ray Stannard Baker wrote about the dishonesty of the railroads. B. J. Hendrick exposed the unethical practices of insurance companies. Samuel Hopkins Adams bitterly arraigned the patent medicine trust. Thomas W. Lawson attacked Amalgamated Copper, H. H. Rogers, and William Rockefeller. Frank Norris exposed the Southern Pacific in his book The Octopus. Upton Sinclair revealed the unsavory conditions existing in the meat-packing plants in The Jungle.

The most successful attack of muckraking journalism was by Ida M. Tarbell, who wrote a series of articles for McClure's on the history of Standard Oil, beginning in November, 1902, and ending in 1904, when the articles were published in book form. Using the voluminous testimony gathered by state and federal authorities, the Congressional Record, court records, newspapers, and interviews, Miss Tarbell told a remarkable story of Standard's rise and development to about 1900. Admitting Standard's efficiency and power, she pointed out how much of its success was due to fraud, coercion, and special privileges. Her articles were read by millions of people, who were deeply impressed.

When Theodore Roosevelt became President in 1901, one of the outstanding issues before the American people was the control of monopolies. With an aroused public opinion behind him, he assumed the leadership of the reform forces and undertook to enforce and strengthen the laws regulating business, secure the passage of new ones where necessary, give merciless publicity to the evil practices of business through the newly established Bureau of

Corporations, and institute suits against various corporations for violating the Sherman Anti-Trust Act.

The first legal attack against the Standard combination, however, was made by the State of Missouri, where complaints had been the loudest. Moved by these complaints, Herbert S. Hadley, attorney general under the reform governor, Joseph W. Folk, began inquiring into conditions. Among other things he found was the fact that refined oil prices had not been reduced in twenty years, yet crude prices had been lowered anywhere from 30 cents to $1.20 a barrel.[1] With the support of three independent oil companies, E. M. Wilhoit of Springfield, the National Oil Company of Kansas City, and the St. Louis Oil Company, Hadley began to gather evidence as to the cause for high prices.

After an exploratory investigation, Hadley instituted *quo warranto* proceedings in the Missouri Supreme Court on March 29, 1905, against three subsidiaries of the Standard of New Jersey— the Waters-Pierce Oil Company, a Missouri corporation, for the forfeiture of its charter, and against Standard of Indiana and the Republic Oil Company, foreign corporations, to cancel their licenses to do business in Missouri.[2] The suit was based on the grounds that they had formed between 1901 and 1905 a pool, trust, combination, or conspiracy in restraint of trade for the purpose of regulating, fixing, and controlling prices paid by retail dealers and others for refined oil products, controlling and limiting trade in refined oil products, controlling, limiting, and preventing competition in the buying and selling of refined oil products, and for deceiving and misleading the public into the belief that they were three separate and distinct corporations, each pursuing an independent business as legitimate competitors. All of this, it was charged, was in violation of the antitrust laws of Missouri.

After the defendants filed their answers, the court referred the case to a special commissioner, the Honorable Robert A. Anthony of Fredericktown, Missouri, to hear testimony and report his findings. The taking of testimony began in St. Louis on June 21st and continued intermittently through 1905 and 1906 in New York, Cleveland, Des Moines, Joplin, and Oklahoma City. Considerable difficulty was encountered in getting information from

1. Hadley told the story of his inquiry and battle to secure evidence against the Standard combination to the Independent Petroleum Marketers Association at St. Louis in 1911. See the *National Petroleum News*, III, No. 3 (May, 1911), 2A.
2. 116 S. W. 907. See Company Encyclopedia: Marketing, I.

some of the principal officers of the defendant companies. When
H. H. Rogers, E. T. Bedford, and E. Carney of the Standard of
New Jersey took the stand in New York, on advice of counsel they
refused to answer practically all of Hadley's questions. It was not
until a court order had been secured that William G. Rockefeller,
John D. Archbold, Wade Hampton, H. M. Tilford, W. C. Teagle,
and other officers of the Jersey company agreed to testify. J. A.
Moffett, P. C. Crenshaw, George W. Mayer, and others appeared
for Standard of Indiana. A court order had to be secured to force
Waters-Pierce and Republic to produce their books, papers, and
documents as to the conduct of their business at 26 Broadway.
H. C. Pierce, President of Waters-Pierce, failed to appear on several occasions, as requested, and finally a court order forced his
appearance. The strength of the opposition and the difficulty of
securing evidence amazed Hadley. "I found," he said, "the most
remarkable combination of money and power, exercising a destructive influence in defiance of the law, never equalled in any
country and by any force, since law was law." [3] He probed every
available source of information to find out about Standard's operations.

After conferring with Ida M. Tarbell, Hadley said, "She didn't
even know the real inside story." Various efforts were made by
Standard's attorneys during the progress of the hearings to settle
the case by paying a large fine, but all offers were refused.[4] By the
time the hearings ended on January 21, 1907, Hadley had taken
testimony from eighty-nine witnesses and put into the record hundreds of exhibits.

On May 24, 1907, the special commissioner submitted to the
Missouri Supreme Court an unprecedented record of the case—
the "Printed Record of Testimony" of three thousand pages, the
attorney general's printed abstract of two volumes of about five
hundred pages each, briefs, and the commissioner's report of three
hundred pages.[5] In his findings the commissioner pointed out

3. *National Petroleum News,* III, No. 3 (May, 1911), 2A; Sherman Morse, "The
   Taming of Rogers," *American Magazine,* LXII, No. 3 (July, 1906), 227-237.
4. *The Chicago Tribune,* December 24, 1908.
5. The following account is based upon the Special Commissioner's findings and
   the testimony of H. Clay Pierce, James A. Moffett, W. C. Teagle, C. L. Nichols,
   P. C. Crenshaw, and other Standard officials as well as many independent
   Missouri oil company officials. See *Report and Findings of Robert A. Anthony,
   Commissioner,* May 24, 1907, and *Pleadings and Abstract of the Testimony,
   History of the Case, Issues Made By the Pleadings, Statement of Facts, Brief
   and Argument,* and *Reply Brief for the State.*

that, in spite of the great diversity and wide range of the evidence, there was little variance between counsel as to the facts proven. The real contention was over the inferences to be drawn from the facts.

Although organized in different states as separate and distinct corporate entities, the defendant companies, according to the commissioner, formed a combination by virtue of the fact that the Jersey company held a controlling interest in each of the companies. Of the total capital stock in the three companies amounting to $1,750,000, the Jersey company owned more than $1,500,000. Two-thirds of the stock, or 2,750 shares, of Waters-Pierce was held by M. M. Van Beuren, a son-in-law of John D. Archbold, as a representative of the Jersey company. Standard of Indiana had been licensed on January 21, 1897, to do business in Missouri, and practically all of its stock was owned by the Jersey company. Organized in New York on June 3, 1901, the Republic Oil Company purchased the oil business and property of Scofield, Shurmer & Teagle and was licensed to do business in Missouri on July 8, 1901. Although the stock of Republic was owned by the Jersey company, it was held in the name of Jersey employees at 26 Broadway. The President, C. L. Nichols, was assistant to L. J. Drake at 26 Broadway.

Through Directors and employees, who served as officers, according to the special commissioner, the business of the three companies was, in a general way, directed and controlled by the Standard of New Jersey from 26 Broadway, New York. Although Mr. Pierce, the minority stockholder in Waters-Pierce, claimed that he had complete direction and control over his company until the spring of 1904, the general policy of the company at all times was directed and controlled from 26 Broadway, especially after 1904. Full and complete reports of their transactions were regularly submitted to the representative of each company in New York. The business of each one was run along definitely established lines laid down by the parent company. Their books were audited under the direction of Wade Hampton, general auditor for all Standard Oil interests. All dividends on the stock of Standard of Indiana and Republic and the dividends on two-thirds of the stock of Waters-Pierce were paid into Jersey's treasury. "The conclusion cannot be escaped," the special commissioner wrote, "that the common ownership of the stock of respondents by an outside corporation is a strong circumstance tending to show them guilty of an agreement, combination or conspiracy to effect the objects stated in the information." [6]

The commissioner found that owing to a division of the marketing territory, the people of Missouri were deprived of any competition between the two largest oil companies in the state. Furthermore, there was no reason for competition, due to common ownership. When the Waters-Pierce Oil Company was organized, there was an understanding between H. C. Pierce and representatives of the Standard of Ohio whereby the former was to market in the southern half of Missouri and the Consolidated Tank Line Company in the northern half and neither company was to market in the territory of the other. When Standard of Indiana purchased the marketing properties in northern Missouri, it continued to respect the understanding and furnish Waters-Pierce with practically all of its oil. Maps with a blue line representing the territorial division were kept in the offices of Standard and Waters-Pierce, and the agents of each company were instructed not to sell in the territory of the other. If orders were received by an agent of Waters-Pierce from a customer residing in the northern portion, it was sent to Standard of Indiana to be filled and vice versa. If these two companies had not been bound together by common stock ownership, according to the special commissioner, they would probably have established and maintained marketing stations at all important points in Missouri and competed. In connection with other circumstances, the failure to compete was a significant factor in the commissioner's findings.

The unfair and deceptive method of competition as illustrated by the operations of the Republic Oil Company was another important factor in the commissioner's findings. The firm of Scofield, Shurmer & Teagle was among the first to engage in refining after the discovery of petroleum in Pennsylvania, and for many years its products were sold throughout the Central West and the Southwest. It was the largest and most aggressive competitor of Standard west of the Alleghenies. It had built up large sales in high-grade Pennsylvania kerosene, greases, and lubricants, which sold at higher prices than Standard's products. The firm's success was also based on the fact that there were some people in every community who preferred to pay a little more for oil sold by an independent than buy from Standard. Feeling the fierce warfare for existence which the firm had been compelled to wage against

6. 116 S. W. 1002.

Standard, the members of Scofield, Shurmer & Teagle sold out in the spring of 1901 to Standard of New Jersey. To operate the property and sell Pennsylvania oils in competition with independent companies, Standard organized the Republic Oil Company. All incorporators and officers were minor employees in Jersey's office at 26 Broadway. Employees of Republic, except for the old employees of Scofield, Shurmer & Teagle, were practically all men transferred from other Standard Oil companies. W. C. Teagle was appointed Vice-President and General Manager of Republic.

Every effort was made to conceal the fact that Republic had any connection with Standard. It was represented to the trade as an independent company. Standard could much more easily secure and hold the "dissatisfied" trade through the operation of a dummy company than it could directly. To further this deception, Republic was supplied for about a year by Standard companies that did not bear the name Standard. Thereafter, practically all of its oil was furnished by Standard of Indiana. As soon as Republic was organized, fierce competition between it and the independents began. Republic was especially effective in those places where Standard of Indiana or Waters-Pierce had keen competition, for it could cut prices and give rebates against a competitor, drive him out, and not suffer as much loss as either of the other two companies. Thus Republic aided in maintaining the price of refined oil for Standard of Indiana and Waters-Pierce. When it was revealed in the hearings before the special commissioner that Republic was a fraud and sham, its usefulness came to an end, and all of its property, except for some in Missouri, was sold to Standard of Indiana in 1906.

Both Standard of Indiana and Waters-Pierce, according to the special commissioner, resorted to every foul and fair means available to keep informed about shipments of oil into their respective territories by independent dealers, which indicated an understanding to monopolize the sale of refined oil. Reports were made to the companies by their salesmen, tank-wagon agents, and railroad employees. So efficient was the system that the destination of oil shipped by a competitor was known as soon as the shipment was delivered to the railroad. This information was then conveyed to Standard's agent at the place of destination, and he was held responsible if the independent oil was sold there. The agent would see the purchaser and endeavor to induce him to countermand the order. If he was not successful in this, the price of oil was dropped in that locality, and by the time the competitive shipments arrived, oil was being sold for less than the competitor's oil cost. Under the circumstances, it was not difficult to appreciate the hesitation with which a local dealer purchased from a competitor of Standard companies.

As a result of this combination of strength and wealth, Standard of Indiana, Waters-Pierce, and Republic enjoyed almost a complete monopoly of the business in their sales territory. They sold at least 90 per cent of all the refined oil in Missouri and about the same proportion of lubricating oil. As long as competitors were satisfied to do from 10 to 15 per cent of the business, they were allowed to operate without molestation. If they attempted to increase their trade, the competing Standard company reduced prices.

After reviewing the evidence, the special commissioner found that the three companies had violated the Missouri antitrust laws as charged by the attorney general. More than a year and a half elapsed after the special commissioner submitted his findings before the Missouri Supreme Court rendered a decision.

On December 23, 1908, the court denounced the three companies in no uncertain terms as having an adverse effect upon competitors and found them guilty as charged.[7] In reviewing the case, Justice Woodson for the court commended the special commissioner for the spirit of justice and fairness of his terse yet full abstract of evidence which was conceded to be substantially correct. "When we view this case in its entirety," Justice Woodson wrote, "we are unable to see how the master could have honestly reached any other conclusion than found in his report filed therein. ... In the case at the bar we have traced every step and carefully considered every act of each and all of these companies from the time of their organization down to the close of the evidence in this case, and they all point to guilt, and are inconsistent with all theories of innocence."[8] The court expressed great regret at having to adjudge the charter of Waters-Pierce and the licenses of the Standard of Indiana and Republic to do business in Missouri forfeited, but "by doing so we are following the plain mandate of the law." The licenses of Standard and Republic were forfeited, fines of $50,000 each plus costs were levied, and each company was

7. For the decision of the Supreme Court of Missouri see 116 S. W. 1006. Also, *The Chicago Tribune*, December 24, 1908.
8. 116 S. W. 1040, 1042.

given until March 1, 1909, to conclude its business.[9] Since the minority interest of Waters-Pierce had done everything it could to prevent the company from entering and becoming a part of the combine, the court took note of this fact, ordered the fine of $50,000 to be paid before March 1, 1909, and issued a stay of execution as to the decree of forfeiture until further action by the court.[10] If Waters-Pierce paid the fine and immediately severed all connection with the other Standard companies and furnished satisfactory proof of its compliance, the court offered to suspend the writ of ouster. If, afterwards, it was shown that the promises and assurances of the company to abide by the judgment had been violated, the suspension of the writ of ouster would be removed and the ouster decree enforced.

Justice Graves concurred in the decision but wrote a separate opinion in which he emphasized that the real offending party, the Standard of New Jersey, was not before the court.[11] It was the parent company, but it was not doing business in Missouri and this precluded action against it. He also felt that the forfeiture of the charter of Waters-Pierce, when those of Standard of Indiana and Republic would not be touched, was excessive. In view of the strong minority interest in Waters-Pierce, those rights should not be slaughtered, and hence he favored a reasonable fine rather than the ouster of the company. Even this, he believed, would be harsh on the minority interest.

Justice Lamm concurred in part and dissented in part.[12] As for Standard of Indiana, Justice Lamm recognized that at Sugar Creek it had a refinery of great value. In so far as it had voluntarily entered into the conspiracy, it deserved punishment, but the ouster order should protect the citizens of Missouri against the dismantling of its refinery. He believed that the ouster order should be suspended during good behavior as in the case of Waters-Pierce. On the other hand, he did not have the same sympathy for the minority interest of Waters-Pierce as the other justices. Although the minority interests had protested joining the combination, they finally consented without any open protest or invoking judicial aid. Lamm favored a fine of $1,000,000 for Waters-Pierce; the fine for Standard of Indiana should be increased, and the ouster made conditional.

9. 116 S. W. 1048.
10. *Ibid.*
11. *Ibid.,* 1050.
12. *Ibid.,* 1051.

Within ten days after the decision, both Standard of Indiana and Republic made motions for a rehearing and asked that the decree be suspended upon such terms as the court might think just and equitable. On February 2, 1909, attorneys for Standard of Indiana filed with the court a proposal that a Missouri corporation be formed to take over all company property in Missouri.[13] If agreeable, arrangements might be made to include the property of Waters-Pierce. All of the stock would be issued for four years to two trustees, one selected by the company and one selected by the state and both approved by the court. These two trustees would run the business. If they disagreed, the court was to arbitrate, and its decision would be final. "Our partnership offer," said Frank Hagerman, one of the attorneys for Standard, "may seem a bit startling, but we can think of no fairer way to convince the state and the people that they are to get a square deal. We have told the state to step in and watch us carefully. If prices don't suit, the state may change them. I hope the court will accept this offer. It would be an important experiment, an unparalleled advance in the management of a great property in which the people are vitally interested. The minority stockholders of the Waters-Pierce Oil Company probably will object, but I believe that will not affect the issue."[14] The novelty of the scheme attracted widespread public attention. It was without precedent. Coming from the most secretive of all corporations, the proposal completely baffled state officials. Many newspapers expressed skepticism as to Standard's real intent.

Why did Standard make this offer? Apparently it was due to the influence of Oklahoma and Kansas producers, who sent a committee to New York to consult with officials of the parent company about the situation.[15] The committee pointed out that to close the Sugar Creek refinery would work a great hardship on the Mid-Continent producers. It would cut off a market for 15,000 barrels of crude oil per day, which they had been selling to Standard, and this meant a loss of about $40,000 a day. Furthermore, the closing of the Sugar Creek refinery would mean an incalculable loss and confusion for a large number of industries using fuel oil throughout its area. Hadley, who had now become governor, and the new attorney general, Elliott Major, seemed to favor the extraordinary

13. *The Chicago Tribune*, February 2, 1909; *National Petroleum News*, I, No. 1 (February, 1909), 14.
14. *The Chicago Tribune*, February 3, 1909.
15. *Ibid.*; *National Petroleum News*, I, No. 1 (February, 1909), 14.

proposal, but it was up to the Missouri Supreme Court to decide.

On March 9, 1909, the court denied motions by Standard and Republic for a rehearing and announced that Waters-Pierce had filed proof of compliance with its order, that these proofs had been approved, and the ouster order against it suspended. Standard's offer to set up a trusteeship with the state as a partner was ignored. Both Standard and Republic immediately appealed to the Supreme Court of the United States. This action served as a stay of execution and permitted Standard to continue business pending a final decision.

While these events were taking place in Missouri, a situation was developing in the neighboring state of Kansas which led to another attack upon Standard.[16] With the market in Kansas flooded with crude oil in 1905, storage tanks full, adequate facilities for transporting oil lacking, and only a few small refineries, crude prices had rapidly declined from $1.38 to 72 cents per barrel in January, 1905. On the other hand, the price of refined oil had not declined. Crude prices continued to fall to 35 cents. On January 1, 1905, the Prairie Oil & Gas Company had 5,714,054 barrels of crude oil in storage, and it was either storing or shipping better than 25,000 barrels a day.[17]

Producers were incensed against the Standard organization because of the lack of competitive buying. Standard of Kansas, Standard of Indiana, and Prairie Oil & Gas, subsidiaries of the Standard of New Jersey, were all chartered or licensed to produce, purchase, refine, and market oil. Instead of each company engaging in all of these phases of the business, Prairie produced, purchased, and transported crude, Standard of Kansas refined crude, and Standard of Indiana, licensed to do business in Kansas in 1903, marketed the refined products. Another cause for dissatisfaction was the fact that Prairie, in buying Kansas crude, paid 15 cents per barrel less for oil north of Neodesha than it paid for oil coming from the south.[18] It claimed that the oil from the north was heavier in quality and yielded less illuminating oil, yet it had previously bought this oil without any discrimination. Producers in the field

16. The attack upon Standard in Kansas provoked much discussion in the current periodicals. For general accounts of the controversy, see Isaac F. Marcosson, "Kansas Oil Fight," World's Work, X (May, 1905), 6155-6166; Ida M. Tarbell, "Kansas and the Standard Oil Company," McClure's Magazine, XXV (September, 1905), 469-481, XXV (October, 1905), 608-622.
17. Isaac Marcosson, "Kansas Oil Fight," World's Work, X (May, 1905), 6166.
18. F. A. Parsons, "What, in Oil, Is the Matter with Kansas?" National Petroleum News, II, No. 11 (January, 1911), 7.

protested the action, and the earlier feeling of good will toward
Prairie turned into bitter antagonism.

To secure relief, Kansas producers sought outlets for crude as
fuel oil and for gas in Kansas City and Omaha, but high freight
rates blocked their efforts.[19] When independent refiners attempted
to enlarge their market, Standard of Indiana cut prices so low
they could not profitably operate. The deep-seated antagonism to
trusts already present was accentuated by the publication of Ida
M. Tarbell's articles on Standard in *McClure's* which revealed a
striking parallel between the situation of the Kansas producers
and that of the early Pennsylvania producers and Standard. Without any dividends on their oil stocks, owing to low prices, 31,000
Kansas investors joined the anti-Standard chorus. Professional
agitators and politicians chimed in, too. S. M. Porter, running for
election as state senator in November, 1904, urged that the state
build and operate a refinery.

Complaints against the Standard organization became so violent
and loud that the new governor, E. W. Hoch, in his inaugural
message in January, 1905, advocated the erection of a state-owned
and operated refinery in order to provide relief from the monopoly. The Kansas Oil Producers Association, organized on January 19th backed the governor's proposal and launched an extensive propaganda campaign in its behalf. A strong majority of the
legislature opposed such a socialistic measure, but the opposition
quickly vanished owing to an ill-timed announcement by Prairie
that, because of the menacing legislation, it was stopping all construction of pipelines and storage tanks within the state, and that
it was discontinuing all purchases of crude oil in Kansas.[20] Under
the circumstances the state legislature with only a few dissenting
votes appropriated $200,000 to build a refinery at Peru as a branch
of the penitentiary. It also passed laws setting maximum freight
rates on oil, prohibiting rebating, making pipelines common carriers, and prohibiting discrimination in the price of refined oil
within the state.[21] These laws were designed, as Governor Hoch
said, "to make the Standard Oil Company decent." [22] The build-

19. *Ibid.*
20. Isaac Marcosson, "Kansas Oil Fight," *World's Work*, X (May, 1905), 6162;
    "Kansas and the Oil Trust," *Outlook*, LXXIX (February 25, 1905), 463.
21. "Kansas and the Oil Trust," *Outlook*, LXXIX (February 25, 1905), 463.
22. F. A. Parsons, "What, in Oil, Is the Matter with Kansas?" *National Petroleum
    News*, II, No. 11 (January, 1911), 7.

ing of a state refinery would afford little relief, for it could take care of only about one-tenth or one-fifteenth of the state's production. It was thought, however, that this action and the other laws enacted might induce independent refiners to come in and help relieve Kansas from its dependence upon Standard's monopoly.

As a result of the war against Standard in Kansas two other important actions were taken. First, Philip P. Campbell, Representative in Congress from the Third District in Kansas, introduced a resolution directing the Secretary of the Department of Commerce and Labor to investigate the relationship of Standard to the Kansas oil field. Secondly, on October 2, 1906, C. C. Coleman, attorney general of Kansas, filed suit in the Kansas Supreme Court against Standard of Indiana, Standard of Kansas, and the Prairie Oil & Gas Company, all subsidiaries of the Jersey company, to oust these companies from doing business in the state for violating the Kansas antitrust laws.[23] Since the Standard of New Jersey, through its stock ownership in these companies, was able to control 75 per cent of the business to retailers, the state asserted that this was an unlawful agreement to restrain trade and fix prices. The court appointed L. W. Keplinger of Kansas City as a special commissioner to take testimony and present his findings.

The war against Standard in Kansas and public agitation in other states resulted in Congress passing a resolution on February 15, 1905, calling upon the Secretary of Commerce and Labor to investigate the relationship of Standard to the Kansas oil field. The investigation was assigned to the recently established Bureau of Corporations.

Since purely local conditions did not determine the price of crude or refined products or provide a proper basis for understanding the petroleum industry, James R. Garfield, Commissioner of Corporations, started an investigation of the whole industry covering crude production, pipelines, refining, competition, foreign trade, transportation and freight rates, ownership, and control of companies engaged in the oil business, and many other phases. Preliminary study indicated that the most important aspect was transportation because freight charges constituted a very large percentage of the total cost of the finished products and a very important factor in competition. Since the domination of the Standard of New Jersey over the petroleum industry was so great,

23. Topeka *Daily Capital*, October 3, 1906; *The Chicago Tribune*, October 3, 1906.

a special study of its relationship to transportation was made. This report was completed on May 2, 1906.[24]

A press release giving a summary of the 512-page report hit the front pages of the newspapers on a Monday morning and attracted nationwide attention. Further publicity was given to the report by President Roosevelt, who submitted it to Congress with a message of transmittal in which he bitterly denounced Standard. The report treated critically many phases of Standard's operations, but the main emphasis was upon Standard's relationships with the railroads and the discrimination in freight rates upon which the monopoly rested and by which competition had been practically eliminated. It struck a hard blow at the Standard organization. Although the officers of the Jersey company had co-operated fully with the Bureau of Corporations in its gathering of data, they immediately denounced the government for issuing such a hasty and one-sided report and for ignoring much evidence.[25] Even though numerous railway executives denied the accusations, they at once undertook to cancel many of the rates condemned by the report and make other adjustments.[26]

The Garfield report provided President Roosevelt and Attorney General William H. Moody with evidence on which to begin a series of prosecutions against various Standard subsidiaries for violating the Elkins Act of 1903. "The Standard Oil Company," declared the Attorney General, "has been sending out its products broadcast over the country, shipping them to and from refining stations and distributing points. The result is there are hundreds of cases where the corporation has been given illegal concessions by the railroads. In each one of these cases the railroad company, the Standard Oil Company, and the officers and agents of both corporations are liable to a fine." [27] Federal district attorneys in Chicago, New York, Boston, St. Louis, Kansas City, St. Paul, Indianapolis, and other places, were instructed to file criminal actions at once in their judicial districts, and two special counsels, Frank B. Kellogg and Charles B. Morrison, were appointed to continue the investigation begun by Garfield.

In June, 1906, the Attorney General held a conference in Washington with Kellogg, Morrison, and various district attorneys to

24. *Report of the Commissioner of Corporations on the Transportation of Petroleum.*
25. Nevins, *John D. Rockefeller*, II, 561.
26. *The Chicago Tribune,* November 18, 1906.
27. *Ibid.,* June 23, 1906.

lay plans for the prosecution. Apparently it was decided to bring the first suit in Chicago since the most flagrant violations of the law seemed to have originated at Whiting. Almost all of the oil sold east of the Missouri River, west of central Indiana, and in all the southern states, except the Atlantic seaboard and Texas, was distributed from Whiting. Chicago's switching area was the largest center of Standard's operations and the reason for attacking first at this point. It was in reality the hub of the "Octopus."

Late in July, Judge Kenesaw Mountain Landis, who had recently been appointed to the federal bench, issued an order for drawing a federal grand jury from the old northern division of the Northern District of Illinois to report in Chicago on August 6, 1906.[28] Since there had been a redistricting of the courts on March 3, 1905, this jury was to consider acts committed prior to this date. It was the 8th before the grand jury was assembled, and after a session of three and a half hours, it returned an indictment of nineteen counts against Standard of Indiana for accepting rebates in the form of nonpayment of storage charges from the Lake Shore & Michigan Southern Railroad to the extent of $8,506 between 1903 and 1905.[29] Commenting editorially, *The Chicago Tribune* asserted that it was high time that Standard was indicted. "There is no reason," it declared, "why the company should not be made to feel the full rigor of the law." [30] It urged that no leniency should be shown, for Standard had been an habitual offender.

The second grand jury, to consider acts committed since March 3, 1905, proceeded with its deliberations on August 16th. On the 27th the two grand juries returned ten indictments against Standard of Indiana containing 6,428 counts for violating the Elkins Act.[31] Each of the counts represented the shipment of one tank car. Standard was charged with receiving rebates aggregating $487,690 from seven railroads. The typed document containing the indictments was reported to be the most voluminous ever presented to any court up to that time and was dubbed "The Government's Thirteen Inch Gun" because it was thirteen inches high and weighed fifty-three pounds.

In view of the ease with which the indictments had been obtained, the Department of Justice seemed quite optimistic and confident about securing a conviction. However, on November

28. *Ibid.*, July 28, 1906, August 6, 7, 1906.
29. *Ibid.*, August 9, 1906.
30. *Ibid.*, August 10, 1906.
31. *Ibid.*, August 28, 1906, November 18, 1906.

10, 1906, general and special demurrers to the indictments were filed by Standard, which precipitated the first battle. These were argued before Judge Landis for several days beginning on December 13th. Standard's plea, argued by John S. Miller, special counsel, was based upon two contentions. First, the indictments were vague and uncertain. Secondly, the indictment of August 27th had been obtained under Section I of the Elkins Act which had been repealed two months previously.[32] The Hepburn Act, repealing Section I of the Elkins Act, was approved by the President on June 29, 1906. On the next day Congress passed an amendment to the effect that the new law should not go into effect until sixty days thereafter. Since Section I of the Elkins Act had not been specifically revived by the amendment, Miller contended that Standard and all corporations accused of receiving rebates could not be lawfully indicted.

Through his fine probing of the law, Miller had raised a very important technical question. If upheld by Judge Landis, it would be a blow to the government and tie its hands in every case started against various corporations and railroads during the past six months for violating the Elkins Act. The Department of Justice admitted that Miller's point was an extremely delicate matter. However, the federal district attorney, Edwin Sims, argued that the Hepburn Act became a law when filed with the Secretary of State and that was on June 30th, the same date as Congress passed the amendment delaying its enforcement for sixty days. The government also insisted that the amendment of June 30th was not a repealing law at all. It merely suspended the operation of the new rate law and automatically revived the old penalties. By virtue of an old common law principle, Section I of the Elkins Act was the law of the land until the amendment of June 30th had expired. This would, of course, cover the period during which the indictments had been made against Standard. On January 3, 1907, Judge Landis overruled Miller's arguments and upheld the government's contention that Section 13 of the *Revised Statutes,* providing that the repeal of a law did not remit offenses committed under the old law unless expressly stipulated, was applicable.[33] Naturally the government attorneys were jubilant, for Landis' ruling validated other pending cases.

32. *Ibid.,* December 10, 11, 14, 15, 18, 1906.
33. *Ibid.,* January 4, 5, 1907.

In October, 1906, a federal grand jury in Jackson, Tennessee, had indicted Standard of Indiana on 1,525 counts involving rebates and rate discriminations.[34] Other Standard companies in Missouri, Louisiana, California, and New York had also been indicted, making a total of over 8,000 counts against Standard interests.[35] Thus, the far-reaching importance of Landis' ruling could not be overestimated.

The government elected to try first the Alton case, beginning on March 4, 1907.[36] Ever since the establishment of Whiting, Standard of Indiana had shipped enormous quantities of oil from Whiting to East St. Louis, the gateway to the Southwest, and to St. Louis, over three different railroads—the Chicago & Alton, the Chicago, Burlington & Quincy, and the Chicago & Eastern Illinois. Oil from Whiting reached the Chicago & Alton line over the tracks of the Chicago Terminal Transfer Railroad at Chappell, Illinois, a junction point. The indictment charged Standard with receiving $223,000 in rebates in violation of the Elkins Act on 1,903 cars of oil shipped from Whiting via Chappell to East St. Louis and St. Louis over the Chicago & Alton between September 1, 1903, and March 1, 1905.[37] Edwin Sims, the federal district attorney, and his assistants, James Wilkerson and H. A. Parkin, represented the government. Alfred D. Eddy, Standard's western counsel, John S. Miller, special counsel, and Virgil P. Kline of Cleveland represented Standard. The big surprise on the opening day of the trial was the appearance for Standard of Moritz Rosenthal, one of Chicago's ablest lawyers, who handled much of the trial work. With amazing rapidity, the trial jury, composed of six farmers or dealers in agricultural products, a banker, a real estate dealer, an iron molder, a manufacturer, and a foreman for a light and power company, was quickly selected. All but one were Republicans. With the swearing in of the jury, the way was now clear to begin the first criminal trial ever started by the government for the violation of the Elkins Act.

The government based its case upon the fact that the rates from Chicago to East St. Louis were fixed by the Chicago and St. Louis Traffic Association to which all railway lines from Chicago to

34. *Ibid.*, October 17, 1906, November 18, 1906.
35. *Ibid.*, January 5, 1907.
36. For accounts of the Alton case, see Company Encyclopedia: Marketing, I; Judge Landis' opinion in 155 F. 306 and the opinion of the U. S. Circuit Court of Appeals in 164 F. 377.
37. *The Chicago Tribune*, March 4, 5, 1907.

East St. Louis belonged.[38] Its latest tariff sheet No. 24, effective May 15, 1899, had been duly filed with the Interstate Commerce Commission. It named rates on classified articles and special rates on certain commodities, but it made no reference to rates on petroleum or petroleum products. However, on the face of the tariff sheet appeared these words: "Governed by the Illinois Classification except as herein noted." By turning to the classification adopted by the Railway & Warehouse Commission of Illinois on September 7, 1899, petroleum and petroleum products were found to be listed in the "fifth" class. Then, by turning back to tariff sheet No. 24, it was found that the rate for the fifth class was 18 cents per hundred pounds from Whiting to East St. Louis and 19½ from Chappell to St. Louis, the extra 1½ cents being the charge for shipping across the river into St. Louis via the lines of the St. Louis Terminal Company. By this process of reference and cross reference, the lawful published rate had been evolved by the government. For years all three of the railway lines running from Chicago to East St. Louis and St. Louis had applied Chicago rates from Whiting, and in more recent years they had filed what were known as "application sheets" specifically stating that Whiting and other suburban points in what was known as the Chicago Switching District took Chicago rates under tariff No. 24. These documents were the only ones filed with the Interstate Commerce Commission. Hence the government contended that the 18 and 19½ cent rate was the only lawful published rate filed and known to the public.

The government introduced evidence to show that the Alton carried oil for Standard for 6 cents per hundred pounds from Chicago to East St. Louis and 7½ cents to St. Louis. Out of the money received from this rate the Alton paid the switching charges of the Chicago Terminal Transfer Railroad for hauling the oil from Whiting to Chappell. These rates were provided for in what was known as special billing orders. The use of the words "billing rates" instead of "tariff" indicated that it was not an ordinary tariff intended for general inspection. It was common custom for railroads to remove particular commodities from the general classification and apply special commodity rates, but, unless filed with the Interstate Commerce Commission, they could not legally be applied to interstate business. In this instance the government claimed that the 6 cent rate had not been filed nor did the appli-

38. *Ibid.,* March 6–10, 12, 14–17, 1907.

cation sheet contain any reference to special billing orders. The government pointed out that the 6 cent rate was far lower than those paid by competitors from points farther east. The rate to East St. Louis from Pittsburgh was 24½ cents per hundred pounds, from Cleveland 19½ cents, and from Toledo 17 cents. Thus the 6 cent rate gave Whiting an enormous advantage over all other competing points.

Extraordinary efforts had been made, according to the government, by the Alton to conceal these rates from other shippers. The government introduced evidence to show that these special billing orders had been kept in separate books and not in the regular tariff files, thus rendering concealment easy. The 6 cent billing orders had not been sent to the local agents of the Alton, which was contrary to custom, but only to the officers in the general office of the railroad and to Standard. The agent at Chappell, not having the 6 cent special billing orders, entered upon the waybills the regular 18 and 19½ cent rate and forwarded the bills to the auditor's office, which made up a monthly statement for Standard. Wilkerson, the assistant federal district attorney, referred to Chappell as a mere "speakeasy on the Illinois frontier—a railroad blind pig maintained for the evasion of the Interstate Commerce Act." [39] The government contended that these methods showed beyond question that the railroad obviously desired to conceal the 6 cent rate.

The government endeavored to show that Standard knew of this false billing practice through its receipt of billing statements from the railway auditor which indicated the rate charged. Even if the company did not originally connive in or bring about the secrecy of the 6 cent rate, the receipt of these bills should have led Standard to make an immediate inquiry. The failure to ascertain that the 6 cent rate was a secret rate not filed with the Interstate Commerce Commission and in conflict with the regular rates could be attributed only to a deliberate connivance in the secrecy. The government emphasized that no experienced traffic officer could be misled into assuming without investigation that these billing orders had been filed with the Interstate Commerce Commission. There was no reason, according to the government, for the Alton to conceal the 6 cent rate from other railroads running between Chicago and East St. Louis—the Burlington and the Chicago & Eastern Illinois. It must have known that these two railroads were

39. *Ibid.*, March 15, 1907.

making the same rate because of the large shipments of oil moving over these railroads. Finally, the government showed that once the Bureau of Corporations in its investigation of 1905 discovered the existence of the 6 cent rate, all three railroads amended tariff No. 24 and substituted a 10 cent rate for the 6 cent rate. This was filed and became legal. In brief, the government's point of view was that the 6 cent rate, including both the failure to file the tariffs with the Interstate Commerce Commission and the secret methods of billing, was devised with the knowledge of and at the suggestion of Standard and primarily for the purpose of concealing the extraordinarily low rates from its competitors.

The last portion of the government's case was devoted to furnishing technical proof of illegal shipments through the identification and verification of waybills for each car and the settlement on a 6 cent basis. More than 2,000 waybills were examined and identified.[40] Record books to show the arrival of the cars at their destination were also examined and verified. Objection after objection was made by the defense to each count in an attempt to get it invalidated. Attorneys jokingly said that each one eliminated meant $20,000 saved for the client. Landis finally invalidated one hundred counts because the cars never reached their destination or else they were clerical errors made by the Alton. The defense raised objections to the introduction of almost every piece of paper and Landis just as promptly overruled the objection. As the trial progressed defense attorneys also frequently objected to Landis' asking questions of the witnesses. Landis finally told the court stenographer: "Let the record show that the defense objects to questions by the Court, that the objection is overruled, and that the defense takes an exception." [41]

The presentation of the government's case was concluded on March 29th. During the trial one hundred and forty-three witnesses, who were for the most part officers of railroad traffic associations and railroad employees, especially of the Alton, had been called. Before the conclusion of the government's case, Miller, special counsel for Standard, moved that certain documents introduced as evidence be stricken from the record and that Landis order a verdict of not guilty. As expected, Landis denied the motion.

On April 4th Standard began presenting its defense. It called

40. *Ibid.*, March 17–29, 1907.
41. *Ibid.*, March 17, 1907.

only seven witnesses. The defense rested its case upon three main points.[42] First, it argued that tariff sheet No. 24 did not provide a legal rate on oil. It made no specific reference to petroleum or petroleum products or to a rate of 18 and 19½ cents per hundred pounds. By an indirect method of consulting several different classification sheets the alleged rate of 18 cents had been evolved. Hence, it was not a binding rate. The defense also argued that tariff sheet No. 24 had been filed prior to the reorganization of the Alton and did not apply to the present company.

Secondly, the defense contended that oil shipments from Whiting to East St. Louis were considered by the railroads as intrastate commerce and that the 6 cent rate was lawful and in no way a violation of the Elkins Act. The Chicago & Alton did not run into St. Louis so shipments over the line were commerce within the State of Illinois. The handling of cars at either end of the line was considered just a switching operation for which the Alton absorbed the cost. To be sure, traffic actually moved from Whiting across the state line to Chappell, but Whiting lay within what was known as the Chicago Switching District. Hence it was intrastate commerce, and there was no obligation to file the 6 cent rate with the Interstate Commerce Commission. Unfiled rates between Chicago and points in Illinois were frequently used on shipments of other commodities from Whiting, Hammond, East Chicago, and similar points in Indiana lying within the Chicago Switching District. There was no common arrangement for the continuous transportation of cars from Whiting to East St. Louis. The defense denied that the filing of an 18 cent rate from Chicago to East St. Louis and the filing of the bridge tariffs at East St. Louis by the Alton constituted the establishment of a through rate and made shipments in interstate commerce.

In the third place, if the lawful rate was not 6 cents, Standard contended that it was issued by the Alton, and the company was justified in believing that the rate was lawful. The company did not knowingly violate or intend to violate the law. It believed that it was using the legal rate. F. S. Hollands, chief rate clerk for the Alton, who had been called by the government as a witness, testified that he had no recollection of telling Edgar Bogardus, Standard's traffic manager, that the 6 cent rate had been filed with the Interstate Commerce Commission. He stated that he regarded the 6 cent rate as the rate between Whiting and East St. Louis and

42. *Ibid.*, April 4-7, 9-12, 1907.

that if he had been asked by Bogardus or anyone else whether there was a rate between Whiting and East St. Louis, he would have answered there was a 6 cent rate and that it was filed.

Bogardus testified that in December, 1902, 1903, and 1904, he went to Hollands, applied for the rate on oil from Whiting to East St. Louis, and that he was given a typewritten sheet—a special billing order—showing that the rate was 6 cents. He also received an "application sheet" applying the Chicago and East St. Louis rates to Whiting and East St. Louis. Bogardus said that each time Hollands told him that the rate had been filed with the Interstate Commerce Commission. Bogardus pointed out that he never knew that his company had been accepting a concession until the Garfield report was made. Although the government forced him to produce original billing orders showing the 18 cent rate, Bogardus said that he had not seen these until 1906.

Attorneys for the defense argued that a shipper could not be held responsible for the violations of the law by a railroad. The company established the fact that the tariff sheets of the Alton were not posted in two conspicuous places in the station at Chappell or in other stations from which Standard shipped, which was required by law. Furthermore, Chappell was not specifically named in the Alton tariffs, which was another violation of the law. The defense claimed that Standard was not under any obligation to see that the railroads filed their tariffs. It was not for the company to question the propriety of whether oil was carried on state tariffs, filed or unfiled. Furthermore, the company had no way of knowing whether the railroads were trying to keep the rate secret. If so, this was not done at the insistence of Standard. The fact that the Burlington billed Standard in the usual manner at 6 cents indicated that it was an open rate. To prove the absence of any motive to accept an unlawful rate, Standard showed, but the evidence was excluded, that a 6¼ cent rate was available over the Chicago & Eastern Illinois Railroad, which had been filed in 1895 on traffic from Dolton, Illinois, a junction near Whiting, to East St. Louis. Under the circumstances Standard believed that it was justified in accepting a 6 cent rate over the Alton and the Burlington even if not filed with the Interstate Commerce Commission, the 6¼ cent rate being equivalent to the 6 cent rate because of a difference in terminal expense. The company also pointed out that the rate between East St. Louis and Toledo, Ohio, three hundred miles east of Whiting, was 17 cents, so it would have been cheaper for

THE STOCK MARKET VERSUS THE AUTOMOBILE MARKET.

The Chicago Tribune, August 16, 1910. Reproduced through the courtesy of *The Chicago Tribune*

GREAT BUSINESS CHANCE FOR MISSOURI.

The Chicago Tribune, February 3, 1909. Reproduced through the courtesy of *The Chicago Tribune*

STILL IN THE PIG BUSINESS.

Drawn by Ralph Wilder, *Chicago Record Herald*

CRUSHING EFFECT OF SUPREME COURT'S STANDARD OIL DECISION.

The Chicago Tribune, March 15, 1912. Reproduced
through the courtesy of The Chicago Tribune

Standard to ship oil to East St. Louis from Ohio rather than use the 18 cent rate from Whiting.

The defense rested its case on the 11th, and closing arguments were made by both sides on April 12th and 13th. Judge Landis charged the jury extemporaneously in what was regarded by some of the lawyers in the court as a masterly effort. The case went to the jury at 6 P.M. on Saturday, the 13th, and at 9:45 P.M. the jury, in accordance with Landis' instructions, found Standard of Indiana guilty as charged on 1,463 counts.[43] The government had won an impressive victory, but the legal battle had not ended. In fact, it was only the first round. Standard's attorneys made motions for a new trial and an arrest of judgment.

Greater emphasis and publicity throughout the nation was given to the guilty verdict when the Bureau of Corporations issued on May 20, 1907, its second report entitled *The Position of the Standard Oil Company in the Petroleum Industry*.[44] In about four hundred pages the Bureau described the domination of the oil industry by the Standard organization and how this was done through railroad rate discrimination and the ownership of 40,000 miles of pipelines. Throughout Standard's entire history, ran the report, the control of transportation facilities had been the keystone of its successes. Another vital element in exercising control over the industry was through its vast marketing system of bulk stations and tank wagons. The Commissioner of Corporations charged that its history and operation over the past thirty-five years showed a substantial monopolization of the petroleum industry, a deliberate destruction of competition, and a control of the industry by less than a dozen men, who had reaped enormous profits.

In considering the punishment that should be meted out to Standard of Indiana, Judge Landis on June 19th submitted a list of questions to its attorneys.[45] What corporation owned the stock of the defendant company? What was the capitalization of the holding company? What were the earnings of the holding company in 1903, 1904, and 1905? These and other questions placed company officials in a dilemma. If they answered, the replies might serve as the basis for the imposition of a huge fine. If they refused, the company would stand convicted before the public. Another

43. *Ibid.*, April 13, 14, 1907.
44. *Report of the Commissioner of Corporations on the Petroleum Industry, Part I: Position of the Standard Oil Company in the Petroleum Industry.*
45. *The Chicago Tribune*, June 20, 1907.

fear was that if the questions were answered, the information might be used against them in other suits.

On June 26th Landis denied Standard's motion for a new trial and again asked if the company would answer the questions submitted. When the request was refused, Landis asked Sims to subpoena those who knew the facts. When Sims asked Miller for a list of employees who knew the answers, Miller, according to a report, said: "I'll see you in hell first." [46] Sims, thereupon, issued subpoenas for John D. Rockefeller, John D. Archbold, H. H. Rogers, William Rockefeller, W. P. Howe, C. T. White, W. H. Tilford, Charles M. Pratt, Moffett, Cowan, Stahl, F. Q. Barstow, H. E. Felton, and others to appear in court on July 6th at 10 A.M. [47] Owing to this most unusual turn of events, Miller asked for a delay in serving the warrants, saying he might be able to supply the answer to Landis' questions. Sims refused, and U. S. marshals started serving the subpoenas. Everyone was served but John D. Rockefeller, who could not be found anywhere. For days the hunt was on. [48] During this time Rockefeller wired Landis from Pittsfield, Massachusetts, saying he understood a subpoena had been issued for him, and if his presence was needed, he would appear. [49] Not hearing from Landis, Rockefeller called in a deputy marshal who served the subpoena.

Rockefeller and the other subpoenaed officials arrived in Chicago on the 5th of July and went into a conference with the officers and lawyers of Standard of Indiana in their new spacious offices at 72 W. Adams in the Commercial National Bank Building. [50] It is said that at this conference Mr. Rockefeller and his associates discussed the question, even at this late date, as to whether or not he should appear in court the next morning. After canvassing the opinion of all the lawyers present and receiving advice against appearing, Mr. Rockefeller turned to the last and newest lawyer in the group, Robert W. Stewart, who had recently joined Eddy's firm. [51] Stewart replied: "Mr. Rockefeller, in view of the opinion rendered by the distinguished legal talent present, I hesitate to express an opinion." "Young man," replied Rockefeller, "I'm paying you to give me your opinion." Thereupon, Stewart said: "Mr.

46. *Ibid.*, January 9, 1909.
47. *Ibid.*, June 27–29, 1907.
48. *Ibid.*, June 30, July 1–3, 1907.
49. *Ibid.*, July 4, 5, 1907.
50. *Ibid.*, July 6, 1907.
51. Interview with Roy J. Barnett, January 20, 1949.

Rockefeller, you are no different from any other citizen before the law, and if I were you, I would appear."

The next morning, when Rockefeller and his associates entered the Federal Building, the corridors were jammed with people curious to get a glimpse of the great industrial tycoon.[52] Waving clubs and pushing back the people, the police opened a passageway for the party. After the doors to the courtroom had been closed, hundreds of people still tried to get inside, until finally the police had to clear the corridors.

When Rockefeller was called to the witness chair, Miller requested that Archbold be allowed to substitute for him, but Landis refused. Twenty questions were put to John D., but he could not provide very much information because he had not been active in the management of the company for about ten years. The spectators were amazed that a man like Rockefeller, who had built up such a great and powerful organization, knew so little about it. Charles M. Pratt, Secretary of the Standard of New Jersey, gave considerable financial data about the Jersey company and stated that a large portion of the stock of Standard of Indiana was held by individuals for the Standard of New Jersey; that the outstanding capital stock of Jersey was about $100,000,000; that the annual dividends of the Jersey company for the three years covered by the indictment were approximately 40 per cent; and that its net earnings for the same period were approximately $200,000,000. Landis adjourned court at 11:25 A.M. and dismissed all the witnesses. The Department of Justice representatives were considerably irritated by the whole affair because Landis, in his grandstand play, had subpoenaed Rockefeller and given him immunity from all criminal prosecution to testify, yet his testimony had been worthless.

The next day Rockefeller and Archbold issued a public statement saying that ever since the enactment of the Interstate Commerce Act in 1887 the Standard Oil Company had carefully observed its provisions and in no case had there been a willful violation. In fact, it welcomed the passage of the law, for the old system of special rates and rebates had been obnoxious and never a source of profit to the company. The statement denied the assertion made so often that rebates were the basis of Standard's prosperity. "Its prosperity has come," they declared, "through its correct apprehension of the possible magnitude and importance of the petro-

52. *The Chicago Tribune*, July 7, 1907.

leum business; through its having provided better and more economical methods for doing the business than have its competitors, and through a better service to the public in price and quality than others have given." [53] Pointing out how the Standard organization had made the petroleum industry great and had held it for this country against foreign competitors, they felt that its downfall through any cause would be a national disaster.

In another hearing on the 8th, Judge Landis wanted Standard of Indiana to produce evidence that it and the Jersey company had not been guilty of violating the Interstate Commerce Act. In a speech that bordered close to contempt, Rosenthal felt that the request was a "situation unheard of in the history of Anglo-Saxon jurisprudence" and declined to submit any evidence.[54] Rosenthal thought Landis should decide the fine on the basis of the evidence submitted during the trial and that he was not within his rights in calling for new evidence. Rosenthal recommended that the court pay "no attention to the gossip of the street or the charges of the mob."

On the morning of August 3rd at 10 A.M. the stately courtroom on the sixth floor of the Federal Building in Chicago was filled to capacity.[55] People stood around the walls two and three deep. Eddy and Miller, attorneys for Standard, were absent in Europe but Miller's partner, Merritt Starr, and Chauncey W. Martyn and Robert W. Stewart of Eddy's firm were present. Judge Landis walked quietly into the courtroom, took his seat, and after a few preliminaries began reading his decision in the Alton case. From the moment that he began reading an almost breathless silence prevailed. Landis reviewed the evidence presented, administered a scathing rebuke to Standard for its methods, expressed his belief that the company was no better than a common thief, held the contentions of the defendant weak at every point, emphasized the fact that guilt had been clearly proven, pointed out that the nominal defendant was Standard of Indiana, a million-dollar corporation, and the real defendant the Standard of New Jersey, a hundred-million-dollar corporation, and ended by levying an unprecedented fine of $29,240,000 upon Standard of Indiana.[56]

53. *Ibid.*
54. *Ibid.*, July 9, 1907.
55. *Ibid.*, August 3, 1907.
56. 155 F. 306; *The Chicago Tribune,* August 3, 4, 1907; Herbert N. Casson, "Is Standard Oil Facing Destruction?" *The New Broadway Magazine,* XIX, No. 6 (March, 1908), 671-679.

For each car of oil, worth about $450, involved in the indictment, Standard had been fined the maximum of $20,000.

Formal motions were made to set aside the court's decision, for an arrest of judgment, and to vacate the judgment. "Overruled," snapped Landis. However, the defense secured a sixty-day stay of execution and immediately filed an appeal with the United States Circuit Court of Appeals in Chicago containing 169 exceptions to Landis' rulings.

Before adjourning court, Landis issued orders for a special grand jury to meet on August 14th to investigate the conduct of the Alton. However, the United States Attorney General Moody had previously promised the Alton immunity from prosecution if it opened its books and otherwise aided the government in securing evidence against Standard. Upon learning this fact, Judge Landis recessed the grand jury and no further action was taken.[57]

The Landis fine upon Standard of Indiana was by far the largest ever assessed in any case in the history of jurisprudence, and never in its history had the Standard organization received such a stunning blow. One of the first reactions heard as soon as the court had adjourned was: "What is the matter with running Judge Landis for President? Surely that opinion is Rooseveltian enough." [58] When asked to comment upon the decision, Sims, the federal district attorney, said: "There isn't much to say. Judge Landis has said about all that is necessary. It was a strong statement of the law. The strongest, clearest, and most up-to-date opinion on the Interstate Commerce act that has been given for a long time." [59] Attorneys Starr, Stewart, and Martyn issued on behalf of Standard a statement saying: "We are convicted for paying from Whiting the lawful rate then in force from Chicago to East St. Louis, although what we did was in accordance with the applicable tariffs, putting shippers at Chicago and Whiting and other points in the Chicago Switching District on an equality, and within the spirit and purpose of the interstate commerce act." [60] Upon hearing about the fine in New York, James A. Moffett, President of Standard of Indiana, issued a long statement and concluded by saying: "For all these reasons the Standard Oil Company asserts that it ought never to have been prosecuted because of the claimed failure of a railroad company—which has neither

57. *The Chicago Tribune*, August 13–16, 1907, September 4, 25, 1907.
58. *Ibid.*, August 4, 1907.
59. *Ibid.*
60. *Ibid.*

been indicted or prosecuted—to file its tariff, and that the prosecution of this defendant under the circumstances of this case is a prostitution of the spirit and high purposes of the Interstate Commerce Act." [61]

Rockefeller was playing golf with some friends in Cleveland when a messenger boy came riding up to Mr. Rockefeller and handed him a yellow envelope.[62] He tore open the envelope, read the contents, folded the paper, and put it in his pocket. Rockefeller then broke the silence by saying: "Well, gentlemen, shall we proceed?" One inquisitive guest asked: "How much was the fine?" "Twenty-nine million dollars," Rockefeller replied. He then went on to play the nine holes in 53, the lowest score he had ever made.

No comment on the decision was made by President Roosevelt, but Secretary of the Interior Garfield in a speech at Riverside, California, said: "The decision and fine are the end of a long fight and will teach the people of this country that no man, big or little, is above the law. The Standard Oil Company and others like that great corporation have gone ahead on the theory that they were so powerful they could do things the ordinary citizen could not. We are showing them that they cannot." [63]

No criminal case up to that time received as much publicity as the Alton case. Judging by the comments, Standard had not only been found guilty by Landis but also by the newspapers and magazines. *The Chicago Tribune* in an editorial declared: "No judicial act will be more popular than that of Judge Landis yesterday in fining the Standard Oil Company. There is no part of the United States where that corporation is not known and detested." [64] In trying to visualize for its readers the meaning of $29,240,000, the *Tribune* pointed out it was a trifle more than half the money coined each year by the United States government. It was about 35 cents for every man, woman, and child in the whole country. It would take 48,730 city street laborers one year to work out the amount. It was the cost of five first-class battleships. It was sufficient to fill 177 flatcars with silver dollars.[65]

Two days after Landis levied the $29,240,000 fine, President Roosevelt made public the third report of the Commissioner of

61. *Ibid.*
62. Nevins, *John D. Rockefeller*, II, 578.
63. *The Chicago Tribune*, August 4, 1907.
64. *Ibid.*
65. *Ibid.*

Corporations on high prices and the enormous profits of the Standard Oil organization and their effect upon consumers everywhere.[66] Digests giving the highlights of the report again appeared in newspapers on a Monday morning throughout the country. Because of the perfect timing in the release of the report, it appeared that Roosevelt was making a deliberate effort to create as much hostile public opinion against Standard as possible. Standard officials were bitter because they had not been given an opportunity to submit any data for this latest report.[67]

Shocked by the huge fine and fearing others in pending cases, Standard officials decided to try negotiations for peace terms with President Roosevelt.[68] Archbold, accompanied by Senator Jonathan Bourne, Jr., and others, visited the White House. Archbold proposed that the government consent to a nominal fine in each of the pending cases and Standard would plead guilty to having received rebates, if they were dropped. For a while it seemed as if a compromise might be possible. Roosevelt believed that if the company pleaded guilty and promised to "sin" no more, nominal fines would be sufficient. Furthermore, if he refused to compromise, it might be said that he was seeking personal revenge because of his enmity toward H. H. Rogers. Representatives of the Department of Justice were consulted, but they opposed any compromise unless each shipment was counted as an offense. After further conferences with Taft, Root, Sims, and others, Roosevelt finally refused a compromise settlement.

Stung into action by the Landis fine and the report on prices and profits by the Bureau of Corporations, Standard issued on August 20th a pamphlet signed by Moffett to editors, stockholders, and employees setting forth a defense of its position. It contained a statement by Moffett and a number of friendly newspaper editorials. Relative to the rebate cases, Moffett emphasized the innocence of wrongdoing in any of the suits recently instituted against the company in federal courts and, in particular, in the Alton case. "The case has been taken on appeal," he declared, "to the higher courts to which we must look for that calm judgment which will rescue the rights of the citizens from the field of public clamor and from the domain of vindictive politics." [69] He pointed out that

---

66. *Report of the Commissioner of Corporations on the Petroleum Industry, Part II: Prices and Profits.*
67. *The Chicago Tribune,* August 6, 1907.
68. *Ibid.,* July 17, 1908.
69. *The Chicago Tribune,* August 21, 1907.

due to political pressure on the federal government it had been difficult to get a fair hearing before the public or in a large portion of the press. Amid the fury of the hour, the company was glad to know that scores of editors on an examination of the facts had forcibly and clearly expressed their opinion that the greatest wrong had been done to the Standard Oil Company. "Thousands of tons of freight," Moffett declared, "have been shipped from these points during the last fifteen years under the same circumstances as the Standard shipment, and if the Standard is guilty in this case, so is practically every other shipper in this great manufacturing territory. Is there a purpose in selecting Standard as a victim?"

On September 24th Landis threw another bomb at Standard. He referred Moffett's remarks to the grand jury and subpoenaed him to appear before that body on October 1st.[70] Landis wanted to know what Moffett meant by "a purpose" and who the other shippers were. When Moffett appeared before the grand jury, he said that he did not know of any actual violations of the law. The next day Hollands and four others from the Alton rate department testified but gave no information or evidence that could be used against other shippers. The grand jury reported to Landis that Rosenthal, not Moffett, had written the controversial statement in the pamphlet. Secondly, there was no evidence to back up the charge.

In December, Herbert Knox Smith, Commissioner of the Bureau of Corporations, upon instructions from the Secretary of Commerce and Labor, issued a statement in which he commented upon Moffett's pamphlet and a series of confidential circular "trade letters" sent out, all endeavoring to throw doubt on the legality and equity of the conviction.[71] He reviewed the 6 cent rate of the Alton and contradicted Moffett's assertion that no rebate was involved. In regard to the statement that others shipped at these rates, Smith called attention to Moffett's inability to produce any evidence before the grand jury in Chicago.

In filing its appeal to the United States Circuit Court of Appeals, Standard petitioned the court to certify to the Supreme Court of the United States the question as to whether the Hepburn Act repealed the Elkins Act.[72] An appeal by the Great Northern Railroad on this point was already pending in the high court. By ask-

70. *Ibid.*, September 25–27, 1907, October 1, 2, 5, 1907.
71. *Ibid.*, December 30, 1907.
72. *Ibid.*, January 12, 1908.

ing for a certification of the question, Standard hoped to get a decision on the moot point at the same time as the court decided the Great Northern case. The request was granted, and the Supreme Court decided on February 24, 1908, that the Hepburn Act did not repeal the Elkins Act for offenses committed prior to its passage.[73] The decision referred specifically to the Alton case and upheld Landis' ruling. The court's opinion was regarded as a severe blow to Standard of Indiana and led some to believe that Landis would be sustained on other aspects of the case. However, the Supreme Court made it clear that its decision on this point did not in any way commit the court as to other features of the Alton case.

The United States Circuit Court of Appeals on July 22, 1908, reversed Landis' decision in the Alton case because of the errors in his rulings.[74] It did not discuss the actual guilt of Standard. The opinion, written by Judge Peter S. Grosscup, was filled with caustic criticisms of Landis and was based on three main points. First, the trial court erred in excluding from the jury the testimony of Edgar Bogardus to the effect that the company did not know that it was accepting an unlawful rate. It had refused his offer to testify that the Chicago & Eastern Illinois had a lawful rate of $6\frac{1}{4}$ cents, which was equivalent to the 6 cent rate. It had excluded the testimony of F. S. Hollands to the effect that he regarded the 6 cent rate as the proper rate between Whiting and East St. Louis, and that it was filed. By excluding this testimony, Landis had deprived the company of the right to have a jury determine whether it had knowledge of the rate as charged. The whole question was fundamental as to whether or not the shipper was guilty. Referring to the 18 cent rate emphasized by the government and how it had been evolved, the court threw doubt upon it, saying: "We are not prepared to say that tariff sheet No. 24 really fixes the rate on petroleum and its products at eighteen cents. The most we can say is, that the question is one upon which judges, after full discussion, might very reasonably disagree."

In the second place, the trial court erred in computing the number of offenses. The computation should have been based upon the number of shipments, not cars. In the Alton case there were 1, 462 cars involving thirty-six different shipments. "The measure adopted by the trial court," declared Judge Grosscup, "was wholly

73. *Ibid.*, February 25, 1908.
74. 164 F. 377; *The Chicago Tribune,* July 22, 1908.

arbitrary—had no basis in any intention or fixed rule discernible in the statute." [75]

Finally, Judge Landis erred in meting out punishment on the ability of the Standard of New Jersey to pay rather than that of Standard of Indiana. There was nothing in the record to show that the assets of Standard of Indiana were in excess of $1,000,000. Furthermore, there was nothing in the record to show that the defendant had ever been guilty of any offense of this character. Except for its relationship to the Jersey company, the fine should have been measured on the basis of these facts. "How can a sentence such as the trial court imposed," asked Judge Grosscup, "based upon reasoning such as the trial court gave, be a sound sentence? Can a court without abuse of judicial discretion, wipe out all the property of the defendant before the court, and all the assets to which its creditors look, in an effort to reach and punish a party that is not before the court—a party that has not been convicted, has not been tried, has not been indicted even? Can an American judge, without an abuse of judicial discretion, condemn anyone, individual or corporation, who has not, in his own person, first been duly indicted, duly tried, and duly convicted? That to our mind, is strange doctrine in Anglo-Saxon jurisprudence. No monarch, no parliament, no tribunal of Western Europe, for centuries has pretended to have the right to punish except after due trial under all the forms of law. Can that rightfully be done here on no other basis than the judge's personal belief that the party marked by him for punishment deserves punishment? If so, it is because the man who happens to be the judge is above the law." [76] For these reasons the Circuit Court remanded the case with instructions to grant a new trial in accordance with this opinion.

President Roosevelt referred to the reversal as, in effect, a miscarriage of justice. Many thoughtful men believed it was unfortunate that any high officer of the government, such as the President, whose opinion would affect public feeling should criticize the courts so as to bring them within the range of popular sentimental judgment.[77]

So far as the government was concerned, it did not have the right of appeal. It could petition for a rehearing or go ahead with a new trial. After a conference of federal attorneys, the government

75. 164 F. 386.
76. *Ibid.*, 388-89.
77. *The Chicago Tribune*, July 24, 1908; "The Great Standard Oil Fine," *World's Work*, XVI, No. 5 (September, 1908), 10633.

filed a petition on August 21st with the Circuit Court for a rehearing. The petition, though couched in respectful language, was a severe arraignment of the court and its decision. Irked by this and other hostile comments, Judge Francis E. Baker issued a statement to the press lashing out at the critics of the decision, claiming that the newspapers had given an incorrect report of the case. He defended the court's position that it was Standard of Indiana which was being tried, not the Standard of New Jersey.[78] Furthermore, he said that the people must realize that the court can only be influenced by laws and precedent, not by what anyone says whether he is President Roosevelt or a bum in the gutter. When the United States Circuit Court refused the government's petition on November 11th for a rehearing, the latter presented a petition to the Supreme Court of the United States for a writ of *certiorari*, but the Supreme Court on January 4, 1909, refused to grant the petition.[79]

With no other alternative open to the government, the case was returned to the District Court for retrial. It would normally have come up for retrial in the same court in which it originated, but Judge Landis flatly refused to preside. Judge Solomon H. Bethea also refused "because he did not want to get mixed up in it." [80] Judge A. B. Anderson of Indianapolis finally consented to preside. The second trial got under way in Chicago on February 23rd.[81] Held in accordance with the principles set forth by the Circuit Court, the trial moved along rapidly and was of short duration. On the basic question of whether or not there was a lawfully filed and published rate of 18 cents over the Alton from Whiting to East St. Louis, the government received a body blow on March 8th when Judge Anderson ruled that the government had not offered sufficient evidence in proof of its contention.[82] Anderson ruled that the 18 cent rate under tariff No. 24 could not be established by using the Illinois Classification. The continuance of the case, Judge Anderson ruled, depended upon the government's ability to submit conclusive proof, which it could not offer. Judge Anderson, therefore, directed the jury to bring in a verdict of not guilty. So, all of a sudden, the famous case came to an end with the government paying the costs. But of a hundred "men on the street"

78. *The Chicago Tribune*, August 26, 1908.
79. *Ibid.*, January 5, 1909.
80. *Ibid.*, January 7, 1909.
81. *Ibid.*, February 23–27, 1909, March 2–6, 1907.
82. *Ibid.*, March 9–12, 1908.

today, more than ninety would probably recall the conviction rather than the exoneration.

After almost three years of bitter litigation, Standard of Indiana had been absolved of violating any law although many people undoubtedly believed the company morally guilty. "I don't care a cent what the public thinks," said Judge Anderson, "I followed the law. I am not running for office. Neither am I on trial in this case." [83] Sims, the federal district attorney, admitted that "we failed in this case because of the law. It is not as if we had failed to secure enough evidence." [84] Moritz Rosenthal, who had been in the thick of the fight all the way, commented: "One of the things that pleases us most is that the judge has shown clearly that no wrong was committed. He indicated plainly that there was no fixed rate, as the government contended. Our victory was therefore complete." [85] Miller, one of Standard's attorneys, expressed a thought that must have occurred to many who had followed closely the famous case. He remarked: "If the government had proceeded under the previous clause of the Elkins Act and had indicted the carrier instead of the shipper I am certain that it could have secured a conviction." [86] The *Boston Financial News* observed: "The decision affords one more illustration, if it were needed, that courts may be depended upon to finally do justice to all interests, notwithstanding public clamor." [87]

A general reaction to the ending of the case was that there would be a return to the vicious practice of rebates unless Congress remedied the defects of the law. Judge Anderson had "blasted an opening in the law that a four-horse rebate team could be driven through." [88] The ruling that a shipper could not be held responsible for an honest mistake brought about by error, intentional or otherwise, on the part of a railroad made it difficult for the government to prosecute successfully under the existing law. Furthermore, the customary and common methods of filing rates with the Interstate Commerce Commission were not sufficient to make them legal. Federal District Attorney Sims and the Interstate Commerce Commission officials said that 95 per cent of the tariffs filed with the Interstate Commerce Commission had been filed in the

83. *National Petroleum News*, I, No. 2 (April, 1909), 14.
84. *Ibid.*
85. *Ibid.*
86. *The Chicago Tribune*, March 11, 1909.
87. Quoted in the *National Petroleum News*, I, No. 2 (April, 1909), 2.
88. *The Chicago Tribune*, March 12, 1909.

same manner as the Alton's, and if the Alton's 18 per cent rate was not legal, none of the others were.[89] Therefore, there was no basis for a criminal prosecution of a shipper for receiving a rebate from the published tariff.

Since Grosscup's and Anderson's decisions were insurmountable, government attorneys, after consultation, decided to drop the remaining indictments against Standard of Indiana for accepting rebates from the Chicago & Eastern Illinois and the Burlington railroads.[90] The adverse decision for the government was, however, beneficial in a sense, for it marked the beginning of an active campaign to remedy and strengthen the rebate law.

So far as Standard of Indiana was concerned, it still had one other indictment, containing 1,524 counts for accepting rebates, pending against it in the United States District Court at Jackson, Tennessee. This suit was considered of equal importance to the Alton case, for the maximum penalty on conviction would amount to $30,084,000. The indictment, based upon evidence gathered by Garfield's investigators, was made on October 16, 1906, shortly after the indictment in the Alton case. It charged Standard with receiving rebates from the railroads on shipments from Whiting to Grand Junction, Tennessee, and points beyond.[91] However, the case did not come to trial until November 9, 1910.[92]

Early in the trial, Judge McCall ruled that an alleged offense against the Elkins Act took place only when a settlement was made, thus reducing the number of counts in the indictment from 1,524 to 46.[93] After eight days of trial and after the government had completed its case, Robert W. Stewart, chief counsel for Standard, moved the court for a directed verdict. In view of the total lack of evidence and the fact that the company had been paying the legal rate, Judge McCall granted the motion, and the jury brought in a verdict of not guilty.[94] With a favorable verdict in this case, Standard of Indiana had been exonerated from all charges of violating the Elkins law.

---

89. *Ibid.*
90. *Ibid.*, March 20, 1909.
91. *The Chicago Tribune*, October 17, 1906; *National Petroleum News*, II, No. 2 (April, 1910), 6.
92. *National Petroleum News*, II, No. 10 (December, 1910), 21; *The Chicago Tribune*, November 8, 1910.
93. *The Chicago Tribune*, November 16, 1910.
94. 183 F. 223.

CHAPTER V
Dissolution and Independence

As a climax to a series of suits filed against Standard Oil companies in different state and federal courts beginning in 1905, the United States government filed a petition on November 15, 1906, against the Standard Oil Company of New Jersey, about seventy affiliated corporations, limited partnerships and co-partnerships, and John D. Rockefeller, William Rockefeller, H. H. Rogers, H. M. Flagler, John D. Archbold, Oliver H. Payne, and Charles M. Pratt in the United States Circuit Court for the Eastern District of Missouri at St. Louis.[1] The petition sought to enjoin the defendants from continuing a combination and conspiracy in restraint of trade in violation of the Sherman Anti-Trust Act of 1890 and asked for a dissolution of the combination. Former Judge Franklin Ferris of St. Louis was appointed special examiner on June 24, 1907, to hear and take testimony. The hearings began in New York on September 3, 1907. Frank B. Kellogg, Charles B. Morrison, and J. Harwood Graves, special assistants to the Attorney General, represented the United States. John G. Milburn, Moritz Rosenthal, John S. Miller, M. F. Elliott, Martin Carey, F. L. Crawford, and Douglas Campbell represented the defendants.

Through the testimony of every important Standard official and others and the production and examination of company records of all kinds, the chief investigator, Kellogg, went into the history of the Standard organization for the past forty years, the relationship of the various companies to one another, their capitalization, earnings, profits, rebates, prices, marketing practices, production, transportation, and manufacturing. The testimony of 444 witnesses was taken and 1,371 exhibits were introduced. When the hearings were completed in January, 1909, a complete transcript of all testimony and exhibits, consisting of twenty-one printed volumes with 14,495 pages, was filed with the court. It was the most comprehensive, thorough, and enlightening investigation of Stand-

---

1. *Transcript of Record, Standard Oil Company Et Al., Appellants, vs. The United States,* A, 5-170.

ard ever made. It provided an invaluable source of information about Standard's operations.[2]

After studying the evidence and hearing arguments, the Circuit Court at St. Louis rendered its decision on November 20, 1909, in which it held thirty-eight Standard companies, including Standard of Indiana, and the seven individuals guilty of conspiring to restrain trade in violation of the Sherman Anti-Trust Act.[3] The complaint against thirty-three of the defendants was dismissed because they were not engaged in the operation or carrying out of the conspiracy. In reaching its decision the court found that from 1899 until the filing of the suit, Standard of New Jersey had controlled and directed the management of the other thirty-seven companies as a single unit. Together these companies produced more than one-tenth of the crude oil of the country, transported more than four-fifths of the oil produced in Pennsylvania, Ohio, and Indiana, refined more than three-fourths of all crude oil, owned more than one-half of all the tank cars, marketed more than four-fifths of all kerosene, exported more than four-fifths of all kerosene, sold more than four-fifths of all naphtha, and distributed more than nine-tenths of all lubricating oil sold to the railroads of the United States. By virtue of the holding company arrangement and the commanding volume of business, Standard of New Jersey was able to prevent competition among the different companies in interstate and international commerce. Furthermore, the seven individual defendants, out of fifteen Directors and about 5,000 stockholders, owned not much more than a third of the stock, held the actual control and direction of all the companies, and were engaged in carrying out the conspiracy in restraint of trade.

As a result of the decision, the court entered a decree prohibiting the Standard of New Jersey from voting the stock in any of the thirty-seven companies and from exercising any control, supervision, or influence over their acts. The subsidiary companies were

2. These volumes have been published under the general title *Transcript of Record, United States of America, Petitioner, v. Standard Oil Company of New Jersey, Et Al., Defendants,* and the individual volumes as *Petitioner's Testimony, Petitioner's Exhibits, Defendants' Testimony,* and *Defendants' Exhibits.* Additional information is to be found in *Brief of the Law for Petitioner, Brief Of Facts And Argument For Petitioner, Summary of The Facts and Brief of the Law for the United States, Brief For Defendants On the Facts, Defendants' Brief On the Facts, Defendants' Brief On The Law,* and *Brief Of The Law On Behalf Of Defendants Standard Oil Company And Others.*

3. 173 F. 177.

enjoined from declaring or paying any dividend to the Jersey company and from permitting the Jersey company to vote any stock or direct the policy or exercise any control whatsoever over their acts. The court enjoined the defendants from carrying into further effect the combination adjudged illegal. Furthermore, they were prohibited from engaging in commerce among the states or territories until the illegal combination had been discontinued. The decree was to become effective within thirty days unless there was an appeal.

The decision was a great legal victory for the government. The "Octopus" had at last been shorn of its tentacles. Thirty-seven companies were to be set free and made independent. The more thoughtful comments upon the decision were not so much concerned about the effect of the decision upon Standard as they were about the effect upon other businesses, for under such a decision it seemed impossible to do business on any large scale without violating the Sherman Anti-Trust Act.[4] The question was: What business, large or small, corporation or partnership, is safe from attack? Standard had been an especially great sinner but that was no reason why innocent businesses should suffer. Many believed that a clear line should be drawn between legitimate and illegitimate combinations.

Within three weeks the defendants filed an appeal with the Supreme Court of the United States citing sixty-five instances wherein the court erred. With a capacity crowd in attendance and spectators standing around the chamber wall, the Supreme Court heard oral arguments in March, 1910. Justice William H. Moody, owing to his previous connection with the case as Attorney General, disqualified himself. Owing to the death of two justices, the case was given a rehearing on two subsequent occasions before a decision could be rendered. Many decisions of the Supreme Court had been awaited with country-wide suspense, but none caused the markets and the whole industrial and commercial world to pause more perceptibly than the case against the Standard of New Jersey. For months the financial markets virtually stood still awaiting the decision.

With very few people in the courtroom late on the afternoon of May 15, 1911, and after many decisions had been read, Chief Jus-

4. "Standard Oil and Other Decisions under the Sherman Anti-Trust Law," *World's Work*, XIX (January, 1910), 12421-3; "Another Blow at the Standard Oil," *Current Literature*, XLVIII (January, 1910), 15-20; A. D. Noyes, "Standard Oil Decision," *Forum*, XLIII (January, 1910), 40-48.

tice White announced in a lazy, half-distinct voice a few unimportant orders and then casually said that he proposed to deliver the opinion in the Standard Oil case.[5] Immediately there was a great stir on the part of those present. A half-dozen men bearing the news rushed through the corridors of the capitol to the telegraph office. Senators and Representatives hastened at once to the Supreme Court chamber, and it was soon filled to overflowing.

After a general review of the case, the Chief Justice took up the government's contention that the language of the Sherman Act embraced *every* contract and combination in restraint of trade, which left no room for the exercise of judgment and required the application of its prohibitions to every case. The court did not seem to be very much concerned about Standard. It was more concerned with how the Sherman Act should be interpreted and applied. The court held that a literal interpretation of the law would prohibit all commercial contracts, each of which to some extent restrained trade. Rigidly and universally enforced, it seemed likely that the law would derange all business. Departing from the ruling in the Trans-Mississippi Freight Association case, the court held that since specific acts were not enumerated or defined in the Sherman Act, judgment in every case should be exercised to determine if a restraint of trade was involved. It held that the interpretation of the Act must be determined "by the light of reason, guided by principles of law." This was the origin of the so-called "rule of reason." There had previously been a great diversity of thought over what the Act meant but now the court had fixed a standard by which a combination might be declared legal or illegal. It gave a more workable though not much more definite meaning to the law. In applying the rule of reason to the Standard Oil case, the court held that the defendants had exercised an unreasonable restraint of trade and had, therefore, violated the law. The Supreme Court upheld the decision of the Circuit Court but made two minor modifications in the decree. One permitted the companies to continue trading in interstate commerce pending the dissolution. The other gave the parent company six months instead of thirty days in which to comply with the decree.[6]

The decision was unanimous, except for Justice Harlan, who concurred in part and bitterly dissented in part.[7] He objected

5. Edward G. Lowry, "The Supreme Court Speaks," *Harper's Weekly,* LV (June 3, 1911), 8.
6. 221 U. S. 1.
7. *Ibid.*

especially to the court's attempt by interpretation to soften and modify what might be regarded as a harsh public policy. It was not the court's function to declare public policy or amend legislative enactments and, in this instance, it had read into an act of Congress words which were not to be found there. Harlan believed that all agreements in restraint of trade were illegal.

Wall Street hailed the decision with enthusiasm. Most of the discussion centered upon the interpretation of the Sherman Act rather than upon the dissolution of Standard. By construing the Sherman Act to prohibit not all restraints of trade, only unreasonable ones, the court had virtually amended the law and established a new rule for determining in the future whether a large industrial organization was legal or illegal. It removed many of the fears and threats of sweeping decisions previously rendered by the lower courts. According to *The Chicago Tribune,* "The wild interpretations had suddenly lost their hold on the community." [8] Despite the favorable reactions, many condemned the court's new interpretation as a usurpation of power. Others asked: What effect will the decision have upon the United States Steel, International Harvester, National Cash Register, and other large-scale businesses?

The lethargy which had hung over business, finance, and the whole country for weeks quickly lifted. Business confidence was stimulated. Stock prices advanced 2 to 6 per cent in the next three days. Transactions on the New York Stock Exchange rose from 143,375 on the 15th to more than a million the day after the decision. Most remarkable of all was the fact that Standard of New Jersey stock, after declining from a low bid of 675 to 665 the next day after the decision, advanced fourteen points on the two succeeding days, reaching the highest price since the middle of 1909. Only thirty shares of the Jersey company were traded on the 15th, but the next day 600 shares changed hands.

While the government had gained a notable victory in bringing about the dissolution of America's greatest monopoly, the decision caused no particular surprise, and there was much skepticism about its ultimate effect.[9] There were many who believed that

8. May 16, 1911.
9. "After the Standard Oil Decision," *The Nation,* XCII (May 25, 1911), 540; "'Jail 'Em,' Is Editorial Opinion in S. O. Case," *National Petroleum News,* III, No. 4 (June, 1911), 40-42; "S. O. Dissolution Will Raise Cost to Public—Now the Cry," *National Petroleum News,* III, No. 6 (August, 1911), 7; "The Standard Dissolves," *The Oil and Gas Journal,* X, No. 8 (August 3, 1911), 1; "What

little would be accomplished by dissolution. "Like the chameleon," declared *The Chicago Tribune,* "the more Standard changes the more it is the same thing." [10] Standard had been through such proceedings previously, and it was predicted that it would find a legal way out. There was a distinct feeling that dissolution and the disorganization of business methods would result in higher prices for the consumer. Business could not be carried on as economically or efficiently by thirty-eight companies as by one.

Independent oilmen, who had been responsible for many attacks and suits against Standard, were now wondering if dissolution was wise. With thirty-eight Standard companies and the officers of each one interested in making a good showing, competition was likely to be keener than ever before. The independents were fearful that increased competition would result in price cuts in order to get the business. The producer had his worries too. From 1899 to 1911 Standard of New Jersey and its subsidiaries had purchased and stored enormous quantities of excess crude oil. Now that it could no longer operate as a unit, would the individual companies have the financial resources to do this? The effect of the decision was watched with great interest and not a little anxiety by the whole oil trade.

A little less than a month after the Supreme Court of the United States upheld the dissolution of the Standard of New Jersey, the special commissioner in the Kansas ouster suit, which had been filed in October, 1906, made his report to the Supreme Court of Kansas. Considering all of the accusations and denunciations which had been levied against Standard in Kansas, the findings of the special commissioner were amazing.[11] Among other things, the commissioner pointed out that in organizing the three defendant companies it was never intended by their creator that they should compete with one another. The general tendency of retail prices of Standard of Indiana in Kansas in the last ten years had been downward, and during the same time the quality of all its products had been gradually improved. Standard of Indiana had not killed off competitors, for in 1900 it had three and in 1912, twenty-

Effect Will It Have," *The Oil and Gas Journal,* X, No. 25 (November 30, 1911), 1; Frank B. Kellogg, "Results of the Standard Oil Decision," *The American Review of Reviews,* XLV (June, 1912), 728-730.

10. May 16, 1911; "The Standard Oil Decision," *The American Review of Reviews,* XLIII (June, 1911), 653-656; T. R. Roosevelt, "Standard Oil Decision—and After," *Outlook,* XCVIII (June 3, 1911), 239-240.

11. *Eighteenth Biennial Report of the Attorney General of Kansas, 1911–12,* 64-91.

two. Prices at which Standard sold kerosene and gasoline in Kansas and Missouri were cheaper than those at which it sold in other states farther removed from refineries. The company sold oil in Kansas at a uniform net price regardless of quantity and did not cut the price in any locality or to any individual for the purpose of getting business. Standard did not restrict dealers in Kansas from handling similar products sold by its competitors. There was no evidence to show that the defendants did anything to influence an increase of railroad rates in 1904. On the contrary, the evidence showed that Standard of Indiana objected to and protested against any increase. The decline in the price of crude oil was largely due to an excess of production over market requirements. The failure of many oil companies in Kansas was not due directly or indirectly to anything the defendants had done. The "manner in which the Indiana Company has transacted its business in Kansas," declared the special commissioner, "so far as shown by the evidence, has been shown to have been beneficial to the people of the State in many respects, and has not been shown to be otherwise in any respect." [12]

The special commissioner found that the evidence relative to many of the plaintiff's allegations was untrue. "By reason of its superior facilities for serving and the extent to which it does now serve the public, the price it charges and the quality of its goods, I find," said the commissioner, "that the exclusion of the Indiana Company would, at least for an indefinite period, be a great detriment to the general public." [13] In further support of his recommendation against excluding Standard of Indiana from Kansas the special commissioner pointed out that it sold lubricating oils of more uniform and satisfactory qualities than anyone else in Kansas. It had 156 tank stations, 341 employees, and an investment of $1,708,726.52 in Kansas. It had not only more tank-wagon stations in Kansas but more efficiently operated ones than its competitors. Its facilities for marketing in Kansas were superior to all other companies.

After Keplinger's report of his findings, the attorney general, John S. Dawson, decided that it would not serve the public welfare to press the case for ousting the companies from Kansas. He began negotiations with the defendants which would give the state everything except a complete judgment of ouster, and they

12. *Ibid.*, 75.
13. *Ibid.*, 91.

agreed to a stipulation of judgment. On June 15, 1911, the Kansas Supreme Court entered a judgment approving the agreement.[14] The decree prohibited Standard of Kansas from selling refined oil at any place except at its Neodesha refinery and to wholesalers. It could not produce or sell crude or have bulk stations or tank wagons, except at Neodesha, for wholesale purposes. Prairie was forbidden to refine or market refined products. It could, however, make and sell gasoline or naphtha from natural gas. Standard of Indiana was prohibited from producing or selling crude, except for fuel or power purposes. It could market products, but it could not sell at different prices in different parts of Kansas, except for equalizing freight charges. It could not make any contract or agreement whereby any persons or firm were bound to refrain from the purchase or sale of petroleum products manufactured or sold in Kansas by any other person or firm. It could not sell under different brands any oil of the same value and quality at different prices for the purpose of destroying competition. All three companies were prohibited from making contracts with each other to restrain trade, competition, or set prices of petroleum products. If Standard of Indiana wished to buy the Standard of Kansas, the court indicated a willingness to approve such a purchase. No fine or imprisonment was involved, except the plaintiffs paid the costs —$16,420.03. To see that the provisions of the decree were enforced and not violated, the court retained jurisdiction over the case.

After the Kansas Supreme Court entered its decree of June 15, 1911, Attorney General Dawson, in accordance with the stipulation that the companies were to pay $25,000, arranged with the county attorneys of about half the counties in Kansas to file civil suits in each county charging restraint of trade and the stifling of competition in order that the money might go into the school fund of the counties where the evidence had been obtained in the antitrust suit.[15] Suits were instituted and settlements made. In most of the counties Standard of Indiana paid the maximum penalty of $500 plus $150 in attorneys' fees to be divided between the office of the attorney general and those of the county attorneys.

14. Topeka *Daily Capital*, June 16, 1911; Topeka *State Journal*, June 16, 1911; *The Chicago Tribune*, June 17, 1911; *National Petroleum News*, III, No. 5 (July, 1911), 35-36.
15. Topeka *Daily Capital*, June 18, 1911; *The Oil and Gas Journal*, X, No. 2 (June 22, 1911), 4, X, No. 8 (August 3, 1911), 10; *National Petroleum News*, III, No. 6 (August, 1911), 8.

For weeks after the decision of the United States Supreme Court in the dissolution suit, not a sound came from 26 Broadway, and all sorts of rumors were rife about what Standard might do. By late July, a plan for conforming to the dissolution decree had been adopted, and on the 28th the stockholders of the Jersey company were informed of its character.[16] About December 1, 1911, shares of stock, which Jersey owned directly or indirectly in thirty-three companies, were to be distributed to the stockholders as of record on August 31st on a proportional basis. The announcement created brisk trading in Standard of New Jersey stock. The number of shares traded jumped from 75 on July 31st to 609 on August 1st, 357 on the 2nd, 862 on the 3rd, and then declined to 677 on the 4th. The amount of stock a holder of one share of Jersey stock would receive in each of the thirty-three companies was announced on November 15th.[17] For example, the holder of one share of Jersey stock would receive 9,990/983,383 of one share of Standard of Indiana stock. The distribution was based upon the capitalization of the Standard of New Jersey, which had 983,383 shares of stock outstanding at $100 per share, and that of each subsidiary.

According to the plan, the personnel at 26 Broadway in New York, the headquarters of the parent company, was to be divided among the thirty-three companies. Moffett, President of Standard of Indiana, was to remain in New York as a Director of the Jersey company. L. J. Drake and H. S. Morton, who had been in New York, and E. J. Bullock, who had been with the Atlantic Refining Company, were assigned to Standard of Indiana. New executive officers for each of the companies were arranged. This was not an easy task because there were so many companies to be staffed. One official said: "We even had to send out some office boys to head these companies." On November 23rd orders were issued for these employees to report to the headquarters of their respective companies, and on December 1, 1911, the career of the most famous holding company in history came to a close.[18] On that day over 200,000 stock certificates were sent out by registered mail to 6,078 stockholders, and Standard of New Jersey and each of the thirty-three companies became separate and independent.

Strange and ridiculous situations developed in apportioning

16. *The Chicago Tribune,* August 1, 1911.
17. *Ibid.,* November 16, 1911; *Chicago Examiner,* November 16, 1911.
18. "Moving Day at Hand," *The Oil and Gas Journal,* X, No. 25 (November 30, 1911), 12.

and sending out the stock.[19] More than half of the 6,078 Jersey
stockholders had less than 51 shares. Many had three, five, or ten
shares. Three hundred held only one share of stock. For one share
of Jersey stock, a stockholder was entitled to 994/983,383 of a
share in the Swan & Finch Company with a face value of 10 cents
and to 7,143/983,383 of a share in the Washington Oil Company
with a face value of 7 cents and so on through the other thirty-one
companies. After the distribution of the stock had been completed,
the small stockholder looked over his assortment and was puzzled.
Yesterday he had one share of Jersey stock, a tangible thing worth
$700. Today he had fractional shares in thirty-three companies,
the value of which was a mathematical mystery. Furthermore, no
stockholder could vote in any company unless he had one full
share.

One effect of the reorganization was that several hundred small
stockholders immediately sold their shares without knowing anything about the real value. Prior to the dissolution suit, Standard
had never published any financial statements. During the trial,
however, it was disclosed for the first time what the assets and
earnings of the various companies were, but this information fil-
tered through slowly to investors. Those who knew or had some
idea of the financial possibilities grabbed the splinters, which resulted in an even greater concentration of stock in the hands of
the larger stockholders. The case of Standard of Indiana is indicative of what happened. On September 1, 1911, the company had
6,081 stockholders holding an aggregate of 10,000 shares of stock;
857 held whole shares and fractional shares and 5,224 held fractional shares only. Seven months later, on April 1, 1912, the company had 5,074 stockholders holding an aggregate of 10,000 shares;
108 stockholders held whole shares only; 773 held whole shares
and fractional shares, and 4,193 held fractional shares only.

On December 6, 1911, at a meeting of the Directors of Stand-
ard of Indiana at 26 Broadway, the resignations of Moffett as
President and a Director, Cowan as Vice-President, and W. C.
Teagle, John D. Archbold, Charles M. Pratt, H. C. Folger, Jr.,
and A. C. Bedford as Directors, were read and accepted.[20] Dr.
Burton, A. D. Eddy, and George W. Stahl were elected Directors.
They, together with Cowan, Drake, and Walter Jennings, consti-

19. Albert W. Atwood, "The Greatest Killing in Wall Street," *McClure's Magazine*,
   XXXIX (August, 1912), 409-419.
20. Minutes of the Board of Directors' and Stockholders' Meetings, I, 225; *The
   Chicago Tribune*, October 1, 1912.

tuted the new Board, which elected Cowan President. Jennings resigned early in January. In this way Standard of Indiana began its independent and separate existence, not under any new and strange officers but under the management of trusted and experienced men, who had long been with Standard of Indiana and had come up through the ranks. Freed from all control by the parent company, they were now in a position to formulate policies best suited to the Middle West, to spend money and develop the business as they saw fit. The dissolution was the first step in making Standard of Indiana a midwestern industrial enterprise.

At the first annual meeting of the stockholders in March, 1913, the number of Directors was reduced from nine to five. It was this small group—Cowan, Drake, Eddy, Stahl, and Burton—who constituted the top management and guided the company in the transition period from 1911 to 1918. Except for Burton, who was about forty-six years old and the youngest, the other four had reached or were very near retirement age. Cowan served as President; Drake as Vice-President. In 1914 Burton was named Second Vice-President. Eddy retired in April, 1915, which resulted in the establishment of the company's Law Department.[21] Colonel Robert W. Stewart, who had been with Eddy's firm since 1907 and closely identified with most of the important legal battles of the company, became General Counsel and a Director to succeed Eddy. Chauncey W. Martyn and Harry A. Daugherty of Eddy's firm became general attorneys in the Law Department. In 1916 the membership of the Board was enlarged to six and Henry S. Morton was added.

All of the Directors elected in 1911 had been closely identified previously with special phases of the company's operations. Burton had been primarily concerned with manufacturing, Drake with sales, Eddy with legal matters, and Stahl with finances. After the reorganization, they not only served as Directors but as the operating heads of these departments. They met regularly in their collective capacity as Directors to discuss and formulate policies. Decisions made were immediately executed by the departmental head affected. This arrangement, a natural outgrowth of conditions, established a strong precedent of having "working" Directors. Unlike many industrial corporations with departmental heads in actual charge of daily operations and a group of Directors

21. C. Henry Austin, "Law Department Important Unit in Company Affairs," *Stanolind Record*, XI, No. 11 (September, 1930), 1-11.

largely drawn from outside the company and without any intimate knowledge of the daily operating problems, the system of having operating heads serve as Directors became a feature in the organization of Standard of Indiana, which remained unbroken until 1929.

The headquarters of Standard of Indiana after 1911 continued without change in the Edison Building and the Marquette Building in Chicago, but in March, 1917, in order to have more space and to bring all officers under one roof, the company purchased the twelve-story Karpen Building at Michigan Avenue and 9th Street for a total of $3,500,000.[22] It was reported to be the largest single real-estate transaction in the history of Chicago up until that time. During the winter of 1917-18 the building was remodeled and improved. In May, 1918, all of the offices were moved to 910 S. Michigan, which has been the company's home office ever since. Seven floors were added in 1925, making it a nineteen-story building.

Other companies went through a reorganization similar to that of Standard of Indiana. Except for the changes in officers and Directors, there was at first little indication that anything had happened. Each company retained its original corporate name, with the result that there were a half-dozen or more "Standard" companies. The name was so well known to consumers that these companies could not afford to change. For this reason, even though the companies were separate and independent, the general public failed to make any distinction and continues to think of them to this day as a single company. The same seven individuals who had held a majority of stock in the Standard of Jersey held a majority of the stock in each of the thirty-four companies. Each of the marketing companies continued to market in the territory originally assigned to it, and for some years they did not actively compete with one another.

The fact that active competition did not immediately develop was due to a number of influential factors. In the first place, there was no particular incentive to invade the territory of another former Standard unit. With the rapidly growing demand, each company had plenty of business available in its own marketing territory. Furthermore, if Standard of Indiana, for example,

---

22. *The Chicago Tribune*, March 3, 1917; "It Takes 124 People Just to Keep House for Us," *Stanolind Record*, VIII, No. 12 (October, 1927), 1-4; *National Petroleum News*, XVII, No. 36 (September 9, 1925), 82.

invaded the territory of another Standard company, the latter probably would have retaliated and created a fierce competitive war at a time when all of them were in a precarious condition. Secondly, as long as Rockefeller men managed the various companies, there was a community of interest, a friendly feeling, which prevented any serious competition or rivalry from developing. Cowan, Drake, and Burton were old Rockefeller men, and they maintained close ties with the Rockefellers and the men of other companies after 1911. Moreover, many of the leading officers and Directors of several companies held stock in two or more former Standard companies. For example, Cowan, President of Standard of Indiana, owned 303 shares ($165,135) in his own company, 420 ($228,000) in the Standard of New Jersey, 320 ($72,000) in the Standard of New York, 256 ($47,872) in the Prairie Pipe Line, 100 ($11,350) in the Indiana Pipe Line, 76 ($33,174) in the Prairie Oil & Gas Company, 64 ($15,040) in the Vacuum Oil Company, 14 ($7,560) in the Standard of Ohio, and 12 ($3,300) in the Continental Oil Company.[23]

Little known or understood by the public, as a factor in keeping each company within its old geographical marketing boundaries, was the trade mark situation.[24] For example, prior to dissolution, Polarine, a lubricating oil, was a brand name registered by the Atlantic Refining. Other Standard brands, probably the majority, were not even registered and constituted common law trade-marks. In either case, each marketing subsidiary had used these brand names in its own territory. When dissolution took place, the question of the ownership of these trade-marks or brands apparently escaped the attention of everyone, and no provision was made concerning them. As a result, each former marketing subsidiary started out selling under old brand names—Polarine, Perfection Oil, Capitol Cylinder Oil, Red Crown gasoline, and others. Under the circumstances, it was very doubtful, for example, that the Standard of Kentucky could legally sell Red Crown gasoline in the territory of Standard of Indiana. A further difficulty lay in the fact that approximately thirty states had some kind of regulation prohibiting a corporation from being organized or licensed to do business in the state under a name that was the

23. Federal Trade Commission, *Report On the Price of Gasoline In 1915*, 145-146.
24. *Stenographer's Transcript of Hearing Before Honorable Charles Martindale, Master in Chancery, 1926, United States of America, Petitioner, vs. Standard Oil Company (Indiana) Et Al., Defendants*, VI, 3253-3256. Hereinafter referred to as *Hearings Before Martindale*.

same or close to that of a corporation previously organized or licensed. Even where no law of this sort existed, the secretary of state in several states had discretionary authority over issuing a charter or licensing a corporation where its name was similar to one already in existence. About the only way, therefore, whereby one of these former Standard companies could invade the territory of another was to adopt a different company name and different brand names. However, the name Standard and the old brands were so well known and established that the various companies were reluctant to change.

The last factor having a bearing upon the lack of competition at first was that freight rates largely determined the extent of the marketing area. How far could a company ship profitably? Inevitably, the shipment of products reached a certain point where, for every mile beyond, freight charges increased while freight charges for another Standard refinery decreased. This continued to be as true after dissolution as it was before, and it acted as a deterrent to invading the marketing area of another company. Obviously the general public, the newspapers, and magazines were not aware of all these factors, and no effort was made by the various Standard units to explain them.[25]

When the new officers of Standard of Indiana took charge in 1911, the company had three refineries. Whiting, representing an investment of about $8,000,000, employed 1,800 men and had a daily refining capacity of 27,400 barrels.[26] It manufactured all grades of naphtha, kerosene, lubricants, road and fuel oil, paraffin wax, candles, coke, and all other petroleum products, except for minor ones like petrolatum. The Sugar Creek refinery had a daily capacity of about 19,200 barrels of crude, employed 350 men, and represented an investment of $1,500,000. It manufactured naphthas, kerosene, road and fuel oils but no lubricants. Wood River represented an investment of $2,225,000, had a daily capacity of 8,200 barrels, and employed 300 men. Twenty-four new stills had been added in 1910 and twelve in 1911. It made naphthas, kerosene, a few grades of lubricants, and crude wax but no candles. The company marketed in nine states of the Upper Mississippi

25. A survey conducted by Elmo Roper in 1943 revealed that only 22 per cent of the public thought of the several Standard companies as individual concerns. *Business Week*, September 8, 1945, 51.
26. This summary of Standard's refining operations is based upon the *Eighteenth Biennial Report of the Attorney General of Kansas*, 1911–12, 71, and a letter from J. C. Documun to Conger Reynolds, December 26, 1952.

Valley, and in this branch of the business it employed 3,641 men, operated 1,331 tank-wagon stations, and had $7,956,508.32 invested. Through these marketing facilities, the company was selling about 85 per cent of the business in its territory.

Financially, the company was in excellent condition. It had a capitalization of $1,000,000, yet its assets amounted to $28,146,-422.26 and its surplus to $24,217, 404.96.[27] In 1911 it paid $2,999,-700 in cash dividends, which was 11.90 per cent upon its total capital assets and 299.97 per cent on the nominal par value of the issued capital stock.

Despite the strong position occupied by the company in 1911, the new officers faced some very serious problems. Unless the United States Supreme Court sustained its appeal in the Missouri ouster case, the company would have to close its refinery at Sugar Creek and withdraw from marketing in Missouri. More disturbing was the fact that the dissolution order left the company with an enormous investment in three large refineries and a vast marketing organization but no crude oil supply, pipelines, or tank cars. So long as crude was available, J. E. O'Neil, President of Prairie Oil & Gas, promised to supply the company.[28]

From the time of the reorganization of the company early in December, 1911, a hunt had gone on for fractional shares of stock in Standard of Indiana although its value was unknown. The stock had never been listed on the New York Stock Exchange, and the management had never voluntarily given out any information about its business or profits. Anyone who had followed the Landis trial or read the Garfield reports or had followed the Kellogg investigation knew the company had an enormous surplus. In the legal battles of 1906 the government revealed that Standard of Indiana had assets of $27,502,089.86 and was earning at the rate of over $10,000,000 per year.[29] The increase in assets and earnings between 1907 and 1911 were huge, far beyond anything dreamed of by the general public. The book value of its stock as of December 31, 1911, was $2,521.74 per share of $100 par value.[30] Late in January, 1912, stock in the company was selling for about $4,000,

27. Balance Sheet, December 31, 1911.
28. Interview with William M. Burton, August 2, 1948.
29. *Transcript of Record, Petitioner's Exhibits, United States of America, Petitioner, v. Standard Oil Company of New Jersey Et Al., Defendants,* 504-505.
30. *High Cost of Gasoline and Other Petroleum Products* (Hearings Before a Subcommittee of the Committee on Manufacturers, United States Senate, 67th Congress, 2nd and 4th sessions, Pursuant to S. Res. 295), I, 765.

which was the most conspicuous increase in the price of stocks of all the former Standard companies.[31]

With a capitalization of only $1,000,000 and assets of $28,146,-422.26 in 1911, the company was obviously undercapitalized, and one of the first actions of the Directors was to equalize assets and capitalization. Suddenly and without any warning on February 6, 1912, the Directors created a sensation by announcing that they had voted to raise the capital stock of the company from $1,000,000 to $30,000,000, an increase of 2,900 per cent, subject to the approval of the stockholders at the annual meeting on March 7th.[32] This declaration was one of the first evidences of the great hidden values in these securities and stimulated considerably the market and public interest in all Standard Oil securities. No one knew from the announcement whether the new $29,000,000 stock issue would be given to stockholders or paid for by them at $100 a share. The stock leaped up and down spectacularly at $100 a jump. On February 9th a $100 share was worth $4,500.[33] Seven days later the management announced that the new stock would be given to the stockholders at the rate of twenty-nine new shares for one.[34] The stock soared to $7,000 a share. When the stock dividend was approved on March 7, 1912, bids on the curb exchanges for the new par $100 stock, when issued, opened at $163 and steadily advanced to $230 on March 14th.

Stock dividends followed leisurely in one Standard company after another in the ensuing months. By the end of March, 1912, it was estimated that in three months' time since the dissolution over $200,000,000 had been added to the market value of the stocks of the different companies.[35] It had been the biggest "killing" in the shortest time in the history of Wall Street. Of the $200,000,000, about one-half was on the stock held by Rockefeller and his six associates.[36] With this situation in mind, Theodore Roosevelt, commenting in 1914 upon the effect of dissolution, wrote: "Not one particle of good resulted to anybody and a number of worthy citizens of small means were appreciably injured.

31. A. W. Atwood, "Greatest Killing in Wall Street," *McClure's Magazine*, XXXIX (August, 1912), 414.
32. *The Chicago Tribune*, February 6, 1911, October 2, 1912.
33. *The Chicago Tribune*, February 9, 1911.
34. *Ibid.*, February 14, 1911.
35. A. W. Atwood, "Greatest Killing in Wall Street," *McClure's Magazine*, XXXIX (August, 1912), 415.
36. "Dissolutions Benefit Stockholders But Not the Consumers," *The Oil and Gas Journal*, July 10, 1924, 130.

No reason has been shown for believing that a better effect would follow success in suits being carried on against the Steel Corporation and Harvester Company." [37]

In a unanimous decision rendered on April 12, 1912, the United States Supreme Court, in the Missouri ouster proceedings against Standard of Indiana and Republic Oil, upheld the Missouri Supreme Court.[38] Republic, therefore, paid the fine, and it was soon liquidated. Officials of Standard issued orders immediately to suspend all construction work at its Sugar Creek refinery and began laying off men.[39] On May 1st attorneys for the company filed a motion asking the Missouri Supreme Court for permission to pay the fine and costs and be allowed to continue in business.[40] It was pointed out that since the dissolution decree of the United States Supreme Court on May 15, 1911, Standard of Indiana no longer had any connection with the Standard of New Jersey. Furthermore, it had in Missouri $3,750,000 worth of property. It did a large business in kerosene, fuel oil, road oil, and oil for heating orchards. It employed several hundred people. However, the court refused early in 1913 to modify the judgment because the time limit for such an action had expired. As a result, the company began shipping oil to Wood River and making other preparations to close the Sugar Creek refinery.

The citizens of Sugar Creek through an attorney filed a plea with the court on February 19th asking for a rehearing in the case and a stay of its ouster order.[41] Out of a population of 500 in Sugar Creek there were some sixty homeowners. Moreover, the citizens had built a $30,000 schoolhouse, two churches, and had made many public and private improvements. If the Sugar Creek refinery were closed, these investments would be jeopardized, the inhabitants would be without work, the state would lose an important and useful industry, and it would leave a monopoly of the business to the old Waters-Pierce company. The Kansas City Commercial Club took the initiative in the movement for legislation to permit the company to remain in business.[42] A bill, introduced in

37. *The Oil and Gas Journal,* September 25, 1924, 82.
38. 224 U. S. 270; *The Chicago Tribune,* April 2, 1912.
39. *National Petroleum News,* IV, No. 2 (April, 1912), 37.
40. *The Oil and Gas Journal,* X, No. 47 (May 2, 1912), 3; *National Petroleum News,* IV, No. 3 (May, 1912), 32.
41. *The New York Times,* May 11, 1913; *National Petroleum News,* V, No. 1 (March, 1913), 16, 33.
42. "Trust Busting vs. Regulation," *Outlook,* CIV (August 2, 1913), 731-32.

the state legislature in April, provided that the company might stay if it paid triple the license fee required of other foreign corporations. Ex-Governor Hadley, who had originally started the suit, publicly endorsed the bill. The bill passed the legislature, but Elliott W. Major, the governor, vetoed it because the terms were too general. Moreover, he believed that the proper method to accomplish the end was through a State Supreme Court order.[43]

The Missouri Supreme Court granted the company's application for a rehearing on May 10, 1913, suspended the writ of ouster, and appointed John Montgomery of Sedalia as special master to take testimony on the company's severance of relationships with the Jersey company.[44] Hearings were held in Chicago and Kansas City where George W. Stahl, the Secretary-Treasurer, W. E. Judd, manager in Kansas City, G. H. Moffett, superintendent at Sugar Creek, and others testified.[45] Montgomery filed his report on June 10th. It was simply a transcript of the testimony without any findings or recommendations. On the basis of the report, arguments, and briefs, the court on June 28th suspended the writ of ouster until further order subject to the following conditions: that the court retain jurisdiction of the case; that the company faithfully observe and obey the laws of Missouri, especially the antitrust laws; that, if the company violated the order, the attorney general might move to vacate the order, take and offer proof but, in such an instance, the company might also offer proof; that the Supreme Court might at any time direct that evidence be taken to see if the company was observing the laws; and that in all investigations proof be limited to things since this order.[46] A policy of regulating business as opposed to a policy of destroying business had finally triumphed in Missouri. After more than four years of litigation, Standard of Indiana had finally won the privilege of remaining in business in Missouri. It has operated since that day to the present under a stay of the ouster order.

43. *The New York Times*, April 10, 1913.
44. *The Chicago Tribune*, May 11, 1913.
45. *The New York Times*, May 17, 20, 1913; *The Chicago Tribune*, May 20, 1913, June 11, 1913.
46. 158 S. W. 601; *The New York Times*, June 29, 1913; *The Chicago Tribune*, June 29, 1913.

CHAPTER VI

Doubling the Gasoline Supply

ONE OF THE MOST URGENT AND IMPORTANT PROBLEMS CONFRONTING the petroleum industry in 1909 was the rapidly growing demand for gasoline. With the coming of the automobile and the greater use of gasoline for lighting and cooking and for gasoline engines, there had been an enormous increase in the sale of gasoline each year after 1900. Between 1903 and 1908 motor car production alone had increased 467 per cent. With the failure of crude oil production to keep pace with the demand, alert refiners realized that, at the rate gasoline was being consumed by 1909, the normal supply would soon be inadequate and prices would skyrocket. The situation was alarming. It was obvious that something would have to be done to increase the supply or else the progress of the gasoline-powered automobile would be halted.

Attempts were made to build automobile engines to run on less volatile fuel, but none were successful. Refiners made every effort to improve the efficiency of their refining methods in order to squeeze out the last drop of gasoline, but the best they could do under the existing refining process was to get a yield of 15 to 18 per cent of gasoline from average crude. M. J. Trumble, W. A. Hall, C. H. Washburn, C. R. Burke, Carleton Ellis, A. M. McAfee, and others were experimenting with new processes for increasing the yield, and applications for patents on processes for this purpose had been filed by C. S. Palmer in 1907, Joseph H. Adams in 1908, and Jesse A. Dubbs in 1909.[1]

As a result of his observations and study, Dr. Burton, by now General Manager of Manufacturing for Standard of Indiana and directly responsible for operations at all refineries, came to the conclusion that his company should go to work on the problem at once. One day in 1909, when he was at Whiting, Burton discussed the situation with Dr. Robert E. Humphreys, a Johns Hopkins

1. For a general account of various inventors and their experiments, see David McKnight, Jr., *A Study of Patents on Petroleum Cracking with Special Reference to Their Present Status.*

140

WILLIAM P. COWAN, PRESIDENT 1911–1918

DR. ROBERT E. HUMPHREYS IN THE RESEARCH LABORATORY
AT WHITING, 1901

FIRST EXPERIMENTAL STILL
USED BY HUMPHREYS IN DE-
VELOPING THE CRACKING
PROCESS

THE SEMI-COMMERCIAL STILL USED IN TESTING THE CRACKING PROCESS

A ROW OF BURTON CRACKING STILLS, WHITING REFINERY

FIRST BURTON-CLARK EXPERIMENTAL TUBE STILL, ERECTED AT
WOOD RIVER REFINERY ABOUT 1914

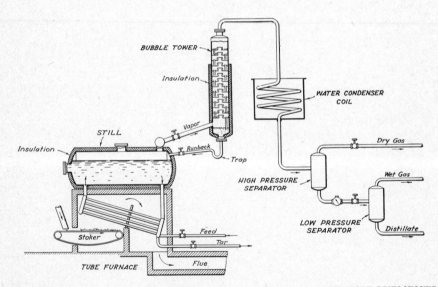

DIAGRAM OF A BURTON CRACKING STILL, SHOWING THE IMPROVEMENTS
OF CLARK, LEWIS, AND COOKE

Ph.D. in chemistry, who had come to Whiting in 1900 and had been chief chemist in charge of the laboratory since 1907.[2] The problem also challenged Humphreys' interest and imagination because it involved basic research in the chemistry of petroleum.

No basic research on the chemistry of petroleum had been done in the Whiting laboratory in the years prior to 1909. Most of the work had been routine—making sulphur determinations, analyzing samples of copper compounds, testing building materials, and examining samples of competitors' greases, motor oils, and other petroleum products which were constantly being sent in from the field by the Sales Department. The management of the company hardly contemplated that a chemist would do more. Dr. Burton had been so bored by the routine that he was glad to leave the laboratory and become assistant general superintendent of the refinery in 1893. In available spare time, which was not much, the other chemists did research on whatever projects were of interest to them personally. Humphreys had worked on the production of hydroxystearic acid from oleic acid for use in stiffening candles, the development of a white oil, the use of wax in treating paper drinking cups, and the manufacture of candles from wax having the appearance and odor of beeswax.[3] Amusing is the story of the efforts to produce in the laboratory a wax-coated metal match, all of which was done in great secrecy. Both Burton and Humphreys now deny any responsibility for the experiment. Nothing had been discovered in the laboratory, however, that was considered by management worth patenting, except the process for making hydroxystearic acid and its use in wax candles.

Without any authorization from New York and without the knowledge of the Directors in Chicago, Burton instructed Humphreys to go to work on the problem of increasing the yield of gasoline from crude.[4] It was the most important assignment ever given the laboratory. At the time, the staff was composed of two chemists, Dr. Humphreys and Dr. F. M. Rogers, another Johns Hopkins Ph.D. Within a year Dr. O. E. Bransky, who had written his doctoral thesis at Johns Hopkins on "The Diffusion of Crude

2. Robert E. Humphreys, "True Confessions of a Member of the Board," *Stanolind Record*, VIII, No. 3 (January, 1927), 34, 38-39, 40.
3. Robert E. Humphreys, "Dr. Humphreys Likewise Becomes Reminiscent," *Stanolind Record*, VIII, No. 6 (April, 1927), 23, 35, 38; Interview with R. E .Humphreys, July 10, 1948, July 17, 1948, August 26, 1948.
4. Interview with William M. Burton, August 2, 1948. For a record of Burton's accomplishments with Standard, see *William Meriam Burton: A Pioneer in Modern Petroleum Technology.*

Petroleum Through Fuller's Earth," joined the staff. There were probably at the time not more than twenty well-trained chemists working in the entire petroleum industry.

Under the general direction of Dr. Burton and with the help of his assistant, Dr. Rogers, Humphreys enthusiastically started to work on the problem. It was difficult to know where and how to begin. Burton suggested that Humphreys start by experimenting with gas oil. Two methods of attack were discussed: first, passing gas oil through hot tubes, and second, distilling gas oil in the presence of anhydrous aluminum chloride. Burton made other suggestions, but his initial ideas were not too concrete.[5] He told Humphreys to tackle the problem and try every conceivable idea. It was Humphreys' responsibility. He was to take the initiative, lay out the work, try various possibilities, and work out a solution to the problem.[6]

If an extended search and study of the literature on the subject or the Patent Office records had been made, Humphreys would have undoubtedly come across the work of Sir Boverton Redwood and James Dewar in attempting to crack oil, which was patented in the United States on April 22, 1890. They were the first to patent a pressure distillation process for the purpose of increasing the yield of kerosene from Russian crude oil, but it had never been applied industrially or on a large scale. This might have given Humphreys a good starting point and saved some time and labor. However, the laboratory possessed a very meager library, and the company did not have any patent department to which one could go for assistance. Humphreys, therefore, started from scratch, working on a few hunches and using the trial and error method.[7]

Gas oil was cheap and abundant. It was a wide cut between kerosene and lubricating oils, which was usually sold to manufacture Pintsch gas. If its large hydrocarbon molecules could be broken down, or "cracked," into smaller ones, more gasoline might be obtained. From his experience in the laboratory and the re-

5. Interview with William M. Burton, August 2, 1948.
6. *Ibid.*
7. The course of investigation is described by Dr. Burton in his address before the Chicago Section of the American Chemical Society on May 17, 1918, upon receiving the Willard Gibbs Medal, and in his address before the New York Section of the Society of Chemical Industry on January 13, 1922, upon receiving the Perkin Medal. See "Chemistry in the Petroleum Industry," *The Journal of Industrial and Engineering Chemistry,* X (June, 1918), 484-486; "Dr. Burton Pays Tribute to His Aids," *Stanolind Record,* III, No. 4 (February, 1922), 7-13.

finery in running reduced crude down to coke, Humphreys knew —and so did other refiners—that the application of high temperature would "crack" molecules with a high boiling point into low-boiling-point fractions, so he commenced to experiment with all processes of cracking gas oil by heat.[8]

Passing gas oil through hot pipes or tubes produced an excess of gas and the gasoline was of an undesirable quality for commercial purposes.[9] Humphreys knew of the Pintsch gas process of heating gas oil to very high temperatures by spraying it on red-hot brick surfaces which actually cracked it mainly to gas rather than gasoline. There were a number of these plants around Chicago making gas for use in homes where commercial gas was not available, but Humphreys' experiments with this process afforded no material help.[10] He also tried aluminum chloride, which was successful in cracking heavy oil, but the substantial loss of oil and the difficulty in recovering the expensive aluminum chloride made this plan unattractive.[11]

Burton visited the laboratory from time to time and inquired how things were going and with what results. Sometimes he would ask Humphreys if he had tried this or that. Otherwise, Humphreys used his own ingenuity. After trying many experiments and not getting anywhere by using heat alone, Humphreys finally decided in despair to try heat and pressure together on the oil. Heating oil in a still was an everyday practice. When this was done, any oil as light as gas oil would distill off when a certain temperature was reached, and there was no cracking. If the gas oil could be held in a still by the use of pressure until a cracking temperature was reached, Humphreys thought it might provide a good yield of gasoline. This had been under consideration by Humphreys almost from the beginning of his research, but the process had never been applied in a practical way and the danger involved caused him to look first at every other promising method. Distilling oil under heat and pressure might seem to present no problem, for water was distilled every day in steam boilers. Why should one hesitate, therefore, to put oil under heat and pressure? The reason was that such a process required temperatures ranging from 650° to 850° F., and there was very little knowledge of the behavior of oil or steel under extreme heat and pressure. It might

8. Interview with Robert E. Humphreys, July 10, 1948.
9. *Ibid.*
10. *Ibid.*, August 26, 1948.
11. *Ibid.*

result in a terrific explosion, injuries, and damages. The practical refiner shivered at the thought of using this method. Refiners and mechanical engineers who were consulted about the matter did not encourage the idea.[12] William E. Warwick, manager of the Whiting refinery, was definitely opposed to any experimental work of this nature.[13] However, Humphreys reached a point where the failure of other experiments and the hope of success led him to try heat and pressure, which was the trail that ultimately led to success.

Over the objections of Warwick but with Burton's approval, Humphreys began experimenting with oil under heat and pressure in a fifty-gallon still made of half-inch steel in the experimental house, the small building in the rear of the laboratory.[14] It was a gas-fired still operated by regular stillmen drawn from the refinery under the direction of a foreman. Little was known about the reaction of hydrocarbons under pressure, so Humphreys proceeded cautiously. He ran the large still day and night for several weeks under a low pressure of five pounds. Some cracking, 3 to 4 per cent, took place, but it was difficult to measure accurately such a small amount.[15]

Simultaneously, Rogers commenced running experiments in the research laboratory with a small pressure still holding a quart of oil. It had several advantages over the larger still. Rogers could make a complete run within a working day. By using different catalysts, he could determine if they had any value in speeding up the cracking process. He could make a greater variety of experiments with the small still than on the large still. He could determine the yield more accurately and govern the distillation process better than on the large still.[16] The two stills complemented one another in the experimental work that was carried on for more than a year.

It soon became evident that heating oil under pressure was the promising process. The pressure on the large still was stepped up to ten pounds for several weeks. Humphreys observed that this

12. William M. Burton, "Chemistry in the Petroleum Industry," *The Journal of Industrial and Engineering Chemistry*, X (June, 1918), 484-486.
13. F. M. Rogers to Giddens, March 1, 1950; Interview with O. E. Bransky, July 14, 1948.
14. There is a difference of opinion over whether this was a 50- or 100-gallon still. Humphreys and Bransky say it was a 50-gallon still. Burton says it was a 100-gallon still.
15. Robert E. Humphreys to Giddens, February 13, 1950.
16. F. M. Rogers to Giddens, March 1, 1950.

small increase in pressure definitely increased the yield of gasoline. When the pressure was increased to fifteen pounds for several weeks, Humphreys secured a 61¼ per cent yield of gasoline.[17] The results made it apparent that very high pressure and temperature would be required to get any significant increase in the percentage of gasoline. Although encouraged by the results, Humphreys had been apprehensive from the beginning that at some elevated temperature the oil would "crack" rapidly, possibly instantly, and explode. Nothing had happened, however, and Humphreys was on the point of increasing the pressure when Burton called a halt.[18] He had come to the laboratory almost daily after the experiments with heat and pressure were started and followed the work through frequent, almost daily, reports from Humphreys.[19] Afraid of an explosion, Burton ordered Humphreys to stop this dangerous work and try other methods.

For several months Humphreys again experimented with other processes.[20] To determine safely the effect of the cracking rate at high pressure and temperature, a two-inch coiled steel pipe was placed inside a heavy-walled heat chamber built of fire brick. Through this, oil was pumped under 150 pounds of pressure and vaporized. The distillation proceeded smoothly, the yield was high, and there was no indication of any explosive tendency. The difficulty, however, was that only one or two runs could be made before the coiled pipe filled up with coke. Humphreys found, however, that oil would crack under higher temperature and pressure without disastrous results. Another experiment was to pass oil vapors from one still through a very hot bed of molten lead to another still under varying pressures. Lead was a very valuable instrument for determining the cracking rate at different temperatures, but the process was not practical. There was not enough lead in the country so that the process could be used on any large commercial scale, and the gasoline had gum-forming tendencies. However, Humphreys learned the minimum temperature and pressure which could be used in a reasonably rapid cracking process.

At this point in the experimental work, Humphreys attended a meeting of the American Chemical Society at Wabash, Indiana, where he learned from Dr. W. B. D. Penniman that he had dis-

17. Interview with Robert E. Humphreys, July 10, 1948.
18. *Ibid.*
19. F. M. Rogers to Giddens, March 1, 1950.
20. Interview with Robert E. Humphreys, July 10, 1948.

\.illed heavy petroleum fractions under pressure with steam up to
fifty pounds without any explosion.[21] Upon returning home Humphreys told Burton of his talk with Penniman. Burton gave
Humphreys permission to resume work with heat and pressure
and made daily visits to the laboratory to confer with Humphreys
as he experimented with oil under heat and pressure. The pressure was boosted to fifty pounds, and the first really encouraging
results were obtained. Gradually Humphreys got the pressure up
to seventy-five pounds, which was sufficient to keep most of the
gas oil from distilling out before being cracked, and there was no
explosion. Pressure distillation of gas oil yielded 20 to 25 per cent
gasoline of a fairly good quality, but it had a strong odor and a
yellowish color. Humphreys also found that the production of coke
was by no means proportional to the production of gasoline. With
a well-fractionated gas oil, 25 per cent or more gasoline could be
made before there was any substantial coke formation. Seventy-
five pounds of pressure was as high as Humphreys could go because the rivets in the still were not tight enough to hold greater
pressure, and welding could not be effectively done.[22] This fact
greatly limited further experimental work. However, the yields
obtained were considered satisfactory for a commercial process.

The idea of cracking oil under heat and pressure was simple but
the difficulty was to make it work successfully at seventy-five pounds
of pressure. One of the problems was the formation of coke on the
bottom of the fifty-gallon still, which tended to insulate the oil
from the heating surface. It precluded running the still long
enough to convert more than about one-third of the gas oil into
gasoline. If the run were continued, the bottom was likely to become red-hot and burst. Humphreys found that if steel plates were
suspended a short distance above the bottom of the still, they
could catch most of the coke, hold it off the direct-fired surface,
and the distillation could be prolonged until about two-thirds of
the gas oil in the still could be cracked.[23]

Another problem arose because the cracking of gas oil under
heat and pressure resulted in the production of gas, which had to
be gradually released at the proper rate to hold the pressure
within the desired limits and maintained with as little variation
as possible. It was of utmost importance that the rate of cracking

21. *Ibid.*
22. *Ibid.*
23. *Ibid.*; Robert E. Humphreys to Giddens, February 21, 1950.

be kept constant, and the proper release of the gas was a significant factor in this. Humphreys found out that if the temperature of the still got too high or the pressure too low, the gas oil would distill without cracking, and a poor distillate would be produced.

It took several months to discover the best method of regulating the temperature and pressure.[24] In operating the fifty-gallon still, Humphreys had an employee keep his eye on the pressure gauge and regulate the intensity of the fire under the still. If the pressure got too high, more gas would be released from the distillate receiver, which operated under still pressure, or the fire would be reduced, or both. If the pressure got too low, the opposite procedure was used—the release of gas from the condenser was cut down, the fire was increased, or both. Skill had to be developed by the stillmen, for it was very important to maintain a uniform rate of cracking throughout the run. This appeared very simple after it was done, but the working out of the method was difficult.

A third difficulty was that all fractions, light and heavy, produced by the cracking process, and some unchanged gas oil passed directly through the condenser into the receiver. How to separate these fractions under pressure so that the light fractions would pass into the condenser and the heavier ones would return to the still was a problem. Humphreys adopted the principle of dephlegmation—the partial condensation of vapors—under pressure.[25] Cooled by atmospheric temperature in an inclined pipe, the gasoline vapors passed through the dephlegmator, were liquefied in a water-cooled condenser, and ran off into the receiver, while the kerosene and heavy oils returned to the still for further cracking into gasoline. Several barrels of gasoline were made using the "run-back pipe," and some was tried in Dr. Burton's automobile.[26] It was probably the first time dephlegmation of petroleum under high pressure was used, and it constituted an exceedingly important element in the successful operation of the cracking process.

Once the problem of dephlegmation had been solved, Humphreys felt that he had really "turned a corner." He was confident that the process would work and could be successfully used on a large commercial scale. After experimenting more than two years

24. Interview with Robert E. Humphreys, July 10, 1948.
25. *Ibid.*, July 17, 1948.
26. F. M. Rogers to Giddens, March 1, 1950.

and spending thousands of dollars, the world's first practical process for producing "synthetic" gasoline by cracking high-boiling-point oil at high temperature and pressure had been discovered. The problem of how to secure a much greater yield of gasoline from crude had been solved.

In contrast to the physical separation of crude oil into various products by the ordinary distillation process, the newly discovered process broke down the heavy hydrocarbons, which had been relatively valueless by-products previously, to create lighter ones. Twice as much gasoline could now be secured from a barrel of crude as before and the heavy hydrocarbons were no longer relatively valueless. The discovery of this thermal cracking process was destined to be one of the great inventions of modern times. It opened a vast, new chemical approach to petroleum refining, and as a result, the petroleum industry was the first big industry to be revolutionized by chemistry.

Burton believed that they should try the process on a larger scale to obtain further data and experience. Therefore, a horizontal cylindrical still made of half-inch steel plate, eight feet in diameter and twenty feet long, capable of withstanding seventy-five pounds of pressure, was built outside near the experimental house.[27] It had a roof over it to keep out the rain. Once the still was completed, Humphreys took charge and began operating it. A foreman and three stillmen on each of the three shifts were on duty day and night. Since the rivets in the steel plates could not be driven tight enough with the air pressure available, leaks began to develop around the rivet heads along the seams. Afraid of an explosion and fire, the regular boilermakers refused to repair the leaks with the still under pressure. Consequently, Humphreys and the stillmen had to climb over the still caulking the leaky spots.[28] Humphreys carried his caulking tools with him all the time, for some spot always had to be caulked. It took about forty-eight hours to run a batch of oil through the still. During two-thirds of the run there was no question of danger, but for the remaining third there was. Stillmen continuously kept an eye on the bottom of the still because it was likely to grow red-hot and bulge due to coke forming on the bottom. Although the first runs convinced Burton that

27. *Ibid.*, July 10, 1948. There is a difference of opinion over the size of this still. Burton says it had a capacity of 6,000 gallons; Humphreys says it was fifty barrels; and Rogers says it was one hundred barrels.
28. *Ibid.*

the process would work satisfactorily on a large scale, they continued the still in operation for the purpose of training stillmen to run the large commercial installations, when completed.

The one big remaining question was: Could they build large equipment that would, in a practical way, secure the desired results and at the same time be durable and reasonably free from the fire hazard? Some of the practical men said, "Yes." More of them said, "No."

Even before the construction of the large experimental still, Burton, owing to the great demand for gasoline, got an estimate from the machine shop on the cost of building one hundred 8,000-gallon pressure stills and sent it to the parent company in New York with a request that $1,000,000 be appropriated to build cracking stills.[29] The Manufacturing Committee rejected the request without giving any explanation or reason. Cowan told Burton later that one of the Directors in New York had said: "Burton wants to blow the whole state of Indiana into Lake Michigan." The rejection of the request was probably due to the fact that the suit for the dissolution of the Standard of New Jersey was pending before the United States Supreme Court, and there was a feeling on the part of its officers that the holding company would probably be dissolved. In view of the uncertainty, why should they appropriate $1,000,000?

Immediately after Standard of Indiana became independent in 1911, Burton, now a Director of the company, presented his revolutionary proposal to the new Board to build one hundred and twenty stills and asked for an appropriation.[30] There was no lengthy debate or discussion, for the Directors knew about the project and had confidence in Burton's judgment. "Uncle George" Stahl jokingly said to Burton: "You'll ruin us." Drake asked: "Bill, do you know what you are doing?" Burton replied: "I do." Then Drake moved that an appropriation of $709,000 be approved, and it was.

Preparations were hurriedly made to start the construction of cracking stills because the gasoline shortage, which had been earlier foreseen, was fast becoming a reality. Manufacturers of gasoline engines were no longer worried about their ability to sell engines. They were more concerned over the fact that their business might come to an end because of a lack of gasoline. The number

29. Interview with William M. Burton, August 2, 1948.
30. *Ibid.; Hearings Before Martindale*, VI, 3282.

of motor vehicles registered had increased from 312,000 in 1909 to 639,500 in 1911. A significant indication of the greater use of motor vehicles was the fact that at the Chicago automobile show in 1911 motor trucks were included for the first time, and fifty-six different truck companies exhibited models.[31] The increase in passenger automobiles and trucks in 1911 alone indicated the need for 80 per cent more gasoline in 1912, and this did not include the output of 1,350 manufacturers of farm gasoline engines or the increased needs of the dry cleaners.[32] With 6,000,000 fewer barrels of crude being produced east of the Rocky Mountains in 1912 than in 1911 and the demand increasing, the country faced a real gasoline famine.

Owing to the shortage of crude from the Illinois fields, one battery of stills was shut down at Standard's Wood River refinery late in 1912.[33] To supply it from the Oklahoma fields, the Prairie Oil & Gas Company began laying late in 1913 a pipeline from its trunk line at Carrollton, Missouri, to the Wood River refinery. In order to conserve its crude supply, Standard of Indiana, according to a report, offered the Frisco Railroad $100,000 to cancel its fuel oil contract, but the railroad refused.[34] Standard increased the offer to include defraying the expense of converting the locomotives to coal burners, but the railroad still refused. A similar effort was made to cancel a contract with the Kansas City Southern Railroad, but it, too, refused. Late in October, 1912, the company announced that after December 1st, it would discontinue the sale of fuel oil and make no new contracts.[35] It was more profitable to refine crude and sell gasoline. The result was that many industrial users of fuel oil in the Chicago area and other cities were adversely affected.

With a world-wide increase in the demand for petroleum products and a diminishing supply, the price of gasoline began to soar. In October, 1911, the price was 9½ cents a gallon. By January, 1913, it was 17 cents. In London and Paris, motorists paid 50 cents per gallon, and in some places in Europe they paid as much as

31. *The Chicago Tribune*, February 5, 1911.
32. "And What of Gasoline," *The Oil and Gas Journal*, X, No. 32 (January 18, 1912), 1.
33. "Tell the Public Why Gasoline Is Advancing," *National Petroleum News*, IV, No. 11 (January, 1913), 29.
34. *Ibid.*, No. 4 (June, 1912), 36.
35. *The Chicago Tribune*, October 25, 1912; *National Petroleum News*, IV, No. 4 (June, 1912), 36.

$1.00 per gallon. The high cost of gasoline was fast becoming a serious menace to the automobile industry and owners; yet in the early years of the petroleum industry, gasoline was in so little demand that much of it had been dumped by refiners. To overcome the shortage and reduce the price, the International Association of Recognized Automobile Clubs at its meeting in Paris in 1913 offered a prize of $100,000 for the production of a motor fuel that could not be cornered by any nation or combination. The Automobile Club of America sponsored tests on substitute fuels but without success. There was some fear that this country might have to use steam and electric automobiles exclusively.

In the meantime at Whiting the drafting room under the direction of "Jimmy" Evans immediately began making blueprints for constructing Burton stills, using the large experimental still as a model. Things took on a livelier tone as the designing of these stills got under way. The "good old days" when the men wore flannel shirts, corduroy trousers, and smoked corncob pipes soon gave way to white shirts, and the drafting department became the Engineering Department.[36]

Once the plans had been completed, the Mechanical Department in charge of William Curtis had the responsibility for constructing the stills. They were built in batteries of ten so that the superfluous gases from some stills could be conducted to other stills, where they would hold needed pressure. They were direct-fired, horizontal, cylindrical stills, eight feet in diameter, and thirty feet long. Their length was limited to thirty feet because that was the longest sheet of steel available. To roll these steel plates, Whiting had a bending machine, but it would not roll thirty-foot lengths, so the workmen at first rolled out shorter pieces and riveted them together. Since welding did not come into general use until about 1918, all of the seams had to be riveted by hand, and no seam was tight enough to hold oil at seventy-five to ninety-five pounds pressure. The cost of construction amounted to about $8,000 apiece.[37]

While plans were being drawn and construction started, the protection of the new process by patent was referred to attorneys for the company. After the results of the first search of the prior art had been studied, it was apparent that valid and broad protec-

36. R. F. Storer, "Reminiscing About Early Days of Whiting's Engineering Dep't," *Stanolind Record*, IX, No. 9 (July, 1928), 5-8.
37. *High Cost of Gasoline and Other Petroleum Products*, I, 805.

tion on the process would be very difficult to obtain. The equipment used in any of the procedural steps in developing the process involved nothing which was intrinsically new. The raw material —middle-to-heavy distillate oils—was available to all refiners. The concept of distilling heavier oils under pressure for the purpose of cracking to increase the yield of kerosene seemed to be an old concept. Holding the still under pressure by a regulating valve on the outlet to the condenser was quite old. So far as the production of gasoline by cracking was concerned, there was voluminous literature proposing or reporting on earlier high-temperature processes of many kinds, some involving pressure, some not.

It was Dr. Burton, under whose general direction the process had been developed, who was responsible for selecting the essential elements out of all the experimental methods used in the laboratory which, taken together, formed a new and patentable combination for the manufacture of gasoline in large amounts by cracking. The principal elements involved the use of a middle-to-heavy distillate type of charging stock capable of being decomposed to yield a fair amount of gasoline without too much coke, a defined operating temperature sufficient to effect the desired thermal decomposition, a defined pressure sufficient to hold the charging stock in a liquid state at the temperature required, and the maintenance of pressure on the liquids and gases produced until after they had been completely condensed or cooled. It was Dr. Burton who supplied the legally indispensable evidence that a new interaction of these elements produced a gasoline of a superior chemical quality.

With these claims as a basis, Burton, who had initiated the research, co-ordinated it, and pushed it in all its ramifications, filed an application for a patent on the basic process on July 3, 1912, in which he assigned his rights to the company. The patent was issued on January 7, 1913.[38] Thus, the cracking process soon became known around the world as the Burton process.

Applications for other patents on various features closely related to the basic process, which had been developed during the course of the experimental work, were also filed by Burton and Humphreys. Burton patented a process for producing asphalt and wax and a method for safeguarding the pressure stills through the use of an improved kind of safety valve. Humphreys patented the use of the coke plates in the bottom of the stills and his "run-back

38. Patent No. 1,049,667.

pipe," or dephlegmation process under pressure. The latter was a procedural step of tremendous significance from a practical standpoint. In the judgment of Standard's patent lawyers and other large oil company officials, Humphreys' patent on the dephlegmation process was regarded as the most valuable single patent on the Burton process. It was the most difficult to avoid or defeat. When fully developed, the Burton process had a value of $70,000,000 according to the United States Board of Tax Appeals.[39]

Sometime in January, 1913, the first battery of pressure stills at Whiting was completed and went into operation under the direction of L. C. Moore. In developing the Burton process and constructing the first battery of cracking stills, the company spent over a million dollars. Each one of these new stills was charged with 8,250 gallons of gas oil, and it took about forty-eight hours to process the batch, clean out the still, and get ready for another run. Since stillmen on the old type of stills were unacquainted with the operation of pressure stills, in which large quantities of oil boiled, they were hesitant about working on these newfangled things. Volunteers were used for a year or two. Humphreys had started training the first group on the large experimental still while the first battery of stills was under construction, and he soon had what seemed like an army of stillmen in training.[40] The men became familiar with all the hazards and learned that if they followed the rules, they were relatively free from danger.

It took a good deal of courage to operate the big stills. At many places along the seams there were leaks, and they frequently burst into flame. It was a most terrifying sight. If the leaks were allowed to go too long without caulking, the fire might soften the steel and cause an explosion. If excessive caulking was done in one place, it might also weaken the steel and result in an explosion. In time, the stillmen found that nature remedied many of the leaks, for coke would form around the rivets and seal the hole. The first stills had riveted seams in the bottom right over the fire and they leaked badly. After several months, the shop secured a bending machine that could roll thirty-foot steel lengths. They could now rivet the plates together, place the seams on the sides above the fire, have a smooth bottom plate over the fire, and thus reduce the number of leaks and the danger. Coke created another problem, for it formed in the threads of pipe connections while

39. 129 F. (2d) 373.
40. Interview with Robert E. Humphreys, July 10, 1948.

expanded under heat and pressure. When the still cooled down between runs, it remained in the threads and kept them expanded. The next run expanded the threads even more and allowed more coke to form. After several runs the threads were so expanded and filled with coke that they sometimes failed to hold and caused accidents. Another danger in operating these stills was that there was no information available as to the tensile strength of steel above about 750°F.

Toward the end of a run, a slight bulging in the bottom of the still was a warning signal, but there was no accurate and scientific means of determining when to stop the run. It was a matter of judgment. When the bottom began to get red-hot, a stillman would watch almost continuously, and he and the foreman would have to determine how red it might get before stopping the run. Stillmen soon got to be experts in judging how long a still should be run under these conditions. According to Burton, "We took some awful risks, and we were awfully lucky not to have any smash-up early in the game." After the pressure stills had been operating a year or two, and there were no serious accidents, workmen lost their fear, and they were eager and interested in working on them. The extraordinary skill and care with which the stills were operated is indicated by the fact that during the first eight years, hundreds of stills were operated before there was any fatal accident.

On February 22, 1913, Standard cautiously announced that it had discovered a substitute for gasoline called "motor spirits," and that as fast as possible its distributing stations would be supplied.[41] The new product resembled gasoline, except that it was yellow in color, and it had a pungent odor. Dr. Burton called it "skunk oil" while Dr. Humphreys applied a more dignified and scientific name to it—"pyrogenous naphtha." Its specific gravity was about 56°. The wholesale price was 3 cents per gallon less than regular gasoline. The company intended it for use primarily in motor trucks, tractors, and stationary gasoline engines, but pleasure car owners soon began using it because of the price. The company claimed that "motor spirits" would give 25 per cent more mileage per gallon than straight-run gasoline. For some time the character of the Burton process was not widely known. It was not until January, 1915, when C. H. Claudy wrote an article based upon an

41. *The Chicago Tribune,* February 23, 1913; *The Whiting Call,* March 12, 1913; *National Petroleum News,* V, No. 1 (March, 1913), 4.

interview with Burton for the *Scientific American,* that the general public learned about it.

By July 1, 1913, Standard's Directors had authorized the construction of two hundred and forty Burton stills: one hundred and twenty at Whiting, sixty at Wood River, and sixty at Sugar Creek.[42] While these were under construction an unexpected opportunity developed in Wyoming for Standard to install pressure stills, increase its gasoline supply, and become a dominant factor in the petroleum industry of that state. After the drilling of the first well on Salt Creek dome in 1908, oilmen and promoters flocked to Wyoming, and the state rapidly came to the front as a new oil field.[43] By 1912 its crude production exceeded 1,000,000 barrels. With the discovery of oil at Grass Creek and Elk Basin and at Big Muddy, Lance Creek, Rock Creek, and Lost Soldier, production increased substantially each year. By 1919 Wyoming was producing 13,580,000 barrels per year and ranked sixth as an oil-producing state.[44]

By the ordinary refining process, Wyoming's dark green crude with a high specific gravity yielded about 18 per cent gasoline, 25 per cent kerosene, and the remainder fuel oil. Both the Midwest Oil Company and the Franco Petroleum Company, the largest refiners and producers in Wyoming, could easily sell all of the gasoline manufactured by their refineries at Casper, but how to dispose of the fuel oil was baffling.[45] Wyoming was an agricultural state; it did not have any industries which could use it as fuel on a large scale, and freight rates made it difficult to compete in the Middle West with fuel oil from the Mid-Continent field. There seemed to be no solution to the problem.

Since Standard had a cracking process by which heavy oil could be converted into gasoline, R. D. Brooks, Vice-President of the Franco Petroleum Company, went to Chicago to see Cowan and Burton about their buying fuel oil.[46] They were interested. However, instead of bringing fuel oil to Whiting to be refined and then shipping gasoline back into the West, it seemed more logical for Standard to build a cracking plant at Casper and distribute

42. Robert E. Wilson, "Fifteen Years of the Burton Process," *The Journal of Industrial and Engineering Chemistry,* XX, No. 10 (October, 1928), 1100.
43. Edward L. Easterbrook, "Finding Oil in Wyoming," *Stanolind Record,* VI, No. 11 (September 25, 1925), 24-25.
44. *Report of the Federal Trade Commission on the Petroleum Industry of Wyoming,* January 3, 1921, 14.
45. *High Cost of Gasoline and Other Petroleum Products,* I, 86-87, 90-91.
46. *Ibid.,* 90.

gasoline from there. On behalf of the Franco Petroleum Company and Midwest Oil, Brooks proposed that if Standard would build some cracking units at Casper, the two companies would deliver each week not less than 7,000 barrels of fuel oil of not less than 26° gravity for 75 cents per barrel for three years.[47] If Standard desired an additional 7,000 barrels per week during the term of the contract, it might have this privilege. An additional 7,000 barrels per week might be obtained if decided upon prior to March 1, 1914.

The proposal presented an excellent opportunity for Standard to increase its supply of gasoline at a relatively low price, supply its marketing territory in the West from Casper, cut freight charges, and make a handsome profit. Standard's officials decided, therefore, to accept Brooks' offer and build some cracking units at Casper. An agreement, embodying the proposal, was signed on July 1, 1913, by Standard, Midwest, and Franco officials. By this action Standard was the first major oil company to recognize the importance of the Wyoming oil fields, and the company soon became a dominant factor in their development.

Even before the contract was signed C. B. Manbeck, representing Standard, had arrived in Casper to look over sites around the town for the cracking units.[48] On July 5th he purchased about eighty-four acres on the west edge of Casper between the town and Midwest's refinery from J. M. Carey and Brothers, paying about $300 per acre. When Carey was requested to make out the deed to Standard, he was terribly surprised to learn the real identity of the purchaser and was considerably disappointed because he had not asked a much higher price.

No sooner did the news concerning the new refinery become public than an even greater boom hit Casper. The Mountain Realty Company ran an advertisement in the local newspaper saying: "What does it mean? It means that when the Standard Oil Company enters a town it increases the price of real estate 200 per cent. It has done it for other towns. It will do it for ours." [49]

A party of Standard officials from Chicago and Whiting arrived in Casper on July 21st to supervise the construction of the new plant. Within a half hour, Manbeck, the general superintendent, had a gang of men at work laying a railroad sidetrack to the re-

47. Minutes of the Board of Directors' and Stockholders' Meetings, I, 104.
48. *The Casper Record*, July 8, 1913; *The Natrona County Tribune*, July 10, 1913; *The Casper Press*, July 11, 1913.
49. *The Casper Press*, July 11, 1913.

finery site; engineers were busy staking out locations for buildings, stills, and tanks; and a crew was clearing the site of sagebrush.[50] The new plant was to be as large as the refineries of Midwest and Franco combined and involved an expenditure of nearly $800,000. Construction progressed rapidly, and by late May, 1914, twenty cracking stills had been completed, and the refinery was ready to operate.[51] To supply the stills with charging stock, fuel oil was pumped through a pipeline from the refineries of Franco and Midwest.

While construction on Standard's refinery was in progress, the Midwest Refining Company, a Maine corporation with a capitalization of $20,000,000, was organized to take over all the assets of the Franco Petroleum Company and certain assets of the Midwest Oil Company.[52] In the main, these assets comprised the pipelines, refineries, contracts for crude oil, and marketing facilities. Production was not included although it was to be supervised by the refining company. In addition, the contract of July 1, 1913, with Standard was assigned to Midwest Refining. The merger of these interests made Midwest Refining the most important factor in the Wyoming oil fields. It had a total daily refining capacity of 12,800 barrels and control over most of the best production at Salt Creek and in the Shannon pool.

Opened at a time when there was a growing shortage of gasoline, which was further intensified by the demand created by World War I, the Wyoming field, owing to its rich yield of gasoline, became exceedingly important to the nation. It yielded 31.9 per cent gasoline from distillation plus cracking in 1916, 43.1 per cent in 1917, 42.4 in 1918, and 44.6 in 1919. Without the use of the Burton process the yield would have been only about one-half as great. Moreover, Wyoming crude was the cheapest available. The market price of Salt Creek crude in 1914, 1915, and early in 1916 was 50 cents per barrel. Beginning in 1916, the price increased to 75 cents and steadily rose from early in January, 1917, through 1920, when it reached $2.75. Except for a short period

50. *Ibid.; The Natrona County Tribune,* July 24, 1913; *The Casper Press,* July 25, 1913; Lewis J. Price, "Hum of Machinery Supplants Hum of Roulette Wheel," *Stanolind Record,* II, No. 11 (September, 1921), 14-16; R. M. Andrus, "The Story of Wyoming Refineries," *Stanolind Record,* VI, No. 11 (September, 1925), 7-11.
51. *The Natrona County Tribune,* March 12, 1914, April 30, 1914, May 14, 1914.
52. *The Casper Press,* March 6, 1914; Ben H. Pelton, "The Midwest Oil Company," *Annals of Wyoming,* XXII, No. 1 (January, 1950), 84-92; D. W. Greenburg, "Midwest, Leader in the Rocky Mountain Region, Company of Romance," *Stanolind Record,* XI, No. 9 (July, 1930), 3-30.

during the first half of 1915, Mid-Continent crude was always 5 cents to $1.00 a barrel higher. Much of the time the differential was greater than 50 cents a barrel.[53]

As new fields were discovered and opened in Wyoming, Midwest rapidly expanded its refining facilities. Owing to the large volume of gas at Salt Creek, the company constructed under the direction of A. W. Peake, field superintendent, a combination compression, refrigeration, and absorption gasoline plant in 1917. About the same time it acquired a refinery at Greybull in the Big Horn Basin and an interest in the Utah Oil Refining Company with a refinery at Salt Lake City. The Utah Oil Refining Company had been operating its plant on refinery "tops," that is, unfinished naphtha distillate, secured from California. During the latter part of 1917 the supply was reduced owing to the wartime demand, so the Utah company turned to the Wyoming field for crude.[54] Simultaneously, Midwest officials realized that they would have to build a refinery somewhere along the Union Pacific railway in southern Wyoming on account of oil developments in Carbon and Albany counties or else acquire the Utah Oil Refining Company. In view of the situation confronting both companies, Midwest purchased a half interest in the Utah company. When oil was discovered in the Rock Creek field, Midwest erected a refinery at Laramie. With the expansion of its interests, Midwest increased its capitalization in 1917 from $20,000,000 to $50,000,000. Owning and controlling four refineries, Midwest was now the fourth largest manufacturer of gasoline in the country.

As Midwest expanded in Wyoming so did Standard. In view of plans for installing ten new pressure stills at its Casper refinery, Standard's contract of July, 1913, with Midwest was amended in March, 1915, to the effect that Standard would take not less than 14,000 barrels of reduced crude or fuel oil and not less than 7,000 barrels of heavy petroleum distillate per week at 57½ cents per barrel for two years. This agreement was superseded in October, 1915, because of plans to build twenty additional stills. The contract of July, 1913, was amended in several respects and extended to March 1, 1919. Deliveries of reduced crude or fuel oil were to

53. *Report of the Federal Trade Commission on the Petroleum Industry of Wyoming*, January 3, 1921, 39.
54. *Ibid.*, 54; *National Petroleum News*, I, No. 5 (July, 1909), 19; "Largest Single Industrial Enterprise in Salt Lake City," *Stanolind Record*, XII, No. 11 (September, 1931), 1-6; John G. Bartram and G. M. Vandaveer, "Long Ago, During Tertiary Times," *Stanolind Record*, XIII, No. 11 (September, 1932), 1-6.

continue at the rate of 14,000 barrels per week for 57½ cents per barrel. Current deliveries of petroleum distillate were to be made at the rate of 7,000 barrels a week for 62½ cents per barrel until the completion of the twenty stills, when they were to be increased to 24,500 barrels per week at a cost of either 57½ or 62½ cents per barrel, depending upon the price of Mid-Continent gasoline. On the other hand, Standard agreed to sell Midwest not less than 2,000,000 gallons of motor spirits at the rate of 2,000 barrels a day for 4¾ cents per gallon and not less than 1,750,000 gallons of pressure-still tar at the rate of 1,500 barrels per day for 57½ cents.

With the extraordinary demand for gasoline in 1913, other refiners were anxious to use the Burton process. Within a few weeks after the first stills were put into operation at Whiting, Standard began receiving inquiries from other companies about the possibility of securing a license to operate under the patent. These inquiries raised a very serious question: Should the company issue licenses or retain exclusive use of the process? Legally, the company had a perfect right to the exclusive use of the process or it could license the process on whatever terms desired. There were grave differences of opinion among the Directors as to what the policy should be.[55] Some of them were opposed to granting any licenses because they wished the company to be the sole beneficiary. If licensed, they were afraid that the use of the process might result in a great Frankenstein which would destroy their business. Others were of the opinion that while the company had a right to the exclusive use of the process, there was more or less of a moral obligation to license it. It would be bad public policy to monopolize it. Moreover, the attractive revenue possibilities from licensing were not to be overlooked. This would be "all velvet." [56] After much serious consideration these conflicting views were finally compromised by deciding to issue licenses for a two-year period, which would provide an opportunity to see what effect doubling the gasoline supply would have upon the company's business. According to Colonel Stewart, the Directors "actually were affected by the belief that it was not right to play the dog in the manger game, and that the industry was entitled to the practice of this process." [57] In making the decision to share the benefits of the Burton process, the Directors established one of the

55. *Hearings Before Martindale,* VI, 3285-87.
56. Interview with William M. Burton, August 2, 1948.
57. *Hearings Before Martindale,* VI, 3291.

most important precedents in the history of American industry.

Once the policy had been determined, Burton and the company's patent attorneys worked out the details of a licensing agreement, which the Directors accepted without much debate.[58] There was one licensing form for all. The agreement included several special features. A royalty of 25 per cent of the net profits made through the use of the cracking process was set. Each licensee was required to recognize the validity of the patents under which it was licensed. Licensees were prohibited from selling cracked gasoline made from the Burton process in the states in which Standard then marketed. Through this provision Standard's executives sought to protect their business against a flood of oil being turned loose within the company's marketing territory by competitors. Any violation of this provision entitled the licensor to cancel the license.

The first license went to the Imperial Oil Company, Limited, of Canada, a subsidiary of the Standard of New Jersey, on January 30, 1914. Standard of Kansas received the second and the Solar Refining Company the third. At this point the question of issuing licenses under the foreign patent rights arose. During 1913–14, Colonel Robert W. Stewart was in Europe on business for the company and was with W. C. Teagle, Vice-President of the Standard Oil Company of New Jersey, a portion of the time. Stewart suggested to Teagle that the Jersey company was in a better position to handle the foreign patents on the Burton process than was his company, for the latter had no foreign operations. Moreover, since Standard of Indiana owned the patents on cracking abroad, it could not export cracked gasoline to those countries without invalidating its patent rights. On the other hand, the Jersey company had refineries and marketing facilities in Europe, Scandinavia, Cuba, Mexico, South America, and Canada. Under the circumstances what was more logical than that Standard of Indiana should assign its patent rights abroad to the Jersey company on a royalty basis?

When Stewart returned to the United States, he pursued the subject with Teagle and the Directors of his own company and, as a result, an agreement was made in April, 1915, assigning the foreign patents in Europe to the Jersey company.[59] A similar agreement was made on May 29, 1919, with the Standard of New York

58. Interview with William M. Burton, August 2, 1948.
59. *Hearings Before Martindale,* VI, 3295.

for using the process in South Africa and the Far East.[60] To protect itself, the company specified in both contracts that no gasoline,
benzine, or naphtha manufactured under these patents in foreign countries could be sold in any of the states of its sales territory in the United States, Canada, or Newfoundland.

Simultaneously, the Jersey company began negotiations with
Standard of Indiana for a license to use the process in the United
States.[61] Even though both companies had been a part of the old
Standard Oil organization and friendly relations existed on the
part of the officers, the negotiations revealed sharp differences and
an unexpected competitive rivalry. When the Jersey company inquired in March, 1913, about the possibility of securing a license,
the Directors of Standard of Indiana had not made any decision
about licensing the process. By May they had come to a decision
and informed the Jersey company that they would be willing to
grant a license for 1 cent per gallon for all stock charged into
the pressure stills.

More than a year passed before the Jersey company made any
further inquiry. In November, 1914, Cowan informed Jersey's
officials that his company would license the process to them on the
same basis as it had been offered to other companies. Jersey preferred to purchase a license for a flat sum rather than upon a profit-
sharing basis, but officials of Standard of Indiana refused to consider such an offer. Early in 1915 Cowan sent the Jersey officials
a license agreement to sign, but they objected to several clauses.
However, the Directors of Standard of Indiana flatly refused to
make any exceptions to the general form of the contract. To make
exceptions might lead to serious difficulties. Realizing that Standard of Indiana would not be moved, Standard of New Jersey capit-
ulated on August 15, 1915, and accepted the company's terms for
a license. The story is told that the most galling thing the President of the Jersey company had to do each month during the next
few years was to sign the big check for royalties payable to Standard of Indiana.

When the licenses for the first two-year period were about to
expire and came up for renewal, the Directors of the company were
not nearly so afraid of the effects of licensing. The licenses were
renewed for the life of the Burton patent, and several important

60. *Ibid.*, 3296.
61. For the correspondence during the negotiations, see *Hearings Before Martindale*,
    VIII, 5545-5572.

changes were made. Instead of a prohibition against the shipment
of cracked gasoline into the sales territory of Standard of Indiana,
a clause was inserted to the effect that the company might, at its
option, cancel the agreement in the event that any of the cracked
gasoline was sold in its territory.[62] If the contract was violated and
notice given to this effect, it could be corrected within thirty days
and the contract continued in force. In requiring 25 per cent of the
net profits made through the use of the Burton process, the company had had constant trouble with licenses because no definite
method of accounting had been provided in the old contracts. The
royalty basis, therefore, was changed to 4/10 of 1 cent per gallon
for all stock charged into the stills.[63] This provided an absolute
method of accounting and, at the same time, the figure represented an effort to get almost 25 per cent of the net profit. Some
old licensees refused to accept the modification, while others did.
All new licenses were issued on this royalty basis.

One exception to the general royalty basis was made in the case
of the Standard of California, which received a license in July,
1919.[64] It spent $500,000 in installing Burton stills, but the process
would not work successfully on California crude. It was a failure,
and the $500,000 was lost. Standard of California spent about
$2,500,000 in experimenting with the basic principle of the Bur-
ton process. Through various developments, the company finally
modified the process so that it would work successfully. Owing to
these difficulties, Standard of Indiana deviated from the general
form of its license and the California company paid a royalty of
$650 per month for each still when in operation with a maximum
of $6,500 for each still.

From 1914 to 1919, Standard licensed fourteen refiners from
whom it received $11,615,506.70 in royalties, which was "all vel-
vet." [65] All of the licensees had been formerly a part of the old
Standard Oil organization. None of them were marketing competitors of Standard of Indiana. Although any company could secure a license, no independent company had. The principal reason
was that the cost of installing a battery of Burton stills amounted
to about $60,000. This expense plus the royalty was beyond the
means of many smaller companies.

62. *Ibid.*, VI, 3287.
63. *Ibid.*, 3305.
64. *High Cost of Gasoline and Other Petroleum Products*, I, 808, 955.
65. *Hearings Before Martindale*, II, 1237.

The development and successful operation of the Burton process was to have profound and far-reaching effects upon the petroleum industry.[66] The most important immediate result was to increase the supply of gasoline. By doubling the amount of gasoline secured from a barrel of crude oil, the cracking process proved to be an exceedingly important factor in alleviating the threatened gasoline shortage, in insuring the future of the automobile, and in keeping the price of gasoline from becoming prohibitive. In addition to increasing the supply of gasoline at a critical time, the Burton process had, in the long run, other important effects upon the industry. Cracked gasoline had a much higher antiknock value than straight-run gasoline, which, in turn, meant more power and made possible the development of higher-compression automobile engines. Many new by-products were ultimately derived from using the cracking process. The use of heat and pressure provided, in time, a greater measure of flexibility in the refining of crude oil, which was something never before possessed by the oil industry. The ordinary refining process merely separated the various hydrocarbons from the crude, and the yield of each fraction could not be appreciably increased or decreased in accordance with the demand. Furthermore, it was always a problem to find a market for some of the less valuable fractions. In using the cracking process the heavy hydrocarbons, which had been less valuable, could now be broken down and made to yield more valuable products in accordance with demand. As a means of conserving the crude oil resources of the country, the Burton process probably contributed more than any other factor. For example, from 1913 to 1928 about 200,000,000 barrels of gasoline were made in Burton stills. To have produced this amount of gasoline by the ordinary distillation method would have required about 1,000,000,000 extra barrels of crude.[67]

The development of the Burton process awakened the oil indus-

66. See several articles by Robert E. Wilson: "Fifteen Years of the Burton Process," *Journal of Industrial and Engineering Chemistry*, XX, No. 10 (October, 1928), 1099-1101; "Pioneers in Oil Cracking," an address delivered before The Newcomen Society of England, American Branch, in Chicago, October 29, 1946; "Research on a Single Reaction and Its Social Effects," Third Annual Arthur Dehon Little Memorial Lecture at the Massachusetts Institute of Technology, November 23, 1948; "What Research on Cracking Has Meant to the Industry and to the Public," an address delivered before the Texas Mid-Continent Oil & Gas Association, Houston, October 13, 1949.

67. Robert E. Wilson, "Fifteen Years of the Burton Process," *Journal of Industrial and Engineering Chemistry*, XX, No. 10 (October, 1928), 1101.

try to the commercial possibilities in bringing about chemical changes in crude oil and created a greater interest in research than ever before. Other companies either established research departments or expanded their existing research staff in order to develop something like the Burton process. The goal was to discover a process using none of Standard's inventions and avoid the payment of royalties or, failing in this, make some improvement that could be traded to Standard in return for a favorable license agreement. To lag behind in technological developments was dangerous. The attitude of practical refiners towards chemists and technically trained men began to change through necessity, if for no other reason. Chemists were needed in the laboratory to experiment with new processes and to supervise the operation of the cracking process. Chemical and mechanical engineers were needed to design and supervise the installation of all kinds of machinery, insure safe and efficient operating units, and devise methods of increasing the yield of products with a high and uniform quality.

In the history of Standard of Indiana there had been an early recognition of the value of the professionally trained scientist when Dr. Burton was promoted from the laboratory in 1893 to assistant general superintendent at Whiting. He became later the superintendent, General Manager of Manufacturing, and finally a Director and Second Vice-President of the company in 1914. The development of the cracking process gave added emphasis to using scientists in important administrative positions. In 1914 Dr. Humphreys became assistant general superintendent at Whiting and later manager. Other scientists, such as Tom S. Cooke, Gentry Cash, O. E. Bransky, M. G. Paulus, and M. R. Schmidt, were soon advanced from the laboratory to responsible administrative positions in the refinery. "The system of this company," declared Russell Wiles, one of its patent attorneys, "is founded on the premise that a scientifically trained man is a good man for any job; the scientific staff does not co-operate with the manufacturing staff—it has become the manufacturing staff." [68] In following such a policy the company pioneered and set a precedent. In time, the Manufacturing Department from top to bottom was largely dominated and controlled by men with scientific training.

So far as Standard was concerned, the development of the cracking process gave the company a great advantage over all other

68. "Standard Oil (Indiana) Revolutionizes Industry," *Stanolind Record*, III, No. 4 (February, 1922), 3.

companies in the manufacturing and marketing of gasoline. By virtue of its discovery, the company acquired a place in the sun. It became the center of attention. The small pioneer laboratory at Whiting emerged as the outstanding research laboratory in the petroleum industry. Financially, the development of the cracking process not only meant an enormous increase in the volume of sales and profits for the company but, in time, handsome royalties.

As for the men who developed the cracking process, Dr. Burton, in recognition of his ability and work, was made a Director of the company in 1911, Second Vice-President in 1914, and President in 1918. He was the first chemist in the country to be elevated to a high executive position in any oil company. In token of their appreciation of Burton's work and the assignment of the cracking patent to the company, the Directors early in 1916 gave him $100,-000. At a conference of Colonel Stewart and Dr. Burton with John D. Rockefeller, Jr., in New York in August, 1918, Mr. Rockefeller mentioned the $100,000 already given to Burton in recognition of his service to the company in connection with the cracking process. As a large stockholder, he felt that Burton was entitled to further recognition and was disposed to recommend to other large stockholders a total payment of $500,000, the remaining $400,000 to be paid at the rate of $40,000 per year for ten years.[69] Nothing further was done in the matter until January, 1919.

Many were the honors bestowed upon Burton by various scientific organizations. In the spring of 1918 the Chicago Section of the American Chemical Society awarded him the Willard Gibbs Medal for his eminent, original work in petroleum chemistry. Burton was the first man from the Middle West to receive this recognition. In 1922 the New York Section of the Society of Chemical Industry awarded him the Perkin Medal. Seldom, if ever, had the award of the medal attracted such widespread interest, for Burton was not only recognized as a distinguished chemist but as a scientist who had become an executive in one of America's great industrial concerns. The National Association of Manufacturers in 1940 cited Burton as one of the "national modern pioneers." The American Petroleum Institute in 1947 awarded him its Gold Medal for Distinguished Achievement.

In receiving the Willard Gibbs Medal, Burton pointed out that,

69. Minutes of the Board of Directors' and Stockholders' Meetings, I, 247; Memorandum of a conference in the office of John D. Rockefeller, Jr., August 12, 1918, with Colonel Robert W. Stewart and Dr. Burton. Rockefeller Papers.

while it happened to be his lot to be in general charge of the research on the cracking process, it could never have been brought to a successful termination without the invaluable suggestions, indefatigable labor, and loyal support of his associates. Dr. Humphreys' ability and work were recognized by the company in promotions to be assistant general superintendent at Whiting in 1914, later manager, and in modest increases in salary. Dr. Rogers became chief chemist in 1914 and continued for many years in charge of the research laboratory.

When Dr. Burton began to receive honors and awards, Dr. Humphreys was disturbed because of the lack of recognition for his contributions to the development of the Burton process. Upon learning that Burton had received $100,000 from the company, Humphreys was more upset and conveyed his feelings through an associate to Colonel Robert W. Stewart, Chairman of the Board, in 1918. "If Humphreys has guts enough to come here and talk," Stewart said, "I shall be glad to hear him." [70] As a result Stewart called a meeting of Burton, Humphreys, and the company's patent attorneys in his office late in 1918. In a carefully prepared statement Humphreys said: "The claims that I shall make are in no sense intended to detract from the proper credit due Dr. Burton. He deserves much from our company for exercising a foresight for the increased demand for gasoline that came within the next few years, a demand that would go far beyond the ability of the methods of those times to supply, and for setting in motion the forces at his command to remedy the impending situation, and for slamming through the business of construction in the face of many difficulties and the prophecies of disaster made by experienced refiners. He placed the problem of supplying the method in my hands as I had charge of the research laboratory at that time. Dr. Burton's supervision did not extend to the practice of saying what method should be tried and, following that, what method should next be undertaken. He permitted us to carry out the work in the way we judged proper. Many methods were tried that he knew nothing at all about." [71] Humphreys then outlined the contributions he had made in developing the cracking process. Upon the basis of this statement he claimed a financial award on equal terms with Dr. Burton.

70. Interview with Robert E. Humphreys, July 10, 1948.
71. Statement read by Robert E. Humphreys at the meeting in Colonel Stewart's office. Humphreys Papers.

After several conferences involving John D. Rockefeller, Jr., several other large stockholders in New York, Colonel Stewart, and Dr. Burton, Rockefeller and his associates recommended that $40,-000 per year be granted to Dr. Burton and Dr. Humphreys for ten years, two-thirds of which should go to the former and one-third to the latter. The recommendation was approved by the Directors in January, 1919.[72] Owing to the imposition of the income tax, the Directors increased the annual payment early in 1921 to $52,-500. By the end of the ten payments in 1927, Dr. Burton had received a total of $433,333.33 and Dr. Humphreys $166,666.68.

Greatly excited and enthused over the discovery of the cracking process and what it meant for the future, Humphreys suggested that many chemists and engineers be employed at once to continue research upon the process. "I felt," Humphreys said, "that we had done a whale of a job. I foresaw that our laboratory was going to be hailed as the laboratory of the Universe. I knew we had done something, and that it had immense possibilities for the future." [73] "Let's pre-empt the whole field of cracking," he urged, "and tackle the problem from all angles." There was a tendency, however, for top management to rest upon its laurels. This might have been due to a feeling that the whole field of cracking had already been pre-empted or to the fact that the value of research was not fully appreciated. The idea of research on a large scale or research of any basic nature was something new in industry, especially in the petroleum industry. Maybe it was a lack of vision. In an address before the American Chemical Society in New York about 1916 Humphreys predicted that the day would come when a barrel of crude might yield as much as 75 to 80 per cent gasoline. Cowan, President of Standard of Indiana, read an account of the speech in the newspaper, and as soon as Humphreys returned to Chicago, he gave Humphreys a "dressing down" for making such a "crazy statement." [74] Humphreys "promised not to do it again."

Whatever the reason for the lag in research, three years elapsed after 1912 before any other chemists were added to the research staff. E. J. Shaeffer and M. G. Paulus came in 1915, R. T. Myrick

72. Minutes of the Board of Directors' and Stockholders' Meetings, I, 568, II, 821; John D. Rockefeller, Jr., L. C. Leyard, Payne Whitney, the Northern Finance Corporation, E. S. Harkness, and Charles M. Pratt to Robert W. Stewart, March 16, 1920; E. S. Harkness, J. D. Rockefeller, Jr., L. C. Leyard, and the Northern Finance Corporation to Robert W. Stewart, April 28, 1921. Rockefeller Papers.
73. Interview with Robert E. Humphreys, July 10, 1948.
74. *Ibid.*

in 1916, and M. R. Schmidt in 1917. All of them had their Ph.D. degrees from Johns Hopkins. Three other chemists were employed in 1919. Much of the time of the research staff was spent on the regular routine work and in research on improving old products and developing new ones because of all kinds of requests from the sales fields and the need to meet competition.

As far as research on the Burton process was concerned, the staff worked primarily on improving the quantity and quality of gasoline, the utilization of pressure tar as fuel, road oil, and asphalt, cracking heavier distillates into gasoline, and on new methods of operating the Burton stills.[75] Practically all of Dr. Paulus' time was spent on the theory of cracking. Rogers and Tom S. Cooke worked out a device for maintaining the pressure constant on the stills. To facilitate the condensation of heavy vapors, "Johnny" Moore, in charge of operating the pressure stills at Whiting, devised and patented a device known as "Moore's harp," which split the vapor line into manifolds so as to get more condensation of heavy ends to flow back to the stills.

E. M. Clark, manager of the Wood River refinery, was a very versatile man whose experimentation resulted in a major modification of the Burton still. Among other contributions, he invented the tube still in the fall of 1914. By adding heating tubes beneath the Burton still, arranging them in a bank inclined somewhat to the horizontal, and connecting them by headers at either end with the still above, the oil was permitted to circulate through the heating pipes. Clark's idea minimized the trouble with hot bottoms, provided greater heat, made possible the use of larger stills, permitted fresh charging stock to be introduced during a run, and enabled a still to run longer between cleanings with greater safety. It was with difficulty that Clark secured the acceptance of his idea by refinery officials, but in April, 1915, twenty tube stills were installed at Wood River. In August, twenty were built at Whiting. Twenty more were added at each place in 1916 and the same number at Sugar Creek in 1917.

To improve the original Burton process, Frank B. Lewis and Cooke applied the fractionating column, or bubble-tower, to pressure distillation and fractionation, which they patented in 1917.

75. For improvements on the Burton process see David McKnight, *A Study of Patents on Petroleum Cracking with Special Reference to Their Present Status*, Chapter II; *Special Master's Report*, December 1, 1927, *United States of America, Petitioner, v. Standard Oil Company (Indiana), Et Al., Defendants*, 65-102. Hereinafter referred to as *Martindale's Report*.

In moving from the still to the condenser, the vapors bubbled through from the bottom to the top of a fractionating column and provided a more accurate means of separating one volatile product from another.

Other individuals and oil companies, in the meantime, had been experimenting with new refining processes, and their results were beginning to appear. The first Adams patent had been issued in 1910 and the Trumble in 1911. Between 1913 and 1920 patents on new cracking processes were issued to A. M. McAfee, W. A. Hall, C. H. Washburn, Carleton Ellis, Walter and Roy Cross, John C. Black, Richard Fleming, J. W. Coast, Jr., U. S. Jenkins, C. S. Palmer, Jesse A. Dubbs, Joseph H. Adams, E. W. Isom, W. F. Rittman, C. R. Burke. Frederick T. Manley, Ralph C. Holmes, W. O. Snelling, and others had applications pending. Through assignment, the Sinclair Refining Company controlled the Isom process, Gulf the McAfee, The Texas Company the Adams, Gasoline Products Company the Cross and Black, the National Hydrocarbon Company the Dubbs,. and the Synthetic Hydrocarbon Company the Rittman.

The Palmer process, patented in 1916, consisted of treating residues which had practically no volatile matter below 575°F. When subjected to 575°F., under certain conditions, about 75 per cent of the residue became volatile and about 20 per cent of this was gasoline. The basis of the process was the interrelated control of temperature, pressure, and time. According to Palmer's attorney, the patent was broad enough to dominate both the Rittman and the Burton processes, for it covered the manufacture of gasoline from hydrocarbons by high pressure and temperature. Furthermore, Palmer's patent was not limited to any special range of temperature or pressure, while the Rittman and Burton patents were. Since Palmer's patent application had been filed in 1907 and constituted a threat to the Burton process, Standard of Indiana purchased Palmer's patent in 1916, and used it regularly in the Burton process as a "digesting step." [76]

Several of the newly patented processes were soon placed in operation on a small commercial scale. Gulf's first 1,000-barrel still for using McAfee's aluminum chloride process was built and put into operation at Port Arthur in 1915. Three years later ten

---

76. *The New York Times,* June 15, 1916; *National Petroleum News,* VIII, No. 5 (July, 1916), 8, IX, No. 7 (September 13, 1917), 24-D; *The Oil and Gas Journal,* XVI, No. 15 (September 13, 1917), 2, XVI, No. 9 (October 11, 1917), 37; William M. Burton to Giddens, March 22, 1950.

1,000-barrel stills were constructed.[77] In 1917 the first Coast stills were installed at the West Tulsa refinery of Cosden.[78] The Texas Company made an appropriation of $570,000 in July, 1918, to install cracking units at Port Arthur.[79] The Holmes-Manley patents, used in conjunction with the Adams and Behimer patents, covered the basic ideas of what came to be known as the Holmes-Manley process. A second appropriation of $2,493,000 was made by The Texas Company in August, 1919, for building additional cracking units, and in February, 1920, the first Holmes-Manley batteries were put into operation. Plans were made for the installation of additional units costing about $14,000,000.

Although the Dubbs process had been used at intervals since 1916 on an experimental basis at the Petroleum Products Company refinery at Independence, Kansas, the installation of the process at the refinery of the Roxana Petroleum Corporation at Wood River starting in 1919 marked the beginning of its commercial use.[80] Sinclair constructed a pilot plant embodying the Isom process in 1917. In 1919 it began building a commercial plant at East Chicago which was in operation before the end of 1920.[81] The Fleming process was installed at the Martinez refinery of the Shell Company of California in the spring of 1920.[82] Even though several of these new processes had been developed and were in commercial use, the Burton process was the only one in operation on a large commercial scale from 1912 to 1920.

In the keen rivalry to acquire new inventions and make discoveries and improvements in the highly complex art of cracking, it was inevitable that aggressive leaders in the field found their paths of endeavor crossing and conflicts of interests arising over the scope, validity, and the ownership of various cracking patents. By 1916 interferences were being declared against pending applications in the Patent Office, notices of infringement served, and infringement suits started.

The first major conflict, which was to be in the courts for years, arose in August, 1916, when the Universal Oil Products Company, successor to the National Hydrocarbon Company and owner of

77. A. M. McAfee to Giddens, February 6, 1951.
78. National Petroleum News, XVI, No. 1 (January 2, 1924), 21.
79. Martindale's Report, 289-290.
80. Paul Truesdell, "Dubbs Uses Dehydrating Patent in Effort to Levy Tribute on Cracking," National Petroleum News, November 29, 1922, 26.
81. Edward W. Isom, "The Cracking of Petroleum" (Reprinted from Quarterly of the Colorado School of Mines, XLV, No. 2A (April, 1950), 8-9.
82. The Oil and Gas Journal, July 24, 1924, 20.

the Jesse A. Dubbs patent, filed suit against Standard in the United States District Court at Kansas City, alleging that the Burton process infringed upon the Dubbs patent.[83] Dubbs had filed a patent application for dehydrating California crude oil in 1909. A year and a half after the Burton patent had been issued and the process was in operation on a large scale, Dubbs filed in 1914 a new set of specifications which broadened the original claims beyond dehydrating oil to include the treatment of oil under autogenous gas pressure. Dubbs' lawyers claimed that an inventor was entitled to the use of his patents for every purpose to which they were adapted and to whatever processes the patents covered, although the claim had not been recited in the original specifications and was unknown to the inventor prior to the issuance of the patent. In the suit against Standard, Universal claimed that the Dubbs patent, issued on January 5, 1915, was the basic patent for cracking and condensing oil under heat and pressure. It asked for all profits made by Standard through the use of the Burton process, punitive damages of not more than three times the sum of the profits, and an order to restrain Standard from further use of the process. Except for the filing of an answer and amended answers, objections and replies, the appearance of new lawyers in the case, and the inspection of the operation of the Burton process by Universal officials, no further action was taken in the case until 1921.

83. "Armour Sues Standard for 'Gas' Process Infringement," *National Petroleum News*, VIII, No. 6 (August, 1916), 16; Paul Truesdell, "Cracking Suit of Dubbs vs. Standard Finally Comes to Hearing in Chicago," *National Petroleum News* (October 4, 1922), 21.

CHAPTER VII

The Competitive Battle Begins

BETWEEN 1912 AND 1918 THE CONSUMPTION OF CRUDE OIL IN THE United States increased from 240,188,000 to 412,273,000 barrels per year. The extraordinary demand was due to several factors.[1] Gasoline engines of all kinds had multiplied with great rapidity. The number of stationary and portable gasoline engines sold jumped from 113,966 in 1913 to 215,623 in 1915. Three hundred thousand motorboats were in use in 1915 and they were increasing at the rate of 30,000 per year.[2] The steep upward rise in farm mechanization, which was so evident about 1910, continued, but it was temporarily slowed down during World War I. Nevertheless, the use of tractors on farms had increased from 8,000 in 1912 to 85,000 in 1918.[3] With the outbreak of World War I during the summer of 1914, petroleum became an essential sinew of war. For the first time in history, tanks, motor vehicles of all kinds, airplanes and oil-burning battleships played a vital role in war, consumed enormous quantities of oil, and placed a heavy burden upon the petroleum industry of the United States. Our export of fuel oil increased from 16,750,205 barrels in 1914 to 28,595,114 in 1918 and gasoline from 4,992,682 barrels to 13,318,306.[4] Moreover, a shortage of coal in 1917 and 1918 created an unprecedented demand for fuel oil for industries, railroads, ships, and home heating. The most important single factor, however, in the great demand for oil was the phenomenal increase in the number of automobiles and trucks. There were 944,000 motor vehicles registered in 1912 and 6,160,448 in 1918.

Alert to the growing demand for gasoline, motor oil, and lubricants and conscious of a broad potential market in the Middle

1. Federal Trade Commission, *Report on the Price of Gasoline in 1915*, April 11, 1917, 28-34.
2. *National Petroleum News*, VII, No. 7 (September, 1915), 70.
3. Martin R. Cooper, Glen T. Barton, Albert P. Brodell, *Progress of Farm Mechanization*, 85.
4. *Report of the Federal Trade Commission on the Advance in Price of Petroleum Products*, June 1, 1920, 42, 48.

DR. WILLIAM M. BURTON (LEFT) AND DR. ROBERT E. HUMPHREYS (RIGHT),
PIONEERS OF OIL CRACKING, AT THE UNIVERSITY CLUB, CHICAGO,
OCTOBER 29, 1946

INTERIOR OF THE RESEARCH LABORATORY, WHITING REFINERY, 1916

From left to right, C. F. Miller, Sam Banazak, janitor, A. W. Hayford, Dr. O. E. Bransky,
Dr. F. M. Rogers, W. C. Smith, and a man named Adams

The Gasoline Story!

Gravity Theory Exploded

The Standard Oil Company of Indiana renders you service of inestimable value.

It delivers to you a motor fuel in Red Crown Gasoline that is uniform at all times—no matter whether it is distilled from heavy or light crude.

So that you may enjoy your car month in and month out, the Standard Oil Company must, to supply you with gasoline, work with many and varied qualities of crude, different sections of the country yielding a different quality.

Just suppose you should receive gasoline that would vary as do the various crudes. You could never know whether you would arrive at your destination or not.

Your carburetor would give you an endless amount of trouble.

You'd be compelled to readjust it every time you filled your tank.

The Standard Oil Company is able to cope with Mother Necessity in delivering to you a uniform gasoline, no matter what they are forced to work with—*because it has gathered together* the best petroleum chemists in the world.

This corps of trained men discovered long ago that the secret of an efficient motor fuel lies absolutely and solely in the adjustment of its range of boiling points.

Gravity has absolutely nothing to do with measuring the efficiency of motor fuel.

If gasoline is produced from heavy crude, without regard to boiling points, the result is a low gravity gasoline.

If gasoline is produced from a light crude, without regard to boiling points, the result is a high gravity gasoline.

If the low and high gravity gasolines are blended without regard to boiling points, the result is excessive evaporation, trouble in starting the engine when cold, jerky power, carbon in the cylinders and on the spark plugs, and innumerable other troubles.

Red Crown Gasoline Is Not a Blended Gasoline

Red Crown Gasoline is not an elementary chemical compound like water.

Red Crown Gasoline is a mechanical mixture of a large number of such compounds, each one having a different boiling point.

Red Crown Gasoline is composed of fractions having low, intermediate, and high boiling points presenting a continuous chain, beginning at about 90 degrees Fahrenheit and ending around 400 degrees Fahrenheit, with no gaps, each one vaporizing at a different temperature.

It contains a sufficient number of low boiling point fractions to insure easy starting when the engine is cold. Too many low boiling points cause, in addition to starting troubles, undue evaporation in storage.

Red Crown Gasoline contains a sufficient number of intermediate, or higher, boiling points to insure smooth acceleration.

It contains a sufficient number of high boiling points to insure a maximum of power. Too many high boiling points cause carbon in the cylinders and on the spark plugs.

Red Crown vaporizes to the last drop and leaves a minimum of carbon deposit.

Every batch of Red Crown is inspected by experts as to boiling points. Every batch is guaranteed to contain the same continuous chain of boiling point fractions.

Red Crown Gasoline is the easiest fuel to obtain. The Standard Oil Company has perfected a comprehensive system of distribution, so that no matter where you happen to be you can always get Red Crown.

Red Crown Gasoline

Everywhere and Everywhere the Same

Standard Oil Company guarantees the uniformity of Red Crown Gasoline at all times, no matter where you buy it.

Red Crown Gasoline is the perfect efficiency motor fuel. In a test run it gave 28.9 miles per gallon on boulevards—accelerated in high gear from 5 to 25 miles per hour in 11 4-5 seconds—developed a speed of 58 miles an hour on country roads.

Red Crown Gasoline gives more power, more speed, more miles per gallon; hence it is the most economical.

Red Crown Gasoline burns with a quick, snappy explosion.

When you need a quick burst of speed to avoid an accident you can get it if Red Crown is in your tank.

Made and Guaranteed by

STANDARD OIL COMPANY (Indiana) 72 W. Adams St., Chicago, U.S.A.

POLARINE, The Perfect Motor Oil, for Correct Lubrication on Any Make Car, at Any Speed or Temperature

The Chicago Tribune, October 26, 1916. Reproduced through the courtesy of The Chicago Tribune

ADVERTISEMENT USED BY STANDARD, EMPHASIZING BOILING POINTS RATHER THAN GRAVITY IN GASOLINE

AN EARLY STANDARD TANK TRUCK

GROUP OF STILL CLEANERS, SUGAR CREEK REFINERY

THE BIG 32-FOOT BENDING ROLLS IN THE WHITING BOILER SHOP WHICH TURNED OUT PLATE FOR THE EMERGENCY FLEET CORPORATION DURING WORLD WAR I

WOMEN AND GIRLS WHO FILLED AND PACKED CANS, WHITING REFINERY, DURING WORLD WAR I

West, Standard, under the aggressive direction of Drake, enlarged its marketing territory, rapidly expanded its marketing organization, and made significant improvements in its products and services. The first enlargement of the company's marketing territory came as a result of the Missouri ouster suit. State officials of Missouri had informed the company that it must either market on a state-wide basis or not at all.[5] Consequently, in the fall of 1913 the company purchased the distributing plant and business of the Purity Oil Company, an independent jobber, at Springfield and began marketing in southern Missouri. Simultaneously, it purchased the Southeast Missouri Oil Company. In taking these steps the company invaded the marketing territory of the Pierce Oil Corporation, one of the former Standard units. In addition to buying jobbers' facilities, the company began building bulk plants in many of the smaller places which the old Waters-Pierce Company would never have thought capable of supporting a station. At about the same time, Standard purchased the properties of the H. A. Williamson Company of Quincy, Illinois, one of its old jobbing firms. In 1913 Oklahoma was added to Standard's marketing territory.[6]

In order to reach consumers throughout the entire marketing area, bulk plants were rapidly built everywhere. Starting with 1,407 in 1911, Drake added, through purchase or construction, 1,438 new distributing stations by 1918.[7] To distinguish bulk plants in the smaller towns from those in the larger ones, the former were designated "B" stations and the latter "A" stations. Agents in charge of an "A" station were on a salary while those in charge of "B" stations usually worked on a commission basis. In towns up to 5,000 inhabitants, the investment was generally under $13,000 although it might run as high as $20,000. In towns between 11,000 and 13,000 inhabitants the investment usually did not exceed $16,500. In a town like South Bend, Indiana, for example, the cost was around $68,000.

To provide better and faster service in the automobile age, the company began using motor-tank trucks to deliver oil and stake-trucks to haul barrels.[8] In 1908 the first motor-tank truck, a Kelly

5. *High Cost of Gasoline and Other Petroleum Products,* I, 778.
6. *Hearings Before Martindale,* VI, 3335.
7. Company Encyclopedia: Marketing, I, Bulk and Service Stations in Operation, 1896–1940.
8. C. Henry Austin, "Sylvan Symphony of Mahn-a-Waukee Transmitted by Man to Busy Bustle of Modern Milwaukee," *Stanolind Record,* VI, No. 5 (March,

truck, was placed in use in the Milwaukee division. The company's first motor-tank truck appeared on the streets of Chicago about 1911. It was a Biddle-Murray truck, a huge and cumbersome piece of mechanism, the only one of its kind ever constructed. Probably its chief value was to break down skepticism as to the feasibility of using motor vehicles in the oil business. A new White motor-tank truck with a capacity for carrying 600 gallons appeared in 1914 at the bulk plant in Aberdeen, South Dakota, and about the same time, the first stake-truck appeared in Duluth, Minneapolis, and St. Paul. A chain drive Peerless was the first motor-tank truck to be used in St. Paul. Soon afterwards a one-ton International tank truck, with high wheels, hard rubber tires, oil lamps, and an open cab with a canopy, was added. Teams continued to be used during the winter and spring when the roads were bad. Gradually, however, the use of horses was discontinued and all deliveries were made by truck. In order that they might cover their territory more quickly and give better service, salesmen were provided with Ford roadsters beginning in 1913. By 1915 the company was the largest individual buyer of Ford cars.

During the fall of 1911 the company began experimenting with shipping oil by barge from the Wood River refinery via the Mississippi and Ohio rivers to the Standard of Kentucky at Louisville.[9] The barge had a capacity of 500,000 gallons and was towed by a chartered towboat, the *Eagle*. It proved so successful that three or four barges were used in 1912.

As a result of the dissolution and reorganization in 1911, the two barges, which had operated on the Great Lakes since 1895, and the large tanker, *Perfection,* which had been put into service shortly after the dissolution decree became effective, were returned to the Standard of New York. Barge "C" with a capacity of 41,867 barrels and the tank steamer, the *Renown,* which was renamed the *Beaumont Parks* in 1930, with a capacity of 43,788 barrels, were acquired.[10] Land was purchased at Bay City and Muskegon, Mich-

1925), 11; "Standard Oil Company (Indiana) Keeps Pace with Amazing Growth of City of Chicago," *Stanolind Record,* X, No. 11 (September, 1929), 35; "Glimpses Into a Pioneering Past and a Future of Pioneering Opportunities," *Stanolind Record,* XX, No. 20 (June, 1939), 2.

9. *The Oil and Gas Journal,* X, No. 18 (October 12, 1911), 2, No. 19 (October 19, 1911), 2, No. 27 (December 14, 1911), 2; *National Petroleum News,* IV, No. 2 (April, 1912), 25.

10. "From the Log of a Tanker Fleet," *Stanolind Record,* XIII, No. 8 (June, 1932), 1-16.

igan, for the construction of water terminals and on the Indiana Harbor Canal for building docks to replace the pier washed away at Whiting during the winter of 1911–12.

The growth of the shipping business carried on by the company on the Great Lakes was astonishing.[11] During 1914 over 78,000,000 gallons of gasoline and kerosene from Whiting were shipped from Indiana Harbor, almost all of which was carried by the *Renown* and Barge "C." In 1915 the total shipped amounted to over 92,-000,000 gallons. Most of the oil went to the company's storage terminals at Superior, Green Bay, and River Rouge at Detroit. In 1915 the company delivered by boat nearly 2,000,000 gallons to the Standard of Ohio at Cleveland.

Establishing company-owned and operated drive-in service stations was the most revolutionary development in Standard's method of marketing. With grocers, hardware dealers, and garages charging whatever the traffic would bear and giving little or no service to motorists, the company recognized that these practices were a major hindrance to the expansion of its sales and business. By establishing company-owned and operated service stations everywhere the company could eliminate the middlemen, provide better service, keep retail prices at a fair and reasonable level, enlarge the volume of business, and offset the losses which it was beginning to feel from the growth of competition. Such a move was in keeping with past policies in establishing tank-wagon deliveries to dealers and farmers. While Standard did not originate the idea of establishing drive-in service stations, it was the first to establish company-owned and operated stations on a large scale in the Middle West. In time, it had more stations than any other oil company in the country.

About 1912 the company began buying or leasing land in towns and cities at strategic locations on which to build service stations. The first one was built at 10th Street and Hennepin Avenue in Minneapolis in 1912 and consisted of a frame office and shed with underground tanks, pumps, and an air compressor for free air, all of which cost $551.83.[12] The company opened its first service station in Chicago in 1913. In 1914 the company had 25 service stations, 68 in 1915, 153 in 1916, 277 in 1917, and 451 in 1918, most of which were in the larger cities like Chicago, where the

11. *National Petroleum News*, VII, No. 6 (August, 1915), 70.
12. Company Encyclopedia: Marketing, I, Methods of Distribution, Through Service Stations, 63.

company had 56. Stations were located in many places where one might well question the business judgment involved. However, with the rapid increase in the number of automobiles, these seemingly out-of-the-way stations soon did a thriving business and the far-sightedness of Standard officials was demonstrated. The scattering of these service stations through the Middle West was a pioneering effort which made possible the more rapid introduction of the automobile. If it had not been for an adequate supply of gasoline and the extensive retail distributing system established by Standard, motorists in the Middle West would have found themselves seriously limited in their travels. On the other hand, the policy of erecting company-owned and operated service stations and the gradual elimination of many dealers naturally resulted in their becoming agents for a competitor, and they did not hesitate to knock Standard products at every opportunity.

In erecting service stations there was at first no uniformity in their style. Each sales field developed its own kind. Usually, however, these stations consisted of a cheap, galvanized-iron building inside of which were installed a couple of pumps with hoses long enough to reach to either side. On both sides of the building were narrow cinder driveways so that two cars might drive in and fill with gasoline at the same time. Free air and water were the first services offered. Not long after the first service stations were opened, signs were posted to the effect that attendants must not crank cars. In trying to give good service, many attendants had cranked balky engines and received broken wrists or arms. About 1917 a type of station was developed at Joliet, Illinois, by Allan Jackson, then manager of that division, which served as a pattern for all those built during the next five years.[13] It consisted of a small brick building with a flat roof and a canopy extending over one of the two driveways in front of the building. The canopy was supported by brick posts that protected the pumps in the center of the driveway from being hit by careless drivers.

Before a service station could be built, many of the larger cities and towns required a building permit or the passage of an ordinance. It was not always easy to secure consent. Occasionally, protests were filed because of the fire hazard, odor, noise, or other objections, real or imaginary. Opposition came from local garages, grocers, hardware and implement dealers who had curb pumps.

13. *Ibid.*, 73.

In erecting a service station, Standard was taking away business which they regarded as rightfully belonging to them. In 1915 the garage association in Chicago bitterly fought the establishment of drive-in service stations by ordering its members to buy oil from only those companies not associated with filling stations.[14] As a result of this fight Standard lost practically every one of its garage accounts—nearly 200—in Chicago to The Texas Company, which had no service stations of its own until about 1921.[15]

While Standard of Indiana was in the process of developing its system of direct marketing through company-owned and operated service stations, it leased some privately built stations and continued to market through privately owned service stations, garages, grocers, and hardware dealers. Originally, the company's policy had been to charge dealers and some automobile customers who filled at bulk plants or had a tank at home, the same price. Soon it became more or less of a policy to sell to all at the same price.[16] No middlemen dealers were necessary in a system of direct marketing. As the dealers' volume of business grew, they began to insist upon a discount. In order to appease the dealers and hold their business, Standard began about 1914 allowing a discount of 1 cent per gallon on purchases of two hundred gallons, which was lowered to one hundred gallons in 1915.

When the marketing of gasoline through service stations became more widespread, the volume greater, and the competition keener, the question of establishing a differential between the tank-wagon price and the service-station price became an exceedingly important issue. Some of Standard's Directors believed the company should sell directly through its own outlets and not make any differential. Establishing a differential would simply invite more people to come into the retail business and compete with Standard's service stations for the business. Others were fearful that, unless one were established, there would be a loss of dealers and business to competitors, who were willing to make concessions of various kinds. In June, 1918, the company announced that hereafter uniform prices would prevail in the sale of refined products; the small buyer would get the same price as the large buyer.[17] Late

14. *National Petroleum News,* VII, No. 4 (June, 1915), 2.
15. Company Encyclopedia: Marketing, I, Methods of Distribution, Through Service Stations, 64.
16. Memorandum written by Allan Jackson to Giddens during the summer of 1948.
17. *The Oil and Gas Journal,* XVII, No. 1 (June 6, 1918), 28; Allan Jackson to Giddens, March 28, 1950.

in World War I, Mark Requa, U.S. Fuel Administrator, established a differential for all resellers.

When Standard began marketing its cracked "motor spirits" in February, 1913, consumers made loud complaints.[18] It was a heavier and somewhat less volatile gasoline than straight-run, and motorists found it difficult to start their cars in winter. It had a gravity of 57° or 58° while ordinary gasoline was about 64° or above. When stored, certain unstable hydrocarbons oxidized, formed gummy materials, which clogged gasoline fuel lines and carburetors. In addition to these deficiencies, "motor spirits" had a vile odor. If some were spilled in filling the gasoline tank under the front seat of a Model T Ford, the odor enveloped the passengers. Owing to its odor and low gravity, "motor spirits" was considered poor-quality gasoline. Public acceptance of "motor spirits" was made even more difficult because competitors took advantage of the opportunity to advise motorists against using it in their cars.

Standard's research men at Whiting went to work on the problem. One immediate result was the perfection of a priming device to make cars start more easily.[19] Since "motor spirits" had been put on the market without treating, the staff worked on various methods to remove the odor and gummy materials.[20] This took considerable time. The goal was to produce a gasoline having as good an odor and quality as that of straight-run gasoline, but in spite of every effort that goal was difficult to reach. They reduced but never did completely eliminate the odor. The one virtue of "motor spirits" was its good antiknock quality, but most people did not notice this in those days of low-compression engines. The complaints continued and were so loud and numerous that the company, within a short time, withdrew the name "motor spirits," mingled cracked gasoline with straight-run gasoline, and offered it to the public as Red Crown gasoline. Even so, it still retained some odor. Moreover, it had a low gravity, which was not of any practical importance but this fact was used by competitors as an argument against "motor spirits."

In the ordinary distillation process of the earlier days, refiners used the Baumé hydrometer, which determined the density of fluids, to control the separation of the various fractions as they

18. *National Petroleum News,* V, No. 2 (April, 1913), 13-14.
19. Interview with Amos Ball, August 17, 1948.
20. Interview with Robert E. Humphreys, July 17, 1948.

came through the condenser. All volatile oils arising from the still when a temperature of 302°F. was maintained were called gasoline, which had an average gravity of about 64° Baumé or over. Hence gravity came to be used to indicate the different grades of gasoline such as 58°, 62°, 64°, and 88°. Even though refiners learned little from the hydrometer about the quality of gasoline, its value as a fuel or ease of vaporation, the high gravity of a gasoline came to be an important sales point. As the petroleum industry moved westward from Pennsylvania, the gravity of refined products of a given quality progressively decreased. In competition with western oil, the jobbers of Pennsylvania oil emphasized high-gravity gasoline and motorists preferred it to gasoline made from western oil.

Many states had laws specifying the quality of gasoline, including its gravity, that could be sold. The laws were based upon gasoline obtained directly from crude oil, which was bright in color and had a pleasant, ethereal odor. Neither "motor spirits" nor any mixture of it with natural gasoline would satisfy these specifications. In North and South Dakota, for example, gasoline with a gravity of less than 63° could not even be shipped into these states, which excluded Standard's gasoline with a gravity of 57°.[21] Consequently, Burton, Humphreys, and Colonel Stewart visited many state legislatures over a period of several years in an attempt to persuade them to modify their restrictions so that cracked gasoline might be sold.

The opposition to using cracked gasoline and the competitive battle for gallonage forced Standard to break with the traditional policy of the old Standard organization and advertise its gasoline. More than $150,000 in 1913 and $283,000 in 1914 were spent in advertising which emphasized power and mileage, not gravity.[22] If the company were to meet the growing competition and overcome the prejudice against "motor spirits," more had to be done. In the fall of 1914 it created an advertising department and made N. H. Reed, formerly with the Sante Fe Railroad, its head.[23] Beginning in 1915, after a long deliberation over policy, the Directors made the first definite advertising appropriation amounting

21. *National Petroleum News,* V, No. 2 (April, 1913), 45, No. 9 (November, 1913), 8.
22. *National Petroleum News,* V, No. 6 (August, 1913), 20, 27; Company Encyclopedia: Marketing, I, Statement of Advertising Expenditures for the Period January 1, 1905, to December 31, 1925, Inclusive.
23. W. L. Gundlach, "Introducing Company's Loud Speaker, Power Type," *Stanolind Record,* XI, No. 2 (December, 1929), 1.

to $235,000, but it was exceeded by more than $137,000.[24] A more comprehensive program was adopted in 1916 involving an expenditure of $429,088. The program was continued on a larger scale in 1917.

Outstanding in the war over the quality and character of gasoline was the fight between Standard and the Wadhams Oil Company of Wisconsin, one of the largest independent jobbers in the country, which marketed in Wisconsin, Minnesota, Iowa, and Illinois.[25] Wadhams' straight-run gasoline, especially in Wisconsin and Minnesota, had a large amount of light ends and a gravity of 65°–70° while Standard's fluctuated from 57°–58° to 64°–65°. In a region where the winters were severe, garages were unheated, and automobile engines were much different from those of today, high-gravity gasoline, because of its quick-starting qualities, had a powerful appeal. For this reason, Wadhams and other competitors of Standard were able to secure the bulk of the gasoline business in Milwaukee. Realizing that 70 per cent of the oil business was in the sale of gasoline and that profits were so low a loss might result from the slightest change in the market, Wadhams decided in 1916 to sell its gasoline for about 5 cents per gallon above that of Standard's Red Crown. It launched an extensive advertising campaign in newspapers and farm journals to convince motorists of the superiority of its product and to justify a premium price.[26] Starting with a $10,000 advertising budget in 1916, Wadhams was spending $125,000 per year by 1922. It was the largest oil advertiser in the four states in which it marketed.

During the spring of 1916 Standard moved its big guns into position in order to increase its gasoline business in Wisconsin.[27] It built six service stations in Milwaukee, each costing $10,000 or more, on very expensive sites. When construction was completed in July, the company opened fire by running a series of full-page advertisements in eight or nine newspapers in which it attacked paying a premium price for gasoline. The general theme was that motorists were paying too much if they paid more than 18.6 cents per

24. Company Encyclopedia: Marketing, I, Statement of Advertising Expenditures for the Period January 1, 1905, to December 31, 1925, Inclusive.

25. "Battled for Success of Independents," *National Petroleum News*, VIII, No. 3 (May, 1916), 10, 12; "S. O. Ads Attack Independents' Quality," *National Petroleum News*, No. 7 (September, 1916), 5, 6, 8.

26. Ward K. Halbert, "Oil Company's Ads in Newspaper Keep Reader Waiting for Next," *National Petroleum News*, XIV, No. 21 (May 24, 1922), 37, 39.

27. "S. O. Ads Attack Independents' Quality Gas," *National Petroleum News*, VIII, No. 7 (September, 1916), 5, 6, 8.

gallon, the price of Red Crown. According to Standard, Milwaukee motorists were being charged $1,000 per day too much for gasoline. Another phase of the war involved two price reductions by Standard so that by September 13, 1916, the price of Red Crown was 16.6 cents. Despite the vigor of its sales campaign, Standard was not able to do more than one-third of the gasoline business in the Milwaukee area.

Wadhams continued to maintain a price of 21 cents for its lowest grade while competitors sold at 17.6 cents. Once a week Wadhams ran in the four Milwaukee newspapers advertisements emphasizing its high-gravity gasoline, and the public continued to buy. Wadhams' advertisements inferred that it had been given an opportunity to buy inferior gasoline made by a commercial cracking process, but it had decided against it in favor of high-quality products. In combating Standard's claims, Wadhams used the "penny wise and pound foolish" slogan most effectively. As cold weather approached, consumers returned to buy from Standard's competitors, for starting a car with Red Crown gasoline was difficult.

Late in the fall of 1916 Standard abruptly stopped its advertising campaign against "quality gasoline at higher prices," for it put on the market a "Special Crown" gasoline, a blended product of 63°–65° gravity with more light ends for winter use, which sold at 19.6 cents while Red Crown sold at 15.6 cents.[28] With "Special Crown" gasoline for sale, Standard could hardly keep up its attack against premium gasoline. It did, however, continue advertising Red Crown and emphasized that gravity had absolutely nothing to do with measuring the efficiency of motor fuel. Standard claimed that the secret of an efficient motor fuel was in the adjustment of its range of boiling points; that Red Crown was uniform in quality at all times; and that on account of the company's comprehensive system of distribution it was the easiest fuel to obtain. Red Crown gave more power, more speed, more miles per gallon, and was the most economical. The fight between Standard and Wadhams lasted for more than six years with Wadhams continuing to advertise against "cheap" gasoline and emphasize the fact that its gasoline was straight-run, that is, contained no kerosene and none of the lower distillates of crude oil as "cheap" gasoline did.

Ultimately, on account of the extraordinary demand for gaso-

28. "Standard Ends Its Milwaukee Advertising Campaign," *National Petroleum News,* VIII, No. 8 (October, 1916), 8.

line the public had to accept cracked gasoline or go without. State legislatures were forced to repeal or modify the restrictive legislation based upon gravity. Motorists soon recognized that although light-gravity gasoline made starting easy it provided less mileage and power than heavy-gravity gasoline, and it had more of a tendency to "vapor lock." Gradually, Standard's position in stressing boiling points of gasoline as an indication of its quality was accepted. In spite of the great prejudice and opposition encountered, Standard's sale of gasoline increased from 156,936,096 gallons in 1911 to 518,102,350 in 1918.[29] It exceeded by far the sale of any other petroleum product both in volume and dollar sales.

Kerosene sales were far from being a thing of the past in the United States. The amount sold by the company steadily increased from 138,555,173 gallons in 1911 to 235,236,282 in 1918, and it ranked next to gasoline in volume of sales.[30] The growing use of tractors on the farms required a greater amount of kerosene. While the use of lamps was considerably less than ten or fifteen years earlier, the great growth of population in the West kept the use of lamps from declining at a rapid rate.[31] It was estimated in 1917 that 3,000,000 oil lamps were being sold per year. There were still many companies manufacturing oil lamps, and one reported that its sales in 1916 were as large as any in its history. Kerosene was being used more than ever before in many sections of the country. For those oil companies handling light oils and marketing in rural areas, kerosene sales were as important as gasoline since there was more profit in kerosene. Many companies did a larger business in illuminating oil than in gasoline. The largest market was in the South, but the West and Northwest also afforded a good market. The sale of oil lanterns was larger than ever before, and there were many places and situations—on the farms, highway construction jobs in cities and rural areas, and on railroads —where nothing could take a lantern's place.

Early in 1915 Standard experimented in St. Louis with selling kerosene directly to consumers in sealed gallon cans especially designed for the purpose and protected by patents.[32] More kerosene was consumed in St. Louis than in most cities because of a large

29. Figures for the Sales Department only. Furnished by M. A. McNulty, Comptroller, Standard Oil Company (Indiana), on May 11, 1950.
30. *Ibid.*
31. "Kerosene Lamps Not Emblem of the Past," *National Petroleum News,* VIII, No. 11 (January, 1917), 50.
32. *Ibid.,* VI, No. 12 (February, 1915), 49-50, VIII, No. 7 (September, 1916), 38.

colored and foreign population and because the gas company required a deposit of $10 and the electric $5 for these services. To prevent the cans from being refilled by competitors, they had an unusual spout which required special machinery to refill the can. The company manufactured the can and controlled the machinery for refilling. The cans resembled those in which lubricating oil was sold, but they were made of much heavier tin to withstand repeated usage. Kerosene in the sealed can sold for 15 cents, 4 cents being a deposit to ensure the return of the empty can. The grocer in turn paid a 5 cent deposit to Standard. Oil in bulk sold for 10 cents a gallon. In introducing kerosene in sealed cans, the company advertised that their use meant uniform quality and the prevention of adulteration.

So successful was the experiment that the National Grocers' Association opposed it largely because of the company's selling direct to the consumer, which took business away from grocers. To some it looked as if the company had adopted the use of the can as a method to drive out competition. Competing oil jobbers could not afford to buy cans or special machinery for refilling or stand the loss in case the cans were not returned. Thus, they were considerably handicapped. However, P. C. Crenshaw, General Manager of Sales, denied the charge and pointed out that it had always been a problem to get the better class of grocers to handle kerosene in bulk. A year later the indications were that the plan was not meeting with any great success. Those who used kerosene in a day of electricity and gas were largely people who could not afford to make a deposit on a can when they wanted kerosene. Most of them had their own cans and could not understand why they had to buy another. It also added to the cost of kerosene in that many of the cans were not returned. Therefore, customers preferred to buy in bulk, and many grocers refused to handle it in cans.

Prior to 1911 many of the lubricating oils sold by Standard were purchased from the Vacuum Oil Company and distributed under its brand names. After the dissolution in 1911, Standard discontinued the distribution of Vacuum's oils and began manufacturing and selling a line of its own under the brand names of Superla, Stanolind, and Stanolex. In order to secure a share in the lubricant business of the railroads, which had previously been handled by the Galena-Signal Oil Company, the company's Railroad Sales Department under W. A. "Commodore" Jones was quickly expanded. Requirements of the railroads were studied and new lubricants and greases developed to meet their needs. In this field the company met strong competition from The Texas Company, which made a specialty of railroad products and had attained a strong position among the railroad companies.[33]

Especially important was the sale by Standard of its old favorite, Polarine motor oil. Even though Pennsylvania motor oils had a paraffin base, wide distribution, and extensive advertising, Standard's Polarine continued to be sold in an ever-increasing amount throughout the Middle West. Sales of this popular motor oil increased from twenty-two barrels in 1908 to 138,532 in 1914.[34] Polarine was used in 1915 by approximately 4,000,000 cars in the Middle West alone. It was a remarkably good motor oil and a great seller. As the demand increased, various grades of Polarine were manufactured and sold. The success of Standard in selling lubricating oils between 1911 and 1918 is indicated by the fact that its volume increased from 34,431,593 to 58,065,388 gallons.[35]

The growth in the number of automobiles and the development of the Burton process combined to emphasize the importance of several other petroleum products. The market for road oil and asphalt for making improved roads steadily expanded. Asphalt was also used in the roofing business. The quantity of light fuel oil available for heating, on the other hand, became less owing to the fact that it could be utilized more profitably in the cracking process to make more gasoline. Considerable coke was formed in the cracking stills, and after a period of operation the stills had to be closed down to remove the coke. It was found that this coke had a high heat value and left little ash. It made an excellent fuel for homes. A limited market was found around the refineries, but as the quantity increased it became a problem. The Sales Department, through P. C. Crenshaw, found a market through coal dealers at a price slightly higher than coal.[36] Since coke was produced in more or less uniform daily quantities and the demand for heating purposes was seasonal, Crenshaw's approach was not satisfactory, and other sales methods had to be devised to get rid of it.

The possibility of putting oil to a new use, although the experiment was a failure, was indicated during the summer and fall of

33. Memorandum written by Allan Jackson for Giddens during the summer of 1948.
34. *The Chicago Tribune,* February 9, 1915, April 1, 1915, October 14, 1915.
35. Figures for the Sales Department only. Furnished by M. A. McNulty, Comptroller, Standard Oil Company (Indiana), on May 11, 1950.
36. Memorandum written by Allan Jackson for Giddens during the summer of 1948.

1912 when the Department of Entomology at the University of Illinois began experimenting to find an effective barrier against chinch bugs in Macoupin and Montgomery counties.[37] It found that the best solution was to pour a line of heavy road oil around a field, and the bugs would not cross the line. During the summer of 1913 hundreds of barrels of Standard's No. 7 road oil, which had proven best in the tests, were ordered by the farmers of the infested area. However, when the farmers poured the oil around their fields, it seemed to soak into the ground and left a slightly discolored line over which the chinch bugs casually crossed. Why it proved ineffective was a puzzle.

Although crude oil production in the United States increased from 265,763,000 barrels in 1914 to a new high of 355,928,000 barrels in 1918, the demand far exceeded the supply and the shortage of gasoline and fuel oil would have been much greater and more serious but for the discovery and use of the Burton process, the opening of new fields in Oklahoma, Kansas, and Wyoming, and large imports of crude.[38] Simultaneously with the oil developments in Wyoming, new fields were opened in 1912 and 1913 at Cushing and Healdton in Oklahoma. Cushing reached its peak in the spring of 1915 when the daily production amounted to about 330,000 barrels and then a swift decline set in. At its height Cushing furnished crude oil for over 50 per cent of the gasoline manufactured in the United States. Healdton reached its zenith a year later with a daily production of about 95,000 barrels. As these fields declined, others were discovered in 1916 and 1917 at Augusta, El Dorado, and Towanda in Kansas. These new sources were so prolific that Kansas production rose from 11,500,000 barrels in 1916 to 38,000,000 in 1917.

The discovery of new sources of crude oil in Oklahoma and Kansas not only helped to avert a gasoline shortage but greatly stimulated the growth of competition in the petroleum industry. At the time Cushing was discovered there were only thirteen refineries in Kansas and Oklahoma, which refined more than 30,000 barrels of crude per day. As the supply of light crude increased and the price decreased, the margin of profit on gasoline sales increased. Consequently, many small refineries were built and they proceeded to skim off the light and more volatile fraction with little regard for the other fractions. By 1915 Kansas and Oklahoma had

37. *National Petroleum News*, V, No. 7 (September, 1913), 61.
38. Imports rose from 6,911,000 barrels in 1912 to 37,736,000 in 1918.

fifty-five refineries processing 75,000 barrels of crude daily.[39] Significant was the fact that between 1914 and 1918 the number of
refineries in the United States increased from 176 to 267. Older
companies, like Gulf, The Texas Company, and Prairie Oil & Gas,
gained a stronger hold in the Mid-Continent field. Others, like
Sun and the Carter Oil Company, a subsidiary of the Standard Oil
Company of New Jersey, entered Oklahoma and began expanding their operations. By the end of 1915 Carter, next to Prairie,
was the largest holder of stored oil in Oklahoma.

Indicative of the "oil fever" which hit the United States was
the fact that between August and December, 1914, seventy-seven
new oil companies were organized. One hundred and ninety-six
were organized in 1915, and two hundred and ten in 1916.[40] The
organization of the Sinclair Oil & Refining Company, the Phillips
Petroleum Company, the Mid-Continent Petroleum Corporation,
the Cities Service Oil Company, the White Eagle Oil and Refining
Company, and the Skelly Oil Company between 1916 and 1919 was
of special importance because they grew rapidly and became powerful competitors of Standard in the Middle West. When the Shell
Company secured control of the Roxana Petroleum Company in
1917, it also became a strong competitor.

Through a consolidation of the properties of the Sinclair Oil
Company, the Chanute Refining Company, the Cudahy Refining
Company, the Milliken Oil Company, and others, the Sinclair
Oil & Refining Corporation was organized in May, 1916. It was
one of the earliest to challenge Standard's supremacy in the Middle West. Producing lands in the Cushing and Healdton fields and
in Texas were acquired and new refineries were started at Houston, Kansas City, and East Chicago. Simultaneously, the Sinclair
Pipe Line Company was organized with a capitalization of $2,000,-
000, and it acquired the pipeline properties of all the consolidated companies. Most of the lines were confined to Oklahoma
and Kansas and constituted a very small system, only about four
to five hundred miles of pipe. In June, 1916, the company started
constructing a pipeline from Drumright, Oklahoma, north via
Kansas City to East Chicago, adjoining Whiting, covering about
the same route as the Prairie line.[41] It was the most ambitious and
aggressive undertaking of any of Standard's competitors. The first

39. Rister, *Oil! Titan of the Southwest*, 135-136.
40. *The Chicago Tribune*, March 3, 1917.
41. *National Petroleum News*, VIII, No. 8 (October, 1916), 6; *High Cost of Gasoline
and Other Petroleum Products*, I, 642-646.

oil reached East Chicago in March, 1918. The effect of building this line to East Chicago was to place Sinclair on an equal competitive basis with Standard so far as transportation costs were concerned. In the spring of 1918 Sinclair built a pipeline from Houston to Healdton and from Healdton to Cushing to connect with the trunk line to East Chicago. When completed, it was the first pipeline to connect the Great Lakes and the Gulf of Mexico.

By the time that Cushing reached the height of its production in the spring of 1915, gasoline was a drug on the market. Refiners were willing to sell at almost any price and the fiercest kind of competition had developed throughout the Middle West. In an effort to get rid of their gasoline and gain a foothold in the trade, refiners either purchased jobbing concerns or marketed through jobbers or did both. Jobbers came into existence by the scores in the North Central States. They established iron-barrel stations in little towns of two to five hundred population and made Standard's tank-wagon trips to these places unprofitable. In other towns, they got coal and lumber firms and ice companies to become dealers and install a pump and storage tank. Where a dealer could not buy them, refiners, in order to secure outlets and increase gallonage, began furnishing them under a lease or loan contract, whereby the dealer paid the nominal sum of $1.00 per year, provided the pump was used exclusively for the sale of company products. Lacking the capital to build service stations costing five to ten thousand dollars each, many small refiners could afford to invest $200 in pump and tank installations. When one company started the practice of leasing or loaning pumps and tanks, others followed. As the fight intensified, there was scarcely any limit to the amount of equipment dealers demanded. If one oil company would not meet the demand, another would.

In the larger places refiners built service stations, but where possible, they interested private parties in building them according to plans furnished, and then they leased them. In this way, refiners secured wider distributing facilities without investing the capital, which they did not have. In 1914 competitors had 18 service stations and 447 bulk plants in Standard's marketing territory. By the end of 1918, they had 356 service stations and 1,375 bulk plants.[42]

42. Company Encyclopedia: Marketing, I, Statement of Other Companies and Individuals Operating Bulk and Service Stations. On the growth of competition see Robert E. Wilson, "Oil Competition in the Midwest," an address before the National Petroleum Association in Cleveland, Ohio, on April 13, 1950.

The most formidable weapon used by refiners and jobbers to secure business was to cut prices under Standard. Many of the jobbers had contracts guaranteeing them a margin of profit of 2 to 3 cents a gallon below any tank-wagon price set by Standard. Hence, they had no particular incentive to fight for the maintenance of prices above the cost of production. They had gasoline to sell and a desire to get as much of the trade as possible. Consequently, Standard began to lose gallonage in those areas nearest the Kansas and Oklahoma refineries. The company's percentage of the gasoline business in 1915 dropped to about 65 per cent.[43] Over much of Standard's marketing territory competitors were making close to one-half of the gasoline sales. In some towns they sold well over half. The more substantial competitors deplored the ill-considered and excessive competition, for prices were already too low. In Kansas City, four competitors of Standard got together, ran large advertisements in the newspapers, and told the public that normal prices were necessary for them to live, and that it was better to pay a moderate price all of the time than a cut price for a little while and an exorbitant price the rest of the time.[44]

To meet competitive practices and promote sales, Standard departed from its traditional policy of selling gasoline and kerosene from the tank wagon for cash and began selling on credit in 1915. To avoid extending credit to thousands of customers for small purchases and increasing the cost of doing business, coupon books containing a thousand coupons were sold for $10.[45] Many books were sold for cash, but where credit was desired, especially by large customers, the use of the coupon books reduced the number of credit entries and the cost of handling. With a great marketing organization scattered throughout the Middle West and the coupon book good at any of its stations, the innovation gave Standard of Indiana a considerable competitive advantage over those who had only scattered distribution.

Beginning early in 1915 Standard made three tank-wagon price cuts on account of the tremendous overproduction at Cushing and a decrease in the cost of crude.[46] However, jobbers alleged that Standard's cuts were aimed at driving the competing refiners and

43. Federal Trade Commission, *Report on the Price of Gasoline in 1915*, April 11, 1917, 9, 144.
44. *National Petroleum News*, VII, No. 5 (July, 1915), 1.
45. Allan Jackson to Giddens, August 30, 1950.
46. Federal Trade Commission, *Report on the Price of Gasoline in 1915*, April 11, 1917, 123.

jobbers out of business and recovering lost gallonage. Standard's first cut of ½ cent per gallon on January 18th was effective principally in North Dakota and Illinois. Another cut of 1 cent was made over the entire territory on February 22nd. In order to hold its business, Standard, which had been allowing a discount of 1 cent per gallon on purchases of two hundred gallons since 1914, now lowered the amount to one hundred gallons.[47] The third cut of 1 cent over the entire territory, effective in June, brought the price down from about 11 cents to 8.5 cents for 100-gallon lots. At some points the tank-wagon price was as low as 7.5 cents. Standard's price cuts created consternation among the more substantial oilmen, who urged the company to raise its prices, for any further cut would mean the closing of independent refineries which had contracts guaranteeing jobbers' margins, and the creation of a monopoly for Standard.[48]

Low crude prices, especially from June until the end of July, discouraged new drillings but enabled Standard to supply its customers with gasoline made from cheap crude, recover gallonage it had lost since 1913, and buy and store large quantities of cheap crude for speculative purposes. In July, 1915, it had 156,630 barrels in storage. By January, 1916, it had 4,288,916.[49] Beginning in August, 1915, there was an extraordinary advance in crude prices due to a decline at Cushing and in other fields, increased exports due to World War I, greater use of oil for all kinds of motor vehicles, the appearance of the "all year" car, better roads, and the accumulation of stocks of crude by major companies. The posted price of Oklahoma crude rose from 25 and 28 cents in July to $1.20 per barrel by the middle of December.[50] To this was added a premium of about 60 cents for Cushing crude, which made the real price $1.80.

Under the circumstances, smaller refiners, whose existence was threatened, were naturally forced to take the lead in raising the price of gasoline. Consequently, the tank-wagon price of gasoline advanced between July and December by 7 to 9 cents per gallon, a rise of 75 to 85 per cent, which brought gasoline to about 15.3 cents. Standard did not follow the advances until the middle of

47. *National Petroleum News*, VII, No. 2 (April, 1915), 54.
48. *Ibid.*, No. 4 (June, 1915), 1-2; *The New York Times*, June 8, 1915; *The Chicago Tribune*, June 22, 1915.
49. Federal Trade Commission, *Report on the Price of Gasoline in 1915*, April 11, 1917, 123.
50. *Ibid.*, 19, 47.

September and then its prices were 2 to 3 cents lower. Competitors took advantage of the differential to proclaim repeatedly that they had better-quality products. After November, Standard's price advanced very rapidly, which meant a large margin of profit on stored crude, and it eliminated the 1 cent discount on 100-gallon quantities, except to garages.

Owing to the fact that so many complaints from all parts of the country were made about the unreasonable high price of gasoline during the latter part of 1915, the Federal Trade Commission launched an investigation. The rise in price and the diminishing supply were alarming. Until 1916 the supply had been ample, but with the demand seemingly insatiable at home and abroad and the price advancing, the use of all kinds of gasoline-burning engines was threatened.[51] Early in 1916 Standard's gasoline production was running 20,000 barrels per month less than its marketing requirements. By March, 1916, the tank-wagon price had reached 18.5 cents. As Healdton reached its peak and declined, the situation grew worse. The Chicago Automobile Club called for an investigation. Judge Landis summoned a federal grand jury to inquire into gasoline prices. O. E. Pagan and Charles Morrison, who had been detailed by the United States Attorney General to watch the Standard companies after their dissolution in 1911, began investigating Standard of Indiana especially and its relationship to high prices.

The Independent Oil Men's Association appointed a committee to develop devices for using kerosene as motor fuel. Many unusual schemes were proposed to make cheap motor fuel, all of which were called "bunk" by the petroleum expert, Professor Charles F. Maberry of the Case School of Applied Science.[52] One of the most widely discussed schemes was that of Louis Enright of Farmingdale, Long Island, who produced a transparent green liquid, a few drops of which, it was claimed, placed in water would run an automobile. In St. Louis, W. H. Stevens made "motorzene" by mixing kerosene with a chemical compound and thus produced a fuel costing 9 cents a gallon. Percy W. Tresidder, also of St.

---

51. Between 1911 and 1915 the demand for gasoline increased over 200 per cent. The number of motor cars manufactured in the U. S. between 1911 and 1915 increased 199 per cent. The increase in 1915 over 1914 amounted to 73 per cent. "Question of Future Oil Fuel Looms Big," *National Petroleum News*, VII, No. 11 (January, 1916), 1-2.

52. "No Substitute for Gasoline Found Yet," *National Petroleum News*, VIII, No. 3 (May, 1916), 14, 16, 16-B.

Louis, blended three chemicals with kerosene and made a substitute for gasoline. In Cleveland a policeman mixed a chemical with kerosene which resulted in a fuel said to be 600 per cent more efficient than gasoline. It cost only 15 cents a gallon. Probably the most fantastic scheme of all was that of Harrison G. Shoupe, who discovered a process of making gasoline out of mixing water and oatmeal.[53] Needless to say, all of these schemes were fakes.

53. *The New York Times*, October 21, 1916.

CHAPTER VIII

World War I Years

WITH THE ENTRANCE OF THE UNITED STATES INTO THE WORLD WAR in April, 1917, the demand at home and abroad for petroleum products placed an even heavier burden upon the petroleum industry. Exports of fuel oil rose from 22,954,520 barrels in 1916 to 28,595,114 in 1918 and motor gasoline from 8,473,102 to 13,318,-306 barrels. Consumption of crude oil in the United States increased from 324,192,000 to 412,273,000 barrels, while production only increased from 300,767,000 to 355,928,000 barrels. In order to meet the extraordinary wartime demand for petroleum products, the oil industry was organized on a war basis in January, 1918, under the direction of the Oil Division of the United States Fuel Administration. The petroleum industry set up the National Petroleum War Service Committee, of which W. P. Cowan, President of Standard of Indiana, was a member, to co-operate with the Fuel Administration.

Through its extensive use and licensing of the Burton process Standard of Indiana made its greatest contribution to the war effort. When the United States entered the war, the company had 336 Burton stills in operation at its refineries.[1] With the installation of thirty tube stills at Standard's Casper refinery in June, 1917, the Midwest Refining Company agreed to supply not less than 4,000 additional barrels of petroleum distillate per day for 25 cents less than the posted price for Mid-Continent crude but not less than 57½ cents per barrel. In return, Standard agreed to sell Midwest finished gasoline equal to one-fourth of the amount of distillate furnished, at 5 cents per gallon less than the tank-wagon price of Red Crown gasoline in Chicago. In the same year Standard installed twenty pressure stills adjoining Midwest's refinery at Greybull and six near the refinery of the United Oil Company, a subsidiary of the Continental Oil Company, at Florence, Colorado. Two more were added at Florence in the

---

1. *Hearings Before Martindale,* II, 1176-1177.

summer of 1918. These stills were operated on a custom basis, that is, Standard processed the oil for so much per barrel but did not own the product. In spite of shortages of labor and building materials, Standard built and placed in operation a total of 128 new stills. In addition to these Burton stills, hundreds were installed and used by Standard's eight licensees.

During the war, refineries of Standard of Indiana ran to capacity in helping to meet the military and domestic demand for petroleum products. The company increased its production of cracked gasoline from 1,218,571 barrels in 1913 to 6,101,672 in 1918.[2] Since the Burton process was the only commercial process in operation on a large scale between 1913 and 1920, Standard and its licensees were largely responsible for increasing the supply of cracked gasoline from 2,028,000 barrels in 1914 to 11,790,000 in 1918.[3] By doubling the amount of gasoline secured from a barrel of crude, the Burton process proved to be a very vital factor in meeting the wartime need for gasoline. "It was solely responsible," according to the *National Petroleum News,* "for averting a gasoline famine during the critical war years and immediately afterward."[4] In addition, Standard increased its production of straight-run gasoline from 4,523,809 barrels in 1915 to 5,285,714 in 1918.[5] Highly refined and with a gravity of about 65°, it was used to power aviation engines.[6]

To aid in increasing the supply of gasoline and improving its quality, Standard in 1916 contracted with the Prairie Oil & Gas Company for the gas coming from its wells in the Cushing field. Gas produced with the crude oil contained a certain amount of light gasoline, and for years it had been allowed to go to waste. It had been discovered about 1903 that a considerable amount of gasoline could be secured by compressing the gas and condensing the gasoline. However, casing-head gasoline, as it was called, was too volatile to be used as motor fuel. Mixed with regular gasoline or cracked gasoline or low-volatile kerosene in proper quantities, it resulted in a high-gravity, quick-starting gasoline. With the in-

2. *Ibid.,* 1180.
3. 33 F. (2d) 621.
4. "Cracking Patents in Hopeless Confusion If Patent Club Decree Is Upheld," *National Petroleum News,* XXII (February 5, 1930), 39.
5. Company Encyclopedia: Manufacturing—Economics, Straight Run Gasoline Production in Gallons at Various Standard Refineries for Each Year 1915 to 1937, Inclusive.
6. Company Encyclopedia: Manufacturing—Gasoline, Motor and Aviation, 9-10.

crease in the number of gasoline engines and motor vehicles and the extraordinary demand for gasoline, considerable impetus was given to the construction of natural-gas gasoline plants in 1916. Standard built five compression plants in the Cushing field where casing-head gasoline was extracted and prepared for shipment to its refineries for blending.[7]

In addition to manufacturing the largest possible amount of gasoline, Standard made several other significant contributions to the war effort. It manufactured and sold to munition makers about 8,000 gallons of toluene from the heavy residue of the coke ovens. From March 18 to December 19, 1918, the company's entire production of its six- and eight-inch candles and coach candles was purchased by the government for use by the Army as trench candles.[8] This required the use of thirty-eight candle machines, which made 500,000 candles every twenty-four hours. During the war the candle factory ran seven days a week, night and day, except for July 4th, and the company shipped 285,000,000 candles from Whiting to France.[9]

When World War I broke out in 1914, France was cut off from its supply of Russian crude oil from which it manufactured and exported medicinal white oil. At the time, the United States was using about 436,000 gallons of medicinal white oil annually of which only 87,400 gallons were of domestic origin. Cut off from the main source of supply, American hospitals and doctors faced a critical situation. How could they secure medicinal white oil? No previous attempt had been made to refine American crude oil to such an advanced stage that it would result in a product that could be taken into the human system. Little information was available on the subject and a process had to be developed.

An appeal was made directly to Standard, and the solution of the problem was assigned to Dr. O. E. Bransky of the laboratory at Whiting in August, 1914.[10] Dr. Humphreys' research experiments in trying to develop a white oil back in 1905, which had been regarded as a novelty, were reviewed in the light of the demand for white medicinal oil. It was found that Humphreys' process did

7. Company Encyclopedia: Manufacturing—Natural Gasoline Plants, 1-2; Donald J. Smith, "Imprisoning the Gas Genii," Stanolind Record, I, No. 6 (March, 1920), 5-7.
8. Company Encyclopedia: Manufacturing—History of Whiting Plant, Candles, 23.
9. The Chicago Tribune, July 15, 1919.
10. "From Darkest Crude to Sparkling White Oil," Stanolind Record, XVII, No. 8 (June, 1936), 8-10; Robert E. Humphreys to Giddens, March 24, 1950.

not work successfully on a large scale. There was some question as to whether superrefining was really necessary. Perhaps Polarine motor oil might serve the purpose. To test the idea, Bransky suggested to Humphreys and Rogers that they appoint themselves members of a "poison squad" and take a dose of Polarine to learn about its reaction on the human body.[11] This experiment became a classic among the chemists at Whiting. Rogers, something of a stoic, was unaffected. It gave Humphreys a stomach-ache shortly before he was to address a meeting of the American Chemical Society in Chicago, but he was able to deliver his speech. Bransky succumbed to a very bad attack of nausea and had to go home. It was obvious that Polarine was not the answer.

Bransky returned to Humphreys' earlier research and worked on the problem of treating viscous oils and by October, 1914, the world's first medicinal white oil refined from American crude oil had been successfully made. It was put on the market under the brand name Stanolax.

The Standard of New Jersey discovered just about the same time how to make a medicinal white oil which it called Nujol. Both Standard of Indiana and Standard of New Jersey spent considerable money in placing literature and samples with physicians in an attempt to create a demand for their new product. In some cases, they sent representatives to call on doctors and endeavored to get them to recommend the product.[12]

Within a year after the outbreak of war, over fifty medicinal white oils under registered brand names were on the market. These were either prepared or purchased by drug manufacturers, who were in the fight for the retail business. The manufacturers also sent literature to physicians accusing the oil refiners of hurriedly making a cheap white oil. They claimed to have a better product, one as good as that produced from Russian crude. Standard of California, having a suitable base stock, secured the information from Whiting on how to make medicinal white oil and nearly ran Standard of Indiana out of the business because the first Stanolax sold brought so many complaints. It was too thin to resist leakage from the body.[13] Soon, however, Standard of Indiana found some special crude in Louisiana which enabled it to produce a highly satisfactory product.

11. Interview with Robert E. Humphreys, July 10, 1948.
12. *National Petroleum News*, VII, No. 6 (August, 1915), 48.
13. Interview with Robert E. Humphreys, July 10, 1948.

As a result of selling Stanolax directly to customers, the company ran into strong opposition from some of the physicians, which led to a change in sales policy whereby Stanolax was only sold under medical supervision. Even so, the sales were not large. Many doctors still opposed Stanolax, and the company's own salesmen were more interested in selling gasoline. As a matter of fact, company officials were not very much interested in developing specialties at this time. Selling gasoline and lubricants was much more profitable because of the large volume.

When the United States entered the war in 1917, there was an urgent need for ships on account of the German submarine sinkings. Standard could not build ships, but the company placed its new mechanical shop building at Whiting at the disposal of the Emergency Fleet Corporation. Within a short time the company was manufacturing parts for ships twenty-four hours a day, seven days a week.[14] From the boiler shop came water and fuel-oil tanks, deck hatches, iron stairways, ship ladders, and other ship equipment. The thirty-two-foot bending rolls, larger than any in Chicago, turned out hundreds of tons of plate for different kinds of war work. The machine shop made rivets by the thousands, bilge pumps, special brass and steel-deck fittings, propeller blades and shafts, boat davits, watertight doors, ventilators, engine jack devices, and brass fittings. The Emergency Fleet Corporation had to wait for nothing. Even special and complicated jobs were ready on time. The work was turned out in the shortest possible time at the lowest possible cost.

With all of the available tank cars carrying oil to the Atlantic seaboard and a need for greater transportation facilities on the Great Lakes, the company in the spring of 1918 added a new tanker, the *W. P. Cowan,* to its fleet. With a carrying capacity of more than 2,000,000 gallons, it was the largest tanker on the Great Lakes. During 1918 the *W. P. Cowan,* the *Renown,* and Barge "C" carried from Whiting to various lake ports 106,328,347 gallons of gasoline and 36,421,480 gallons of kerosene, which equaled 17,844 tank cars of 8,000 gallons capacity, or 446 trains of forty cars each.[15]

In order to meet the wartime demand, Standard purchased large quantities of gasoline and fuel oil from oil brokers and smaller

14. R. F. Storer, "Helping Uncle Sam Treat 'Em Rough," *Stanolind Record,* I, No. 5 (February, 1920), 9-15.

15. R. C. Curtis, "Standard Oil Flag on Great Lakes," *Stanolind Record,* I, No. 3 (December, 1919), 7-9.

refining companies in the Mid-Continent field from 1917 to 1919.[16]
These purchases were made largely through the Western Petroleum
Company, an oil brokerage firm in Chicago, headed by Thomas
S. Black and Ernest L. Hughes, which virtually acted as the purchasing agency for Standard of Indiana and other Standard companies.[17] Black had been in charge of sales for the Cudahy Refining
Company from 1911 to 1916, when it was consolidated with Sinclair. Hughes, a stepson of Dr. Burton, gained his first oil experience as a salesman with Standard of Indiana in 1910–11. In 1916
Hughes and Black formed the Oil Marketing Company of Tulsa,
a brokerage firm. After being with the Oil Marketing Company
a very short time, Black contemplated returning to Sinclair.
Hughes, however, wanted to go into the oil business for himself
and discussed the matter with Black and Dr. Burton. The latter felt
that Hughes did not have either the experience or capital. Anxious
to help Hughes, Burton told Black, according to the latter's testimony before the La Follette Committee, that if he would go into
partnership with Hughes, Standard would permit them to do a large
part of its crude oil purchasing and use its influence with other
Standard companies to do the same. Black and Hughes, therefore,
organized in October, 1916, the Western Petroleum Company for
the purpose of purchasing and selling all kinds of oil in tank-car
lots. Shortly thereafter they began buying from various independent refiners in the Mid-Continent field for Standard of Indiana
and other Standard companies on a commission basis, receiving
a commission of 3 cents per barrel. Black handled the account of
Standard of Indiana and Hughes those of other Standard companies. Their volume of business ranged from $35,000,000 to
$45,000,000 a year. To enhance the profits of their business, ac-
cording to Black, they were given advance notice a great many
times either by Burton or Seth C. Drake, the General Manager of
Sales for Standard of Indiana, of price increases or decreases in
gasoline as long as the firm was in business. Occasionally, they got
advance verbal notices from Burton on changes in crude prices.[18]

16. *High Cost of Gasoline and Other Petroleum Products,* II, 1305-1306.
17. *Ibid.,* II, 1239-1246, 1348-1354.
18. In his testimony in February, 1923, before the Senate Subcommittee of the Com-
    mittee on Manufacturers, which was investigating the high price of gasoline,
    Black related the activities of the Western Petroleum Company. Black's testi-
    mony was strongly corroborated by his brother, W. C. Black, and R. A. White-
    head, former Sales Manager of fuel oils of the Western Petroleum Company.
    Immediately Standard asked to be heard. Both Colonel Robert W. Stewart,

Confronted with an enormous demand for gasoline and fuel oil, it was quite clear to officials of Standard that they must acquire their own source of crude in order to insure the future of their refining and marketing investment. Since the dissolution proceedings in 1911, the Prairie Oil & Gas Company had furnished most of its crude, but owing to the great demand from Atlantic seaboard refineries, Prairie became less and less able to supply Standard. In order to produce crude oil, it was necessary to amend the company's charter, for it had been incorporated as a refining and marketing corporation. As amended on March 23, 1917, the articles of incorporation enabled the company to engage in practically every branch of the oil business. The amendment was exceedingly broad in its scope.

The first step taken in creating the company's own crude supply was the purchase in July, 1917, of the producing properties of John A. Bell, Jr., in Montgomery, Chautauqua, and Butler counties, Kansas, consisting of 3,133 acres of producing leases and 4,359 acres of undeveloped leases at a reported price of $1,500,000.[19] At the time of purchase, these properties contained 121 producing wells with an approximate production of about 508 barrels per day. Although the production was negligible, there was hope of increasing it. Before Standard of Indiana could engage in production in Kansas, it was necessary to secure from the Kansas Supreme Court a modification of its decree of June 15, 1911. Therefore, on October 17, 1917, the company filed a petition asking the court for a modification.[20] Removing the ban, the company urged, would materially help in providing the United States and its Allies with more oil, which was desperately needed, and it would also be beneficial to the business development of Kansas. Within two weeks

Chairman, and Dr. William M. Burton, President, testified and branded Black's testimony as false, but the subcommittee declared that the "denials were not persuasive." Hughes testified that he could not recall any details of the conversation with Dr. Burton about his going into the oil business; that he could not recall going with Black to talk with Dr. Burton about going into the oil business; that he knew of no understanding between Black and Burton over the latter's helping to get business for the firm; and that he did not know about Black's getting advance notices of changes in prices. *High Cost of Gasoline and Other Petroleum Products*, II, 1295-1302, 1303-1314, 1318-1327, 1372-1380.

19. *The Chicago Tribune*, September 11, 1917; Company Encyclopedia: Production—Purchase and Transportation by Pipe Line of Crude, 175.

20. Topeka *Daily Capital*, October 18, 1917, November 2, 1917; E. W. Evans to Robert W. Stewart, November 2, 1917.

the Kansas Supreme Court modified its decree and opened the way for the company to begin development work.

Owing to the opening of new fields in Kansas at Augusta, El Dorado, and Towanda and in Oklahoma at Blackwell, Ponca, and other places, Standard made plans to build a refinery near these developments. The Chamber of Commerce at Wichita announced on January 20, 1918, that Standard would build a $2,500,000 refinery with a daily capacity of 20,000 barrels in that city.[21] Several hundred acres had already been purchased at the edge of the city along the Arkansas River, and construction was to begin in the spring. When completed, the refinery was to be the largest in the Mid-Continent field. However, the refinery was never built because it was found that the refinery of the Standard of Kansas at Neodesha and that of Standard of Indiana at Sugar Creek could adequately handle the crude and supply the market in that area.[22]

Standard's determination to acquire its own crude supply at the earliest opportunity was re-enforced in February, 1918, when it had to shut down 110 stills at Whiting owing to the fact that most of the available crude was being sent to Atlantic seaboard refineries to fill government orders.[23] As a result, Whiting got only about 18,000 barrels of crude daily compared with its normal supply of 55,000.

In its efforts to provide the maximum of petroleum products during the war years, another of the company's chief difficulties was the lack of an adequate supply of coal. In 1917, when it was increasingly difficult to get coal and the price was prohibitive, E. M. Clark, manager of the refinery at Wood River, proposed that the company buy a coal mine and mine its own coal.[24] Moreover, with a crude oil shortage, some thought the company might be forced into low-temperature distillation of coal or oil shale and, in that event, the ownership of a coal mine would be advantageous. The Directors liked Clark's idea and after an investigation of various mine fields they selected an area at Carlinville, Illinois; it was near Whiting and Wood River and freight rates would be cheaper than from other sites. It was also located on the

21. *National Petroleum News*, X, No. 4 (January 23, 1918), 6, No. 5 (January 30, 1918), 11; *The Oil and Gas Journal*, XVI, No. 34 (January 24, 1918), 43, No. 39 (February 28, 1918), 45.

22. William M. Burton to Giddens, March 22, 1950.

23. *National Petroleum News*, X, No. 10 (March 6, 1918), 13.

24. Interview with William M. Burton, August 2, 1948.

main line of the Chicago & Alton Railroad from St. Louis to Chicago.

After drilling several test holes in the northeastern part of Macoupin County which indicated a very good seam and grade of coal for boiler purposes, the company purchased the coal rights to about 24,000 acres.[25] Late in 1917 a contract was let to Robert W. Hunt & Company, an engineering firm, to construct and equip two complete mines which would produce 5,000 tons of coal every eight hours. The company also purchased the Carlinville Coal Company, which had a small mine producing about 500 to 600 tons per day. Since this mining property was in poor shape, considerable money was spent to put it in a first-class condition so that it would produce 1,000 or 1,200 tons per day.

Before the company's mines at Carlinville were in full operation, the coal shortage grew worse, partly due to a very severe winter, and in January, 1918, numerous plants and packing houses in the Chicago area were forced to shut down for the lack of coal, making 150,000 workers idle. Fuel Administrator Garfield ordered a five-day shutdown of virtually all factories between January 18th and the 22nd and on the nine succeeding Mondays, but the Whiting refinery was exempted from the orders.[26] The steam boilers, however, were run on oil in order to save coal. The Whiting refinery closed down for a few days, not because of a coal shortage but on account of a raging blizzard. With the roads practically impassable and the fire apparatus unable to function in case of fire, operations were suspended for the first time since Whiting began in 1890 rather than run the risk of a disaster.[27] Fires were pulled in the stills and the employees were put to work shoveling snow. At the Sugar Creek refinery, the Fuel Administration seized 178 cars of coal to be turned over to the packing houses in Kansas City, but the seizure did not affect refinery operations since oil was being used for fuel and the coal was only being held in storage.[28] At Casper, Midwest Refining and Standard installed coal burners under the stills and boilers, because coal was plentiful in Wyoming and several mines were shut down for the lack of a market.

Preparations were made in March, 1918, to sink two mining shafts northeast of Carlinville. In order to secure labor, which was

25. Company Encyclopedia: Manufacturing—Coal Mining Department, 1-11.
26. *The Chicago Tribune,* January 15, 17, 19, 1918.
27. *The Whiting Call,* January 18, 1918.
28. *National Petroleum News,* X, No. 4 (January 23, 1918), 29.

very scarce, the company built and operated boarding and lodging facilities for three or four hundred men. Since facilities for housing permanent operating employees in Carlinville were poor and insufficient, the company contracted with Sears Roebuck & Company to build 168 small houses. When completed, they were sold to employees at prices ranging from $3,370 to $4,060 on an installment plan with ten years in which to pay. After an inspection trip covering all the mining towns in Illinois, Oscar Hewitt of *The Chicago Tribune* wrote of Carlinville, "This town has a reputation for having the best miner's houses in Illinois." [29]

The first shaft to be completed, called the Berry Mine, went into operation in 1919 and produced a maximum of 2,800 tons per day. Owing to the fact that railroad coal cars were very scarce and the Chicago & Alton Railroad was in receivership and did not have the money to purchase rolling stock, Standard purchased five large freight locomotives and five hundred coal cars to aid the Alton in transporting the coal to company refineries.[30] The second, called the Schoper mine, one of the largest shafts in Illinois, began mining operations in 1920 and produced about 4,500 tons per day, although it could have produced 8,000. About seven hundred men were employed at each mine.

After the opening of the two large shafts, the small mine in Carlinville was abandoned early in 1921. Late in 1923 the company shut down the Berry mine and two years later the Schoper mine because it could purchase coal much cheaper than producing it. Those who had purchased company houses and became unemployed were allowed to continue living in them without making further payments until they vacated them of their own volition. No one was evicted. Some families lived in the houses for as long as three years without making any additional payments. Eventually all of the houses were vacated, except five. Since it was expensive to maintain the houses and pay taxes each year, the company offered them for sale in 1935 at bargain prices. In about two months all of the houses at Carlinville had been sold.

The ownership and operation of the coal mines tided the company over a difficult time, but they were operated at a loss. It was an expensive venture for which the company spent over $6,000,-000. As a result of the experience, top management officials learned

29. *The Chicago Tribune,* November 3, 1919.
30. *The Oil and Gas Journal,* XIX, No. 40 (March 4, 1921), 6.

that they were oil refiners, not coal operators. Those who recall this experience regard it as an episode better forgotten.

Like other industrial concerns, Standard suffered from a shortage of labor during the war. Of nearly 20,000 employees, more than 15 per cent either volunteered for military service or were drafted.[31] To meet the emergency, women and girls replaced men where possible. At Whiting nearly three hundred women and girls were employed in the candle factory, can house, grease works, and other places. Additional employees were secured by running a bus every day between Whiting and Chicago, where men were picked up along West Madison Street, "Skid Row," and brought to Whiting. Without adequate boarding and lodging facilities in the town to care for these transient laborers, the company erected a men's camp during the summer of 1918. However, the practice of hiring men off the streets of Chicago was far from satisfactory, for they were not particularly interested in working.

As the scarcity of labor increased, living costs rose, and labor unrest developed in many quarters of the country, Standard adopted and put into effect many measures for the benefit of employees. Following the lead of the Standard of New Jersey and Gulf Oil, Standard of Indiana responded to the current agitation throughout the country against the twelve-hour day and on October 1, 1915, put into effect an eight-hour day without loss of pay at all of its refineries.[32] It meant the addition of some four hundred new employees in order to operate three shifts. In taking this pioneer step, these oil companies showed great wisdom in anticipating the inevitable trend and making the concession in a liberal manner. Thus, they avoided a conflict when the question became the center of political and industrial agitation in 1918 and 1919.

With the competition for labor keen and the maintenance of the best in working conditions important, Standard's method of employing and handling labor proved to be far from satisfactory. Having department heads or their representatives appear at the entrances to the plant and pick men haphazardly for jobs out of a crowd, though common with industrial firms, did not always secure the most desirable employees. Moreover, leaving the hiring

31. "Called to the Colors," *Stanolind Record*, I, No. 1 (October, 1919), 23; "Our Women Workers," *Stanolind Record*, I, No. 2 (November, 1919), 21.
32. *National Petroleum News*, VII, No. 6 (August 15, 1915), 32, No. 8 (October 15, 1915), 59; "8-Hour Day for 10,000 Standard Oil Workmen," *Survey*, XXXV (October 16, 1915), 59.

and firing of employees to foremen sometimes resulted in favoritism, corruption, injustices, and fear, which had a demoralizing effect upon subordinate officials and workmen. New employees were not always properly informed about hours, wages, and conditions of work, which also resulted in trouble. When work fell off in one department, employees were discharged without knowing whether or not their services could be utilized in some other part of the refinery. There was no method by which an employee could be transferred from one department to another without being discharged and rehired. If an expert switchman was working at some other kind of a job in the plant and an expert switchman was badly needed, there was no means of finding him.

Conscious of the need for placing its labor relations upon a sounder basis, the company established an employment bureau at Whiting in September, 1917, under the direction of J. W. Curry, who had been the principal of the Whiting High School. Curry spent six weeks or more studying employment practices and policies of other companies in the Chicago area, drew up a plan as to how the employment office should function, and began putting it into effect.[33] It marked the beginning of an intelligent and sympathetic approach to improving the conditions of labor. Under Curry's guidance, the Employment Bureau centralized and systematized the hiring and firing of all employees at Whiting. It soon became a real personnel office.

To aid the monthly salaried employees in meeting the rising cost of living, the company, for the first time in its history, authorized in December, 1916, the payment of a 10 per cent bonus to all receiving not more than $250 per month or receiving in the aggregate for 1916 not more than $3,000. A general wage increase of 10 per cent for all became effective in January, 1917. In June the Directors voted another 10 per cent bonus but limited it to those not receiving more than $125 a month or an aggregate of not more than $750 for the first six months of 1917.

Prior to 1918 accidents at Standard's refineries were regarded as one of those things bound to happen, about which little could be done. If a man was injured, no matter how, it was his own hard luck. However, in view of the need for conserving manpower, the heads of departments at Whiting early in 1918 began discussing ways and means of preventing accidents. An accident prevention

33. Interview with J. W. Curry, May 25, 1949; Company Encyclopedia: Manufacturing—Personnel, Labor Relations.

campaign appeared to be an experiment worth trying, and they recommended the idea to top management. To give the experiment a fair chance of success, they also recommended that a safety department be established and placed in the hands of a competent person to work with plant executives, department heads, foremen, and workmen. The Directors approved the recommendations and launched a direct, uncompromising attack upon the refinery accident toll. It was good business, for accidents meant a loss of time and for employees a loss of wages, suffering, and family worries.

The establishment of a safety department at Whiting on July 8, 1918, marked a major pioneer development in the history of the petroleum industry. Standard was the first oil company to establish a regular organized safety department.[34] Unusual care was taken to find the right person to head this department, for it required a man of strong character, an enthusiasm for the job, a man of finesse and diplomacy, and one who could take a lot of punishment. He would need all of these qualities to succeed. In C. W. Smith, an Indiana public school administrator, they found such a man, and he became the first safety director of the company.

Management embarked upon the program with the full realization that if the idea of safety was to be sold to the employees, the company must first prove its good faith and sincerity by putting its own house in order. Employees would never enter into the spirit of safety if they observed all about them evidences of failure on the part of management to do its part. The campaign began, therefore, with the installation of safeguards of all kinds within the plant and the elimination of all dangerous situations. As rapidly as possible, the company provided various mechanical protective devices for machines, railings for stairways, improved ladders, goggles to protect the eyes in certain departments, heavy shoes to protect the feet where needed, and a multitude of other things. Codes for scaffold building, electrical work, and fire protection were devised and strictly followed. This part of the safety program was relatively easy to execute.

While the company was spending large sums of money to eliminate hazards about the plant, Smith formulated and began exe-

34. C. W. Smith, "Safety Reduces Refinery Accidents 38 to 80 Per Cent," *Stanolind Record*, III, No. 12 (October, 1922), 1-9, 14-15; Robert E. Humphreys, "Department Head Responsible for Workers' Safety," *Stanolind Record*, IX, No. 1 (November, 1927), 1-5.

Moffett, Chicago

L. J. DRAKE, PRESIDENT 1918

Russell, Chicago

COLONEL ROBERT W. STEWART, CHAIRMAN 1918–1929

DR. WILLIAM M. BURTON, PRESIDENT 1918–1927

COLONEL STEWART, MEMBERS OF THE BOARD, AND OTHERS INSPECTING
CARLINVILLE COAL MINE

Standing, left to right: C. W. Clark, Edward G. Seubert, W. M. Burton, Charles Manbeck,
Colonel Robert W. Stewart, T. J. Thompson, W. E. Warwick, Tom Paul
Kneeling, left to right: John McMillan, Allan Jackson, E. J. Bullock, R. H. McElroy,
Rollin Smith

National Petroleum News, August 30, 1944. Reproduced
through the courtesy of the *National Petroleum News*

"THE BIG FOUR" OF THE MEXIA OIL BOOM

Left to right: Colonel A. E. Humphreys of the Humphreys Oil Company, Colonel Robert
W. Stewart of the Standard Oil Company (Indiana), James O'Neil of the Prairie Oil
Gas Company, and Harry Sinclair of the Sinclair Oil Company

cuting an educational program to make employees "safety minded" and to get them to "Do this work safely." The object was to develop an attitude and spirit of safety in every phase of their work. This was the most important, though the most difficult and tedious, part of safety work, and it required unremitting and untiring effort. The safety director devoted more than half of his time to training heads of departments and foremen to be safety teachers. They, in turn, taught the workmen on the job. Foremen were made to realize that safety was a plant policy and that the teaching of safety was a regular part of their duties. There were not very many printed rules or regulations, for it was impossible to cover everything. Furthermore, even if there had been a handbook of rules, foremen and the workmen would have become dependent upon it, instead of thinking safety. However, a few regulations were issued, many of which are still in effect today. Bulletin boards were put up in each department and on these were posted literature of all kinds to emphasize safety.

In every department of the refinery a safety committee, composed of the head of that department and two employees appointed by him, was organized. Its function was to make inspections in their department once a month, investigate serious accidents and make reports, instruct and warn employees against dangerous practices, meet regularly every week with the safety director to discuss safety measures, and receive suggestions from employees as to how accidents might be prevented. The membership of these committees was frequently changed so that many of the employees could receive the value of this training. All committee work was done on company time. The main feature of the safety policy was to get suggestions from employees as to how accidents might be prevented. These suggestions determined very largely the course which was followed in the safety program. During the first year over 3,000 suggestions came from the employees and 97 per cent of them were accepted by management and put into effect.

The effectiveness of the whole safety program showed in marked results very early. During the last six months of 1918 the number of accidents at Whiting was reduced 20 per cent. At the end of one year's trial there was about a 30 per cent decrease in the number of accidents over the preceding year. Success in safety work was not accomplished by spectacular publicity stunts but by the steady application of safety methods which were worked out from day to day. At the heart of the whole program was the sincere application of a simple principle—the company did not want its employees to be injured. When employees became convinced that everyone from top to bottom was honestly trying to follow this principle, success in the safety work was assured.

Closely related to the safety program was the expansion of the company's facilities to care for injuries when they occurred. Prior to 1912, members of the staff in the research laboratory at Whiting stopped whatever they were doing when an accident occurred in the plant and rendered first aid. Aware of the fact that success in business was closely related to the healthy minds and bodies of its employees, the company organized a medical department in 1912 under the direction of Dr. Frank R. Morton.[35] It was one of the first large corporations in America to establish such a department. Three years later a full-time nurse was employed at Whiting to administer first aid. Originally organized to handle cases of injured employees, the functions of the Medical Department were in time expanded to include the examination of applicants for jobs, aid to those in temporary need of medical care, examination of applicants for annuities, the maintenance of sanitary conditions in the plants, supervision of industrial conditions connected with hazardous occupations, advising employees on dental and medical care, co-operating with schools in towns where refineries were located, in the care of children of employees, and many other activities.

With the inauguration of the safety program, a first-aid room was set up in the tin shop at Whiting on November, 1918, with a full-time physician in charge. Similar stations were also established at Wood River, Sugar Creek and, later, at the other refineries, with a full-time nurse and a part-time physician in charge. One further step was taken in December, 1918, when a completely equipped hospital was opened at Whiting. The establishment of plant medical service was of utmost value in gaining the respect of the employees for the safety program.

The progressive character of the company's labor relations program was further expressed by the adoption of a new and more liberal annuity system made effective July 1, 1918. It provided

35. Company Encyclopedia: Manufacturing—Medical, 1-2; "Prevention Rather Than Cure Comes First in Work of Medical Department of This Company and Subsidiaries," *Stanolind Record*, XI, No. 6 (April, 1930), 20-29; M. R. Schmidt, "Whiting Observes 20th Anniversary of Safety Dep't and Plant Medical Service," *Stanolind Record*, XIX, No. 9 (July, 1938), 1-4.

that for each year in service, an employee on his retirement would receive 2 per cent of his average annual remuneration for the ten years immediately preceding retirement. The minimum annuity to be paid was $300 per year and the maximum 75 per cent of the average annual remuneration for the ten years immediately preceding retirement.[36] Employees now eligible for pensions were of two classes: one, those men sixty-five years old or women fifty-five years old who had given twenty years of continuous service; and two, those men fifty-five years old and women fifty years old who had given thirty years of continuous service. Special provision was made for those who had given ten years' continuous service and were incapacitated or because of advancing years found it difficult to work, to retire on a regular or special allowance. A new feature of the plan was the inclusion of a death benefit. If an employee had worked for the company five or more years and died, the Directors might, at their discretion, grant to the heirs or dependents a sum not less than $500 and as much as $2,000. No part of any employee's pay was withheld to pay for these benefits. The company assumed all expense. In the first fifteen months after July 1, 1918, the company paid out $90,956.94 to ninety-eight retired employees with the average amount paid nearly $77 per month. The average length of service for the group was twenty-seven years and six months.[37]

Owing to the company's policy of paying good wages and adopting many measures for improving the employees' welfare before they became an issue in the industrial world, there were no strikes or labor disturbances to interrupt operations during the war. However, there was some unrest and agitation in certain quarters. Consequently, the company in 1918 employed private detectives from the Corporation Auxiliary Company, a strike-breaking and labor-detective organization, to safeguard property, prevent stealing, stimulate production, and check on "radicals" and "agitators" in its refineries.[38] They reported daily to their own organization which, in turn, sent a daily letter to the plant manager. Detective J-94 reported to the manager at Whiting and J-111 reported to the manager at Wood River. Detectives continued to be employed in all of the principal refineries until 1923, when the practice

36. Minutes of the Board of Directors' and Stockholders' Meetings, I, 482.
37. "Faithful Employees Get Huge Sum," *Stanolind Record*, I, No. 2 (November, 1919), 5-7.
38. Industrial Relations Staff, Curtis, Fosdick & Belknap, "Report on Industrial Relations in the Standard Oil Company (Indiana)," 1923, II, 94-95.

was abandoned. From a reading of their reports, it appears that they rendered but slight service. Their reports consisted largely of their opinion about certain individuals with whom they had been working. Many errors in the names of the men and apparent misrepresentations of facts were made.

During July, 1918, Mr. Cowan, the President of Standard, who was seventy-two years old, had a stroke, and the doctors reported that he would never be able to resume his responsibilities. John D. Rockefeller, Jr., one of the large stockholders, asked Colonel Robert W. Stewart, Dr. Burton, and L. J. Drake to come to New York for a conference.[39] Rockefeller suggested to them that, in the event of Cowan's death, Drake should succeed him as President. In the event of Drake's death, since he was seventy-two, Mr. Rockefeller said to Stewart and Burton: "You two are to run this company." [40] Burton was to become President and concern himself especially with manufacturing, and Colonel Stewart was to be the chief executive and Chairman of the Board, a new position to be created at the proper time. While Drake, Burton, and Stewart were in New York, Cowan died on August 14, 1918. Five days later Drake was elected President. At the same time, his son, Seth C. Drake, General Manager of Sales, was elected a Director. L. J. Drake served less than two months, for he died on October 10th. In accordance with the suggestion previously made, the bylaws were amended, creating a chairman of the Board. Stewart was elected Chairman and Burton President.

The death of Mr. Cowan and Mr. Drake brought to a close an era in the history of Standard of Indiana. Both men had come up through the ranks in the Rockefeller organization and had served with distinction, one as a construction and refinery man and the other as a dynamic sales leader. As top executives of the company after 1911, they and their associates on the Board of Directors had ably guided the course of the company through the first years of its independence. Many outstanding things had been done—the installation and successful operation of the Burton stills, the formulation of a licensing policy for the Burton process, the rapid extension of the tank-wagon delivery system, the inauguration of company-owned and operated service stations on a large scale, the beginnings of a policy to acquire production, the adoption of

39. Memorandum of a conference in John D. Rockefeller's office on August 12, 1918, with Stewart, Burton, and Drake. Rockefeller Papers.
40. Interview with William M. Burton, August 2, 1948.

some progressive measures in the handling of labor relations, the gaining of a foothold in Wyoming which was to have significant consequences, and the rendering of outstanding service to the nation and to the people of the Middle West during World War I.

From a financial point of view, the plant investment between 1911 and 1918 had increased from $19,598,098 to $79,744,699, assets from $28,146,422 to $145,428,034, and the surplus from $10,216,045 in 1912 to $87,509,465.[41] The net earnings per share had been excellent every year, especially in 1915, 1916, and 1917, when they reached $53.33, $100.15, and $146.03 respectively.[42] The net earnings of $43,808,931 for 1917 were the greatest in the history of the company to that time and exceeded those of 1916, the next best year, by $13,765,316. Cash dividends per share ranged form $12 to $32 per share. In 1917 the company paid an income and excess profits tax amounting to approximately $17,000,000. At a time when heavy expenditures were being incurred for constructing Burton stills, extending bulk plants, and building service stations, the company followed a very conservative policy of retaining a high percentage of the net earnings in the business. The amount retained in the business in 1912 was 72.13 per cent, in 1913, 34.64 per cent, in 1915, 77.50 per cent, in 1916, 88.02 per cent, and in 1917, 83.56 per cent. However, in 1914 dividends paid exceeded net earnings by 13.8 per cent and in 1918 by 48 per cent.

After 1915, in view of the large net earnings and growth in assets, the declaration of a stock dividend was freely predicted in many quarters and the market value of the company's stock boomed.[43] It rose from $593 on July 27, 1916, to $725 on September 8th. By January 20, 1917, it was selling for $865 and two days later for $915. The stockholders voted on March 1, 1917, to increase the capital stock from $30,000,000 to $100,000,000, but the issuance of the stock was postponed pending a decision of the United States Supreme Court as to whether or not stock dividends were taxable as income. By the fall of 1917 Standard's stock stood at $945 per share.

41. Balance Sheets of December 31, 1911, and December 31, 1918; *High Cost of Gasoline and Other Petroleum Products*, I, 767-769, 793-794.
42. Statement of Net Earnings, Dividends, Etc., for the Years 1892 Through 1929. Furnished by Robert E. Wilson, Chairman, Standard Oil Company (Indiana), September 30, 1949.
43. *The Chicago Tribune*, July 27, 1916, September 9, 1916, January 23, 1917, October 30, 1917.

CHAPTER IX

Stewart Creates a Crude Oil Supply

THE ELECTION OF COLONEL ROBERT W. STEWART AS CHAIRMAN of the Board of Standard of Indiana and the chief executive officer represented in a sense a break with tradition. He had been neither a driller, rigger, tank-wagon driver, a refinery man, nor a salesman. He had never had a day of practical oil field experience like the heads of many other oil companies. On the other hand, he was a lawyer who had come up through the ranks of the organization. Impressed by his reputation as a lawyer in South Dakota, Alfred D. Eddy's law firm in Chicago, which handled all of Standard's legal business, employed Stewart as a general attorney in 1907. From that time until 1918, he was active in practically every important legal case involving Standard of Indiana. With an inveterate thirst for facts, Stewart quickly learned all about the operations of the company and the petroleum industry. In 1915, when Eddy retired, Colonel Stewart succeeded him as General Counsel and on the Board of Directors. Recognized as an exceedingly able and aggressive businessman and executive, he was elected, at the suggestion of John D. Rockefeller, Jr., as Chairman of the Board at the age of fifty-two.[1]

Under Cowan and his associates the company had made progress since 1911, but the times required younger and more vigorous leadership. Stewart, who was richly endowed with physical strength, stature, personality, mind, and spirit, seemed to be tailormade for the top executive position. He was an intelligent, shrewd, and able lawyer with an unusual knowledge of the oil business. Physically, he was a fine-appearing man, more than six feet tall and weighing about 250 pounds. His erect and handsome military bearing, which he acquired as a member of the "Rough Riders" in the Spanish-American War and as an officer in the South Dakota National Guard, made him a commanding figure wherever he

1. For sketches of Stewart, see *The New York Times*, April 12, 1925, February 19, 1928; *Chicago Daily Journal*, January 23, 1929; *System*, XL (December, 1921), 699-701.

went. Stewart immediately attracted attention as an important personage. His tremendous physical strength and boundless energy enabled him to carry burdens and fight battles which would have wrecked an ordinary man. From the time of his youthful days on an Iowa farm, he had known what it was to work long and hard. This was obvious to anyone who tried to keep up with the Colonel. Despite the terrific pace Stewart set, he could relax. He liked to attend prize fights, swim, play poker, bridge, golf, and hunt and fish, but no matter what the game or sport might be, Stewart always liked to win whether in sports or business. He loved competition, but he hated to lose. In business, Stewart was exceedingly ambitious not only for himself but for the company. He fought vigorously for supremacy in the petroleum industry. He took the attitude that he was working for a lot of people who expected him to make a good showing. Possessing an active and restless spirit, Stewart loved to do things and bask in the glory of the accomplishments.

Stewart's charming personality, hearty, frank, and outspoken manner, ability as an inspiring and persuasive speaker, wonderful poise, democratic way, great capacity for friendships and showmanship, and his sense of fairness in dealing with people made him a colorful and dynamic leader. He was a man's man, and everybody looked up to "Colonel Bob," as he was affectionately called. Blessed with many fine qualities of leadership, Stewart soon made his influence felt throughout the organization from top to bottom and created an excellent *esprit de corps*.

Elected President at the same time as Colonel Stewart was made Chairman, Dr. William M. Burton became the second top-ranking executive. From his start with the company as a chemist at Whiting in 1890, Burton had rapidly advanced, owing to his scientific background and administrative ability, from one position to another in the Manufacturing Department until he became General Manager of Manufacturing in 1903. At his instigation and under his general supervision, research had been started at the Whiting laboratory that led to the development of the Burton cracking process, which brought distinction to him and the company. Elected a Director after the dissolution in 1911, Burton was responsible for securing the appropriations and constructing hundreds of cracking stills at the company's refineries. From 1914 to 1918 he had served as Second Vice-President.

Associated with Stewart and Burton in the direction of company affairs in 1918 were the other members of the Board of Directors: H. S. Morton in charge of Lubrication Sales, Seth C. Drake, General Manager of Sales, George W. Stahl, Treasurer, and Charles Gano. The membership of the Board was increased to seven in 1919, nine in 1921, and eleven in 1923. As retirements, resignations, and death created vacancies and the membership of the Board was increased between 1918 and 1929, men from the ranks were elevated to directorships. William E. Warwick, Beaumont Parks, and Edward G. Seubert were elected in 1919, Allan Jackson in 1920, Robert H. McElroy, E. J. Bullock and T. J. Thompson in 1922, John D. Clark in 1923, Amos Ball in 1926, Robert E. Humphreys in 1927, and L. L. Stephens and C. J. Barkdull in 1928. Upon Dr. Burton's resignation as President in 1927, Edward G. Seubert was elected to the position.

The first to feel the effect of Stewart's vigorous leadership was the Board of Directors. Every Director was an active, operating executive in charge of some department engaged in the company's business on a full-time basis. Sitting collectively, they constituted the Board, which met regularly three times a week and sometimes more than once a day. There were numerous committees, like the Manufacturing Committee, which governed the detailed work of a department. If any new policy was contemplated, it was first considered by the proper departmental committee and a recommendation was made to the Board. There was always an opportunity in Board meetings to discuss policies and problems, but if the matter related, for example, to the Sales Department, it usually resolved itself into a discussion between the Colonel and the head of that department.[2] Since the other men were specialists in their fields and knew little about sales they sat, listened, and "doodled." When it came time to vote, the members could do little else than follow the recommendations of the Colonel or the head of the Sales Department.

Whenever an important matter came before the Board, the Colonel would usually say: "Here's what we are going to do. What do you think about it?" [3] Such an approach made it exceedingly difficult for his fellow Directors, who might think differently. It was a tough job to oppose Stewart when he thought he was right.[4] However, beneath the surface he appreciated intelligent opposi-

2. Interview with Robert E. Humphreys, July 17, 1948.
3. Interview with William M. Burton, August 2, 1948.
4. Interview with Amos Ball, August 17, 1948.

tion and if one could show him to be wrong, he was quick to admit it. To outpoint the Colonel was not easy because of his over-all knowledge of the business and his careful and thorough investigation of all the facts on any proposed line of action. On account of his mastery of any given situation and the high quality of his leadership, which inspired great confidence, the Directors accepted his word for almost everything. The net effect was to make Stewart a benevolent despot and the Board members largely "yes" men. As new Directors were added to the Board, they tended to be even more "under his thumb" because he was responsible for their advancement.

Upon becoming Chairman, Stewart and the Board began formulating, initiating, and executing simultaneously several policies which broke many precedents and radically altered the character of the company. Their major objectives were to improve the position of the company in its relations with the public, bring management and labor closer together, improve the conditions of labor, secure an adequate and independent source of crude, build pipelines to cut transportation costs, expand the marketing organization, manufacture new and improved petroleum products, and provide stockholders with a profit upon their investment.

The new management team came into office on the eve of a decade of unprecedented expansion in the petroleum industry. Between 1918 and 1929, crude oil production in the United States increased from 355,928,000 to 1,007,323,000 barrels per year, crude run to stills from 326,025,000 to 987,708,000 barrels, and the total demand for petroleum products from 427,409,000 to 1,015,391,000 barrels.[5] Motor fuel consumption increased from 2,747,030,000 to 15,051,036,000 gallons. This unparalleled expansion was chiefly due to the astounding increase in the number of motor vehicles, tractors, and other types of gasoline-burning engines. Between 1918 and 1929 motor vehicle registrations in the United States increased from 5,554,952 to 23,060,421. In 1920 there were 246,083 tractors in use; by 1929 there were 920,021.

The use of gasoline for cooking and heating where gas and electricity were not available, and for lighting became more important in the 1920's due to the sales efforts of manufacturers.[6] Two of

5. *Petroleum Facts and Figures,* Ninth Edition, 2-3, 152, 222.
6. J. C. Chatfield, "Growing Use of Gasoline Stoves, Heaters Offers New Market for Oil," *National Petroleum News,* XX, No. 7 (February 15, 1928), 58; "The Coleman Story," *Standard Torch,* III, No. 5 (May, 1950), 21-22.

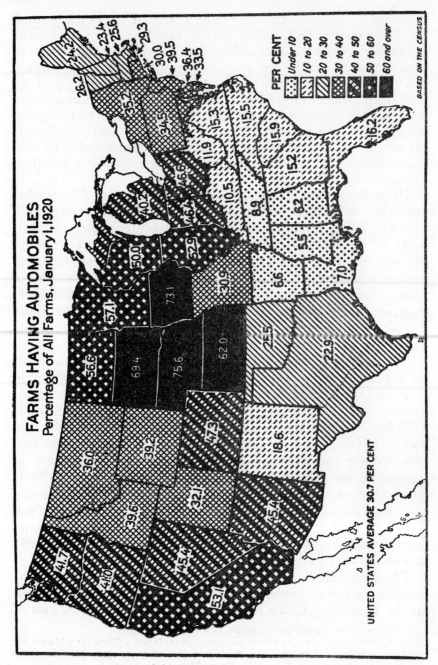

FARMS HAVING AUTOMOBILES
Percentage of All Farms, January 1, 1920

PER CENT

Under 10
10 to 20
20 to 30
30 to 40
40 to 50
50 to 60
60 and over

BASED ON THE CENSUS

UNITED STATES AVERAGE 30.7 PER CENT

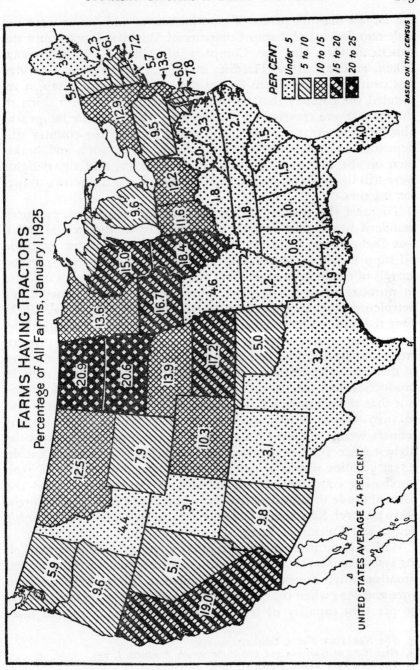

FARMS HAVING TRACTORS
Percentage of All Farms, January 1, 1925

PER CENT

Under 5
5 to 10
10 to 15
15 to 20
20 to 25

BASED ON THE CENSUS

UNITED STATES AVERAGE 7.4 PER CENT

the largest manufacturers of gasoline stoves and lamps were the Coleman Stove and Lamp Company of Wichita, Kansas, and the American Gas Machine Company of Albert Lea, Minnesota. When, on the death of Harding in 1923, Vice-President Coolidge was sworn in as President by the light of a kerosene lamp, it reminded the country that the use of kerosene was not a thing of the past. If one traveled off the beaten paths, kerosene lamps still abounded in great numbers, and many parts of the country still depended entirely upon them for light.[7] Watchmen and brakemen on the railroads still carried oil lanterns, and signal lights were still lighted with kerosene. Moreover, it was the principal fuel for tractors.

To meet the steadily rising demand for petroleum products, Standard was almost entirely dependent upon the Prairie Oil & Gas Company and the Prairie Pipe Line Company for its crude oil supply. Before World War I, Prairie had close to 49,000,000 barrels of crude in storage. With the rapid and enormous increase in number of motor vehicles, plus the additional demand for petroleum products created by World War I, Prairie's crude stocks were reduced to about 8,000,000 barrels by January, 1920, the lowest amount on hand between 1915 and 1920.[8] While the price of crude during the war had remained relatively constant, the cost of drilling wells, building storage tanks, and everything used in production had increased from 300 to 1,000 per cent, with the result that there was practically no drilling being done by the end of 1919. Consequently, the country faced an oil famine. Many refiners were unable to get crude. The price of gasoline was the highest since 1913, and predictions were freely made that within a year gasoline would be 40 or 50 cents per gallon.[9] Early in 1920 purchasing companies in all sections of the country raised the price of crude to stimulate drilling until Pennsylvania oil brought $6.10 a barrel, Kansas and Oklahoma $3.50, Salt Creek in Wyoming $2.75, and California $2.15.

With a huge investment in refineries and an extensive marketing system and no crude supply of its own, Standard faced a critical situation when Stewart became Chairman. There were times in 1920 and 1921 when the company's refineries were operating at only 50 per cent capacity or less, which made it impossible to meet

7. *The New York Times,* February 15, 1925.
8. *High Cost of Gasoline and Other Petroleum Products,* I, 249.
9. *The New York Times,* March 11, 1920.

the demand for refined products.[10] In the Eastern Division of the Sales Department, which included the states of Michigan, Indiana, and Illinois exclusive of Chicago, Standard had about 1,000 bulk plants. From January 1 to August 31, 1920, 574 or 57.4 per cent of these stations were out of kerosene for 6,848 days, or an average of twelve days per station, and 945 or 94.5 per cent were out of gasoline 11,597 days, or an average of twelve days per station.[11] Competitors faced the same kind of shortage, but a greater percentage of Standard stations were out of stock and for a slightly longer time. Shortages not only meant an immediate loss of business for Standard but the growth of competitors.

To meet the emergency, Colonel Stewart scoured the country trying to buy crude oil.[12] In Louisiana, he bought at one time 3,000,000 barrels of crude and had it hauled by rail to the refineries. In order to deal directly with producers and refiners rather than depend upon oil brokers as in the past, he established a company buying office in Tulsa early in 1919. Millions of barrels of gasoline were bought from various refiners to meet the needs of the company. A five-year contract was made with the Midwest Refining Company in April, 1919, by which Standard agreed to build forty additional pressure stills at Casper for processing Midwest's petroleum distillates.[13] In return, Standard had the privilege of purchasing one-third of all the gasoline but not less than 1,500,000 fifty-gallon barrels per year produced for Midwest. Gasoline under this contract was shipped to Standard's outlets in the Dakotas, Minnesota, and Iowa. Other contracts were negotiated whereby Cosden & Company sold Standard about 60 to 75 per cent of its output, the Sapulpa Refinery Company about 60 per cent, and the Standard of Kansas sold all of its output. Standard purchased from these and other refiners 2,471,376 barrels of gasoline in 1919, 4,368,468 in 1920, 5,773,261 in 1921, and 4,390,557 in 1922.[14]

Obviously, the only safe course for Standard was to acquire as rapidly as possible an adequate crude supply of its own. The first

10. *High Cost of Gasoline and Other Petroleum Products,* I, 772; *Leases Upon Naval Oil Reserves* (1929), 212.
11. Report on the Eastern Division, Stations Out of Stock January 1st to June 30, 1920, With the Competitive Situation. The same for July 1st to August 31, 1920. Furnished by Allan Jackson.
12. *High Cost of Gasoline and Other Petroleum Products,* I, 772.
13. *Ibid.*
14. *Ibid.,* 776.

step in this direction, though a minor one, was the purchase of the Dixie Oil Company, Incorporated, which had been organized on September 14, 1917, by Frederick H. Wickett, a Chicago lawyer, to take over the Dillon lease in the Caddo field not far from Shreveport, Louisiana. Within a little over a month after Dixie had been organized, Wickett sold all of the stock, except for fifty shares. Prominent among the large stockholders was a group of men from Denver—H. M. Blackmer, R. D. Brooks, K. C. Schuyler, F. G. Bonfils.[15] Colonel Robert W. Stewart, C. H. Pforzheimer, E. A. Howard, C. G. Burnham, F. B. Brown, E. M. Brown, Jr., and F. L. Dyer were also heavy investors.

Under a contract drawn in October, 1919, Wickett, acting as agent for other stockholders, agreed to sell Standard 90 per cent of Dixie's 6,000 shares, par value $100.[16] Wickett was to secure, if possible, the other 10 per cent of the stock, which he did. For all the shares, Standard paid $1,650,000, or $275 per share. On November 20th Dixie transferred 5,745.795 shares of stock to Standard. Colonel Stewart surrendered his 254.205 shares on January 5, 1920, to Standard for $275 per share ($69,906.37) plus interest at 4½ per cent from November 20th.[17] W. E. Warwick, Dr. Burton, Edward G. Seubert, Beaumont Parks, H. S. Morton, Seth C. Drake, and Stewart were elected Directors of Dixie, and Wickett became President.

By acquiring Dixie, Standard secured either a full interest or part interest in leases on about 27,000 acres of oil land in Louisiana and Arkansas, an interest in a pipeline from the Dillon lease to Gilliam, Louisiana, the loading rack at Gilliam, and all boilers, tanks, gathering lines, engines, and buildings on the Dillon lease. At the time of purchase, Dixie had a production of about 500 barrels of heavy crude per day.[18] Its annual crude production in the Caddo field, however, steadily increased from 234,400 barrels in 1920 to 388,685 in 1922. The average daily production was about 1,000 barrels, but it never exceeded 1,500 barrels during these years. Except for about 400 barrels of the daily production, which was low cold-test oil shipped to Whiting, most of the pro-

15. List of Dixie Stockholders from September 14, 1917, to December 19, 1919. File No. 2,000. Office of the Secretary, Standard Oil Company (Indiana).
16. Memorandum of Agreement, October 31, 1919. File No. 2,000. Office of the Secretary, Standard Oil Company (Indiana).
17. Memorandum on Stewart's sale of Stock. File 1,006. Office of the Secretary, Standard Oil Company (Indiana).
18. *High Cost of Gasoline and Other Petroleum Products,* I, 762, 770-771.

duction was sold to the Caddo Central Refining Company. In 1926 all of the crude-oil producing properties of Standard of Indiana in Kansas were sold to Dixie. By 1928 it had more than 105,000 acres of promising oil lands in Louisiana and Texas and in the Mid-Continent field, which produced about 10,167 barrels per day.[19]

Of major importance in securing a crude supply was Standard's acquisition of The Midwest Refining Company in Wyoming. Ever since 1913, when Standard established a cracking plant at Casper adjoining Midwest's refinery, there had been close and friendly relations between the officers of the two companies. In fact, Standard had no sooner established its refinery at Casper than the general gossip was to the effect that Midwest was a part of Standard. With a rapidly increasing production of high-grade crude, rich in gasoline content, at Salt Creek, Midwest had become the dominant factor in the Wyoming field. It seemed, therefore, logical and natural for Standard to acquire Midwest, if possible.

Certain large stockholders of Midwest had offered on several occasions to sell their stock to Standard for various reasons. While the company's development had been remarkable, it had reached a point where experienced oilmen were needed in the management instead of financiers and stock promoters, and greater financial resources were required. Furthermore, with a large refining capacity located a long distance from markets, Midwest needed marketing outlets. Those acquainted with its situation felt that it would be wise to tie in with a strong, well-established company. In the summer of 1920 these large stockholders made another offer to sell. If Standard did not want the stock, they would offer their holdings to some other company.

Afraid that Midwest might be acquired by another company and Standard's supply at the Casper refinery would be cut off, Colonel Stewart got busy. He and Burton conferred with Henry M. Blackmer of Denver, President of Midwest, and worked out a private agreement in August, 1920, not with Midwest but with a few of Midwest's large stockholders.[20] Standard agreed to exchange one share of its stock for four shares of Midwest, provided Blackmer and such associates as he wished to include would deliver a minimum of 175,000 shares and not more than 225,000. Midwest had a capitalization of $50,000,000 with 624,081 shares,

19. *Stanolind Record*, IX, No. 6 (April, 1928), 13.
20. *High Cost of Gasoline and Other Petroleum Products*, I, 85-87, 444-445, 451-452, 771-772.

par value $50, outstanding and assets of $61,737,529. Standard's stock had a par value of $100. Midwest's stock had a book value of $105.08 and Standard's $594.11. Prior to August, Standard had purchased some Midwest stock, and in the first exchange it got 68,193 shares. Among those who held Midwest stock and exchanged it for Standard stock in August, 1920, were R. H. McElroy (20 shares), Frank R. Morton (130), George W. Stahl (100), E. J. Bullock (50), E. G. Seubert (180), Allan Jackson (25), and John L. Carter (9), all of whom were employed by Standard. By August 27, 1920, Standard had acquired 156,886 shares of Midwest, most of which were certificates of a voting trust which had been created in 1917.[21] By late December, Standard had acquired 205,053 shares or about 33 per cent of Midwest's stock, which was sufficient to give it control of Midwest's operations and policies.

Through its stock interest in Midwest, Standard secured control of a company that consumed about 86 per cent of all the crude oil refined in Wyoming.[22] There was little competition in the region, and the nearest large refineries were six hundred to a thousand miles distant. Furthermore, Midwest had twenty-year contracts running until 1934 with practically all the principal producing companies at Salt Creek to supply it with crude. By stock ownership in other companies and through these long-term contracts, Midwest interests controlled about 65 per cent of Wyoming's production, which amounted to 16,831,000 barrels in 1920. Midwest also owned and controlled about 46 per cent of the pipeline mileage. Standard stood to benefit enormously from Midwest's control of crude production and from its production of refined products because Standard was marketing approximately 16,000,000 barrels of motor gasoline annually, yet it produced only about 11,000,000.

In October, 1920, Standard declared a stock dividend of 150 per cent, and in December it reduced the par value of its stock from $100 to $25, so that by these two moves stockholders had their number of shares increased in the ratio of 12 to 1. Standard's Directors authorized its officers in May, 1921, to make further exchanges in the ratio of two new shares of Standard for one of

21. Statement of Midwest Refining Company Stock to be Exchanged on Ratio of Four Shares of Midwest for One Share of Standard. Voting Trust File—Midwest. Office of the Secretary, Standard Oil Company (Indiana).

22. *Report of the Federal Trade Commission on the Petroleum Industry of Wyoming,* January 3, 1921, 8.

Midwest.[23] This was less favorable to Midwest stockholders than the original offer, due to an easing of the shortage of crude and refined products. Midwest's stock at the time had a par value of $50, a book value of $101.03, and a market value of $150. Standard's had a par value of $25, a book value of $53.25, and a market value of $75. As a result of the second offer 11,747 shares of Midwest were acquired, making a total of 238,080 shares or about 38 per cent.

In order to acquire a majority interest in Midwest, Standard's stockholders at a special meeting in June, 1921, increased the company's capitalization from $100,000,000 to $140,000,000, divided into 5,600,000 shares with a par value of $25. Notices were sent to all Midwest stockholders offering to exchange two shares of Standard, plus 73 cents in adjustment of dividends, for one share of Midwest. With the country in a depression and the price of crude low, Midwest's stock on the market had just declined to a new low level of $131. When it became known that the original exchange with Midwest's large stockholders had been made on the basis of one share of Standard for four of Midwest and that they had benefited from Standard's stock dividend of 150 per cent declared in October, 1920, and the reduction in its par value in December, there was considerable resentment among many stockholders of Midwest. However, under the offer of June 15th Standard brought its holdings up to 99.5 per cent of Midwest's stock by 1923. The exchange or purchase of stock continued until, by the end of 1928, Standard held 99.93 per cent.

In addition to acquiring control over the physical assets of Midwest in 1920, Standard was able in time to draw upon Midwest's human assets to strengthen the parent company. Experienced oilmen, such as A. W. Peake, Frank O. Prior, John D. Clark, Leon C. Welch, Herbert G. Naylor, Robert S. Ellison, John F. Cullen, and many others, were gradually brought into Standard's organization from Midwest. Peake and Prior, who later became Presidents of Standard, were responsible for the great strides Standard made in developing a crude oil supply of its own after 1930. Both men were graduates of Stanford University. Peake became associated with Midwest as field superintendent in 1916. Prior started with Midwest as a roustabout in the Salt Creek field in 1919.

Shortly after Standard first acquired a stock interest in Midwest,

23. Minutes of the Board of Directors' and Stockholders' Meetings, II, 873.

the postwar depression and an overproduction of crude oil at Salt Creek created a critical situation in Wyoming. By April, 1921, Salt Creek was producing 34,000 barrels per day, and Wyoming refineries were swamped. Fifty thousand barrels per day could have been easily produced if there had been adequate refining capacity. The problem was further aggravated by the fact that Wyoming refineries were far removed from large consuming centers. Freight rates made it impossible for Wyoming oil to compete with Mid-Continent oil. The refineries at Laramie and Greybull alone could supply the local marketing area, but Casper, with a capacity of about 50,000 barrels, was badly in need of a market. To aggravate the situation, a country-wide shortage of oil which prevailed in 1920 had quickly become a country-wide surplus due to new discoveries.

Colonel Stewart, officials of Midwest, and executives of the Chicago, Burlington & Quincy Railroad conferred in Casper in April, 1921, on possible means of providing relief for producers in Wyoming and Montana.[24] The problem was to provide the producers with sufficient refining capacity without making a heavy investment that might later become valueless. Some thought was given to building a pipeline from Wyoming to the main trunk lines leading north from the Mid-Continent field but that was shelved. The cost would require more production to warrant such an investment. The best solution seemed to be for Standard and Midwest to enlarge their Wyoming refineries and especially to erect storage tanks.

As conditions grew worse, crude prices were slashed, wages cut, and men laid off at the refineries. In June, Midwest limited the amount of crude it would take daily from Elk Basin and Grass Creek to 50 per cent of the production and from Salt Creek to 40 per cent. During the summer of 1921, Standard built a Burton cracking plant at Glenrock alongside the Mutual Oil Company refinery, a subsidiary of the Elk Basin Consolidated Petroleum Company, in which Midwest had an interest. A new battery of stills was installed at Greybull and the storage capacity doubled owing to the increased production at Cat Creek in Montana, which was about 25,000 barrels per day. At Casper, Standard constructed forty-five 80,000-barrel storage tanks. The company considered building a gasoline line from Casper to Sioux City, Iowa, but re-

24. "Officials Say Casper Plants to Be Enlarged," *The Oil and Gas Journal*, XIX, No. 46 (April 15, 1921), 92.

jected the idea owing to the high cost of construction. Midwest made plans to triple the capacity of its natural gasoline plant at Salt Creek so that it could produce 100,000 gallons of gasoline per day.

The greatest boon to the depressed Wyoming oil industry was the negotiation of a contract in November, 1921, between Standard of Indiana and Standard of Louisiana, whereby the latter agreed to purchase 2,000,000 barrels of export naphtha at Casper in fairly equal monthly quantities at a price 50 cents per barrel below the Louisiana company's selling price.[25] The announcement of this news was wonderful since it had seemed for a while that the lack of a market would surely cause a shutdown of all refineries and create widespread unemployment in Wyoming. Beginning in January, 1922, Standard shipped every week three solid trainloads of gasoline, composed of about sixty cars each, from Casper to Baton Rouge. The huge order for export gasoline kept the Wyoming refineries operating at full capacity. Between 1921 and early in 1927, when the contract was canceled, about 10,000,-000 barrels of gasoline were shipped in accordance with the contract.[26]

Although it proved valueless, another move toward acquiring a crude supply was Standard's purchase of the Chicago-Montana Oil & Gas Corporation.[27] J. Q. Adams, who had been connected with the Chicago & Milwaukee Railroad, had at one time purchased considerable property in South Dakota and Montana. He sold it to different parties but retained the mineral rights. Upon his death, B. S. Adams, his son, went out to see about his father's interest in 1920 and found considerable excitement over the possibilities of oil in the Cat Creek field of Montana, which had just been opened. He asked Standard to finance and explore the territory. The negotiations finally resulted in young Adams, K. M. Hancock, and Frederick H. Wickett organizing the Chicago-Montana Oil & Gas Corporation. They secured oil and gas leases for the company on more than 31,000 acres in Musselshell and Golden

25. Exhibit No. 72. Reply to a questionnaire of the Bureau of Investigation, Department of Justice, dated December 21, 1923. Office of the Secretary, Standard Oil Company (Indiana).

26. M. A. McNulty, Comptroller, Standard Oil Company (Indiana), to Giddens, July 25, 1952.

27. *High Cost of Gasoline and Other Petroleum Products*, I, 763; Minutes of the Board of Directors of the Chicago-Montana Oil & Gas Corporation, January 3, 1921, and January 9, 1929. Office of the Secretary, Standard Oil Company (Indiana).

Valley counties in Montana. In January, 1921, Standard bought all of the stock in the Chicago-Montana company, 1,500 shares for $150,000, and, as compensation for their efforts, gave Adams 225 shares, Wickett 200, and Hancock 25. Geologists were employed to explore the leases, but nothing ever came of the venture. In January, 1929, all of the company's leases in Montana were terminated.

Of greatest importance in the history of Standard's efforts to secure a substantial crude supply and a pipeline system was its acquisition of a half interest in the Sinclair Pipe Line Company and the organization of the Sinclair Crude Oil Purchasing Company. Since the dissolution in 1911, Standard of Indiana had depended upon the Prairie Oil & Gas Company for crude and its transportation to its refineries. During World War I, however, Prairie had to supply the refineries along the Atlantic seaboard to keep them operating at capacity for military purposes. The result was that Prairie could not adequately supply inland refineries.

After the spring of 1918, a substantial portion of Standard's crude oil purchases in Kansas and Oklahoma was delivered through the newly built Sinclair pipeline, which ran from Drumright, Oklahoma, to East Chicago. It had a capacity of 20,000 barrels per day. Whiting was so large that, when running to capacity, it could easily consume all of the oil that the Sinclair line was capable of carrying, plus what it received from the Prairie line. When Sinclair increased its pipeline charges, Standard stopped using the line and its Directors either in 1920 or 1921 decided to build a line from the Mid-Continent field to Chicago.[28] Since the Sinclair line was not running to full capacity and the parent company, the Sinclair Consolidated Oil Corporation, needed cash for expansion purposes, Sinclair offered to sell a half interest in the line. To build a second line at a time when there was one already laid and not used to capacity would be an economic waste. If the capacity of the Sinclair line were increased, Standard agreed to buy the half interest. This looked like an attractive proposition to Sinclair because the cost of increasing the capacity would be relatively small and comparatively little would be added to the operating expense.

After many conferences between Colonel Stewart and Harry F.

28. *Prices, Profits, and Competition,* 41. A report of the Federal Trade Commission dated December 12, 1927. See Senate Document No. 61, 70th Cong., 1st Sess.

Sinclair and in spite of the fact that they were the bitterest of competitors, Standard purchased on February 9, 1921, a half interest or 142,500 shares in the Sinclair Pipe Line Company for which it paid $16,390,000 in cash.[29] The price was based upon the actual cost of the line according to Sinclair's books. The sale in no way involved Sinclair's manufacturing, producing, or marketing facilities. Considering the length of the line and all of its facilities, the purchase price was generally regarded as cheap. Through the purchase, Standard secured a half interest in a company that owned and operated 2,900 miles of trunk and tributary lines extending from the Ranger field in north Texas through Oklahoma and Kansas to Chicago. It had connections with almost 6,000 wells. For Standard, the purchase meant the elimination to a large extent of shipments of crude by rail and a reduction in freight costs. More important was the fact that Standard could increase its supply by 10,000 barrels a day. It also meant increasing the importance of Standard as a purchaser in the Mid-Continent field. From a long-range point of view, it marked the beginning of Standard's efforts to develop its own independent transportation system.

The acquisition of a half interest in the Sinclair Pipe Line did not in itself increase Standard's crude supply one barrel. A pipe-line without crude was useless. Therefore, in order to get crude to fill the line, Standard and the Sinclair Consolidated Oil Corporation organized on February 9th the Sinclair Crude Oil Purchasing Company with a capitalization of $20,000,000, par value $100, to purchase crude for the two companies.[30] Each of the two companies owned a 50 per cent interest in the new enterprise.

The Sinclair Crude Oil Purchasing Company immediately started buying and storing crude oil. New connections were made with wells in the Mid-Continent field, and it was soon buying about 110,000 barrels a day. The Sinclair Pipe Line ran about 65,000 barrels of oil daily, of which 40,000 went into storage. Of the deliveries made to refineries, those of Sinclair got 67.6 per cent and Standard 32.4 per cent.[31] The Sinclair Crude Oil Purchasing Company soon had 11,586,320 barrels in storage and was adding at the rate of about 1,000,000 barrels per month. During 1921 it purchased 21,495,639 barrels.

In the fall of 1921 the Sinclair Crude Oil Purchasing Company

29. *High Cost of Gasoline and Other Petroleum Products*, I, 642-643, 781.
30. *Ibid.*, 650, 801-803.
31. *Ibid.*, 650, 659, 678.

became involved in one of the largest and, at the same time, one of the most unusual and mysterious oil deals in history. It was a result of the opening of the Mexia field in Texas. In November, 1920, Colonel Albert E. Humphreys, one of the most picturesque wildcatters in the oil business, brought in his first well in the Mexia field.[32] Two other wells were completed in August, 1921, one flowing 18,000 barrels per day and the other 24,000 barrels per day. The striking of these two sensational gushers started a mighty boom at Mexia. Whether the field would provide a large production no one knew, but Humphreys was convinced that he had opened a 100,000,000-barrel field. During 1921 the production was nearly 5,000,000 barrels. Mexia was the "World's Wonder Field." The Humphreys Mexia Company and the Humphreys Texas Company owned about a third of the daily production. At a time when there was an unprecedented demand for gasoline and a shortage of crude, the discovery of this sensational field caused a mad scramble among oil companies to buy either the oil or the property of Colonel Humphreys.

Henry M. Blackmer, President of the Midwest Refining Company and a long-time friend of Humphreys, knew that Standard was short of crude, so he arranged for Colonel Stewart and Colonel Humphreys to meet in the spring of 1921 at Cheyenne, Wyoming.[33] Humphreys wanted to take the Mexia properties, evaluate them, and exchange them for Standard stock. Stewart said he could not make a deal like that, for the Mexia production might or might not be a continuing one. He did, however, say that he would like to buy the oil when, as, and if produced, and he would pay a good price, but there would be no exchange of stock unless his Directors insisted upon it. Humphreys held to his notion all through the summer and saw Stewart at different times in Chicago about the matter. Blackmer tried to influence Stewart to trade Standard stock for the Mexia property, but Stewart refused.

Blackmer took a very active part in trying to get Stewart to buy the oil. He had E. L. Estabrook, petroleum engineer for Midwest, make a survey of the Mexia field. A copy of the report was forwarded to Stewart, who sent it to the research laboratory at Whiting for study.[34] The analysis indicated that Mexia crude was par-

---

32. Rister, *Oil! Titan of the Southwest,* Chapter XIII.
33. *Leases Upon Naval Oil Reserves* (1929), 164-167. This reference contains the hearings before the Senate Committee on Public Lands and Surveys in 1928 upon the Continental Trading Company.
34. *Ibid.,* 130-131, 175.

ticularly well suited for a company which extensively employed the cracking process. After studying the report, Blackmer wrote Stewart in September, 1921, that "we" should take advantage of the opportunity to tie it in some way to "our interests." [35] He believed that "we" should have a conference at an early date with James E. O'Neil, President of Prairie Oil & Gas, present, and that Sinclair or Prairie should extend its pipeline to Mexia and bring the oil up to "our" refineries. "All I can say," Blackmer wrote, "is that we have Mr. Humphreys ripe for a trade." If Stewart wanted to push the matter, it should be done immediately. Blackmer pointed out that Humphreys would not be satisfied until "we" go south, and if "we" go, Humphreys would be pleased and more willing to meet in a future conference. Stewart had made a splendid impression on Humphreys in the spring, according to Blackmer, and Humphreys was very anxious to deal with him personally. O'Neil was also a type of man who appealed to Humphreys. Hence, a little further personal contact would be good, so Blackmer thought.

Blackmer, O'Neil, and Stewart immediately went to Mexia to see Humphreys.[36] They drove all over the property with Humphreys and J. Julius Fohs, his chief geologist, watched the wells in operation, smelled the oil, and talked. During the course of a barbecue party, Humphreys again offered to sell his interests to Stewart in exchange for Standard stock at its market price. In insisting upon trading for stock, Humphreys was encouraged by competitors for the purchase of Mexia oil, who confidently expected Stewart would refuse, and then they might be able to get the oil. Stewart told Humphreys that he would very carefully consider a proposal if Humphreys wanted to sell the properties or the oil, if and when produced. They did not get to first base on trading Standard stock, according to Stewart, "because he was as stubborn in one direction as I was in the other." Upon Stewart's return to Chicago he told his Directors about the proposition, but none was disposed to trade stock for the properties.

In October, the Pure Oil Company purchased a one-third stock interest in the Humphreys Texas Company and a one-eighth stock interest in the Humphreys Mexia Company, which netted the companies about $7,500,000 in cash.[37] Learning of Pure's acquisi-

35. *Ibid.*, 136.
36. *Ibid.*, 172-173.
37. *Ibid.*, 226-228.

tion of an interest in these companies, other oil companies renewed their efforts to get a share of the oil. Humphreys discussed the matter with Beaman G. Dawes, President of Pure, who was interested in purchasing all of the oil produced, provided the amount was not too great. It was finally agreed that Pure would take one-half the oil produced up to 40,000 barrels a day, leaving the other half to be sold to other companies. Pure was to get its oil on the same terms as the other 50 per cent sold for.

Late in October, A. E. Humphreys, Jr., President of the two Humphreys companies, went east with several people, including Blackmer. They stopped for several days at French Lick where Blackmer and young Humphreys talked further about the Mexia field. Blackmer asked him if his father would be interested in the sale of a large amount of oil. Young Humphreys sent several telegrams to his father about the matter with the result that Colonel Humphreys came to New York early in November prepared to sell his oil.

Humphreys met Blackmer alone in New York on November 15, 1921, and the latter offered to buy 30,000,000 barrels of oil at $1.50 a barrel. After considering the offer for a few minutes, Humphreys accepted the proposal. Whether Blackmer was acting for himself as a broker or acting as a representative of an unnamed group of individuals is one of the unsolved mysteries. It is clear, however, that Humphreys thought Blackmer was making a deal for the oil for Prairie and the Sinclair Crude Oil Purchasing Company. In any event, having bought the oil, it was up to Blackmer to sell it to someone who could run pipelines to Mexia. Prairie and the Sinclair Crude Oil Purchasing Company were the logical ones to whom he should turn; they had the pipelines and were in need of crude.

The next day Harry F. Sinclair and James E. O'Neil, who had apparently been invited by Blackmer, Humphreys, his attorney, C. S. Thomas, and Blackmer met for lunch in one of the private dining rooms at the Bankers Club. According to Sinclair, Blackmer informed them that he had purchased from Humphreys some 30,000,000 barrels of oil and that a number of people were interested in purchasing the oil.[38] The wells were coming in rather large, and he would like to interest Prairie and Sinclair in the repurchase of that oil. It would require the building of tanks immediately and the extension of pipelines to the field as soon as

38. *Ibid.*, 1058.

possible. Sinclair's impression was that the whole affair was a deal
between Blackmer and Prairie and the Sinclair Crude Oil Purchasing Company. They discussed various aspects of the deal, and
finally the representatives of the two companies agreed to buy the
oil. About 2:30, when the meeting was on the point of breaking
up, Thomas asked Sinclair and O'Neil who represented them in
New York, saying he thought he could put in the afternoon working on the preparation of a contract. Colonel Humphreys broke
into the conversation by saying: "Gentlemen, I wish you would
make this contract for 33,333,333⅓ barrels of oil because that will
make the consideration $50,000,000 and I have some pride in
wanting to be a party to a contract of these dimensions." [39] To this
they agreed. In reply to Senator Thomas' question about their
attorney, one of the gentlemen said that while the contract was of
tremendous size, the details were comparatively simple, and it was
not necessary for Thomas to see another attorney. Blackmer was
an attorney of experience, and if they needed any counsel, he and
Thomas could settle any differences. The conference broke up
about 3 P.M. with the understanding that they would meet the
next morning at 10 in Blackmer's suite at the Vanderbilt Hotel.

Having learned that Humphreys had sold a stock interest in his
companies and one-half of the oil to Pure and that Humphreys
was in a position to sell the other half, when and if produced,
the Directors of Standard asked Stewart to go to New York,
meet Humphreys, and see if they could buy the balance.[40] Upon
Stewart's arrival in New York, on the 17th, he telephoned Humphreys at the Waldorf-Astoria and asked for a conference to talk
about buying the oil. Humphreys said that matters were at a point
where he was going to meet some gentlemen at Blackmer's room
at the Vanderbilt Hotel that morning, and that he was not in a
position to sell any oil to Standard, but that he would like to
have Stewart at the conference.

At ten o'clock the same persons as were present at the luncheon
on the previous day met at Blackmer's suite. In addition, there
was Colonel Stewart, Beaman G. Dawes, and young Humphreys.
Stewart was surprised to see Sinclair present, for he had not been
previously involved. The negotiations of the previous day were
resumed with conferences being held in various rooms by different
people in an effort to work out the details. Early in the day, in

39. *Ibid.*, 145.
40. *Ibid.*, 177-178.

one of these conferences with Sinclair and O'Neil present, Blackmer told Colonel Stewart that there was no chance of Standard
getting the oil; that the Continental Trading Company was going
to get the oil at $1.50; that Humphreys wanted to sell the oil in
some way to the two companies having pipelines down there—
Prairie and Sinclair; and that if these companies wanted the oil,
they would have to pay $1.75 a barrel.[41] If they did not, there
were plenty of others who would take it. According to Colonel
Stewart, this was the first time he had ever heard of the Continental Trading Company. Without making any inquiry about the
Continental Trading Company or asking why they had to pay an
extra 25 cents, Stewart acted quickly and indicated that he still
wanted the oil, even though somebody—presumably Blackmer—
was getting a brokerage fee of 25 cents per barrel. If Humphreys
produced the oil and the contract was fulfilled, someone stood to
make $8,000,000. Stewart had no definite information as to who
was getting the commission on the deal, did not inquire, and did
not care. Stewart knew they were getting the oil at $1.75 when
the posted price was $2.00. Stewart also knew that premiums of
25 to 50 cents per barrel were being paid for oil.

About 2 or 3 P.M. agreement on a tentative basis was reached.
Senator Thomas said that, as far as he was concerned, he had all
the information necessary, and he would go into the next room
and draft a contract. Up to this point there had been no mention
of who the purchaser was to be. It was assumed, at least by Beaman
G. Dawes, Senator Thomas, and the two Humphreys, that the purchasers were Prairie and the Sinclair Crude Oil Purchasing Company. However, as Senator Thomas prepared to leave the room,
Blackmer said to him: "The party of the second part in this contract, Senator, is the Continental Trading Company of Canada." [42]
Humphreys turned to Thomas and asked: "How is that, Governor?" Thomas replied that this introduced an entirely new
feature into the transaction, and they could not go ahead until
they learned something about the status, character, and responsibility of the corporation. Humphreys and Thomas had never
heard of it. Sinclair said that this was the first time he had heard
of it, too.

Someone suggested that the difficulty could be overcome if there

41. *Ibid.*, 178, 180, 183, 217. For a brief history of the Continental Trading Company,
    see 1171-1183, 1185-1204.
42. *Ibid.*, 9, 146-147, 179, 186. On the Continental Trading Company, see 5 F. (2d)
    330, 72 Law. Ed. 137, 14 F. (2d) 705.

was a guarantee of performance for Continental. In discussing the matter with Sinclair and O'Neil, Stewart said: "I don't see very much in this guarantee." Even though they professed no knowledge of Continental, they agreed that no great liability or risk was involved in guaranteeing the contract, and they were anxious to get the oil. The oil was to be paid for by the month and settlement was to be made on the 15th of the succeeding month. In the event of Continental's failure to pay, Humphreys could stop delivering the oil, and there would be no more than a month's supply of oil in the tanks of Prairie and the Sinclair Crude Oil Purchasing Company, which could be used to meet the obligation. After a brief conference, Sinclair spoke up and said: "Why, we will guarantee that contract. We receive the oil, and we pay for it." When Thomas asked who was going to execute the contract for Continental, Blackmer said H. S. Osler would be present the next day for that purpose.

While the negotiations in New York were in progress on the 15th and 16th of November, H. S. Osler of the law firm of Osler, Hoskin & Harcourt of Toronto was called to New York on business by a "client" who was negotiating for the purchase and sale of a large quantity of oil from Humphreys.[43] The "client" emphasized the confidential character of his business and did not wish his name disclosed under any circumstances. "He also told me," said Osler, "that he had associates who were interested with him in the matter, and whose names he desired me not to disclose." According to Osler, "They then, according to my understanding, became my clients." The "client" informed Osler that arrangements had been made for the resale of the oil at an advance of 25 cents to the Prairie Oil & Gas and the Sinclair Crude Oil Purchasing Company. Osler was to act as counsel in preparing and settling the contracts. Since Humphreys had imposed some very onerous conditions as to delivery, storage, and transportation, litigation with Humphreys was obviously possible, so the "client" wanted Osler to take charge of the receipt and payment of all moneys in order that he might be on the alert to avoid litigation.

Osler felt that if litigation occurred, his position might be difficult and embarrassing unless the business was incorporated. He so advised his "client." As a result, Osler gave instructions by telephone from New York to his office in Toronto to incorporate the Continental Trading Company of Canada. It was organized

43. *Leases Upon Naval Oil Reserves* (1929), 14-19, 33-34.

and an application was made for incorporation on November 16, 1921, which was approved on the 17th. Osler was President and all of the officers and directors of the corporation were members or employees of Osler's legal firm. It was a unique and peculiar corporation. The company was, in effect, merely a corporate clerk in Osler's office. Osler remained in entire charge of affairs as effectively as if no company existed. Coupon sharing warrants, transferable by delivery, were issued, as was permissible in Canada, instead of certificates of stock. The company had no list of stockholders or stock warrant holders, in fact, nothing to show who the stockholders were.

The next morning, November 18th, the group assembled at Blackmer's rooms at the Vanderbilt Hotel for the formal closing of the deal. There, for the first time, Thomas and Humphreys met Osler. The first contract to be signed was between the Continental Trading Company and the Humphreys Mexia Company and the Humphreys Texas Company. Under its terms the Humphreys companies were to deliver in their field tanks "in the vicinity of" 33,333,333⅓ barrels of crude for $1.50 a barrel at the rate of 50 per cent of their production from their field operations when, as, and if produced.[44] Continental was to accept the oil in the field tanks and furnish facilities for taking out the oil as fast as produced. Settlement was to be made for the oil in cash by Continental on the 15th day of each month for the oil delivered during the preceding calendar month. Osler signed for Continental and, after signing, he reached into his pocket, brought out a silver-plated seal and affixed it to the contract. O'Neil signed the guarantee of performance as President of Prairie, and Sinclair and Stewart signed as "Directors" of the Sinclair Crude Oil Purchasing Company.

Before signing the guarantee, however, Sinclair discussed privately with Blackmer the commission of 25 cents per barrel that someone was receiving.[45] He assumed that Blackmer was the Continental Trading Company, for he had purchased the oil and injected the Continental Trading Company into the picture. Sinclair said that he felt the 25 cent commission on each barrel was exorbitant. Furthermore, Sinclair said that if he signed the guarantee, he would expect for his company a fair share of the 25 cent commission. Blackmer agreed, and said that his company or Sin-

44. *Ibid.*, 5-6.
45. *Ibid.*, 1070.

clair for the company would receive a fair portion of the commission.

A second contract was executed between the two Humphreys companies and Prairie and the Sinclair Crude Oil Purchasing.[46] It provided that the Humphreys companies would sell, at the posted price, to Prairie and Sinclair 50 per cent of all oil that they might produce at Mexia, but this contract was not to take effect until after the contract with Continental had been fulfilled. This was signed by Sinclair and Stewart "for the Directors" of the Sinclair Crude Oil Purchasing Company.

A third contract provided that Continental would sell to the Prairie Oil & Gas and to the Sinclair Crude Oil Purchasing Company the 33,333,333⅓ barrels of oil purchased from the Humphreys companies, when, as, and if produced, at $1.75 per barrel or at the field price for Mid-Continent crude as posted from day to day less 40 cents a barrel, whichever should be higher, up to but not exceeding a maximum of $2.50 a barrel.[47] Prairie and Sinclair were to accept the oil in their field tanks and assume the obligation of Continental for furnishing facilities to take the oil from the field tanks and proceed with reasonable diligence to furnish the facilities necessary for taking out the oil. They were to pay for the oil in United States currency at the Dominion Bank of Canada in New York on the 10th of the month for the preceding month's supply. Though signed by Sinclair and Stewart, as representatives of the parent companies, the contracts were purely tentative. They had to be approved by the Directors of Prairie and the Sinclair Crude Oil Purchasing Company.

Stewart returned to Chicago the next day and called a meeting of the Directors of Standard for the 19th to present the contracts. At the meeting, he laid the contracts upon the table and stated that he had been able to make an arrangement for the Sinclair Crude Oil Purchasing Company to purchase oil at Mexia, Texas, for $1.75 a barrel. Furthermore, the Colonel informed them that someone had bought the oil for $1.50 and was selling it for $1.75. "It is perfectly apparent," Stewart told them, "that somebody is making 25 cents a barrel out of this thing. If that is material, don't take these contracts. Give them up. If you want this oil at this price that is the price I am told you have got to pay

46. *Ibid.*, 6.
47. *Ibid.*, 9-10.

for it and I believe that is what you will have to pay for it." [48]
There was a little discussion, but no one made any inquiry about
the commission or who was getting the commission or Continental
and how it got the contract rather than Stewart or why it was
necessary to guarantee the contract with Continental. The fact
that someone bought the oil for $1.50 and, on the same day, sold
it for $1.75 did not seem significant to the Directors.[49] "We had
no interest in that," said Seubert, "because we were told by the
Colonel the best price for which Sinclair could purchase oil was
$1.75 a barrel." Because of implicit confidence in Colonel Stewart,
which no outsider can fully appreciate, the Board was willing to
accept his word. In spite of the price, the Board felt that it was
a good buy, for crude of like character in the Mid-Continent field
was selling for more than $2.00 a barrel. Standard's nominees on
the Board of the Sinclair Crude Oil Purchasing Company were
advised to accept the contract.

The Directors of the Sinclair Crude Oil Purchasing Company
met in Chicago on November 26th. The Directors of the Sinclair
Pipe Line Company met at the same time because, if the contracts
were approved, these officials would have to execute the terms.
Prior to the formal meeting of the Board of the Sinclair Crude
Oil Purchasing Company, there was a general meeting of the two
Boards and other officials. Stewart and Sinclair attended, and one
or the other presented the contracts made in New York, discussed
their desirability, and passed the contracts around for examination. After the general meeting and discussion, the Board of the
Sinclair Crude Oil Purchasing Company held a very perfunctory
meeting and approved the contracts.[50] Once the contracts were
approved, Stewart, Sinclair, and officials of the Sinclair Pipe Line
and Sinclair Crude Oil Purchasing Company left for Mexia to
arrange for extending the pipeline from Ranger to Mexia and
building storage tanks. Other events arising out of these contracts
will be discussed later.

By the summer of 1922 Casper, Wyoming, was being hailed as
"The Oil Capital of the World." A gigantic oil boom was in full
progress and there was a flood of oil. Salt Creek had a producing
area about eighteen miles long and three to five miles wide. It was
considered the greatest potential field in the country and 75 per

48. *Ibid.*, 179.
49. *Ibid.*, 138-144, 153, 155-157, 160-162, 164, 232-235, 242-243.
50. *Ibid.*, 117-118, 236, 238-240, 270-275.

cent of its acreage was controlled through contracts by Midwest. There were about 380 producing wells with a potential production of 180,000 barrels a day but the production was less than one-third because of prorationing. Crude oil production in Wyoming in 1922 amounted to 26,715,000 barrels, an increase of 38 per cent over 1921.

Limited by its refining facilities and the market, the only way Midwest could keep its refineries from being swamped and the price of crude at a reasonable figure was to prorate the production and accept only about 35 per cent. It purchased about 75,000 barrels per day and stored about 25,000. In 1922 the average daily crude run at Standard's Casper plant was 44,329 barrels, which exceeded that of Whiting for the first time.[51] From the point of view of the volume of gasoline produced, Standard's Casper plant was reported to be the largest in the world.[52] About 615,000 barrels of gasoline, 170,000 barrels of kerosene, 2,500,000 pounds of paraffin wax, and 5,000 tons of coke a month were manufactured in 1922 and for the year 30,000 barrels of lubricating oil, to say nothing of fuel oil, gas oil, asphalt, and engine distillate. At Salt Creek, Midwest's natural gasoline plant, the largest in the world, added to the gasoline supply. In 1922 a second and in 1923 a third unit was added so that it could handle 30,000,000 cubic feet of gas per day and produce 60,000 gallons of gasoline per day. Midwest's gas supply was further augmented in 1922 through an agreement with the Producers & Refiners Corporation whereby the latter piped its natural gas from the Ferris, Mahony, and Wertz oil fields to Casper.[53] Midwest agreed to purchase a minimum of 30,000,000 cubic feet of gas a day for ten years. Gasoline production reached such large proportions that it flooded the Middle West and sold beneath that of independent refiners to an almost disastrous extent. Operating the Burton stills in Wyoming on stock from crude costing 50 to 75 cents per barrel, Standard could ship from Casper into the Middle West and sell for less than Mid-Continent refiners. During the summer of 1922 a trainload of Cat Creek crude from Montana was shipped every other day to Whiting for Standard.[54] Cat Creek crude had

51. Company Encyclopedia: Manufacturing—Past and Present Curtailment of Manufacturing Operations at Casper, 2.
52. *The Casper Herald*, January 1, 1923.
53. *Chicago Journal of Commerce*, August 30, 1921, September 2, 1921.
54. *The Oil and Gas Journal*, XX, No. 12 (August 17, 1922), 46.

the highest gravity of any in the country. It yielded about 60 per cent gasoline.

The great expansion of the oil industry in Wyoming had a significant effect upon both the Sinclair Pipe Line and the Sinclair Crude Oil Purchasing Company. On April 7, 1922, the Secretary of the Navy, Edwin Denby, and the Secretary of the Interior, Albert B. Fall, for the United States government, signed a five-year lease granting to Harry F. Sinclair's Mammoth Oil Company the right to drill and take oil and gas from the Naval Oil Reserve No. 3, better known as Teapot Dome, in Wyoming.[55] The reserve, which was on a structure adjacent to and rather similar to Salt Creek, was estimated to have 150,000,000 to 200,- 000,000 barrels of oil. When production reached 20,000 barrels a day, Mammoth was obligated to build a pipeline from Teapot Dome east to connect with the main trunk lines from Kansas City to Chicago and to the Gulf in order to run the government's royalty oil. Even before Mammoth leased Teapot Dome, Colonel Stewart had proposed that the Sinclair Pipe Line build a pipeline to Wyoming in order to offset high freight costs. Inasmuch as the Sinclair Pipe Line was already planning to build a line, Mammoth, which was without any facilities, designated the pipeline company as its nominee under the contract of April 7th to carry the oil from Teapot Dome and the Sinclair Crude Oil Purchasing Company as its nominee to buy the oil and erect storage tanks.

The leasing of Teapot Dome to Mammoth was regarded by some as another step in the development of the Sinclair-Standard "entente." However, the Sinclair Pipe Line and the Sinclair Crude Oil Purchasing Company had nothing to do with the leasing of the Teapot Dome. Their only connection was that their contractual rights were derived from Mammoth. Also, Standard had nothing to do with the leasing of Teapot Dome, and neither did Colonel Stewart. Standard was only indirectly involved in the affair because of its stock interest in the Sinclair Pipe Line, the Sinclair Crude Oil Purchasing Company, and the Midwest Refining Company. Furthermore, there was no connection whatsoever between the Teapot Dome lease and the Continental Trading Company deal. They were two separate, different, and unrelated transactions.

In the fall of 1922 the federal government announced that bids would be received until November 15th for the purchase of its

55. 5 F. (2d) 330, 72 Law. Ed. 137, 14 F. (2d) 705.

AIRPLANE VIEW OF MIDWEST HOME CAMP, WYOMING, AND THE
SALT CREEK OIL FIELD

GREAT FIRE AT THE CASPER REFINERY CRUDE OIL TANK FARM

THE TUG *OUTAGAMIE*

THE *STANOLIND*

royalty oil at Salt Creek. Owing to the scarcity of crude, many oil companies were interested in buying this oil. Representatives of The Texas Company, Producers & Refiners, and others went to see Secretary Fall about the oil even though it was a bidding proposition. Because of this situation, Stewart, at Blackmer's suggestion, visited Fall at his home in Three Rivers, New Mexico, early in November.[56] Blackmer and Sinclair were also there. Thirteen companies finally submitted bids. On December 22nd Secretary Fall announced that he had accepted the bid of the Sinclair Crude Oil Purchasing Company. Under a contract of that date, the company agreed to buy for five years the government royalty oil at field tanks furnished by the lessee, beginning on January 1, 1923.[57] An option to renew the contract for an additional five years was included. The government was to receive the highest market price paid either in Salt Creek for the majority of the oil purchased or in the Mid-Continent field, whichever was the higher, for oil of the same gravity. The Sinclair Crude Oil Purchasing Company was willing to make this price arrangement, even though Salt Creek prices were sometimes below Mid-Continent prices, because it wanted the oil badly. All other bidders wanted a differential of 25 to 40 cents a barrel less for Wyoming oil than for Mid-Continent.

As a result of the contracts for the purchase of Mexia crude and the developments in Wyoming, there was a tremendous expansion of the Sinclair pipeline system and the operations of the Sinclair Crude Oil Purchasing Company. Plans were immediately made to increase the capacity of the pipeline from Drumright to Whiting from 20,000 to 40,000 barrels per day, build a 20,000-barrel line from Mexia to Sinclair's refinery at Houston, build a line from Teapot Dome to join the main Oklahoma-Whiting line at Freeman, Missouri, and construct tanks for the storage of oil from Teapot Dome and Salt Creek. Indicative of the rapid expansion of the purchasing company was the fact that its capitalization of $20,000,000 in 1921 was increased to $63,000,000 by 1923.[58] In addition, the purchasing company had sold $70,000,000 in gold notes to the public by March, 1923. The success in floating these loans marked a significant change in the attitude of bankers and the general public toward the oil business. A new era of public

56. *Leases Upon Naval Oil Reserves* (1929), 1042-1045, 1303.
57. *High Cost of Gasoline and Other Petroleum Products*, I, 671-673, 802.
58. *The Oil and Gas Journal*, XXI, No. 39 (February 22, 1923), 52; *Chicago Journal of Commerce*, April 20, 1922, November 27, 1923.

participation in the development of the petroleum industry had started.

In January, 1923, the Sinclair Crude Oil Purchasing Company bought seventeen storage tanks built or under construction at Teapot Dome and made preparations to receive additional oil from Teapot Dome and Salt Creek by starting construction on ninety 80,000-barrel storage tanks at Clayton, Wyoming, about thirty miles east of Casper and south of Teapot Dome. Soon there were 150 built or under construction.

Commencing at Clayton, the Sinclair Pipe Line Company began in the spring the laying of a line of eight- and ten-inch pipe southeast to the Wyoming state line, across Nebraska to Kearney, then southeast to Freeman, Missouri, near Kansas City, a distance of 717 miles. With the completion of the line in March, 1924, Wyoming, long handicapped in the marketing of oil by high freight rates, now had an outlet for its crude. It was now possible for Wyoming crude oil to come into direct competition on a large scale with Mid-Continent and eastern crude for the first time in history.

The completion of the Wyoming line increased the total mileage of the Sinclair Pipe Line to 5,625 miles. It now operated in eight states and was the most extensive pipeline system in the world. With its trunk lines extending from Houston to Chicago and westward to Wyoming and connecting with the principal producing, refining, and export centers, except in the East and on the Pacific Coast, crude could be easily piped from one place to another as needed. The development of such a large purchasing organization and pipeline system was the most outstanding event in the history of the petroleum industry between World War I and 1923. The Sinclair-Standard combination was now in a position to contest the supremacy of the Prairie Oil & Gas Company, which had been the dominant purchaser and pipeline carrier in the Mid-Continent field since 1911.

Wyoming reached the peak of its production in 1923, when it produced 44,785,000 barrels, an increase of 68 per cent over 1922. During the year Standard increased the operating capacity of its Casper plant to 55,000 barrels, an increase of 5,000 barrels over 1922. Its average daily crude runs amounted to 50,035 barrels, which for the second time exceeded that of Whiting.[59] With the

59. Company Encyclopedia: Manufacturing—Past and Present Curtailment of Manufacturing Operations at Casper. 2.

decline of flush production in Texas and Louisiana in 1922, there was a greater demand for Wyoming oil in the East. Refiners in Pennsylvania, lacking sufficient crude, began experimenting with shipping crude from Wyoming. Wyoming crude cost 70 cents per barrel and Pennsylvania oil $3.00. It was found that a car of Wyoming crude could be delivered in the Pittsburgh area for $573.62 while the same amount bought at Oil City cost $600. Consequently, Wyoming crude began moving to Pennsylvania by the trainloads.

During 1921 the Sinclair Crude Oil Purchasing Company bought more than 21,000,000 barrels of crude and in 1922 over 26,000,-000.[60] Of the pipeline deliveries in 1922, the Sinclair refineries took 6,623,300 barrels, or 66 per cent, and Standard 3,412,151, or 34 per cent. The company also had in storage about 29,000,000 barrels along the line from Mexia to Kansas City. Under the contract with the Continental Trading Company of Canada, the company had received 3,971,711 barrels of Mexia crude and Prairie 4,761,195 barrels by May 23, 1923.[61] By March, 1924, the purchasing company had received under its contract with Mammoth 1,430,024 barrels.[62] Its purchases of government royalty oil from Salt Creek averaged in excess of 20,000 barrels per day. By the end of 1924 the company had in storage 40,000,000 barrels of crude, not including 10,000,000 barrels at Clayton in Wyoming.

Further efforts to increase Standard's crude supply led to negotiations to purchase Cosden & Company, Marland, and other oil companies. During the summer of 1921 Stewart launched negotiations for what would have been one of the greatest mergers in oil history, the purchase of the Gulf Oil Corporation. Gulf was one of the richest petroleum companies outside the Standard group. Although an integrated company, it was particularly strong in production and oil reserves, which Standard badly needed. Neither company competed with the other to any great extent, and in a merger they would complement one another. There was also much speculation over the fact that Stewart saw in the proposed merger an opportunity to become the most dominating figure in the petroleum industry and for Standard of Indiana to become a more important factor than any other Standard company. Gulf officials manifested an interest in merging because

60. *High Cost of Gasoline and Other Petroleum Products,* I, 650, 659, 678, 1311.
61. *Leases Upon Naval Oil Reserves* (1929), 124, 249.
62. *Standard Oil Company (Indiana) v. Commissioner of Internal Revenue,* 129 F. (2d) 363.

Standard had extensive marketing and refining facilities and a long experience in manufacturing, which would benefit Gulf. It might be a good financial move, too, if satisfactory terms could be agreed upon.

Each company made a careful survey of the properties and equipment of the other. When the surveys were finished, there were several meetings between Gulf and Standard officials in 1922 in an effort to reach an agreement. However, the deal failed to materialize. Colonel Stewart's rough-and-ready method of horse trading led him to depreciate Gulf's values with the result that the two parties could not agree upon the relative value—to the annoyance of Andrew Mellon—of Gulf and Standard properties.[63]

Failing in several efforts to buy other companies, Stewart turned his attention in another direction. For some time he and his Directors had been considering the acquisition of Pan American Petroleum & Transport Company, one of the largest crude oil producers in the world.[64] In the meantime, Blair & Company of New York had been formulating plans for the organization of a world-wide corporation interested in producing oil and marketing petroleum products. It had investigated many oil companies and properties and finally secured an option to buy a controlling interest in Pan American Petroleum & Transport. In January, 1925, Standard unexpectedly secured from Blair & Company a sixty-nine-day option to buy an interest in Pan American, which would expire on March 31st. Working against time, Stewart, Frederick H. Wickett of Dixie, and a party of technical men left immediately for Mexico and South America to survey the physical assets, actual and potential, of Pan American. It was a job of great magnitude considering the extensive and far-flung character of the properties. They traveled thousands of miles, and worked day and night going over various details. Upon the completion of the survey, it appeared desirable that Standard should acquire an interest with a view to ultimate ownership. As soon as Stewart returned to New York on March 27th, he agreed to buy an interest in Pan American, which had 1,001,558 shares of Class A stock and 2,400,000 shares of Class B, or nonvoting stock.

Four days later one of the greatest and most sensational deals in oil history was consummated when a syndicate composed of

63. J. F. Drake, Chairman, Gulf Oil Corporation, to Giddens, June 28, 1949.
64. "Standard of Indiana Assumes Impregnable Position Among World's Oil Companies by Purchase, With Its Associates, of Controlling Interests in Capital Stock of Pan American," *Stanolind Record*, VI, No. 7 (May, 1925), 1-4.

Colonel Stewart, Blair & Company, the Chase Securities Corporation, and certain British interests headed by Lord Inverforth purchased from Edward L. Doheny and his family a majority of the voting stock, 501,000 Class A shares of Pan American, for $37,-575,000.[65] Doheny retained his California oil properties, which were segregated and put into the Pan American Western Corporation. The deal, which was equivalent to a merger of Pan American, exclusive of its California properties, with Standard of Indiana, was the largest oil consolidation in the history of the industry and represented a phase of the keen competition for the control of the oil resources of the world. Their combined assets were valued at about $584,000,000 with securities rated on the open market at $787,000,000.[66]

To buy and hold the 501,000 shares of stock, the syndicate organized the Pan American Eastern Petroleum Corporation on March 27th with a capitalization of $25,000,000 with 250,000 shares of preferred stock, $100 par, and 10,000,000 shares of common stock, no par.[67] Elisha Walker and Hunter S. Marston, partners in Blair & Company, E. R. Tinker, Jr., President of the Chase Securities Corporation of New York, Lord Inverforth, Managing Director of the British-Mexican Petroleum Company, Ltd., Colonel Stewart and John D. Clark of Standard, and Frederick H. Wickett, President of Dixie, comprised the Board of Directors. Walker became Chairman of the Board and Wickett President. The company issued 133,584 preferred shares, par value $100, of which Standard of Indiana purchased 30,000. Pan American Eastern also issued 550,000 shares of voting common stock, no par, at $10. The British interests took 110,000 shares, Blair & Company 193,334, and the Shermar Corporation 96,666. Standard wanted the other 150,000 shares, but the attorneys of Blair & Company opposed it on account of their fear of the antitrust laws. In order to overcome this objection and keep the stock in friendly hands, Stewart personally subscribed for 150,000 shares and gave his note to the Chase National Bank for $1,500,000. The voting stock of Pan American Eastern was placed in a ten-year voting trust with Walker, Stewart, and Wickett as trustees to exercise all rights and

65. Minutes of the Board of Directors of Pan American Eastern Corporation, April 1, 1925. See also, "From Jobbership to Integration," *National Petroleum News*, August 25, 1954, 31-34.
66. *The New York Times*, April 2, 1925.
67. *Chicago Journal of Commerce*, April 2, 1925; *The Oil and Gas Journal*, XXIII, No. 45 (April 2, 1925), 23, No. 46 (April 9, 1925), 142.

powers of absolute owners of the stock covered by the agreement.

Stewart informed the Directors of his company about the arrangements and invited them to subscribe personally to a portion of the 150,000 shares he held in Pan American Eastern. In order to further the company's effort to acquire ultimately Pan American Petroleum & Transport, they agreed to accept Stewart's offer.[68] Burton took 2,500 shares, Seubert 5,000, Warwick 5,000, Parks 5,000, Jackson 5,000, McElroy 2,500, Bullock 2,500, Clark 5,000, and Thompson 2,500. Though not a Standard Director, Wickett took 5,000 shares. Stewart held the remainder—110,000 shares. Although Standard's ownership of stock in Pan American Eastern represented only a minority interest, it was to exercise management control over Pan American Petroleum & Transport.

With two Standard Directors about to retire, the question arose as to what should be done with their stock. In order for Standard to control this stock, it was necessary to keep it in a block. To accomplish this purpose, Seubert, Jackson, and Ernest W. Stephens incorporated Panamex on September 22, 1926, in South Dakota, with a capital of $1,500,000 and 150,000 shares.[69] Stewart, Seubert, Jackson, Bullock, and Ernest W. Stephens composed the Board of Directors. Panamex stock was then exchanged, share for share, for the 150,000 shares of Pan American Eastern held by Stewart and the other Standard Directors. By this method Pan American Eastern stock was held intact and voted in the interest of Standard.

For an investment of $3,000,000 plus $1,500,000 by its Directors, Standard secured an interest through Pan American Petroleum & Transport in some of the finest oil fields in the world.[70] The deal included about 1,500,000 acres of producing or prospective producing properties in Mexico which had a settled production of about 150,000 barrels a day equally divided between heavy and light crude. Pan American interests controlled a substantial share of the phenomenal production of the so-called "Golden Lane," where wells flowed 100,000 barrels per day unless shut in. The Mexican field was considered at the time one of the

68. L. L. Stephens to Bruce Johnstone, September 25, 1933. Wilhelmi File.
69. *Ibid.; The Chicago Tribune,* September 17, 21, 1933.
70. "Standard of Indiana Assumes Impregnable Position Among World's Oil Companies by Purchase, With Its Associates, of Controlling Interests in Capital Stock of Pan American," *Stanolind Record,* VI, No. 7 (May, 1925), 1-4; N. O. and L. M. Fanning, "Effects of Indiana-Doheny Merger," *The Oil and Gas Journal,* XXIII, No. 46 (April 9, 1925), 22.

most important and valuable in the world. In Venezuela the Lago Petroleum Company, a subsidiary of Pan American, had a concession covering 3,000,000 acres around and under the waters of Lake Maracaibo with a production of about 45,000 barrels a day. The British Equatorial Oil Company, another subsidiary, had a concession in the Maracaibo Basin. Pan American was also one of a group of five United States oil companies which owned a quarter interest in the Iraq Petroleum Company. To transport crude, Pan American had one of the largest tanker fleets in the world. It was valued at $10,000,000 and had a carrying capacity of about 3,000,000 barrels. Pan American interests had the largest refinery in Mexico at Tampico with a topping capacity of about 130,000 barrels a day and more than 500 miles of pipeline, loading terminals, and a railroad. A refinery at La Salina in Venezuela manufactured refined products for local consumption. A skimming and asphalt refinery at Destrehan near New Orleans, Louisiana, had a capacity of about 30,000 barrels a day. It was advantageously situated for barging oil up the Mississippi River into the middle section of the country.

The marketing facilities of Pan American had not kept pace with its production and manufacturing interests, yet they were extensive. Moreover, they were located in areas never before served by Standard, and they did not duplicate in any way its existing marketing facilities. Subsidiaries had established a large number of bulk stations for marketing fuel oil and a few service stations along the Atlantic seaboard, the Gulf Coast, and in South America at Cristobal, Buenos Aires, Montevideo, and in several cities in Brazil. Through the British-Mexican Petroleum Company, Pan American had large marketing facilities in Great Britain for supplying the transatlantic trade with marine oil. It was the pioneer and largest marketer of bunker oil on the Atlantic seaboard, where its deliveries ran from 15,000,000 to 20,000,000 barrels a year. Naphtha and gasoline were sold especially to the Standard Oil Company of New York. With the completion of a $2,000,000 refinery at Tampico for finishing gasoline, it had discontinued its contract for selling crude gasoline to the Standard of New York and entered the retail marketing field in 1923 in California, the New Orleans area, the Middle Atlantic states, and the South along the seaboard to Georgia.

Pan American marketed gasoline in the East largely through the American Oil Company of Baltimore, which had been organized by Louis Blaustein and his son, Jacob.[71] Prior to 1922, the Blausteins were retailing gasoline and kerosene in Pennsylvania, Maryland, the District of Columbia, and Virginia under the name of the American Oil Company. In 1922 they incorporated the American Oil Company and began retailing their products through a wholly owned corporation, Lord Baltimore Filling Stations, Inc. Their business increased so rapidly that they had difficulty in securing products and competing with integrated oil companies. At the outset, most of their supplies were purchased from the Standard of New Jersey, their greatest competitor. Consequently, the Blausteins sought an alliance with some company in order to compete on more favorable terms.

In 1923 Pan American was an integrated oil company but weak in marketing. Its retail and wholesale marketing was, in the main, the sale of fuel oil. On the other hand, American sold little fuel oil and much gasoline. Since Pan American was an independent oil company, it appeared that an affiliation with American would be mutually advantageous. Therefore, in June, 1923, American and Pan American entered into a contract, whereby the latter agreed to supply American's gasoline needs until December 31, 1933, at a fixed and rather wide margin below the Baltimore tank-wagon price. In return, the Blausteins sold Pan American a 50 per cent interest in American and Lord Baltimore Filling Stations, Inc. Pan American received all of the Class A stock and the Blausteins the Class B with the right to elect the president, vice-president, and general manager of American. As a result of the deal, American expanded its marketing facilities into other states and prospered as never before.

The acquisition of an interest in the Pan American Petroleum & Transport by Standard was considered the most significant event in the oil world since the dissolution of Standard Oil in 1911. By one stroke it placed Standard in the front rank as a world oil power and made it a vastly greater factor in the petroleum industry than ever before. It was surpassed only by the Standard of New Jersey in the United States and abroad in the extent of its operations, petroleum reserves, and resources. "Those who know the intense ambitions of Col. R. W. Stewart," the *National Petroleum News* commented, "to make his company a vital factor

71. For a brief background of the American Oil Company and its relation to Pan American, see Judge Samuel I. Rosenman's opinion in the Blaustein case, Supreme Court, New York County, June 8, 1940. See also, "From Jobbership to Integration," *National Petroleum News*, August 25, 1954, 28-31.

in the petroleum world, and the extent to which he controls the board of directors of his company, can well appreciate this latest move in the working out of plans he has carried on his mind for a long time." [72] The transaction gave enormous strength to Standard in its weakest spot—the lack of crude. With Pan American's vast crude supply behind it, Standard occupied an impregnable position among the oil companies of the world. It was the capstone in Stewart's efforts to acquire a crude supply for his company. In interpreting the event to Standard employees, Colonel Stewart in his Christmas message in 1925 proudly wrote: "Through the acquisition of great producing properties and of remarkable facilities for transport, the last twelve months have seen us bulwark the foundations of our industrial home and raise its superstructure to such heights that the industrial edifice of no other oil company in all the world may look down upon it." [73] The acquisition of an interest in Pan American not only elevated the position of Standard but placed Stewart alongside the two or three top executives in the petroleum industry. Some put him at the head of the list. "If petroleum is to have another Rockefeller or, more modestly, another Harriman or Jim Hill," wrote R. L. Duffus in *The New York Times,* "Stewart may play the role." [74]

Standard's acquisition of an interest in Pan American created widespread interest and led to immediate speculation on at least three features. What would the effect be upon the Mid-Continent market? Middle western refiners and producers manifested considerable anxiety over the turn of events. To allay any apprehension, Standard announced that it would continue its present activities in the Mid-Continent market, and that its middle western refineries would operate on Mid-Continent crude. Secondly, what effect would that portion of the Mexican constitution of 1917 providing for the nationalization of its mineral resources have upon Standard's interests in Mexico? Through Pan American, Standard was now among the largest United States companies operating in Mexico. Within a very short time after the acquisition of the Mexican oil properties, the question flared up and jeopardized Standard's interests. Fortunately for the company, it had in Stewart "the one man who might be assumed to be the

72. Roger B. Stafford, "Indiana Standard Completes Deal for Mexican Petroleum Properties," *National Petroleum News,* XVII, No. 13 (April 1, 1925), 33-34.
73. *Stanolind Record,* VII, No. 2 (December, 1925), 36-37.
74. *The New York Times,* April 12, 1925.

best fitted, both by natural qualifications and training, to handle such a situation." Thirdly, with the acquisition of fuel oil marketing facilities and gasoline service stations along the Atlantic Coast, in the South, and in Europe, Standard now came into direct competition with the Standard of New Jersey, Kentucky, New York, Louisiana, the Atlantic Refining Company, and the Magnolia Petroleum Company for the first time. East of the Rocky Mountains, only the Standard of Nebraska and the Standard of Ohio seemed to be free from competition with Standard of Indiana.

With the sale of majority control, Doheny retired as Chairman of the Board of the Pan American Petroleum & Transport, and Frederick H. Wickett was elected Chairman, Herbert G. Wylie President and General Manager. Stewart, Seubert, and Clark of Standard, Elisha Walker, Hunter S. Marston, George N. Armsby, and Edward F. Hayes of Blair & Company, E. R. Tinker, Jr., of the Chase Securities Corporation, Harold Walker, Paul H. Harwood, J. J. Cotter and Frederick Ewing of Pan American were elected Directors. There were no immediate changes in the operating management. Owing to differences between the new and old management, Wylie resigned in August and Wickett assumed his position. Robert G. Stewart, son of the Colonel, became Vice-President. Stewart, Wickett, Clark, and Burton of Standard were elected Directors of the Mexican Petroleum Company, Ltd., of Delaware, a holding company, and the same group, except Burton, was elected to the Board of the Huasteca Petroleum Company. Although it owned only a minority of the stock, these changes put Standard and its men in active control of the management of Pan American. The full impact of Standard's aggressive managerial control over Pan American, effective May 1, 1925, was quickly felt in all phases of its operations.

In the summer of 1925 Pan American Petroleum & Transport sold all of its controlling stock in the British-Mexican Petroleum Company of Great Britain to the Anglo-American Oil Company, Ltd.[75] Anglo-American and British-Mexican competed in many parts of England, but the latter did not have the economical marketing methods of the former. Hence, it seemed advisable to sell rather than try to compete. The sale, however, did not include Pan American's stock interest in the Southern Crude Oil Purchasing Company, the Southern Pipe Line Company, Lago Petroleum Company, and Lago Oil & Transport Company, Ltd.

75. *National Petroleum News*, XVII, No. 34 (August 26, 1925), 100.

Another part of the general reorganization was that Stewart and his associates in the syndicate immediately started to acquire enough stock in the Lago Petroleum Company, which owned the concession in Venezuela, in order to have majority control. By November 4, 1925, this had been accomplished and the stock placed in a newly organized company, the Lago Petroleum Corporation.[76] Stewart, Wickett, Walker, Armsby, and Tinker were elected Directors. Wickett became Chairman of the Board. In the reorganization, James W. Stewart, a son of Colonel Stewart, became Vice-President of the Lago Petroleum Corporation and President of the Pan American Petroleum Exploration Company.

Owing to a change in plans for developing a world-wide petroleum organization, Blair & Company and the Shermar Corporation offered their Pan American Eastern common stock for sale in May, 1927. Standard bought their 290,000 shares for $23 per share.[77] With these stockholders eliminated, the way was now cleared for Standard to secure complete control of Pan American Petroleum & Transport. A special meeting of stockholders was called for September 9th to vote on raising the capitalization of Standard from $250,000,000 to $375,000,000 and 15,000,000 shares with a par value of $25. The notice of the meeting contained no reference, however, to the fact that the Directors of Panamex proposed to sell their stock in Pan American Eastern to Standard.

After the stockholders had approved the increase in capitalization, Colonel Stewart explained that he and those who were Directors in April, 1925, were involved in Panamex and that they wanted to sell their stock in Pan American Eastern Petroleum Corporation to Standard.[78] Since they were personally interested, he felt that they should take no part in the deliberations. Consequently, they withdrew from the meeting. With Amos Ball presiding, C. W. Martyn, Standard's General Counsel, made a detailed statement relative to the 150,000 shares of Pan American Eastern held by Panamex. The proposal was: Should Standard acquire these shares? The stockholders voted to exchange one share of Standard (market price $73.78) for four shares of Pan American Eastern (subscription price $10). The profit on the transaction was $33.78 on each four shares, or about $1,250,000 on the 150,000

76. On December 31, 1923, Pan American owned 1,497,869 of the 4,000,000 outstanding shares in Lago. It assumed managerial control of the company on that date.
77. L. L. Stephens to Bruce Johnstone, September 25, 1933. Wilhelmi File.
78. Minutes of the Board of Directors' and Stockholders' Meetings, III, 1549.

shares.[79] On this basis, Panamex's holdings in Pan American Eastern were exchanged for 37,500 shares of Standard stock.[80] At this rate, Panamex's stock was secured on a more favorable basis than that from Blair or Shermar. Later, Standard acquired the British interests in Pan American Eastern on practically the same exchange basis as that with Panamex. By the end of 1928 Standard had acquired 28 per cent of the preferred stock and 50.02 per cent of the common stock of Pan American Eastern.

With the acquisition of additional stock, Standard consolidated its managerial control over Pan American Petroleum & Transport by moving more of its personnel into executive positions. All of the banking group representatives resigned from the Board, except Walker. Wickett continued as Chairman, Robert G. Stewart became President. Bullock, Parks, McElroy, and Humphreys, all Standard Directors, became Directors of Pan American.

When Pan American passed payment on its regular quarterly dividend in December, 1927, it caused considerable comment. The dividend had been earned, but it seemed wise to retain the cash in view of plans for expansion. Some stockholders suspected that Standard intended to offer an exchange of its stock for Pan American and desired to scare out stockholders, so that the exchange might be made on a more favorable basis. Whatever the reason, the passing of the dividend was a bitter disappointment to both American and British investors. No dividends were paid until 1931.

In their efforts to obtain crude oil for Standard, Stewart and the Directors had been eminently successful. Between 1918 and 1929 they had acquired the Midwest Refining Company, which controlled through contracts the great oil resources of Wyoming, a half interest in the Sinclair Pipe Line Company and the Sinclair Crude Oil Purchasing Company, which enabled Standard to draw more easily upon the oil resources of Wyoming and the Southwest, an interest in a contract for 33,333,333⅓ barrels of Mexia oil, a half interest in the purchases of oil from Teapot Dome and from

79. Burry, Johnstone, Peters & Dixon to L. L. Stephens, September 21, 1933. Wilhelmi File.

80. On September 16, 1933, Frederick W. Wilhelmi of Duluth, Minnesota, who owned twenty-two shares of Standard stock, filed a suit in the United States District Court for the Northern District of Illinois, Eastern Division, against Standard and seventeen past and present Directors, charging a breach of trust in connection with the purchase of Panamex's stock and seeking a recovery of profits made from the sale for the company. Before the case came to trial, a settlement was made. Wilhelmi File.

the government's royalty oil from Salt Creek, and a majority interest in Pan American Petroleum & Transport Company and its vast crude resources. By virtue of these moves, they had changed Standard from a strictly refining and marketing organization to an integrated company with a crude supply and pipeline facilities of its own and from a purely domestic oil company to one with international interests in oil.

Actually the amount of crude produced by the parent company in 1929 was relatively small compared to its requirements. Starting with a production of 96,615 barrels in 1919, Standard in 1929 had under lease 1,967,071 acres of oil land on which it had 829 producing wells with a gross production of 7,276,163 barrels.[81] Next to the Standard of New Jersey, Standard of Indiana was the largest purchaser of crude oil among the major oil companies with purchases amounting to 71,183,504 barrels. In addition, it was one of the three heaviest importers of crude with imports amounting to 12,674,456 barrels. Purchases of gasoline totaled 4,530,809 barrels.

81. *Investigation of Concentration of Economic Power* (Hearings Before the Temporary National Economic Committee, Congress of the United States, 76th Cong., 2nd Sess.) Part 14-A, 7770, 7780, 7783, 7786, 7811

CHAPTER X

Refinery Expansion and Cracking Litigation

OWING TO THE EXTRAORDINARY GROWTH IN THE DEMAND FOR GASO-line, Stewart and his Directors showed the same aggressive spirit in expanding refining facilities as in acquiring a crude supply. New pressure stills were built, new refineries constructed, and other companies with refineries were purchased. In 1918 the company had 548 Burton stills in operation. Between 1918 and 1922 the Stewart administration built 107 pressure stills at Whiting and Sugar Creek.[1] The company's refining capacity was further enlarged in 1920 through its acquisition of the Midwest Refining Company, which gave it control over refineries at Greybull, Laramie, Casper, and Salt Lake City with an aggregate daily refining capacity of 64,000 barrels. By the time this deal had been consummated, Standard had completed forty additional Burton stills at Casper, which marked the beginning of its No. 2 plant.

With a crude oil supply in Wyoming assured, Standard made plans to add 135 Burton stills and other facilities to its original refinery, or No. 1 plant, at Casper. Midwest contracted in November, 1920, to furnish Standard with 19,500 barrels of fuel oil daily beginning on July 1, 1921. Midwest had the privilege of supplying 6,000 barrels of wax distillate and reduced crude. The price was $1.50 per barrel for the fuel oil with an allowance for a fluctuation in price. The price for the distillate was to be $1.10 above the price of fuel oil. In order to have homes for its operating personnel due to the big expansion program, Standard purchased in 1920 forty acres of land on the west side of Casper and, later, laid out 245 lots and streets, put in sewers and water lines, and offered lots at modest prices to employees on which to build homes. In addition to the expansion at Casper, Standard built twenty Burton custom stills at Midwest's refinery in Laramie and eight at Continental's refinery at Glenrock. The large expansion program in

1. For the number of cracking units Standard installed at its different refineries to 1925, see *Hearings Before Martindale*, II, 1176-1177.

Wyoming between 1920 and 1924 resulted in building a total of 203 new cracking units.

A step looking toward Standard's ultimate absorption of Midwest Refining was the negotiation of a contract whereby Standard was to operate all Midwest refineries on a cost basis plus 5 per cent for supervision.[2] Effective October 1, 1921, T. S. Cooke, superintendent at Whiting, became manager of all Standard and Midwest refineries in Wyoming, and Standard took over more than two thousand Midwest refinery employees and added them to its own payroll. The consolidation made the Casper works second only to Whiting in size and in point of capacity. Other experienced refining officials from the Whiting plant were sent to Wyoming to improve Midwest's efficiency and methods. No change took place in Midwest's executive organization except that Ralph D. Brooks, the Vice-President, resigned and John D. Clark, General Counsel, became his successor. Midwest continued through its own organization to explore, produce, transport, and purchase crude for its refineries and to sell wholesale as previously. The ties between Standard and Midwest became closer in 1923 when Clark was made a Director and a Vice-President of Standard and Assistant to the Chairman.

One of the difficulties encountered in manufacturing lubricating oil by 1920 was the scarcity of Fuller's earth with which lubricating oils were treated. Existing mines in Florida and Georgia, the chief producing states, could not meet the demand. Standard even considered erecting silos to store any surplus over current requirements when available. Early in 1920 deposits of Fuller's earth were discovered in Pulaski County near Olmstead, Illinois. Since they were close to Standard's refineries, the company took an option on 154 acres. Exploratory tests were made which resulted in a decision in July, 1920, to purchase the property and construct a mill.[3] The clearing of the land and construction of buildings was completed and the first clay put through the mill in March, 1921. Shipments to Standard's refineries ran as high as 2,500 tons per month.

From the Whiting refinery an increasing amount of petroleum products was shipped by tankers on the Great Lakes during the

2. "Standard of Indiana Takes Over Midwest Refineries," *Stanolind Record*, II, No. 12 (October, 1921), 1-2.

3. Company Encyclopedia: Manufacturing—Clay Mining Department, 1-5; "Fuller's Earth For Filtering Mineral Oils," *Stanolind Record*, XIII, No. 2 (December, 1931), 10-12.

1920's. In 1918 more than 3,441,000 barrels were carried. By 1929 the amount exceeded 8,200,000 barrels. As business increased in the Great Lakes region, new water terminals were built in Michigan at Muskegon in 1920 and at Bay City in 1923. Standard's fleet was augmented in 1920 by the purchase of the tug *Outagami* for exclusive use in towing. A much more important addition was the tanker *Robert W. Stewart,* which was launched late in 1927. It had a carrying capacity of 50,542 barrels and cost about $1,000,000.

The appointment of Robert E. Wilson, Director of the Research Laboratory of Applied Chemistry and Associate Professor of Chemical Engineering at the Massachusetts Institute of Technology, as assistant director of research for Standard in 1922 gave a new impetus to research in a highly important period in the history of the company. Studies were continued on various chemical problems. More attention, however, was given to chemical engineering in approaching refinery problems. During the 1920's the research staff devoted its attention to studying distillation and cracking, corrosion, evaporation losses, gasoline recovery, other cracking processes, protective coatings for refinery equipment, antiknock gasoline, the deterioration of turbine oils during use, crankcase dilution, oils to prevent transmission chattering in Model T Fords, synthetic lubricating oils, carbon formation, utilization of gases from vapor phase cracking, and other problems.[4] In order to test and develop motor fuels and oils, Standard planned and constructed at Whiting during the winter of 1924–25 the first complete automotive laboratory building for this specific purpose.[5] As aviation became increasingly important, the company installed at Whiting in 1928 the first full-scale aviation engine for fuel testing ever employed by a petroleum company. This was closely followed by the installation of the first full-scale single-cylinder fuel test engine ever used by an oil company. The expansion of research activities and the adding of new laboratory equipment stimulated the improvement of old products and processes, the development of new ones, and more efficient operation of the refineries.

Early in 1929 the Development and Patent Department was organized. Wilson was transferred to Chicago and made head of

---

4. Company Encyclopedia: Manufacturing—History of Research, 4-6.
5. D. P. Barnard and A. H. Fox, "Standard Oil Co. (Indiana) Builds Complete Automotive Laboratory," *The Oil and Gas Journal,* March 27, 1941, 82-84.

the department and assistant to the Vice-President in charge of Manufacturing. The new department not only had over-all responsibility for the general research policy, but also the responsibility for obtaining patents on new inventions, protecting the company's patent rights against infringement, gathering and disseminating information on new developments, negotiating contracts with inventors for the purchase of their inventions, maintaining contacts with various chemical, legal, and engineering experts in the petroleum industry, negotiating licenses for new processes and methods, licensing the company's patented developments, and guarding against the infringement of patents of others. It was also charged with looking after the patent affairs of subsidiaries.

When Standard purchased a stock interest in Pan American Petroleum & Transport Company in 1925, its refining capacity was further enlarged. It acquired a refinery at Tampico, Mexico, with a topping capacity of about 130,000 barrels a day, another at Destrehan, Louisiana, with a capacity of about 30,000 barrels, and a third at La Salina, Venezuela, which manufactured only for local consumption. With a production of 100,000 to 125,000 barrels of crude per day in Venezuela, crude was shipped to Destrehan and refining centers along the Atlantic seaboard, where it was topped under contract and the bunker oil and the gasoline marketed by Pan American. The company was a leading factor in the heavy fuel oil business, marketing between 15,000,000 to 20,000,000 barrels of bunker oil annually against less than 5,000,000 barrels of gasoline. To supply the demand for asphalt, the Mexican Petroleum Corporation (Maine) built a modern asphalt refinery with a capacity of 365,000 tons per year at Baltimore in 1926.

When a new source of crude was discovered in 1925 at Saginaw, Michigan, and the annual production reached some 94,000 barrels in 1927, Standard decided to build a 2,000-barrel refinery at Zilwaukee, a small town near Saginaw.[6] It contracted with two of the largest producers in the pool to supply the crude. Late in 1927 the Muskegon field was opened, which increased Michigan's annual production to about 439,000 barrels. The refinery at Zilwaukee, the first to be established in Michigan, began commercial operations early in 1928.

In the same year as the Zilwaukee refinery was built, the Dixie

6. *Chicago Journal of Commerce,* March 4, 1927.

Oil Company, Inc., acquired a small refinery at Superior, Louisiana.[7] It was reconditioned and modernized under the supervision of Standard officials from the Sugar Creek refinery. When placed in operation in 1928, the refinery had a capacity of 3,000 barrels per day.

By 1927 Standard's refineries and those of Midwest had a crude capacity of 160,000 barrels per day, which constituted about 7 per cent of the total refining capacity of the United States. Combined with that of Pan American, Standard's refining capacity amounted to about 300,000 barrels. The extent to which Standard expanded its manufacturing facilities between 1918 and 1929 can be illustrated in two ways.[8] The investment at its principal refineries increased from $37,746,171.27 in 1918 to $99,356,149.04 in 1929. These refineries consumed 13,022,955 barrels of crude in 1918 and 68,428,000 in 1929.

On account of the huge crude production from the Lago properties in Lake Maracaibo, Pan American, late in the fall of 1927, decided to build a large refinery. After several months spent in considering sites, the coral island of Aruba in the West Indies, a Dutch possession, four miles wide, twenty miles long, and about twenty miles from the mainland of Venezuela, was selected. While Aruba was not an attractive tropical island, it afforded an excellent spot on which to build a refinery. It had a good, deep harbor. There was a native population of seven or eight thousand. Most of the men were forced to migrate yearly to Cuba to work in the cane fields in order to obtain money. Another important factor in selecting Aruba as the site of the new refinery was a desire to avoid the political uncertainties in Venezuela. Since Aruba was more or less barren, it was necessary for the company to import not only everything to build a refinery but everything for the care and comfort of its employees. All of the technical and supervisory personnel for constructing, also operating, the huge refinery came from Standard.

The first construction material arrived in May, 1928, and by January 1, 1929, the first refinery units were in operation. The last were completed in December. The refinery, one of the most modern plants in the world, had an initial capacity of about

7. G. H. Moffett to O. E. Bransky, August 10, 1938. Company Encyclopedia: Manufacturing.
8. The following figures are taken from: Company Encyclopedia: Manufacturing—Economics; *Investigation of Concentration of Economic Power*, Part 14-A, 7800; *Prices, Profits, and Competition*, 84.

110,000 barrels.[9] It was both a topping and cracking plant operating mainly on heavy crude from wells under Lake Maracaibo. The oil was pumped to shore tankage, loaded into shallow-draft tankers, and moved to Aruba. It had an asphaltic base, a high sulphur content, and was heavier in gravity and more viscous than most of the crude produced in the United States. Since the crude came from one source, it had been possible to design and build a plant at Aruba of more than ordinary efficiency. Upon the completion of the refinery, the company was in a position to manufacture a large volume of gasoline, which necessitated the expansion of its marketing facilities in the United States and abroad.

With a large demand for asphalt in Europe, a new German subsidiary, the Ebano Asphalt-Werke, Aktiengesellschaft, built and placed in operation a new asphalt refinery at Hamburg in 1930. It was the most complete refinery in existence for the manufacture of asphalt, with a capacity of 250,000 tons per year. Tankers, carrying crude oil from Mexico, supplied the refinery. Another German subsidiary, the Ebano Asphalt Gesellschaft m.b.H., marketed the product through Central Europe. The Ebano Oil Company, Ltd., a subsidiary with considerable British capital invested, was organized in England in 1929 to supply the rapidly expanding asphalt market in the British Isles. Another asphalt refinery was started in 1929 at Savannah, Georgia, with a capacity of 200,000 tons per year. By 1930 Pan American ranked second among American asphalt producers.

In order to make the Burton process available to more refiners, Standard made a significant change in its policy of licensing in 1920 for several reasons. First, the growth in the number of new and improved processes necessitated a change in order to meet competition. Between 1918 and 1921 patents on the Coast, Jenkins, Fleming, Cross, Rittman, McAfee, Tube and Tank, Dubbs, and Holmes-Manley cracking processes were issued, and commercial installations were made during this period or shortly thereafter. Secondly, while some of Standard's licensees had violated the restriction in their contracts and sold millions of gallons of cracked gasoline in Standard's marketing territory, the company had found it either impractical or inexpedient to enforce the provision. Hence, it was ineffective. Thirdly, in view of the company's litigation with the Universal Oil Products Company over the

9. *The Oil and Gas Journal*, March 21, 1929, 140, 150, May 2, 1929, 138, 152, August 8, 1929, 174; *World Petroleum*, July, 1931, 415-420.

Dubbs patents, it wanted to be in a position to show that the Burton process had been made available to all. The new policy involved granting licenses without any restriction on the sale of cracked gasoline in its marketing area.[10] However, the licensee must sell to Standard, if it desired to buy, one-third of the licensee's output of cracked gasoline at a fixed price below the tank-wagon price at the time of sale. The clause was a safeguard, a precautionary measure. It gave Standard access to a supply in case of a scarcity.

Early in 1920 Colonel Stewart conferred with the Secretary of the Western Petroleum Refiners Association, an organization that represented most of the refiners in the Mid-Continent field, informed him of the change in policy, gave him a printed form of the licensing agreement without the territorial restriction clause, and sent notices of the change in policy to the press and trade journals.[11] After this no more licenses were issued with the territorial restriction, except for one where the clause inadvertently slipped into an agreement made with the Standard of California.

The White Eagle Oil & Refining Company was the first independent refining company to secure a license. Although Standard was willing to license anyone, only four additional companies were licensed during the next two years: The Aetna Refining Company, Lion Oil and Refining Company, Tidal Refining Company, and the Galena Signal Oil Company of Texas. There were several reasons why more licenses were not issued. First, the cost of installing Burton units was staggering for small refiners. A still cost $40,000, and one needed to install a battery of ten to make the process profitable. This factor put the process beyond the reach of the smaller refiners. For this reason, the Cross and Fleming processes were the most popular. Secondly, the fact that Standard insisted upon an option on one-third of the gasoline produced on sixty days' notice, and its refusal to protect licensees from any damages that might be suffered in any infringement suits acted as a deterrent. Lastly, by 1922 the Burton process was obsolete.

Progress in research on the cracking process and the installation of new units during the 1920's was greatly hampered by the development of an extremely complicated and serious conflict over patents among the leading refiners. The first major clash had come

10. *Hearings Before Martindale*, VI, 3287-3288, 3291-3292.
11. "Refiners Consider Standard's Offer to License Burton Process," *National Petroleum News*, XII, No. 11 (March 17, 1920), 39.

in 1916 when the Universal Oil Products Company filed suit against Standard of Indiana, alleging that the Burton process infringed its Dubbs patent. The second major conflict developed in 1920 between Standard of Indiana and The Texas Company. Upon the issuance of the Adams patents in 1919 and 1920, The Texas Company came to the conclusion that the Burton process infringed these and some of its other patents. At the same time, Frank A. Howard, Manager, Development Department, Standard Oil Company (New Jersey), recognized that Adams' principal patent constituted a very serious threat to the Burton patent which his company was using. He immediately took up the matter with the officials of Standard of Indiana and told them that they must remove the cloud upon Jersey's continued operation of the Burton process.[12] If The Texas Company proceeded against them, Howard insisted that Standard of Indiana would have to be responsible for Jersey's losses. Russell Wiles, patent attorney for Standard of Indiana, denied any responsibility for Jersey's fate, but he agreed that the company would do its best to aid in the event of any trouble.

In July, 1920, The Texas Company notified Standard of Indiana that the Burton patent constituted a direct infringement of its patents and requested a discontinuance of the infringing operations.[13] A comparison of some of the claims of Adams and Burton by Standard officials indicated a serious conflict. Standard knew that Adams' application antedated Burton's. On the other hand, Standard's study of the situation revealed that, in some respects, the Holmes-Manley process infringed the Burton and other patents.

At the first conference between officials of the two companies, representatives of Standard charged Texas with infringing some of its patents.[14] Upon further study the Texas officials reached the conclusion that, in some respects, the charges of Standard were true. Under the circumstances, if either company sued the other for infringement, they would hesitate to use their cracking processes pending the outcome since the possible penalties would be great. However, to stop operations would contribute toward creating a motor fuel shortage because the demand for gasoline was increasing by leaps and bounds. Furthermore, protracted litiga-

12. *Hearings Before Martindale*, VI, 3224-3226.
13. *Ibid.*, VIII, 5528.
14. *Ibid.*, V, 3113.

tion would be costly, harassing, annoying, and have a bad effect upon operations and profits.

Both companies were confronted by a very practical situation. Standard had been operating the Burton process since 1913 and had a heavy investment in stills. It had licensed a dozen or more companies which had made similar investments. All were liable to suit by The Texas Company. Standard wanted to grant more licenses and have protection in its operations. It also wanted the right to install the Holmes-Manley process, a continuous type of process, which was recognized as superior in certain respects to the Burton process. On the other hand, The Texas Company had also made a heavy investment in Holmes-Manley cracking stills and was planning an even greater investment. It had issued no licenses, but it was hopeful. It needed a general release and the right to sublicense under Standard's patents. Under the circumstances, the sensible thing for both companies to do was to come to some agreement.

After long negotiations, involving the most strenuous horse trading and a fight for the best arrangement each could make, Texas and Standard signed a contract on August 26, 1921, which provided for a general settlement.[15] This agreement marked the beginning of what was popularly known as the "Patent Club." Since the two companies were about equal in size and in operations, each agreed to license the other to use its process without royalty payments. They also agreed to an exchange of immunities under their patents, past and future, for the cracking operations of each company and its subsidiaries. Owing to the fact that George T. Rogers had filed a suit in New York in December, 1920, against Joseph H. Adams and The Texas Company, claiming an interest in Adams' patents, and the outcome was uncertain, Standard of Indiana insisted that Texas warrant its title to its patent rights, which it did, and Standard reciprocated with a similar warranty as to its patent rights. Since Standard of Indiana had nineteen major United States refiners as licensees and Texas had none, Standard agreed to pay Texas 25 per cent of its future royalties on the operations of the first thirteen of these licensees, who were licensed prior to January 6, 1920, and 50 per cent of its future royalties on the operations of the remainder of these nineteen licensees as well as any other additional United States licensees. After 1936 Texas' share of the royalties from the first thirteen

15. *High Cost of Gasoline and Other Petroleum Products,* II, 1532-1534.

licensees increased from 25 per cent to 50 per cent. Standard agreed not to alter existing licenses so as to fix the royalty at less than $\frac{3}{10}$ of 1 cent per gallon without the consent of Texas. Texas in return agreed not to sue the licensees so long as they paid their royalties to Standard under the existing contracts, in which royalties Texas was to share. If either party granted licenses under the patents of both parties, it was obliged to charge the same royalty—$\frac{4}{10}$ of 1 cent per gallon of charging stock—as had formerly been charged by Standard under its own patents, and the royalty was to be evenly divided. In other words, a license could be issued by either party under the patent rights of both for the same royalty as was then being charged by Standard for licenses under its own patents. Since Standard had no regular and reliable source of crude oil by which it could fill contracts for gasoline, it inserted a provision, Section 13, giving Standard an option to buy one-third of the cracked gasoline manufactured by Texas in the retail marketing area of Standard under certain contingencies. Neither company expected that the option would be exercised, but it insured Standard against any shortage of cracked gasoline.

The agreement was advantageous to both companies, the public, and the industry. It removed the threat of costly litigation, eliminated the possibility of paying large damages, enlarged the freedom of each company to manufacture, license, and conduct research on cracking without restraint, and made possible an ample supply of gasoline at reasonable prices. It also gave Standard the benefit of the research on cracking of The Texas Company and the opportunity to use the Holmes-Manley process if it desired.

With the settlement of the Texas-Standard controversy, only Universal's suit against Standard remained. On November 25, 1921, Holmes Hall of Sedalia, Missouri, was appointed special master by the court to hear evidence and present his findings. The hearings opened in Santa Barbara, California, in February, 1922, and continued intermittently over the next several years at various places.

A great deal of research and experimental work had been done at Whiting to improve the operation of the Burton process, but owing to high operating costs in producing antiknock gasoline, excessive coke, and other disadvantages of an essentially batch type of operation, when compared with newer patented processes, the attempts to correct some of its shortcomings were abandoned. After a study of the newer processes by Wilson and his associates,

Standard of Indiana began installing the Holmes-Manley continuous process of The Texas Company in 1925.[16] This marked the
first departure from the company's policy of confining its cracking
operations to the Burton process. The Holmes-Manley process was
considered to be the best embodiment of the art of pressure bulk
distillation. Whereas a large Burton unit enabled an operator to
handle 20,000 gallons of cracking stock in a cycle of two days and
secure 30 to 35 per cent gasoline, a Holmes-Manley unit handled
70,000 gallons per day, or seven times as much as the Burton
process, made around 40 per cent gasoline, and ran for a period
of fifteen to thirty days, and frequently longer, before having to
shut down because of coking. Of course, the Holmes-Manley units
cost many times as much as the Burton units.

As a result of the increase in the number of cracking processes
and patents, a third major conflict developed in 1922 between the
Gasoline Products Company, The Texas Company, Standard of
New Jersey, and Standard of Indiana. Several events happened
almost simultaneously to produce the conflict. The Texas Company discovered in the spring of 1922 that the Cross process, owned
by the Gasoline Products Company, was very similar to the
Holmes-Manley process.[17] In fact, the Gasoline Products Company
was asserting the ownership of the clean circulation feature in
cracking which Texas claimed to have developed. At about the
same time, The Texas Company discovered that its Holmes-
Manley process was seriously threatened by some patents on the
Tube and Tank process which Standard of New Jersey had developed. In May, 1922, the Jersey company sent notices to several oil
companies using the Cross process, saying that it controlled the
Tube and Tank patents which dominated the Cross and Holmes-
Manley processes, and requesting that all infringements cease.
When the suit of George T. Rogers against Adams and The Texas
Company came to trial in May, 1922, The Texas Company received another jolt.[18] The lawyers of Standard of New Jersey
appeared in Rogers' behalf, and The Texas Company learned for
the first time that the Jersey company, not Rogers, was the real
party of interest in the suit.

As officials of The Texas Company considered a possible suit
by the Jersey company, they experienced another rude awakening.

16. Company Encyclopedia: Manufacturing—History of Whiting Plant, Light Oils,
     13-14.
17. *Hearings Before Martindale*, V, 3117, 3120-3121.
18. *Ibid.*, VI, 3223-3224, 3227-3228, V, 3116.

They had dealt with Standard of Indiana in August, 1921, on the theory that the Jersey company was simply a licensee of Standard of Indiana. Under the licenses which Standard of Indiana had granted, the licensees were not limited to the use of any specified process. By its contract with Standard of Indiana, Texas had extended licenses to those licensees under all its patents, present or future, so long as they paid their royalties on the Burton process. Thus, Jersey was free from attack by Texas, provided it paid its royalties at the Burton rate on any process it chose to employ. On the other hand, The Texas Company had inadvertently bargained away everything it had to trade. It was imperative, therefore, that Texas settle with the Jersey company and Gasoline Products if it wished safety for itself and its licensees. The Texas Company felt itself not only bound to negotiate with Gasoline Products for safety against infringement but to ally itself with someone like Gasoline Products who had not already largely released Jersey and whose claims, if pressed, might result in an injunction against Jersey and Texas operations.

Infringement notices sent by Jersey and the filing of a suit in July, 1922, against Pure Oil created a critical patent situation for Gasoline Products.[19] It was obligated to defend its licensees against any infringement suits and, under some earlier licenses, to indemnify and hold the licensees harmless against all judgments rendered. Although Gasoline Products had licensed thirteen refiners to use the Cross process, the licensees, owing to the suit, hesitated to install the units. By the end of 1922 only a few Cross cracking units, aggregating about 6,000 barrels a day capacity, had been built, and the royalties amounted to only $26,251. Under the circumstances the sensible and businesslike thing for Gasoline Products to do was to settle, if possible, the suit with the Jersey company and adjust its difficulties with The Texas Company. The development and profits of its business were dependent upon licensees being free from infringement. Unless it could offer the licensees freedom from suit and such improvements as would enable them to compete effectively with other refiners, the revenue of Gasoline Products would cease and its very existence be jeopardized. Officials of Gasoline Products immediately sought,

19. *Main Brief for Primary Defendants. Standard Oil Company (Indiana), Standard Oil Company (New Jersey), Texas Company, Gasoline Products Company, et al., vs. United States of America.* In the Supreme Court of the United States, October Term, 1930, 14-16, 76-77.

therefore, to adjust their differences with The Texas Company in order to have assistance in defending Jersey's suit against Pure Oil.

The Texas Company was more anxious than ever to make a settlement because on July 21, 1922, the Rogers suit was decided against The Texas Company, and a very drastic decree entered.[20] Rogers not only received a 40 per cent interest in Adams' basic patents, past, present, and future, but was awarded a 40 per cent interest in all past, present, and future profits derived from the use of the process. To make matters worse, Texas had warranted its title to the Adams patents to Standard of Indiana. The court order made Texas liable for 40 per cent of whatever profits Standard had made from the use of Adams' patents. Standard looked to The Texas Company to make good on its warranty, which the latter agreed to do. In jeopardy from all sides, The Texas Company hastened to make peace with Gasoline Products "rather than let him slip over to the enemy."

To complicate the cracking situation still further, Dr. Burton in August, 1922, sent letters to Cosden & Company, Sinclair, National Refining, Sterling Refining, the American Gasoline Company, Milliken Refining, and the Marland Refining Company notifying them of the cracking patents owned by Standard, warning them that they were infringing these patents, and offering to grant a license.[21]

Oilmen believed that the sending of these notices and the filing of infringement suits were the first steps on the part of Standard to attack every competitive cracking process and to control all cracking by heat and pressure. The general feeling was that the time had arrived for the entire oil industry, the public, and the government to give some thought toward clearing up the confusion relative to the cracking patents.[22] Only a complete showdown on the entire situation could clear the air. Some urged that the matter be investigated by the Senate Subcommittee on Manufactures headed by Senator Robert M. La Follette. This committee had been appointed in June to investigate prices of petroleum

20. *Hearings Before Martindale*, V, 3116.
21. *High Cost of Gasoline and Other Petroleum Products*, II, 1360.
22. Warren C. Platt, "Development of Valuable Art of Cracking Into Gasoline Held Back by Patent Tangle," *National Petroleum News*, September 6, 1922, 17; Paul Truesdell, "Suit to Annul All Basic Cracking Patents Would End Confusion That Retards Progress," *National Petroleum News*, September 13, 1922, 17; Warren C. Platt, "Eastern Refiners Pledge Action to End the Cracking Patent Snarl," *National Petroleum News*, September 27, 1922, 19.

products and the profits of oil companies. Others urged the United States Attorney General to bring suit to define the basic patents, give every claimant a hearing, and settle the rights of all rather than have numerous suits which might drag along for years and be terribly expensive. This approach was based on the theory that the Patent Office had granted scores of claims for patents, more or less conflicting, on the same thing.

As a result of the negotiations between The Texas Company and Gasoline Products, they signed an agreement on January 26, 1923, whereby the latter acquired an immunity for its existing and future licensees under the patents of The Texas Company. Gasoline Products agreed not to make any infringement charges against Texas on its licensees because of their use of the Holmes-Manley process.[23] The Texas Company agreed to open negotiations with Standard of Indiana and the Jersey company to acquire for Gasoline Products an immunity under the patents of those companies. If Texas failed to get assent from Standard of Indiana within sixty days, Texas was to pay Gasoline Products $250,000. As a result of the settlement, litigation between The Texas Company and Gasoline Products was avoided. Gasoline Products secured for itself and its licensees an immunity from attack by The Texas Company. On the other hand, The Texas Company secured a share in the royalties of Gasoline Products, removed the threat of any infringement suit, and made an alliance against a common enemy, the Standard of New Jersey.

The Burton process was not under any threat from Gasoline Products, but it was obvious that the process would soon be displaced even in Standard's operation by either the Holmes-Manley or Cross processes. Thus, Standard of Indiana had an urgent need for immunities under the patents of Gasoline Products. Hence, it agreed in March, 1923, to an immunity for Gasoline Products and its licensees in return for the use of the Cross process. Shortly thereafter, Gasoline Products improved the Cross process by embodying the inventions of The Texas Company and Standard, and the Cross stills were more than twice as profitable to operate as the original stills. By the end of 1923 twenty-two refineries with forty-six Cross stills had been licensed. The Texas-Gasoline Products agreement put Standard of Indiana in a strong strategical position with reference to a long list of patents. It also brought into the "Patent Club" one of Standard's strongest competitors.

23. *Main Brief for Primary Defendants*, 16, 79.

Furthermore, it placed all three parties in a strong position to settle the questions at issue with the Standard of New Jersey.

Simultaneously with the negotiations between Gasoline Products and The Texas Company, the latter negotiated with the Jersey company during the spring and summer for rights under the Ellis patents and for Jersey's 40 per cent interest in Adams' patents and profits. In the negotiations Jersey occupied a very strong position. It had a license under all of the patents of Standard of Indiana, present and future, which it could employ as it saw fit, provided the royalties were paid at the Burton rate. It had acquired a like privilege under all the Texas patents. On the other hand, there were certain vulnerable spots in Jersey's position.[24] Proceedings were then under way in the Patent Office looking to an interference involving The Texas Company, Gasoline Products, and the Jersey company, the outcome of which might result in a patent to Gasoline Products which would completely dominate and result in an injunction, unless there was a settlement, against Jersey and Texas. Furthermore, Standard of Indiana was insisting that Jersey ought to pay royalties on the use of the Tube and Tank process because it contained inventions of Burton, Palmer, and Clark. Jersey was also infringing upon a product patent of Standard of Indiana. There was a possibility, too, of a reversal of the Rogers decree on appeal. Jersey had early recognized the commercial possibility of high antiknock motor fuel and had started on a definite program for developing such a fuel. However, W. A. Hall's patents, dominating the making of such fuel by pyrogenic cracking, had been acquired by The Texas Company, and the field was fairly well blocked for Jersey. The Jersey company was, therefore, anxious to secure freedom to develop better antiknock fuel.

With the business of each of the four companies in jeopardy for one reason or another and injunctions, damages, and a loss of business possibilities, the representatives of the four companies started negotiations in the spring of 1923 which resulted in the outline of a fair and equitable agreement on all points in dispute. In agreeing to the settlement, Standard of Indiana was not only interested in being protected against infringement suits, but in the benefit it might derive from the Jersey company's research on cracking. In June, 1923, the Appellate Division of the Supreme

24. *Ibid.*, 80-81.

Court of New York affirmed the Rogers decree, which immeasurably strengthened Jersey's position and weakened the position of all the others. Since the negotiations had reached a point where the proposed contract had been reduced to writing and assurances given by all that they were willing to complete the contract along the lines outlined, Jersey felt obliged to go ahead with the settlement.

Under the agreements made in September and October, 1923, Standard of New Jersey assigned to Texas its interests in Adams' patents and obtained for itself and its subsidiary, Standard of Louisiana, the right to use the Burton process at a reduced royalty rate until 1931, after which time no royalty was to be paid.[25] The Jersey company licensed Standard of Indiana and Texas under its Tube and Tank patents and authorized them to grant sublicenses in the use of their own patents. Jersey received a license and the right to sublicenses under the patent rights of Standard of Indiana, Texas, and Gasoline Products in order to protect itself and licensees in the use of its Tube and Tank process. The Texas Company was not required to pay any royalty for using the Holmes-Manley process nor was Jersey for its use of the Tube and Tank process. However, Jersey was to pay Standard of Indiana one-half of its royalties, or 5 cents a barrel, from licensees using the Tube and Tank process, and Gasoline Products was to pay Texas a part of its Cross royalties from licensees. If Standard of Indiana and Texas desired to use the Tube and Tank process, Jersey was to receive 5 cents a barrel on all charging stock. If Jersey used the Holmes-Manley process, Texas and Standard of Indiana were to receive 8.4 cents per barrel. The settlement provided for Jersey's licensing Gasoline Products and its licensees to use the Tube and Tank process and for Gasoline Products' licensing Jersey and its licensees to use the Cross process royalty-free in each case. This was done in fulfillment of Texas' obligation to Gasoline Products. Mutual releases for past infringements were exchanged by the four parties. Following the negotiation of the settlement, Jersey's suit against Pure Oil was dismissed.

As a result of the settlement, Standard of New Jersey became a member of the "Patent Club." The four companies were relieved from the danger of costly and tedious litigation, the possibility of paying heavy damages, and some, if not all, might have

25. *Ibid.*, 87-88.

lost substantial rights and a large investment in plants. Each was now free to use its own cracking process and offer it to the industry without fear of infringement. There was no increase in royalty rates to users, even though many more patents and many improved processes were made available. Furthermore, the threat of a possible interruption in the gasoline supply had been removed.

Although the various agreements had been made at different times and for different reasons in order to settle a real conflict of interests over cracking patents, many in the industry felt that the "Patent Club" had been deliberately formed as a part of a plan to put the fear of God into the hearts of the owners and licensees or prospective licensees of other cracking processes. Members of the "Patent Club" controlled all of the important successful commercial cracking processes in use, except the Dubbs, Jenkins, and Fleming. Everything else was so well covered by patents and applications covering so many types and phases of equipment and processes that it was hard to imagine any process operating with heat and pressure that could not be attacked from some angle.

In its report on the *High Cost of Gasoline and Other Petroleum Products,* submitted to the United States Senate in March, 1923, the Subcommittee of the Committee on Manufactures, better known as the La Follette Committee, among other things, recommended that the Department of Justice should immediately institute a thorough investigation into all claims for basic patents on pressure-still processes used in the production of gasoline. "There is no doubt," the report declared, "that as a result of these patents, now largely controlled by Standard Oil Companies, the production of gasoline is greatly limited.   If any such patents were obtained by misrepresentation, or unlawfully, or improperly, or are being used through baseless threats of suit or otherwise to limit the production of gasoline, suits should be instituted by the Government to declare such patents void and thus permit the process now claimed by such patents to be covered by such patents to be thrown open to general use."

After a long and exhaustive study of the cracking patent situation, the United States Attorney General, Harlan F. Stone, in his first important act, filed a civil suit on June 25, 1924, in the Federal District Court for the Northern District of Illinois against the members of the "Patent Club"—Standard of Indiana, The Texas Company, Standard of New Jersey, Gasoline Products Company —and forty-six other oil companies for violating the Sherman

Anti-Trust Act.[26] The four companies owning patents covering the cracking processes were named primary defendants, while their licensees were named secondary defendants. The government charged an illegal combination to create a monopoly and restrain interstate commerce in the production and sale of cracked gasoline. Control over the supply of cracked gasoline, it asserted, had been achieved by means of seventy-nine contracts relating to seventy-seven patents on the art of cracking. The principal targets, however, were the three main contracts negotiated by the primary defendants. The government asked the court to do away with certain clauses in the contracts, particularly those of Standard of Indiana restricting the production of cracked gasoline, imposing higher royalty rates as more gasoline was made, and limiting the territory in which cracked gasoline could be sold. No damages were asked, although the petition sought such general relief as the nature of the case might require and the court deemed just. The fact that the suit had been filed in a presidential election year, at a time when the Democratic National Convention was in session, and when Senator La Follette was in the act of launching his own presidential campaign, led many to question the government's motive in filing the suit.

The announcement of the government's sensational action by the daily newspapers and magazines without any accompanying statement by the defendants led the general public to believe that the oil business had been "caught with the goods." Commenting upon this angle, *The Oil and Gas Journal* declared: "It is already indicted and convicted and only awaiting sentence at Chicago in the minds of a large bulk of the people." [27] In almost every legislature and political convention the oil industry was violently denounced. Politicians used the action to further their own ends and increase public prejudice against the petroleum industry. Scarcely a voice was raised in its behalf. Emphasis was given in the publicity to the huge royalty payments. No thought or consideration was given to what cracking had meant to motorists and the general public. Publicity for the oil industry could have shown that, instead of restraining the supply of gasoline and gouging the public, the cracking process had greatly increased the available supply, avoided a shortage, conserved oil reserves, and saved mo-

---

26. *Chicago Journal of Commerce*, June 26, 1924; Warren C. Platt, "Suit Is Step Toward Clearing Patent Situation," *National Petroleum News*, July 2, 1924, 27.
27. "A Lost Opportunity," *The Oil and Gas Journal*, July 10, 1924, 34.

torists hundreds of millions of dollars per year. Colonel Robert W. Stewart, Chairman of the Board of Standard of Indiana, issued a statement welcoming the investigation, defending his company's contracts, and offering to present every contract to the court for adjudication as to their propriety and equity.[28] The Universal Oil Products Company ran full-page advertisements in *The Oil and Gas Journal* and other trade magazines in July with just one sentence: "The license contracts of the Universal Oil Products Company for the use of the Dubbs Cracking Process are *in promotion of trade* and *not in restraint of trade,* especially for the independent refiner."

All defendant companies filed answers to the suit before December 1, 1924, denying the government's allegations, but very little appeared in the newspapers about their replies, except in the case of Standard of Indiana. A twelve-hundred-word résumé of Standard's answer, devoid of as much legal phraseology and as many technical terms as possible, was prepared in advance. On the day Standard filed its answer, copies of the résumé were sent to the press and trade papers with the result that Standard's position finally received widespread publicity.[29]

At a conference in Washington, D.C., on July 10, 1924, between Attorney General Stone and a committee representing the National Association of States Attorneys General, Stone offered to place in the hands of the states the results of the federal investigation on cracking should any of them desire to institute proceedings for violations of their state antitrust laws.

Immediately upon returning from Washington, Jesse W. Barrett, attorney general of Missouri, who had a reputation as a "trust buster" and who had secured more convictions than any of his predecessors, not excepting Herbert S. Hadley, declared war upon the "Gasoline Trust." He demanded an immediate price cut by Standard of Indiana and other oil companies operating in Missouri. Barrett likened the price structure in Missouri to a gigantic circus tent with Standard representing the tent poles holding up the canvas. His idea was to take out the poles and see if the tent would stay up without them. Failing to secure a reduction in prices, Barrett, acting under the Missouri Supreme Court order of June 28, 1913, which had suspended the ouster of Standard of Indiana from the state, filed a motion in July before the Mis-

28. *Chicago Journal of Commerce,* June 26, 1924.
29. *The Oil and Gas Journal,* April 23, 1925, 126.

souri Supreme Court to investigate Standard. The motion charged Standard with discrimination in prices, allowing secret rebates for the purpose of destroying competition, and combining with other companies in maintaining the price of gasoline and restricting its sale. The court appointed DeWitt C. Chastain of Butler, Missouri, special commissioner to take testimony to determine whether or not the company had been observing its order of 1913. Several Standard officials were subpoenaed as well as various company records, including the contracts relating to the licensing of the cracking process.

The hearings began at Jefferson City on August 11th and were attended by a score or more of independent oil dealers and a large number of Standard officials—Dr. W. M. Burton, John D. Clark, L. L. Stephens, Edgar Bogardus, George M. Cook, H. A. Lewis, T. B. Clifford, H. C. Griffen, and C. H. Wagner.[30] The most important part of the hearing came on August 20th when twenty-six contracts which Standard had negotiated with other companies in licensing the Burton process were introduced.[31] This was the first time that all of the licensing arrangements had been made public, and the terms of the contracts aroused great public interest. Six of the older contracts contained a clause prohibiting the licensee from selling cracked gasoline made by the Burton process within the marketing territory of Standard of Indiana, which included the State of Missouri. By his questioning of John D. Clark and Dr. Burton, Barrett brought out the pertinent facts relative to the licensing agreements and the "Patent Club." He tried to secure from Clark and Burton an admission that the restrictive clauses had been instrumental in keeping large quantities of gasoline out of Missouri and had tended to hold up prices to the public. Both men testified, however, that those clauses were "dead letters," that they had never been enforced, and that no attempt had ever been made to enforce them.

At the request of Standard, another hearing was scheduled for September 10th in order that Colonel Robert W. Stewart, Chairman of the Board, might testify. At that time Stewart made an able defense of the company's position.[32] He declared that the company had always been conscious of the fact that it had been

30. "Missouri Investigates Gasoline Prices," *The Oil and Gas Journal*, August 14, 1924, 23, 142.
31. *Chicago Journal of Commerce*, August 22, 1924.
32. "Colonel Stewart Answers Missouri Suit," *Stanolind Record*, VI, No. 2 (December, 1924), 1-7.

permitted to remain in business in Missouri since 1913 on the condition that it observe the state antitrust law. It had endeavored to make its trade practices clean, defensible, public, and open. The greatest effort had been made to observe every law of the state in both the letter and the spirit. In any investigation, it had never denied to any board, officer, or public official having authority access to its books, papers, and records for examination purposes. Stewart now offered the State of Missouri this privilege to prove that his statements were true.

In defense of the company Stewart gave a comprehensive view of its operations not only in Missouri but over its entire marketing area. He pointed out that in 1913 the company operated sixty sales stations in Missouri. In 1924 there were 316 bulk stations and 289 service stations. In 1913 Standard had more than 75 per cent of the business in its territory, in 1924 only about 30 per cent. In Missouri it did no more than 45 per cent. In 1913 the company employed only 149 people; in 1924, 1,614. The Sugar Creek refinery, the only substantial refinery in Missouri, had a capacity of about 5,000 barrels in 1913 and employed 250 men. In 1924 it had a capacity of 13,000 barrels and employed 626 men. In 1924 Standard used about 70,000 barrels of crude oil per day at Sugar Creek, Whiting, and Wood River but produced only about 3,000 barrels of crude. The balance was purchased in the open market in competition with other refiners. In 1913 Standard was paying about 95 cents per barrel for crude. In 1924 it paid an average of $1.66, this being the field price at the wells. The average tank-wagon price charged by Standard in 1913 was 14.8 cents; in 1924, with much higher crude costs, 17.2 cents. Hence, there had been no profiteering by Standard in Missouri during the period of the suspension of the writ of ouster. The annual payroll of the company in Missouri amounted to $5,150,000 a year. In addition, the company spent from $1,500,000 to $2,000,000 annually in increasing its sales and in building new bulk and service stations. Moreover, the operation of the refinery at Wood River, Illinois, where the payroll was several millions per year, had contributed to the prosperity of the St. Louis district.

Owing to the fact that the Missouri Supreme Court in 1913 was concerned over whether his company had actually severed relations with other Standard companies, Colonel Stewart emphasized the fact that the company was independent, with no man or associated group owning enough stock to give them a dominating voice.

The company had 4,600 stockholders in 1918; 49,000 in 1924, of which twenty-five hundred were from Missouri. No stockholder held more than 5¼ per cent of the stock.

Regarding the licensing agreements, Stewart pointed out that the contracts had been prepared by eminent counsel, who had assured the company that they were legal, valid, and not contrary to the law of any state. For more than ten years they had gone unchallenged by public officials until the recent suit instituted by the United States Attorney General, who questioned the legality of only certain parts of the contracts, the provisions of which never had been enforced.

According to Stewart, Standard was far from being a monopoly. Since it had no crude supply of its own, the company had to compete with others in the open market for practically all of its crude. In refining Standard was outranked more than ten to one by its competitors; 260 competing refineries had an aggregate capacity of approximately 800,000 barrels of crude per day while Standard's capacity amounted to 70,000 barrels. Its service stations in Missouri competed with 728 service stations and 546 bulk stations owned by competitors.

After Stewart had made his statement, Standard officials tried to avoid suit by offering to revise the contracts and eliminate the restrictive clauses. Barrett insisted, however, that Standard admit the illegality of its contracts, which it refused to do. They had been drafted after careful consideration by company lawyers, who believed that the company was within its rights.

On September 11th, Barrett filed a motion with the Missouri Supreme Court to vacate its order of June 28, 1913, and oust Standard from Missouri.[33] The action was based solely upon the restrictive clauses in Standard's licensing agreements. They were, according to Barrett, *prima facie* evidence that it had tried to limit competition in Missouri. Barrett contended that Standard had a right to restrain others from using the Burton process, and it might sell an undivided interest in the patent or license its use in a given territory but, having sold an interest or licensed its use, Standard could not restrict the sale either as to price or territory.

Standard denied all of the allegations and, in defense of its posi-

33. *Motion To Vacate Order Suspending Writ of Ouster. State of Missouri on the information of Herbert S. Hadley, Attorney-General, Informant, v. Standard Oil Company (Indiana), Waters-Pierce Oil Company and Republic Oil Company, Corporations, Respondents.* In the Supreme Court of Missouri, En Banc, April Term, 1924.

tion, cited much of the material already presented by Colonel Stewart.[34] In addition, its reply pointed out that through the Burton licensing agreements other oil companies had been aided, their trade opportunities had been enlarged, and the public good served. From time to time the licensing policy had been liberalized and extended. Instead of restraining trade, the licensing agreements had increased and promoted competition by increasing the supply of gasoline and making methods of production more efficient and economical. Although the contracts prohibited the sale of cracked gasoline in Missouri by licensees, it was pointed out that the White Eagle Oil & Refining Company, the Lion Oil & Refining Company, and The Texas Company, licensees of the Burton process and competitors of Standard, were selling cracked gasoline regularly in Missouri.

Attorney General Barrett's term expired in January, 1925, and he was succeeded by Robert W. Otto, who freely admitted that the suit against Standard was a "white elephant." There was little evidence aside from the licensing contracts which, Standard admitted, contained territorial restrictions that had never been enforced. The elevation of Otto to the Missouri Supreme Court bench relieved him from taking any further action.

North T. Gentry, Otto's successor, inherited the case. If the charges against the company were sustained, the court had no choice except to oust Standard. Under the circumstances, Gentry felt that the court would be reluctant to find the company guilty, so he moved on December 12, 1925, to dismiss the case, which was done.[35] At the same time Gentry started *quo warranto* proceedings against Standard of Indiana, The Texas Company, Standard of Kentucky, and White Eagle on virtually the same charges as listed in the original suit. The attorney general asked that all be ousted from doing business in the state and their property confiscated or, in lieu thereof, a fine imposed. In filing this suit, Gentry evidently believed that it would be wiser and more popular just to squeeze a good fine out of the defendants, which would not have been possible in the original suit, rather than oust them. Everyone was puzzled over why the list of defendants had been increased and especially why Standard of Kentucky had been included, for it had no license to do business in Missouri.

34. "S. O. Indiana Declares Burton Licenses Open Field To Competitors," *National Petroleum News*, XVI, No. 42 (October 15, 1924), 79.

35. "Withdraw Ouster Case; New Suit Filed," *The Oil and Gas Journal*, December 17, 1925, 23.

For months the defendant companies were prepared to submit evidence to the special commissioner appointed to hear the case, but the suit dragged along through 1926 and 1927 without any action being taken. Although the delay was attributed to lack of funds for prosecuting the case, the attorney general's office was frankly pessimistic over the outcome if it came to trial, on account of the lack of evidence. Finally, Attorney General Gentry presented a motion for the dismissal of the suit, which was granted on July 11, 1927. Outside of the widespread publicity, the long-winded statements denouncing "price hikes," flamboyant charges of combinations, price fixing, and division of markets, nothing had been accomplished by the suit.

In the meantime, after months of legal skirmishing, the United States government prepared to get under way with its suit against the "Patent Club." The Attorney General under Paragraph I of the Expediting Act of the Sherman Act, as amended, filed a certificate of general public importance on February 24, 1925, and the case was assigned for hearing before Judges Evan A. Evans, George T. Page, and Albert B. Anderson of the United States Circuit Court of Appeals in Chicago. Inasmuch as it appeared that months would be required to take evidence and the business of the court would not permit the withdrawal of three judges for so long a period, the court appointed Charles Martindale of Indianapolis as special master in chancery to take evidence and report his findings.

The taking of testimony began on October 12, 1925, in New York.[36] In regard to the patents, the government offered exhaustive expert technical testimony by Professor Ralph H. McKee, Professor of Chemical Engineering at Columbia University, to impeach their validity and scope on the ground that the cracking process had been known for at least sixty years, and the original patents covering these inventions had long since expired. In other words, the government contended that there was no basic cracking patent. The defendants' patents merely related to unimportant or minor improvements on the cracking process.

On the second contention, regarding the huge profits derived from royalties, the government introduced extensive testimony and records to show that the profits derived from royalties constituted an unreasonable reward, which resulted in increasing manufacturing costs and adversely affected the price of gasoline. More

36. *Hearings Before Martindale.*

than $30,000,000 had been paid in royalties to members of the "Patent Club" in the eleven years from 1914 to 1924 inclusive. Of this, $26,868,407.88 had been collected by Standard of Indiana, $2,858,148.67 by The Texas Company (1921–24), $519,861.49 by Standard of New Jersey (1922–24), and $528,271.28 by Gasoline Products (1921–24).

On the third issue, the government endeavored to show that these patents for minor or unimportant improvements in the cracking process had been pooled by the three principal agreements to accomplish a restriction, which no one company alone could have achieved. The procuring and treating of these patents as valid had been brought about by a desire to lend the color of legality to the combination, conspiracy, and monopoly. No one, according to the government, could practice the commercial processes of the primary defendants without running afoul of the patents on indispensable features embodied in them. The government considered the agreements as if they were made about the same time and under the same circumstances. They were claimed to constitute a series of interrelated or causally connected agreements to form a "system of contracts" entered into with the full knowledge of a plan and of other agreements made or to be made. As a result, the defendants were able to restrain trade and commerce, secure huge royalties by means of restrictive clauses in the licensing agreements and, in effect, fix arbitrarily the price of gasoline and kerosene. The government contended that numerous onerous and oppressive restrictions in these agreements went beyond what was necessary to protect legitimate rights and enabled Standard of Indiana especially to have a virtual monopoly in its marketing territory.

Under the skillful questioning of Russell Wiles, Robert E. Wilson, expert technical witness for the defense, presented the defendants' side of the case beginning October 12th and continuing until the 19th. In clear and simple language, which amounted to a comprehensive lecture on cracking, Wilson discussed the background of the refining process, the evolution of the Burton process, the development and different characteristics of the Holmes-Manley, Cross, Tube and Tank processes, and the patents by Burton and others which constituted real inventions and valid patents, not mere adaptations of old processes and apparatus in the art of cracking. Whenever a knotty problem arose that puzzled the master, Wilson took a piece of chalk and illustrated the point on a blackboard.

Lacking any scientific training in organic chemistry, the special master made an earnest effort to understand the experts, appraise their apparent knowledge or want of it, and their fairness in interpreting the description of the apparatus, process, or product and the theory of the inventor. Without intending any disparagement of the learning of Dr. McKee, the government's expert witness, the master indicated that in his effort to show want of novelty, McKee's interpretation of the prior art disclosure was quite beyond any reasonable construction of the description. On the other hand, the master stated that he was so impressed with the candor, fairness, and superior practical knowledge and experience of Wilson in dealing with all of the prior art references that, where there was irreconcilable conflict, he adopted the testimony of Wilson as much more reasonable and accurate.[37]

W. C. Teagle, President, and Frank A. Howard, Manager, Development Department, Standard Oil Company (New Jersey), R. C. Holmes, President of The Texas Company, Colonel Robert W. Stewart, Chairman of the Board of Standard of Indiana, Frederick Osborn, President of Gasoline Products, Joseph H. Adams, and others testified for the defense on other aspects of the case. The collective testimony of these witnesses served as an exhaustive textbook on the development of the art of cracking and the reasons for the various contracts.

The defense contended that the suit was based upon a complete misunderstanding by the government of the effects and results of the licensing contracts. Every patent granted by the United States was legally a monopoly for seventeen years and a lawful burden upon commerce. Every patent owner had the right to use his patent exclusively or license it upon whatever terms might be imposed. If Standard had refused to license the Burton process, there would have been a vast shortage of gasoline from 1913 to 1921. In order to avert such a shortage, Standard licensed every refiner who desired to use the process, charging not over 25 cents of each dollar net profit for the use of the process, and imposed no conditions that were unreasonable. Standard contended that every contract complained of, in place of restraining trade, gave the parties greater freedom in making and selling gasoline and tended gradually to break down the patent monopoly granted by

37. *Martindale's Report*, 145-146.

the government. As a result of patent conflicts arising among the primary defendants, the problem was solved by the companies' agreeing not to sue one another and permitting each other to use and license others to use its process without fear of litigation. The companies were entitled to the commendation of the public, the defendants contended, rather than criticism and assault in the courts.

The three main agreements had been made in good faith and without any ulterior purpose in order to prevent confusion and to avoid long-drawn-out litigation and expense. They also gave much more freedom and protection to all licensees at no greater cost. There had been no concealment of the facts, for both the Department of Justice and the La Follette Senate Committee had been apprised of all the facts. The defendants denied that the agreements had been made as the result of any plan or conspiracy but entered into from time to time to settle very real conflicts of interest. They contended that the validity of each agreement must be considered separately, and its legality determined without regard to its effect upon any of the other defendants.

Even if the paying of royalties added to the cost of manufacturing and the price of gasoline, the defendants contended that the cost would have been far greater if licensees had developed their own process, designed, and constructed their own apparatus. Under the licensing agreements, a licensee not only secured the privilege of using the process but received expert guidance in its installation and operation. The fact that the licensees continued to adhere to their contracts and had not made any complaints of excessive royalties was the best evidence that they profited by using the license and had not found the royalty onerous.

To support the government's case, testimony was offered to show that two patents secured by Joseph H. Adams and subsequently assigned to The Texas Company had been obtained through the filing of false affidavits. The government also sought to show that The M. W. Kellogg Company had conspired with the primary defendants to injure competitors who were engaged in licensing the Fleming process.

More than three years after the filing of the suit, the hearings came to a close in December, 1926. The evidence and testimony, including 655 exhibits, filled ten stout volumes with more than 4,300 pages. From an examination of all the evidence, the special master on December 1, 1927, recommended that the government's petition should be dismissed.[38] He found that the patents of each defendant were of great utility. Excepting not more than five or six, they were not for minor improvements but for substantial, valuable, and highly useful improvements which had made possible the manufacture of gasoline in commercial quantities, increased the yield of gasoline from a barrel of crude, and enabled the supply to meet the demand. They were not the same processes as those known and employed long prior to the application for those patents but useful, new, and patentable inventions. They had been processed in a regular and lawful manner and acquired in good faith for the laudable purpose of producing gasoline at a critical time.

As for the government's charge that the primary defendants sought "to realize huge profits by extorting from all concerns engaged in the manufacture of cracked gasoline large sums in the guise of royalties," the master reported that the evidence "wholly fails to support these charges." The royalties and conditions imposed by the licensing contracts were reasonably within the reward which the respective patentees were entitled to secure.

The master found that none of the defendants had monopolized or attempted to monopolize or combined or conspired with any person or persons to monopolize any part of the trade or commerce among the several states or with foreign nations. In support of this finding, the master pointed out that there were in 1924 and 1925 in the United States a very large number of refiners manufacturing cracked gasoline in competition with the primary defendants and not under license from them. None of the defendants in the suit manufactured or controlled as much as 30 per cent of the total annual production of cracked gasoline in the United States. The aggregate cracking capacity of all the defendants was about 55 per cent. Competition between each and all was actual and genuine, and marketing rivalry keen. The rivalry of the so-called "independents," users of twenty-one competitive cracking processes, was of such volume and the competition so extensive that the defendants had no control over the supply or the market price. There was no evidence of the defendants' attempting to suppress competition, control the supply, fix prices, or allocate marketing territory. The diversity of interests of the several defendants was such as to make any such effort—were they inclined to so do—impractical. The evidence showed that the re-

38. *Ibid.,* 351-384.

lationship of the volume of sales of Standard of Indiana to total sales in its retail territory had been constantly decreasing in percentage by reason of shipment of gasoline into its territory by its own licensees as well as by the manufacturers of cracked gasoline under processes not owned by the primary defendants.

The master found that the various agreements made by the primary defendants over conflicting patents, which was the keystone of the government's case, were "beneficial to the public in that it removed the threat of interruption of the supply of gasoline and the consequent increase in price, and offered the prospect of a wider use of the cracking processes with a consequently larger supply, and probable reduction of prices, which, since the close of the testimony in this case, as a matter of current public history, has become a realization."

Regarding the Adams patents, the master found that the government had failed to prove that they were obtained by fraudulent and deceptive affidavits and statements. Moreover, he found that The M. W. Kellogg Company had not conspired with the primary defendants to suppress the Fleming process.

The special master's report was a sweeping victory for the defendants in their three-year fight against the government's charges of conspiracy to restrain and monopolize trade and fix prices. The fight, however, was not ended. It was only the first round, for the government filed a motion to recommit the report together with 273 exceptions and appealed.

While the case was on appeal, Standard of Indiana, The Texas Company, and The M. W. Kellogg Company contracted for the purchase of the Gasoline Products Company.[39] In 1924 Kellogg had contracted with Gasoline Products to take over the licensing of the Cross process. At the same time, Kellogg secured an option on a part of the stock, which it subsequently exercised. In 1928 Texas obtained through Kellogg an option on all the stock and assets of the company. Standard and Texas had come to the conclusion that the business prospects of Gasoline Products were sufficiently good to constitute an attractive investment. Consequently, they formed the Gasoline Products Company of Delaware, which took over the assets of the old company.

On June 11, 1929, in an opinion written by Judge Evans, the United States District Court for the Northern District of Illinois, by a two-to-one decision, sustained the government and reversed

39. Company Encyclopedia: Manufacturing—Cracking, 9.

the master in the "Patent Club" case.[40] Although the court found that none of the patents was basic and that they covered only improvements, it was unwilling to disturb the master's finding that they were valid. Even though the court refused to recognize the patents as basic, it did not follow that the inventors had not made a real contribution to the art. Regarding the validity of the various agreements pooling the patents, the court declared that the ownership of a patent unquestionably carried with it certain rights monopolistic in character, but its use was subject to the same antimonopoly tests as other property rights. The defendants might license the use of their patents, but two competing companies could not enter into agreements the effect of which was to extend the monopoly beyond the limitation of the patent. The court took the position that the licensing agreements transcended what was necessary to protect patents, and that they were outside the limits of lawful monopolies which arose from the issuance of the patents. In answering the defendants' contention that the agreements were made in good faith in order to avoid litigation, the court did not question the argument but held, much to the amazement of the well-informed, that the principal patents could be practiced without infringing upon one another.

In sustaining the government's contention that these agreements restrained commerce and trade, created a monopoly, and violated the law, the court directed its attack at several provisions in the agreement between Standard of Indiana and The Texas Company. In requiring licensees to acknowledge in advance the validity of all present and future patents and all inventions acquired as late as January 1, 1937, the court held that the primary defendants were attempting to fasten upon the public burdens which it was not the purpose of the patent law to impose. Such agreements violated the letter and spirit of the patent law and were contrary to public policy. Section 13, requiring The Texas Company to sell Standard of Indiana a portion of its cracked gasoline under certain conditions, was also declared a violation of the Sherman Anti-Trust Act. The court attacked especially those sections in the agreements relating to the fixing of royalties and their division. Under these, the primary defendants not only fixed royalties as between themselves but for the sublicensees as well and provided for a division of the royalties among themselves. This was in effect a method of fixing prices of cracked gasoline and resulted in

40. 33 F. (2d) 617.

monopoly. In fact, the court believed the evidence justified find-ing that such royalties nearly equaled and sometimes exceeded the profits of outside refiners.

For these reasons the three-judge court, with Judge Anderson dissenting, found the seventy-nine cross-licensing and sublicensing agreements null and void. The court upheld the master's finding that the Adams patents had not been obtained by fraud, and that The M. W. Kellogg Company had not conspired with the primary defendants against the Fleming process.

The defendants appealed the decision to the United States Supreme Court. In its appeal, Standard of Indiana contended that the Circuit Court's decision was so vague and ambiguous that the defendants did not know what was or what was not forbidden. The decision had created a chaotic condition. It made uncertain the rights of the primary defendants and deprived the secondary defendants of immunity granted to them and for which they had paid. It opened the way for innumerable suits for patent infringe-ment. It made for war, not peace, and for free development it substituted a condition little short of absolute paralysis. The con-tinuation of the agreements in some form not in violation of the antitrust laws was essential to an adequate production of gasoline. Counsel for the companies joined in urging the high court, be-cause of the public interest in the outcome, to expedite its decision.

The United States Supreme Court in a unanimous decision delivered by Justice Brandeis on April 13, 1931, reversed the Fed-eral District Court, upheld the special master, and dismissed the bill against the defendant companies.[41] The long, hard fight, ex-tending over almost seven years, had finally ended in victory for the defendants, who had been subjected to much undeserved criticism for nearly a decade.

There was still one dark and threatening cloud on the horizon for Standard of Indiana, and that was Universal's suit claiming that the Burton patent infringed its Dubbs patent.

41. 283 U. S. 163.

CHAPTER XI

The Country's Largest Gasoline Marketer

WITH A MARKETING TERRITORY CONTAINING MORE THAN ONE-THIRD of the population of the United States, more than 50 per cent of the motor vehicles registered in the country, and more than 50 per cent of the tractors, Standard of Indiana had the greatest potential market in the world for petroleum products during the 1920's. Under the vigorous leadership of Colonel Stewart, Standard proceeded to capitalize upon the extraordinary demand of this rich market. The Sales Department embarked upon the greatest program of building bulk and service stations ever seen. Starting with 2,845 bulk plants and 451 company-owned and operated service stations in 1918, the Sales Department literally peppered the vast plains region with new distributing facilities. Service stations sprang up everywhere. Standard's service stations were neither large nor costly, and none had rest rooms. Most of them were of a uniform design—the Joliet type—with the ground about the building neatly seeded and a few shrubs planted. Everything was in a first-class condition. There were no lubrication facilities, except for an outside oil drain pit. Owing to the relatively low mileage and speed traveled, only infrequent greasing of cars was necessary. Moreover, in the early 1920's Ford was the only large producer of cars, and since Fords were equipped with grease cups, an owner could do his own greasing. All he needed to do was to give the grease cups a turn or two and refill them when empty. Otherwise, greasing was done by automobile dealers and repair shops.

In the early 1920's the Alemite Corporation developed a method for lubricating the chassis which replaced grease cups on cars and forced grease into the bearings by means of a special fitting.[1] It meant faster and more complete lubrication, smoother operation, and longer life for the chassis bearings. Alemite tried to get various oil companies to develop chassis lubricants to use in its fittings

1. Company Encyclopedia: Marketing, I, Methods of Distribution, Through Service Stations, 69-72.

but they, including Standard of Indiana, believing that their cup grease was satisfactory, were reluctant to change their products. Alemite finally succeeded in getting a manufacturer to make a suitable grease for its fittings with the result that Alemite went into the grease business on a large scale and sold to garages and automobile dealers. As Alemite became popular, greasing racks sprang into existence on vacant lots, especially in the cities. Standard's Polarine Cup Grease had been in use since before 1910, but as automobile chassis lubrication became more important, the company increased its Polarine grease line in 1927 by adding special chassis lubricants ranging from fluid lubricants to hard greases. However, Alemite's big start early in the 1920's gave it a prestige in the market that was difficult to overcome.

The Sinclair Refining Company was one of the earliest oil companies to inaugurate lubrication service at its service stations.[2] It began by erecting on a lot near its service stations in Chicago four wooden racks with awnings over them. By the fall of 1926 Sinclair had erected three "Greasing Palaces" and was at work on seven others. These "Greasing Palaces" had pits for greasing six cars at a time. Motorists were cordially invited into the pit to watch the greasing. The "Palaces" had toilet facilities and waiting rooms for men and women where they could wait during the twenty to twenty-five minutes required to grease the chassis, clean the inside of the car and the windshield, and check the battery.

Beginning in 1927 Standard offered customers a greasing service at its service stations, but mainly at the less busy stations. Greasing was done by regular attendants in their spare time. No special equipment was provided because the work was done at outside oil drain pits. In inaugurating this service the company denied that it was planning any extensive greasing service at its stations like Sinclair's. However, in the summer of 1928 Standard had a change of heart and went into chassis lubrication on an "experimental" basis.[3] It built four greasing stations in Chicago and about twenty-four in the rest of its territory. Those in Chicago were similar to Sinclair's but less pretentious. They were built of red brick. Inside was a row of four pits where greasing was done from a working level below grade. The pits were very roomy and had two levels, the lower one for the driver to watch, if he desired, and an upper

2. W. K. Halbert, "Sinclair Opens 'Greasing Palaces' in Chicago," *National Petroleum News*, XVIII, No. 36 (September 8, 1926), 58.
3. *Ibid.*, XIX, No. 3 (January 19, 1927), 26, XX, No. 20 (July 18, 1928), 21-22.

one for the greaser. Practically all greasing was done by air pressure, which furnished air for the spring sprays and grease guns. A greasing station like this cost $10,000 to $15,000. There was no lounge room, and no car washing or other service was given. There were no gasoline pumps, for these greasing stations were not located at service stations. Each Standard service station within a mile of a greasing station had big signs indicating where a motorist might have his chassis lubricated. Some of the greasing stations outside of Chicago had lifts for raising the car. Some were housed and others were in the open.

By the late 1920's Standard service stations had evolved into stores for the sale of petroleum products instead of simply being gasoline filling stations.[4] Station operators had a quota of motor oil in packages to sell. They were expected to sell a number of fifteen-gallon drums of Polarine or Iso-Vis each month to customers for delivery to their homes. They also had a quota of Semdac, Standard's auto and furniture polish, to sell and attendants were expected to give demonstrations when business was slack. To women customers, they were expected to sell Finol, Standard's household oil for clocks, vacuum sweepers, sewing machines, phonographs, and other things. These and other products were prominently displayed at the station and the windows were full of advertising matter. Outside near the gasoline pumps was a rack that held twelve different pocket-sized booklets on various products, Standard's marketing organization, and other subjects.

Service-station attendants constituted the most important link between the public and the company. If they were friendly, courteous, and rendered efficient service, regular customers could be held and new ones acquired. If they were not, a loss of customers and business would result. It was essential, therefore, in the keen competition for business that service-station attendants be trained to give superior service. Recognizing the importance of having trained personnel, Standard started its first service-station training school in Chicago early in 1924. Out of about one thousand applicants for jobs, Standard selected ninety-five to attend the school. Of the ninety-five, almost all were high school graduates, and thirty-three were college men. Personality, education, experience, aggressiveness, courtesy, and inherent possibilities were factors considered in making the selections. Their intensive week of training included instruction in the history and organization of the

4. *Ibid.*, XIX, No. 3 (January 19, 1927), 51-52.

company, the employees' stock purchase plan, the annuity plan, the history of the petroleum industry, the quality of various Standard products, audits, inventories, reports, and methods of handling customers. Upon completing the course of training, the men were put to work among 163 service stations in the Chicago Sales Division.

To assist those who could not attend the service-station school, the company issued its first Service Station Manual about 1926. Employees were instructed to be prompt, honest, accurate, and courteous in all dealings with customers. They should keep the station clean and orderly. They should tactfully call the attention of the customer to other company products apart from gasoline. Suggestions were made as to how to remember names and faces. Employees were carefully instructed against accepting any tips. The manual emphasized service rather than sales. Many pages were devoted to operating rules and regulations, the maintenance of equipment, accounting procedure, and other matters. As a result of giving greater care to the selection of service-station attendants and greater emphasis to rendering prompt and courteous service, Standard pioneered in setting a high standard for service-station operation.

With new equipment and machinery being continually developed by industry, it was apparent that a technically trained group of men was needed in the Industrial Sales Department of the company to advise sales personnel as to product application and recommend requirements for manufacturing. Consequently, Standard's management decided in 1922 to set up a training program. Early in 1923 Dr. A. M. Kinney of Harvard University and O. G. Miller, then a "smokestack" salesman in the Detroit field, were given the opportunity to study the company's products and basic manufacturing methods at the Whiting refinery. Late in that year they were commissioned to set up a course of instruction for sales engineers. When their work was completed, the first Sales Engineering School was opened at Whiting on January 3, 1924. Lasting for four to six months, these schools were held regularly at first and then at such intervals as more trained men were needed. They supplied many men who became leaders in the Sales Department as time went on.

As its automobile lubrication service expanded, Standard began training lubrication engineers in January, 1927. Twenty-six men from its service staff in the sales field were given a week's training in Cleveland at the plant of the White Company, studying truck and bus production and the relationship of proper lubrication to the successful operation of trucks and buses. These men then returned to the sales field better prepared to advise the owners of fleets of trucks and buses on their lubrication problems.

In the East, Pan American rapidly expanded its marketing facilities. The Mexican Petroleum Corporation (Maine) was already doing retail marketing in New England, New Jersey, and New York. The 50 per cent owned American Oil Company and its subsidiary, Lord Baltimore Filling Stations, Inc., had stations scattered along the seaboard from Pennsylvania to Georgia, but they were concentrated in Baltimore and Washington. In building bulk plants and service stations on a formidable scale after 1925, Pan American joined the parade of other big companies like Sinclair, Pure, Texas, and Sun in invading the marketing territory of the Standard of New Jersey, Standard of New York, Tidewater, and Atlantic Refining, which had been in progress for two or three years. The improvement in roads, increased motor car sales, and the influx of thousands of new residents into the South, and Florida especially, created a race among oil companies to tap this expanding market.

In January, 1926, the name of the Mexican Petroleum Corporation of Louisiana, Inc., a subsidiary of Pan American which had been refining at Destrehan and marketing in Louisiana, Mississippi, and Alabama, was changed to Pan American Petroleum Corporation, sometimes called "Papco," with headquarters in New Orleans. A new trade name "Pan-Am" was adopted. Late in 1926 the company began establishing a marketing organization in Tennessee and then in Georgia and Florida. This expansion continued until 1930, when the company was rated as one of the major oil companies in the South.

In the drive to increase the company's volume of business, the introduction of new products played an important role. Solite gasoline, Ethyl gasoline, and Iso-Vis motor oil were the major products introduced. The introduction of Solite was a continuation of the old fight between Standard and its competitors over high-gravity gasoline. In attempting not only to hold but increase its business, Standard at first through large newspaper advertisements asserted that Red Crown was the best that could be made; that the claims for high-gravity gasoline were false because motor fuel efficiency depended upon boiling points. When motorists paid more for gasoline than Red Crown cost, according to the advertisements, they were wasting their money. Better gasoline than Red Crown could not be made, and paying premium prices was like paying a premium for gold dollars.

Failing to make much of any headway against high-gravity, premium gasoline, Standard finally made a radical change and introduced in October, 1922, a premium gasoline called Solite, "the perfect gasoline," in Minneapolis, St. Paul, Milwaukee, and other places, which sold for 3 cents above Red Crown.[5] To the petroleum industry, Standard's move came as a distinct surprise, for the company had always sold only one grade—Red Crown. Advertisements introducing Solite did not belittle Red Crown. The latter was still referred to as a gasoline giving "maximum power at minimum cost." However, Solite was a light gasoline with a gravity of 62°, an initial boiling point of 107°F., and an end point of 412°F. In offering it to the public, the company contended that Solite was the first high-gravity gasoline to be manufactured which its engineers considered economically sound. In the past, light gasolines had been wasteful of power, and the company had been unwilling to sell a luxuriously volatile fuel, even at a premium price, which it considered to be a sacrifice of valuable fractions of crude.

Solite was no sooner introduced than C. C. Stoll, President of the Stoll Refining Company of Louisville, Kentucky, informed Standard that his company had used the name Solite for a high grade of kerosene oil in the Middle West ever since the establishment of the company in 1896, and it valued the brand name highly. Stoll expressed the hope that Standard would discontinue using the name for its gasoline. Rather than abandon the name, Standard officials negotiated with Stoll and purchased the brand name.[6]

Solite, "Red Crown's little brother," intensified the battle for gallonage in the Northwest. The weapons consisted of harsh words hurled back and forth by Standard and its competitors through full-page newspaper advertisements in the Twin Cities, Milwaukee, and elsewhere.[7] Pure Oil hailed the "stranger" with hoarse

5. "A Perfect Gasoline," *National Petroleum News,* XIV, No. 43 (October 25, 1922), 24, 32.
6. "Challenges Use of 'Solite' Name by Standard of Indiana," *National Petroleum News,* XIV, No. 44 (November 1, 1922), 19.
7. "Solite, Red Crown's Little Brother, Gets Rocks for Birthday Cards," *National Petroleum News,* XIV, No. 50 (December 13, 1922), 59, 61-62.

hoots. It printed earlier statements made by Standard when it had but one child—"how foolish it was to pay more for premium gasoline," "a better gasoline than Red Crown can't be made," and "one grade, one quality best by test." The inconsistency of Standard's position was hammered hard. Pure emphasized straight-run gasoline as the best gasoline and condemned the artificial means employed by Standard to make its gasoline. Wadhams and Bartles-Maguire launched similar attacks. Standard rushed to the defense of the legitimacy and pedigree of both Red Crown and Solite. It took cognizance of the ugly rumors spread about cracked and casing-head gasoline and pointed out that the Burton process was approved by scientists and sought by the best refiners. Cracked gasoline was even more efficient than straight-run, and he who condemned cracking was living in the dark ages of the oil industry.

The controversy aroused by Solite was soon overshadowed by the introduction of another new product, Ethyl gasoline. Beginning about 1916, Charles F. Kettering, President of the General Motors Chemical Company, assisted by Thomas Midgley, Jr., and T. A. Boyd, started studying the tendency of automobile engines in burning ordinary gasoline to "knock" or "ping" at high-combustion pressure. When knocking took place, the power of an automobile engine was appreciably reduced and overheating resulted. Knocking also limited the progress and development of higher-compression automobile engines. Little, if anything, was known as to the causes of knocking. For years it had been ascribed to the presence of carbon in the cylinders. Midgley found, contrary to general belief, that knocking was dependent on the chemical composition of gasoline. Consequently, he began looking for a chemical compound that could be put into gasoline to overcome its inherent tendency to knock. Thousands of different compounds were tried with little success. Finally, after years of research, it was dicovered by the spring of 1922 that a mixture of tetraethyl lead with gasoline was the best to prevent knocking. Unable to interest any of the larger oil companies in the East in marketing gasoline with tetraethyl lead, or Ethyl gasoline as it was called, Midgley got the Refiners Oil Company, a jobbing company at Dayton, Ohio, to introduce Ethyl gasoline at its service stations in Ohio early in 1923.

Robert E. Wilson, assistant director of research for Standard of Indiana and a friend of Midgley's since 1917, had, through fre-

quent meetings, closely followed his research on antiknock gasoline and had suggested an approach that led to the discovery of
tetraethyl lead.[8] When Ethyl was ready for commercial use, Wilson
persuaded Midgley to come to Chicago and talk with officials of
Standard about marketing it. Midgley told Dr. Burton that he
hardly expected a large oil company to incur the expense or risk
its prestige in something that might result in failure. Burton
interrupted this line of talk to say that "Standard of Indiana was
not afraid to pioneer anything if it felt that the venture was technically sound." As a result of the conversation, Wilson was given
the assignment of determining the soundness of Ethyl gasoline and
spent several weeks exploring all aspects. Allan Jackson studied
the sales possibilities. It was found during the course of the investigation that Standard's cracked gasoline had better antiknock
qualities than straight-run gasoline and required less tetraethyl
lead to meet a given antiknock standard than the ordinary gasoline
of the day. Both Wilson and Jackson made favorable reports and
recommended that the marketing of Ethyl gasoline was something
in which their company should participate.

Foreseeing the possibilities that Ethyl held for automotive
progress, Standard's management asked Wilson and Midgley to
work out the details of a contract.[9] If Standard pioneered the marketing of Ethyl in the Middle West, it wanted exclusive distributing rights in its marketing territory. The principal argument
was over the length of time the exclusive contract should run.
Wilson wanted it for a long enough period so that the experiment
might have a complete test—at least five years.

On September 29, 1923, a group of Standard and General
Motors Chemical officials met at Standard's office in Chicago to
sign the contract. Allan Jackson, Vice-President in charge of Sales,
signed for Standard, and Charles F. Kettering, President, signed
for the General Motors Chemical Company. The contract gave
Standard exclusive rights to market Ethyl in its eleven-state territory for eighteen months. Standard was to pay 1 cent per cubic
centimeter for tetraethyl lead with the provision that not more
than three cubic centimeters per gallon should be used. Standard
had the right to extend the contract from April 1, 1925, to September 30, 1927, upon request. If the contract were extended, the

8. Robert E. Wilson, "Early Recollections of Tom and Ethyl," *Ethyl News*, Feb-
    ruary, 1928, 11-14; "Gasoline At Its Best," *Ethyl News*, January–February,
    1953, 3-5.
9. "Ethyl's First Big Customer," *Ethyl News*, September, 1948, 10-11.

company had exclusive sales rights, except that the General Motors Chemical Company might sell 5 per cent of the quantity sold to Standard to others during the first six months, 7½ per cent during the next year, and 10 per cent during the last year of the extension.

Standard of Indiana was the first major oil company to sign a contract for the marketing of Ethyl gasoline, and the arrangement worked to the mutual advantage of both companies. By distributing through Standard in the Middle West, the General Motors Chemical Company would not have to create a large sales force and carry on extensive promotional work. This was of tremendous value in the initial success of Ethyl, for the product would go on sale as soon as possible at more than 2,100 Standard service stations. For Standard, the contract meant that it would be able to market exclusively a gasoline with a higher antiknock value than any other company and increase its gasoline sales.

Once the formalities of signing the contract were over, Standard lost no time in equipping its service stations and getting Ethyl gasoline on the market. C. C. Inglefield, superintendent of service stations in Chicago, was assigned to promoting and distributing Ethyl. The problems of marketing were numerous, and Standard went through all the growing pains one experiences in marketing any new product. The first thing was to get tetraethyl lead, but the supply was limited because the compounding plant at Dayton, Ohio, had a very small capacity. To avoid the installation of additional tanks and pumps at service stations for dispensing Ethyl, Midgley devised a small metal container called an "Ethylizer" to hold and meter Ethyl fluid.[10] These were attached to the retail gasoline pumps and discharged a small quantity of Ethyl fluid into the gasoline as it was pumped into a car. The device was unsatisfactory in many respects, but it made possible the introduction of Ethyl without requiring a heavy investment in duplicate tanks and pumps. Service-station operators naturally had to be given some training in mixing Ethyl and gasoline.

The first Standard service station to dispense Ethyl gasoline was in Richmond, Indiana. Red Crown Ethyl, which sold for 3 cents above the regular grade of Red Crown, was introduced in other eastern and southern Indiana towns, and then distribution gradually spread north and west from Ohio River points during

10. C. C. Inglefield to Thomas Yates, July 12, 1948; C. C. Inglefield to Giddens, May 22, 1950.

the winter. Towns in the hilly regions received preferential treatment because the demand was greatest there. The demand was so great, in fact, that it was impossible to secure Ethyl in sufficient quantities to supply everyone.

News of the signing of the contract became public on October 12th and created considerable apprehension among the marketing competitors of Standard. Independent jobbers were fearful that General Motors would redesign several of its motors and take advantage of the greater compression made possible by Ethyl, which would make it extremely difficult for them. The *National Petroleum News* advised competitors not to be dismayed by Standard's exclusive contract for Ethyl, for they had had a long experience with Standard in selling premium gasoline.[11] Ethyl was just another premium product, and independents could continue as heretofore to sell premium gasoline as well as Standard. The only thing about the new gasoline, according to the *News,* was that it silenced the engine knock. It had no other advantages. Meeting Standard's competition in the sale of Solite had not been particularly difficult for jobbers, and Ethyl should not be any harder. The same intensive selling methods used in years past would enable them to hold their share of the business no matter what Standard did. It was pointed out that competitors could convince drivers of low-compression cars they did not need Ethyl. Regular fuel was good enough. Drivers of high-compression cars could get rid of the knock by other means than using Ethyl. So far as carbon was concerned, Ethyl did not remove that, and the cost of Ethyl was more than if you had the carbon periodically removed. The thing to stress was "Clean out the carbon."

While Midgley and Wilson were working on the marketing contract, Wilson urged that General Motors consider making Standard of Indiana a partner in the manufacture and sale of Ethyl because the company could render a special service in solving marketing and other problems. At the time, General Motors was not interested, but Midgley promised to let Wilson know if there was any change in attitude. After the passage of several months, Midgley told Wilson that General Motors was interested in a partnership with an oil company, and asked him to sound out Standard. Wilson talked with Dr. Burton, who said Standard was definitely not interested in a "sideline" of this kind.[12]

11. October 24, 1933, 15.
12. Robert E. Wilson, "Early Recollections of Tom and Ethyl," *Ethyl News,* February, 1948, 14.

About two months later, Colonel Stewart telephoned Wilson at Whiting to ask if he knew anything about the proposed partnership of General Motors and Standard of New Jersey to produce and market Ethyl. Wilson informed Stewart of his conversation with Dr. Burton, about which Stewart had not known. The Colonel immediately got Mr. Alfred P. Sloan, Jr., on the telephone. Stewart learned that a deal had just been made with Standard of New Jersey, and the only way Standard of Indiana could be included was to get Jersey to agree. Stewart hurried to New York for a conference with the Jersey officials. "Anyone who thinks that there is not competition between the Standard Oil companies," wrote Wilson, "should have sat in on that meeting." Stewart wanted either a third interest in the partnership or a quarter interest with Jersey. The Colonel was told that the deal had been agreed upon and that Jersey was not willing to reopen it. In August, 1924, it was announced that General Motors and Standard of New Jersey had formed the Ethyl Gasoline Corporation with a capitalization of $5,000,000 to take over the General Motors Chemical Company. Thus, opportunity had knocked at the door of Standard of Indiana and passed. It would now have to pay tribute to the Standard of New Jersey as the latter had been doing for the use of the Burton process.

The marketing of Ethyl gasoline was hardly under way before it became known that one man had died and four others were hospitalized due to breathing concentrated tetraethyl lead vapors in the research laboratory of the Standard of New Jersey at Elizabeth, New Jersey, which was manufacturing tetraethyl lead by a new process. As more men died and others were hospitalized, city, state, and federal officials began investigations. The Ethyl Gasoline Corporation announced on May 4, 1925, the withdrawal of the product from the market until a report could be made by a conference called at Washington by the United States Public Health Service. Standard of Indiana discontinued the sale of Ethyl fluid on May 5th.

After an exhaustive study, a committee of distinguished scientists reported to the United States Surgeon General, H. S. Cummings, that Ethyl was safe to market if certain conditions were observed. The only real danger was in handling concentrated tetraethyl lead and not ethylized gasoline. The committee recommended, and Ethyl accepted the recommendation, that Ethyl gasoline be mixed only at main distributing centers and in not less than tank-car lots. All mixing devices at service stations were to be scrapped. By virtue of these recommendations the sale of Ethyl was confined to concerns with refineries. It also meant that those who sold Ethyl would have to provide additional pumps and tanks or discontinue one of their grades of gasoline.

Standard hailed the return of Ethyl to the market with full-page newspaper advertisements in June, 1926.[13] On the day Ethyl Red Crown went on sale, cardboard signs were tied around gasoline pumps at its service stations, tacked to the walls of service stations and fences, and posted in windows with the wording: "Ethyl is back." At its service stations Standard now had three pumps: one for Red Crown at 21 cents, one for Ethyl at 24, and one for Solite at 24.

Owing to the lengthy interruption of sales and the fact that General Motors had been unable to perform certain parts of its original contract, Standard's exclusive contract was extended to March 1, 1929, and then renewed for two more years. Ethyl gasoline sales by Standard amounted to 56,321,944 gallons in 1926, 105,689,100 in 1927, 162,977,700 in 1928, 293,398,984 in 1929, and 405,556,000 in 1930.[14] Approximately one-third of Standard's gasoline sales were Ethyl. All Red Crown gasoline was ethylized to a lower antiknock standard beginning in 1933, and sales of ethylized gasoline increased from 406,580,900 gallons to 1,241,153,634 in 1940. Owing to the fact that Standard sold a relatively large amount of cracked gasoline, which had a higher antiknock value than ordinary gasoline, it was able to meet Ethyl's standard with only a little over two cubic centimeters of tetraethyl lead, which made the venture all the more profitable.

The introduction of Ethyl gasoline forced those refiners without Ethyl contracts to turn their attention toward producing high antiknock premium motor fuel. More and more turned to cracked gasoline, natural gasoline and, in some cases, benzol to produce a competitive fuel for higher-compression engines, since all automobile manufacturers were working on smaller, lighter, and higher-compression engines. In July, 1925, Gulf announced that it had perfected No-Nox, a new motor fuel offered at a premium of 3 cents over the regular grade. The Texas Company, in a spectacular publicity campaign beginning in May, 1926, introduced its "new and better gasoline" in Chicago and the West. During

13. *National Petroleum News*, XVIII, No. 24 (June 16, 1926), 22.
14. Robert E. Wilson to Giddens, May 19, 1950.

that summer Chicago was swept by a huge advertising campaign as Sinclair introduced its new H-C gasoline. To compete with Standard's Ethyl, the Roxana Petroleum Corporation began marketing a new premium antiknock motor fuel called "Super-Shell." Nearly every refiner in the country was offering at a premium during the summer of 1926 a "high test," or some kind of antiknock motor fuel.

Following the resumption of the sale of Ethyl gasoline, Standard, in keeping with a policy of constantly improving the quality of old products and adding new ones, introduced a new line of motor oil. Heralded by one of the most intensive advertising campaigns ever made, Standard introduced the new line on December 8, 1926, under the trade name Iso-Vis, meaning constant viscosity.[15] Declared to be unique and to some extent revolutionary in lubrication engineering, Iso-Vis represented the culmination of three years of intensive research in the company's automotive laboratory under the direction of Robert E. Wilson. It had been developed as a result of a study of the causes and methods of preventing the dilution of crankcase oils with the heavy ends of gasoline, especially during winter operations, which constituted an outstanding problem in the lubrication of automobile engines. Research in the automotive laboratory had shown that the most serious dilution in the average car in winter operations occurred in the first 150 to 200 miles of operation after new oil had been put into the crankcase, when it picked up about 15 per cent of the heavy ends of gasoline. The undesirable feature of this 15 per cent diluent was that it reduced the viscosity, or "body," of the oil to about a third of its original value, which was a very serious reduction. However, after this 15 per cent or so of dilution took place, it reached a sort of equilibrium, varying somewhat with operating conditions.

A long series of tests were made to determine what viscosity an oil should have in the crankcase to give satisfactory winter operation. Having found this, the next problem was to get an oil that would maintain that viscosity during winter driving. Research men took an oil which would be too heavy to give satisfactory operation in cold weather and diluted it initially so that it would maintain a relatively "constant viscosity" in cold-weather operations. This was the basic feature of Iso-Vis. It was a prediluted oil. The new line of oil was made from specially selected crudes

15. "The Story of Iso-Vis Motor Oil," *Stanolind Record*, VIII, No. 6 (April, 1927), 20.

to give a very low pour and carbon test and a good color. Made
in several grades, Iso-Vis was put on the market as a premium oil.

As a result of Standard's advertising, motorists rushed to fill
their crankcases with Iso-Vis. Within a short time, one of the
coldest winter snaps suddenly hit the Middle West. Cars filled
with Iso-Vis and left in a cold garage would not start. Scores of
users complained to dealers, garagemen, Standard service stations,
and to the General Office in Chicago.[16] Some dealers asked the
company to come and get the oil. As time passed, other brickbats
were thrown at Iso-Vis. It was charged that its consumption was
excessive over that of Polarine or some other oils. It attracted
more moisture in the crankcase than regular oil. In a long, hard
drive, when the engine was well warmed up, the light ends of
Iso-Vis boiled off too rapidly, leaving a relatively heavy oil which,
if the car stood all night in the cold, stiffened so that it could not
be started in the morning. The introduction of Iso-Vis probably
caused more discussion, debate, and speculation than any other
product that ever appeared on the oil industry's horizon, with the
possible exception of Ethyl gasoline.

Competitors were quick to capitalize upon the situation and
assist in creating prejudice against Iso-Vis. They had been irritated
at the outset because Standard got the newspapers in which it
advertised the introduction of Iso-Vis to write the oil dealers of
their community and ask them to stock Iso-Vis in order to meet
the demand. This action naturally brought a flood of protests
from competitors to the newspapers involved. After Iso-Vis was
introduced, salesmen of competitors would fill their cars with
Iso-Vis, drive around the block, and return to the station scream-
ing and demanding that the dealer drain the oil before it ruined
the car. They aided in circulating all kinds of stories, some true,
others false. One of the widely circulated stories was that Standard
paid out thousands of dollars in damages caused by Iso-Vis. This
was untrue. The company paid out less than $700 in damages, and
even in these cases Standard engineers who investigated were not
sure that the damage was the fault of Iso-Vis. Speaking of these
experiences, the Sales Department reported: "It was a major
catastrophe in the motor oil marketing experience of the Standard
Oil Company of Indiana, and it took years to overcome that set-
back. It was years before a Standard Oil salesman could walk into

16. *National Petroleum News*, XIX, No. 12 (March 23, 1927), 7, 18, 20; Company
    Encyclopedia: Marketing, I, 123.

an automobile dealer's place of business without hearing some derogatory remark about Iso-Vis." [17] With some changes in formula, however, Iso-Vis became a well-established brand.

As the number of automobiles in the Middle West grew, Standard met formidable competition from Pennsylvania premium oils. Vacuum's Mobiloil was one of the oldest Pennsylvania oils marketed, but Quaker State, Pennzoil, and Kendall came into the field strongly after 1924 when there was more money to spend and people were willing to pay a higher price. This gave the 35-cent-a-quart Pennsylvania oils an opportunity on which they were not slow to capitalize through increased sales promotion and national advertising under brand names and by the Pennsylvania Grade Crude Oil Association. Impressed by the quality claims made for these oils, motorists demanded these products. Quaker State motor oil especially became a serious competitive problem for Standard. It was not uncommon for motorists to buy gasoline at Standard's station and drive around the block to another station to get Quaker State or some other Pennsylvania oil. No small part of this demand for Pennsylvania oils was due to car dealers who liked to handle national brands because they were higher priced and more profitable. Car dealers also liked to handle national brands not so generally available at filling stations. They would get more frequent calls from car owners and have more opportunities to get service business. The demand was also due to the fact that car dealers and some manufacturers, too, felt that Pennsylvania oils resulted in better performance.

Many Standard resellers soon recognized the situation, and more and more they began to handle a nationally advertised brand of Pennsylvania motor oil. In fact, from time to time, even some of the company-operated service stations were found with Pennsylvania oil hidden somewhere around the station because employees felt that they would lose business and commissions if they "did not give their customers what they wanted." The problem resulted in an immense amount of discussion over what should be done because from 1925 to 1929 Standard motor oil sales steadily declined, despite its increase in gasoline sales.[18]

Standard also developed in its laboratories and put on the market during the 1920's many other new petroleum products for a wide variety of purposes. For example, Stanolind Furnace Oil,

17. Company Encyclopedia: Marketing, I, 124.
18. "Motor Oil Merchandising, 1937."

a new fuel oil for heating homes, was introduced in 1922. Stan-olind Aero Motor Oil for aviation came out in 1923. Nonpareil White Mineral Oil appeared in 1924. The fuel and lubricant needs of diesel engines were met at first with the conventional petroleum products, but in 1924 Standard developed Nonpareil Diesel Lubricating Oil and in 1928 Diesel Locomotive Fuel. In 1925 a line of greases for high-speed and heavier locomotives was first made at Whiting. Later, this was expanded to include greases for rod cups and journal lubrication. About 1926 Nonpareil Tur-bine Oil began to be marketed. Increased boiler pressures and temperatures necessitated the use of improved cylinder lubricants, which were developed between 1928 and 1930 and known as Stanocyl Cylinder Oils.

Numerous specialty products dealing with flies and bugs were developed. Bovinol, a tasteless, odorless, and colorless cattle spray, which was fly-repellent, was first marketed in 1923. In that year the company sold 23 gallons; in 1924 it sold 186,000 gallons. "New Bovinol," introduced in February, 1928, had fly-killing as well as a fly-repelling value. Kip, a household insect spray, was developed in 1926. Three years later the name was changed to Kosak because Standard of New Jersey brought suit against Standard of Indiana complaining of the similarity to the name of Flit. It was soon discovered, however, that the name Kosak had been used by a manufacturer of polishing cloths for some time. Consequently, in December, 1929, the name of the product was changed again to Superla Insect Spray. Dendrol Dormant Spray Oil for trees ap-peared in the same year as Kip, and Verdol Summer Spray Oil in 1929. Standard brought out a new product called Stanisol in 1926 for use in dry cleaning. It was better than cleaners' naphtha, for it had less odor and was safer. The fire hazard was practically eliminated if ordinary precautions were taken. For the purpose of marketing all petroleum specialty products such as Stanisol, Kip, Bovinol, and others, Superla Laboratories, Inc., a new 100 per cent owned marketing subsidiary, was organized in July, 1927.

Significant was the growth in Standard's sale of asphalt prod-ucts. The asphalt manufactured by Standard was a better grade than that imported from Trinidad. The company placed on the market in 1922 an asphaltic oxidizing road oil that appeared to be the oil for which the country's road builders had been looking. Heretofore, asphalt required heating tanks, hot rollers, hot treat-ing drums, and other equipment which increased the cost so that only large cities could afford to use it. The great value of Standard's road oil was that it could be applied at ordinary summer temperatures and with very little expense. When applied to a road during normal conditions and temperatures, the oil was very liquid, and it penetrated the road for a depth of several inches. The sun and air oxidized it and formed a rubberlike substance which bound the particles on the surface of the road into a compact mass that was waterproof.

While used extensively in building roads, Standard's asphalt was used for a great variety of other purposes. For example, every Ford car that was manufactured in the early 1920's had in its coil box, in order to waterproof and insulate it, one-half pound of asphalt furnished by Standard. Every carton of Uneeda Biscuits had an inner lining of Standard asphalt which prevented moisture from entering.

Although the coming of electricity and gas killed the use of candles as a practical source of light, the home consumption of candles increased almost 230 per cent between 1914 and 1923. The growing popular demand was ascribed to the fact that during World War I Americans saw in England and France how candles were used for ornamental purposes. As a result, the market for decorative candles in the United States, especially during the holiday season, rapidly expanded. While Standard did not maintain an art department in connection with its candle factory to paint candles, it sold great quantities to firms like the Peacock Candle Company of South Bend, Indiana, which painted and resold candles. From 1925 to 1928 Standard manufactured and sold four outstanding models of Christmas candles that were in every sense of the word hand-decorated. These tapers were rich in color, graceful in form, and all about the same shape but widely different in color and character. The greatest demand, however, was for practical white candles used by miners, milkmen, and plumbers, and for emergency lighting on Pullman cars, in hotel rooms, and in homes. The small candle, three-eighths of an inch or an inch in diameter, was still popular and made in three styles —the birthday, the Ehanukak, which was used exclusively for Jewish holidays, and Christmas-tree candles made in five colors. Still another model, which was used exclusively in Roman Catholic churches, was the Votive. In fact, about 15 per cent of all wax made into candles by Standard was used in religious ceremonies— church worship, weddings, funerals, death watches, and as altar lights. As a result of the demand for all kinds of candles, the candle factory at Whiting more than doubled its capacity between 1923 and 1928. It was using about 1,000,000 pounds of wax per month in 1928.

In sharp contrast with its early record, Standard embarked in 1919 upon a gigantic advertising program designed to accomplish two things: first, boost the sale of its products as more and more competitors came into the field; second, humanize the company and tell its story in an effort to improve its relations with the public. As a result, Standard's advertising expenditures increased from $1,110,232.06 in 1919 to $4,168,138.20 in 1926, which was the largest amount spent for advertising in any one year in the history of the company until 1946.[19] In 1927, 1928, and 1929, advertising expenditures fell off to around $3,500,000.

Standard used all forms of advertising—newspapers, billboards, signs painted on barns along the highways, posters, direct mailing, hanging disc signs, road maps, station identification signs, car and bus, movies, and radio. Throughout the 1920's expenditures on newspaper advertising were the heaviest. Standard was one of the nation's largest newspaper advertisers and the largest newspaper advertiser among oil companies.[20] In 1924 Standard, along with Liggett & Myers Tobacco Company, ranked fifth in the amount of money spent for newspaper advertising. The Ford Motor Company was the largest, with an expenditure of $2,000,000. Standard spent $1,500,000, which was far beyond the amount spent by any oil company. Standard ranked ninth among the 227 largest newspaper advertisers in 1925. In that year it spent about $1,275,000, which was $500,000 more than any oil company, the second highest oil company being the Standard of California, with an expenditure of about $750,000.

Using a new medium of communication, Standard first went over the radio air waves in June, 1922, when the Standard Oil Band of Whiting gave a "radiophone" concert over KYW in Chicago. No further use of radio was made by the company, however, until the fall of 1928, when it began sponsoring one of the outstanding radio programs, the Chicago Symphony Orchestra under the direction of Dr. Frederick Stock. Heard on Sunday eve-

19. Company Encyclopedia: Comparison of Advertising Expenditures With Sales of Petroleum Products, 1907 to 1940, Inclusive.
20. *National Petroleum News,* XVII, No. 3 (April 1, 1925), 118; XVIII, No. 13 (March 31, 1926), 96; XIX, No. 15 (April 13, 1927), 100; XXIII, No. 30 (July 29, 1931), 81.

ning over eight stations in the Middle West, the concerts were given for twenty-six consecutive weeks. At the same time, the company started sponsoring a popular program, the "Iso-Vis Hour," once a week, featuring the Iso-Vis orchestra and the Iso-Vis tenor. In 1924 the company made two educational motion pictures for the United States Bureau of Mines, one *The Story of Gasoline* and the other *The Story of Lubricating Oils*. Both were based upon operations at Whiting.

Since the company did not have a uniform color scheme in effect in 1918, it was felt that some distinctive color scheme would be advantageous in advertising. After much study and experimentation, a decision was made to use a red, white, and blue combination, which was attractive and made for good visibility. The color scheme was extended to the service stations in a repainting program in 1926 and gradually introduced in all packaging.

Believing that a new trade-mark for the company was also desirable for advertising purposes a letter was sent in the spring of 1926 to the sales representatives in the field explaining what was wanted and asking for ideas. The general suggestion was made that the trade-mark should be one useful in handling small or large packages and effective when printed on paper, burned into wood, stamped in metal, painted on bulletin boards, or built into electric signs. Scores of suggestions were received, but no single one seemed to have all the good points. Working with all the ideas received, a number of designs were prepared, studied, changed, and put in proper shape for further examination. Out of these, one was selected because it met three fundamental requirements. It was pleasing to the eye. It was simple and dignified. It symbolized ideals basic to Standard's policies and practices. Placed in use in June, 1926, the general outline, a perfect circle, typified strength, stability, and dependability. A white band inside, containing the company's name, was intended to typify that complete cycle of service ever present, never ending, which the company so successfully rendered. The disc at the center, with the word "Service" across it, was symbolic of the will to render service, which was the heart and bone of the company. The torch in the foreground was a symbol which lighted the way to bigger and better things. In a word, the design symbolized progress backed by service.

During 1926 and 1927 more than 14,000 nine-foot Red Crown gasoline and Polarine motor oil signs were placed along the highways. At the same time, single and double hanging disc signs, which could be illuminated at night, were installed to identify company and dealer stations. Beginning in 1929 the hanging disc signs were replaced by larger but less artistic identification signs, four by eight feet, with the name "Standard Oil Company" on both sides.

One of the greatest and most spectacular achievements in advertising the company in the Middle West was the purchase of an airplane for the use of its executives.[21] Late in 1925 W. B. Stout of the Stout Metal Aircraft Division of the Ford Motor Company talked with Allan Jackson, Vice-President in charge of Sales, about Standard's buying a plane for company use. Jackson had already made three flights between 1920 and 1922 and was interested in Stout's suggestion, but he did not believe a single-motored plane was either safe or suitable. When Ford developed a tri-motored metal plane in 1926, Jackson became more interested and suggested to Colonel Stewart that the company buy one. At the time, the petroleum industry had a surplus of gasoline, prices were fairly low, and it seemed to Jackson that aviation was in about the same position as the automobile in 1905. Instead of waiting for aviation to develop in a normal way, Jackson believed that its development might be hastened if Standard took the leadership by purchasing a plane. It would enable the Directors and other company officials to make safe, fast, and comfortable business trips to widely scattered refineries and sales offices. It would stimulate public interest in aviation and aid in the development of airports. It would increase the demand for petroleum products. It would also result in a large amount of free advertising and good will for the company.

Colonel Stewart had flown in 1925 from Baranquilla to Bogotá in Colombia and returned in about eight hours, a trip normally requiring about fourteen days by water and land. He appreciated, therefore, the value of aviation for business purposes. Since he, too, saw the vast possibilities in purchasing a plane for the company, Colonel Stewart enthusiastically supported Jackson's idea. After an investigation of its safety, necessity, practicability, and economy, Jackson proposed the idea to the Directors and they approved. An order was given to Stout, and the firm delivered to

21. The following account is largely based upon a history of Standard's role in pioneering aviation in the Middle West written by Allan Jackson, Vice-President in charge of Sales, dated May 8, 1939.

Standard the sixth tri-motored plane ever constructed and the first ever built for the use of the executives of any large company.

The *Stanolind,* as the giant 600 HP monoplane was christened, cost $47,709.48.[22] There were larger and faster planes, but there was none finer or safer or better fitted for the work intended. It carried two pilots and a mechanic. It was equipped with a complete set of double controls. Powered by three air-cooled motors with a maximum speed of 110 miles per hour, the all-metal plane could carry eight passengers and 4,000 pounds of baggage. The interior was royally furnished with observation seats, a desk, and Pullman-type berths for sleeping, the first berths used in any airplane. It had all the conveniences of a Pullman-car drawing room.

Stanolind made its first flight from Detroit to Chicago on May 21, 1927. Colonel Stewart, Allan Jackson, R. E. Humphreys, Amos Ball, N. R. Grimshaw, W. B. Stout, and William B. Mayo of the Ford organization were aboard. The flight marked the beginning of the "big business era" in aviation, the acceptance of the airplane by business institutions as a means of fast, safe, and comfortable transportation for executives. As the plane approached Chicago, it flew along the south shore of Lake Michigan, over Whiting and Gary, and up the lake front. When a locomotive engineer at the south end of the lake noticed the plane in the air, he blew his whistle. This was done by other locomotive engineers and boats in the harbor all the way up to the 12th Street railroad station in Chicago. As the plane flew along the lake front, the demonstration surpassed all expectations, and those in the plane were a bit puzzled. The noise continued even after the plane reached and circled Standard's General Office Building at 910 S. Michigan and for some minutes after it landed at the Municipal Field at 63rd and Cicero. Upon disembarking, the passengers learned that just about the time their plane was opposite 910 S. Michigan a "flash" had been received that Charles A. Lindbergh had landed at Le Bourget field in Paris, and a part of the demonstration in Chicago was in honor of Lindbergh's epoch-making flight.

Much of *Stanolind's* time during the first two months was spent in flying to scores of cities within Standard's marketing territory on good-will tours under the direction of Allan Jackson. Many invitations were received from cities and towns in the Middle West ask-

22. "Stanolind to St. Louis For Lindbergh Greeting Carrying Chicago Men," *Stanolind Record,* VIII, No. 9 (July, 1927), 37-40; "Company Orders Giant New Plane; To Sell Stanolind," *Stanolind Record,* X, No. 2 (December, 1928), 12-14.

ing that *Stanolind* visit their communities. Since many of them did not have an adequate landing field, they were advised to lay out an airport and *Stanolind* would pay a visit. Everywhere large and curious crowds gathered to see the plane. They were as large at midnight as at noon. Wherever the plane went, Jackson usually spoke on aviation at some luncheon meeting of the Chamber of Commerce or other civic body. During the day the local celebrities were invited to take a ride. Not more than ten were taken at a time. Usually eight trips a day were made. In almost all instances, those who rode in the *Stanolind* had never flown before, and it demonstrated the smoothness, swiftness, and comfort of flying. Within a short time, it was known by sight to people in almost every city in the Middle West.

When not on good-will tours, *Stanolind* carried company executives everywhere on business trips. The first flight for business purposes exclusively was made on July 24th when it carried Stewart, Jackson, McElroy, and Bullock to Denver to attend a meeting of the Board of Directors of the Midwest Refining Company. Some of the trips were spectacular and gained considerable publicity. For example, on one trip to inspect an oil field in Texas, the Board of Directors covered 2,900 miles in thirty-three hours of flying time. To have covered the same route by train and auto would have required ten days. The use of the *Stanolind* effected an enormous saving of time which more than offset the expenses of operation and made it an economical method of travel. Furthermore, with 50 to 80 per cent of the Directors, who controlled the destiny of a great corporation, flying together on many of these trips, it inspired public confidence in the airplane.

As further evidence of the faith of Standard in the future of aviation and its desire to keep pace with aviation developments, the company purchased in 1927 a second plane, a Laird biplane, which was christened *Stanolind Junior*.[23] This small, open ship, with a cruising speed of 120 miles per hour and a maximum speed of 138, carried a pilot and had room for two passengers. It was used by Standard's representatives to solicit aviation gasoline accounts in the Middle West. The chief advantage of *Stanolind Junior* was that it could land in less space than the big plane.

Foreseeing the growth of aviation, Standard began early studying the oil requirements for airplane motors, and by 1924 it had

23. "S. O. Company Buys Second Airplane, The Stanolind Junior," *Stanolind Record,* IX, No. 5 (March, 1928), 1.

perfected three products, Stanolind Aviation Gasoline, Superla Aero Oil, and Stanolind Aero Oil. With the acquisition of the large Stanolind plane, Standard started stocking aviation gasoline and lubricating oil at most of its important stations. By November, 1927, these products were stocked at 4,200 bulk stations. Even the most remote station carried a sealed 55-gallon drum of Stanolind Aviation Gasoline and a five-gallon can of Stanolind Aero Oil in case any plane had to make an emergency landing. Agents were instructed to see that aviators were supplied with oil and gas at any hour of the day or night, regardless of the cost and distance, because company officials were looking ahead to the bigger volume that would come.

Standard gave further assistance to the development of aviation by painting on the roofs of its bulk plants in 1,500 towns on established air lines, in the largest possible letters and in appropriate colors, the name of the town, arrows indicating north and south, and a direction sign to the nearest airport. In time, all 4,200 bulk plants were similarly marked. Since this was long before radio directional beams, what Standard did in airway identification was of utmost importance to early aviators.

As a tribute to the growing importance of aviation and in keeping with the company's progressive aviation policy, Standard erected in 1929 the first air-earth outdoor advertising sign, calling attention to Standard's products, on the main highway near the Ford airport at Detroit. In order that it could be plainly read by motorists as well as aviators, the sign was placed at a 45-degree angle. Hundreds of passengers in planes arriving and departing from the big airfield could read it clearly at 700 feet in the air. Owing to the curiosity the sign aroused among motorists, a legend at the bottom of the board read: "This is the first bulletin board erected advertising to the people who travel by air."

After twenty months of missionary service, the *Stanolind* was sold early in 1929, and another larger, faster, and more powerful plane, *Stanolind II,* was purchased.[24] It was so badly damaged in June, 1929, by a windstorm at Wichita, Kansas, that it was replaced by *Stanolind III*. After being used for a little over two years, this plane was sold, and the company's pioneering efforts in behalf of aviation came to an end.

24. "Stanolind II, Larger, Faster, Better Equipped Than Stanolind, Makes Maiden Flight from Detroit to Omaha To Pick Up Allan Jackson, Vice President," *Stanolind Record,* X, No. 8 (June, 1929), 19-20.

During more than four years of flying, Standard's planes had flown more than 200,000 miles, had landed in every community in the Middle West where time and airports permitted, and had carried aloft free of charge more than 25,000 passengers.[25] The Directors had flown together on business trips in the three planes a total of 87,436 miles. Allan Jackson, Vice-President in charge of Sales, personally flew more than 100,000 on some 250 trips. Except for Lindbergh, Standard had done as much as any organization or individual in popularizing aviation and making people of the Middle West air-minded. It had helped to establish confidence in the safety, speed, and comfort of air travel. No doubt hundreds of airports built in the Middle West got their original impetus from an anticipated visit of the *Stanolinds*. From the company's point of view, the value of the *Stanolinds,* as a timesaver for busy executives and as agents of good will, was invaluable. Many people took their first flight in one of Standard's planes, which made many friends for the company. Much actual new business which developed was traceable to the friendships formed. It was estimated that the value of the free publicity given Standard in connection with the visits of its planes exceeded a million dollars.

Owing to the seemingly insatiable market for petroleum products and the fact that no one company was big enough to meet the growing demand, the keenest kind of competition in marketing developed in the Middle West. Either through building, purchasing, or leasing service stations, or purchasing distributing companies, or acting through jobbers, hundreds of oil companies invaded the marketing territory of Standard during the 1920's in order to get a share in the lucrative business. "I have never known in my business experience," Colonel Stewart declared in 1926, "any competition that approaches it. . . . It is one of the most fiercely competitive districts that I have ever seen." With an abundance of crude oil, especially after 1922, and an unprecedented demand for gasoline and other petroleum products, it would have been impossible for Standard, or any other company, to maintain a monopoly or near monopoly of the market. Among those who became major factors in the competitive struggle were Sinclair, The Texas Company, Cities Service, Mid-Continent, White Eagle, Roxana (Shell), Marland, Tidewater, Phillips, Pure, National Refining, and Indian Refining. Several units of the old Standard Oil Company—Vacuum Oil, Prairie Oil & Gas, Con-

25. Company Encyclopedia: Marketing, I, Aviation.

tinental, and the Ohio Oil Company—broke out of their old marketing territories and began invading that of Standard of Indiana. Late in the 1920's a new kind of competition began to appear—the oil co-operatives.

In attempting to establish themselves in Standard's territory, most of the companies at the outset relied upon jobbers to secure distribution. Jobbers were the middlemen, the wholesalers, who stood between the refiner and dealers. They usually bought to sell through retail outlets owned or operated. Sometimes jobbers sold through their own outlets and conducted a wholesale business as well. They might sell under their own brand name, or buy and sell branded gasoline, or buy branded gasoline and market it unbranded. Jobbers could buy gasoline on the open market at spot tank-car prices, but they generally had a definite source of supply and bought on a contract basis. Generally speaking, gasoline sold under such contracts guaranteed the jobber a fixed margin of profit, that is, he paid so many cents below the established tank-wagon price of Standard or so much above the tank-car spot market. Where necessary, refiners seeking wider distribution made loans or extended exceptional credit to jobbers, for this enabled the jobbers to extend their operations more rapidly than their own limited resources would permit. Additional aid was given jobbers through sharing some of their operating expenses, assisting in sales plans, paying a portion of their advertising costs, providing equipment, and making other concessions.

With a wide margin between the tank-wagon price and the tank-car market, particularly from 1920 to 1930, it opened the way for jobbers with low selling costs to come into the market and take volume and profit from Standard. With long and generally fixed margins, jobbers could cut prices, give better discounts in order to secure dealer outlets, extend as much credit as they desired, lease or give away pumps and tanks, and make special concessions of almost any kind. In case of a price war, jobbers still got the same margin of profit and the refiners absorbed the loss. If they encountered insurmountable financial troubles, they usually sold out to their refiner, who got a ready-made distribution system over a certain area.

Even though it was well known as a dependable source of petroleum products, had established brands, an expert research staff, and laboratory-tested products, Standard was particularly vulnerable to the cut-price competition from jobbers and tank-car sellers of other refiners because it marketed directly over a vast territory, had the greatest number of retail outlets, and transacted the largest percentage of the business. When jobbers cut prices and passed the cut to dealers, Standard was soon forced to cut prices. Whenever conditions permitted, Standard would usually restore the price toward normal. This was not a happy public relations situation, for the public soon learned that price cutting was always started by others, and it was Standard that usually started the price rise.

Another troublesome aspect of jobber price cutting for Standard was that jobbers on fixed-margin contracts were able to cut prices much more readily and quickly than Standard. They operated in a relatively small territory and could lower the price without suffering the loss Standard faced in lowering prices over an entire state. In order to protect itself against prosecution under the antidiscrimination laws, Standard made it mandatory for sales representatives who wished to meet a local price cut to gather evidence of a competitor's cut and send it to the General Office in Chicago.[26] A sales ticket of an actual purchase from a competitor, or a photograph of a posted cut-price sign, or a sworn statement was required. Upon the evidence submitted and collateral information, the Sales Department then made a decision as to whether the price should be cut. The result was that a competitor might have the advantage of a price cut for as much as two or three weeks and gain new customers before Standard could take action.

In the race to secure business those refiners who did not have the capital to invest or did not want to build service stations began installing pumps and underground tanks at hardware and grocery stores, garages, and at privately built service stations. This method had the advantage of securing extensive retail outlets without requiring any great investment in land or buildings. Where a dealer did not have the money either to buy or rent the equipment, refiners, in their zeal to acquire outlets, offered to furnish it either free or on a very nominal rental basis. Pump and tank manufacturers, eager for business, urged dealers to ask oil companies to furnish the equipment. When one company started the practice of furnishing equipment free or on a nominal rental basis in order to increase its gallonage, others were forced to follow until it became widespread and a perennial problem in marketing. As the battle for gallonage increased during the 1920's, there was almost no limit to the amount of equipment and concessions dealers

26. Company Encyclopedia: Marketing, I, Major Competition, Price Cutting.

demanded. If one company would not meet the demand, others would. Furthermore, one supplier would no sooner install his equipment and improve the station than another would offer the dealer a greater inducement, and the dealer would switch his account. It was a regular rat race to secure dealers.

To meet competitors' practices of leasing and loaning equipment, Standard could not profitably erect a service station in every town, irrespective of size. On the other hand, it wanted to hold and increase its business. Therefore, while adhering to its policy of marketing directly through its own service stations, Standard developed over the objection of some members of its Marketing Committee three general leasing forms which could be applied to resellers whoever they might be—hardware and grocery stores, garages, or privately owned service stations.[27] The Commission Agency Agreement form was entered into with a party who already owned a tank and pump. According to the terms of the agreement, the equipment was to be used for dispensing Standard's products. The owner acted as the company agent. He was paid a commission of $1\frac{1}{2}$ to 2 cents per gallon. He made reports similar to the agents of company-owned and operated service stations and accounted for the gasoline sold. Under the Tank Rental Agreement the company furnished an underground tank or pump or both to a reseller at an annual rental equal to 10 per cent of the selling price of the equipment. The dealer agreed to sell through the equipment only Standard gasoline, which was paid for on delivery and sold as the dealer's gasoline. The Pump and Property Lease was entered into with parties operating a garage or other business. Its use was bitterly protested by some members of the Marketing Committee because it violated the policy of "direct from producer to consumer" and was likely to result in a demand for a wider margin of profit. However, it was adopted in 1920 to meet a particular competitive situation in North Dakota and then extended over the territory. If the dealer owned a pump and tank, Standard rented the equipment together with the land on which they were located at a specified rental. If the dealer had no pump, the company leased the ground, installed a pump and tank, and paid a rental for the use of the ground. The dealer was then employed as the company's agent on a commission basis of $1\frac{1}{2}$ to 2

27. *High Cost of Gasoline and Other Petroleum Products*, I, 817-821; Recommendations made by Allan Jackson, Vice-President in charge of Sales, on the Marketing of Gasoline, January 25, 1922. Jackson File. Hereafter referred to as Jackson's Recommendations, January 25, 1922.

cents per gallon. The company kept the tank filled, set the rental price, and as the gasoline was sold the money was turned over to the company. Standard used this kind of setup in communities where business did not warrant the establishment of a service station of its own in order to give its customers the advantage of service-station prices.

Owing to complaints over the leasing of tanks and pumps upon the condition that only the lessor's product be stored and sold through the leased equipment, the Federal Trade Commission investigated the situation in the spring of 1918 and filed a complaint against Standard but postponed a hearing because of World War I.[28] Following a hearing in June, 1919, the Commission issued a cease and desist order against the company on the ground that this restriction violated the Clayton Anti-Trust Act. Within a few days similar complaints were filed against thirty of the largest marketers, and in July, 1920, cease and desist orders were issued against sixteen. Several of the companies, but not Standard, petitioned the United States Circuit Court of Appeals for the Second, Third, Sixth, and Seventh Circuits to set aside the order. The courts upheld their petitions and overruled the orders. On April 9, 1923, the United States Supreme Court affirmed the decisions of the Circuit Courts.

Standard of Indiana did not indulge in the practice of giving away or nominally leasing anywhere near as many pumps and tanks as other companies, especially some of the Standard companies in the East. Its policy was to market directly through its own service stations and not through dealers. However, the applications for appropriations for equipment became so numerous and for such large amounts that the Sales Department made an analysis of the situation, which revealed the following: [29]

INVESTMENT IN EQUIPMENT AS OF DECEMBER 21, 1921

Division	Commission Agency Agreement	Tank Rental Agreement	Pump and Property Lease
Eastern	$7,319.73	$ 89,676.98	—
Western	—	97,631.19	$126,682.42*
Northern	—	75,633.88	80,802.59
	$7,319.73	$262,942.03	$207,485.01

* Not including Chicago.

28. Company Encyclopedia: Marketing, II; 67 Law. Ed. 747.
29. Jackson's Recommendations, January 25, 1922.

When the extent to which Standard had gone into these three types of leasing was realized and the effects noted, a halt was called on making new agreements and efforts were made to cancel the old contracts.

In the battle for business one strange episode occurred during 1920 which was interpreted by observers as a secret move on the part of Standard and Sinclair to drive competitive dealers in Chicago out of business. It centered around Henry B. Sewell, a shrewd promoter and organizer, who was a man about fifty years old, a good talker, an excellent dresser, handsome, and one whose demeanor inspired confidence. Sewell, accompanied by George Whalen, secretary to the Vice-President of Standard of Indiana, visited Standard's office in Milwaukee in June, 1920, where he met Robert G. Stewart, son of the Colonel, who was manager of the Milwaukee division. Sewell told Stewart that he might be able to help Standard secure some gasoline business since he was purchasing agent for the Munger Laundry Company in Chicago. He would be glad to do this because of his friendship for Whalen. And he did. This marked the beginning of a unique and mysterious venture in oil.[30]

Shortly thereafter, Sewell began buying from young Stewart gasoline coupon books, often in lots of 100 at a time, and he paid the full market price of $10 for each. Within three months' time, Stewart was personally loaning Sewell money, all the way from $700 to $3,000 without any notes or written security. However, it was all repaid with interest at 25 to 30 per cent. When Robert Stewart was married in December, 1920, Sewell acted as his best man. Sewell also became acquainted with James W. Stewart, a younger brother of Robert, and the two became very friendly. In fact, James became an officer and stockholder in two of Sewell's companies.

Simultaneously, Sewell began purchasing gasoline coupon books from Sinclair in Chicago. Through his large purchases, Sewell became an important customer of both companies. In a little while, Francis M. Baker, city sales manager for Sinclair, was making trips personally to Sewell's office to deliver the coupon books ordered. Sewell sold the $10 gasoline coupon books to an exclusive circle of favored friends at $7.50 each, taking a loss of $2.50 on

30. "Chicago's Leading Price Cutter Is A.W.O.L. Court Action to Follow," *National Petroleum News*, XIII, No. 11 (March 16, 1921), 27-28; Chicago *Herald and Examiner*, February 18, 1921.

each one. To those to whom he sold the books he urged the greatest secrecy. His customers got the idea that he was within the inner circle of both Standard and Sinclair, which made it possible for him to purchase coupon books at a reduction. Customers saw Baker and Sewell together a great deal, and they came to think of Sewell as a Sinclair representative. The same was true of customers who bought from Standard, for Sewell talked glibly of his relations with Stewart's sons.

Sewell gradually increased the number of his customers, and when hundreds of them were thoroughly imbued with the idea that he had the inside track with Sinclair and Standard, he proceeded to open negotiations on furnishing gasoline to large consumers below the market price. The first sales were for relatively small lots, 2,000 to 5,000 gallons. Standard, Sinclair, or the Union Petroleum Company would make the deliveries and at the end of the month bill the consumer at the regular tank-wagon price. Sewell paid the consumer the difference between his price and the tank-wagon price, and the consumers would then send their own check to Standard, Sinclair, or Union. In some instances, Sewell took the invoice and settled with the oil companies in the customer's name. Sewell lost the difference. Where he got the money to finance such operations is a mystery.

As sales increased, Sewell increased the amount of gasoline sold to a customer "because the price was going up." He would offer a customer 30,000 or 50,000 gallons at 22 cents, or 5 cents under the market. Sears Roebuck & Company, the Wieboldt Department Store, many big garages, automobile dealers, and trucking companies became Sewell's customers. On one occasion he called to his home the head of one of the city's biggest garages and said: "Colonel Stewart took dinner with me last night. He gave me credit for 100,000 gallons of gasoline. I'll let you in on this deal. I'll give you the gas at 3 cents under the market price, but I must have $10,000 cash now." As the orders increased in size, Sewell insisted upon payment in advance and was able to secure advance payments of $25,000 to $40,000 from some of the large companies.

Since it was losing orders from large customers, in most cases to Standard, The Texas Company became suspicious. Sinclair also realized that something was wrong in the spring of 1920 because it was losing large customers. Standard started an investigation for the same reason as Texas and Sinclair. With the oil companies hot on his trail, Sewell disappeared from Chicago on February 3, 1921, with $200,000 to $300,000, without paying for the gasoline which had been delivered by the three companies.

The Chicago *Herald and Examiner* on February 18th broke the news of Sewell's operations with a big, black, front-page headline: "$300,000 Oil Gusher Gone." The story clearly implied that Standard was cognizant of the details of Sewell's business; that through his acquaintanceship with Colonel Stewart, Sewell was able to buy large quantities of gasoline at a substantial discount; and that because of this friendship, he was given unusual credit. The next day Standard ran large advertisements in all of the Chicago papers in which the Board of Directors categorically and without reservation denied the allegations. The advertisement was signed by Henry S. Morton, Vice-President.

A committee of 150, representing about 5,000 retail dealers in Standard's territory, conferred with the United States district attorney in Chicago on September 6th and demanded an investigation of the charges that Standard and Sinclair had conspired through Sewell to force the independents from Chicago.[31] The committee charged that sixteen independent companies had been forced out of business through the reduction in gasoline prices, and the committee wanted the district attorney to determine the connection of Sewell with the two companies. Nothing further came of the episode, however, except embarrassment for Standard and Sinclair.

As a result of various competitors, like The Texas Company, Sinclair, Indian Refining, Roxana, and others, offering differentials of 2 and 3 cents in order to secure dealer outlets, hundreds of inexperienced men with little capital rushed into the oil business, put in curb tanks and pumps, and built service stations. As the competitive battle for business developed along a broad front, they soon found it difficult to make ends meet. Price wars, rebating, and other uneconomic practices developed. Unless garage owners and other resellers were allowed a 2 cent margin of profit, those not having service stations would soon be forced out of business.

Confronted with the possibility of losing the business of resellers if it did not increase the margin from 1 to 2 cents, Standard referred the matter to its Marketing Committee for study. The question posed one of the most momentous problems ever presented for consideration. The Marketing Committee finally rec-

31. "Sewell Case Made Basis of Conspiracy Accusation By Independents," *National Petroleum News*, XIII, No. 36 (September 7, 1921), 17.

ommended the establishment of a 2 cent differential, chiefly on the ground that it would create a better feeling on the part of the garage owners toward the company and aid in not only holding their business but in increasing it. However, Allan Jackson, Vice-President in charge of Sales, and N. R. Grimshaw, Assistant General Manager, radically disagreed with the recommendation, and they made a very strong case against it.[32] They argued that the policy of Standard had always been to get closer to consumers. Encouraging the middlemen, according to Jackson and Grimshaw, would divert trade to the resellers, increase their number, restrict the growth of Standard's service stations, violate the policy of "direct from producer to consumer," increase the cost to the public, and increase the cost of marketing, for it cost more to market by tank wagon than through service stations. They doubted if the garage owners were antagonistic toward the company, for it was already getting approximately 51 per cent of their business. The reason it was not getting more was due to the fact that the company would not make some of the concessions made by competitors. Even if the resellers got a 2 cent differential from Standard, they, in turn, would get more from competitors and favor them. The 1 cent differential had helped to build up uneconomic and unprofitable bulk and service stations, and if a 2 cent differential were allowed, the situation would only be made worse. Both Jackson and Grimshaw believed that the 1 cent differential plus the profits on motor oil was a substantial remuneration for the resellers. Their plight was due not so much to the company's depriving them of their livelihood as it was to the appalling increase in their numbers.

Early in March, 1922, Colonel Stewart called a meeting of all the Directors and the top sales executives to discuss the recommendation. More than twenty-five men were present to discuss whether or not Standard should allow dealers a 2 cent differential. As a result, all, including Grimshaw but not Jackson, voted in favor of making the change. At the conclusion of the meeting, Jackson went to the office of Colonel Stewart and said: "Colonel Stewart, as a result of the action just taken wherein not only every member of the Board but my own sales people voted against my proposed policy, I feel I should resign." [33] The Colonel looked up with a smile and replied: "Allan, if you resign, I will too. I believe you were right, but the Board of Directors decided they wanted

32. Jackson's Recommendations, January 25, 1922.
33. Allan Jackson to Giddens, March 28, 1950.

more business to make more money, and I decided to go along with them and give them the chance." Thus, after a long campaign, the company put into effect on March 13, 1922, throughout all its territory the 2 cent differential between the tank-wagon and service-station price.

In the meantime, Standard's policy of discontinuing the leasing and loaning of pumps and tanks, announced in December, 1921, had completely broken down, owing to the competitive situation. While the amount invested in Pump and Property Leases declined from $342,172.14 on January 1, 1922, to $89,594.50 on January 1, 1923, the investment in Tank Rental Agreements for the same period had increased from $438,179.56 to $801,445.05.[34] In an effort to protect itself against the great turnover in dealers and, at the same time, bring dealer stations up to the standards of company-owned and operated service stations, Standard adopted in October, 1922, a general plan for leasing private service stations to supplement its own distribution system.[35]

Various lease forms were used. One method was simply to lease a service station from the owner for a year and put in a salaried employee or sublease it to a private individual for operation as a dealer on a commission basis. This arrangement was classified as a Privately Owned Service Station Leased, or a POSSL station. Another method was to lease the station from the owner and make him the company agent or operator. This was known as a Private Drive-In Service Station Leased, or a PDISSL station. Under this form, the dealer entered into two agreements with the company. One was a lease of the property for a flat annual rental to be paid on a monthly basis. The lessee paid the general and special taxes, water, light, heat, and any other expenses charged against the property. The other was the Authorized Agent's Agreement, whereby the owner became the operator of the station. In some cases the agreement was written with someone other than the lessor. Company products were to be handled exclusively. All gasoline was to be purchased from the company at regular dealer prices, sold at the established price, and handled on a commission basis. Where the company furnished a part or all of the dispensing equipment, another contract was executed, leasing or loaning the equipment to the dealer. When these three agreements were used,

---

34. *High Cost of Gasoline and Other Petroleum Products*, I, 817.
35. Company Encyclopedia: Marketing, I, Methods of Distribution, Through Service Stations, 77-84.

the arrangement was called the triple "A" agreement, i.e., lease, agency, and loan. The AAA and PDISSL were forms of the well-known Lease-and-Agency Agreement used by so many oil companies late in the 1920's and early 1930's. With the leases running for a year, the company saved the expense of putting in equipment and taking it right out when a competitor offered greater concessions. When the lease expired, the supplier was forced to pay higher rentals due to competition, and it was expensive, but it was nothing compared to the mad scramble prior to the use of leasing forms. The leasing of private service stations under the AAA and PDISSL forms started immediately, but the leasing of POSSL stations did not begin until 1928. Other companies saw the advantage of having some degree of permanency and soon adopted the lease system with variations.

Two sensational attacks were made upon Standard during 1923 on account of its price policies. The first was the result of a marked increase in gasoline prices beginning about April, 1922, when the service-station price of gasoline in Chicago was 21.5 cents a gallon. Sometimes Standard led the advance in prices, at other times it followed the lead of competitors. Coming at a time when the industry had accumulated the largest stocks of gasoline in its history, with the daily production greater than ever and the price of crude on the decline, the advance in gasoline prices aroused much public agitation and discussion. Most oil companies attributed the rise in prices to the tremendous increase in the consumption of gasoline and the relatively small demand for other petroleum products. The more gasoline produced by the ordinary distillation process, the greater was the quantity of residuum left which had to be utilized in order to hold down the price of gasoline. Major refiners with a cracking process had an enormous advantage, for they could convert much of the residuum into gasoline. Refiners without a cracking process had a greater quantity of residuum to utilize in by-products, and their gasoline had to pay for whatever was lost on the by-products. These refiners were losing money at 23 cents per gallon. Their economic condition necessitated raising prices if they were to continue to operate. In May the price was advanced to 24 cents. Since Standard could not possibly supply the entire market, it preferred to sell less at higher prices, and it led in making the price advance late in June to 25 cents, the highest for the year. Out in South Dakota, where freight rates were higher and the population scattered over a large area, the service-station price was

29 cents including 1 cent tax. While Standard was making money with gasoline at lower prices because of its huge marketing system, large volume, and the cracking process, it had gone along with the advances rather than undersell competitors and possibly bring ruin to many.

Owing to the advance in prices, the United States Senate in June, 1922, authorized its Committee on Manufactures to make a sweeping investigation of the oil industry covering the years from 1920 to 1922. Pursuant to the resolution, the committee met and designated a subcommittee with Senator Robert M. La Follette as chairman to conduct the investigation. The subcommittee held hearings for a brief period in August, 1922. Commencing again on December 14, 1922, daily sessions were held intermittently until February 28, 1923. The top executive officers of nineteen oil companies, including Stewart, Burton, Bullock, and Bogardus of Standard of Indiana, as well as representatives of the leading trade organizations were orally examined, more than fifty in all. Voluminous records and documents relating to the industry were subpoenaed for the committee's consideration. All phases of the petroleum industry—the extent of control over the industry exercised by the Standard companies, profits, crude and refined prices, salaries, earnings, subsidiaries, production, pipeline transportation, the cracking process, naval oil reserve leases, railroad freight rates, and refinery operations—came within the scope of the investigation.

In a report containing 1,500 pages of testimony and documents, submitted on March 3, 1923, the committee made a blistering attack upon the Standard Oil companies.[36] "The dominating fact in the oil industry today," it declared, "is its complete control by the Standard companies. Standard Oil today fixes the price which the producer of crude oil receives at the well, the price which the refiner receives for his gasoline and kerosene, as well as the retail price paid by the consumer.... A careful examination of the evidence taken in this investigation will show that in respect to the above matters and others which led to the outlawing of the Standard Oil monopoly the same conditions exist as existed when the decree of the Supreme Court was entered, and that in some respects the industry as a whole, as well as the public, are more completely at the mercy of the Standard Oil interests now than they were when the decree of dissolution was entered in 1911." If a few

36. *High Cost of Gasoline and Other Petroleum Products*, I, 1-69.

great oil companies were permitted to manipulate oil prices for
the next few years as they had been doing since January, 1920, the
people of this country, according to the report, must be prepared
before long to pay at least $1 a gallon for gasoline. The subcom-
mittee recommended, as immediate remedies, that a uniform system of bookkeeping be required of all oil companies doing an
interstate business. A compulsory system of monthly reports
should be made to the government on crude oil on hand by all
companies doing an interstate business. Pipelines should become
real common carriers. Changes in freight rates should be made to
enable Mid-Continent refiners to compete in the East. The expor-
tation of petroleum should be prohibited. A grand jury investigation should be made of price manipulations and prosecutions instituted, if warranted. Further investigation should be made to
see if the dissolution decree of 1911 had been violated. Finally, the
Department of Justice, as previously mentioned, should immediately institute a rigid investigation into all claims for basic
patents on pressure-still processes.

The next day, after the report was released, Colonel Stewart
issued a statement pointing out that it was unjust to Standard of
Indiana in many particulars. "The Standard Oil Company of
Indiana," he said, "is an independent corporation and it neither
owes nor acknowledges allegiance to any other corporation or
organization. It has no understanding or arrangement of any kind
or character with any other of the so-called Standard Oil Companies." [37] He emphasized that the competitors of his company had
practically all of the crude production in the Mid-Continent field,
which was its main source of supply. These same competitors had
as many bulk stations as Standard of Indiana, double the number
of service stations, and five times the refining capacity. In fact,
there were 126 refineries in the Mid-Continent area which turned
out 32 per cent of the total gasoline in the United States. Under
the circumstances, Standard of Indiana could not arbitrarily put
the price of petroleum up or down. Although Standard was the
"biggest frog in the puddle, we are not the puddle," Stewart said.
Competitors made prices without domination by Standard, and
there was no agreement to fix prices. Stewart vigorously denounced
the committee hearings because they were *ex parte* in character,
that is, witnesses were examined along the lines chosen by the

37. *The New York Times,* March 5, 1923; "Dollar Gasoline Would Wreck Standard
    Oil," *Stanolind Record,* IV, No. 6 (May, 1923), 1-9.

committee's attorney, and they were not allowed to bring forward or submit to the committee or the public anything in behalf of the oil companies. Only one side of the case had been presented. The result was a mass of half-truths.

The La Follette Committee had no sooner made its report than a situation developed in the Middle West that led to a second attack upon Standard of Indiana. While there had been a steady increase in the domestic crude production in the United States prior to 1923, that of 1923 broke all records with an output of 732,407,000 barrels, an increase of 31 per cent over 1922. It was not only the peak year of production in Wyoming but one of flush production in California. For the first time since 1914, production in the United States in 1923 was greater than consumption. Moreover, stocks of crude had increased from 291,630,000 barrels in 1922 to 374,512,000 in 1923, a quantity sufficient to supply the domestic consumption and the export trade for about 172 days. To aggravate the general situation, the gasoline shortages of 1919 and 1920 had proved to be a great stimulus to building refineries and had caused an overexpansion. In 1917 there were 176 refineries in the United States; by 1922 there were 325. Furthermore, keen competition among refiners had resulted in an extravagant overexpansion of service-station facilities. With the remarkable increase in service stations, observers wondered how any of the oil companies were going to make any profit. Many predicted that the day would come when the number of retail outlets would be burdensome to the companies and profits would suffer.

As a result of all these factors operating together, the price of crude fell drastically in 1923, resulting in a thorough demoralization of the entire oil industry. Between February 17th and September 1st, the price of Mid-Continent crude declined from $1.85 per barrel to $1.25. Light California crude dropped from $1.95 in January to 75 cents in October. The competition between California and Mid-Continent crude created a real conflict of interest among former units of the old Standard Oil in a way that was almost unbelievable.[38] The eastern group, led by Standard of New Jersey, with little production of their own and with immense refining and marketing facilities, either stopped or reduced their purchases in the Mid-Continent field and moved California crude east through the Panama canal. Oil backed up in the Mid-Continent field and many wells were either capped or "pinched in"

38. *Prices, Profits, and Competition*, 172-173, 199.

due to the lack of a market. The middle western group, headed by Standard of Indiana, Prairie Oil & Gas, and the Sinclair Crude Oil Purchasing Company, had millions of barrels of high-priced crude in storage and large producing interests in the Mid-Continent field. The middle western group, therefore, viewed the fall in crude prices with dismay.

As the eastern group continued to import California crude and cut Mid-Continent prices, the middle western group refused to follow. In an effort to stabilize the crude market and protect crude in storage, Prairie on May 12th pegged the price of crude at $1.45 per barrel and kept it there until in September. Commenting upon the situation, Ida M. Tarbell wrote: "It certainly looks very much as if the Standard Oil Company might be crumbling—crumbling from within; as if something had happened to it which the great dissolution suit had not been able to bring about. The parent company making a price for oil and its strong young relative in the West refusing to follow is something that has not happened in forty years." [39]

Standard of Indiana proceeded to base its tank-wagon price upon this artificial crude price and permitted a wider and wider margin to develop between the tank-wagon price and the open refinery price as the latter declined. Obviously, some adjustment downward in tank-wagon and service-station prices should have been made, but the companies involved were more concerned with stabilizing the market and protecting an enormous investment in stored crude than in lowering tank-wagon and retail prices. The maintenance of this artificial price by Standard served to hold up the price structure in its entire marketing area because 46 per cent of the purchases of jobbers in the Middle West were made under contracts allowing them a fixed differential below Standard's tank-wagon price.

In spite of Prairie's pegging the price of crude, Mid-Continent producers were forced to accept prices much below $1.45 and refiners, especially the smaller ones, were obliged to sell their gasoline at almost any price in order to raise money to meet their financial obligations. As the Mid-Continent refinery price of gasoline declined, wider and wider became the margin between it and the established tank-wagon price in Chicago. By May 1st the spread was 10.2 cents and by August 11th, 11.5 cents. Throwing

39. Ida M. Tarbell, "Is Standard Oil Crumbling," *New Republic*, XXXVI (November 14, 1923), 300-301.

"distress" gasoline, as the surplus was called, upon the market enabled jobbers without contracts and fixed margins to buy at low refinery prices, sell much below Standard's retail price, and make a handsome profit.

Governor W. H. McMaster of South Dakota knew that his state was buying "distress" gasoline for state vehicles at 14 cents a gallon, freight included, when the retail price in many parts of the state was 26.6 cents, including 2 cents tax. This meant nearly 100 per cent profit which, to him, was unreasonable, unfair, and unjust. Early in August, on his way east to attend President Harding's funeral, McMaster stopped in Chicago to see Colonel Stewart about the situation.[40] The Colonel showed him piles of figures and told him that the company could not afford to sell gasoline any cheaper in South Dakota.

McMaster told Stewart that if Standard could not, the state could and would. Stewart asked him what he wanted, and Mc-Master replied: "A five cent cut in price today." The Colonel said he would never sell gasoline in the State of South Dakota for less than 26 cents, even if he lost his job.

Characterizing the price of gasoline in South Dakota as "nothing more or less than highway robbery," Governor McMaster bought 160,000 gallons of distress gasoline at the lowest possible price and placed an order for 500,000 more. On August 7, 1923, he declared war on Standard and precipitated a general collapse of the market by ordering the state highway warehouse at Mitchell to sell gasoline at 16 cents a gallon, including the state tax, a drop of 10.6 cents per gallon in the retail price.[41] The established tank-wagon price had been 24.6 cents and the service-station price 26.6 cents. McMaster announced that he would establish fuel depots in other parts of the state just as soon as possible. Moreover, he requested the chief executives of other states to join in the fight and wage war to the bitter end.

McMaster's dramatic action created a situation which had no parallel in the history of the oil industry. It was a most drastic step and its effects were far-reaching. Telegrams and letters flooded state officials at Pierre asking for information on which to base demands for reductions in other states. Governors, automobile clubs, mayors, and publicists demanded a cut in other parts of

40. "How I Twisted Standard's Tail—By Mac Hunself," *National Petroleum News* XVI, No. 9 (February 27, 1924), 23.

41. Pierre *Daily Capital Journal*, August 7, 8, 9, 10, 1923.

Standard's territory. Governor Charles W. Bryan of Nebraska threatened to follow McMaster's action if the oil companies did not cut prices. He also telegraphed the Attorney General at Washington demanding a federal investigation. Governor William E. Sweet of Colorado and Governor R. A. Nestos of North Dakota asked oil companies in their states to meet South Dakota prices. The Chicago City Council petitioned Governor Len Small to permit state agencies to sell gasoline. Senators Lynn J. Frazier of North Dakota and Henrik Shipstead of Minnesota forgot about the price of wheat and began to shriek about the high price of gasoline.

To meet Governor McMaster's price, Standard on August 10th reduced its service-station price from 26.6 cents to 16 cents. L. V. Nicholas, President of the National Petroleum Marketers Association, bitterly assailed Standard for meeting McMaster's price. Although favoring a reduction in both tank-wagon and crude oil prices, Nicholas declared that prices in South Dakota had been reduced to a point where they would "force an incalculable loss on the independent oil industry of that state and place it irrevocably at the mercy of the Standard Oil Company." [42] Dealers could not exist at McMaster's price. McMaster admitted that 16 cents was not enough to insure dealers a profit but, he said, the state did not need a profit. With Standard's reduction in price, Governor McMaster announced that the state would not sell any more gasoline unless current prices again increased to an unreasonable figure. Therefore, the sale of gasoline at Mitchell was discontinued on the 11th.

After the drastic cut in Standard's retail price in South Dakota, a cut in the rest of its territory was inevitable. It was necessary to forestall other states and municipalities from going into the gasoline business. On the night of August 13th Standard announced that effective on the 14th its gasoline prices would be cut 6.6 cents throughout its entire marketing area, except in South Dakota and in Indiana, where the cut was only 5.6 cents on account of a new state tax, but it was equivalent to the 6.6 cent cut. This brought the service-station price in Chicago to 15.4 cents and the tank-wagon price to 13.4 cents. This cut was, according to Ida M. Tarbell, "the most drastic slashing of gasoline prices ever known to business."

In making the price reduction, Standard asserted that the new

42. *Chicago Journal of Commerce*, August 13, 1913.

price was way below the cost of production and distribution.[43] Since McMaster was buying "distress" gasoline and distributing it without respect to cost and since Standard's policy was that its customers should never be compelled to pay a higher price than that fixed by a competitor, quality and service duly considered, Standard had no alternative. The company made clear that in establishing such a price it was not endeavoring to injure any of its competitors because it felt that competitors were necessary to the successful conduct of its business. Standard only wanted a change in attitude by all parties which would result in a reasonable profit for all.

Complaints of small refiners, distributors, and dealers piled in on Governor McMaster, and he invited Colonel Stewart, Allan Jackson, Vice-President in charge of Sales, and George M. Cook, Director of Public Relations, to Pierre on August 29th to discuss the situation.[44] Stewart offered to keep the price at 16 cents, even though it did not reflect the cost of production, refining, and distribution plus a reasonable profit. He told McMaster that whatever the people of South Dakota wanted to do about the price would be all right with him. After an all-day conference the Governor asked that the 16 cent price be allowed to stand for the time being as it was just about right, and he publicly announced that he took the responsibility for the decision, and no one was to charge Standard with being responsible for the price. With this agreement, the gasoline war temporarily came to a close, but it meant a ruinous competitive price and the possible elimination of much competition. To many, it seemed as if Governor McMaster was acting in collusion with Standard.

When Standard advanced the price to 18 cents in South Dakota in November in an effort to equalize prices with those in other states, the gasoline war broke out anew, and McMaster resumed the sale of gasoline at state stations. Furthermore, he and Governor Bryan of Nebraska requested President Coolidge in February, 1924, to take action to prevent "profiteering" in gasoline. The President promptly requested the Federal Trade Commission to investigate. The fever for establishing state or city-owned service stations spread and gained momentum, especially in Nebraska, which resulted in price wars, all kinds of litigation, and a hectic time in general for the oil industry. The gasoline war in South

43. *Ibid.*, August 14, 1923.
44. Pierre *Daily Capital Journal*, August 29, 30, 1923.

Dakota did not finally come to an end until October, 1925, when the South Dakota Supreme Court on the petition of the White Eagle Oil & Refining Company enjoined the state from selling gasoline with funds derived from the taxation of gasoline for road purposes.

In the meantime, the Federal Trade Commission reported early in 1924 that in so far as oil profits were concerned, the average rate of profit in 1923 was 6.8 per cent, while that of the Standard companies was 7.7 per cent.[45] No evidence was discovered of disproportionate accumulations of or any corner on crude during 1923–24 either by the Standard companies or large independents as a group. It found that Standard of Indiana, Prairie, and other Standard companies did exercise a very decided price leadership during 1923 and 1924 which was responsible for the failure of both crude and gasoline prices to respond to the conditions of excess supply prevailing in the Mid-Continent field in the summer of 1923. This price leadership was also responsible for the advance in gasoline prices in December, 1923, and in January and February, 1924, which was effected in spite of a continued increase in gasoline stocks during those months. The Commission made several recommendations, most of which had been previously made by the La Follette Committee.

Tank-wagon prices in Standard's marketing territory underwent a gradual downward revision during 1924. There was, however, little or no pattern of a price structure, for price wars were taking place all over the territory. It was a free-for-all with each man making his own price to suit his own ideas, locality, and convenience. The flooding of eastern markets with cheap California gasoline and the creation of a surplus in the Mid-Continent field were the main cause behind the rampant price cutting in all parts of the Middle West.

By 1925 the growth of competition forced Standard to make a revolutionary change in its price policy on gasoline. Many inside and outside of the company contended that the price structure in the industry was archaic and did not meet current conditions. For one thing, the 2 cent differential between the service-station price and the tank-wagon price prevailed in about twenty-seven states, and in the remainder—the Pacific Coast area, Gulf Coast, and the East—it was even greater. Secondly, Standard had been soliciting

45. Letter of Transmittal and Summary Report on Gasoline Prices in 1924, June 4, 1924.

all classes of trade at the same price for the same class of service. A trucker who required twenty to thirty gallons of gasoline paid the same price as a buyer who required only one gallon. The farmer, far out in the country on bad roads, paid the same for his twenty gallons as the owner of a garage or station who took deliveries every day and often by the truckload. To serve this "high cost" type of trade—small deliveries and long-distance hauls —the company depended upon some of the less expensive type of trade to equalize the costs of distribution. The most desirable and least expensive kind of business was: first, those who bought large quantities delivered at one time; second, those who took regular deliveries at assured intervals; and third, the most attractive customers, those who took large dumps frequently and without solicitation. In this last group were the resellers, garages, and consumers with fleets of trucks such as department stores, bus companies, and taxicab companies.

With the great growth in the number of gasoline marketers, the only way an ambitious company could grow and expand, aside from the natural increase in the use of gasoline, was to find new ways of securing customers from companies already established in the territory. Vigorous efforts were made to get as much of the "attractive" business as possible. Price cutting, secret rebates, and other concessions were given to preferred tank-wagon and service-station customers. It was apparent that, unless some definite marketing policy was soon effected, all low-cost or attractive business of a company maintaining a single price schedule would be lost, and it would have only high-cost business to handle.

In a study of the situation, Standard's Marketing Committee found that in 1924 Standard's sales through service stations, in which the company had an investment in excess of $37,000,000, was 28.7 per cent of the total and sales to resellers 34 per cent.[46] The shrinkage in the percentage of sales through service stations and the growth of sales through the resellers, or dealers, was significant. Under the circumstances, something had to be done to protect the growing, profitable trade through the more permanent outlets—the service stations—rather than market through resellers, who were always open to overtures from the oil company willing to make the lowest price.

In June, 1925, the Marketing Committee made various recom-

46. Unanimous Recommendation by Marketing Committee as to Marketing Policy on Gasoline, June 19, 1922. Jackson File.

mendations to the Board.[47] While accepting full responsibility for the price policy pursued since 1920, the committee frankly stated that the policy had not been economically sound from the point of view of maintaining the company's position. The widespread margin between the cost of goods and prices realized by competitors at certain periods had increased Standard's competition, had been a direct cause for its loss of business, and had increased the cost of marketing. However, no one on the Marketing Committee wanted to abandon the 2 cent differential inasmuch as the reseller and large consumers were now important factors to be recognized. However, to protect the service-station trade, the committee recommended that the company make certain price concessions to large buyers. If the recommendations made were adopted and persistently followed, the company should be able to stem the tide and regain its position.

Much to the surprise of its competitors, Standard on July 1, 1925, announced the Quantity Discount Agreement Plan. It was based upon the principle that the larger the order for gasoline, the greater the discount. Written contracts were to be made with gasoline customers for one year. Under these, resellers and large tank-wagon customers were allowed monthly and yearly discounts from the tank-wagon price on specified quantities of gasoline purchased and certain discounts were to be made to service-station customers. Effective July 1st, the following monthly gallonage discount schedule was offered: [48]

MONTHLY GALLONAGE DISCOUNT

Tank Wagon Contract	Service Station Contract
Over 1,000 gallons per mo. $\frac{1}{2}$ cent	Over 300 gallons per mo. 1 cent
Over 2,000 gallons per mo. $\frac{3}{4}$ cent	Over 600 gallons per mo. 2 cents
Over 3,000 gallons per mo. 1 cent	
Over 6,000 gallons per mo. $1\frac{1}{2}$ cent	

CUMULATIVE GALLON DISCOUNT

Tank Wagon Contract	Service Station Contract
Over 12,000 gallons per year $\frac{1}{2}$¢	Over 3,600 gallons per year 1¢
Over 24,000 gallons per year $\frac{3}{4}$¢	Over 7,200 gallons per year 2¢
Over 36,000 gallons per year 1 ¢	
Over 72,000 gallons per year $1\frac{1}{2}$¢	

47. *Ibid.*
48. Company Encyclopedia: Marketing, II, Quantity Discounts; Ward K. Halbert, "Standard's Quantity Discount System Met By All Competitors," *National Petroleum News*, XVII, No. 41 (October 14, 1925), 33-37.

This was Standard's answer to price cutting, rebating, gift giving, and other concessions made by competitors, especially to Standard's larger and more profitable accounts. In taking such a step, the company pioneered in establishing the open discount system, which came to be of outstanding importance in the marketing of gasoline.

Although other refiners were skeptical of the effect, the new QDA policy met with widespread approval even among Standard's competitors because its basic principles were the same as those used in practically every other industry. Several of its major competitors, Sinclair, Texas, Roxana, Pure, Magnolia, and a considerable number of independent jobbers prepared at once to fall into line. The Minnesota Petroleum Association and the Indiana Independent Oil Jobbers Association formally endorsed the new plan. On the other hand, some, like the Missouri Oil Men's Association, disapproved of the plan as unethical and demoralizing.

Simultaneously, Standard dropped its long-standing policy of giving away equipment indiscriminately for the sake of increasing its gallonage. This striking departure from past policy was regarded as the most important single development in marketing in years. It even transcended the importance of the QDA. Taken in conjunction with the QDA, the two policies constituted the greatest single advance in business methods made at one time in the history of oil marketing. Together they seemed to open the way for business based on merit, quality of products, enterprise, good salesmanship, and sane business building. The new policies struck a blow at irregular dealers without descending to their level and waging battle upon their terms.

As the competitive conflict sharpened between 1926 and 1928, owing to an abundance of crude oil and the overexpansion of marketing facilities, price wars increased. The market was flooded with cheap, unbranded gasoline. Service-station operators began offering premiums as an inducement to purchase gasoline. Sofa cushions were sold at cost to regular customers who accumulated a certain number of coupons given with each purchase of gasoline. Sales of cushions reached huge proportions and had a definite effect upon increasing gasoline sales. Other stations offered flashlights, auto robes, and chinaware as premiums.

To eliminate uneconomical marketing practices and bring order out of chaos, the American Petroleum Institute initiated a movement in June, 1928, to formulate rules which marketers of petroleum products might apply uniformly and lawfully, with the Federal Trade Commission's approval, to the conduct of their operations. Hundreds of refinery and marketing executives participated in discussions which resulted in the drafting of "The National Code Practices for Marketing Refined Petroleum Products." Upon its completion, the code was submitted to the industry at the ninth annual meeting of the Institute at Chicago in December. Following the Federal Trade Commission's approval, the Directors of the American Petroleum Institute approved the code and recommended its acceptance by the members as of August 31, 1929.[49]

The rules of the code covered three types of marketing practices: those known to be in violation of the law, those generally agreed to be unethical, and those which, though neither unlawful nor unethical *per se,* were, nevertheless, regarded generally by the industry and the Federal Trade Commission as bad business practices. Among its provisions, the code declared the practice of loaning or leasing gasoline pumps, tanks, and other equipment unsound and recommended that it should be discontinued at the earliest possible moment. No company should paint over any sign of another company until it had communicated with the company whose signs were involved to see if any written contract was involved. Attempts to induce a breach of contract between competitors and customers by any false or deceptive means and the selling of goods below cost with the intent to injure a competitor were declared unfair trade practices. Lotteries, prizes, wheels of fortune, and other games of chance should not be used in connection with the sale of gasoline or motor oils. No oil or other thing of value was to be given away or special inducements granted on opening days, special sale days, or other occasions. Coupon books or scrip of any nature, if used, should be sold and redeemed at face value without any discount.

Between August 31, 1929, and July 28, 1930, about 15,800 separate and distinct units marketing refined petroleum products in the United States signed the agreement. Standard of Indiana signed the code wholeheartedly and without reservation and publicly pledged itself to assist in restoring order within the industry. Despite the good intentions of all concerned, the whole thing fizzled out with the coming of the depression.

The competitive struggle of the 1920's even resulted in an

49. Revisions of the code delayed its final approval until 1931.

attempt on the part of competitors to capitalize upon Standard's own trade-mark. In the spring of 1925, for the purpose of carrying on a national advertising campaign and selling oil under a common brand in order to attract tourist trade, the Independent Oil Men of America adopted the "Red Hat" emblem as its trade-mark. It consisted of two concentric circles. In the space between appeared the words "Red Hat Gasoline." Within the smaller circle, there was a conventional stovepipe hat, red in color with a blue band on which there were white stars, one similar in appearance to the hat used by the mythical Uncle Sam. Formal application was made to register the Red Hat emblem with the Patent Office in June. Soon Red Hat emblems began to appear everywhere. By fall, more than two-thirds of the members were distributing Red Hat gasoline. In 1926 the sign of the Red Eagle, the insigne of the Association, was flying in more than 4,000 towns.

Standard of Indiana filed an opposition with the Patent Office to the registration of the Red Hat emblem on the ground that it infringed Standard's Red Crown trade-mark, which the company had used exclusively for almost forty years in advertising and marketing gasoline.[50] It involved the use of two concentric circles with the words "Red Crown Gasoline" in the space between. Within the smaller circle, there was a red crown of royalty with jewels of white. The concentric circles, the color scheme, the use of the adjective "Red," the fact that a crown and hat were worn on the head and that the emblem applied to gasoline, made the two emblems very similar and confusing. Upon its advertising of Red Crown and the experience of its customers, Standard had built a successful business. It appeared that the use of the Red Hat emblem stemmed from a desire to secure an advantage for the new trade-mark at the expense of Red Crown.

After a hearing upon Standard's opposition, the Examiner of Interferences of the Patent Office made a preliminary decision in favor of Standard and gave IOMA until October 30th to file a complete answer.[51] After a hearing and a rehearing of the case, the Examiner of Interferences decided in February, 1927, in favor

50. "Standard Units Oppose Registration of 'Red Hat' Trade Mark," *National Petroleum News*, XVII, No. 39 (September 30, 1925), 140.
51. "Psychologist Figures Confusion in Red Hat and Red Crown," *National Petroleum News*, XVIII, No. 10 (March 10, 1926), 109; "Present Claims of Standard in Red Hat Trade-Mark Dispute," *The Oil and Gas Journal* (October 28, 1926), 138; "Patent Office Sustains Standard in Red Crown Trade-Mark Case," *The Oil and Gas Journal* (February 24, 1927), 130.

of Standard. IOMA appealed to the Commissioner of Patents, and on August 9th the First Assistant Commissioner of Patents reversed the decision of the Examiner on the ground that there was no proof of actual confusion. Standard appealed to the Court of Appeals of the District of Columbia in January, 1929, and that court reversed the Commissioner's decision.[52] It held that the two trade-marks were deceptively similar. According to the court, this was a case where the likelihood of confusion could have been readily avoided if IOMA had selected an emblem not closely similar to that of a competitor. The opportunity for selecting a trade-mark being as limitless as the imagination, the court questioned the motive prompting the adoption of a trade-mark previously applied by Standard to like goods.

By 1926 Standard of Indiana was operating 4,126 bulk plants and 3,116 service stations, the largest number of any oil company in the country.[53] The next largest was The Texas Company with 1,152 bulk plants and 130 service stations. Standard not only had the largest number of service stations, but it was also the largest marketer of motor fuel in the country. It was selling 11.81 per cent of all gasoline consumed. Standard of New Jersey was second with 9.46 per cent, and Standard of New York third with 9.09 per cent.[54]

GASOLINE SALES IN THE MARKETING TERRITORY OF STANDARD OF INDIANA IN 1926

Company	50 Gallon Barrels	Percentage of Total Sales of Gasoline
Standard Oil Company (Indiana)	21,620,438	35.5
Sinclair Consolidated Oil Company	5,887,795	9.7
Roxana Petroleum Corporation	5,269,790	8.7
The Texas Company	2,324,866	3.8
Pure Oil Company	1,651,995	2.7
Tidewater	829,630	1.4
Producers & Refiners Corporation	683,372	1.1
Total	38,267,886	62.9
All Other Companies	22,540,274	37.1
Grand Total	60,808,160	100.0

During the period 1926–29 Standard not only increased the number of its marketing facilities but also enlarged its marketing

52. 30 F. (2d) 996.
53. *Prices, Profits, and Competition,* 56.
54. *Ibid.,* 59, 226.

territory in 1928 by establishing through the Midwest Refining Company retail outlets in Colorado, Wyoming, and Montana. In anticipation of this move, Midwest had earlier purchased the marketing properties of the Arro Oil & Refining Company of Lewistown, Montana, consisting of three bulk and forty-five service stations, eighteen bulk and service stations of the Aero Oil Company of Cheyenne, Wyoming, and seventy-five service stations of the Vickers Petroleum Company in Colorado and New Mexico. Midwest expected to erect its own service stations as required. By virtue of this extension into the Rocky Mountain region, Standard invaded the marketing territory of an old Standard unit, the Continental Oil Company, upon which Midwest had largely depended in previous years for the distribution of its products. Counting all kinds of marketing outlets—company-owned and operated service stations, AAA and PDISSL, and POSSL dealers—Standard in 1929 had 7,535 outlets and 4,205 bulk plants under its control.[55]

While the development of Standard's marketing system during the 1920's had been remarkable, the growth in the number of competitors and their marketing facilities was even more striking. Starting with 672 oil companies selling gasoline through about 615 service stations in the marketing territory of Standard of Indiana in 1920, the number of competitors had grown until by 1929 there were 15,421 oil companies, large and small. In the aggregate, they had 9,027 bulk stations and 24,246 service stations. With such an amazing growth of competition, it is not surprising that Standard's percentage of the total business had declined by 1929 to about 30 or 40 per cent. Despite the decline in its percentage of the business, the significant fact was that Standard's sales had shown a steady increase in volume and value. The volume had increased from 1,169,978,511 gallons in 1919 to 2,154,469,499 in 1929 and the value from $221,969,793.23 to $317,991,771.14.[56] Sales of gasoline, the leading product in volume and value, had increased from 674,984,782 to 1,428,009,128 gallons. Refined oils, which ranked second, remained fairly constant. Striking was the increase in the sale of asphalt products. In 1919 they ranked sixth in volume, but in 1929 they were in third place. Sales of gas oil, distillates and fuel oils, lubricating oil, and motor oil ranked fourth, fifth, and sixth, in the order named, in 1929.

55. Stations in Operation ending December 31st For The Following Years. Company Encyclopedia: Marketing, I.
56. Figures for the Sales Department only. Furnished by M. A. McNulty, Comptroller, Standard Oil Company (Indiana), on May 11, 1950.

CHAPTER XII

Humanizing the Company

THE MOMENT THAT COLONEL STEWART BECAME CHAIRMAN OF THE
Board of Directors revolutionary changes were made in the relationship of the company to its employees and the public. The
first notable change, which marked a complete reversal of early
practices and policy, was in Stewart's relations with the press.
Under the old regime, when newspaper men came to Standard's
office to find out about affairs of the company, they were given to
understand that these matters were strictly private, and the curiosity of the press was definitely resented. Consequently, the company was unpopular with the press and in a hundred ways, directly
and indirectly, the public mind was poisoned against Standard.
"A permanent attitude of secrecy is a confession of weakness,"
Stewart declared, "for it implies that the management has policies
of such a character as to make secrecy necessary. A well-managed
company has no such policies, and secrecy is unnecessary except
relating to plans still in the stage of development. Secrecy en-
courages suspicion, and suspicion among either customers or employees hinders a business; it never aids it." [1] With nothing to
conceal, Stewart welcomed the press and announced that the door
to his office would "always swing in." He would see anyone who
wanted to see him and tell anything within reason about any
business which engaged his attention. By being open and frank
with the newsmen, Stewart not only created good will but took
advantage of the opportunity to give the public the facts about
company affairs rather than have gross distortions and untruths
published.

Stewart not only gave newsmen information when requested
but deliberately sought publicity for the company. "I am firm in
my conviction," he said, "that the personnel of a business organization, as well as its policy, its purposes, its current activities, its
volume of business, and its products all are matters of public

1. Colonel Robert E. Stewart, "It Pays Us To Tell Our 'Business Secrets,'" *Stanolind
Record*, III, No. 2 (December, 1921), 2.

interest, and that these matters should be given as wide publicity as possible. In short, I believe the management of a business should devise ways and means to give the public any information about the business which the public may care to have—the only exception to this rule being the publication of future plans of the organization, the details of which have not matured." [2]

Stewart, believing that his company had a story to tell, launched in March, 1919, one of the greatest programs of institutional newspaper advertising ever seen in the country. It was the first of its kind in the advertising and business world. Costing about $100,000 per year, large advertisements were run regularly in the newspapers throughout Standard's marketing territory. The campaign was not about the products Standard manufactured and sold but about the details of its business. Under such captions as "Who Owns The Standard Oil Company (Indiana)?" "Who Manages The Standard Oil Company (Indiana)?" "The Function of The Standard Oil Company (Indiana)," "The Policy of The Standard Oil Company (Indiana)," "The Facilities for Distribution of The Standard Oil Company (Indiana)," "Democracy in Industry," "The Standard Oil Company (Indiana) and Its Competitors," the policies, principles, profits, practices, prices, operations, and other phases of the company's business were freely and frankly discussed week after week. Such a policy was unheard of in the practice of large corporations and Standard in particular. For ten years these friendly messages to the public were published. Steadily, though slowly, Stewart lessened the gap between his company and the public.

Stung by the unfairness of the La Follette Committee Report in the spring of 1923 and aware that Standard loomed large in the public mind as a manifestation of Big Business, Colonel Stewart was fighting mad. Putting on his old campaign hat, he started on March 18th on a "barnstorming" trip to visit the cities and towns of the Middle West and tell the citizens the truth about Standard of Indiana.[3] With him, in a private Pullman car, went the Directors. They visited nineteen of the sales division offices, the refineries, and met about 8,000 company employees. Between March 18th and May 15th, they traveled more than 6,000 miles, and Stewart addressed forty-one audiences—Chambers of Commerce,

2. *Ibid.*, 1.
3. "Colonel Stewart's Tour Opens New Sales Policy Independents Must Heed," *National Petroleum News*, XV, No. 23 (June 6, 1923), 23; Neil M. Clark, "How Standard of Indiana Wins Public Approval," *Forbes* (June 23, 1923), 361-363.

Rotary clubs, Kiwanis clubs, Lions clubs, and other business and professional groups—in twenty-two cities of the Middle West and Northwest.

Once Stewart had been presented to an audience, he would, first of all, point to his Directors sitting about the table and say: "They and they alone run the business; they make the policies." Then he would introduce each one. "Stand up, Jackson, I want these men to know our Vice-President in Charge of Sales." He would then tell briefly how Jackson started with the company as a stenographer in 1896 and worked his way to the top. The same informal but effective method was used in introducing "Doc" Burton, "Eddie" Seubert, "Monty" Parks, and the Directors who had started with the company as an office boy, timekeeper, common laborer, draftsman, or in some other lowly capacity. Stewart would then ask his audience: "Do these men look like dirty, crooked businessmen?" For the first time in history in these cities and towns, the ordinary citizens got a glimpse of the "top brass" of Standard. Many were, no doubt, much surprised to find Standard's Directors ordinary, hard-working human beings just like anyone else.

With the introductions over, Colonel Stewart, as an "unashamed representative" of Big Business, would launch into an inspiring address upon the policies, motives, and ideals of Standard. "I told them," said Stewart, "the story of Standard Oil. I told it plain and straight. I gave them the intimate facts." What the company had done for its employees, the growth in stock ownership, the lack of any connection between the various Standard Oil companies, management's concern for a fair return for stockholders, competition in the Middle West, how competitors were essential to good business, the services rendered by Standard, wages, taxes, and dividends provided the Colonel with plenty to say, and he effectively said it. Everywhere he spoke on the absurdities and untruths in the La Follette report. He not only told the company's side of the story but that of the entire oil industry. When he stopped talking, many a time, his audience would yell: "Go on! Tell us some more! We want to hear the rest." It was the greatest one-man show the Middle West had ever seen.

While visiting one of these cities on the tour, the members of the host club at a luncheon for Stewart and the Directors improvised a song to the tune "Tammany" and sang it for the guests. It ran:

THE CHIEF DRAWBACK ABOUT BEING GENEROUS IS THAT IT ATTRACTS SO MUCH ATTENTION

National Petroleum News, May 5, 1926. Reproduced through the courtesy of the *National Petroleum News*

BLIND MAN'S BUFF AS PLAYED IN SOUTH DAKOTA

National Petroleum News, September 2, 1925. Reproduced through the courtesy of the *National Petroleum News*

The Facilities for Distribution of the Standard Oil Company (*Indiana*)

THE service which, at all times, the Standard Oil Company (Indiana) is prepared to render its patrons, rests securely upon a solid foundation of complete distribution.

To perfect a system which shall make every product manufactured by the Company instantly available to anyone, anywhere, any time, has been the goal toward which this Company has been working since the day of its organization.

As yet this ideal has not been achieved; but the system as it stands is conceded to be the most perfect of its kind in the world.

The present equipment for distribution, including grounds, buildings, storage tanks, motor trucks wagons, etc., represents an investment of more than $30,000,000.

There are 27 main stations where complete stocks of all products are kept on hand. Supporting these are the bulk stations located at 2881 carefully selected points in 11 states. These stations are equipped with storage tanks having a combined capacity of 86,113,650 gallons of gasoline, 66,115,300 gallons of kerosene, and 4,300,000 gallons of lubricating oils.

It is necessary to carry this tremendous stock—total 156,528,950 gallons—at all times to insure quick, convenient service to the patrons of the Standard Oil Company (Indiana) wherever they may be, regardless of transportation difficulties or weather conditions.

To enable the Company to fulfill its obligations to patrons, and deliver to them the products they require, it is necessary to maintain a fleet of 3700 motor trucks and a caravan of 8500 horse-drawn wagons, either active or in reserve. These tank wagons are so organized that they, at regular intervals, can reach 75% of the homes in the territory at present served by this company.

Supplementing the wagons, an equipment of 530,000 iron barrels, representing an investment of more than $7,000,000, is kept in service to insure the safe delivery of oils and gasoline, even to those remote places where the dark-green tank wagon never has penetrated.

For the convenience of the motoring public, a chain of 1300 service stations has been organized and many others are in the course of construction. These stations are prepared at all times to supply the motorist with his requirements of gasoline and lubricating oils in any quantity and at the lowest prices.

This, in outline, is the distribution system upon which the service of the Standard Oil Company (Indiana) rests.

It is the hope of the Company that the time is not far distant when no person in the territory served will be more than five or six miles from a Standard Oil Company (Indiana) service station if he lives in the country, or more than one mile away if he lives in a town or city.

Standard Oil Company
(*Indiana*)
910 So. Michigan Avenue - Chicago, Ill.

1908

The Chicago Tribune, March 24, 1919. Reproduced through the courtesy of *The Chicago Tribune*

ONE OF STANDARD'S INSTITUTIONAL ADVERTISEMENTS

Standard Oil, Standard Oil,
Turns the darkness into light;
Makes the customers feel all right.

Standard Oil, Standard Oil,
Curse it, damn it,
You can't do without it,
Standard Oil!

Through the years, Colonel Stewart spoke before scores of business, professional, and civic groups telling the story of Standard, championing the cause of Big Business, and defending the oil industry against malicious attacks. Never before had any chief executive of Standard of Indiana or any other Standard company or any oil company made such an effort to bring about a better public understanding of his company or the oil industry. It certainly was a new and effective approach to an old problem.

In a large corporate organization such as Standard, Stewart recognized that it was also good public relations—and good business—to bring management and employees closer together. The top was too far from the bottom. In order to reduce the gap, many significant innovations were introduced. In making these changes, Stewart declared: "I would rather leave as a heritage to my four sons that I tried to do something for the 27,000 employees of the company, than establish a nation-wide reputation as a business man." [4]

The first move in such a program was the establishment of the Industrial Relations Plan, one of the most notable experiments in industrial democracy in the country, under which the labor relations in the Manufacturing Department of the company were conducted from 1919 until 1937. In developing and putting into operation such a plan, the company was one of the pioneers. The initial impetus to the adoption of the plan came from W. L. MacKenzie King, Director of Industrial Relations for the Rockefeller Foundation, who had been studying labor relations since 1914 in various industrial corporations in which John D. Rockefeller, Jr., and his family had substantial stock interests. At the request of Standard of Indiana, Mr. King made a study of labor relations in its refineries and coal mines in 1918.

After an intensive study, Mr. King made a formal and compre-

4. *The Oil and Gas Journal*, XXII, No. 15 (September 6, 1923), 65.

hensive report on February 14, 1919.[5] This became the Magna Carta in guiding the company in its labor relations program. King's investigation disclosed an enlightened policy and efficient administration with respect to terms of employment and working and living conditions. So far as working conditions in the refineries were concerned, King reported: "It would be difficult, if not impossible, to surpass, in America or elsewhere, the conditions in some of the shops and departments. There was ample space, good lighting and ventilation, and a regard for cleanliness." The company had shown great wisdom in adopting the eight-hour day and in anticipating the inevitable trend. The maintenance of wages at all times comparable with and even better than the rates paid for similar work within the competitive area, supplemented by the company's past record, made any comment by King unnecessary. The establishment of the Employment Bureau was cited as further evidence of an enlightened policy. The methods followed appeared to be efficient and comprehensive. The Annuity Plan was "generous in its conception and provisions." While the company had made provision for pensions, King pointed out that it recognized no obligation and made no provision at all for sickness or disability payments. Since the death benefit was paid at the discretion of the Directors, the report indicated that the plan should be modified to remove all uncertainty. The safety program and plant medical service received warm commendation. It was suggested that physical examinations of all applicants for employment might be added to the precautions already introduced by the Medical Department. Both as to policy and administration, King declared, "The Company will be entitled to a foremost place in any comprehensive industrial audit."

King suggested that the company give further consideration to the long-run policy of employing women. The war had brought women into many industries where they had not worked before, and the natural tendency was to continue them in their jobs. King called attention to what the effect of such a policy might be in view of the unemployed, returned soldiers. If the company continued women as employees, there should be a matron to supervise all that pertained to their welfare, and consideration should be given to appointing women as foremen. The company was commended for adopting a policy of equal pay for equal work so far

5. W. L. MacKenzie King, "Report on Labor Relations of Standard Oil Company (Indiana)," February 14, 1919.

as women were concerned and for making payment by the hour instead of by the piece.

Company policy in erecting houses for permanent employees at Wood River and the Carlinville mines and their sale to employees had been eminently wise, for it encouraged labor to be thriftier, steadier, and more contented. The class of houses erected was excellent. What had been done at Carlinville was worthy of the highest commendation. King questioned the practice of the company in departing from its regular policy on housing to create a men's camp at Whiting. While necessitated by the war and done as a temporary measure, its retention was likely to have an unsettling effect upon labor permanently employed. King found that there was a special need where refineries and mines were located for something in the way of a social center or community building where employees and their families might meet in social intercourse. Since these communities could not be counted upon to undertake such ventures, the company should consider doing so.

In reviewing the company's policy toward labor unions, King found that, while the company was not hostile, it recognized them only in so far as it was necessary to secure labor in the different trades, and where recognized to this extent, it avoided, if possible, any formal contract with unions. Memoranda of terms and conditions of employment or letters of agreement formed the basis for existing arrangements between the company and those unions. The extent of recognition accorded varied considerably. At Whiting and Wood River only two of three trades were involved. At Sugar Creek recognition had been extended to a number of unions representing virtually all labor employed. At Carlinville there was a complete recognition of the United Mine Workers, except that there was no formal contract. King recommended that the company make it clear to labor that it was not opposed to collective bargaining, but it was prepared to foster and encourage that method of dealing with labor where it could be shown that such a relationship was likely to prove mutually advantageous.

In concluding his report, King recommended that the company strengthen what it was already doing. It should make an effort to secure a fuller appreciation of its industrial welfare program on the part of employees and the public. Machinery should be established by which a wider measure of democratic control might be secured for workers regarding terms of employment, working and living conditions, medical service, and other matters. It already had the nucleus of such an organization, but of all the things that the company was already doing for the welfare of its employees, King pointed out that "probably not one person in five of the Company's employees has any knowledge, or one person in a thousand in the State." In order to achieve the objectives set forth, King recommended the establishment of an employee representation plan to permit some joint relationship on all matters of mutual concern. "The reason labor has appreciated so little, and often appeared ungrateful," King declared, "is that things which have been expected to win the appreciation or gratitude of workers, have been done *for* them, not *with* them." Employees might be made to feel the full significance of all these measures, take more pride and interest in them, and become more intelligent and loyal if allowed to participate in the inauguration and administration of such measures and have some knowledge of the financial and other obligations involved. It was necessary to harmonize industrial with political development and to bring the government of industry more into accord with the democratic spirit of the day. The underlying idea should be to make industry a partnership in which each of the contributing parties—capital, labor, management, and the community—would share in a knowledge and understanding of the enterprise as a whole and of each other's rights and duties, worked out on the principle of round-table conferences effected through some device of representation.

King believed that postwar readjustments and the serious industrial unrest throughout the world rendered more imperative than ever the adoption of the plan suggested. A step so significant, taken by a great corporation like Standard of Indiana, according to King, could not fail in the critical times ahead to assist materially in maintaining the harmonious relationships which had hitherto existed between the company and its employees. "It should do more than this," King said, "it should serve, on the part of the company, as a contribution toward the reorganization of industry in America, upon lines calculated permanently to improve relations between the several parties to industry. It is still within the power of directors of large industries to determine whether the method of further change shall be that of evolution or revolution. The change itself is inevitable."

After giving careful consideration to King's report and various plans for employee representation already in operation, like that of Hart, Schaffner & Marx, Standard's Directors concluded that if such plans were sound in principle and successful in operation, they should inaugurate such a system. They did not believe that the company had been neglectful in its relationships with employees, but every Director had come up through the ranks and recognized the extreme importance of keeping in close touch with the needs, desires, and wants of employees. Therefore, under the guidance of King, an industrial relations plan was drafted in keeping with the principles enunciated and suited to the particular needs of the company.[6] It incorporated the strength of those plans already in operation in other companies and the weaknesses of none. When drafted and adopted, the plan was considered the broadest, fairest, best, and most efficient yet devised.

The purpose of the Industrial Relations Plan was to provide an effective means of contact between management and employees on matters pertaining to industrial relations, give employees a voice in matters pertaining to their employment and working conditions, establish regular facilities for access by employees' representatives to management and for consultation by the management with representatives of the employees, and promote the common interests of employer and employees. Nothing was intended to abridge or conflict with the right of employees to belong to any legitimate society, lodge, fraternity, labor union, or other organization.

To carry out these objectives, the plan provided for the creation of a department of industrial relations under the supervision of a director, who was to be directly responsible for the operation of the plan and the maintenance of just and harmonious relations between all persons in the company. Assistant directors were to be appointed at each refinery, who were to report to the director. Within the department, divisions relating to employment, safety and accident, health and welfare, workmen's compensation, statistics, and publication were to be organized. Managers, superintendents, and employees were to be free to communicate in person or by letter with the director of industrial relations at any time. All officials of the company were to be charged with giving full co-operation to the work of the Department of Industrial Relations.

A joint general committee was to be established at each re-

6. "Report on Industrial Relations in the Standard Oil Company (Indiana)," 1923, I, 35-42; Company Encyclopedia: Manufacturing—Labor Relations, Industrial Relations Plan, 17-33.

finery. These committees were to be composed of representatives elected by the employees and an equal number appointed by management. In the larger refineries, there was to be one representative to about every two hundred employees; in the smaller plants, one to about every one hundred and fifty. The employees in each plant were to be divided into natural and convenient divisions for electing representatives so that all departments and crafts might be fairly represented. Representatives were to be elected for a term of one year but were eligible for re-election. They could be recalled at any time, too, by a two-thirds vote of the employees. Company officials and employees having the power to hire, discharge, or discipline an employee were ineligible for election as employee representatives. Regular primaries were to be held for nominating candidates, and a few days later the general election was to be held. All employees in the refinery might vote for employee representatives except company officials and employees in a supervisory capacity, provided the employee had been in the service of the company for at least sixty days prior to the primary. Elections were to be held annually on days to be set by the director of industrial relations, who was to supervise the elections and see that they were conducted in such a manner that management and employees would have confidence in them. All voting was to be by secret ballot, with the ballot boxes under the supervision of tellers appointed by the employees and management.

The Joint General Committee was to have power to elect its own officers, arrange its own procedure, and appoint such subcommittees as might be necessary. Regular meetings were to be held once a month and special meetings when necessary. Representatives of the employees and management were to alternate in presiding over the meetings. Minutes were to be kept of all proceedings and not only placed on file at the refinery and in Chicago but distributed among the employees at the plants. A change or amendment to the plan, subject to the approval of the Board of Directors, could be made at any time by a petition signed or concurred in by two-thirds of the employees' representatives. Every representative was protected in the discharge of his duties, without fear of his individual relations with the company being affected in the least degree by any action taken by him in good faith, in his representative capacity. For time lost while occupied in attending meetings called during working hours, employees were to receive compensation at their regular rates of pay. Moreover, the company was to provide suitable places for meetings and defray all expenses involved in operating the Industrial Relations Plan.

The Joint General Committees were to have jurisdiction over wages, hours, employment, working conditions, safety and accidents, sanitation and health, recreation, and any other matters which might be brought before them by representatives of either management or employees. They might make any recommendations to management. Likewise, management might refer any questions to them for study and report. If a committee made a recommendation to the plant management and it was not accepted, an appeal could be made directly to the President of the company and ultimately to the Secretary of Labor in Washington, by whose decision both employees and management were to abide. The right of appeal was the keystone of the whole plan. Management did not have the final word and the employees always had the opportunity of obtaining redress from a disinterested agency. On account of this fundamental feature, there was never any reason for a strike.

In addition to the Joint General Committees, the plan provided for holding an annual conference to be attended by all representatives, the Chairman of the Board, the President, and such other officers as they might designate.

In order to protect employees against unjust or arbitrary treatment by foremen who tried to be little autocrats, or any unfair or undesirable condition of their employment, the plan included a list of specific offenses for which an employee might be suspended or dismissed without further notice. For offenses not listed, an employee could not be discharged without first having been notified that a repetition of the offense would make him liable to dismissal. Furthermore, any employee who felt he had been unjustly treated or subjected to any unfair condition had the right of appeal to the superintendent of his department and the assistant director of industrial relations in the order named. If the matter could not be satisfactorily adjusted, the employee could appeal to his Joint General Committee. This unusual procedure guaranteed every employee fair and just treatment, and no one could be fired because of some whim or caprice of a supervisor or foreman.

Preparatory to inaugurating the Industrial Relations Plan in the Manufacturing Department, the Directors created the Department of Industrial Relations on April 16, 1919, and appointed as its director J. W. Curry, who had been in charge of the Employment Bureau since 1917. Mr. Curry was sent to Hot Springs for a three- or four-day conference with John D. Rockefeller, Jr., Mr. King, and a number of associates, who discussed the background of the plan, how it should be operated, and the results to be attained.[7] Assistant directors were appointed for Whiting, Wood River, and Sugar Creek. On June 5, 1919, the plan was announced to the employees through printed notices posted at each refinery in which Colonel Stewart invited the employees to participate in the plan by nominating representatives for the Joint General Committees on June 11th and by electing candidates on June 16th.[8] At the same time, booklets outlining the plan in detail were widely distributed among all employees.

Owing to the fact that the plan was new, unique, and different from anything the employees had ever known, it was not received with much initial enthusiasm. Many of the men were suspicious of the motives of the company in launching such a plan. Others were indifferent. There were not very many around the refineries who had any confidence in the plan. To many of the more serious-minded employees, what the company had done was unbelievable. It was the fulfillment of a dream. As the plan was read, studied, and better understood, more employees became interested. When two or three or more got together, they talked about the plan and possible candidates to represent them.

For purposes of employee representation and voting, Whiting was divided into eleven divisions and given twenty-two representatives, Wood River into six with eight representatives, and Sugar Creek into eight with twelve representatives. The whole-hearted interest of the employees in the plan was indicated by the fact that of the 6,100 employees at the three refineries, 97.4 per cent voted in the primary election. They nominated one hundred and sixteen men to represent them: sixty-six at Whiting, twenty-four at Wood River, and thirty-six at Sugar Creek. Until the primary election, there had been little political activity, but the next morning after the names of the nominees were known, the political pot began to boil. The fight was on to see who would be finally elected. Placards and bulletins in favor of different

---

7. Interview with J. W. Curry, May 25, 1949.
8. "The Primaries and The Elections," *Stanolind Record*, I, No. 1 (October, 1919), 7-8; "Voters Kick Over the Dope Bucket," *Stanolind Record*, I, No. 4 (January, 1920), 6-9.

candidates were posted on tanks, trucks, fences, and other places. Meetings were held at the refineries where the candidates appeared, talked, and tried to win votes. Interest in the election was rather universal and created considerable excitement. Early on election day, June 16th, ballot boxes, two tellers, and a polling desk appeared in various divisions of the refineries, and every employee was given an opportunity to vote. This continued until evening. When the ballots were counted, it was found that 98.1 per cent of those eligible to vote had voted.

In the first regular election held in December, 1919, there were some sweeping changes among the employee representatives. Favorite candidates were unseated and "dark horses" were elected in all four plants. More than half of the previously elected representatives went down to defeat. Some candidates thought they saw evidence of influence being exerted by the company to bring about their defeat, but after a thorough investigation, it was found that the rumors were baseless. As a matter of fact, management officials were always exceedingly careful not to do anything that would violate the freedom of choice.[9] To have exerted influence in favor of or against any candidate would have immediately destroyed the effectiveness of the plan. "Should I learn that any major or minor executive of this company," declared Colonel Stewart, "had in any way sought to influence the election or defeat of any candidate, I would ask immediately for his resignation." There was a distinct trend during the first nine years to reject candidates with experience and inject new blood into the Joint General Committees. In spite of the trend, there were some, such as Henry Behrens, Nick Scholl, Dan Gallagher, and Oliver Thibedeau of Whiting, L. G. Harrison of Sugar Creek, and William E. Kelley of Wood River, who were re-elected year after year. It was not until 1928 that the employees elected more candidates with experience than without. This indicated a growing appreciation of the value to employees of having representation by experienced men.

An organization meeting of the Joint General Committee at Wood River was held on June 18th.[10] Similar meetings were held at Whiting and Sugar Creek two days later. It had been expected that the Industrial Relations Plan would go into effect simultaneously at all plants, but due to the newness of the whole affair and

9. Interview with J. W. Curry, May 25, 1949.
10. Company Encyclopedia: Manufacturing—Personnel, Labor Relations, 20-21.

the enormous volume of detail involved, it was necessary to postpone the inauguration of the plan at Casper until fall. Nominations and elections were held there on September 17th, the election on the 22nd, and the first meeting of the Joint General Committee on the next day.

In some plants, like Sugar Creek, the force was 100 per cent union labor. Even after the Industrial Relations Plan had been adopted, the policy of the company was to confer with union representatives, but to make no formal agreements. However, it had "understandings" as to wages and working conditions which represented practical compliance with regular union agreements. The company preferred these to signed contracts, but during the depression of 1921 all union agreements except those with the teamsters' and miners' unions were dissolved and practically all "understandings" were eliminated by 1923. If union members desired a change in wages, hours, or conditions of labor, they followed the regular procedure and took up matters with their Joint General Committees. Some union members were members of these committees. In fact, some of the strongest support of the system came from union members of the Joint General Committees despite the adverse attitude of their own unions.[11]

Within two weeks after the plan was instituted at Sugar Creek the common laborers' union went on strike partly for the recognition of their union and partly for an increase in wages.[12] After two weeks, the entire plant closed down for two more weeks. By the end of the month the shiftmen, who were members of the Oil Field, Gas and Refinery Workers' International Union, brought the matter to the attention of the United States Secretary of Labor, who sent a conciliator. Upon investigating, the conciliator advised the common laborers to return to work and use the Joint General Committee, which they did, and the plant resumed full operation.

Within five months' time after the establishment of the Industrial Relations Plan, the Joint General Committees were flooded with petitions asking for major and minor improvements in working conditions.[13] The petitions covered a wide range of subjects:

11. *The Chicago Tribune,* January 10, 1920.
12. "Report on Industrial Relations in the Standard Oil Company (Indiana)," 1923, I, 54-55.
13. "A Recipe For Happiness," *Stanolind Record,* I, No. 1 (October, 1919), 32; "See the Wheels Go Around," *Stanolind Record,* I, No. 2 (November, 1919), 8-9; "See the Wheels Go Around," *Stanolind Record,* I, No. 3 (December, 1919), 10.

wages, sanitation, seniority, safety measures, working conditions, erection of new buildings, and many others. Little things which had annoyed workmen for years were brought up for consideration. Some things could be done at little cost, others involved large sums. The Joint General Committees went to work in earnest, studying each petition thoroughly and with a determination to be fair to all. By October 13th two hundred and thirty-six matters had been considered at all refineries, and one hundred and fifty-four were satisfactorily settled. In nearly every instance where a committee reported in favor of a petition, the action of management was favorable and prompt. The results were little short of amazing, and they more than justified the existence of the committees. Employees began to believe that possibly the Industrial Relations Plan was the best thing ever devised for the rank and file. Some began to feel, too, that, in turn, they must give the company an honest day's work for a day's pay.

Although not a formal part of the Industrial Relations Plan, Stewart decided that he and his Directors should visit Whiting, Sugar Creek, Wood River, and Casper to inspect the plants, meet with each Joint General Committee, establish more intimate contacts with the employees, and talk over problems of mutual interest. Therefore, in July, 1919, Stewart and the Directors started out. The usual procedure at each place was for Stewart to stand on a truck or some improvised platform in the refinery yard before the assembled workers. He would then introduce the Directors one at a time, calling them by their first names and telling how each one had come up through the ranks after starting as a stenographer, timekeeper, or a machinist's helper. "Because we control the policies and direct the operations of this corporation, with which you have tied up your fortunes," Stewart continued, "we believe that you have a right to an accounting of our stewardship. I am here to make that accounting, to report to you what we have been doing." He would then launch into one of his inspiring discussions of wages, finances, profits, expenses, volume of sales, the Industrial Relations Plan, and other aspects of company business of interest to the assembled workers. In order to reach every worker, Stewart and the Directors would appear several times during the day in the larger refineries. Stewart's frank, fair, and forceful manner made a profound impression and inspired confidence. Employees were soon convinced that as long as he directed the affairs of the company they were assured of a square deal. There is no doubt that the personal influence of Stewart in his contact with the employees through these meetings and in other ways contributed largely to the success of the Industrial Relations Plan.

At noon or in the evening Stewart and the Directors had lunch or dinner at the plant with the members of the Joint General Committee. A spirit of earnestness and enthusiasm pervaded the meeting. Dispensing with all formality, everyone sat down at the table without regard for rank or position. The visiting executives deliberately scattered themselves among the employees in order to talk and get the employees' point of view. Meeting the Directors and talking with them about problems of mutual interest resulted in their appearing to employees less and less like devils and more and more like human beings. According to one participant, "These meetings went farther towards dispelling any existing feeling of antagonism and suspicion from the minds of the employees than any action of the Joint General Committee." After the meal, there were informal talks by the plant manager, Stewart, other officials, and employee representatives. In time, the employees became very outspoken in presenting complaints at these meetings. Speaking at a meeting of the Directors and the members of the Joint General Committee at Whiting on July 10, 1928, Colonel Stewart with pride asked: "In what other company in the world comparable in size to ours, with its 30,000 employees, would an employee ever have the opportunity of so voicing his complaint in the presence of the company's chief executive and its Board of Directors and that without prejudice to his position? A finer example of the workings of our Industrial Relations Plan, a greater proof of its success could not be offered."

Each year, as long as Stewart was Chairman, he would charter a private Pullman car, get his Directors aboard, no matter how busy they were, and off they would go on their annual visit to confer with the Joint General Committees. Summarizing the experiences of these trips, Seubert said: "We had a hell of a time all day long, shaking hands, making speeches, attending meetings, and listening to complaints. However, it was a good experience for all of us." [14] While the benefits resulting from these annual visits cannot be definitely measured, there is no question that they became a most effective means of establishing friendlier relations between the top and the bottom and of creating *esprit de corps* among employees.

14. Interview with Edward G. Seubert, August 31, 1948.

To report on the various activities of the Industrial Relations Plan and the company and to help create a greater community feeling among employees, a monthly magazine, the *Stanolind Record,* was started in October, 1919. Beginning in November, 1920, the size of the magazine was increased from thirty-two to sixty-four pages in order that items about activities in the Sales Department might be included. In addition to news relating to the Industrial Relations Plan, the *Record* ran feature articles by the Directors on appropriate subjects, biographical sketches of executive officers, and stories on all phases of the company's business, the petroleum industry, towns in which the company did business, styles, diet, health, and a host of other subjects. Photographs and news items about employees, recreational events, and other happenings at the different refineries and in the sales field occupied a large amount of space. Distributed free to employees, the *Record* became an increasingly important medium in helping to create *esprit de corps* among the vast army of Standard employees.

The first annual conference of the Joint General Committees was held in December, 1919, at the Hotel La Salle in Chicago.[15] This was the first industrial assembly of its kind ever held west of the Allegheny Mountains and in the field of labor relations it was an historic occasion. Each Joint General Committee had previously designated a representative to serve on the program and nominating committees. These committees met early on the day of the conference to arrange the order of the program and to select a presiding officer. As soon as the conference was organized, each subcommittee of the Joint General Committees presented a report on the activity at its plant. The painstaking care with which these committees did their work indicated the importance which they attached to the Industrial Relations Plan. Also, one was impressed by the fairness of mind and the ability of American workmen to solve their own problems, if given an opportunity. The reports emphasized the fact that the settlement of every problem had been based upon facts obtained by a careful investigation of each situation.

At the banquet in the evening, brief speeches were made by delegates from each of the refineries. The remarks of Daniel J. Gallagher, the employees' fighting representative from Whiting,

15. "Colonel Stewart Stirs Convention," *Stanolind Record,* I, No. 4 (January, 1920), 3-5.

represented the sentiments of many when he declared: "When we employees meet the management as men to men, and deal with each other fairly and squarely, we both get a lot out of it. It's for the good of both of us, and the results have already proved that this Industrial Relations Plan is going to be of enormous benefit to the employees, the management, the stockholders, the public and everybody."

The climax of the evening's program came when Colonel Stewart addressed the group. Speaking frankly and man to man, he emphasized the fact that there was no paternalism in the company's policy of dealing with its employees; that the Industrial Relations Plan was a business proposition on both sides, but a business proposition founded on a policy which, it had been proved, would work to the benefit of both the employees and the company. Without divulging what was being considered, Colonel Stewart indicated that the Directors were at work on a proposition which would eventually make it possible for all employees to exercise an even greater influence in company affairs.

In the minds of many, the holding of this conference marked the beginning of a new epoch in the industrial history of the Middle West. It demonstrated the success of the Industrial Relations Plan in a manner so convincing as to be almost startling. Everyone was sorry that the day was over, for it had been a stimulating experience. The general reaction was expressed by one participant who said: "It is without exaggeration to say that every man who had the good fortune to attend the first annual conference left the meeting with the feeling that corporations are neither soulless nor heathens, and with a determination to preach to his fellow workers the gospel of the Industrial Relations Plan."

The Industrial Relations Conference continued to meet annually in Chicago, except for 1925, when it met in Casper. Beginning in 1923 the program was changed to consist of general reports by each Joint General Committee rather than by each subcommittee of each Joint General Committee. In addition, papers were prepared in advance on designated topics by various members for presentation. "Every Employee a Salesman and Booster," "The Principles of Fair Dealing Between Management and Employees," "Free Medical Service to Employees," "Vacations With Pay for Hourly Paid Employees," and "Unemployment Insurance" were representative of the subjects presented. At the conclusion, there was always a period for the general discussion of these and other problems of mutual interest.

With the conclusion of the first annual conference in December, 1919, all of the machinery of the Industrial Relations Plan and procedures under which it operated had been established. Only minor changes were made in the plan between 1919 and 1929. For example, in 1921 the date for holding the annual conference was changed. In 1922 a requirement that members of the Joint General Committee must be American citizens was adopted. More significant was the fact that the plan was extended to include the employees of Midwest Refining in 1921, the General Office, and the Chicago Sales Division in 1924.

Only those directly and intimately associated with the inauguration and the early history of the Industrial Relations Plan knew the heartbreaking difficulties of putting the plan into operation and making it work. Many a time they were so discouraged about ever getting the spirit as well as the letter across to the men that they would have given up had it not been for the personal encouragement and backing of Colonel Stewart. Several of the Board of Directors and many of the operating officials at the refineries did not believe either in the theory or practice of the plan. Only one Director and a few plant officials were outspoken in their support of the plan. Foremen resented the restrictions upon their power to hire and fire. Frequent conflicts occurred between the managers of the refineries and the assistant directors of industrial relations over authority in settling local grievances. There was a desire on the part of a minority of the employees for too much hasty action on highly important matters. The great majority, however, recognized the need for a slower pace and backed their committees in taking time to make a careful and thorough study of the problems presented. Some representatives found it difficult to adjust themselves to the "give and take" feature of the plan. A few representatives failed to appreciate the necessity of impartially considering all questions, and there were instances of a tendency to trade votes—"log rolling." On important matters there was also a tendency for management representatives to line up on one side of a question and employee representatives on the other. Generally speaking, the finest spirit and the best of cooperation prevailed, although, at times, members of the Joint General Committees got too personal in their remarks.

In practically every plant there were local situations which tended to create distrust of the plan. In the Wyoming refineries there was still a great deal of fear of the company and opposition to any schemes presented by management. Also, the refusal of the Directors, after being petitioned, to restore an overtime rate for common labor did not promote confidence in the plan. At Sugar Creek the bitterness of the old fight with unionism lingered among the Mechanical Department employees. A bank failure at Wood River during the depression of 1921–22, in which hundreds of employees lost their savings, undermined confidence in the company because several local plant officials had held prominent positions in the bank, and the company would not make good the losses. At Whiting, there was a lack of co-operation by the leading officials in backing up the plan, and this fact was well known not only to department heads and foremen but also to many employees. A general 10 per cent cut in wages for all employees in the Manufacturing Department ordered by the Board in February, 1921, without any previous conference with or discussion by the Joint General Committees, led many employees to believe that the Industrial Relations Plan was "just damn junk."

In spite of all these obstacles, confidence in and loyalty to the Industrial Relations Plan slowly and gradually developed, and by 1923 a majority of the employees were sold on it.[16] This was due, to a large extent, to some of the accomplishments under the plan. In 1920 the Whiting Joint General Committee initiated a move for a six-day week for shiftmen. Until 1915 shiftmen had worked twelve hours, seven days a week. In that year the company adopted the eight-hour day with no loss of pay, but the seven-day week was continued. Upon receiving the request, Stewart asked the Joint General Committees to work out a scheme which would make a six-day week practicable. As a result of a study of the situation, a plan was recommended to the management which was approved and became effective March 1, 1920. Under the arrangement shift workers received thirty-two consecutive hours off each week. At about the same time, the Joint General Committee at Whiting petitioned for an annual vacation with pay, but the Directors believed that a more equitable thing would be to provide annual vacations for all employees. On April 3, 1920, the company announced that all employees in continuous service of

16. "Report on Industrial Relations in the Standard Oil Company (Indiana)," 1923, I, 57.

the company for twenty years or more would be entitled to an annual vacation of two weeks on full pay.

An important part of the Industrial Relations Plan was an organized program for the prevention of accidents, and the Joint General Committees made many recommendations for the adoption of additional safety measures. Gratified by the results of the safety program at Whiting, the Directors decided in the spring of 1920 to extend the organized safety program to all other refineries. Since the development of the accident prevention program at Whiting to its high degree of efficiency had been largely due to the efforts of "Safety" Smith, he was made supervisor of safety work in all refineries, also assistant to Curry, director of the Industrial Relations Department. The organization and techniques used at Whiting were, in time, extended to the other refineries.

After the inauguration of the safety program there was almost a continuous reduction in the frequency of accidents every year in the Manufacturing Department, and Standard began to make impressive safety records.[17] In 1926, for the first time in fourteen years, Whiting, the largest of Standard's refineries, went through the year without an industrial fatality. This was an outstanding achievement in view of the fact that the average number of full-time workers was 3,773. Lost-time cases per thousand workers per month averaged only 1½, which was the lowest record for all Standard refineries. The year 1927 was the most successful since the establishment of the Safety Department. During the year, every refinery bettered its record of the previous year, and the Manufacturing Department as a whole showed a reduction in accident frequency rate of 38 per cent as compared with 1926. In 1928 Whiting made one of the finest accident prevention records in the history of American industry. It operated sixty days or 2,000,000 man-hours without a lost-time accident. Such a record would have been considered impossible ten years previously. Also, in 1928, the Laramie refinery, the company's smallest plant, set a record of two years without a lost-time accident. Safety contests among the company's refineries to see which one could have the

17. "Whiting Leads All S. O. Refineries in Safety in '26," *Stanolind Record*, VIII, No. 4 (February, 1927), 30-31; "Refineries Reduce Accidents 38 Percent in Twelve Months as Laramie Wins 1927 Safety Race by Making Perfect Score for Fourteen Months; Whiting's Record Remarkable," *Stanolind Record*, IX, No. 4 (February, 1928), 31; "Two Million Man Hours Without A Lost Time Accident Is Whiting's Remarkable Accident Prevention Record," *Stanolind Record*, X, No. 3 (January, 1929), 18, 20.

lowest accident record each year proved to be an effective stimulant for employees to practice safety.

About 1921 the Sales Department inaugurated a safety program under the direction of F. C. Singleton.[18] Rules of safety suitable for the sales fields were made without regard to expenses. A safety committee, composed of employees, was appointed in each of the twenty-seven sales divisions to supervise the work. To reduce the number of accidents involving motor equipment, the company created in each sales field a "Safety Court" composed of employees which met weekly. Any employee, whether a manager or truck driver, who had been in an accident had to appear before this court with his immediate superior as his attorney. If the investigation showed that the employee had been guilty of carelessness in observing traffic laws, the Safety Court fixed the punishment, which was often as novel as the plan itself. For example, a truck driver might be removed from his position and "sentenced" to work for two weeks in the company's warehouse as a common laborer.

When automobiles were first used for delivering oil products, there were occasional deaths and accidents at railroad crossings. With six deaths in 1922 and seven in 1923, the company inaugurated in 1924 a policy of requiring all company vehicles, even those of Directors, to make a full stop before crossing any railroad tracks. This meant spending thousands of dollars in time. During 1924 company vehicles made 85,000 railroad crossings a day or 31,000,000 in the year without a single crossing accident. In the ten states of Standard's marketing area there were 5,494,405 automobiles registered in 1925 and there was one fatality at railroad crossings for every 9,172 cars registered. Standard had only one accident among its 12,500 cars, which traveled about 192,000,000 miles.

In five years of safety work, accidents in the Sales Department decreased more than 51 per cent. In 1927 all safety work of the company was brought under the supervision of "Safety" Smith, but Singleton continued as the director of safety for the Sales Department. Despite the safety measures taken, the Sales Department accident records for 1926 showed a frequency of 7.24 per million man-hours worked. Not only was the personal injury rate

18. "Safety's Arch Enemy Is Day Dreaming, Oil Company Figures Show," *National Petroleum News*, XVIII, No. 28 (July 14, 1926), 77-78; *Chicago Journal of Commerce*, June 20, 1922, October 13, 1925.

high but also the property damage. At the end of 1928, after a full year of safety work under Smith's supervision, the frequency rate was reduced to 6.72, and to 2.47 in 1933.

During the first nine years of the operation of the Industrial Relations Plan 1,816 adjustments were made by the Joint General Committees. Of the 1,393 classified as important subjects, 661 related to wages, 524 to working conditions, and 208 to conciliation.[19] Of the recommendations made by the Joint General Committees, 87.2 per cent were approved in full or in part by management and only 11.4 per cent were rejected. Only six appeals were made to the Secretary of Labor at Washington; one-half of these decisions favored management, the other half the employees. The record on appeals indicated that there were very few matters on which employees and management could not agree when the problem was approached with a determination on both sides to solve it in a just and equitable manner in the light of all facts. While the Industrial Relations Plan never worked perfectly, it consistently and effectively improved the working conditions of employees, brought management and labor closer together, demonstrated the inherent fairness, good faith, and square dealing of the American workingman, and developed an exceptional *esprit de corps* within the company.

Probably the greatest influence in bringing about better cooperation between employees and management was the launching of an employee stock purchase plan in 1921. The idea had its inception shortly after Stewart became Chairman in 1918, when a proposal was made in the Board of Directors that a bonus system, as an answer to petitions for wage increases, should be established by the company.[20] After a full discussion of the matter, a bonus system did not seem desirable. Most bonuses were paid at Christmas time, they were soon spent, and there was no lasting benefit. Furthermore, the granting of a bonus smacked of paternalism. It was a gift, and understanding people did not want gifts of this kind. The Directors preferred something that had a permanent value, something that would encourage thrift, something that would stimulate employees to take a greater interest in the com-

19. "Big Decline in J. G. C. Business Over Nine Year Period Shows Success of Industrial Relations Plan in Company's Refineries and General Offices," *Stanolind Record*, IX, No. 10 (August, 1928), 26-27.
20. "Illness or Death Only Excuse For Stock Sale," *Stanolind Record*, VII, No. 5 (April, 1926), 8.

pany. An employee stock purchase plan seemed to fulfill these requirements and tie in closely with the objectives of the Industrial Relations Plan for giving employees a voice in determining matters of vital interest to them. Through a stock purchase plan, employees could become partners in the business. Such a plan would also contribute to Colonel Stewart's ambition to have 100,000 stockholders in his company. "I want them right here in the Middle West," he said emphatically. Every stockholder was a potential customer. As Stewart saw it, increasing the number of stockholders was also good public relations.

In order to increase the number of stockholders, there had to be an adjustment in the capital stock structure of Standard. The amount actually invested in the business approximated $185,-000,000 instead of $30,000,000 as indicated by the company's capitalization. Owing to the disparity between the capitalization and the actual investment from plowing back earnings, a single share of $100-par Standard stock sold for about $700 in August, 1920. This made it difficult for stockholders to dispose of their stock and for small investors to buy. Furthermore, the low capitalization created an impression of exorbitant earnings and aroused public resentment. Rumors of a stock dividend and the purchase of a stock interest in Midwest's refinery caused Standard's stock to soar from $700 per share early in September, 1920, to $810 per share on October 28th.[21] On the next day, the Directors declared a stock dividend of 150 per cent. News of the action reached New York just before 3 P.M., and when the market closed Standard's stock stood at $805. Trading in the new stock, when issued, began on the 29th with $315 to $320 per share bid.

While the declaration of a stock dividend automatically reduced the market value of Standard's stock and put it more within the reach of the small investor, it was still high. At a special meeting of the stockholders on December 9, 1920, the par value of Standard's stock was reduced from $100 to $25, and the number of shares increased from 1,000,000 to 4,000,000.[22] This reduced the market value of the new stock to about $74. The way was now cleared for the stockholders at the annual meeting on March 3, 1921, to approve the proposed employee stock-purchase plan.

The plan, similar to one already adopted by the Standard of

21. "Standard Oil Company of Indiana Declares 150 Per Cent Stock Dividend," *National Petroleum News*, XII, No. 44 (November 3, 1920), 35.
22. Minutes of the Board of Directors' and Stockholders' Meetings, II, 812.

New Jersey, was to run for five years beginning March 31, 1921.[23] Any employee who had been in continuous and exclusive service of the company for more than one year was eligible to purchase an amount of stock not in excess of 20 per cent of his annual compensation. Regular deductions from the employee's pay were to be made and deposited by the company to his credit in a special fund. The company also paid into the fund to his credit a sum equal to 50 per cent of his deposit. Standard's Directors designated trustees to receive the funds, purchase the stock, and administer the plan. In order to avoid the fluctuations of the market and enable employees to know how much stock was being purchased, the price was to be fixed by the Directors on March 31st of each year during the five-year period. The price represented the average market price of the stock for the six months previous but in no case was it to be fixed below the par value of the stock. No employee was to receive his stock before the termination of the five-year period, except as provided for in the provisions for withdrawals. At the end of the five years, the trustees were to distribute all stock and any cash which was not enough to buy a full share. In case any employee went on strike or for any reason quit his employment without the company's consent, he forfeited all rights to participate in the annuity plan, the stock-purchase plan, and all other rights.

The announcement of the plan attracted widespread interest for several reasons.[24] In the first place, here was a great industrial corporation, which had been held up to the extreme point of public contumely in the "muck-raking" days, calmly taking a step toward making its employees partners in industry. The action surpassed any similar steps taken by any first-ranking industry in the United States. It was significant in showing that a younger generation of leaders with ideas differing from those of the older generation had come into control. The younger leaders were applying themselves to the ever-necessary and difficult task of marching with the times. Secondly, the employee stock purchase plan was put into effect in the early stages of one of the most severe industrial depressions and periods of deflation ever experienced. In spite of this and at a time when many companies were retrenching in the industrial relations field, Standard of Indiana not only carried out the pro-

23. "Oh, Boy! We're Almost a Standard Oil Stockholder," *Stanolind Record*, II, No. 6 (April, 1921), 1-8.
24. *Chicago Journal of Commerce*, December 1, 3, 1920.

posed plan but maintained and advanced the entire range of its industrial relations activities. Thirdly, the liberality of the terms of the plan caused considerable surprise. Few companies had gone so far as to add 50 per cent to all stock purchased by employees. Only a highly successful organization of great financial strength could establish and carry through a plan as liberal as Standard's. Fourthly, few common stocks were stable enough to offer the employees an investment such as Standard was able to do. Lastly, and most important, the employee stock purchase plan was one of the great achievements in modern industrial history in bringing about co-operation between employee and employer.

Thirteen thousand employees were eligible to subscribe for stock on April 1, 1921, and by April 15th, when the first deductions were made, 6,100 employees had grasped the unparalleled opportunity to become stockholders at $73 per share.[25] Many employees were unable to subscribe to the plan during the first month but gave notice that they wished to do so in the future. When the first five-year period came to an end on May 20, 1926, 15,325 or about 70 per cent of the eligible employees scattered over the Middle West and the Rocky Mountain region received 384,638 shares of stock worth $34,350,000, for which they had paid $11,800,000.[26]

Upon the receipt of their stock, a wave of enthusiasm, probably without parallel, swept through the ranks of the employees.[27] Letters and telegrams by the hundreds poured into Colonel Stewart's office conveying expressions of appreciation. Desiring to tell the world how they felt, Standard's Wood River refinery employees prepared and paid for a full-page advertisement in the St. Louis *Globe-Democrat* on May 22, 1926. Carrying the names of about six hundred employees who shared in the plan, the open letter to Colonel Stewart and the Directors expressed their appreciation and thanks for the liberal stock purchase plan which had just terminated. The editor of the *Globe-Democrat* referred to the advertisement as one of "the most singular full-page advertisements within the memory of many newspaper men of experience." The enthusiasm was heightened on June 15th, when the em-

25. "Two And One-Half Million Wage and Salary Increase, Affecting All Departments of Company, Ordered," *Stanolind Record*, IV, No. 8 (June, 1923), 1-2.
26. *Stanolind Record*, VII, No. 7 (May, 1926), 31; VIII, No. 8 (April, 1927), 8.
27. "Stock Certificates, Dividend Checks Stir Enthusiasm," *Stanolind Record*, VII, No. 9 (July, 1926), 29-31.

ployees received their first dividend of 62½ cents per share plus an extra 25 cents.

The Second Employee Stock Purchase Plan, authorized to begin on March 31, 1926, was similar to the first, except for the fact that it ran for only three years, the amount an employee could subscribe was reduced from 20 per cent to 10 per cent of his annual salary, and a subscriber must have retained at least two-thirds of the stock purchased under the first plan unless relieved by the Board of Directors. If employees sold their stock shortly after receiving it, the purpose of the plan would be nullified, for the objective was to stimulate employees to take a greater personal interest in the welfare of the company and to encourage thrift.

Every effort was made by management to encourage employees to hold on to all of their stock under the first plan, which most of them did. With the development of the speculative stock boom in 1928, certain employees began pledging their Standard stock from the first plan as security with brokerage houses. In some instances brokers required an immediate transfer of ownership. Therefore, in September, 1928, the management warned all employees that if they put up their stock as collateral and it had to be sold, they would lose their right to participate in any future stock buying. By the end of the Second Employee Stock Purchase Plan in May, 1929, approximately 239,750 shares of stock worth $14,385,000 were distributed to 15,022 employees who had paid $6,606,000 for it.[28] The employees now owned approximately 4½ per cent of the outstanding stock of the company.

Obviously, Colonel Stewart was tremendously happy and pleased over the amazing success of the plan. Speaking to the employees of the Chicago Sales Division in the spring of 1926, the Colonel proudly asserted, "In our company we have the world's greatest democracy. . . . Someday, and it is my wish that it be so, the Chairman of the Board of Directors and all of the Directors of the Standard Oil Company (Indiana) may be elected by a vote of the employees. There is nothing that would give me greater pleasure, a keener satisfaction, than to have won your confidence to such an extent that you would name me the Chairman of your board of directors and executive head of your company." [29] When Stewart finished speaking, C. F. Hatmaker, manager of the division, took

28. "125.7% Maximum Profit to Participants in Stock Plan," *Stanolind Record*, X, No. 7 (May, 1929), 1-2.
29. " 'Hold On To Your Stock,' Col. Stewart Urges," *Stanolind Record*, VII, No. 7 (May, 1926), 34.

the floor and asked the employees whom they had in mind to elect as Chairman when they had control. A thundering chorus shouted: "Stewart." The Colonel smiled broadly and bowed.

With the establishment of the Employee Stock Purchase Plan and the growth in stock ownership, the appearance of the company's annual financial report began to change. Prior to 1924, the financial statement was either typed or dittoed upon a small sheet of white paper and handed out to stockholders at the annual meeting. It simply listed the assets and liabilities. In 1924 the company began printing the statement. With the adoption of the Employee Stock Purchase Plan, the financial statement was published for the first time in the *Stanolind Record* in April, 1926. Beginning with the financial statement for 1927, a four-page folder printed on plain white paper was used which not only provided the bare figures but a descriptive analysis of the statement by Stewart.

Another advance in the development of a more progressive labor policy was the adoption in June, 1924, of an employees' death benefit plan.[30] All employees, except those in the coal mining department and those who had less than one year's continuous service, were eligible to participate. Under the plan, actual dependents were to be allowed sums ranging from $500 to $2,000, depending upon the employee's length of service with the company. If workmen's compensation were involved in any death case, the company would not pay unless the amount received was less than the amount which would have otherwise been paid under the plan. For those who did not have actual dependents, a death benefit not exceeding $200 was provided to pay funeral expenses. The company paid the benefits and for the administration of the fund without any expense to the employees.

While many notable advances were made during the 1920's in labor relations, company policy in granting pensions under its plan of 1918 grew more conservative in administration because of mounting costs.[31] It became increasingly difficult to secure a pension before reaching the age of sixty-five. The depression of 1921 put industrial pension systems to their first great test. As profits vanished, so did many of the pension plans, few of which were funded or even based on actuarial studies. Despite a more con-

---

30. Minutes of the Board of Directors' and Stockholders' Meetings, II, 1181-1185.
31. Walter G. Whitman, "The Annuity Plan," *Stanolind Record*, XI, No. 1 (November, 1929), 5-6, 8.

servative policy of granting pensions, Standard's annuity payments in 1928 were 40 per cent greater than in 1924. Without restrictions, the increase would have been greater. The number of annuitants in 1928 was 371 when employees numbered 26,000, or 14.3 per thousand employees. This was close to the figure of 15 annuitants per thousand found by the Pennsylvania Old Age Pension Commission in a survey of over one hundred pension plans. Age and service features of Standard's plan were about the average of those of other industrial firms. The size of its annuity payments, when compared with the usual industrial plans, was rather striking. Of fifty-nine plans studied by the United States Bureau of Mines, fifty-three showed the average payments to be less than those of Standard and only four higher. The average of industrial pensions was lower than $500 per year per man, yet the average pension paid by Standard in 1924 and 1928 was approximately $1,000. Standard's allowance of 2 per cent per year of service was generous when compared with the vast majority of industrial plans. Most of the industrial pension plans in 1929, like Standard's, were financed entirely by the employer out of current earnings.

In his survey of Standard's labor relations, MacKenzie King pointed out the need for a social center or community house in the towns where the company had refineries. The new management, under Stewart, studied the matter, conferred with the directors of the Whiting Community Service Association, and in April, 1920, announced that the company was prepared to turn over to the City of Whiting a tract of land to be used as a site for a community service house.[32] In addition, the company was prepared to make available for building purposes a cash fund of $450,000, of which the company had appropriated $300,000, John D. Rockefeller $100,000, and John D., Jr., $50,000. The object was to provide facilities and activities for mental, moral, and physical growth, fellowship and recreation, civic service, and the enjoyment of the arts. In making the announcement, Stewart emphasized the fact that there was nothing paternalistic in the company's taking this action; that the company was making its contribution as a citizen of Whiting, not as an employer; and that the planning, erection, furnishing, and administration were squarely up to the

32. "Whiting Gets Community Service House," Stanolind Record, I, No. 8 (May, 1920), 14; "Whiting Dedicates Beautiful Memorial Community House," Stanolind Record, V, No. 2 (December, 1923), 15.

citizens of Whiting. The company did not propose to suggest how
the building was to be put up or on what plan it was to be operated
after erected. The gift of the company represented an extension of
the Industrial Relations Plan. The gifts of the Rockefellers expressed the interest they still felt in the people of the community
where one of their oldest and largest refineries had been located.

In appropriate ceremonies under the auspices of the American
Legion, the formal opening and dedication of the Community
House at Whiting as a memorial to Standard employees who
served in World War I took place on November 12, 1923. Mayor
Walter Schrage proclaimed a holiday, and thousands of people
attempted to crowd into its auditorium for the program. Colonel
Stewart and Dr. Burton were the principal speakers. Colonel
Stewart's speech stressed the efforts of the company to better the
working conditions of its employees because it was the rank and
file of employees who had made Standard what it was. This building was placed in their hands to develop a community service
whereby the life of the people might be broadened and lightened.
The company would not interfere with its management or operation, Stewart said, but it would watch with interest its use. In his
speech, Burton, with a gifted touch, struck a responsive chord in
the hearts of all old-timers present by comparing the social opportunities in Whiting thirty years ago and now.

The Community House was a two-story, red brick building
patterned after southern Italian architecture. Besides the lobby
and general administrative offices, there was a completely furnished billiard room, reading room, refreshment lobby, club room
for the American Legion, an auditorium with a seating capacity
of about 1,100, a social room, gymnasium, lockers, showers, and
swimming pool. It was the finest, most complete, and beautiful
community house in America. A board of eleven, composed of
five employees of Standard at Whiting and six citizens of Whiting,
was set up to supervise and administer the center for the city.
Maintained by annual membership dues and company contributions, the Community House became "the pride of Whiting" and
an important factor in the social and civic life of the town.

After considering suggestions as to what type of a community
project would be most useful to the citizens of Wood River,
Stewart and the Directors for the company provided $100,000 in
1926 to construct a recreational center and outdoor swimming

pool for the city.[33] The largest portion of the money went into the swimming pool, which was 200 x 300 feet. It was equipped with everything found on a modern beach.

Consideration was given to building a community house for the small village of Sugar Creek, but local citizens pointed out their inability to support such an enterprise. In view of this and the fact that the company annually had to help maintain the Whiting Community House, because it never became self-sustaining as anticipated, the project for Sugar Creek was abandoned.

While Colonel Stewart was trying to bring the top and bottom personnel of the company closer together, he also tried to develop better teamwork and co-operation among the top executives. He decided that the best means of doing this was to have them play together, so he sent a scout into northern Wisconsin to find a place which could be used to accomplish his purpose. As a result, in the spring of 1922 the company purchased an estate on a high spot overlooking Trout Lake a dozen miles north of Woodruff and within a mile of a golf course. By the expenditure of a few thousand dollars, the main lodge and boathouse were enlarged and remodeled to accommodate fifty people. In June and September selected groups of the top executives and the Directors would go via train from Chicago to Red Crown Lodge, as the place was named, for week-end outings.

From the time each party arrived until it left, Stewart had every minute of the day planned, what each individual was to do, and with whom he was to do it. In the morning there was golf with the foursomes prearranged. Those who did not care to play golf went fishing. After lunch everyone played horseshoes and softball. Even though one did not care to fish or play horseshoes or softball, he did. It was customary before the dinner hour for all to gather on the porch of the lodge and hold one of Stewart's "vesper services." Bridge, poker, and conversation occupied the evening. It was a highly regimented and strenuous outing, as those who have attended these outings can relate. This was due, in part, to the personal vigor of Stewart and, in part, to his belief that if executives played together and became better acquainted, they would work together better. When these outings were not being held, Red Crown was open to Directors and certain other officials and their families for vacationing at a nominal daily charge.

33. "Wood River Opens Community Center, Gift of S. O. Co.," *Stanolind Record*, VII, No. 10 (August, 1926), 29-35.

Through the vigorous leadership and strenuous efforts of Colonel Stewart, Standard of Indiana in 1929 meant something radically different to the employees, stockholders, and the general public from what it did in 1918. The difference lay in the fact that in the course of a decade Stewart had humanized the corporation and increased its popularity.

CHAPTER XIII

The Continental Trading Company

SHORTLY AFTER THE MAMMOTH OIL COMPANY LEASED TEAPOT DOME on April 7, 1922, the United States Senate asked Secretary of the Interior Albert B. Fall for all documents and papers relating to the leasing not only of Teapot Dome but also the naval oil reserves No. 1 and 2 in California to Edward L. Doheny, and it authorized its Committee on Public Lands and Surveys to make an investigation. Nothing sensational developed in the committee hearings until late in November, 1923, when witnesses from New Mexico testified to the unusually large expenditures Fall had made upon his ranch properties. Edward L. Doheny testified that he had "loaned" Fall $100,000 on November 30, 1921. Colonel J. W. Zevely, attorney for Harry F. Sinclair, testified that Sinclair had loaned Fall $25,000 in the summer of 1923; that it had never been repaid; and that no interest had ever been paid. When Fall was called to appear before the committee, he refused on the ground that its authority had expired. Sinclair also refused to testify, which practically marked the end of the committee investigation early in 1924.[1] As a result of the sensational disclosures, the Senate instructed President Coolidge to employ special counsel, begin suits to cancel the leases of the naval oil reserves, and to institute criminal action against the parties involved. Coolidge appointed Atlee Pomerene of Ohio and Owen J. Roberts of Pennsylvania as special prosecutors.

On March 12, 1924, the special prosecutors filed suit in the name of the United States against the Mammoth Oil Company, the Sinclair Pipe Line Company, and the Sinclair Crude Oil Purchasing Company in the United States District Court at Cheyenne, Wyoming, to cancel the agreement of April 7, 1922, and the supplemental lease of February 9, 1923, relating to the leasing of

1. *Leases Upon Naval Oil Reserves* (Hearings before the Committee on Public Lands and Surveys, United States Senate, on S. Res. 282 and S. Res. 294), 1924; Robert L. Owen, *Remarkable Experiences of H. F. Sinclair With His Government,* 1929.

Teapot Dome, on the ground that the United States had been defrauded by Fall and Sinclair and that the lease was executed without authority in law. The government asked for a restraining order, a decree nullifying the agreement, the appointment of receivers, a final injunction against the defendants, a decree for accounting, and a decree for ousting both the Sinclair Crude Oil Purchasing Company and the Sinclair Pipe Line Company from Teapot Dome. The two Sinclair companies had been made defendants because their rights were derived from Mammoth, and the government alleged that both were trespassers. The court issued a temporary restraining order, appointed receivers, and set the trial for December 20th. The purchasing company continued buying oil from Teapot Dome after the appointment of a receiver, who impounded the proceeds pending the outcome of the suit.

In preparing for the trial at Cheyenne, Pomerene and Roberts investigated the records of certain banks in the West in which Secretary Fall had accounts, and they found reference to 3½ per cent United States Liberty Bonds, the numbers of which were noted. Through the Treasury Department, these bonds were traced to the Continental Trading Company, which had purchased a total of $3,080,000 through the New York branch of the Dominion Bank of Canada. Inquiry revealed that the Continental Trading Company had been organized by H. S. Osler in 1921 and dissolved in 1923. This was about all the information the government had about the Continental Trading Company.

In an effort to secure information about Continental, the special prosecutors found that James E. O'Neil had resigned as President of the Prairie Oil & Gas Company in September, 1923, and gone to Europe. Henry M. Blackmer had also left for Europe in February, 1924. Colonel Stewart testified in September, 1924, before a grand jury which was considering evidence for the purpose of filing criminal charges against Sinclair, Fall, and Doheny, but he did not throw any light upon the Continental Trading Company.

Government counsel then filed an affidavit in the Canadian courts in an attempt to obtain a process to compel H. S. Osler, the President of the Continental Trading Company, to testify. Osler took refuge in the plea of privilege of counsel and refused to answer the questions submitted. However, in a deposition dated November 24, 1924, he made a carefully guarded statement relative to the Continental Trading Company.[2] In addition to the facts already noted about the origin of the company, Osler said that the business of the company did not require more than a half hour's work per month, and it related primarily to keeping the accounts. Remittances were made monthly by the Prairie Oil & Gas Company and the Sinclair Crude Oil Purchasing Company to Continental's account in the New York branch of the Dominion Bank of Canada, and monthly remittances were sent to the Humphreys companies by the bank on instructions from Osler. After paying the Humphreys companies, the Dominion Bank had instructions to use the balance to buy $3\frac{1}{2}$ per cent United States Liberty Bonds whenever $10,000 or more had accumulated and hold them for the account. From time to time Osler would take out 2 per cent for his commission and divide the balance among his clients.

By the spring of 1923, Osler pointed out, the oil situation had changed considerably from that which existed in 1921 when the Humphreys-Continental deal took place. The general shortage of crude and the consequent rise in price had not taken place as anticipated. On the contrary, there was a flood of oil owing to new discoveries, and the price had fallen. The Humphreys-Continental contract had become onerous from the point of view of the purchasing companies. Moreover, the prospect of litigation over the contract had become alarming. Humphreys had made many threats to sue Continental, alleging that the oil was not being taken according to the original contract. Furthermore, production at Mexia was decreasing considerably; the wells were beginning to pump water, and there was apparently no possibility that anything like the original stipulated amount of oil would ever be secured. Under the circumstances Osler advised his clients to sell the contract, if possible, to Prairie and the Sinclair Crude Oil Purchasing Company.

Once the contract had been sold, the business of the company came to an end, the charter was returned to Ottawa, what few papers and records existed were destroyed, and the life of one of the most intriguing and mysterious business organizations came to an end in 1923. No meeting of the stockholders was ever held except to organize and liquidate the company. No files or records existed because they had been destroyed in the ordinary course

2. *Leases Upon Naval Oil Reserves* (1929), 33-48.

of business. No distribution of assets ever took place, for there were none.

Osler's statement was wholly unsatisfactory inasmuch as he did not disclose who his clients were, who the actual owners of the company were, and other pertinent points. Persisting in his refusal to answer specific questions, Osler was cited for contempt of court, but he appealed. Hoping that Osler might be compelled to testify, the special prosecutors asked the court at Cheyenne for a postponement of the trial until March 9, 1925. Government counsel then issued letters rogatory to any judge or tribunal having jurisdiction of civil cases in France to take the testimony of Blackmer and O'Neil, but both men refused to testify, and compulsory processes could not be resorted to in France against recalcitrant witnesses.

It was expected that Colonel Stewart would be the star witness at the Cheyenne trial, for he was the only one in a position to tell the story of the Continental Trading Company since Sinclair was under indictment on criminal charges. However, when the United States marshal went to subpoena Stewart he was gone. Business associates and his family were reported as not knowing his whereabouts. Consequently, the marshal and his deputies started a nationwide search for the Colonel, but their efforts were in vain.

When the trial opened at Cheyenne in March, John D. Clark, Vice-President of Standard and assistant to the Chairman, issued a statement reluctantly admitting that Stewart was out of the country bound either for South America or Mexico on a business deal so important that Standard wanted to keep his movements secret. Clark reported that his business might keep him away for a month or more.[3] Owen J. Roberts, one of the special prosecutors, commented that he was not surprised since Blackmer and O'Neil had also quit the country. Despite Colonel Stewart's desire to keep the nature of his business secret, it came out that Stewart and Wickett, together with a technical staff, were on a trip inspecting the oil properties of Pan American Petroleum & Transport in Mexico and South America to determine whether or not Standard and a syndicate should buy them.

Three days after the trial opened in Cheyenne, the Appellate Division of the Supreme Court of Ontario ruled that Osler must testify, but by this time he had departed for Egypt on a hunting trip. With all roads apparently blocked in their quest for evidence

3. *The New York Times*, March 10, 1925.

COLONEL STEWART ADDRESSING REFINERY WORKERS

ELECTIONEERING FOR A REPRESENTATIVE ON THE
JOINT GENERAL COMMITTEE AT WHITING, 1923

FIRST BANQUET OF THE ANNUAL JOINT GENERAL COMMITTEE
CONFERENCE, CHICAGO, DECEMBER 4, 1919

THE WHITING COMMUNITY HOUSE

THE WOOD RIVER RECREATIONAL CENTER

about the Continental Trading Company, the special prosecutors went ahead and presented the government's case against Mammoth. M. T. Everhart, Fall's son-in-law, was the government's one hope of finding out how the bonds of the Continental Trading Company came into Fall's possession, but when called to testify he refused to answer on the ground that what he might say would tend to incriminate him, and the court sustained him. Senator Thomas, Colonel A. E. Humphreys, H. L. Phillips, a Director and Vice-President of the Sinclair Crude Oil Purchasing Company, and others testified, but they knew relatively little about Continental. Conclusive proof that the bonds received by Fall came from Sinclair was lacking because none of those who had any connection with Continental were in court.

During the course of the trial at Cheyenne the New York *World* and other newspapers began a bitter editorial attack upon John D. Rockefeller, Jr., and those who held large interests in the companies whose leaders were involved in the oil scandals. At the end of a lengthy editorial on March 23, 1925, the *World* asked: "But where today do the boards of the great oil companies with which Stewart, Blackmer, and O'Neil have been connected stand in this national oil scandal? Where do the directors as individuals stand? Where are the men who act and speak for rich and respectable interests controlling these companies? What have they done and what are they doing for the protection of their own reputations and their personal honor. . . . It is time for an accounting all along the line. It is time to let in the light from top to bottom. It is time to clean house. . . . John D. Rockefeller, Jr., is a large stockholder in the Prairie Oil and Gas Company. So is the Rockefeller Foundation. The General Education Board is a large stockholder in Prairie Oil and Standard Oil of Indiana. Both are supported from Rockefeller endowments. Mr. Rockefeller breakfasts at the White House and discusses law enforcement with the President. But how much has he contributed toward the enforcement of the law as it affects the oil company in which he is heavily interested. When does he propose to begin and what does he intend to do in the case of his own company, where officers and directors have failed in their duty toward the Government."

Stung into action by blistering newspaper attacks, Mr. Rockefeller sent a telegram on March 23rd to Dr. Burton, President of Standard of Indiana, requesting him to forward it to Stewart. It read: "Your absence from the country at this time, although we understand on business for the company, also with Blackmer's absence, are being publicly misconstrued and are bringing criticism on yourself, your company, and your larger stockholders especially named, including myself, the General Board of Education and the Foundation. I strongly urge your taking immediately such action as may be necessary to remove any just ground for criticism." [4] Three days later, Rockefeller issued a statement to the press saying he had no definite knowledge of the facts, and that he had urged Stewart to take immediate steps to see that any just grounds for criticism be removed.

When Stewart returned to New York on March 27th, he was served with a subpoena, but the trial at Cheyenne had ended the previous day. Commenting upon the situation, Stewart said that at the time he went to South America he had no reason to believe he was wanted to testify. Moreover, he had previously appeared before the La Follette Committee and "told all he knew about the Teapot Dome matter." While in New York, Stewart saw Mr. Rockefeller and showed considerable resentment over Rockefeller's telegram which implied that he was purposely absent from the country when he was wanted as a witness. [5] He told Mr. Rockefeller that so far as he and Standard of Indiana were concerned nothing had been done in the Continental transaction that was improper. Furthermore, he thought the deal had been a thoroughly good one for his company, the best that he could make. Considering the mood and attitude of Colonel Stewart, it was impossible for Mr. Rockefeller to discuss the matter further, and he accepted the Colonel's statements as true.

Judge T. Blake Kennedy of the Federal District Court of Wyoming, on June 19, 1925, upheld the validity of the leases relating to Teapot Dome. [6] They appeared to be good leases for the government, and the court found no fraud in connection with their execution.

The government appealed Judge Kennedy's decision, and on September 28, 1926, the United States Circuit Court of Appeals, Eighth District, held that the leases were procured through fraud and corruption and should be canceled. [7] Although there was no evidence of the actual transfer of the bonds of Continental by Sinclair to Fall, the court held that "proper and reasonable infer-

4. *Leases Upon Naval Oil Reserves* (1929), 313.
5. *Ibid.*
6. 5 F. (2d) 330.
7. 14 F. (2d) 705.

ences and presumptions from the accrual of incidents" supplied the "fatal missing link." According to the court, "The entire Continental Trading Company deal bears the earmarks, either of a swindle of the stockholders of these companies which, of course, is not a question before us, or a scheme to create a fund to be used in a way the government claims the profits of the Continental Trading Company, Limited, were in part used, *viz.*, for a sinister or unlawful purpose or both." [8] The Circuit Court instructed the District Court to enter a decree canceling the lease and contract as fraudulent, enjoining the defendants from further trespassing on the reserve, and providing for a general accounting by Mammoth for the value of all oil taken from the reserve under the lease. The defendants appealed the decision, and on October 10, 1927, the Supreme Court sustained the Circuit Court.[9]

A week after the Supreme Court's decision the trial of Harry F. Sinclair on criminal charges of defrauding the government in leasing Teapot Dome began before the Supreme Court of the District of Columbia. Colonel Stewart was present and expected to testify, but the trial suddenly ended on November 2, 1927, in a mistrial because of Sinclair's shadowing the jury. Owing to the fact that he had to make a very important trip to Venezuela and did not know when the Sinclair case would again come to trial, Colonel Stewart conferred with Owen J. Roberts of government counsel, and Roberts informed him that Sinclair's second trial was scheduled to begin on January 16, 1928. If the Colonel could get back by January 23rd and not later than the 24th, Roberts agreed that he might make the trip.[10] Because of a postponement of the trial date, Pomerene and Roberts wired Stewart on January 9th that he need not appear until April 2nd.

After the ending of the first Sinclair trial in November, Paul Y. Anderson, Washington correspondent for the St. Louis *Post-Dispatch,* called on John G. Sargent, the Attorney General, to see if the Department of Justice had made any attempt to trace the $3,080,000 in Liberty Bonds bought by the Continental Trading Company, but Sargent refused to discuss the matter.[11] Anderson

8. *Ibid.*
9. 72 Law. Ed. 137.
10. Owen J. Roberts to Colonel Robert W. Stewart, December 17, 1927; Atlee Pomerene and Owen J. Roberts to Stewart, January 9, 1928. Albert L. Hopkins File.
11. Transcript of Testimony, United States vs. Robert W. Stewart, Supreme Court of the District of Columbia, IV, 443-444.

then called on Senator George W. Norris of Nebraska and told
him about Sargent's attitude. Norris was surprised and amazed that
President Coolidge had not ordered the Justice Department to investigate. Unless action were soon taken, the statute of limitations
would prevent any prosecutions in case fraud was involved. Since
the Department of Justice was not taking any action, Norris introduced a resolution on January 4, 1928, calling upon the Senate
Committee on Public Lands and Surveys to continue its investigation and trace all of the bonds of the Continental Trading
Company to ascertain the beneficiaries. Without debate or a dissenting vote, the Senate adopted Norris' resolution. Rather than
designate a subcommittee to conduct the investigation, the Committee on Public Lands and Surveys decided that the whole committee should act with the Chairman, Senator Gerald P. Nye,
presiding, and Senator Thomas J. Walsh conducting the inquiry.

Since Stewart was the only one of the guarantors of the Continental Trading Company contract available, the committee asked
him to appear, but Stewart was out of the country. L. L. Stephens,
an attorney for Standard of Indiana, in a conversation with Senator Nye on January 12th explained that Stewart had sailed for
Venezuela on December 28, 1927, with the permission of the special
prosecutors.[12] Stephens told Nye that Stewart's business would
keep him out of the country until about March 1st. Though the
committee would like to have him appear immediately, Stephens
got the impression from Nye that his appearance about March 1st
would be satisfactory, and he cabled Stewart to this effect.

Contrary to this understanding, Nye wired the Standard Oil
Company in Chicago on January 14th stating that the Senate Com-
mittee desired Stewart's appearance at the earliest possible time.
Nye expressed the hope that Stewart's return would not be delayed
longer than late in the month in accordance with his original plan.
Stephens replied on the 16th setting forth the agreement with
Roberts and Pomerene, and said that he would endeavor to get in
touch with Stewart and advise Nye of the date of his return. Plans
were being made by Standard for the erection of a refinery at
Aruba, and the controversy between the Mexican government
and the oil companies over the nationalization of the oil lands

12. Gerald P. Nye to Standard Oil Company (Indiana), January 14, 1928; L. L.
Stephens to Gerald P. Nye, January 16, 1928; Gerald P. Nye to Standard Oil
Company (Indiana) January 17, 1928. Albert L. Hopkins File.

had become more critical. These matters required Colonel Stewart's immediate personal attention.

Upon receiving this information from Stephens, Senator Walsh wrote John D. Rockefeller, Jr., appealing for his active aid in persuading Colonel Stewart to appear before the committee and tell the whole story of the Continental Trading Company.[13] Mr. Rockefeller had been watching the situation ever since the opening of the Teapot Dome trial at Cheyenne in March, 1925. As subsequent events in the oil scandal unfolded, more and more pressure was placed on him by the press led by the New York *World* to oust Stewart inasmuch as he was a large stockholder in Standard of Indiana. In a memorandum to Mr. Rockefeller on April 16, 1927, Raymond B. Fosdick noted that the attack was coming from far more papers than the *World*. "Isn't this a matter," he asked, "in which the directors of the Midwest or the Indiana or the Prairie companies ought to make some public statement? My concern is from the standpoint of the Boards, which are heavy stockholders." [14] The attacks by the New York *World* and the St. Louis *Post-Dispatch* upon Mr. Rockefeller for not doing anything about Stewart became so great late in 1927 and early in 1928 that Mr. Rockefeller and Thomas M. Debevoise,[15] his personal attorney, went to see Ralph Pulitzer. Rockefeller expressed his loyalty to Stewart, and said that he was not sure that Stewart had done the things of which he was accused. He explained that they were gathering data and weighing the evidence. He wanted to be fair. If the evidence at any time warranted his taking action, Rockefeller said he would not hesitate to act.

In reply to Senator Walsh's plea for aid, Mr. Rockefeller on January 19, 1928, emphasized that all the facts regarding the Continental Trading Company should be brought to light in order that the guilty might be punished and those who had acted uprightly protected.[16] "The present uncertainty," he wrote, "is harmful to the entire oil industry, as well as disquieting to the public." He was confident that Colonel Stewart would return in a few days and be available. "It is my belief," he continued, "that when the facts are known it will be evident that any part he took in the matters in question reflects in no way on him or his company." Mr. Rockefeller was not clear as to how Senator Walsh thought

13. Thomas J. Walsh to John D. Rockefeller, Jr., January 16, 1928. Rockefeller File.
14. Raymond B. Fosdick to John D. Rockefeller, Jr., April 16, 1927. Rockefeller File.
15. Interview with Thomas M. Debevoise, December 1, 1948.
16. John D. Rockefeller, Jr., to Thomas J. Walsh, January 19, 1928. Rockefeller File.

he could be of help and asked to be advised. Walsh replied that Rockefeller could make it clear to Stewart that the stockholders expected him to come forward and tell the whole story of the Continental Trading Company.[17] Stewart had professed to Roberts and Pomerene his entire ignorance of the whole affair, but Walsh contended that Stewart and other Standard officers must know all about the transaction.

Rockefeller wrote Stewart on January 24th and said: "Because of the complete confidence which I have always had in your integrity, based upon a business acquaintance extending over many years, the assurance you gave me several years ago, when the transactions of the Continental Trading Company were first questioned, satisfied me that your record in the matter was clear." However, the present situation, according to Rockefeller, was such that nothing short of the fullest statement of all facts could clear the skirts of those who had no improper connection with the transaction in question and remove the cloud of suspicion which now overhung the entire industry. Stewart owed it to himself and associates, stockholders, and the public to help bring these transactions to light. "No desire, however praiseworthy," Rockefeller wrote, "to protect those who may have been guilty of wrongdoing, justifies the withholding of any slightest fact that will clean up the situation." Rockefeller vigorously urged Stewart "not to wait for an invitation from the Senate Committee, much less a subpoena, but to wire Walsh at once, offering to appear and tell all." [18] On the same day, Rockefeller wrote Senator Walsh that Colonel Stewart had long known how he felt about the situation.[19] Furthermore, he said that he had just written Stewart urging him to offer immediately to appear and tell all he knew. "My confidence in Colonel Stewart's integrity is such," Rockefeller wrote, "that I count on for his sake and the sake of his company the earliest and most complete public statement from him."

The Senate Committee hearing got under way on January 24th. The first witness was M. T. Everhart, Fall's son-in-law, who testified that $233,000 in bonds had been delivered to him in May, 1922, in Sinclair's private railroad car. The bonds were for a one-third interest in the Tres Ritos Cattle & Land Company, which was owned by Fall and Everhart. Of the $233,000 in bonds,

17. Thomas J. Walsh to John D. Rockefeller, Jr., January 23, 1928. Rockefeller File.
18. John D. Rockefeller, Jr., to Colonel Robert W. Stewart, January 24, 1928. Rockefeller File.
19. John D. Rockefeller, Jr., to Thomas J. Walsh, January 24, 1928. Rockefeller File.

$200,000 had been purchased by Continental. Everhart used a portion of the bonds to pay the debts of the company and the balance was placed to the credit of Fall in banks at Pueblo, Colorado, El Paso, Texas, and Carrizozo, New Mexico.

On the next day Senator Walsh at the committee hearing asked L. L. Stephens to explain Stewart's failure to appear on the 24th as requested. Stephens repeated that Stewart was in Havana, Cuba, and that he was about to leave there for South America on business of an urgent nature and would not be back until March 1st. Walsh then produced Havana papers showing that Stewart was not too busy, for he was reported as attending the races, dinners, and other social functions. Walsh requested Stewart's immediate return. That very day Senator Nye wrote Stephens acknowledging that Stewart was away with the consent of the special government counsel, and his departure was prior to any knowledge that his appearance before the committee was desired.[20] Nye admitted that the committee had misunderstood as to when Stewart would return. Yet, in fairness to Colonel Stewart, neither Nye nor any of the committee ever publicly corrected the inference made in the press that he was purposely away.

Stephens talked by telephone on the evening of the 25th with Stewart, who said he was sailing for Vera Cruz to confer with Ambassador Morrow and Pan American executives, and he would not return until his business was finished. The next day Colonel Stewart received a telegram from John D. Rockefeller, Jr., repeating the contents of his letter of the 24th and adding: "Unwilling believe morning paper statement you have declined appear until completion business engagements no duty to company or stockholders comparable to your immediate appearance only such action will justify confidence your friends and business associates have in you please wire." [21] Upon receiving this communication, one wonders if Stewart recalled the advice he gave to John D. Rockefeller, Sr., more than twenty years earlier, when Judge Landis wanted the latter to testify. In any event, Colonel Stewart replied that he was canceling some very important engagements and returning at once.

On February 2, 1928, at the age of sixty-two and at the height of his career, Colonel Stewart, a tall, broad-shouldered, massive,

20. Gerald P. Nye to L. L. Stephens, January 25, 1928. Rockefeller File.
21. John D. Rockefeller, Jr., to Colonel Robert W. Stewart, January 26, 1928. Rockefeller File.

genial man, took the witness stand in a crowded room in the Senate Office Building. "With a handsome roll of fat at the back of his neck," wrote Frank R. Kent, "a full blown bosom, tortoiseshell spectacles, lightly compressed lips, he is the perfect picture of the Super-Babbitt. . . . He fairly exudes prosperity and it is quite easy to see he is used to pressing buttons and having battalions of wage slaves bruise each other in the rush to do his bidding." [22] Under the questioning of Senator Walsh, who had known Stewart from their early days in South Dakota, Stewart told of his negotiations with Colonel Humphreys to buy Mexia oil, the events which took place at Blackmer's apartment in the Vanderbilt Hotel, his learning of the Continental Trading Company for the first time, the necessity for paying $1.75 a barrel, his awareness that someone was getting a brokerage of 25 cents a barrel, the guaranteeing of the contract, and the meeting of the Standard's Directors to approve the contracts. [23] There was no orderly line of questioning but a constant shifting from one subject to another. Most affable, Stewart from time to time would remark: "I will be delighted to give you an answer," or "Oh, bless your heart, Senator, I don't know anything about it," or "Thank you, Senator, thank you." On many occasions, Walsh repeatedly asked questions wanting Stewart to "imagine," "assume," or "interpret" something or testify as to what he had "heard" or "understood," but Stewart stubbornly refused to deviate from the facts. His refusal to give hearsay information won the favor of some observers.

When Walsh questioned him about his guaranteeing the Continental contract, the first blood was drawn. "It looks," said Walsh, "as if you had some good reason for signing that guarantee." The massive Stewart half rose from his seat in the witness chair, pointed a husky arm and a long forefinger at the Montana Senator and shouted: "No, sir, except what appears upon the face of it. If you are intimating by that I ever made a dollar out of that personally you are absolutely mistaken. . . . I never made a dollar personally out of that transaction in any way, shape or manner." [24]

Walsh asked if Stewart had read in the newspapers about the testimony of Everhart, and if this was the first information he had about the bonds going to Fall. [25]

22. Brooklyn *Eagle*, February 6, 1928.
23. *Leases Upon Naval Oil Reserves* (1929), 164-198, 205-226.
24. *Ibid.*, 189.
25. *Ibid.*, 192.

STEWART: I do not know at this time whether any bonds went to Secretary Fall.

WALSH: What, if anything, do you know about any of the bonds purchased by the Continental Trading Co.?

STEWART: I never had anything to do with the Continental Trading Co.'s distribution of any bonds.

WALSH: That is not an answer to the question, Colonel.

STEWART: I think it is.

WALSH: The question is what do you know about them, whether you had anything to do with them?

STEWART: Well, I didn't know anything about it.

WALSH: Now, let us get to this transaction by which the Sinclair Crude Oil—

STEWART: (interposing) I never had anything to do with the distribution by the Continental Trading Co. of any bonds.

WALSH: Do you know anything about the matter?

STEWART: I don't know anything about it.

WALSH: What is that?

STEWART: I don't know anything about it, that is, I don't remember anything about it.

By alternately blarneying and bulldozing Walsh, Stewart pushed aside his effort to pin him down and upset Walsh so much that he was unable to wring out of him any other information about Continental. Speaking of Stewart's manner, Frank R. Kent wrote: "It is not an exaggeration to say no more truculent, patronizing, contemptuous and blandly superior witness ever has been seen in Washington. Instead of the committee going after Stewart, Stewart went after the committee. In loud tones he lectured it, told it what he thought it could do and what he thought it could not do." [26] Walsh went on to other questions about the purchase of Continental's contract by the Sinclair Crude Oil Purchasing and Prairie Oil & Gas, and whether Stewart had seen or talked with Blackmer and O'Neil in Europe. As the frustrated Walsh came to the end of his examination, he said to Stewart: "That is all."

Paul Y. Anderson, Washington correspondent for the St. Louis *Post-Dispatch,* who was sitting at the end of the committee table, exclaimed: "Great God! They are letting him off without asking him just the things I wanted them to ask him." [27] Anderson had

26. Brooklyn *Eagle,* February 6, 1928.
27. Transcript of Testimony, United States vs. Robert W. Stewart, Supreme Court of the District of Columbia, IV, 667, 673, 675, 676.

a suspicion from the beginning that Colonel Stewart had some of the bonds, but if not, he knew who did. "I felt," Anderson said, "he was getting away with something. I thought—it looked to me like he had been a pretty tricky witness all through his examination, and I wanted to see that point blank question asked him, to find out if he did know who got them and if he did know who it was because that was what I wanted to know—who got them."

Anderson hastily scribbled two questions on a slip of paper and passed them along the table to Senator Nye. Without a moment's hesitation, Nye put the two questions directly to Stewart.[28]

NYE: Mr. Stewart, do you know of anyone who received these bonds that the Continental Trading Co. is reported to have dealt in?

STEWART: Senator Nye, I did not personally receive any of these bonds or make a dollar out of them; I personally did not make a dollar out of this transaction.

NYE: That was not the question.

STEWART: I have said that to you to make way for something else. I am a witness in a case which is now pending between the Government of the United States and some defendants I have been interrogated in regard to these subjects by the counsel appointed to represent the United States in that case. From their interrogation of me I am of the opinion those are the issues which are going to be tried in that case, and I do not think that the line of interrogation by this committee is within the jurisdiction of the committee under the laws of the United States. I do not think that the question is entirely pertinent to this inquiry, even.

NYE: You understand, of course, that the Senate has specifically directed that we make inquiry into the transaction of the bonds?

After a brief attempt at evasion, Stewart threw away all pretense and defied the committee and the Senate.

STEWART: I have read the resolution under which you gentlemen are operating. Now, furthermore, there are others interested in this matter, and I regret it exceedingly—and I am really not doing it through any lack of respect to Mr. Walsh, or to

28. *Leases Upon Naval Oil Reserves* (1929), 196-197.

you, or to any of the members of this committee—but I have
to decline to answer.

NYE: You would not desire to say you did or did not know?

STEWART: No; I will have to content myself with this statement, by
saying that personally I have never made a dollar out of
this transaction; and second that I have never given any
bonds of any description to any representatives of any
political party, or to any public officer of the United States,
or of any State or Territory, or any municipality inside it.

NYE: Just one more question, Colonel Stewart. Have you discussed any of these bond transactions with Mr. Sinclair, or
has Mr. Sinclair discussed any of these bond transactions
with you?

STEWART: Well, for those same reasons, I have to decline to answer
that. I will say to you that I think that it is not material to
any of the issues, that I knew anything about.

NYE: That will be all.

Until Anderson gave Nye the two questions, everything had
gone along fairly well for Stewart, but during the last ten minutes
of the hearing, he found himself backed into a corner. "One of the
most soothing sights in the world," wrote Frank R. Kent, "is to
see a large, dominant, self-assertive, blustering person with a bel-
ligerent, not to say bullying manner, caught in a jam just at the
time he thinks he has got away with it. It is the sort of thing that
happens too rarely. Usually they do get away with it. . . . It was
quite plain that 'Colonel' Stewart's view of himself—at least up
until the last of the hearing—was a highly complimentary one,
but . . . it is doubtful whether any one else present shared that
view." [29]

Following Stewart's refusal to answer the two questions, the
Senate Committee adjourned at 1:12 P.M. and asked Stewart to
appear the next morning at 10 A.M. Walsh immediately wrote
Rockefeller saying that the press the next morning would advise
him of how well his admonition to Stewart had been observed. [30]
Walsh expressed the hope that it would not be necessary to call
Mr. Rockefeller before the committee for interrogation over what
Stewart had told him, but he would lay the correspondence be-
tween them before the committee to determine whether or not

29. Brooklyn *Eagle*, February 6, 1928.
30. *The New York Times*, February 9, 1928.

Rockefeller should be called. Rockefeller replied that Stewart's testimony on the 2nd covered all the information which Stewart had given him and confirmed the statement made to him that Stewart had not personally profited from the transaction. He did not feel that Stewart failed in his duty to his company and the stockholders, but he was sorry that Stewart did not answer all the questions.

The next morning Walsh resumed his questioning of Stewart. Senators Bratton, Kendrick, and Cutting also asked questions. Most of the questions Stewart readily answered, but it was a stormy session. The greatest explosion came while Senator Cutting was questioning Stewart about his willingness to pay the 25 cents per barrel or $8,000,000 brokerage fee on the Mexia oil.[31]

CUTTING: It did not occur to you whether Mr. Blackmer was doing anything odd or Colonel Humphreys was doing anything odd or you yourself were doing anything odd?

STEWART: I am always doing odd things, Senator.

CUTTING: Well, Colonel, the thing is, knowing your business ability—

STEWART: Let us pass that up.

CUTTING: We are very reluctant—

STEWART: Let us pass that.

CUTTING: Well, passing that, we might assume that you are an imbecile. That is possible.

STEWART: Absolutely.

CUTTING: And one we are very reluctant to take.

STEWART: You can have it if you want it.

CUTTING: There is another logical assumption, that you are committing perjury.

STEWART: You say there is a logical assumption that I am committing perjury?

CUTTING: A possible assumption.

For a moment it looked as if Stewart and Cutting might come to blows.

STEWART: (shouting) I say there is no possible assumption that I am committing perjury, and I am not here to be insulted, and I say you have no right. I do not mean to be insulted, and I shall leave the room instantly if this goes on.

31. *Leases Upon Naval Oil Reserves* (1929), 220. That part of the official record omitted may be found in the Transcript of Testimony, United States vs. Robert W. Stewart, Supreme Court of the District of Columbia, II, 289-291.

WALSH: I think the remarks should be withdrawn.

CUTTING: I move to withdraw that from the record. I did not mean to insult you. We are anxious to assume that you are telling the truth. We are also anxious to assume that you were in full possession of your faculties when you acted as you did at that meeting.

Toward the close of the session Senator Nye repeated the two questions he had asked the previous day.[32]

STEWART: Mr. Nye, now in all fairness, do you think the Senate of the United States wants you to interrogate me as to whether I accept a newspaper story or not?

NYE: Not at all; but the Senate expects us to interrogate you with respect to whether or not you knew anything of the transaction in Liberty-Loan bonds. With that purpose in mind, I am now going to repeat my question of yesterday. "Do you know of anyone who received any of these Liberty bonds in which the Continental Trading Co. is represented to have dealt?"

STEWART: Senator, again, with the greatest reluctance and with great respect for the committee and for the reasons which I have already given in the course of my testimony and for other reasons which might appear later, I will have to respectfully decline to answer that question.

NYE: Very well; I shall also repeat that question of yesterday as to whether or not you have had any conversation with Mr. H. F. Sinclair with regard to this transaction in Liberty-Loan bonds or with regard to the Continental Trading Co.'s transactions?

STEWART: For the same reasons, I shall have to decline to answer.

NYE: Have you had any conversation with Mr. O'Neil with regard to any of these transactions in the Continental Trading Co.'s Liberty-Loan bonds?

STEWART: Not to my best remembrance. I have not seen Mr. O'Neil in a great many years.

NYE: Have you had any conversation with Mr. Osler with regard to the Liberty-Loan bond transactions?

STEWART: I have not seen Mr. Osler in a great many years.

NYE: Have you had any conversation or any knowledge which

32. *Ibid.,* 224-225.

would lead you to believe that any individual or any organization, political or otherwise, was the recipient of any
of these Continental Trading Co. bonds?
STEWART: No, sir.

With the conclusion of his testimony, Colonel Stewart was
excused but requested to stay in Washington until the next day.

The committee went into executive session about 2:15 P.M.
and unanimously voted that Walsh should prepare a report for
the Senate and a resolution directing the arrest of Stewart for
contempt. It was 5 P.M. when Walsh reached the Senate chamber.[33]
The galleries were packed, and there was a full attendance of
Senators. Walsh read his report and resolution without objection
or debate and, with the air of the Senate tense, the resolution was
adopted. The whole proceeding took just seven minutes. Five
minutes later David S. Barry, sergeant at arms of the Senate, and
his deputy, John J. McGrain, were on their way to the Willard
Hotel to arrest Stewart.

When Barry and McGrain arrived, Stewart shook hands with
them, smilingly remarked that he was at their service, and they
notified him that he was under arrest. For the first time in more
than fifty years a person who had refused to answer questions put
to him by a congressional committee was held a prisoner by direct
action of the Senate or House. Usually such a matter was referred
to the district attorney for presentation to the grand jury. Barry
informed Stewart that he would have to be held in custody until
his appearance before the bar of the Senate at noon the next day.
Instead of going to jail overnight, Stewart remained at the Willard
with McGrain on guard. L. L. Stephens secured the legal assistance
of Jesse C. Adkins, head of the District of Columbia bar, and
Frank F. Nesbit, and the three of them worked all night preparing a petition for a writ of habeas corpus to present at court the
first thing in the morning.

When the Senate convened at noon on the 4th, the floor and
galleries were filled to capacity. A great spectacle was about to
take place—the appearance of Stewart before the bar of the Senate. Just before Stewart was to appear, Justice Jennings Bailey of
the Supreme Court of the District of Columbia issued a writ of
habeas corpus, and Stewart secured his release on a $1,000 bond.
Thereupon, the Senate directed that the facts be presented to the

33. *The New York Times*, February 4, 1928.

district attorney for action by a grand jury, and it authorized the employment of counsel to represent the Senate.

While the habeas corpus proceedings were taking place, the Senate Committee succeeded in locating more of the Continental bonds. On February 4, 1928, W. S. Fitzpatrick, Chairman of the Board of Directors of the Prairie Oil & Gas Company, revealed that James E. O'Neil had received some of the bonds.[34] O'Neil had resigned as President of the Prairie Oil & Gas Company on September 13, 1923, and had left for France early in 1924. Sick and advised by his doctor that he only had about eighteen months to live, O'Neil returned to Montreal in 1925. He telegraphed Fitzpatrick, Clark H. Kountz, who had been his secretary and kept his private books for some time, and Judge Flannelly, Prairie's General Counsel, to meet him in Montreal. At the conference, O'Neil showed no disposition to make a full disclosure about the Continental deal, but he told them he had received a share in the profits which, he thought and always had thought, belonged to Prairie, and that he had kept the profits intact. These bonds were in the custody of his son, Wayne, in New York. By inadvertence or a slip, part of the interest coupons had been cashed, but he had put enough additional bonds to the account to cover the interest he had drawn. O'Neil wanted to right this matter before death came.

When the conference was over, Fitzpatrick and Kountz went to New York with an order from O'Neil on his son to deliver the bonds. On May 20, 1925, Wayne O'Neil turned over to them $800,000 in 3½ per cent Liberty Bonds. These were taken to Independence, Kansas, the home office of the company. A Board of Directors meeting was called. Fitzpatrick told them the story, and he turned over the bonds to the Treasurer. Fitzpatrick informed the Directors that he had accepted the bonds in settlement of any claim against O'Neil, and if the government made any claim for income tax, the company would either defend or pay it. Once Prairie had the bonds, it did not cash any of the interest coupons in accordance with O'Neil's request.

Through the testimony of Earl W. Sinclair, a brother of Harry F. Sinclair and President of the Sinclair Consolidated Corporation, Charles E. Crawley, Vice-President, George H. Taber, Jr., Vice-President, and Kenneth Porter, Assistant Treasurer, and H. L. Phillips, President of the Sinclair Crude Oil Purchasing Com-

34. *Leases Upon Naval Oil Reserves* (1929), 247-267.

pany, on February 6th, 7th, and 8th, the details of the purchase of the Continental Trading Company contract in May, 1923, by the Sinclair Crude Oil Purchasing Company and Prairie Oil & Gas were revealed.[35] Somehow or other James E. O'Neil learned in the spring of 1923 that Continental wanted to sell the contract made in 1921. At a conference with Earl W. Sinclair, O'Neil informed him that the Continental Trading Company contract could be purchased for $400,000. Sinclair called Edward J. Bullock, a Standard representative on the Board of the Sinclair Crude Oil Purchasing Company, explained the situation, and Bullock approved the purchase. Sinclair also got in touch with H. L. Phillips, President of the Sinclair Crude Oil Purchasing Company, and had him come to New York.

Upon arriving in New York, Phillips wired Osler to meet him within a day or two. Osler came on May 26, 1923, and brought with him an executed assignment of the contracts in which the figure $400,000 was included; each company, Prairie and the Sinclair Crude Oil Purchasing Company, was to pay half. Phillips and Osler discussed the assignment but made no changes. Prairie and the Sinclair Crude Oil Purchasing Company approved the purchase, which became effective on June 1st. Everyone seemed to feel that it was a good deal. C. W. Martyn, one of Standard's representatives on the Board of the Sinclair Crude Oil Purchasing Company, was suspicious as to why "someone was bearing us gifts" and thought that perhaps the yield was falling off appreciably. However, the runs from May to August removed his distrust, and it was apparent that within three or four months the $400,000 would be recovered. Under the contract with the Humphreys companies, 20,596,594 barrels of oil were still to be delivered, which represented a profit of approximately $4,000,000 for Continental if the contract had not been sold. By the end of 1927 a total of approximately 28,000,000 barrels had been delivered. It was a "wonderfully profitable" contract for Standard of Indiana. The company got crude, got it cheap, and made several million dollars. Under it the Sinclair Crude Oil Purchasing Company had received by the end of 1927 about 11,500,000 barrels of crude.

While the testimony about the purchase of Continental's contract was being heard, Stewart called on Mr. Rockefeller in New York on February 6th. Rockefeller expressed surprise and disappointment over the fact that Stewart had been evasive in his

35. *Ibid.*, 9, 11-13, 118, 124, 150, 152, 192, 240-243, 260-262, 276-281, 304-305, 307-308.

testimony and had refused to answer the questions put by the committee.[36] It appeared as if Stewart were holding back or hiding something. The impression created was so bad as to cause a loss of confidence in Stewart, his company, and the oil industry. Colonel Stewart stoutly defended his position and said nothing could change his decision. Colonel Stewart reiterated the statements made to Rockefeller in 1925 after the Teapot Dome trial, and said "that he did not wish to embarrass in any way the stockholders of his company, and that they could have his resignation whenever they desired it." "This is a question," Mr. Rockefeller said, "which the stockholders should, of course, and will naturally consider as the matter develops." In fact, Stewart went on to say, according to Mr. Rockefeller, that he would resign at any time on Rockefeller's own personal request.

Senator Walsh made public his correspondence with John D. Rockefeller in regard to Stewart on February 8th. At the same time, he subpoenaed Rockefeller to appear before the committee on February 11th. Rockefeller told Walsh that he greatly regretted the situation and was frankly at a loss to know what more he could do. Since Stewart had refused to discuss the case any further, Rockefeller pointed out that he was still without any information which had not already been submitted to the committee.

Mr. Rockefeller, upon being questioned before the committee, revealed his stock holdings in Standard of Indiana.[37] Personally, he held 402,280 shares or a little more than 4½ per cent: Rockefeller held 140 shares in his own name, 137,900 in H. P. Fish's name, 130,000 in A. H. Bates' name, 130,000 in Robert W. Gumble's name, and 4,240 in Butler Herrick Marshall's name. In addition, the Rockefeller Foundation held 460,760 shares or a trifle over 5 per cent, the University of Chicago 30,000 shares or ⅓ of 1 per cent, and the Equitable Trust Company of New York 500,000 shares for Rockefeller's two sisters. All these holdings amounted to just under 15 per cent of the capital stock.

Even if he had held as few as one hundred shares in his own name, Mr. Rockefeller testified that his sense of responsibility and obligation to aid in uncovering this unfortunate situation would have been the same. "I have in view," he said, "the important public interests which are at stake here. But more than that I have personally, as well as relation in other ways as an officer

36. John D. Rockefeller, Jr., to Thomas J. Walsh, February 8, 1928. Rockefeller File.
37. *Leases Upon Naval Oil Reserves* (1929), 311-323.

in these funds, a large investment in the oil industry. More than that, my father was one of the pioneers in the development of the industry. The family name has for over 50 years been connected with the oil industry. I have these additional reasons for being more eager than you gentlemen can be to do everything in my power to bring to light all the facts in this unfortunate matter. . . . This situation, Senator, and gentlemen of the Committee, is far reaching. It affects certain individuals, but far beyond that it affects the whole industry. The oil industry is under suspicion because of the facts that have not yet been brought to light. The business structure of the country is under suspicion for these reasons. The cynic is saying: 'Is there any such thing as basic integrity in business?' "

In his testimony Mr. Rockefeller reiterated his belief in the integrity of Colonel Stewart, yet he wanted to co-operate in every way in exposing a wrong which apparently had been done. Furthermore, as a stockholder in a great many corporations, he was always desirous of using his influence in support of able and trustworthy management. At the same time, he was prepared to withdraw his support from management that no longer justified his confidence.

Following his appearance before the committee, Mr. Rockefeller spoke the next evening over Collier's Weekly Radio Hour and vigorously condemned business dishonesty. Without mentioning the oil industry specifically and with a ring of determination in his voice, he enumerated the high standards which corporations and individuals should follow. Integrity, obedience to the law, clean living, and loyalty were four fundamental qualities underlying character. His address was a sermon on the necessity for character in personal and business relationships.

Mr. Rockefeller's testimony before the Senate Committee, the publication of the Rockefeller-Walsh correspondence, and his radio address met with universal favor. The New York *Evening World* declared that Rockefeller deserved "the compliments of the nation." William Allen White of Emporia collected scores of clippings from Kansas newspapers endorsing Mr. Rockefeller's efforts. "I have never seen in a dozen years," he wrote to George E. Vincent, President of the Rockefeller Foundation, on February 18th, "such splendid response as Mr. Rockefeller has had to his position before the Senate Committee. I have been reading the American press carefully, looking for editorial expression, and I have found in every quarter worth considering the most cordial support of his attitude and the most flattering personal words for his courage." [38] Scores of personal letters congratulated Rockefeller upon the dignity with which he had made a clear, frank, and fearless statement.

To aid the Senate Committee in locating other bonds of the Continental Trading Company, the Brooklyn *Eagle,* the St. Louis *Post-Dispatch,* and other newspapers published in February a list of the serial numbers of the Liberty Bonds purchased by Continental. Mr. Rockefeller checked the investments of all companies and their subsidiaries in which he, his father, and the Rockefeller Foundation were interested. About one hundred and forty-four companies were canvassed, but no Continental bonds were found.

The briefs in the habeas corpus proceedings in Stewart's behalf were filed on February 17th. On the 23rd, Justice Bailey discharged the writ and remanded Stewart to the custody of the Senate sergeant at arms. Stewart was under arrest for a few minutes until his lawyers conferred, noted an appeal to the Court of Appeals of the District of Columbia, and then he was freed on bond. Once again Stewart was saved from appearing before the bar of the Senate.

Further disclosures about the Continental Liberty Bonds were made before the Senate Committee by Karl C. Schuyler of Denver, attorney for Henry M. Blackmer, on February 23, 1928. [39] In a striking statement, Schuyler told of Blackmer's return to Montreal, Canada, in July, 1926. At Blackmer's request Schuyler met with him at the Mt. Royal Hotel for two or three days. After attending to some business on which Schuyler had been previously working, Blackmer told Schuyler that the chief reason for wanting him in Montreal was to secure his advice as to certain Liberty Bonds "which he had received for services in the purchase and resale of the Mexia and other Texas oil of the Humphreys companies" in the Continental transaction. Before accepting the employment offered by Blackmer, Schuyler asked whether to his knowledge Continental ever had any deals with any public officials of the United States, whether the company had been used as an agency or instrumentality to induce the granting of the Teapot Dome lease and, generally, whether any funds or bonds purchased by the Continental Trading Company had been used for any un-

38. William Allen White to George E. Vincent, February 18, 1928. Rockefeller File.
39. *Leases Upon Naval Oil Reserves* (1929), 357-375, 1158.

lawful purpose. According to Schuyler, Blackmer answered, in the most unequivocal manner, that he had no such knowledge. Schuyler said he believed Blackmer then, and that he had no subsequent reason to doubt his honesty or the good faith of his answer.

Blackmer informed Schuyler that he had received from Continental 3½ per cent Liberty Bonds amounting to approximately $750,000, and that he had kept the bonds intact awaiting developments. Interest coupons for 1922 had been cashed, though not those for 1923, and reinvested in Liberty Bonds which, in turn, had been placed and kept with those received from Continental. Blackmer had retained one bond for himself as reimbursement for his personal expenses in connection with the matter. These bonds were now in a safety deposit box in the Equitable Trust Company in New York.

Schuyler suggested that Blackmer should place the bonds beyond the possibility of his control by turning them over to what might be called a trustee pending the determination of title; that such action ought to place his good faith beyond question. Blackmer requested that Schuyler hold the bonds as trustee, and Schuyler consented, provided the powers were expressed in terms acceptable to him. Schuyler prepared a letter expressing the powers and obligations of the trustee, which Blackmer signed. Schuyler then went to New York, secured $763,000 in bonds, and placed them in a safety box at the Equitable Trust Company. They were still in the box at the time of Schuyler's testimony.

Will H. Hays, former Chairman of the Republican National Committee, appeared on March 1st and the 13th and testified that in addition to a $75,000 contribution, which was in Continental bonds, Sinclair had loaned the Republican National Committee $185,000 in Continental bonds in November, 1923. He further testified that $100,000 had been returned to Sinclair, so that Sinclair's total contribution was $160,000, all of which had been paid in Continental bonds.

While these events were transpiring, notices were mailed in February regarding the annual meeting of the stockholders of Standard of Indiana to be held at Whiting on March 1st. The management requested proxies in favor of re-electing Stewart and all the other Directors. This raised the question of Colonel Stewart's future relationship to the company, and there was great interest and speculation over what position Rockefeller would take. It was assumed that he would oppose Stewart's re-election. William Allen White, editor of the *Emporia Gazette* and one of the trustees of the Rockefeller Foundation, believed that the Foundation should use all of its influence quietly if possible, and publicly if necessary, to oust Stewart. "We cannot afford to be a large holder of stocks," he wrote on February 11, 1928, to George E. Vincent, "under the executive control of a man who is an obvious abettor of swindles and who publicly scorns his country when it is asking only for the truth that he can, if he will, reveal." Vincent believed it would not be wise to do anything until after the Sinclair trial. If Stewart then remained obdurate and refused to testify, the Foundation should withdraw its support of Stewart's leadership.[40]

In a letter to Colonel Stewart, Rockefeller suggested that the annual meeting be postponed thirty days and preferably sixty.[41] This would allow time for the Sinclair trial and give Stewart a chance to testify. Without showing Rockefeller's letter to the Board of Directors or submitting the question, Stewart replied that he was not in favor of postponing the annual meeting.[42] The year 1927 had not been a favorable one in the oil industry, and the earnings of the company were substantially smaller than in 1926. Since 18,000 employee stockholders and others were interested in and waiting for the financial statement, such a move in Stewart's opinion would arouse suspicion and cause tremendous harm. "In my opinion," he wrote, "it would be infinitely preferable that the stockholders should vote against my selection as a director at this Annual Meeting, than to adjourn the meeting. I believe this adjournment would work incalculable harm to the Company, and above all else in this entire matter, I place the good of the Company and its stockholders and the public it serves far ahead of my individual good." Mr. Rockefeller appreciated the Colonel's point of view, but he still felt that a postponement was desirable.[43] He suggested holding the meeting as scheduled and transacting all business except electing the Directors. If the Colonel did not agree with this, then Rockefeller's only alterna-

40. George E. Vincent to William A. White, February 16, 1928. Rockefeller File.
41. John D. Rockefeller, Jr., to Colonel Robert W. Stewart, February 20, 1928. Rockefeller File.
42. Colonel Robert W. Stewart to John D. Rockefeller, Jr., February 21, 1928. Rockefeller File.
43. John D. Rockefeller, Jr., to Colonel Robert W. Stewart, February 23, 1928. Rockefeller File.

tive was to ask to have his proxies returned inasmuch as he was not prepared to vote for Directors at this time. The Finance Committee of the Rockefeller Foundation voted on February 23rd that if satisfactory arrangements were not made for a postponement of the meeting, the Treasurer of the Foundation should withdraw its proxies already signed in favor of the Stewart management.

Owing to the situation which had developed, Colonel Stewart left for New York on the 24th to see Mr. Rockefeller. In his absence from the city, Stewart talked with his associates, Thomas M. Debevoise and Bertram Cutler, and expressed strongly his conviction that a postponement of the meeting would be detrimental to the best interests of Standard.[44] It was much wiser for stockholders to vote or not vote than to force a postponement. Relying upon Stewart's repeated promise to resign, if requested, Rockefeller finally withdrew his request for a postponement of the annual meeting and instructed the Proxy Committee to vote his stock for the re-election of all Directors except Stewart. The Finance Committee of the Rockefeller Foundation voted to do likewise. It also instructed the Chairman to write to the Board of Directors of Standard and ask, as one of the stockholders, for Henry M. Blackmer's resignation as a Director of Midwest, and that they seek advice of counsel in the matter of Blackmer's liability to Standard and Midwest for the profits from Continental.[45] Upon the receipt of this communication, the Board asked C. W. Martyn, its General Counsel, for his opinion on Blackmer's liability.

The annual meeting at Whiting on March 1, 1928, had all the elements of a drama because of the breach which had developed between Colonel Stewart and Mr. Rockefeller. The general public had no idea as to what the Rockefeller interests would do. When the hour of the meeting arrived, Colonel Stewart, always known for his constant smile and jocular manner, opened the meeting with a grim expression. "It is usual," he began in a slow and precise voice, "for the president of this company to preside at the stockholders' meetings when the chairman of the board is not present. In order that my presence will give no embarrassment to any stockholders or to myself, I will absent myself from the room

44. Interview with Thomas M. Debevoise, December 1, 1948.
45. John D. Rockefeller, Jr., to the Board of Directors, Standard Oil Company (Indiana), February 27, 1928. Rockefeller File.

and Mr. Seubert will take over this meeting. I will be in the adjoining room and available when sent for." [46]

After making the annual report, Stewart excused himself and
Mr. Seubert presided. All of the old Directors were renominated
for re-election. Before balloting, Seubert said he would like to
read a communication. The atmosphere became tense. Seubert
proceeded to read a letter to the Proxy Committee from Rockefeller dated February 27th in which he enclosed proxies for 402,280
shares. The letter said that he was not prepared to vote his stock
either for or against Colonel Stewart's re-election as a Director,
but his stock and that of the Rockefeller Foundation was to be
voted for the re-election of all other Directors. The balloting resulted in the re-election of all the Directors except Burton, who
retired. All eight Directors received 6,320,275 votes except Stewart,
who received 4,980,355. No votes were recorded against Stewart.
The vacancy created by Burton's retirement was not filled nor
was a new directorship created by the stockholders. The Board
was authorized to fill these places when it saw fit. At the Board
meeting following the stockholders' meeting, Stewart was re-
elected Chairman and Seubert President.

The day following the annual meeting, Mr. Rockefeller issued
a statement saying that since Colonel Stewart had offered to resign
from the company at any time on request, nothing would have
been gained by opposing his election.[47] Whenever he felt that
Colonel Stewart should resign, Rockefeller said that he would not
hesitate to ask it in so far as his stock was concerned. In the meantime, he would continue to seek the facts.

On the same day a grand jury in Washington presented an
indictment to Justice F. L. Siddons of the Supreme Court of the
District of Columbia against Stewart, charging him with contempt
of the Senate. Stewart appeared before the court in Washington
on March 15th, pleaded not guilty, and was released on $5,000
bail. Stewart left shortly thereafter with his two sons, Robert and
James, for a brief trip abroad.

In the meantime, Rockefeller asked Standard's Directors if they
had sought advice of counsel on the liability of Sinclair to the
Sinclair Crude Oil Purchasing Company or Standard of Indiana

46. *Chicago Journal of Commerce*, March 2, 1928; *The New York Times*, March 2, 1928.
47. *The New York Times*, March 3, 1928.

for his share of the profits in the Continental deal.[48] Again, the Directors referred the matter to Martyn for an opinion. Martyn informed the Directors that he found nothing to show that Blackmer was acting in any other way than for himself in the Continental deal, and that he was not liable to either Standard or Midwest for any of the profits.[49] As a result of pressure exerted on Standard's Directors by Rockefeller, Blackmer's resignation as a Director of Midwest was secured on March 20th. About the same time, Colonel Stewart resigned as Chairman of the Dixie Oil Company, but no reason was given for this action. Mrs. Norma M. Hancock, Vice-President of Dixie, also resigned, and she was succeeded by A. W. Peake of the Midwest Refining Company. Because of Dr. Burton's resignation, effective on March 1, 1928, Mr. Rockefeller inquired of Seubert if this was the result of some recent or unexpected development or a step which he had contemplated.[50] Seubert replied that Burton had planned to retire, and for this reason he had not been re-elected.

Not having heard from the Directors of Standard about the liability of Blackmer and Sinclair, Rockefeller submitted the question to his own counsel, Murray, Aldrich & Roberts. Their opinion indicated that all of those involved in the Continental deal were jointly and severally liable for damages as a result of conspiracy.[51] A tentative draft of a complaint to be filed by Rockefeller and other stockholders against Sinclair, Blackmer, O'Neil, Stewart, and Osler to recover $1,540,000 with interest and costs for the Sinclair Crude Oil Purchasing Company was drawn. Felix T. Graham, Secretary of Standard, reporting for the Directors, informed Mr. Rockefeller on April 17th that if Blackmer and Sinclair were liable, it was primarily to the Sinclair Crude Oil Purchasing Company.[52] The latter company was awaiting further information as it developed in the Sinclair trial, then in progress, before coming to any definite conclusion. On the advice of counsel, the Directors of Midwest adopted a resolution on April 28th

48. John D. Rockefeller, Jr., to the Board of Directors of the Standard Oil Company (Indiana), March 2, 1928. Rockefeller File.
49. C. W. Martyn to the Board of Directors of the Standard Oil Company (Indiana), March 8, 1928. Albert L. Hopkins File.
50. John D. Rockefeller, Jr., to Edward G. Seubert, March 26, 1928; Edward G. Seubert to John D. Rockefeller, Jr., March 28, 1928. Rockefeller File.
51. Murray, Aldrich & Roberts to John D. Rockefeller, Jr., April 17, 1928. Rockefeller File.
52. Felix T. Graham to John D. Rockefeller, Jr., April 17, 1928. Albert L. Hopkins File.

declaring that the company had no claim to the $763,000 in Liberty Bonds of Blackmer.

The second trial of Sinclair on criminal charges began on April 19, 1928. During the trial the government held Colonel Stewart as a witness, but he was never called to testify. Government counsel had been unable to learn anything previously from Stewart regarding either the Continental Trading Company or Harry T. Sinclair as the source of the Liberty Bonds found in Fall's possession. Stewart had been from the first not only an adverse and reluctant witness but, at all times, most unco-operative in aiding the government. He was held under subpoena by government counsel in the hope that something might break at the trial which would make it advisable for the government to call him as a witness.[53]

Once the Sinclair trial had ended and Sinclair was acquitted, Stewart no longer had any ground for not answering the questions put to him by the Senate Committee, which was still holding hearings. Stewart, in company with Stephens, consulted Albert L. Hopkins, Stewart's personal attorney, and Stewart told the story of the Continental Trading Company deal.[54] Hopkins advised Stewart to tell his story immediately to the Directors of Standard and testify. Stewart hoped that the Senate Committee would call him. If not, he was prepared to volunteer.

In the meantime, the Senate Committee had sent a subcommittee to Chicago, where it examined Colonel Stewart's bank deposits in 1922 and 1923, which were extremely interesting in view of the disclosures about Fall, O'Neil, and Blackmer.[55] Photostatic copies of Stewart's deposit slips covering the period when the Continental Trading Company was active were obtained showing that in 1922 and 1923 Stewart had deposited the interest from coupons of $3\frac{1}{2}$ per cent Liberty Bonds. These deposits indicated that Stewart had in his possession approximately $750,000 in bonds. In view of this evidence, Senator Nye wired Stewart on April 20th to appear before the Senate Committee on the 24th. Roy J. Barnett, tax commissioner for Standard of Indiana, was also subpoenaed.

53. George S. Chandler to Giddens, June 10, 1949. Mr. Chandler assisted Owen J. Roberts from the beginning in the prosecution of the Teapot Dome cases.
54. Interview with Albert L. Hopkins, May 26, 1949.
55. Chicago Journal of Commerce, April 21, 1928; The New York Times, April 24, 1928.

Stewart's and Barnett's testimony before the committee disclosed the following facts.[56] As soon as the Continental Trading Company contracts had been approved in November, 1921, Stewart, Blackmer, O'Neil, Sinclair, Osler, and various officials of the Sinclair Pipe Line, Sinclair Crude Oil Purchasing Company, and Prairie Oil & Gas arranged to leave Chicago for Mexia on the night of November 26th to arrange for running pipelines, building tanks, and terminal facilities. On Saturday morning, the 26th, Osler arrived in Chicago to join the party. While in Stewart's office that morning, Osler told the Colonel, "very much to his surprise," that a part of the profits from the contracts would be given to him. "This was the first time," Stewart said, "that I knew that there was going to be a disposition on the part of anyone to give me any part of the profits." Stewart told Osler: "I don't care to have any of these profits; I don't think I am entitled to them." There was no reason, according to Stewart, why any of the profits should come to him. "Well," replied Osler, "you can do what you want about this matter of expending the money." Stewart was not informed what other people were to receive profits or in what form the profits would come. While Stewart and Osler were talking, Roy J. Barnett, Standard's tax commissioner, walked into the Colonel's office.[57] Seeing that Stewart was engaged, he backed out, returned to his own office, and prepared to leave for the day. Before he could depart, he received a telephone call from Stewart to stand by for a while.

Osler's remarks raised a question as to Stewart's right to use these profits if they came to him. After pondering the matter, Stewart made a quick decision to trustee any profits that might come for three reasons. First, he was not sure as to what company the profits might belong. If Sinclair turned over his share of the profits to the Sinclair Crude Oil Purchasing Company, Stewart in equity should do likewise. If Sinclair did not, Stewart's share should go direct to Standard. Secondly, if Stewart turned the profits immediately to one or the other of the two companies, there might be some question raised or resentment created that would prevent the execution of the highly profitable contract. And Stewart wanted the oil badly. Thirdly, turning over the profits to either company would necessitate recording the matter in the books, which might result in some publicity. The problem,

56. *Leases Upon Naval Oil Reserves* (1929), 973-980, 984-1005, 1026-1047.
57. Interview with Roy J. Barnett, January 25, 1949.

as Stewart saw it, was not an ordinary one. The company was getting a highly profitable contract, and Stewart's immediate concern was to see that the contract was executed. By creating a trust with the two companies as the beneficiaries, both companies would be protected and the matter kept private. Moreover, by creating a trust the payment of an income tax could be avoided until the final disposition of the profits was decided. Therefore, Stewart telephoned Barnett to come to his office.

Stewart told Barnett that he had made a deal for some oil. He had just been informed that someone was going to turn over some of the profits to him. Stewart did not know why, and he did not know what form the profits would take. He was in a position where he did not want to upset the deal because the company needed the oil badly. If any profits should come, would Barnett act as trustee? "Trustee of what?" Barnett asked. Stewart said he did not know exactly. Barnett asked to whom the profits belonged. Stewart said they did not belong to him but to either Standard or the Sinclair Crude Oil Purchasing Company. The whole thing naturally struck Barnett as a queer transaction. It appeared to him that Stewart was in some kind of a game and "had to play his hand out." Consequently, Barnett agreed to do what the chief executive of his company requested and become the trustee.[58] He could not very well refuse.

Since Stewart did not want anyone to know about the matter, no stenographer was called in to type the trust agreement. Stewart sat down and wrote out a trust agreement with an indelible pencil which he usually carried, while Barnett read the form from a book on income tax trusts. It was an ordinary trust agreement in which Stewart conveyed to Barnett as trustee all his rights, interest, and any profits that might accrue from the contracts signed with the Humphreys companies, to be held in trust for Standard and the Sinclair Crude Oil Purchasing Company.[59] Any profits arising were to be invested in Liberty Bonds. In case of Stewart's death, the trustee was to turn over the bonds to the two companies and, in case they could not agree as to ownership, the trustee was to divide them equally. The trust agreement could be terminated at any time by Stewart, but in case of termination, the agreement provided that Barnett was to turn over all funds to Standard of

58. *Ibid.*
59. *Leases Upon Naval Oil Reserves* (1929), 1016.

Indiana and the Sinclair Crude Oil Purchasing Company in such parts as Stewart should direct.

When the agreement had been written, Stewart signed the document, gave it to Barnett, who hurriedly read it and signed. Handing him the trust agreement, Stewart asked Barnett what he was going to do with it. Barnett said he would have to put it in a safety deposit box or something. On second thought, Barnett said, "Here, you keep that, because if there is a copy of it lying around, and I lose it or anything, or if you are down there and anything should happen to the copy I would be to blame; so here, you take care of it." [60] As the Colonel put the agreement in his pocket, he said to Barnett: "Now, I don't want you to talk about it to anybody until I have talked to you, and I promise you that I won't talk to anybody about it until I have told you."

About a month later, the subject of the trust agreement came up. Barnett asked the Colonel as to its whereabouts. Stewart pulled it out of his pocket, handed it to him, and asked if he had a safety deposit box in which to keep it. Barnett had one in a bank on the North Side, but he did not want to put it in his personal box. "Haven't you got a box?" asked Barnett. Stewart said he had one at the Continental & Commercial National Bank. Barnett told him to put it there. Barnett raised the question of having a copy which Stewart agreed to give him but, on second thought, Barnett said: "Never mind." If the Colonel wanted to keep the matter a secret, Barnett decided it was wise from his own personal point of view not to have a copy.[61] If anything happened to him, the agreement would surely come to light. Furthermore, if word about the agreement got out, it might prove personally embarrassing to Barnett. As a result of the conversation, the Colonel went to his desk, got an envelope, put the trust agreement inside, sealed it, and wrote on the outside: "To be opened in case of my death by my executors or administrator in the presence of the then Treasurer of the Standard Oil Company of Indiana and the Sinclair Crude Oil Purchasing Company." It was then placed in the Colonel's safety deposit box at the bank.

Several months passed before any profits were received. In April, 1922, Osler met Stewart at the Belmont Hotel in New York and handed him a package. Without unwrapping it, Stewart carried the package to Chicago and, upon reaching his office, he sent

60. Interview with Roy J. Barnett, January 25, 1949.
61. *Ibid.*

for Barnett who opened it. It contained 3½ per cent Liberty Loan Bonds in $1,000 denominations. Barnett did not recall the exact amount, but there were probably $100,000 or more, some of which had the interest coupons clipped. "What are you going to do with them?" the Colonel asked. "What do you want me to do with them?" Barnett replied. "You are the trustee," declared the Colonel. "Trustee of what?" Barnett inquired. Then the Colonel reminded him of the trust agreement. "Well," asked Barnett, "is this all of them?" "I don't know," the Colonel said. Barnett thought that they should be put in some safe place. He would have to get a safety deposit box. "Do you know how long I am going to have these?" asked Barnett. The Colonel did not know. "Haven't you got a place around here where I can keep them?" asked Barnett. The Colonel suggested cleaning out the small safe in his office and giving Barnett the combination. "Well, if it is just temporary," said Barnett, "we might as well put them in the safe here." Therefore, Colonel Stewart cleaned out his private safe and the bonds were placed in it. The safe was then moved to a vault near the Directors' room.

On four or five subsequent occasions Stewart received packages of bonds from Osler in New York, brought them to Chicago, had them opened by Barnett, counted in the same manner as the first ones, and Barnett put them in the safe. Barnett kept no formal record of the transactions. He made a memorandum of the total amount of bonds on a little slip of paper on each occasion and put this with the bonds in the safe. Each time bonds were added, he would tear up the old slip, make a new one, and put it back in the safe. Barnett thought that this was just a temporary affair, and it might be closed out any time, so there was no need to keep a complete record. Because it was a queer transaction and in order to protect himself, Barnett kept a private record of the serial numbers of some of the bonds in code and a slip of paper with the total amount of bonds, both of which he carried on his person.[62] Furthermore, Barnett did not give the Colonel any receipt. He did not think about it, and the Colonel never asked him for one. The last delivery of bonds was made to Colonel Stewart in May or June, 1923, which brought the total to $759,500. Thus, according to Stewart, "I have never had those bonds in my possession as the owner of them at all. I have not been in the possession of them, except as a mere conduit from Mr. Osler to the trustee, and those

62. *Ibid.*

are the facts so far as I know them with regard to these bonds. I assume that these bonds which Mr. Osler turned over to me must have been connected with the Continental."

When the interest came due each quarter, Barnett clipped the coupons in Stewart's presence. Sometimes both Barnett and Stewart clipped coupons. When the first coupons were clipped, Barnett said he was not interested in how the coupons were handled. He would buy some additional bonds with the interest as the trust agreement provided. The Colonel said he had some bonds and would exchange his for the coupons. On only one occasion did Barnett have to wait three or four days for the Colonel to turn over the bonds. There was usually a little difference between the amount of coupons clipped and the bonds exchanged. Sometimes the Colonel was short, and sometimes he was long. Stewart always took the coupons, deposited some in the bank to his personal account, and turned some of them in for cash.

Sometime after December, 1923, and before June, 1924, Colonel Stewart asked Barnett not to clip any more interest coupons. Colonel Stewart said, "There was a great deal of newspaper notoriety about this proposition at the time and I thought it best not to do it. . . ." Although Barnett was the trustee and Stewart had no legal control over the bonds, Barnett followed Stewart's instructions. He assumed that the Colonel was in some sort of a jam, so he asked no questions and clipped no more coupons. Barnett first learned of the Continental Trading Company through the newspapers reporting on the trial at Cheyenne. He immediately began acquiring information about it, especially from his friends among the government agents.

One day in the fall of 1924, when the Colonel was preparing to leave on an extended trip, he sent for Barnett and told him he wanted to tell L. L. Stephens, one of Standard's attorneys, about the trust agreement. That was all right with Barnett. Stewart called Stephens to his office and, in Barnett's presence, said he wanted to give him some information on a highly confidential matter. The Colonel then told Stephens about the negotiations for the Mexia oil, the profits, the making of the trust agreement, where it was, where the bonds were, and that no one knew of this except Barnett. Stewart pointed out that he had called him in to tell him this in case anything happened to him or Barnett. "Is that plain to you?" asked Stewart. "Yes," said Stephens, "I think it is quite plain."

While government agents were investigating Stewart's bank account in Chicago in April, 1928, they tapped the telephone lines to the offices of Stewart, Barnett, and Bullock. They also shadowed Barnett. On one occasion, Barnett was tipped off to the fact that they were planning to search various company offices on a certain night.[63] Barnett informed the Colonel, so their desks "were in order." Without Stewart's knowing it, Barnett took the Continental bonds out of the safe, put them in a wastebasket in his office for overnight keeping, and returned them to the safe the next day. How the government agents got by the night watchman and the cleaning people into the desks of Stewart, Bullock, and Barnett, no one ever knew. As the investigation got hotter, Barnett brought in an expert safe man while the Colonel was out of town and, unknown to the latter, had the combination on the safe in the vault changed.

The bonds remained in the safe and vault of Standard until April 21, 1928. When the Sinclair case went to the jury in Washington, Stewart returned to Chicago and called a special meeting of the Board of Directors for the 20th. Prior to the meeting, Stewart, along with Seubert, Martyn, and Barnett, went to the Continental & Commercial National Bank, got the trust agreement out of Stewart's safety deposit box, and brought it to the Directors' meeting. Stewart told the Directors the story, broke the seal to the trust agreement, read it, and said: "I hereby terminate this trust." The fact that the Colonel was involved in the profits of the Continental deal came as a bolt of lightning to his Directors. They were appalled. The Board members were taken to the vault to see the bonds. Stewart started to open the safe but hesitated and asked Barnett to do so. After seeing the bonds, they returned to the Board room and decided that the bonds should be turned over to the Sinclair Crude Oil Purchasing Company. The next day Barnett delivered to its Treasurer and General Counsel $759,500 in Liberty Loan Bonds plus $38,000 in bonds exchanged for interest coupons.

After Colonel Stewart had told his story and had been questioned about the transaction, the Senate Committee recessed at noon on April 24th. Just before the recess, Colonel Stewart asked if he might be heard.[64]

63. *Ibid.*
64. *Leases Upon Naval Oil Reserves* (1929), 1004-1005.

STEWART: I want to say to you gentlemen before you adjourn that I will be glad to answer either of these questions. I have now answered the first as to what I know about the bonds, and I would be glad to answer the committee on the other question which they have propounded, which I declined to answer at the time on the ground that I was going to be a witness and would probably be interrogated in a court of law.

NYE: I do not think that a committee of the Senate can hear for the Senate your answer to this question.

STEWART: I am rather inclined to think that if you want to do it you can. I imagine that the Senate will back you.

WALSH: We will be glad to hear Colonel Stewart's statement as to what he may want to say if you care to answer the question that was propounded before.

NYE: Will you return at 2 o'clock?

WALSH: Let us take it up now and get through with this part of it.

STEWART: You asked me two questions, and I think you will consider that I have answered one of them. I know nothing else about the bonds with the exception of what I have told you this morning.

In regard to the second question which was whether I had had any conference or talks—what was that second question, Senator Walsh? You have it there.

WALSH: This is the question, probably, that was addressed to you by the chairman:

Just one more question, Colonel Stewart. Have you discussed any of these bond transactions with Mr. Sinclair or has Mr. Sinclair discussed any of these bond transactions with you?

STEWART: In answer to that I will say that I do not remember any talk that I have had with Sinclair in regard to those bonds. I have had many meetings with Mr. Sinclair and have talked with him a great deal about many different matters of policy, such matters that come up on the oil business, but I do not remember—and it may be Mr. Sinclair might say he had a conversation with me, and I would not deny it positively, but I do not remember any conversation of any kind or character I have had with Mr. Sinclair with regard to these bonds or any part of them.

WALSH: Could you say the same thing with respect to any profits accruing by reason of the Continental Trading Co. transaction?

STEWART: Yes; we never discussed that.

WALSH: You never talked with him about that subject?

STEWART: Not to my remembrance did I ever discuss that with him in any way, shape, or manner.

During the course of his testimony Stewart gave the committee the serial numbers of the bonds turned over to the Sinclair Crude Oil Purchasing Company. Stewart's list was checked against those purchased by the Continental Trading Company, and all of Stewart's bonds were on Continental's list, except one hundred and twenty-five $1,000 bonds. Also, all of the coupons cashed by Stewart checked with the bonds purchased by Continental.

In view of the seemingly irreconcilable discrepancies in Stewart's testimony in regard to the Continental Trading Company given on February 2nd and 3rd and again on April 24th, the Senate Committee on April 25th agreed to ask the Senate to certify certain parts of Stewart's testimony to the district attorney of the District of Columbia to determine whether or not charges of perjury should be made. At the same time, there was a discussion over whether or not the committee should recommend that the warrant ordering Stewart's arrest, after his refusal to answer the two questions on February 2nd and 3rd, should be dismissed. Nye and Cutting opposed such a move. Walsh contended that Stewart had purged himself before the committee.

Walsh's report on Stewart's testimony was read to the Senate on April 26th. He recommended that the warrant of arrest issued by the Senate for contempt be vacated and that the district attorney be directed to determine if Stewart had committed perjury. A fiery debate on the report lasted for nearly two hours, during which time Senator Norris made scathing attacks upon Stewart. The Senate finally voted to vacate the warrant for arrest, but it refused to reverse its position on the contempt indictment and voted to send the record to the district attorney to study. Apparently, only the statute of limitations prevented Roberts and Pomerene, the special prosecutors in the oil scandal litigation, from seeking Stewart's indictment on perjury because he had lied to them and to the grand jury about his knowledge of the Continental bonds.[65]

65. *Nation*, CXXVIII (March 6, 1929), 280.

In view of the sensational disclosure made by Colonel Stewart as to his relationship to the Continental Trading Company and the previous assurance given to Mr. Rockefeller that nothing improper had been done in making the deal, Mr. Rockefeller wrote Stewart on April 27th: "Your testimony before the Senate Committee leaves me no alternative other than to ask you to make good the promise you voluntarily gave me some weeks ago, that you would resign at my request. That request I now make." [66] On account of Stewart's receiving one-fourth of the profits in the Continental deal, his attitude toward his company, public authority, and the general public, Rockefeller had lost confidence in Stewart's leadership. Stewart's actions had not only cast a cloud over Standard of Indiana but over the oil industry and all Big Business. Rockefeller had no information showing that Stewart originally intended to keep the Continental bonds for his own personal use, but he felt that public confidence in Standard of Indiana had been seriously impaired. It could not be restored without a change in leadership. From the beginning, Rockefeller had been eminently fair to Colonel Stewart and had loyally supported him until his disclosure on April 24th. Then, after careful deliberation and with the utmost regard for the feelings of all concerned, he decided that it was time to act in such a way as to leave no doubt or question that Standard of Indiana stood, and stood only, for the highest standards of business integrity. Rockefeller's decision to act represented a marked departure from his general policy of not interfering with the management of those companies in which he had a stock interest and was due to the moral issue involved.

Since Sinclair had been acquitted of charges of conspiracy on April 21st, the Senate Committee ordered him to appear on May 1st. He testified concerning his efforts to buy Mexia oil from Colonel Humphreys in 1921, Blackmer's purchase of the oil, the negotiations in New York in November, 1921, the guaranteeing of Continental's contract, and his receipt of Continental bonds.[67] Some of the Continental Bonds were delivered to Sinclair by Blackmer and some by messenger. When Blackmer gave him the first package, Sinclair was asked not to clip the interest coupons and to hold the bonds intact. Sinclair kept a personal memo-

66. John D. Rockefeller, Jr., to Colonel Robert W. Stewart, April 27, 1928. Rockefeller File.
67. *Leases Upon Naval Oil Reserves* (1929), 1057-1124, 1129-1155; Robert L. Owen, *Remarkable Experiences of H. F. Sinclair With His Government*, 1929.

randum of the amount of bonds as they were received to the effect that he had "received bonds to the amount of so much for the benefit of my company from Mr. Blackmer, in reference to the commission referring to the contracts, the Mexia interest, and so forth." He put them in the vault or safe at his home with other Liberty Bonds. Sinclair did not advise his company about the bonds, for he felt that sooner or later it would be advised. However, he treated the bonds as his own, for he gave some to Fall and others to the Republican National Committee. Sinclair's personal memorandum regarding the Continental bonds, as they were delivered to him, was destroyed ten days prior to his appearance before the Senate Committee. Moreover, after the Sinclair conspiracy trial and on April 27, 1928, Sinclair sent a communication to the Board of Directors of the Sinclair Crude Oil Purchasing Company explaining that profits had been derived from the Mexia deal which he had held for the company until the end of the agitation in Congress, the civil suit against Mammoth, and the criminal proceedings against himself. Since the litigation had now been settled, Sinclair turned over, through E. H. Chandler, his attorney, bonds to the amount of $757,000 and accrued interest of $142,808.75.

With the conclusion of Sinclair's testimony, the Senate Committee had traced the ownership of all the Continental bonds and completed its work. Senator Walsh for the committee made a report to the Senate on May 29, 1928. Senator Nye filed a separate report.[68] In concluding his report Senator Walsh said: "It is unnecessary to dwell upon the facts leading to the conclusion that no one of the four conspirators had at the outset any purpose to make the company each respectively represented the beneficiary of the Continental transactions. If this judgment is harsh the parties affected, whose testimony given directly or vicariously was characterized in no degree by candor, are themselves to blame. It is impossible to offer any sane reason for taking the pains or going to the expense of organizing the corporation device or for paying Osler commissions amounting to $60,000 for conducting its affairs if there was an honest intention that the companies should have the profits." Walsh said that the committee had been directed to resume its work because of a widespread belief that the fund accumulated by the Continental Trading Company was to be devoted, and perhaps had been devoted, to corrupt uses.

68. *Leases Upon Naval Oil Reserves* (1929), 1171-1183, 1185-1204.

"It seems now, however, to have been," he said, "the ill-gotten gains of a contemptible private steal, the speculation of trusted officers of great industrial houses, pilfering from their own companies, robbing their own stockholders. . . ." Senator Nye took a different point of view. He said: "Whether the purpose of the company was that of winning quietly a neat profit for the four participants, a profit that others need never know about, or whether the purpose was that of creating a fund to be used to corrupt and influence elections and public officials like Albert B. Fall, or other 'slush' purposes, is a question for debate. However, in view of what Sinclair did with his share of Continental Trading Co. profits and the interest of all the men and their companies concerned, it is much easier to believe that it was the purpose of the Continental Trading Co. to create a huge slush fund to be available for such purposes as have been suggested. . . ."

As the hearings of the Senate Committee were brought to a close, the Federal District Court at Cheyenne made an accounting in the case against Mammoth at Teapot Dome. Final judgment was entered on August 17, 1928, and Mammoth was ordered to pay the government $2,294,597.74 for 1,430,024.7 barrels of crude taken from Teapot Dome to which it was not legally entitled. By this time Mammoth had largely evaporated, and the only assets found by the government consisted of some office equipment and other items, which were seized and sold. During the accounting, it was discovered that Midwest Refining had purchased from Mammoth some natural gas and a small amount of gasoline which had been produced on Teapot Dome. The aggregate claim amounted to about $28,000, but it was settled for a figure less than this.

On October 22, 1928, the Attorney General of the United States pronounced illegal the contract under which the Sinclair Crude Oil Purchasing Company was buying the government royalty oil at Salt Creek, and it was annulled. Therefore, the Sinclair Pipe Line Company suspended the operation of its pipeline from Casper to Freeman, Missouri, leaving the Sinclair Crude Oil Purchasing Company with around 10,000,000 barrels of crude in storage in the Salt Creek area.

After it was discovered that Mammoth was unable to pay more than $3,509.19 on the judgment, the government filed suit in the Federal District Court of Delaware in December, 1928, against the Sinclair Crude Oil Purchasing Company, as the purchaser of the oil from Mammoth, for $2,294,597.74 (less the $3,509.19 paid by Mammoth) plus 7 per cent interest.[69] This was notwithstanding the fact that full payment for the oil had already been made by the Sinclair Crude Oil Purchasing Company to Mammoth. The government also claimed title to seventeen fifty-five-thousand-barrel storage tanks and the equipment which had been erected and paid for by the purchasing company on Teapot Dome. The suit to compel the company to pay a second time was based upon the theory that Mammoth never legally acquired title to the oil and it could not convey title. The Sinclair Crude Oil Purchasing Company was, therefore, responsible under the law for the oil illegally extracted. No fraudulent intent was attributed to the company other than the Supreme Court charged it with knowledge of fraud because of the activity of Harry F. Sinclair in negotiating the original contract between Mammoth and the government, plus the fact that, at the same time, Sinclair was in control of Mammoth and President of the Sinclair Crude Oil Purchasing Company.

Before the case came to trial, the Sinclair Crude Oil Purchasing Company officials and government counsel reached a settlement in April, 1930, subject to approval by Congress. Under the agreement, the government agreed to pay the company $170,000 for the seventeen steel storage tanks on Teapot Dome. On the other hand, the company agreed to pay $2,906,484.32, and place that sum in escrow in the Chase National Bank of New York for sixty days pending acceptance by the government. Congress approved the settlement on May 8th, and five days later President Hoover signed the bill authorizing the settlement. The company consented on May 28th to the entry of a judgment of confession for $2,906,484.32 in favor of the United States and paid not only the claim in full but all expenses of the litigation.

At the same time as this settlement was made, an out of court settlement was made with the Sinclair Crude Oil Purchasing Company for the government royalty oil it had taken from Salt Creek in 1928.[70] The government claimed, and the company agreed to pay, $375,081 for 1,527,765 barrels of crude which had been taken from Salt Creek between January 1, 1928, and October 21, 1928.

In filing its income tax return for January 1 to September 21, 1930, the Sinclair Crude Oil Purchasing Company showed a net loss or bad debt item of $2,906,484.32, which was the amount of

69. 129 F. (2d) 363.
70. *The New York Times*, April 8, 1930.

the judgment entered against it on May 28, 1930. Standard of Indiana filed a consolidated return for the balance of the year, carried forward the net loss, and claimed this amount as a legal deduction. When the Commissioner of Internal Revenue disallowed the deduction, Standard appealed to the United States Board of Tax Appeals, which sustained the Commissioner. The case was then appealed to the Circuit Court of Appeals, Seventh District, which upheld the Commissioner on June 12, 1942.[71] In rendering the decision the court pointed out that it had not found any case which permitted a taxpayer to claim a deduction for a sum paid to the government by way of damages arising from a charge of fraud and corruption upon the government.

In concluding the story of Teapot Dome, it is ironical to note that in the end Colonel Stewart and Standard of Indiana, neither of whom had any part in the affair, really suffered the most by it.

71. 129 F. (2d) 363.

CHAPTER XIV

Rockefeller Ousts Colonel Stewart

AFTER RECEIVING MR. ROCKEFELLER'S REQUEST THAT HE RESIGN, Stewart had dinner with Rockefeller at the latter's home on the evening of May 8th. Thomas M. Debevoise came in after dinner. During the conversation that ensued Stewart suggested that Standard of Indiana give him a leave of absence until the next annual meeting with the expectation that he would not stand for re-election, but Mr. Rockefeller was adamant.[1] He insisted upon Stewart's resignation. Unable to secure this, Rockefeller issued a statement the next day saying that he had lost confidence in Stewart and made public copies of his correspondence requesting Stewart's resignation.[2] The Colonel was en route to Chicago as the news broke. Along the way, some reporter boarded the train, located the Colonel, and sought a statement. Always cordial in his relations with the press, the Colonel, when pressed for a statement, became angry, lost his temper, raised his cane as if about to strike a blow, and told the reporter to "get the hell out of here."

Deciding to use more pressure, Rockefeller wrote to the Directors of Standard on May 23rd requesting that they ask for Stewart's resignation at once or exercise their power under Article II of the company's bylaws which provided that the officers held office during the pleasure of the Board or call a special meeting of stockholders as provided for in Article I in order that they might express their views.[3] The Board carefully considered the matter and replied that it was not justified in asking the Colonel to resign as Chairman, which, under the bylaws, was all that they could legally do, and that no justifiable reason existed for calling a special meeting of the stockholders.[4] The refusal of the Directors to demand Stewart's resignation was not surprising to Rockefeller

1. John D. Rockefeller, Jr., to Edward G. Seubert, May 8, 1928. Albert L. Hopkins File.
2. *Chicago Journal of Commerce*, May 10, 1928.
3. John D. Rockefeller, Jr., to the Board of Directors, Standard Oil Company (Indiana), May 23, 1928. Rockefeller File.
4. Edward G. Seubert to John D. Rockefeller, Jr., May 31, 1928. Rockefeller File.

or his associates because the Colonel was their leader, and the Directors were loyal to him.

Debevoise thought the Rockefeller people should keep the Board in uncertainty as to their next move.[5] He suggested that they start an investigation of various charges made against Colonel Stewart and the Directors which had come to them from many sources. They should exercise the right to examine the company's books without letting the Directors know for what purpose. They should also request a list of stockholders as an indication of their intent to call a special meeting. Winthrop W. Aldrich of the law firm of Murray, Aldrich & Roberts, counsel for Rockefeller, agreed with the proposed plan of action.

On May 31st the trial of Stewart for contempt of the Senate got under way in Washington, D.C. Efforts had been made to get Justice F. L. Siddons of the Supreme Court of the District of Columbia to bar the indictment for contempt on the ground that Stewart had purged himself by answering the two questions on April 24th, but the court ruled that the case must be tried.[6] Stewart was ably represented by Jesse C. Adkins, Frank Nesbit, Albert L. Hopkins, John L. Hopkins, and Frank J. Hogan. The latter did most of the trial work.

In defending Stewart, Hogan endeavored to establish the fact that Stewart had answered every committee question that was "pertinent" to the matter under consideration. The Continental deal was a private affair into which the committee had no right to inquire. Moreover, Stewart was under subpoena to testify in the Sinclair trial and could not be expected to answer more than he did. Furthermore, the two questions which Stewart had declined to answer were not questions by the committee but ones put at the request of a newspaper reporter. Hogan also stressed the fact that the members of the committee were never polled to decide whether or not Stewart should be compelled to testify, and that Stewart was never notified that the committee demanded an answer. Hogan struck a hard blow at the government's case by thoroughly discrediting the official printed record of the testimony before the committee on account of its numerous inaccuracies. Under Hogan's questioning, both Senators Nye and Walsh made poor impressions as witnesses for the government. The bomb that

---

5. Thomas M. Debevoise to Winthrop W. Aldrich, June 4, 1948. Rockefeller File.
6. For a record of the contempt case, see Transcript of Testimony, United States vs. Robert W. Stewart, Supreme Court of the District of Columbia.

wrecked the government's case was the introduction of evidence that there were no more than three Senators—Nye, Walsh, and Bratton—actually present at the committee hearing when Stewart declined to answer the questions. Under the rules of the Senate, at least six members of the committee must be present in order to have a quorum. Hence, the committee had not been legally in session. In less than three hours, Hogan thoroughly discredited the whole committee proceedings and created doubt in the minds of the jurors about Stewart's guilt.

The case went to the jury on June 13th about 1 P.M., and the next morning about 10 the jury returned a verdict of "not guilty" on all counts. As Stewart, a haggard, drawn-looking man, heard the verdict, he slumped in his chair for a moment but quickly recovered his composure to accept the congratulations of friends.[7] It is impossible to say what factors influenced the jury in acquitting Stewart. Some insight into the thinking of the jurors, however, came from Erwin R. McIntyre, one of the jurors, who said afterwards that they were impressed by the "slipshod methods followed by the Senate Committee and the Senate itself"; that there was no quorum present; that the minutes of the committee of February 2nd and 3rd had not been transcribed until May 30th; and that Colonel Stewart had been arrested without any warning that he was to be cited for contempt. They believed that an individual could delay his testimony if the Senate could delay action on national matters for long periods of time, which was especially true in Colonel Stewart's case when he had been subpoenaed as a witness in a trial. "There was," McIntyre said, "in our minds very grave doubt that there was any violation of the law. . . ."

Senator Norris bitterly denounced the verdict and the judicial system in general. "It is an outrage," he said, "against justice. It demonstrates clearly that if you have money enough to hire lawyers you will not be found guilty, even though you admit you are guilty."[8] Aroused by Norris' attack, the foreman of the jury wrote a letter to the Washington *Evening Star* in which he defended the verdict and pointed out that the jury gave considerable attention and weight to the "unbelievable methods" practiced by Norris and his colleagues.[9] While a few Senators wanted to impose the penalties of the law on Stewart, the foreman added, they paid little

7. *The New York Times,* June 15, 1928.
8. Baltimore *Evening Sun,* June 18, 1928.
9. June 18, 1928.

attention to what their own rules and the law prescribed regarding committee meetings and procedure.

Shortly after the conclusion of the contempt trial, Stewart was indicted by a federal grand jury for perjury on three counts.[10] The first count was that he denied having anything to do with or knowledge of the distribution by Continental of bonds which that company had purchased and distributed, yet he had received $759,500 in bonds of that company. The second charged that he deliberately, intentionally, wilfully, and corruptly swore falsely that he did not receive any bonds, whereas he had received $759,500 in bonds. Thirdly, Stewart swore that he had no knowledge of any kind of the recipients of these bonds. Stewart pleaded not guilty to the charges in the Supreme Court of the District of Columbia on June 26th, and the trial was set for October 8th.

While the contempt trial was in progress, Mr. Rockefeller requested that his representatives be given an opportunity to examine the account books of Standard and that a list of stockholders be provided. After a conference of Aldrich, William Roberts, Seubert, and Stewart in Chicago on July 2nd, these requests were granted. The books were examined under the direction of Roberts. For what purpose? It was simply a "fishing" expedition.[11]

Because he did not seem to be accomplishing anything in ousting Stewart, the Brooklyn Eagle on May 30, 1928, ran an editorial entitled "Has Rockefeller Backed Down?" It commended Rockefeller for using his influence to get Stewart to testify and in asking for his resignation, but it asked: Did he intend to leave matters as they stood? Had he abandoned his fight to force Stewart out and clean up that industry? If so, the demand for Stewart's resignation and the many statements issued by Mr. Rockefeller had no more meaning than pious gestures. The public expected, according to the editorial, more than this from the most powerful figure in the oil industry and the one man who could restore confidence in that badly smeared business. The Eagle continued its attacks and other papers joined in the hue and cry. In another editorial on "Rockefeller Prefers Retreat to Fight," the Philadelphia Record asserted that having failed to interest other stockholders in ousting Stewart, Rockefeller seemed content to dispose of his

10. The New York Times, June 26, 27, 1928.
11. Interview with Thomas M. Debevoise, December 1, 1948.

holdings.[12] This reflected a rumor current in Wall Street that the Rockefellers were selling their stock in Standard of Indiana. A few days later Mr. Rockefeller issued a statement stating that neither he nor his father contemplated selling or otherwise disposing of their investment in Standard of Indiana.[13] Not one share of stock had been sold nor had the question of sale been considered. Furthermore, while no reply had been received from Stewart about his resignation, Mr. Rockefeller stated that he would continue to take such steps as appeared practicable.

During the summer Rockefeller cabled Burton, who was vacationing in Europe, requesting him to return at once in order that he might have the benefit of his advice and counsel. Upon meeting Rockefeller in New York, Burton said that Rockefeller was the most upset man he had ever seen. He was still groping for all the information he could secure in addition to that which had come out of the Walsh investigation, but Burton could not add much to that already known.[14]

Owing to a crowded docket and an insufficient number of judges, Stewart's trial for perjury did not get under way until November 12th.[15] In attempting to prove that Stewart had sworn falsely and made statements contrary to what he knew to be the facts, the prosecution again relied heavily upon the officially printed record of the committee hearings and the testimony of Walsh and Nye. Hogan again attacked the inaccuracies of the official record. To discredit the officially printed record and show that it could not be depended upon to reveal what Stewart actually said before the committee on February 2nd and 3rd, Hogan had the official reporters compare their original shorthand notes with the printed record. They found 330 errors not counting instances of where they used "was" for "were."

In examining Senator Nye, Hogan brought out the fact that Stewart had been requested to reappear before the committee on April 24th; that he was not sworn again on that date; that the Senate Committee was functioning under the authority of the same Senate Resolution in April as in February; and that separate reports on the whole hearing had been made by Nye and Walsh

12. June 20, 1928.
13. *Chicago Journal of Commerce*, June 25, 1928.
14. Interview with William M. Burton, August 2, 1948.
15. For the record in the perjury case, see Transcript of Testimony, United States vs. Robert W. Stewart, Supreme Court of the District of Columbia.

on May 29, 1928. In view of these facts, if Stewart had earlier made statements which were later corrected in the same hearing, he had not committed perjury.

Under cross-examination by Hogan, Senator Walsh again made an exceedingly poor witness for the prosecution. He could not even recall that Congress had adjourned on May 29th. Owing to Walsh's poor memory, Hogan asked: "Then, Senator, let me ask you this question—I am sure that your initials were given, but to be sure, you are the Senator Thomas J. Walsh of Montana?"

Hogan then put on a highly interesting show. He called an impressive array of character witnesses—George M. Reynolds, Chairman of the Board, Continental National Bank and Trust Company of Chicago, Harry M. Gage, President of Coe College, Malcolm M. Harris of Chicago, President-elect of the American Medical Association, Captain Joseph B. Binder, a Spanish-American War veteran and a "Rough Rider" with Stewart, Emil Buticofer, Stewart's chauffeur since 1908, Mrs. Celia McWiginney, Stewart's housekeeper and cook since 1919, Elizabeth Chambers, chief telephone operator for the company in Chicago, Ernest R. Graham of Chicago, an architect, William Kelly, a mason's helper at the Wood River refinery, Charles "Chick" Evans, Jr., famous golfer and Stewart's golf caddy twenty years ago, and others. All of them testified that the Colonel's reputation for honesty, integrity, and truth was of the very highest.

In a brilliant closing argument, Hogan emphasized the inaccuracies and omissions in the officially printed record, the fact that Stewart had not been asked one question on which the perjury charge was based, the poor memory of Senator Walsh, the importance of the character witnesses, the lack of a committee quorum, the taking of Stewart's testimony out of its context and using it in reporting to the Senate, the Colonel's association with the "Rough Riders," and the fact that Stewart had answered all questions asked before the close of the hearing.

The outcome of the trial was foreshadowed when Justice Bailey, in his instructions to the jury, ruled that a quorum of the Senate Committee had to be actually present when Stewart testified.[16] Actually, there had been only three and sometimes five. The case was given to the jury at 2:35 P.M. on the 20th. Before even discussing the case, the jury took an immediate ballot and all twelve

16. *The New York Times,* November 20, 1928.

jurors voted for acquittal.[17] Some of the jurors had even been ready to vote "not guilty" before the defense put in any evidence or the judge's charge to the jury. It was apparent to them that the government had no case against Stewart and that there was no need to consider the question of whether or not a quorum had been present at the committee hearing. The whole affair impressed several of the jurors as a plain case of political persecution— nothing else. In deference to the court and the importance of the case, the jurors felt that they should not return immediately, so the indictment was read to kill time. Then they sat around for a little while. Finally, at 3:25 P.M. the jury filed in and rendered a verdict of "not guilty."

Commenting upon the verdict, the Brooklyn *Eagle* declared: "The acquittal of Colonel Robert W. Stewart, Chairman of the Board of the Standard Oil Company of Indiana, adds still another miscarriage of justice to the long legal travesty that has followed the oil scandal." [18] In an editorial entitled "That Potent Technicality" *The Chicago Daily News* said that apparently the jurors had no choice but to acquit Stewart on a technicality; he escaped a conviction but received no moral vindication.[19] The editorial made Stewart furious. He sent for one of his close friends and wanted to know how such things could be stopped.[20] The friend suggested that the Colonel issue a statement. Whereupon the Colonel replied: "With the fight I am going to have with Mr. Rockefeller for the control and management of the company, I am not going to make a statement." Reflecting another point of view, the Indianapolis *World* said: "The verdict of the jury was just and should end the persecution of Colonel Stewart. . . . We rejoice in the verdict in Colonel Stewart's case and protest against any further proceedings in this line, for after all the achievements of Colonel Robert W. Stewart and his breed of men are the very essence of our economic well being." [21] *The New York Times* said it was highly doubtful if Colonel Stewart could have been or should have been convicted of perjury. "His real offense," according to the *Times*, "was in its essence moral, or

17. See statement of Charles E. Henderson, foreman of the jury, in *Ten Years of Accomplishment 1918–1928.*
18. November 21, 1928.
19. November 22, 1928.
20. Memorandum from Raymond B. Fosdick to Thomas M. Debevoise, November 26, 1928. Rockefeller File.
21. November 23, 1928.

anti-social. For a long time he did his best to hinder an important investigation by the government into a complicated case of fraud affecting the public interest. If he did not swear falsely to the Senate Committee, he at least misled it, and sought to throw it off the trail it was pursuing toward the mysterious transactions of the Continental Trading Company." [22] Of this editorial, Ivy Lee, Rockefeller's public relations representative, said: "I have read a great many editorials on this subject but I think this sums up the general feeling."

Owing to widespread press reports that Stewart's acquittal had been due to a technicality, all members of the jury signed a statement on December 6, 1929, denying the allegation.[23] In regard to the technicality, the statement said: "This is not a fact. We considered the charges on their merits and acquitted the defendant thereof. It was our intention that our verdict should stand as a vindication of Colonel Stewart. Our verdict was not based upon a lack of quorums in the Senate Committee. It was based on our belief after hearing all the evidence, that Colonel Stewart had not testified falsely as charged."

Strengthened by the fact that he had been acquitted of contempt and perjury, Colonel Stewart, instead of resigning, prepared to stand for re-election as a Director of Standard at the annual meeting of the stockholders on March 7, 1929. Mr. Rockefeller's only alternative, therefore, was to depart from his general policy of not interfering with the management of companies in which he held a stock interest and wage a proxy fight to secure enough votes to oust Stewart. Consequently, the opening gun in what was to be the most spectacular proxy battle in American corporate history up to that time was fired on January 9th when the Rockefeller proxy committee, composed of Mr. Rockefeller, Winthrop W. Aldrich, and William Roberts (of the law firm of Murray, Aldrich and Roberts) mailed a letter to all stockholders asking for their proxies to vote to terminate Stewart's connection with the company. All of the other Directors were to be re-elected. The enclosed proxy covered any stockholders' meetings which might be held in 1929 for the election or removal of Directors. The letter emphasized the fact that under the leadership of Seubert and his associates the interests of the company would be fully protected and its business well handled without Stewart. Commenting upon Rockefeller's appeal

22. November 22, 1928.
23. *The New York Times*, January 12, 1929.

for proxies, *The Chicago Tribune* said: "A generation can bring about astonishing changes. No one would have believed twenty-five or thirty years ago that a Rockefeller would ever have to appeal for public support to gain control of an oil company bearing the name 'Standard,' or, indeed, of any oil company, whatever its name. No one would have believed that a Rockefeller would be engaged in such a struggle and fighting on the side of a more scrupulous business morality. That is what has happened; no one has said that Mr. Rockefeller is anything but sincere, and no one is likely to say it. Time and their own acts have softened public opinion toward the Rockefellers, father and son." [24]

At a meeting of all Standard sales managers and other company officials at the Lake Shore Athletic Club early in January, 1929, Colonel Stewart reviewed the history of the whole controversy and, at the conclusion of his address, he accepted Mr. Rockefeller's challenge. "If the Rockefellers want to fight," Stewart shouted, "I'll show them how to fight." [25] Even though Stewart realized that he did not have a chance to win, he elected to fight.[26] He was not the kind to quit under fire. His decision to fight, however, placed his fellow Directors in an exceedingly difficult position.

Fully prepared, the Stewart proxy committee, composed of Stewart, Seubert, and Felix T. Graham, sent a letter on January 10th to all employee stockholders asking for their proxies for the re-election of all Directors. Within a few days, proxies were mailed to all other stockholders. The appearance of Seubert's name as a member of the proxy committee occasioned considerable surprise and indicated that he was not as neutral as was thought. Seubert issued a statement on the 14th in which he made it clear that he would cast his vote for Stewart; that there had never been the slightest doubt as to his attitude; and that he had so informed Mr. Rockefeller several months ago.[27] At the same time the members of the Board of Directors expressed their complete confidence in Stewart, saying that his retirement would be detrimental to the best interests of the company. Although many of them had individual doubts about Stewart's having done the right thing in handling the Continental bonds, they gave him their unqualified support because he had done so much for the company. These statements by Seubert and the Directors set at rest all rumors

24. *The Chicago Tribune,* January 16, 1929.
25. *Ibid.,* January 11, 1929.
26. Interview with Albert L. Hopkins, May 26, 1929.
27. *The Chicago Tribune,* January 15, 1929.

that Standard's management would split in its support of Stewart. A great many stockholders inquired of Mr. Rockefeller what his support of Seubert and the other Directors meant and raised doubts about placing the leadership of the company in Seubert's hands. Mr. Rockefeller believed that the statement by the Directors had been forced by Stewart, but he did not see how they could have done otherwise.[28] He did not hold the statement against them or take it to mean that they would be any less loyal to the company if Stewart were defeated.

One of the first effects of the proxy fight was to stimulate the purchase of Standard stock.[29] Beginning on January 15th, the company's stock advanced nearly $9 per share over that of the previous two days, bringing it to almost $100, and 70,800 shares changed hands. On the next day, with the shares at $103½, a new high, 95,800 shares changed hands. The battle for stock raged furiously. Traders fought each other on the curb floor, while brokers from nearly every house vied with each other executing orders. Blocks of five hundred were dealt in frequently. The New York Stock Exchange, which exercised jurisdiction over curb members, injected new zeal into the fight by ruling that in certain cases brokers might vote the stock which they held for customers who had not requested proxies. The battle did not last long, however, because February 1st was the latest one could buy shares in New York and have them recorded in Chicago by the 5th. Except for a few shares of stock Rockefeller purchased in order to qualify the members of a new Board of Directors, if that became necessary, neither he nor Stewart increased their personal holdings. On the other hand, there was nothing to prevent their partisans from buying and voting their proxies. Others, probably a majority of buyers, purchased the stock as a matter of good business in order to advance their own personal interest.

In order to avoid abuse and embarrassment which he knew would arise in connection with the fight, Mr. Rockefeller sailed for Egypt on January 9th. Many of his friends and supporters were highly critical of his leaving the country; it looked as if he were running away from the fight. Moreover, it gave the Stewart forces an opportunity to say that Rockefeller was not deeply concerned or interested in the outcome. With Rockefeller's departure, the

28. John D. Rockefeller, Jr., to Thomas M. Debevoise, February 8, 1929. Rockefeller File.
29. The Chicago Tribune, January 16, 17, 1929; Chicago Journal of Commerce, January 17, 1929.

direction of the proxy fight was left in the hands of trusted associates, Thomas M. Debevoise, Winthrop W. Aldrich, Bertram Cutler, William Roberts, Ivy Lee, and Raymond B. Fosdick, who constituted a campaign committee. They devoted their full time to securing proxies. Charles E. Hughes of New York was retained as general counsel and H. H. Hornbrook of Indianapolis acted for the committee in Indiana. When Mr. Hughes' appointment was announced, the Wichita, Kansas, *Eagle* on January 31st declared that "Stewart is a terrible, double-fisted fighter. The farm soil of Iowa still shows on his boots. He makes the old rich families nervous just to look at him. So they call in Hughes. He makes them comfortable."

Working as a team, the Rockefeller campaign committee met every morning to plan, consult, and receive reports.[30] It was impossible to consult Mr. Rockefeller on every move in the campaign, so the members simply went ahead, hoping that the results would justify what they had done. By cable and letter, however, Rockefeller was kept informed of general developments. The committee made lists of stockholders residing in twenty-four of the largest cities of the country. A separate list of all those holding more than five hundred shares in these cities was then prepared. From this list a volunteer committee of fifteen in each place was formed in so far as possible to canvass local stockholders and encourage them to send in their proxies. Where necessary, various lawyers and law firms across the country were retained to direct the solicitation for proxies. Aldrich and Roberts looked after the formation of the committees and acted as adviser to Lyman Rhoades who received the proxies. Debevoise and Lee handled the publicity. Debevoise also handled the correspondence with stockholders.

Colonel Stewart, L. L. Stephens, and Albert L. Hopkins directed the management's campaign for proxies. Members of the Board of Directors worked actively, writing personal letters to stockholders, making speeches, and directing the solicitation by employees. With a vast marketing system covering the Middle West, employees in the sales divisions were especially active in soliciting proxies. They were given lists of stockholders with instructions to drop everything and get proxies. Proxies came first, business second. Colonel Stewart had an unusually wide acquaint-

30. Memorandum of the Campaign Committee Plan, January 14, 1929. Rockefeller File.

ance in the Middle West and knew thousands of stockholders personally. Aroused by Rockefeller's attack, many of them volunteered to assist the Colonel and worked at their own expense interviewing stockholders and soliciting proxies.

There was much speculation by the public at the outset as to which side could muster sufficient votes to control the election. There were predictions that the contest would be close. Some felt that Mr. Rockefeller had made a mistake in starting the fight with the "Rough Riding" Colonel. Tremendously popular everywhere in the Middle West and with thousands of friends, Stewart could be counted upon to wage a hard fight. Stewart also had the loyal support of all the Directors and their opinion of what was best for the company carried weight. Furthermore, under Stewart's brilliant leadership a record of achievement unparalleled in the history of the company had been made, which was a source of pride to all in any way connected with it. The employees owned about 400,000 shares, and it was expected that most of them would vote for Stewart. Although Stewart's integrity had been assailed, the fact that he had been re-elected a Director of the National City Bank of New York, the Continental National Bank and Trust Company of Chicago, the Boulevard Bridge Bank of Chicago, and the Hanover Fire Insurance Company also carried weight.

Rockefeller, likewise, had several important advantages. He entered the fight with a nucleus of more than 15 per cent of the stock. He owned 402,800 shares personally, the Rockefeller Foundation 460,760 shares, and Rockefeller's family about 500,000, making a total of 1,364,700 shares. Through personal connections it was expected that he would be able to secure proxies for large blocks of stock held by the Whitney, Harkness, Flagler, Brewster, Rogers, and other old Standard families. Waging his fight on the basis of a moral issue had already brought him tremendous public support from leaders of Big Business, newspaper and magazine editors, ministers, teachers, and people from all walks of life.

The campaign for proxies resembled a presidential election campaign in many respects. Stewart's campaign office in Chicago took on the appearance of a national political party headquarters. Large pictures of Stewart were on the walls and attached were hundreds of signatures under a large statement: "We're with you, Col. Stewart, 100 per cent." Statements were issued to the press from time to time by each side. Pamphlets of different kinds were printed and were mailed to stockholders. Mass meetings and demonstrations by employees were held. Full-page advertisements appeared in middle western newspapers. When some especially large stockholder cast his lot with one side or the other, announcement of this appeared in the press. Reprints of articles from periodicals on the controversy were bought and circulated freely by both sides. Clergymen spoke and wrote on the issues involved. Senators Nye and Norris made savage attacks upon Stewart in speeches on the Senate floor. Oswald Garrison Villard, editor of the *Nation*, who found himself at the opposite extreme on many political issues from Rockefeller, made a radio appeal over Station WMCA in behalf of Rockefeller.

Through the issuance of statements to the press and the publication of letters in reply to inquiries made by stockholders and others, the Rockefeller campaign committee consistently emphasized that the fight was an opportunity to clean house and show the public that Big Business in general and the petroleum industry in particular would not countenance the course of conduct followed by Stewart in his appearance before the Senate Committee and through his participation in the Continental Trading Company deal. The committee refrained from rehashing the Continental deal because the facts were well known, and Rockefeller did not want to engage in a mud-slinging campaign. With Mr. Rockefeller, it was not a question of Colonel Stewart's efficient and able leadership, his brilliant record, or the prosperity of the company. It was a question of Colonel Stewart's conduct in connection with the Continental transaction and his attitude toward his company, the public, and toward public authority, which had seriously impaired confidence in Standard of Indiana and all Big Business. Stockholders were assured that Rockefeller had their interests at heart and would use the proxies to insure the continued prosperity of the company under leaders who would have the confidence of the public. If he won the fight, the policies of the company with regard to management, dividends, and other matters would continue undisturbed. Considerable emphasis was given throughout the campaign to the promises Colonel Stewart had given to Mr. Rockefeller on two different occasions to resign at his personal request.

Colonel Stewart waged his fight against Mr. Rockefeller in his characteristic manner, answering every criticism directed against him as rapidly as they appeared. Regarding the oil scandals, Stewart denied that he ever had anything to do with the leasing of Teapot Dome or the Elk Hills naval oil reserves. Of the Continental Trading Company, he denied that he ever had any connection with it, that he was ever an officer or director, and that he personally ever made a dollar out of the deal. On the other hand, Standard of Indiana honestly and legitimately made several millions. Stewart stated that he refused personally to receive the bonds and immediately created a trust for the two companies, and one of them now had the money. Furthermore, he had answered the questions of the Senate Committee, except for two which it had no power to ask because they were judicial questions. In this he had been vindicated by two regularly constituted courts and juries and not on any legal technicalities.

Regarding the promises that he would resign at Mr. Rockefeller's personal request, which was a main point in the controversy, Colonel Stewart said: "I haven't the slightest doubt in the world that Mr. Rockefeller, Jr., and his attorney, Mr. Debevoise, honestly believe I gave him the promise he claims, but I am just as honest in the assertion that my every thought and intention was to tell them that the stockholders alone and not Mr. Rockefeller, Jr., individually, were to have the right to demand my resignation." [31] Speaking of his conference with Debevoise and Cutler in February, 1928, Stewart continued: "Undoubtedly, in the conversation, I spoke kindly of Mr. Rockefeller, Jr., but it was never my intention in that conversation or any time to make Mr. Rockefeller, Jr., the sole arbiter of my future or of the future welfare of the company, and in justice to Mr. Rockefeller, Jr., I may state that I do not believe at that time he wished to occupy any such position." Stewart contended that he would not argue over the veracity of either Rockefeller or Debevoise, for both were men of high character and would not wilfully misstate the facts.

Stewart's chief appeal to the stockholders was based on the progress and prosperity of the company under his administration. It was an impressive record, comparable to that of but a few corporations in the country. He had made the company one of the outstanding successes in the annals of American finance. In 1918 it had net assets of $117,509,000; in 1928 it had $460,000,000.[32] In 1918 the company owed banks $35,000,000; at the end of 1928 there were no outstanding liabilities and the cash amounted to

31. *Statement to Stockholders.*
32. *Ten Years of Accomplishments, 1918–1928; Chicago Daily Journal,* January 25, 1929.

$112,000,000. In 1918 the company owned no crude oil properties; in 1928 through Midwest, Dixie, Pan American, and Lago it had a supply second to none. In 1918 there were only 4,622 stockholders; in 1928 there were 57,000. In 1918 one share of stock had a market value of $535; in 1928, stock resulting from the splits of this one share had a value of $1,760. In 1918 the total market value of Standard's stock outstanding was $219,000,000; in 1928, it was $840,000,000, or an increase in ten years of approximately 300 per cent. During Stewart's ten-year administration cash dividends of $213,000,000 had been paid, while in the seven years previous they amounted to only $42,000,000. In addition, two stock dividends had been declared, one of 150 per cent in 1920 and another of 100 per cent in 1922. By comparison, Standard of Indiana had made greater progress under Stewart's leadership than any of the Standard companies and, as a result, it was in a strong independent position. It was one of the largest money makers and a liberal dividend payer.

An unofficial financial report in January, 1929, indicated that Standard's net earnings for 1928 would be approximately $80,000,000, or about $9.00 per share, which would make it double that of 1927 and a third larger than that of 1926.[33] Actually, Standard earned about $6.00 per share and Midwest about $3.00 per share. Furthermore, Midwest's dividend of $21,821,870 did not represent 1928 earnings but an accumulation of two or three years. The earnings for 1928 were $5,743,670. The Rockefeller committee was aware of this situation but did not say anything in order to keep from having its cause branded with the dollar sign.[34] Irrespective of how the earnings were attained, many believed that the stockholders would be dazzled by the $9.00 per share profit and cast their votes for Stewart.

With the growth and expansion of Standard of Indiana, Stewart's love of competition had brought the company into conflict with several old Standard Oil units—Standard of New Jersey, New York, Louisiana, Kentucky, and California, Atlantic Refining, Continental, and Prairie Oil & Gas. Because Mr. Rockefeller was more heavily interested in the prosperity of some of these companies than in Standard of Indiana, many people especially in the Middle West thought the "moral issue" was a pretense or camouflage for his wanting to curb and restrict the expansion of the

33. *Chicago Journal of Commerce*, January 15, 1929.
34. Thomas M. Debevoise to Thomas Allen III, February 7, 1929. Rockefeller File.

western company. They looked upon the fight as a contest between the East and the West for the control of the oil industry.

It had been assumed that John D., Sr., who was in Florida, backed his son in the proxy fight, yet there had been no statement from him to this effect. Late in January, Debevoise wrote John D., Sr., that there was a feeling in Chicago that he favored Stewart because of his business policy while his son opposed him because of his unethical conduct.[35] In view of the fact that Colonel Stewart was basing his campaign on the dollar standard, Debevoise, for the campaign committee, advised John D., Sr., to make a statement, if he would, since it would have an effective influence upon stockholders and public opinion, even though he owned no stock in Standard of Indiana. On January 31st John D., Sr., issued a statement giving his unqualified endorsement to his son's efforts to oust Stewart.[36] He said he did not see how his son could have done otherwise than request Stewart's resignation. Stewart wrote John D., Sr., the next day saying that he believed that the loyal and honest support Rockefeller had given him and his associates for so many years and through the most trying time would have prevented him from opposing his re-election.[37]

A special effort was made under the direction of Frank V. Martinek, manager of personnel for Standard's Sales Department, to secure the proxies of 7,918 employee stockholders for Stewart. Mass meetings in the sales field were held and addresses were made by the Directors in behalf of Stewart. Resolutions and testimonials pledging support to the Colonel were adopted both in the sales fields and refineries. Full-page advertisements, bought and paid for by the employees, appeared in various newspapers with a picture of Stewart and a caption "He's For Us—We're For Him." Within various departments, supervisors and foremen were given lists of employee stockholders within their jurisdiction to canvass. No one was overlooked. There is no doubt that there was a tremendous amount of spontaneous and genuine enthusiasm for Stewart. Left alone to make their decisions, probably the majority would have supported him without any canvassing. On the other hand, there was considerable evidence of quiet opposition. Early in the contest Stewart announced that coercion was not being used,

35. Thomas M. Debevoise to John D. Rockefeller, Sr., January 25, 1929. Rockefeller File.
36. *Chicago Journal of Commerce*, February 1, 1929.
37. *Ibid.*, February 2, 1929.

and none would be used. However, letters in the Rockefeller files from employees in the sales offices at Minneapolis, Milwaukee, St. Louis, Indianapolis, and from the refinery at Casper indicated that at numerous points coercion was used. Some employees were made to feel that, unless they voted for Stewart, they might lose their jobs. The situation was aggravated by baseless stories to the effect that the plant would be shut down or wages would be cut or other dire things would happen if Stewart lost. Debevoise pointed out that if it were generally known how many letters his office had received from employees who regretted the necessity of signing their proxies for Stewart, the character of his "employee support" would be better understood.[38] According to Debevoise, Stewart's boast of employee support meant little.

Almost from the beginning, stockholders in the East, West, and South wrote to Mr. Rockefeller complaining about the amount of time used by the employees not only of Standard but of the American Oil Company and Pan American Petroleum & Transport Company in soliciting proxies. In many places the office force was turned into "proxy hunting scouts." They would call not only once or twice on a stockholder but in some cases as high as five times. It seemed to the Rockefeller proxy committee as if the employees were spending all of their time in what practically amounted to a house-to-house canvass. Many letters written by managers on company stationery and on company time to stockholders soliciting proxies were forwarded to Mr. Rockefeller's office. While the Rockefeller proxy committee appreciated the position of the employees, it felt that the company was put to an enormous expense through the loss of time in having employees make the canvass. The proxy committee seriously considered filing suit against the officers of the company for damages after the fight was over but dropped the idea in order not to disrupt company affairs.[39]

Without consulting the "large stockholders" in the East, Stewart, in a dramatic move, played his ace card on February 4th, when Standard's Directors voted a regular quarterly dividend of 62½ cents, an extra dividend of 50 cents per share, and a 50 per cent stock dividend.[40] It was the greatest stock and cash dividend ever

38. Thomas M. Debevoise to Julius Rosenwald, March 19, 1929; Thomas M. Debevoise to R. J. Hanna, March 19, 1929. Rockefeller File.
39. Interview with Thomas M. Debevoise, December 1, 1948.
40. *Chicago Journal of Commerce*, February 5, 1929; *The Chicago Tribune*, February 5, 1929.

declared in the company's history. The stock dividend involved the
issuance of approximately 4,616,000 shares of additional stock.
The action graphically brought to the attention of all shareholders the immense profits which the company had made under
Stewart. The use by Colonel Stewart of his absolute control over
Standard's Directors to declare the stock dividend to show stockholders what he was accomplishing and could accomplish in their
interest seemed outrageous to Rockefeller, Sr. To take such important action on his sole initiative and solely in his own interest
seemed far from fair to the real owners of the company.[41] Since
the stock books were closed on the 5th, none of the new stock
could be voted on March 7th. However, the declaration of a stock
dividend might cause some to revoke the proxy given to Rockefeller and file a new one for Stewart. It might also prove influential with those who were still wavering. In any event, the over-
all psychological effect seemed to be beneficial to Stewart's cause.

As a result of Standard's declaring a stock dividend, investors
and speculators attempted to capitalize upon the event and a
runaway market, unparalleled in recent years, developed in New
York on the 5th.[42] Traders specializing in Standard stock on the
curb exchange were buried under an avalanche of orders. It was
sensational. Orders from all over the country and from abroad
had poured in during the night of the 4th. The next morning
orders were placed for 70,000 shares when trading opened even
though the price had not been fixed. Specialists dealing in Standard securities held a conference to determine the price, and it
was not until after 1 P.M. that trading in Standard stock began
at $100.25 per share. These 70,000 shares involved more than
$7,000,000. It was the greatest monetary turnover in curb history.
Nearly 130,000 shares changed hands that day. Frenzied trading
took place in Chicago, where the curb price for a brief period
went as high as $108 or $109. Owing to the confusion in New
York, many traders transferred their orders to Chicago. Another
factor in favor of buying stock in Chicago was that it could be
transferred in time to be entered before the stock books closed on
the 5th.

The Rockefeller campaign committee sent to the stockholders on
February 10th a "final message," a seventy-two-page brochure

41. John D. Rockefeller, Jr., to Bertram Cutler, February 4, 1929. Rockefeller File.
42. *Chicago Journal of Commerce*, February 6, 1929; *The Chicago Tribune*, February 6, 1929.

signed by Winthrop W. Aldrich. Most of it was simply excerpts from documents and testimony of the Senate Committee hearings on the Continental Trading Company. Albert L. Hopkins, Stewart's personal attorney, branded the publication as "untrue in many places" and a "cunningly drawn document to deceive the stockholders and the public." [43] He called it "nothing short of a cowardly and dastardly libel." Furthermore, Aldrich had printed extracts from the official transcript which contained more than six hundred errors. The contents of the brochure made Stewart furious, and he scored the document as a "grossly unfair deception—unfair because it was largely insinuation rather than accusation—a deception of omission as well as of statement." [44] He attacked Aldrich for selecting only parts of the testimony to paint "a sinister and unwholesome picture" and for including irrelevant material on Teapot Dome and Elk Hills with which Stewart had nothing to do. "I cannot believe," said Stewart, "that Mr. John D. Rockefeller, Junior, ever gave his approval to the publication of such a slander." Later, when Rockefeller received a copy, he cabled that he had read the able, statesmanlike seventy-two-page letter with utmost satisfaction and pride.[45]

The issuance of the brochure seemed to be a last straw, for Colonel Stewart's lawyers immediately addressed a letter to Rockefeller, Aldrich, Roberts, and Lee requesting them to "forthwith publicly disavow, retract, and deny the false allegations and statements concerning Stewart contained in three publications, which they had printed and circulated." [46] As a result, Aldrich issued a statement to the press saying that the three pamphlets contained excerpts from editorial comment to show the trend of newspaper opinion. They were not to be construed as the editorial comment of the Rockefeller campaign committee.

Rockefeller received tremendous support from newspapers all over the country throughout the campaign. Ivy Lee gathered 428 editorials on the fight from newspapers in forty-five states and the District of Columbia during January and February, and the overwhelming majority endorsed Rockefeller.[47] Unfavorable comments

43. *The Chicago Tribune,* February 11, 1929.
44. *Ibid.,* February 21, 1929.
45. John D. Rockefeller, Jr., to Thomas M. Debevoise, March 18, 1929. Rockefeller File.
46. Hopkins, Starr & Hopkins and Leonard W. Guiler to John D. Rockefeller, Jr., Winthrop W. Aldrich, William Roberts, and Ivy Lee. Albert L. Hopkins File.
47. Ivy Lee to John D. Rockefeller, Jr., April 2, 1929. Rockefeller File.

were confined for the most part to newspapers in the Middle West. A few scattered editorials from other sections disagreed with Rockefeller. One widely quoted editorial phrase was: "Rockefeller never served his country better than he is serving it now in his fight with Colonel Stewart."

In the course of the campaign it was natural that anyone who had any grievance, founded or otherwise, against Colonel Stewart should bring it to the attention of Mr. Rockefeller. Many letters were received from individuals raising questions about various deals and making complaints. One person who had contacts with oil well supply people alleged that Stewart would do no business with these companies unless "he got his." Another alleged that when the Dixie Oil Company was organized, Frederick H. Wickett peddled the stock for a long time before anyone would buy it. Stewart wouldn't even let Wickett into his office. All of a sudden Stewart changed his mind and bought Dixie for Standard when the value of the company was questionable. Still another complained of the "dirty" deal that the small stockholders got in the exchange of stock between Midwest and Standard. John D., Jr., was advised to inquire into the Sewell affair of 1921. A stockholder in Council Bluffs, Iowa, asked: "Do you know the record of Colonel Stewart's son in New York? If not, please look it up. It will be a revelation." Most of the complaints related to Stewart and his management of Pan American Petroleum & Transport Company and Lago.

During the first two weeks or more of the proxy campaign, strenuous efforts were made by the Rockefeller committee to line up large blocks of stocks held by trust companies and other large stockholders. From these it received powerful support. By January 15th proxies for 2,440,548 shares had come in, which was about 26 per cent.[48] In reporting to Mr. Rockefeller in Egypt, Mr. Debevoise indicated that the fight had been won. Within another week the committee had more than 38 per cent.[49] Efforts were then made to get the proxies of the small holders.

Proxies for Stewart likewise poured into the Chicago office, but the bulk came from small holders. Some unidentified person, apparently employed by Standard in the Chicago office and de-

48. Thomas M. Debevoise to John D. Rockefeller, Jr., January 16, 1929. Rockefeller File.
49. Thomas M. Debevoise to John D. Rockefeller, Jr., January 23, 1929. Rockefeller File.

tailed to counting proxies, sent two communications to the Rockefeller committee reporting on activities in that office. Whoever it was, reported that on January 23rd Stewart had proxies for about 1,260,000 shares representing about 18,000 stockholders. No proxies covering any large amounts had come in. It was "mostly piker stuff."

By January 25th, within two weeks after the campaign began, the outcome of the battle was practically determined, but the general public was not aware of the situation. The Rockefeller committee had 43½ per cent of the shares, which was enough to control the stockholders' meeting.[50] These facts were kept strictly confidential because the Rockefeller committee was afraid that early knowledge of defeat might make Stewart desperate and lead to mud-slinging. On January 28th Debevoise issued a statement saying that the Rockefeller committee now had enough to swing the election, but he did not indicate the percentage. Even though sufficient votes had been quickly secured to control the meeting, the objective of the Rockefeller committee was to make the election outcome as decisive as possible. Stewart countered with a statement to the effect that the activity of the Rockefeller agents throughout the country belied these claims; there was only one purpose for the claim and that was to make it appear that the "band wagon is trundling their way." They were not getting as many votes as they expected. "We have the Colonel licked," Debevoise wrote to Thomas B. Lockwood of Buffalo on February 4th, "and wish you were here to enjoy the fun." On February 7th Aldrich announced that the Rockefeller committee had proxies for more than 51 per cent. By the 15th they had 54⅜ per cent with 15,000 shareholders who represented over 5,000,000 shares. Still fighting hard, Stewart claimed he had a large majority of the stockholders on his side and that thousands of proxies originally given to Rockefeller had been revoked and new ones made out to the management. On February 27th the Rockefeller proxy committee had 57 per cent of the stock, representing about 16,000 shareholders. Stewart claimed the proxies of 32,000 stockholders.[51] With victory certain, Charles E. Hughes, general counsel for the Rockefeller proxy committee, left for a vacation in Bermuda.

Early in February, when it was apparent that the battle had

50. Thomas M. Debevoise to John D. Rockefeller, Jr., January 26, 1929. Rockefeller File.
51. *Chicago Journal of Commerce*, February 28, 1929.

been won, many stockholders were asking the Rockefeller committee to reveal the names of its candidates for the Board of Directors. Originally, it was Rockefeller's intent to re-elect all Directors except Stewart. Basic in his thinking was the desire not to disrupt company affairs any more than was absolutely necessary. As the proxy fight progressed, the Rockefeller campaign committee decided to replace L. L. Stephens, who had been "unwarrantedly partisan" in the canvass for Stewart proxies. While the other Directors were openly and actively supporting Stewart, the committee was convinced that their first loyalty was to the company. Rockefeller believed that it would be very unfortunate to select an entirely new Board. It was agreed that Dr. Burton should be brought back temporarily as Chairman. A cable to Burton in Europe indicated the desire of the proxy committee to make him a Director, and it was believed that the Board would elect him Chairman.[52] Would he accept a directorship and, if the Board so desired, the chairmanship even if only temporarily to help out? Burton agreed to the proposal, provided it did not affect his annuity, but asked that his name as Chairman be withheld until the new Board had been elected.[53] Furthermore, he desired full approval of the Board as Chairman. If he were to serve as Chairman, he expressed a preference to act with his old associates and thought it advisable that they should be re-elected. With this assurance, the proxy committee went ahead with its plans. If a new leader for the company was required, Rockefeller suggested K. R. Kingsbury, President of the Standard of California, or Otto D. Donnell, President of the Ohio Oil Company, to the committee for consideration.[54]

To replace Stephens, confidential inquiries were made in Chicago as to some banker best qualified for the place.[55] Howard W. Fenton, President of the Harris Trust & Savings Bank, received favorable consideration, but the general consensus was that the outstanding figure among commercial bankers was Melvin A. Traylor, President of the First National Bank. For his bank, the proxy fight had raised a delicate and embarrassing problem. Stewart carried his personal account with the Continental National Bank and Trust Company and was on its Board, but he kept a fabulous

52. Cable to William M. Burton, February 15, 1929. Rockefeller File.
53. Cable from William M. Burton, February 18, 1929. Rockefeller File.
54. John D. Rockefeller, Jr., to Thomas M. Debevoise, February 22, 1929. Rockefeller File.
55. Chauncey Belknap to Thomas M. Debevoise, February 23, 1929. Rockefeller File.

company deposit with the First National which for years had run
between fifteen and thirty million dollars. In addition, he was an
intimate golfing pal of Frank Wetmore, Chairman of the Board.
Under these circumstances, the officers decided that they must
take their chances on keeping the deposit if Stewart were defeated. They could not turn down Stewart's request for the bank's
proxies. Traylor did not like Stewart's conduct, but his bank,
"merely for business reasons," felt obliged to support Stewart.
Even though Traylor was on Stewart's side, the Rockefeller committee agreed on Traylor as the replacement for Stephens.

Assured of victory, the Rockefeller party, headed by Winthrop
W. Aldrich, Thomas M. Debevoise, William Roberts, Richard E.
Dwight (law partner of Charles E. Hughes), and others left New
York in a private car on Sunday night, March 3rd, for Chicago.
On arriving in the city, they established their headquarters at the
Drake Hotel. Seventeen steel filing cases containing their proxies,
which they had brought with them, were loaded into taxis and
taken to the General Office at 910 S. Michigan and turned over
to a joint committee under the direction of Felix T. Graham, the
Secretary, to count and check. All of their proxies were compared
with those of Stewart's and the one dated the last, in case of any
conflict, was certified. Not one proxy was disputed. Debevoise and
Hornbrook conferred with Seubert as to the procedure to be
followed at the meeting. On the 5th Aldrich announced that his
committee was certain of about 59 per cent of the votes. Even
though Stewart, Stephens, and Hopkins had known for at least
three weeks that the battle had been lost, Stewart never conceded
defeat and maintained an outwardly confident attitude.[56] Within
the last three or four days, his fellow Directors were aware of the
fact that the fight had been lost.

While the Rockefeller proxy committee had agreed on a tentative slate of Directors, no final decision was reached until the 6th.
The committee talked with Traylor, asked him to go on the
Board, and he agreed. Seubert was asked to a conference on the
night of the 6th to discuss the situation in a confidential way, but
he refused to do so until he first consulted with the Directors and
had their approval.[57] It was at this conference that Seubert actually
learned that all of the Directors except Stewart and Stephens were
to be re-elected, Burton and Traylor elected, and that he, because

56. Interview with L. L. Stephens, August 30, 1948.
57. Interview with Edward G. Seubert, August 31, 1948.

of his honesty and loyalty to the company, was to be retained as President. In the event that the Directors might resign if Stewart were ousted, the proxy committee had a list of new Directors in reserve.

On the morning of March 7th, the day of the annual stockholders' meeting at Whiting, Colonel Stewart was at his office as usual. Even though the morning newspapers predicted his defeat, Stewart gave no visible evidence of the fact. He was calm and unruffled. He visited with several persons in their offices and shook hands as he left but never once did he say "Good-by." Before leaving for Whiting, he gave out copies of the 1928 financial report to newspapermen who had gathered in his office. Shaking hands with financial editors and other newsmen, he passed out cigars and asked: "Now boys, any questions you would like to ask?" He declined comment on all queries about the proxy fight, but promised them a statement after the meeting.

The day was raw and cold.[58] Even so, Whiting had taken on a holiday atmosphere. It presented the appearance of a town about to celebrate a county fair. Merchants had prepared for a crowd of 1,500 to 2,000 people. There was some expectation that the stockholders' meeting might last several days, so special lunch rooms had been opened, extra supplies laid in, and everything made ready for a rush of business. The Whiting police force, augmented by firemen sworn in for special duty, reported earlier than usual in order to handle the traffic. Drawn by curiosity, a large crowd of local inhabitants, nearly all Standard employees, gathered early in front of the Community House. Stockholders and spectators soon began arriving early by automobile, bus, street car, and train. As trains carrying persons to the meeting came to a stop in Whiting, one conductor was heard to shout: "All out for the Standard Oil rumpus."

The annual meeting was scheduled to start at 12 o'clock in the Administration Building at the refinery, but because of the anticipated crowd arrangements had been made to adjourn the meeting to the auditorium of the Whiting Community House, which held about a thousand people. In case of an overflow, other rooms, connected to the main auditorium with loud-speakers, were

58. For general accounts of the day and meeting, see *Chicago Daily Journal*, March 7, 1929; *Chicago Evening American*, March 7, 1929; *The Chicago Tribune*, March 7, 8, 1929; *Chicago Journal of Commerce*, March 8, 1929; Chicago *Herald and Examiner*, March 8, 1929; *The Chicago Daily News*, March 7, 1929.

in readiness. Telegraph lines had been strung into the basement pressroom under the main stage, and special telephones had been installed in order that the news might be flashed to all parts of the country. The orchestra pit had been equipped for the use of newspapermen, who had ready access to the telegraph and telephones. On the large stage were tables, one for the presiding officer, one for the Directors, and others for officials in charge of the voting records.

Once past the police at the entrance of the Community House, stockholders found themselves inside a spacious lobby which was lined with tables. At each of the ten tables sat three men, one a clerk of the stock recording department armed with a ledger against which all stock must be checked. Banners on tall standards bearing different sections of the alphabet aided stockholders in finding their places. A second clerk inspected the credentials, and a third pinned on badges. Badges were of four colors: white for stockholders who expected to vote their stock, blue for those voting proxies, buff for ushers, and red for reporters. Since newspapermen were not stockholders and technically could not attend, they were given badges designating them as members of the "house staff." It was the first time reporters had ever attended a Standard stockholders' meeting. Properly badged, stockholders were allowed to pass beyond the lobby into the lounging room, lunch room, auditorium, or any other place in the building.

Upon entering the auditorium, their credentials were again checked by the ushers. The right side of the auditorium was given over to women, the left to men. In spite of the care exercised in admitting people to the auditorium, apparently there were some gatecrashers, for two of the stockholders, one of whom was in the Rockefeller party, had their pockets picked during the meeting.

About 10:20 A.M. a squad of motorcycle police pulled up in front of the Community House with several limousines behind. It was the Rockefeller proxy committee party of some twenty-five people headed by Winthrop W. Aldrich, the generalissimo and floor leader. Suspense deepened as the Rockefeller army filed in. Other stockholders, in the meantime, streamed through the doors and took seats or stood talking in little groups. Newspaper reporters sat in the orchestra pit smoking, working, and chatting as the zero hour approached. A press attaché notified reporters that two statements would be made after the meeting, one by the "new executive director" and another by Colonel Stewart. A special messenger who had left New York the night before bringing a new lot of one hundred and seventy-five proxies for Rockefeller, arrived and delivered the proxies.

As twelve o'clock approached, the Rockefeller party left the Community House and drove to the Administration Building at the refinery. Stewart and the Directors were at lunch when Aldrich and his party arrived. A minute or two before noon Stewart and the Directors came into the Directors' room of the Administration Building. Stewart shook hands with the Rockefeller men, and everybody smiled and exchanged greetings. "Has the whistle blown yet?" Stewart asked. Just then the 12 o'clock whistle blew. Stewart stood up, called the meeting to order, and announced that the meeting would adjourn to the Community House. Everybody, including a small regiment of newspapermen and photographers, entered automobiles and drove the short distance to the Community House.

Assembled in the main auditorium of the Community House were about five hundred stockholders, a number far below the number expected. Probably the coldness of the weather and the certainty of Stewart's defeat accounted for many vacant seats. On their arrival at the Community House about 12:10 the Rockefeller party walked down the aisle and took front seats reserved for them on the left side in front of the stage. The crowd of stockholders was silent. About 12:30 Mr. Seubert and the other Directors appeared on the stage and stood beside the long Directors' table and smilingly acknowledged the applause. For a moment there was a pause, then Stewart strode in from the back of the stage. As he entered, a majority of those present stood and gave him an ovation rarely accorded to any person. For four minutes the stockholders applauded, shouted, whistled, and stamped their feet on the floor. There was no doubt about its being a Stewart crowd.

It was a dramatic moment, doubly dramatic, for there stood Stewart ready to preside over his own defeat. Holding his head high, knowing exactly what was coming and bitterly disliking the taste of it, Stewart continued to smile as the crowd applauded. When the applause had subsided, Stewart, with all the dignity befitting the leading actor in a widely heralded financial drama, picked up the gavel, rapped for order and said: "We are here for the fortieth annual meeting of the stockholders of our company. The first order of business will be the reading of the notice of

EDWARD G. SEUBERT, PRESIDENT 1927–1944

EDWARD G. SEUBERT HANDS CHECK FOR $72,500,000 TO EARL W. SINCLAIR

With the delivery of this check, Standard acquired the half interest of the Sinclair Consolidated Oil Corporation in the Sinclair Pipe Line and the Sinclair Crude Oil Purchasing Company

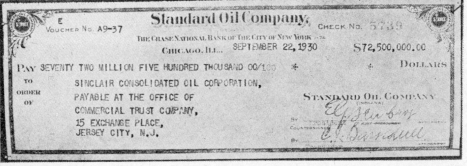

National Petroleum News, September 24, 1930. Reproduced through the courtesy of the *National Petroleum News*

the meeting." His voice was firm, pleasant, and commanding. There was not even a trace of nervousness in it. After the reading of the notice and the minutes of last year's meeting, Stewart read in a precise and businesslike manner the annual report, which was by far the most detailed document ever presented to the stockholders. In his presentation Stewart pounded home the fact that this had been Standard's greatest year, a most stupendous year, with earnings far ahead of any in its history. His voice grew in volume as he read the statement that the company's net earnings after a reserve for taxes in 1928 were $77,337,166, an increase of $47,204,710 over 1927. The 1928 net earnings represented a profit of 16.76 per cent on the capital invested. Included in the 1928 net earnings was an extra cash dividend of $21,821,870 declared by Midwest Refining. Aside from Midwest's dividend, the tremendous increase was due to greater profit on sales, decreased manufacturing and marketing costs per barrel, and a greater volume of sales which totaled 35,432,806 barrels as against 33,131,975 barrels in 1927. The reserve—$114,867,962—in cash, securities, and investments in other companies was the largest in history. At the conclusion of Stewart's reading, there was another prolonged period of applause. Once more the crowd cheered, whistled, sang, and stamped their feet—except in the Rockefeller corner. Stewart stood smiling and nodded to the little group of Rockefeller men down in front. The proposal of a third employee stock purchase plan was then presented and readily passed.

At this point Stewart told the stockholders to be at ease until the tellers could check how many shareholders were present and voting and the number of proxies received. While this was being done, the Rockefeller party sat quietly eating sandwiches which they had brought with them. Others in the audience did likewise. Stewart visited with the Directors and other friends. While he was having his picture taken, some friends approached, shook Stewart's hand, and asked if he saw any chance of his re-election. Stewart shook his head and said: "No hope." After a few minutes Stewart stood up and said: "You might as well meet your Directors while we wait. I'll introduce them." As each Director stood up, Stewart gave his name, nickname, and added some personal touch about each, finishing with "Eddie" Seubert, "whose impulse is for the good of the company, for the good of the stockholders, and for the good of the public." Stewart's manner was almost festive. It was able, courageous acting.

As soon as the checking was done, Stewart called the meeting to order. Felix T. Graham, the Secretary, announced that 8,446,-120 shares of stock out of 9,284,000 shares outstanding were represented at the meeting. This broke all records and demonstrated the thoroughness with which the work of corralling proxies had been done. Stockholders owning 817,410 shares were present in person; the rest were represented by proxies.

The moment for nominating Directors had now arrived. Stewart smiled at the five hundred stockholders before him and said: "The next order of business brings up the election of directors. I feel just a bit embarrassed over this situation." According to the bylaws, he was empowered to preside, he said, "until somebody thinks I am not doing it right." Most of the audience cheered him wildly. With a smile, he continued: "In view of the fact that there are gentlemen from eastern cities here who are very deeply interested in this election, I suggest that Mr. Debevoise come up and assist me." Debevoise stood up and genially declined, saying he appreciated the honor and spirit of the suggestion but he didn't think Stewart needed any assistance. Stewart then invited Aldrich, who also politely declined.

At this point the audience became intensely serious as Albert L. Hopkins, a Chicago lawyer and Stewart's personal attorney, arose and nominated the management ticket which included Stewart and all the incumbent Directors plus Dr. Gentry Cash and T. S. Cooke, who were nominated to succeed John D. Clark, who had resigned, and Beaumont Parks, who had died on February 25th. Stewart asked if there were other nominations. Aldrich rose, introduced himself, and nominated the same slate, except for Stewart and Stephens, and added the names of Dr. Burton and Melvin A. Traylor. The nomination of Traylor created special excitement, for the Rockefeller group had previously refused to divulge its slate of candidates and had indicated that there would be no drastic changes.

Stewart asked for further nominations. Mr. J. P. Hayes, one of the smaller stockholders, rose and said that inasmuch as there were already two vacancies on the Board, he moved that they re-elect the present Board and then select two at large, one to be selected by shareholders having 500 shares or less, the other to be selected by shareholders having more than 500 shares. In support of his motion, Hayes argued that if you are "going to give mere money representation it is only just that men of numbers be represented as well as the mere aggregation of money." The motion was seconded, and they were about to vote on it when Aldrich got up and protested that the motion was clearly out of order, that neither the bylaws nor the laws of Indiana provided for any such procedure, and that he would be forced to vote his proxies against it. A voice in the audience asked if the stockholders could not amend the bylaws. Stewart replied that the stockholders were the supreme power, of course. His statement brought a round of applause. When Stewart announced that he was about to put the motion, Mr. Aldrich rose again, demanded to know whether the vote was to be by the number of stockholders or the number of shares. Stewart replied: "Now just leave that to me and I think you'll be satisfied, Mr. Aldrich." With a broad smile on his face, Stewart chose to give his followers another chance to shout and called for the vote. There was a mighty roar of "ayes." He then called for the negative votes, and a dignified chorus of "noes" came from the Rockefeller group. There was a tense moment until Stewart spoke. "The 'noes' seem to have it," shouted Colonel Stewart. "The motion is lost." Mr. Aldrich settled back in relief, and there was another roar of laughter.

Stewart asked that the ballots be distributed. There were blue ones for the Rockefeller slate and white ones for the management. Nearly an hour elapsed while the ballots were being distributed, marked, and counted. When the meeting was again called to order, a resolution on the death of Beaumont Parks was read and adopted. This was the one solemn moment in the meeting. At this point one of the stockholders suggested that both Stewart and Rockefeller or Aldrich be elected to the Board, at which there was laughter and applause but Stewart, laughingly, ruled it out of order. Turning grave, Stewart finally said: "Well, then. Let's have the news. It may be bad news to some of us, but I'm sure we'll all take it standing up." Felix T. Graham, the Secretary, read the report of the inspectors. Without a tremor in his voice, Stewart announced the winners. The Rockefeller slate had decisively won. All of the Rockefeller nominees received 8,465,276 votes except Burton and Traylor, who received 5,510,313, Stewart, who received 2,954,986, and Stephens, who received 2,954,963.[59] Rockefeller's ticket polled about 60 per cent and Stewart's about 32 per cent with about 8 per cent of the stock not voted.

Upon the announcement of the results, Mr. Seubert moved that

59. Minutes of the Board of Directors' and Stockholders' Meetings, III, 1701.

the meeting adjourn. Aldrich interrupted to express the thanks of the Rockefeller proxy committee to Stewart for the fair manner in which he had conducted the meeting and for the help of the employees of the company who had aided them in checking their proxies. "Why," Stewart replied, "that's the kind of people these boys out here are." Someone moved that Aldrich's remark be placed in the record. By a tumultuous oral vote it was done, and the meeting adjourned after being in session about two hours.

When it was all over, Stewart was still smiling though tears trickled down the cheeks of many in the audience. The Colonel obligingly posed for news photographers and stood talking with friends who had come forward to shake hands. Presently, he left the stage, walked down to where his wife was sitting in the front row, embraced her, gave her a kiss, and they walked out of the auditorium with the applause of both supporters and adversaries ringing in their ears. Thus, one of the most historic struggles ever known in American business history came to an end and Colonel Stewart, who had risen from an obscure country lawyer in South Dakota to the top position in one of the largest business enterprises in the world, had been deposed. It also marked the end of a colorful and brilliant era in the history of Standard of Indiana.

As soon as the meeting was over, Stewart released a prepared statement. "It would be idle," he said, "for me to say that I leave the Standard Oil Company of Indiana without regret. For years its welfare has been my deepest concern. Its affairs have been my very life. I have seen it grow under the present administration from a $167,000,000 corporation with 4,620 stockholders to practically a billion dollar corporation with 56,203 stockholders. One cannot disassociate himself from such an intimacy without a wrench." [60] He thanked all the men and women who had so loyally supported him in the proxy campaign and, even in defeat, he drew great comfort from the fact that 31,336 stockholders had voted for him as against 15,204 for his opponents. In the states in which Standard marketed, there were 19,409 stockholders participating in the election, of whom 15,051 voted for Stewart. Of the 7,918 employee stockholders only 17 had voted against him. Commenting upon these facts, Stewart said: "It was a magnificent testimony both to the company and to our administration from the people who know it best." In concluding his remarks, the great leader requested all employees in the company to work as

60. *The Chicago Tribune*, March 8, 1929.

hard for the new management as they had for him, for the "Stand-ard Oil Company of Indiana must still go forward." He refused to be interviewed, stating that he wanted the turmoil to cease and Standard to continue on its business course.[61]

Immediately after the stockholders' meeting at Whiting, the Directors met for nearly an hour and re-elected Seubert President and the chief executive officer. Dr. Robert E. Humphreys was elevated to the vice-presidency created by the death of Beaumont Parks. Stephens was re-elected general counsel even though he had been defeated as a Director. The chairmanship remained vacant with the expectation that Burton would be elected upon his return. Traylor's election to the Board marked a radical de-parture from past practice. It was the first time in the history of the company that a person from outside the active management had been elected a Director.

The fact that Stewart had been supported by 31,336 stock-holders while only 15,204 voted with the Rockefeller interests on the "moral issue" was widely commented upon by the newspapers. The general tenor was that the average small investor did not care whether corporation heads were honest or crooked so long as they received their dividend checks. On the other hand, it was generally assumed that large stockholders, men of wealth, with important interests to guard, were more honest and scrupulous in matters of business. So many elements entered into the giving or withhold-ing of proxies that it is impossible to say that small stockholders were less scrupulous about the management of a company than large ones. For example, the feeling that Rockefeller's fight repre-sented an attempt on the part of the eastern Standard Oil com-panies, through Mr. Rockefeller, to gain control of Standard of Indiana in order to curb its growth and expansion certainly weighed heavily with some stockholders. Some were pro-Stewart because whatever he had done was no worse or as bad as some of the Rockefeller practices of the early days. This feeling was ex-pressed by some newspapers and in several letters to Mr. Rocke-feller. "If you will look up the record of your father," one party wrote to Rockefeller, "in the early days of the old Standard Oil Co. you will find it pretty well smeared with black spots ten times

61. After working for Standard for twenty-one years, Stewart retired from the company on March 8th with a pension of $50,801.94 per year. On January 1, 1939, when all pensioners above $1,200 per year were cut, Stewart's pension was reduced to $36,462.68.

worse than the charges you lay at the door of Col. Stewart. . . .
There is not enough soap in the world to wash the hands of the
elder Rockefeller from the taint of fifty years ago. Only people
with clean hands should undertake to blacken the character of
other and better men." [62] Other stockholders would have been
anti-Rockefeller on any issue because the name Rockefeller had
long been a symbol of monopoly.

John D. Rockefeller, Jr., was immediately notified of the victory and its extent. By cable from Palestine, he sent word that he
was very proud of Debevoise, Aldrich, and all who had worked
so ably for the victory.[63] "Deeply sympathetic," ran the cable,
"with opponent who for years past we have tried our best to save
from this." In so far as his knowledge went, Rockefeller expressed
his approval of all that had been done in the proxy fight. He was
well pleased with the way his associates had handled everything
and expressed regret that he had not been able to share the burden of the fight.

Stewart's defeat was a great personal victory for Mr. Rockefeller, who had dramatized the issue of business morality and
focused public attention upon it. He received hundreds of con-
gratulatory messages from ministers, newspaper editors, wage earners, industrialists, public school and college teachers, lawyers, and
others from all over the country. "No endowment of a college
nor support of a piece of research," wrote one college teacher,
"could have done more it seems to me to educate the public toward
honest business." Representative of the editorial comment was
that of the New York *Evening World,* which had been so influential in bringing pressure on Mr. Rockefeller to make the fight.
"This was an event of the first importance," declared the editor,
"in that it denotes an awakening in high business circles to the
necessity of keeping business clean and straight. It was, then, first
of all a triumph for American business. But too much credit cannot be given to Mr. Rockefeller, who made the demand and directed the fight that has brought victory." [64]

While the defeat of Colonel Stewart was a great personal triumph for Rockefeller, it had not been easily accomplished. Starting
with an initial advantage of having a nucleus of about 15 per cent

62. E. A. Stowe to John D. Rockefeller, Jr., January 11, 1929. Rockefeller File.
63. John D. Rockefeller, Jr., to Thomas M. Debevoise, March 9, 1929. Rockefeller
   File.
64. March 8, 1929.

of the stock, Rockefeller's associates had worked long and hard to acquire about 60 per cent of the proxies. Moreover, in spite of the fact that they received the enthusiastic support of a large number of volunteer workers all over the country, the campaign expenses were heavy. In the end, it cost Mr. Rockefeller personally several hundred thousand dollars to make the fight.[65]

The general public was, of course, not aware of how difficult and expensive a task it was for Mr. Rockefeller and his associates to oust Colonel Stewart. In the minds of a large majority who did not look below the surface, the incident simply confirmed their belief that the Rockefellers still dominated Standard of Indiana and it was not free and independent as Colonel Stewart had, through his extensive public relations program, been trying to prove. On the other hand, the financial community and most well-informed individuals realized that Mr. Rockefeller could not have won the fight had it not been for the widespread newspaper support and a moral issue on his side. In other words, the extensive and expensive efforts he had put forth in order to get proxies really proved that he no longer dominated Standard of Indiana.

The retention of the old Board of Directors, with the addition of Burton, Cash, and Cooke, removed much of the basis for believing that eastern stockholders with interests in rival companies desired to curb the expansion of Standard of Indiana. Although Traylor was added to the Board as an outside Director, the fact that he was widely known as a leading Chicago businessman and had been a long-time friend of Standard's management kept him from being generally considered as essentially a Rockefeller representative. If an Easterner or one from some other Standard Oil company had been placed on the Board, it would have been more disturbing, both to the employees and to the company's reputation for independence.

65. Interview with Thomas M. Debevoise, December 1, 1948.

CHAPTER XV

The Seubert Regime Begins

THE ELECTION OF EDWARD G. SEUBERT TO BE THE CHIEF EXECUTIVE officer of the company continued the tradition of selecting men from the ranks for top executive positions. The story of his rise to the presidency of one of America's great corporations reads like an Horatio Alger story.[1]

Moving with his parents in 1891 to Whiting, when his father became head of the pipe department at the refinery, the fifteen-year-old Seubert also secured a job at the refinery as a mechanic's helper. Within a year he was given a chance to transfer to the main office. His avidity for figures, appetite for work, and ability to get things done made him outstanding. During the next six years he was advanced from junior clerk through several grades to become cashier at Whiting. In 1898 Seubert was transferred to the General Office in Chicago at a salary of $50 per month, and before long he was the right-hand man of "Uncle George" Stahl, the Secretary-Treasurer of the company. Between 1902 and 1920 Seubert served as bookkeeper, chief clerk, and auditor of the Manufacturing Department, Assistant Secretary and Treasurer, and Secretary-Treasurer. As an accountant and one who knew and understood figures, Seubert was a genius. In recognition of his ability, he was elected a Director in 1919 and a Vice-President in 1920. Owing to his wide knowledge of the business, he was responsible for countless details in administering the finances of the company. When Burton resigned as President in 1927, Seubert was elected to that position. The Rockefeller decision in 1929 to retain him as President and make him the chief executive officer was not only a tribute to his loyalty and service to the company for thirty-eight

1. For sketches of Seubert's career, see "E. G. Seubert Promoted," *Stanolind Record*, I, No. 3 (December, 1919), 5; "Dr. Burton Resigns; E. G. Seubert Is President," *Stanolind Record*, VIII, No. 6 (April, 1927), 6; "Edward G. Seubert Is Executive Head of Company," *Stanolind Record*, X, No. 6 (April, 1929), 1, 4; "Two Score Years of Service," *Stanolind Record*, XIX, No. 8 (June, 1938), 2; David Lawrence, "American Business and Business Men," *The Saturday Evening Post*, CCIII (September 13, 1930), 50.

years but a recognition of his honesty, integrity, ability, and administrative experience. In view of the situation created by the Stewart affair, Seubert seemed to be just the type of man whose leadership and experience could restore the prestige of the company, strengthen the morale of the employees, and provide a steady hand as the company sailed into the uncharted waters ahead.

At the age of fifty-three, Seubert was a big man physically, and a more prodigious worker than Colonel Stewart. Seubert had worked hard all his life and he expected everyone else to do the same. Once asked about "big moments" in his life, Seubert remarked: "There haven't been any big moments. My life has been a steady experience of prosaic hard work."

While Seubert had many sterling qualities, he was far less effective as a leader than Colonel Stewart. Without any formal education and none of the charm, tact, or sociability of Stewart, Seubert was a "diamond in the rough." He spoke with a loud voice, was brusque in his manner and rough in his methods. Although he could be gracious and agreeable when he desired, he was noted for his biting remarks, roars and bellows, scowls and scoldings, and domineering attitude. While Seubert made some speeches mainly before the employees, he did not make many public addresses like Stewart. He was not a gifted or inspiring speaker, but he had a way of challenging men to do things.

Seubert's point of view in planning and administering company affairs was that of an accountant who was primarily interested in saving money, having money in the bank, and paying good dividends. Stories about Seubert's own personal economizing while chief executive of the company, even though he was a well-to-do bachelor, are both numerous and priceless. While he fought waste in every form and scrutinized proposals for expenditures with the greatest care, there was a natural reluctance, strongly reinforced by the coming of the depression, to expand in any direction.

As chief executive, instead of delegating responsibilities, Seubert gathered the reins tightly in his own hands and involved himself in the details of everything. Much of the determination of policies was done informally by Seubert, Stephens, and Barkdull, who went over various problems, prepared recommendations, and presented them to the Board for discussion and approval.[2]

The selection of a Chairman of the Board had been deferred

2. Interview with L. L. Stephens, July 18, 1948.

until Burton returned from Europe. As soon as he landed in New York on March 11th, he and Debevoise discussed the possibility of amending the company's bylaws so as to make it possible for Burton to be elected Chairman and made the titular head, without interfering with the position of Seubert as the chief executive officer. When this and other problems could not be satisfactorily solved, Debevoise regretfully had to inform Dr. Burton that they could not go ahead with the contemplated plans.[3] Therefore, on March 15th Burton tendered his resignation as a Director to take effect at the pleasure of the Board. It was accepted on April 10th and upon the recommendation of Melvin A. Traylor, Bruce Johnstone of the law firm of Burry, Johnstone, Peters & Dixon of Chicago was elected to fill the vacancy.

Seubert's assumption of office marked the beginning of an administration which was to last until 1945, the longest in Standard's history. Associated with him as leaders and administrators in company affairs were the members of the Board of Directors. During the ensuing decade there were various changes in personnel due to retirements, deaths, and resignations. In 1930 Alonzo W. Peake, formerly President of the Dixie Oil Company, was elected a Director to succeed Thomas S. Cooke. He was also made Vice-President in charge of Production. L. L. Stephens, General Counsel and formerly a Director, and Robert E. Wilson, Director of Research, head of the Development and Patent Department, and Assistant to the Vice-President in charge of Manufacturing, were elected Directors in 1931. M. G. Paulus was elected to the Board early in 1932 and, after Robert E. Humphreys retired at the end of the year, Paulus became Vice-President in charge of Manufacturing. At the same time, Wilson became Vice-President in charge of Research and Development. In May, 1933, Charles J. Barkdull, who was Vice-President in charge of Finance and Accounting and Treasurer, became Executive Vice-President. In 1935 Wilson resigned to become Vice-Chairman of the Board of Pan American Petroleum & Transport and Harry F. Glair succeeded him as a Director. To fill the vacancy on the Board of Directors created by the death of Melvin A. Traylor in 1937, Judson F. Stone of Chicago was elected. Stone was a Trustee of the McCormick Estates and a Director of the International Harvester Company, Poor & Company, the Chicago Title & Trust Company, and the Continental Illinois National Bank and Trust Company of Chi-

3. Interview with Thomas M. Debevoise, December 1, 1948.

cago. Roy F. McConnell, Assistant General Manager of Sales, succeeded Robert H. McElroy, who died in 1938. Edward J. Bullock, Vice-President in charge of Purchasing, retired in 1939. In the same year, Amos Ball succeeded Allan Jackson, Vice-President in charge of Sales, who was given other duties, and McConnell became General Manager of Sales. All of the new Directors, except Traylor, Johnstone, and Stone, had come up through the ranks and were full-time operating heads.

Immediately after assuming office, Seubert issued a statement addressed to the employees in which he pointed out that the 1929 stockholders' meeting was now a thing of the past and the new administration was already busy with company affairs. He emphasized that there need not be the slightest uneasiness or apprehension about the future. Nothing must be permitted to stand in the way of the future development of Standard. The interests of too many people—stockholders, employees, and customers—were in volved for that. Seubert on behalf of the Directors stated that nothing would be closer to the heart of the management than the welfare of the employees. Since employees, management, and stockholders had but one supreme interest, the continued success and development of Standard, Seubert concluded by saying, "Let us all get to work."

For a short time at the beginning of Seubert's administration, he often referred to "the big stockholders in the East" and was reluctant to undertake anything of importance without conferring with the Rockefeller representatives in New York. This was natural for a number of reasons. Seubert had been retained in office and placed in charge of the company by them. Another chastening factor was that their proxies were good for a year and if anything went wrong, the management could be easily voted out. An early but minor incident illustrated Seubert's sensitiveness to Rockefeller influence. Within six days after the annual meeting at Whiting, Seubert received word from Debevoise to the effect that Allan Jackson had left with Stewart for a vacation in Florida. Debevoise asked if this were true and if any other Directors or employees were with Stewart and, if so, who. Seubert immediately got in touch with Jackson in Florida and insisted upon his immediate return to Chicago.[4] This episode had its effect upon all other executives of the company, and for some time they carefully

4. Thomas M. Debevoise to Edward G. Seubert, March 13, 1929. Rockefeller File. Interview with Allan Jackson, July 23, 1948.

avoided seeing or being seen with the Colonel. Once several matters left over from the Stewart affair had been disposed of, the Rockefeller group discouraged Seubert from coming in to confer so frequently and told him to go ahead and run the company.[5]

In view of the unsavory reports which had come to the attention of the Rockefelier committee during the proxy fight about the mismanagement of the Pan American Petroleum & Transport Company and especially the Lago Petroleum Corporation in Venezuela, the committee insisted that the charges be carefully investigated and, if they were true, a thorough house cleaning be made. In order to find out what had been going on in Venezuela, Seubert, Robert G. Stewart, President of Pan American Petroleum & Transport and son of the Colonel, and F. T. Graham, Secretary of Standard, met with Arthur A. Holland, who had been Vice-President and General Manager of the Lago Petroleum Corporation until April 14, 1926, in New York on March 26th.[6] Asked if the presence of Colonel Stewart's son, Robert G. Stewart, embarrassed him, Holland said: "No." Seubert then asked him to speak frankly regarding Lago. Among other things, Holland pointed out that the Fitzsimmons Drilling Company had been given a drilling contract in Venezuela in 1926 to drill for $6.00 per foot when Holland had been paying $2.00 to $2.30 a foot. In addition, Lago, contrary to past practice, was paying all of the expenses of Fitzsimmons' men and making other new and unnecessary disbursements. Some $2,000,000 worth of drilling tools had been purchased for Fitzsimmons, but they were just lying around on the ground rusting. Holland considered the overhead about four times greater than it had previously been.

After the conference, Holland wrote Seubert: "When I met you in New York and found Robert Stewart present at the meeting, I felt I had stumbled into a hostile camp. As a result I confined my discussion to the Fitzsimmons Drilling Contract." He said nothing about Colonel Stewart's ordering in 1926 that all future drilling be done by contract or about Robert G. Stewart's interference with sales or irregularities in the purchasing of supplies.

Seubert told Debevoise regarding his conference with Holland

5. Interview with Thomas M. Debevoise, December 1, 1948.
6. Memorandum of Seubert's conference with A. A. Holland at the Biltmore Hotel, March 26, 1929. For charges made against the management of Pan American, see letter of A. A. Holland to William M. Burton, March 15, 1929. Rockefeller File.

and, in turn, received a polite rebuke because he had taken
Stewart along.[7] Debevoise was sure that Seubert would have received more information if he had gone alone. "The more I hear
of Pan-American and Lago," wrote Debevoise, "the more clear it
seems that a thorough investigation of their affairs (not simply the
books) should be made, and the more likely it seems to me that
such an investigation will result in a thorough housecleaning. I
doubt that you will wish to retain either of the Stewarts. On
general principles it would be better not to have any of the father's
family affiliated with the company, but you will probably find
ample ground to make a change for the purpose of securing better
management."

To make a full, complete, and impartial investigation of Pan
American and Lago, Seubert sent Frank V. Martinek as his personal representative on a secret mission to Venezuela and Mexico.
After about nine months of investigation Martinek made his report, which confirmed Holland's charges and more about gross
mismanagement of the Lago Petroleum Corporation.[8] As a result,
Standard recovered for Lago $425,000 from the Fitzsimmons
Drilling Company for the profits made in connection with the
drilling contracts of 1926 and 1928.[9]

One of the first and most popular moves made by the Seubert
administration was the extension of the company's vacation plan
to a greater number of employees. Ever since the question of
vacations with pay for hourly paid employees was first raised in
1919 by the Joint General Committee of Sugar Creek, it had presented one of the knottiest internal problems ever to confront
management. It had been denied repeatedly by the company on
the grounds of impracticability. However, Seubert and his Directors tackled the problem and quickly and successfully resolved it.
At the annual Industrial Relations Conference in Chicago on
October 7, 1929, Seubert announced a revised vacation plan effective January 1, 1930.[10] Hourly paid employees who had been
employed for five years and less than ten were to get one week's
vacation with pay and employees who had been employed for ten
years or more, two weeks. Approximately 5,000 employees who

7. Thomas M. Debevoise to Edward G. Seubert, April 5, 1929. Rockefeller File.
8. Interview with Frank V. Martinek, November 23, 1948.
9. Minutes of the Board of Directors' and Stockholders' Meetings, III, 1824.
10. "Grant Vacations with Pay for Hourly Paid Employees of All Departments—
President Seubert Keeps Pledge of March 7," *Stanolind Record*, XI, No. 1
(November, 1929), 1-2, 4.

had not been previously eligible for vacations were affected. Of these, 3,500 were in the refineries and 1,500 in the sales fields. A total of approximately 11,000 men and women employees of the company were now eligible for annual vacations with pay.

The strengthening of Standard's crude oil supply continued to be a major objective during the Seubert regime. Under the direction of Peake the company continued to buy crude as in the past, but increasing emphasis was placed upon buying and developing crude-oil producing properties in order to have a backlog for the future. In 1929 the Dixie Oil Company purchased from the Amerada Petroleum Corporation a half interest in leases on 490,000 acres of land located in Oklahoma and Kansas for $10,-000,000.[11] The purchase was more important because of its potentialities than for the actual production. It foreshadowed a program of greater aggressiveness on the part of Standard in the Mid-Continent field. A second significant move was Standard's purchase in 1930 of the McMan Oil and Gas Company, one of the most successful producing companies, for 200,000 shares of Standard stock.[12] McMan's gross production in Texas in 1929 approximated 10,000 barrels per day. The company's best holdings were located in the Yates field in Pecos County, Texas, with some in the Mid-Continent field.

The new Michigan oil fields continued to increase in production, and by the fall of 1929 the daily production amounted to around 30,000 barrels. Dixie bought about 8,000 barrels a day from the Dundee field, most of which went to Standard's refinery at Whiting.[13] In the spring of 1929, it leased one of Pan American's 16,000-barrel tankers in order to carry a greater quantity to Whiting.

An outstanding event in Standard's effort to improve its crude supply was the acquisition of complete control of Pan American Petroleum & Transport Company. A special meeting of the stockholders in August, 1929, approved an increase of Standard's capital stock from $375,000,000 to $450,000,000 and the shares from 15,000,000 to 18,000,000 at $25 per share. The stockholders also

11. *Chicago Journal of Commerce,* July 16, 1929; "Standard of Indiana Buys Mid-Continent Acreage," *National Petroleum News,* XI, No. 29 (July 17, 1929), 48.
12. "Standard of Indiana May Buy McMan Oil & Gas," *The Oil and Gas Journal* (April 17, 1930), 158.
13. *Chicago Journal of Commerce,* May 20, 1929; Ward K. Halbert, "Demand for Muskegon Crude Improves: New Refineries Are Projected," *National Petroleum News,* XXI, No. 23 (June 5, 1929), 31.

approved the acquisition of all or a part of the outstanding shares of common stock, Class A and B, of Pan American Petroleum & Transport on the basis of seven shares of Standard for six of Pan American.[14] The minority English interests, represented by Lord Inverforth, offered in November to sell 108,000 shares of preferred stock and 110,000 shares of common stock in Pan American Eastern to Standard for $14,084,281. Standard accepted the offer. By the end of November, Standard owned all of the preferred and common stock of Pan American Eastern which, in turn, owned 501,000 shares of common voting stock of Pan American Petroleum & Transport. In December Pan American Eastern exchanged its Pan American stock with Standard on the basis of seven shares of Standard for six shares, Class A and B, of Pan American Petroleum & Transport. Thus Standard got 501,000 shares of Pan American common stock which Pan Eastern had acquired in 1925. By the end of 1929 Standard owned 91.28 per cent of the Class A stock and 75.82 per cent of the Class B stock of Pan American.[15] To complete the acquisition of Pan American's stock, Standard in 1930 increased its capitalization from $450,000,000 to $500,000,000 and the number of authorized shares from 18,000,000 to 20,000,000 at $25. Pan American Eastern was dissolved in October, 1930, with Standard, the sole stockowner, taking over all of its assets and assuming its liabilities, including notes given for Pan American stock. By the end of 1932 Standard owned 97.37 per cent of the Class A stock and 95.96 per cent of the Class B stock of Pan American Petroleum & Transport.

At the time Standard acquired control, Pan American had some twenty-seven subsidiaries. From a production point of view, these subsidiaries held in fee and leases approximately 2,500,000 acres in Mexico and about 3,000,000 acres in Venezuela. The average daily crude production in Mexico amounted to 26,000 barrels and in Venezuela 105,000 barrels. Its refining capacity in Mexico was about 120,000 barrels a day and in Aruba 100,000.

In view of the possibility that Congress might levy an embargo or duty on the importation of foreign oil, Pan American expanded its foreign markets by buying in June, 1930, the Tide Water Export Corporation, a subsidiary of the Tide Water Associated

14. Minutes of the Board of Directors' and Stockholders' Meetings, III, 1743, 1781.
15. For an over-all view of Pan American's operations, see the *Stanolind Record*, XI, No. 8 (June, 1930).

Oil Company, which marketed chiefly in Brazil and Argentina. About a year later, it purchased the Petroleum Storage and Finance Company of England, a holding company for a number of British oil marketers. In 1931 it purchased a 270-acre tract near Texas City on the Houston ship channel on which to build a domestic refinery.

On account of the fact that Pan American had practically no voice in the management of the Near East Development Corporation and its interest yielded only 2,900 barrels daily, it sold its 16⅔ interest, which had been acquired in 1928, to Standard of New Jersey.

Another outstanding event in the effort to make the company independent with respect to crude production and transportation was the purchase of the other 50 per cent stock interest in the Sinclair Pipe Line Company and the Sinclair Crude Oil Purchasing Company in the summer of 1930.[16] Standard paid the Sinclair Consolidated Oil Company $42,500,000 for its interest in the Sinclair Pipe Line Company and $30,000,000 for its interest in the Sinclair Crude Oil Purchasing Company, or $72,500,000 in cash for both. Standard also assumed the other half of the bonded indebtedness amounting to $53,000,000. Through the purchase, Standard acquired gross assets with a book value of approximately $162,000,000 as of May 31st. There had been larger oil deals, but this was the largest cash transaction ever made in the history of the petroleum industry. Moreover, no outside financing was necessary because of the tremendous cash resources of Standard. Its treasury as of December 31, 1929, contained cash, government securities, and miscellaneous investments of $122,692,246. The original investment of Standard in the two companies plus the cash consideration involved in the transaction brought its total investment to about $118,700,000. The purchase was regarded as an event of major importance in the petroleum industry because it involved the ownership of key crude-oil buying and transportation properties in the heart of the Mid-Continent field and in Wyoming. As a result of it, Standard gained full control over one of the largest pipeline systems and crude-oil buying agencies in the country. It was a notable step in decreasing Standard's depend-

16. A. E. Mockler, "Directors Approve Sinclair Sale," *The Oil and Gas Journal* (July 24, 1930), 31; "S. O. (Indiana) Acquires Complete Ownership of Sinclair Pipe Line and Crude Oil Purchasing Companies," *Stanolind Record*, XI, 10 (August, 1930), 12.

ence upon others and in making Standard a fully integrated company.

The Sinclair Pipe Line Company had about 6,878 miles of pipelines extending from Wyoming to Chicago and from Houston to Chicago. In 1920 the line carried 12,503,000 barrels of crude; in 1929 it carried 40,576,615. The carrying capacity of the system was about 135,000 barrels a day and the delivering capacity at its terminus on Lake Michigan was about 75,000 barrels a day. The Sinclair Crude Oil Purchasing Company was a major factor in buying, storing, and reselling crude in Wyoming and the Mid-Continent area. It was second to the Prairie Oil & Gas Company in the volume of buying. As of December 31, 1929, it owned 45,000,000 barrels of steel tankage, and it had in storage 36,445,940 barrels of crude. Its Wyoming tank farm alone had a capacity of 12,000,000 barrels with 11,500,000 barrels of crude in storage. Even though Standard now transferred the transportation of crude from the Mid-Continent field to Whiting from Prairie to its own line, which was nearly sufficient to take care of Whiting's needs, it continued to purchase some 18,000 barrels a day from Prairie. The loss of Standard's business and the competition which developed proved to be a hard blow to Prairie and helped to bring about its merger with the Sinclair Consolidated Oil Corporation in 1931. In the fall of 1931 steps were taken to increase the capacity of the Sinclair pipeline from Healdton to Whiting from 75,000 to 90,000 barrels per day.

Owing to the cancellation of the Mammoth Oil Company's lease of Teapot Dome, that part of the pipeline running from Wyoming to Freeman, Missouri, had been idle since late in 1928. Shortly after Standard became the owner of the entire system, one of the stockholders wrote an open letter to President Seubert suggesting how the pipline from Wyoming to Freeman could be profitably used.[17] According to the plan, Wyoming was full of jackrabbits, and there was a big demand for these in centers of population like Kansas City, Chicago, and St. Louis, where they appeared on the menu under such names as chicken salad, veal pie, and goose liver sausage. Owing to high freight rates, it was difficult to supply the market. Since the pipeline was large enough to accommodate half-grown jackrabbits moving under their own power, the stockholder suggested that they be run through the line from Wyoming

17. L. E. Smith, "The Mid-Continent Sky Line: An Open Letter," *National Petroleum News*, XXII, No. 32 (August 6, 1930), 35.

to Kansas City, which would take about three days. To keep lazy jackrabbits moving, it was suggested that Standard install a device for dropping small amounts of a fluid known as "high-life" on the rabbits. This would have to be timed properly in order not to drop it on the rabbit's nose and cause him to go into reverse. This was a problem, according to the author of the letter, which Robert E. Wilson of the Development and Patent Department could solve. If this were done, the stockholder was sure that the "Standard Rabbit Transportation Company" could be one of the more profitable subsidiaries. In 1931, however, Stanolind leased the west portion of the Wyoming line to the North Central Gas Company and the east portion to the Kansas Pipe Line & Gas Company to be used for transporting gas.

Effective January 1, 1931, the names of the Sinclair Pipe Line Company and the Sinclair Crude Oil Purchasing Company were changed to the Stanolind Pipe Line Company and the Stanolind Crude Oil Purchasing Company, respectively, newly organized and 100 per cent owned subsidiaries of Standard. At the same time, all of the assets and liabilities of the Midwest Exploration Company in Texas, the Dixie Oil Company, and the McMan Oil & Gas Company in all states where they were domesticated and operating were absorbed by another newly organized subsidiary, the Stanolind Oil and Gas Company, under the direction of Frank O. Prior. On July 1, 1931, the Southern Crude Oil Purchasing Company and the Southern Pipe Line Company, originally organized by Pan American Petroleum & Transport, were consolidated with Stanolind Oil and Gas. The purchase of the Southern Crude Oil Purchasing Company was based upon an appraised value of more than $7,700,000. Through its acquisition, Stanolind acquired a net daily average production of 7,409 barrels and net recoverable reserves amounting to more than 19,250,000 barrels.

While these developments were taking place, aggressive efforts were made by the new management in expanding the company's retail marketing system. During the summer of 1929 Midwest Refining organized a retail sales department under the direction of Frank L. Cochran of Standard's Sales Department. The names of various retail companies which Midwest had previously purchased were changed and the name of Midwest and its slogan "Mountain Made for Mountain Trade" appeared all through Wyoming, Montana, and Colorado. Midwest also handled Standard's brands.

In order to attract tourists from its own marketing area, simplify administration, and effect economies in operations, Standard purchased Midwest's marketing organization and began marketing directly under its own name in the Rocky Mountain region on April 1, 1930.[18] An office was opened in Denver, and the Midwest marketing organization now became Standard's Rocky Mountain Sales Division. Standard signs were placed on 250 bulk and service stations of Midwest, and a full line of Standard products was stocked. *The Midwest Review,* the company's magazine for employees, was discontinued after December, 1930, and the *Stanolind Record* was furnished thereafter to all employees of Midwest. By absorbing Midwest's retail distribution system, Standard now marketed directly in thirteen states. Moving into the Rocky Mountain region put Standard into direct competition with the Continental Oil Company, the major marketer and one of the old Standard Oil units. Through the enlargement of its marketing territory and building, purchasing, and leasing, Standard increased the number of its service stations and dealer outlets to 11,307 and the number of its bulk plants to 4,282.[19]

Shortly after Standard of Indiana began marketing under its own name in the Rocky Mountain area, it came into conflict with the Standard Oil of Colorado, Inc.[20] The latter was chartered by that state in 1922 to produce, transport, refine, and market oil. Owing to the fact that the charter had not been used, Colorado canceled it in 1926. The company was reincorporated in 1927, and its name was changed in 1930 to the Standard Oil Company of Colorado with offices in Denver. By the fall of 1930 the promoters of the Standard Oil Company of Colorado were flooding the country by mail with circulars offering 400,000 shares of common stock no par at $10 per share, and it reaped a harvest from small investors.

Standard of Indiana had no knowledge of the company until November, 1929, and no information as to its business until the fall of 1930 when many letters intended for the Standard Oil Company of Colorado were received by the offices of Standard of

18. "S. O. (Indiana) Takes Over Marketing Facilities of Midwest Refining Company, Creating Three New Sales Divisions Under Frank L. Cochran," *Stanolind Record,* XI, No. 6 (April, 1930), 9, 14; D. W. Greenberg, "Midwest, Leader in the Rocky Mountain Region, Company of Romance," *Stanolind Record,* XI, No. 9 (July, 1930), 3-30.

19. *Investigation of Concentration of Economic Power,* Part 14-A, 7819.

20. "Right of Colorado Promoters Challenged To Use 'Standard Oil' in Name," *National Petroleum News,* XXII, No. 53 (December 31, 1930), 27-28.

Indiana in Chicago and Denver. On the other hand, some of the company's mail went to the Standard Oil Company of Colorado, thus indicating that the public believed that the latter was connected with Standard of Indiana. Early in 1931 Standard of Indiana filed suit in the Federal District Court at Denver against the Standard Oil Company of Colorado to restrain it from calling itself the Standard Oil Company of Colorado or Standard Oil or Standard or any similar name. The court sustained Standard's suit but Standard of Colorado appealed. In 1934 the Circuit Court of Appeals sustained the lower court's decision.[21]

To introduce Standard's new line of motor oil, President Seubert on the evening of March 12, 1930, went on the air in a special radio program.[22] The broadcast over fourteen stations of CBS in the Middle West was unique in two respects. It was the first time that an executive officer of the company had gone on the air. Secondly, it was one of the most expensive broadcasts, for it featured three of the topflight entertainers of the country: Will Rogers, Louise Homer, and Sousa's Band. Although the new line of motor oils retained the old names, Polarine and Iso-Vis, they were entirely different in appearance and characteristics. A feature of the new oils were their color—a clear amber. The new oils were made from 100 per cent distillate stock. No residual stock had been blended with lighter distillates. The stock produced oils with low carbon deposit, and they resisted oxidation in the crankcase. The company attempted to eliminate the confusion as to the meaning of the grade designation by prominently using the SAE viscosity numbers, such as Polarine 50 (special heavy) or 60 (extra heavy) as a part of the names. All grades, save Polarine 20, had their viscosity index raised to the highest point within the SAE specifications.

To enable several of the former Standard Oil units to compete effectively with nationally advertised automobile products, a most important development in service-station merchandising occurred in 1929. Colonial Beacon and Standard of New Jersey, Ohio, Kentucky, Nebraska, California, and Indiana organized the Atlas Supply Company for the purpose of determining specifications and acting as purchasing agent for automobile tires and other accessories to be sold on a nationwide basis under the brand name

21. 72 F. (2d) 524.
22. J. C. Chatfield, "Standard of Indiana Announces New Line of Motor Oils," *National Petroleum News*, XXII, No. 11 (March 12, 1930), 24.

Atlas.[23] Each company owned stock in the Atlas Supply Company, had representation on its Board of Directors, and was to receive a percentage of the profit. The program for the sale of tires and other automobile accessories meant that these companies were departing from the long-established policy of merchandising only petroleum products, and that their service stations in the future would become retail outlets for tires, batteries, flashlights, spark plugs, bulbs, wrenches, and all kinds of automotive merchandise.

The first product to be marketed was Atlas tires. These were purchased according to Atlas' specifications from various tire manufacturers. Each of the companies was the sole distributor in its own territory. Atlas tires were of first-line quality, and they sold at a uniform price which was between mail order prices and standard tire prices. They carried a twelve-month guarantee for passenger tires and a six-month guarantee for commercial cars. In the event of a breakdown before the expiration of the guarantee, repairs were made free of charge or else the tire was replaced by a new tire with a price adjustment. Arrangements were made among the participating companies so that service and guarantees for tires purchased from any one company could be serviced by the others.

The inauguration of the new merchandising policy raised many questions. Would tire manufacturers and dealers retaliate by going into the gasoline business? What effect would the handling of tires have on gas and oil sales, the principal business? Would it hurt gallonage? Would it not increase the investment necessary to go into the service station business? Would it be possible to secure station personnel who could combine service and salesmanship without letting the service suffer? These and other questions could only be answered in the light of experience. The adoption of such a policy proved, however, to be the forerunner of similar movements on the part of other marketers of petroleum products.

While Standard of Indiana had previously sold some accessories at its service stations, it had not done so on any large scale. In September, 1930, the company announced that about 1,000 of its service stations in 550 cities would sell and service Atlas tires and the usual accessories.[24] This move was in keeping with the trend of increasing the usefulness of company service stations and meet-

23. Company Encyclopedia: Marketing, I, Origin of Atlas, 127-129; *National Petroleum News*, XX, No. 38 (September 17, 1930), 28.
24. "Standard Oil of Indiana Enters Tire Business," *Stanolind Record*, XI (October, 1930), 32-33.

ing the demand of the motorist for more complete service. Just as rapidly as possible the service was extended to all company-owned or controlled service stations, garages, and stores dispensing its products. To promote the sale of tires and other accessories as they were added, Standard of Indiana selected a group of men, gave them intensive sales training, and put one in each sales field as a TBA specialist.

In the winter of 1931 Standard of Indiana began selling and servicing Atlas batteries on an experimental basis at its service stations in the Chicago area. Gradually, it extended the sale to all of its marketing territory. In 1932, Atlas added a number of accessories—windshield wiper blades, radiator cleaner, lamp bulbs, spark plugs—to its line of products. As Atlas expanded its line, Standard of Indiana tested many of the items recommended and put them on sale.

Standard's investment in Atlas increased from $90,100 in 1930 to $856,300 in 1940. Standard's TBA sales also increased from $3,197,135 in 1930 to $8,341,000 in 1940. Sales and profits on tires might have been larger after 1937 if the inventory of stock had not been reduced. With the sales fields short of stock, dealers could not make prompt delivery to customers. Consequently, the sale of tires fell off from 800,000 in 1936 to 650,000 in 1939. During the period from 1930 to 1940 Atlas' sales to Standard amounted to $45,658,065.27 while Standard's TBA sales amounted to $62,-882,566 with an estimated gross profit of $20,058,758 and a net profit of $9,978,204.49.

With the development of large air-cooled engines for airplanes and the expansion of commercial air lines, there was a growing demand for better aviation products. In order to supply uniformly high-grade aviation fuels and lubricants and, at the same time, secure national distribution for their products, Standard of Indiana, California, and New Jersey established in May, 1929, the Stanavo Specifications Board, Inc., for the purpose of studying and writing specifications for aviation fuels and lubricants.[25] The organization of the Board marked the first co-operative effort on the part of several large oil companies to bring order out of the

---

25. Paul Truesdell, "Three Standard Companies Join To Offer Lubrication to the Flying World," *National Petroleum News*, XXI, No. 35 (August 28, 1929), 27; Paul Truesdell, "Aviation Fuel Specifications Are Next Before 3-Company Stanavo Board," *National Petroleum News*, XXI, No. 36 (September 4, 1929), 31; "Standard Companies Recommend Products for Aviation Industry," *The Oil and Gas Journal* (August 29, 1929), 350.

chaos which had marked the development of petroleum products for the aviation industry. This seemed to be a sound and forward-looking move at the time because of the anticipated rapid development of aviation in the United States and throughout the world. Under the direction of expert chemists and engineers drawn from each of the three companies, exhaustive tests of fuels and lubricants were made, specifications prepared, and brand and grade names adopted for the identification of products. The Board's decisions were final, and it required that member oil companies rigidly adhere to the specifications. Each company manufactured its own aviation products according to the specifications and sold them under the trade-mark Stanavo. The Board also required that all lubricants bearing the name Stanavo be marketed in sealed packages. Early in 1931 Standard of Indiana shipped its first Stanavo 74-octane gasoline. In the ensuing years the Board made substantial progress in the development of uniform products for aviation. It also secured national and world-wide recognition of its standards and the quality of the products. Stanavo products were soon found along all the well-recognized air routes and in many of the out-of-way places in the world. The work of the Board constituted an unusual and important development in the history of the petroleum and aviation industries.

Various new measures were taken by the company to stimulate sales. Quin Ryan, favorite football announcer in the Middle West, began broadcasting the outstanding football games of the region each week for Standard over WGN, Chicago. This feature was soon broadened to include the professional games of the Chicago Bears and the Detroit Lions. Another innovation was Standard's arrangement in 1930 with the Postal Telegraph whereby it accepted telegrams from its customers for sending. Telegrams were received by station attendants, the charges collected, the message telephoned to the nearest Postal Telegraph office, and for this the station attendant received a small commission. Still another development was the establishment of a Service Station Department for the purpose of co-ordinating service-station sales and operating procedure throughout the company. The improvement of service, the development of sales quotas, compensation for service-station employees, and the selection of sites for service stations were also important functions.

Although Standard was not ready or prepared to use the process, its acquisition of rights to use the German-developed hydrogenation process in 1930 appeared to be desirable insurance for the future.[26] Discovered about 1913 by Friederick Bergius of Germany, the process for the synthetic production of gasoline by liquefying coal and applying hydrogen under pressure to the resultant liquid converted heavy oils almost completely into gasoline. While the petroleum industry knew of this development, it was assumed that the process would require a long period of experimentation, and that it would not become a factor in commercial production for many years. About 1926 Standard of New Jersey acquired the rights to use the Bergius process under the United States patent rights from the I. G. Farbenindustrie.[27] These rights were taken over by a company organized as the Standard-I. G. Farbenindustrie Company in which Jersey owned 80 per cent of the stock. Extensive laboratory work upon the application of the hydrogenation process to petroleum was started in 1927 at its Baton Rouge refinery, and in 1930 two commercial plants were completed by the Jersey company, one at Baton Rouge and the other at Bayway, New Jersey. The industry as a whole was securing 40 to 42 per cent recovery of gasoline from crude and under the most favorable conditions up to 75 per cent. By the catalytic hydrogenation process, however, the yield could be brought to 100 per cent though at a rather high cost. At the moment, the use of the hydrogenation process was unnecessary owing to an ample supply of gasoline and the need for other petroleum products. Its chief value lay in its possible use in case of any future necessity.

Early in 1930, the Jersey company organized the Hydro Patents Company to take over the patent rights of the hydrogenation process and to promote and facilitate the licensing of the process. At the time, Jersey held all of the stock. The oil industry was then invited to inspect the process and join Hydro. Officials of Standard of Indiana and other oil companies studied the matter and were impressed by the possibilities. On July 12, 1930, Standard signed an agreement to purchase 1,660 shares of Hydro at $53 per share plus an option to obtain complete participation in the Hydro Patents Mutual Licensing Plan by increasing its holding to 16,600

26. Company Encyclopedia: Manufacturing, Hydrogenation.
27. *Chicago Journal of Commerce*, July 5, 1929; C. E. Kern, "Hydrogenation Will Assure Consumer of Adequate Supplies," *The Oil and Gas Journal* (July 24, 1930), 138; Paul Truesdell, "Hydrogenation Process To Be Used First in Conversion of Heavy Fuel Oil," *National Petroleum News*, XXI, No. 28 (July 10, 1929), 27-29.

shares prior to September 1, 1931. Standard's decision to participate was based upon the fact that the cost of entry was low, and it
wanted to avoid being in an unfavorable position when it might
decide later to use the process. Altogether, seventeen oil companies, representing approximately 80 per cent of the refinery
capacity of the United States, joined the Hydro Patents Company
to get the right to use the process. Apart from Jersey's plants, no
large-scale developments took place immediately. Construction
costs were high and the costs of producing and compressing hydrogen were very substantial.

One of the most important problems inherited by Seubert was
the litigation between the Universal Oil Products Company and
Standard over their patents on the Dubbs and Burton processes.
Since the filing of the original suit by Universal against Standard
in 1916, other suits and countersuits had been filed. Universal also
became involved in suits with The Texas Company, the Gasoline
Products Company, the M. W. Kellogg Company, and Standard of
New Jersey. In addition, there were pending in the United States
Patent Office in 1929 eighteen interferences involving patent applications or patents of Universal and patent applications or patents
of Standard of Indiana, The Texas Company, and Gasoline Products. For a while Universal's suits against Standard had not interfered with the latter's business or royalties, but by 1929 they had
practically stopped further licensing by Standard.[28] Faced with a
loss in royalties and harassed with suits which might result in
heavy damages, Standard was naturally interested in a reasonable
settlement.

Various efforts had been made on the part of different oil companies to make a settlement with Universal but without success.
In 1929, L. L. Aitken, President of Salt Creek Producers, a personal friend of Ogden Armour, the principal stockholder in Universal, and several of the oil company executives involved in the
cracking litigation, attempted to settle the dispute. The stockholders of Universal indicated a willingness to sell their stock for
$25,000,000. If Standard of Indiana, Standard of New Jersey, and
The Texas Company purchased a paid-up license, the price would
be about the same as for purchasing the company itself, hence it
was better that they should consider buying Universal and take
a chance on recovering a part of their investment through licens-

28. Company Encyclopedia: Manufacturing, Cracking—Dubbs, 12.

ing. Therefore, in November, 1929, Standard's Directors approved in principle a plan for the purchase of Universal's stock.[29]

About one-half of Universal's royalty came from Shell and the Standard of California, the only two large companies which had secured licenses. Shell's royalties amounted to about $3,000,000 a year and those of Standard of California to about $1,000,000. Under the circumstances, it seemed advisable for them to join in purchasing the stock of Universal. Shell indicated its willingness to put up as much as $11,000,000 for a paid-up license.

As a result of the negotiations among these companies, arrangements were made in June, 1930, for organizing a holding company, the United Gasoline Corporation, to purchase and hold the stock of Universal.[30] It was agreed that the voting stock of United should be held by Shell and Standard of California in equal amounts. As licensees of Universal, these companies were familiar with Universal's business, and they had no other patent relations which would interfere with the proper management of United Gasoline. Universal was to continue functioning as previously with the same management and personnel but with Standard of California and Shell representatives on the Board.

Toward the purchase price of $25,000,000 for Universal's stock, Shell was to pay $10,000,000, Standard of California $5,330,000, Standard of Indiana $3,334,000, Standard of New Jersey $3,-334,000, and The Texas Company $3,000,000. Each was to receive, in return, A notes or income notes of United for $3,000,000. All net income was to be paid on these notes as interest or interest plus retirement of the principal, and none of the income was to devolve to dividends until the notes had been retired. At the last minute in the negotiations The Texas Company refused to put up any money toward the purchase. It believed that its patent position was so strong that it was entitled to secure a license from Universal without paying any money. The old stockholders of Universal agreed, therefore, to take The Texas Company's share of A notes in lieu of cash, and $3,000,000 in subordinated B notes were issued to The Texas Company in recognition of its patent position. Standard of California also changed its position because it had such an equity against Standard of Indiana on account of an old license contract that it refused to pay $3,000,000 for A notes without a guarantee that they were good. Standard of Indiana,

29. Minutes of the Board of Directors' and Stockholders' Meetings, III, 1796.
30. Company Encyclopedia: Manufacturing, Cracking—Dubbs, 14-23.

therefore, agreed that within a certain time the California company would recover $2,000,000 in cash on the A notes purchased.
Five million dollars in C notes were to be issued equally to Standard of Indiana and the Jersey Company for license rights under
their patents and as a bonus for purchasing A notes. They were
entitled to one-half of the net income of Universal after the retirement of A and B notes. The other half of the income was to be
paid in dividends to participating nonvoting stock, of which Shell
held 60 per cent, Standard of California 20 per cent, and the old
Universal stockholders 20 per cent.

As for patents, Standard of Indiana granted to Universal and
all of its present licensees an immunity under its patents, and
Universal reciprocated. The same arrangement was made between
Universal and all other parties to the agreement. Shell and Standard of California would not enter into any agreement that did
not involve the acquisition of a license under the cracking patents
of Gasoline Products and Kellogg, so Kellogg conveyed licensing
rights under its patents to Gasoline Products and Gasoline Products exchanged immunity grants with Universal, Shell, and Standard of California on the same basis as with Standard of Indiana.
As a part of the settlement, the parties agreed to drop all litigation,
except The Texas Company's suit against Warner-Quinlan, a
Dubbs licensee, which was to be appealed, and settle all Patent
Office interferences.

Standard's Directors on January 5, 1931, agreed to purchase
$3,000,000 in A notes and $2,500,000 in C notes of the United
Gasoline Corporation. They also approved the agreement between
the United Gasoline Corporation on the one hand and Standard
of New Jersey, Standard of Indiana, Shell, and Standard of California on the other.

After several years of negotiations the settlement which had been
worked out was signed on January 6, 1931.[31] One month later
the Atlantic Refining Company and the Gulf Oil Corporation
entered into an exchange of patent immunities with all of the
parties to the January 6th settlement. These two companies purchased one-half of the block of $3,000,000 of A notes which had
been held in trust for the benefit of the original stockholders of

31. J. C. Chatfield, "Cracking Patent Peace Pact Is Signed: Dubbs Sells to Oil
Companies," National Petroleum News, XXIII, No. 2 (January 14, 1931), 27;
"Development of the Dubbs Process," The Oil and Gas Journal (January 15,
1931), 65; Minutes of the Board of Directors' and Stockholders' Meetings, III,
1914.

Universal. Contemporaneously, Atlantic purchased a fully paid license from Gasoline Products, and Gulf purchased from The Texas Company a fully paid license.

With the conclusion of the "Peace of 1931," as the settlement was called, the long and costly war between Universal and Standard came to an end. During the fifteen years of litigation Standard alone had spent more than $1,000,000 in the defense of its patents. The settlement removed the uncertainty that had hung over the whole art of cracking, and the way was cleared to utilize existing processes without litigation. A concerted attack could now be made upon the problem of perfecting the best cracking process for a given situation without fear. The settlement had no pronounced immediate effect upon the licensing situation largely because of the economic depression. While there was active competition for business among all parties, there was little business.

The momentum gained by Standard during the 1920's and the aggressiveness of the new management carried the company through 1929 in a highly successful manner with a large increase both in volume and earnings.[32] The Sales Department in 1929 marketed 39,432,806 barrels as compared with 35,432,806 in 1928. Net earning after taxes amounted to $78,499,754, an increase of $1,162,588 over 1928 and the largest in the history of the company. The reserve in cash and securities was also the largest in the history of the company.

32. *Annual Statement Year Ending December 31, 1929.*

CHAPTER XVI

Fighting the Depression

EARLY IN 1930 THE DEMAND FOR GASOLINE WAS SURPRISINGLY HIGH and the outlook ahead seemed good, but the petroleum industry was about to enter upon the most disastrous period in its history. The stock market crash of 1929 and the world-wide business depression which followed only served to aggravate an unfavorable situation which had been developing in the petroleum industry for several years. For the past decade the industry had attracted more capital than was required, resulting in an overexpansion of all phases of the industry.[1] Producers had frantically drilled new wells and produced more and more oil. New refineries had been built everywhere as a result of the producers' need to find an outlet for their crude. They crowded their refined products onto the market regardless of the economic consequences. As long as consumption increased, there was enough business for all. Long margins of profit as well as other concessions induced thousands of people to install pumps and tanks and build service stations. As gasoline consumption moved toward what seemed to be the saturation point in the late twenties, too much oil was being produced. There were too many refineries and too many marketing outlets. One writer estimated that 70 per cent of the new marketing facilities and about 90 per cent of the new refining facilities built in the 1920's were the result of overproduction and not demand.[2]

As this overexpansion developed, the fight for gallonage and survival became fierce. The practice of giving rebates, premiums, and cutting prices resulted in declining profits and losses for all. The demoralizing effect of low crude prices and resultant price wars led President Hoover in June, 1929, to call an oil conserva-

1. "Excessive Capital in Oil Business Cause of Distress—Teagle," *National Petroleum News*, XXIII, No. 20 (May 20, 1931), 23; W. T. Holliday, "Marketing Returning to Narrow Margins in Sales of Oil Products," *The Oil and Gas Journal* (June 2, 1932), 42.
2. "Unrestrained Crude Production Is Source of Our Marketing Ills," *National Petroleum News*, XXIII, No. 17 (April 29, 1931), 40-45.

tion conference to see what might be done to regulate production, but there was no immediate action.

As the petroleum industry wrestled with the problem of over-production and unsettled markets, the largest oil field in history was discovered in East Texas in October, 1930. It threatened the whole industry with disaster.[3] The scramble to produce oil from under a neighbor's land before he did the same quickly brought the East Texas production to a daily average of 300,000 barrels in 1931. It came at a time of flush production in California, at Greater Seminole, at Oklahoma City, and in West Texas, and the market was soon flooded with oil. A tidal wave of cheap third-grade gasoline with an octane rating less than 65 began rolling to distant markets, causing greater indiscriminate price cutting. Gasoline sold in Chicago for 14 and 15 cents per gallon, including a tax of 3 cents per gallon, early in 1931.

Early in December, the Prairie Oil & Gas Company created a sensation and more of a crisis when it announced its withdrawal as a purchaser of crude oil in the Mid-Continent field effective January 1, 1931.[4] Competitors and especially Standard of Indiana, it said, had taken away its markets. Prairie's deliveries to refineries had declined during the last four months to less than 40 per cent of what its shipments had been the previous year. If producers had a definite buyer, Prairie offered to transport their crude. For more than twenty years Prairie had been the dominant buyer in the Mid-Continent area, and its withdrawal from the market was a particularly hard blow to thousands of small producers in Oklahoma and Kansas. In Sedan, Kansas, residents of the town organized and agreed not to buy petroleum products from any company unless that company was buying crude produced in the area. The boycott plan rapidly spread to other towns. In a conference of pipeline and crude-oil buying representatives sponsored by the American Petroleum Institute at Tulsa in December to consider relief measures, A. W. Peake, Vice-President in charge of Production for Standard, defended his company against accusations that it was to blame for Prairie's plight.[5] He placed the responsibility squarely upon Prairie. Peake pointed out that Prairie had enjoyed the profits of gathering and selling crude from stripper wells in

3. Rister, *Oil! Titan of the Southwest,* Chapter XXII.
4. *Chicago Journal of Commerce,* December 6, 1930.
5. "Indiana Standard Will Co-operate in Relief—Peake," *National Petroleum News,* XXII, No. 53 (December 31, 1930), 35-37.

past years, and it had a responsibility for continuing to help purchase the oil rather than to create an emergency for other companies to face. On the other hand, Peake pledged Standard's assistance in any relief measures which might be agreed upon.

The Stanolind Pipe Line Company took the lead in arranging immediate relief for 3,500 small wells in Nowata and Rogers counties in northeastern Oklahoma by extending its lines to all favorable production within reasonable reach.[6] To relieve those wells not served by pipelines, the producers and Stanolind worked out a plan whereby the producers in a given area would build short gathering lines to a central point and from here Stanolind would lay a lateral to its trunk line. Through these measures and others, Standard began buying about 16,000 barrels daily of "distress" crude oil production which Prairie had formerly purchased. A similar plan was adopted for several hundred wells in Chautauqua County, Kansas, which provided relief at the rate of about 750 barrels daily.

When Harry H. Woodring became Governor of Kansas in January, 1931, he sent Seubert, President of Standard, a telegram blasting the company for not doing its part in the crisis.[7] He warned that Kansas would not idly stand by and become a victim of foreign imports or of a controversy "between the present subsidiaries of the old parent Standard Oil Company." The state would take action, if necessary, to save Kansas. Woodring urged Standard to increase its crude oil purchases and that Kansas stripper wells be connected to some pipeline not later than February 10th. Astonished by Woodring's singling out Standard, when it had been doing everything possible to aid the stripper-well owners, Seubert said in a sharp reply that his company had co-operated and was co-operating. It deserved credit and support for what it was doing rather than to be requested to do impossible things. Further relief would have to come from others concerned. Standard could not buy more oil directly from Kansas producers because the wells were too distant from its gathering lines. It had tendered an order for an additional 3,000 barrels daily from Prairie to be supplied from Kansas producers even though it meant paying a substantial premium because of the marketing,

6. "Stanolind Preparing to Handle Oil From Oklahoma Stripper Area," *The Oil and Gas Journal* (January 22, 1931), 32.
7. "Kansas Governor Demands Stripper Well Relief by Feb. 10," *National Petroleum News*, XXIII, No. 5 (February 4, 1931), 49-50; *Chicago Journal of Commerce*, January 4, 1931.

gathering, and trunk line charges, but Prairie had refused the order. No other company, said Seubert, had done anywhere nearly as much, and Standard could not settle the problem alone. Why didn't Woodring call upon other oil companies to give relief as Standard had done? As for imports, Seubert pointed out that gasoline in Kansas came from Kansas refineries using Kansas labor and Kansas crude, hence foreign imports did not affect the Kansas situation as Woodring implied.

Despite the sharp exchanges of communications, Standard officials conferred with Governor Woodring at Topeka, and the company agreed to tender an order to Prairie for 300,000 barrels of oil at the rate of 6,000 barrels daily over the next sixty days for delivery at Wood River.[8] The crude should not be of Prairie's own production but from Kansas "distressed" wells. This order was for more than the estimated amount of "distress" crude in Kansas. Prairie was the only company which had served these producers, and it was economically impossible for any other company to connect with them. Even though the transaction involved paying a premium for the oil and was "pure velvet" for Prairie, it was the only way by which Prairie was willing to gather and deliver the oil. Standard tendered the order to Prairie, which it accepted, and crude began running about February 13, 1931. Governor Woodring felt that this action would temporarily take care of the situation until he could present the problem to other companies and work out a permanent solution. He finally issued a statement saying that Standard was certainly doing all he could ask to relieve the producers.

By July, 1931, the price of crude oil in some areas had dropped to as low as 10 cents a barrel. Producers all over Oklahoma, Kansas, and Texas were shutting down their wells. The Texas legislature was called into special session on July 14th to pass legislation to enforce conservation measures. With overproduction wrecking the markets and causing widespread waste, Governor W. H. Murray of Oklahoma ordered out the militia on August 4th to control the supply at the Oklahoma City pool until the price of oil rose to $1 per barrel. The Texas Railroad Commission ordered a curtailment of production in East Texas, but the order was ignored or evaded until Governor R. S. Sterling on August 17th sent troops to enforce it. Even with troops in control of the oil fields, the flow

8. "Kansas Distress Oil Offered Outlet By Indiana Standard," *The Oil and Gas Journal* (February 12, 1931), 40.

SEUBERT AND OTHER STANDARD MEN AT RED CROWN LODGE

Second row, left to right: ——, Dr. B. B. Reeve, O. M. Perrenot
Front row, left to right: Amos Ball, Edward G. Seubert, Allan Jackson, E. J. Bullock, G. H. Moffett

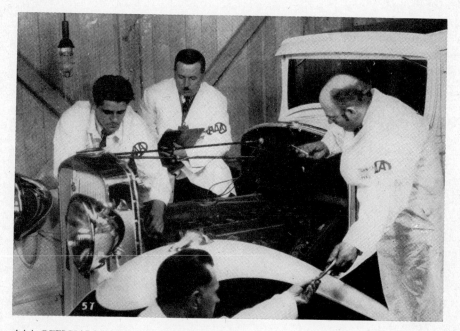

AAA OFFICIALS CHECKING AN ISO-VIS TEST CAR, INDIANAPOLIS SPEEDWAY

A METHOD USED IN EVADING THE GASOLINE TAX

Gasoline was hauled in a 400-gallon tank in this sedan to service stations
where it was dumped into tanks after dark

PROPANE DEWAXING PLANT, WOOD RIVER REFINERY

of "hot oil"—oil produced in excess of quotas set by state regulatory bodies—continued.

With more crude than the market could possibly absorb, some of the producers in the Mid-Continent and Gulf Coast areas particularly began agitating in 1929 for the imposition of a tariff duty of $1 per barrel on crude oil.

U. S. CRUDE OIL IMPORTS AND EXPORTS 1928–1932

	Imports	Exports
1928	79,767,000 barrels	18,966,000 barrels
1929	78,933,000 barrels	26,401,000 barrels
1930	62,129,000 barrels	23,705,000 barrels
1931	47,250,000 barrels	25,535,000 barrels
1932	44,682,000 barrels	27,393,000 barrels

Source: *Petroleum Facts and Figures*, Ninth Edition, 1-3.

Pan American, Shell, Gulf, Tidewater, and Standard of New Jersey were importing crude oil and gasoline in large quantities from Venezuela. Many persons were of the opinion that within a short time more Venezuelan crude would be used in the East than domestic. The House Ways and Means Committee held hearings on increasing the tariff, but the efforts to keep oil on the free list were successful.

As the depression deepened in severity, domestic producers increased their pressure for a tariff or an embargo. Since Pan American Petroleum & Transport was the principal target, independent producers petitioned Seubert to use his good offices to bring about a reduction of oil production in South America to conform to the program of voluntary limitation and prorating in the United States. Strenuous efforts were made again in 1931 to have Congress enact a tariff on oil. Pan American set up an office in Washington under the direction of Harold Walker, a Pan American Director, to oppose before the Ways and Means Committee the passage of any tariff. Although the campaign to enact a tariff failed again, it was apparent that unless oil industry conditions promptly righted themselves the passage of a tariff was inevitable. To prevent Congress from taking action, Standard of New Jersey and Gulf proposed to Standard of Indiana in February a voluntary reduction of 50 per cent in Venezuelan imports, but the latter was against it. In March, Secretary of Commerce Robert P. Lamont requested major importers to reduce their imports and all except Pan American agreed. To restrict imports would mean a heavy financial loss for Pan American and interfere with the obligations laid upon it by the terms of its concessions in Venezuela. Secretary Lamont and W. C. Teagle, President of the Standard of New Jersey, especially were very angry over the attitude of Standard of Indiana and Pan American.

The seriousness of the situation was discussed by several members of the Pan American Board on March 19, 1931, when Seubert pointed out that the question of curtailing imports "involved the most important question that had ever come before the Board." [9] He stated that the interests of Pan American must be primary. Any action taken must not be predicated upon the effect it would have upon Standard of Indiana. He also emphasized that the rights of the minority stockholders, possible violations of the law, and action by the Venezuelan government must be considered. On the other hand, the President of the United States had indicated that Pan American should co-operate with others to limit imports. All of these angles and the consequences, if Pan American refused to co-operate, were discussed.

In order to forestall the passage of any tariff and comply with the government's request, Gulf and Standard of New Jersey announced on March 25, 1931, that they would curtail crude imports by 25 per cent. Shell agreed to reduce its gasoline imports by at least 50 per cent for 1931 as compared with 1930. A few days later Pan American agreed to curtail its production 10,000 barrels per day and its crude imports and refined products from Venezuela by 23 per cent from April 1 to May 31, 1931.[10] While the action would result in a severe reduction in income for Pan American, there seemed to be no alternative.

With an abundance of cheap third-grade gasoline available at almost any price, an era of wild, unrestrained, and ruthless competition developed. Motorists operating low-compression automobiles under favorable conditions secured satisfactory performance in using third-grade gasoline. In rural areas, where there were many old model cars and cheap gasoline was used for lighting, heating, and cooking, there was a large market for it. Small marketing companies, trying to get a foothold in the business, became increasingly important as competitors. That some broke them-

9. Minutes of an informal meeting held by Messrs. Seubert, Walker, et al., March 19, 1931.
10. The Minutes of the Board of Directors of Pan American Petroleum & Transport Company, May 13, 1931.

selves while they broke the market did not help. Independent jobbers, with guaranteed margins of profit and the ability to buy from 1/2 to 1 cent per gallon under refinery tank-car prices established by the majors, took advantage of the situation to secure new outlets and enlarge the volume of their business through giving dealers longer margins of profit, providing free tanks and pumps, offering generous loans, painting service stations, paving driveways, and other concessions. To secure good dealer outlets or to assist dealers in improving facilities, loans to dealers to build new stations became a common practice among refiners. These were often made as a competitive measure where good business practice did not justify them. With longer margins of profit, dealers, in their zeal to secure gallonage, offered rebates, discounts, and gift premiums of all kinds. By 1931 it was hard to buy gasoline without being offered a premium—candy, cigarettes, ash trays, dolls, chinaware, cigarette lighters, clothes brushes, and a host of other items—with the purchase. Many were outright gifts, not merely items to be purchased with coupons given with each sale.[11]

Many of the price cutters were trackside stations, where gasoline was pumped from the tank car directly into the customer's auto at less than the posted retail price. Demurrage paid on the tank car saved the cost of installing pumps and underground tanks. Since the operators had little money invested and rendered none of the ordinary service-station services, they could easily undersell regularly established marketers. Their business flourished solely because of price appeal. Ironical was the fact that many people filled their gasoline tanks at trackside stations, then drove to a regular service station to secure free air, water, and other services. Some trackside operators installed storage tanks and pumped from these into the customer's car. As they found business profitable, some acquired outlets not always along the tracks, supplied them by tank wagon, and sold at the same price as the trackside station. These price cutters rapidly gained a large share of the retail business with a corresponding loss in gallonage for Standard and other regular marketers. In all of the large consuming areas of the Middle West, price cutters were getting from 10 to 40 per cent of the total gallonage. By January 1, 1931, there were 691 trackside stations in operation in Standard's territory, and they were in-

11. Company Encyclopedia: Marketing, I, Other Competitive Methods, Premiums, 245-251.

creasing in number.[12] Generally speaking, they furnished the worst form of competition Standard had to meet.

In the mad scramble for business, unscrupulous operators earned extra profits by collecting the gasoline tax but avoiding payment to the state. With the average tax in 1930 about 5 cents per gallon, profits of $300 to $500 could be made on a tank car of gasoline and $50 on a thousand-gallon truck by evading the tax. Those who evaded the tax and cut prices not only defrauded the state of revenue but caused a further demoralization of the market. Legitimate marketers could not compete effectively.

The extent to which the gasoline tax was evaded and the methods used were forcibly called to the attention of the petroleum industry and the general public by *The Chicago Daily News* in 1930. It reported in June that a former president of a small oil company had been kidnaped and held for ransom in Chicago. A few days later he reappeared unharmed but offered no explanation or protest. Police paid little attention to the episode and would have closed the incident except for *The Chicago Daily News,* which assigned Dan Gallagher, one of its top reporters, to the story.

After two months of investigation, the *Daily News* ran a series of articles in August, 1931, by Gallagher on the kidnaping. Among other things, Gallagher revealed that the kidnaping was an incident in the operations of a gigantic bootlegging gasoline ring in Chicago in which the kidnaped man and several others had been playing important parts. Gallagher also disclosed that the oil industry was a prey to night riders, armed convoys, counterfeiting, thefts from pipelines, forgery, and collusion between state officials and tax evaders. It was estimated that the State of Illinois alone had been defrauded of $9,000,000 in gasoline taxes in a year and a half, and similar thefts were believed to be going on in practically every state where Standard operated. Though no one knew definitely, it was estimated that in the Mississippi Valley the sale of bootleg gasoline amounted to more than 10 per cent. Whatever the actual percentage, it was large enough to break legitimate distributors.

Competition in the Middle West in the early 1930's was terrifically increased by the appearance of new marketers and con-

12. Company Encyclopedia: Marketing, I, Other Competition, Trackside Stations, 200.

solidations among older companies.[13] The Phillips Petroleum Company began expanding its retail marketing system in 1929 through building new service stations and purchasing others. Its invasion of the market created considerable alarm among Standard's officials because its gasoline was heavily blended with well-stabilized casing-head gasoline, of which Phillips had an abundance. The Bartles-Maguire Oil Company and the Wadhams Oil Company, two well-established marketers, merged in 1929. Standard of New York, in a drive to strengthen its refining position and attain national distribution for its products, became an important factor in marketing in the Middle West in 1930 through its acquisition of the White Eagle Oil & Refining Company, one of the most successful refining and marketing organizations in the region. With the acquisition of White Eagle, Standard of New York came into direct competition with Standard of Indiana. At about the same time, the Vacuum Oil Company, another old Standard unit, purchased the Lubrite Corporation of St. Louis and the White Star Refining Company of Detroit. As a climax to a series of consolidations, Standard of New York and Vacuum merged in 1930. The result was that Socony-Vacuum became the second largest oil company in the United States with a vast network of marketing facilities and twenty refineries. In 1930 Sinclair acquired the facilities and business of seventy-two marketing concerns. The Continental Oil Company, another old Standard Oil unit, began moving into the Middle West in 1932. Shell, The Texas Company, Barnsdall, Pure, and Skelly were also most aggressive in extending their marketing systems.

A new type of competitor was beginning to rear its head in the early 1930's—the co-operative oil company. The rise in prices during World War I and the introduction of farm machinery on a large scale provided a strong impetus for groups of farmers to organize, buy a tank car of gasoline, and distribute it among the purchasers at a lower price than the established price. The exceptionally wide margins prevailing in the 1920's and exemption from federal and state income taxes stimulated the rapid growth of co-operative oil companies. In the 1920's, according to the *National Petroleum News,* "the co-ops made their great growth in the Middle West largely because the then management of the Standard of Indiana, as did some other majors, held to a false theory of price structure which resulted in unreasonably high margins despite the

13. Robert E. Wilson, *Oil Competition in the Midwest.*

open and violent protest of the independents. The Standard of Indiana held high a fine large umbrella under which co-ops and many other competitors crowded who never would have entered the oil business had margins been narrower." [14] The oil co-operatives were so strong and important that Standard began keeping a record of the number of companies and outlets in its territory. By the end of 1931 there were 1,002 co-operative companies with 1,168 outlets in its marketing area.[15] In 1933, in order to combine the purchasing power of the regional co-operative associations, the National Co-Operatives, Inc., was organized. Through this, seven regional associations combined their purchasing power on gasoline, kerosene, greases, tires, and tubes. Lower selling prices, the patronage dividend, and exemption from certain state and federal taxes made them a serious threat to the established marketer.

Competition was further intensified through the growth of trucking and the building of gasoline pipelines. In the early 1930's the trucking of gasoline and kerosene rapidly spread from Kansas to Nebraska, Iowa, Missouri, and Colorado.[16] Almost every company arranged for truck transportation from either its refinery or terminals direct to its service stations or dealers. This resulted in the bypassing of bulk stations, the elimination of the jobbing function of marketing in many instances, and a reduction in freight charges.

The most revolutionary development, however, was the building of gasoline pipelines, which provided an extremely economical method of shipping. The new era in the transportation of gasoline by pipeline began in the East in 1929 when the Tuscarora Oil Company, Ltd., a subsidiary of the Standard of New Jersey, cleaned out its old crude oil pipeline running from Bayonne, New Jersey, to the Ohio-Pennsylvania line near Pittsburgh and used it to deliver gasoline.[17] It was the first long pipeline to transport gasoline from the refinery to market. With a carrying charge far below railroad freight rates, gasoline could now be shipped into the Middle West via the Ohio River and the Great Lakes and have a

14. *National Petroleum News*, XXXVIII, No. 36 (September 4, 1946), 11-12. For a survey of the growth of farm co-operatives, see Kenneth S. Davis, "A Bigger Role for Farm Co-ops," *The New York Times*, January 4, 1953, Section 6, 17.
15. Company Encyclopedia: Marketing, I, Other Competitors, Co-operatives, 204-214.
16. Company Encyclopedia: Marketing, I.
17. A. E. Heiss, "Gasoline Pipe Line Competition Creates Excitement in Railroad Circles," *National Petroleum News* (November 20, 1929), 31.

profound competitive effect upon the price of gasoline from Wood River, Whiting, and other Mid-Continent refineries.

Proposals to build gasoline pipelines from the Mid-Continent field through the heart of the upper Mississippi Valley had been made on several occasions since 1925, but many regarded such a project as impossible and impracticable. As competition for gasoline markets became increasingly keener, there was a renewal of the agitation. The Phillips Pipe Line Company, a subsidiary of the Phillips Petroleum Company, was the first to build a gasoline pipeline from Texas and the Mid-Continent field into the Middle West. Beginning at Borger, Texas, the line was laid in 1931 to Kansas City and St. Louis, a distance of 800 miles. With water terminal facilities in St. Louis, Phillips barged oil northward to Minneapolis and St. Paul, where the company had a large market, south to Memphis and New Orleans, and east via the Ohio River to Louisville and Pittsburgh. The line served over 8,000 Phillips outlets.

In February, 1930, the Barnsdall Oil Company decided to build a gasoline pipeline from Oklahoma into the heart of the Middle West.[18] Rather than duplicate facilities, the Continental Oil Company joined with Barnsdall to form the Great Lakes Pipe Line Company and build the largest and longest gasoline pipeline in the world. By late summer, Pure, Skelly, Mid-Continent Petroleum, and Phillips, all with refineries in Oklahoma and distributing facilities in the Middle West, had joined in the project. Beginning at Barnsdall, Oklahoma, the line was to run north to Kansas City, Des Moines, and the Twin Cities. From Des Moines a line was to run west to Council Bluffs and Omaha and east to Chicago. The first gasoline reached Kansas City early in February, 1931. With its own line completed to Kansas City in May, Phillips connected with the Great Lakes Pipe Line. By 1938 The Texas Company, Sinclair, and Cities Service had joined the other companies in the ownership of the Great Lakes Pipe Line Company. With the extension of the Great Lakes line into the Middle West, it placed all of these companies in a more advantageous position to compete with Standard and enabled them to pass on the savings in transportation costs to their customers. It marked the end of large profits per gallon in many of Standard's best markets.

18. L. E. Smith, "30,000-Barrel Gasoline Pipe Line From Oklahoma Announced," *National Petroleum News,* XXII, No. 29 (July 16, 1930), 31-32; *Chicago Journal of Commerce,* August 28, 1930.

Confronted with a severe business depression, oceans of cheap crude and gasoline, price wars, gasoline tax evaders, keener competition, the building of gasoline pipelines, and increased trucking of gasoline into the Middle West, Standard curtailed refining operations, made drastic retrenchments, and fought hard to hold its business. The construction of new refinery equipment was stopped, except where it was absolutely necessary. With the largest stocks of gasoline on hand in the history of the industry, the Federal Oil Conservation Board early in 1930 appealed to the oil industry to curtail crude runs one-seventh by operating refineries on a six-day week basis instead of seven. Standard curtailed its production and was running only enough crude for current requirements. Its refineries operated at times in 1931 at as little as 50 per cent capacity.[19] In 1932 the refineries at Zilwaukee, Michigan, and Laramie, Wyoming, were closed.

To avoid layoffs at Standard's refineries, employees were transferred, where possible, to construction and repair work, and part-time work schedules were provided for others.[20] Where necessary, those with short-term employment records were the first to be laid off. The rest of the employees were classified and in further layoffs consideration was given to the service record, value to the company, and the number of dependents. By the end of the summer of 1931, the number of layoffs had considerably increased.

Instructions were given to sales managers in the fields in the spring of 1931 to make immediate and drastic cuts in marketing costs, so 797 employees were dropped from the payroll.[21] From January 1, 1930, to July 31, 1931, Standard did not open any new bulk stations. However, 226 service stations were built and 2,156 Authorized Agent's Agreements were added. For the same period, competitors put into operation 1,449 bulk plants and 5,309 service stations. Also, a great many of their stations were of the super-service type, yet Standard built few of them. Thirty-one bulk stations and 666 service stations were closed by Standard in 1932. Even though the advertising budget for gasoline amounted to

19. *Stanolind Record*, XII, No. 8 (June, 1931), 16. Despite the curtailment of refining operations, Standard imported an increasing amount of gasoline. It imported 2,272,812 barrels in 1929, 7,403,939 in 1930, 8,081,986 in 1931, and 3,736,867 in 1932.
20. S. K. Botsford, "The Relationship Between The Standard Oil Company (Indiana) and Its Employees During a Period of Depression," *Stanolind Record*, XIII, No. 1 (November, 1931), 5-8.
21. Marketing Policies Proposed by Allan Jackson on December 1, 1931. Jackson File.

$662,000 in 1931, all expenditures were deferred until later in the year. The company disposed of its Stanolind airplanes and stopped this form of advertising which had been so successfully used.

No wage cuts were made during 1931, but the Board appointed a committee to study the matter. "We want, if possible," Seubert told the employees in October, 1931, "to weather this storm and be able to say that we were among the corporations that did not cut the wage scale. . . ." However, a 10 per cent reduction in wages and salaries for all employees of Standard and its subsidiaries became necessary in view of the competitive situation, and was made effective on April 1, 1932. The fact that the announcement of the cut was made by different executives personally appearing before the employees at the several refineries and explaining the situation created a favorable impression. Effective at the same time was a 10 per cent reduction in annuity payments, but this did not apply to those receiving less than $1,500 per year nor did it reduce any annuity to less than $1,500.

In order to distribute the work equitably among employees not laid off at Whiting, a short-week schedule was made effective on September 1, 1932.[22] At the time there were 400 part-time employees, and unless something were done to alleviate the situation, this number would shortly be increased to 850 or 1,000. It was considered better to have all working on a short week. The new schedule plus the 10 per cent wage decrease amounted to about a 25 per cent cut for the majority of the employees. Even with a short-week schedule, by October about one-third of all the plant workers were on a half-time schedule.

To aid the less fortunate victims of the depression, Standard's employees in the Chicago area subscribed during the early winter months of 1930 approximately $25,000 to the Cook County Emergency Relief Committee, and the company contributed enough to bring the total to $50,000. In the winter of 1931 they subscribed $39,413.32. The company matched the amount and agreed to cover any losses resulting from the inability or failure of an employee to pay his subscription. During the third winter, 1932, the employees contributed $22,906 and the company $28,000.

Some retrenchment policies, though involving what seemed to be relatively small things, greatly impaired morale. In Board meet-

22. "Share-Work Policy Enunciated by President Seubert," *Stanolind Record*, XIV, No. 1 (November, 1932), 1-2.

ings both Seubert and Barkdull repeatedly made disparaging remarks about the expense of research and the small service it was
rendering. Seubert finally demanded a list of chemists and laboratory men to be discharged as surplus. Pressure was brought
to bear to force employees to retire. The practice of supporting
the Whiting refinery band was discontinued. In Colonel Stewart's
time, the Directors were provided with cars which were maintained
by the company. In the retrenchment program all of the Directors
except Seubert were forced to buy their cars and assume the
maintenance expense. Also in Stewart's time, the company provided lunch for all department heads at Whiting. This practice
had been inaugurated years before to stimulate consultation and
discussion of problems of mutual interest over the lunch table.
The value derived was considered far greater than the cost. This,
too, was abandoned as an economy measure. The company also
discontinued the practice of giving retiring Directors a year's salary
after their retirement became effective.

As the severity of the depression increased and bank failures
became more numerous, Standard took action to prevent its employees in the Calumet industrial area from losing their savings.
The company subscribed $50,000 to aid in the reorganization of
two Riley banks in East Chicago in March, 1931, and $26,500 for
the reorganization of the Indiana Harbor National Bank early in
December.[23] About the same time, it became known that the
First National Bank of Whiting and its affiliate, the First Trust
and Savings Bank of Whiting, were about to be closed. Since this
would precipitate the closing of other banks in the vicinity and
bring disaster to Standard's employees, the company organized on
December 11, 1931, a new bank, the State Bank of Whiting, with
a capital and surplus of $63,750. Seubert, Barkdull, Humphreys,
and W. R. Smith, all Standard men, became Directors with
Seubert as President and Smith Vice-President and Cashier. The
new bank took over the First National Bank and the First Trust
and Savings Bank.

Much of the time of the Directors' meetings was naturally
devoted to discussions of sales problems because the sales records
from day to day showed "red from top to bottom." Speaking of
the Sales Department, one Director summarized the situation in
March, 1931, by saying: "Competitors have them on the run.
They are scared stiff because they are losing volume, prestige,

23. Minutes of the Board of Directors' and Stockholders' Meetings, III, 2026-2027.

position, money—everything, including their shirt." [24] Even though Standard seemed to be losing its shirt, there was one slight consolation. Every other company was losing its shirt too. The situation got so bad that by July Seubert was urging that the Sales Department make a house-to-house canvass to increase sales. The percentage of the total gasoline business done by Standard had dropped to about 25 per cent, and it was increasingly difficult to hold it at profitable prices.[25] All efforts to raise prices were resisted by both little and big companies. To Humphreys, Vice-President in charge of Manufacturing, Standard of New Jersey and Shell appeared to be acting in collusion to hamstring Standard of Indiana.[26] He wondered if Pan American's invasion of the East had resulted in reprisals.

The fact that Seubert was Chairman of the Marketing Committee of the American Petroleum Institute placed a special responsibility upon him and his company to lead in maintaining "ethical" practices, but it only seemed to lead to a further loss in business. Seubert believed that the company had been too "ethical" and declared that it should meet competitors on their own ground in order to preserve its business. Humphreys favored paying less attention to the Law Department until the Directors got into jail. To aid the Board in formulating sales policies, it established a Sales Research Department in the fall of 1931. Its functions were to study marketing conditions, make consumer surveys, and recommend sales policies.

To avoid indiscriminate price cuttings, the question facing Standard was whether its price policy should be based upon maintaining earnings at a sacrifice of volume or maintaining volume at a sacrifice of earnings or a policy somewhat in between.[27] The Sales Department preferred an in-between policy but, above all, it wanted a fixed policy, one that did not change from day to day or week to week. The department was too large and too scattered an organization to be responsive to quick changes of policy. Some of the Board believed that volume should be preserved at all cost. Seubert and the majority believed, however, that it was better to maintain the price and sacrifice gallonage. The Sales Department begged frantically early in 1931 for a 2

24. Diary of Robert E. Humphreys.
25. Marketing Policies Proposed by Allan Jackson on December 1, 1931. Jackson File.
26. Diary of Robert E. Humphreys.
27. Marketing Policies Proposed by Allan Jackson on December 1, 1931. Jackson File.

cent reduction in the price of gasoline, but this could not be done without cutting the price of crude, which Seubert refused to do because the tariff situation in Congress might be adversely affected.

To boost motor-oil and tire sales the company launched a most dramatic and unusual advertising campaign in the spring of 1931. It centered upon a series of tests of Iso-Vis motor oil and lubricants at the Indianapolis speedway under the direction of the American Automobile Association Contest Board.[28] The object was to secure information relative to the consumption of motor oil and fuel at various speeds and data as to the comparative deposition of carbon and engine wear in relation to the speed of the car. Thirteen sedan stock cars of different makes were purchased from dealers. All were equipped with Atlas tires, except the Cord, and special instruments for measuring data on which information was sought. The bodies were painted white, the wheels red, and lettering on both sides indicated that they were Standard test cars.

After giving the test cars a 2,000-mile run at different speeds in order to put them in good running order, they were given six test runs of 1,000 miles each. The first two were at 30 miles per hour and the last four at 55. After every 1,000-mile run, the engines were taken down and observations made to determine engine wear, carbon formation, oil and fuel consumption, tire wear, and chassis lubrication. As the cars finished the last laps of the test on the evening of April 9th, the roar of racing motors was broadcast in a gala radio program. Barney Oldfield, veteran racing driver, and T. E. Allen, Secretary of the AAA Contest Board, spoke directly from the speedway while Sousa's Band alternated with Mario Chamlee in entertaining radio listeners. On the following morning full-page advertisements announced to approximately 12,000,000 newspaper readers that the greatest and most complete study of motor oil, lubricants, and tires had been finished.

As a result of the speedway tests, the correctness of the Iso-Vis motor oil principle was clearly demonstrated. The oil did not thin out, and carbon deposits and wear were negligible. In both the 30- and 55-mile-an-hour tests, Iso-Vis showed a substantially heavier

28. "Indianapolis Speedway Scene of Gigantic Lubrication Study," *Stanolind Record*, XII, No. 6 (April, 1931), 34; "Radio Broadcasts Completion of Indianapolis Track Tests; Cars to Start 5-Month Road Tours," *Stanolind Record*, XII, No. 7 (May, 1931), 29-30; "Test Cars Off to 'Meet the Public,' Visit Dealers and Gather More Data for Lubrication Study," *Stanolind Record*, XII, No. 8 (June, 1931), 21-23, 25; "Test Cars on Tour Tie Up New Iso-Vis and Tire Accounts," *Stanolind Record*, XII, No. 11 (September, 1931), 25-27.

body at the end of the 1,000 miles than at the start. Speed was one factor, if not the principal one, in controlling oil consumption. Carbon deposits averaged one-third more per cylinder at a speed of 30 miles per hour than at a speed of 55 miles per hour. Wear per cylinder for the entire 9,000 miles of driving averaged less than $\frac{1}{1000}$ of an inch, which was an excellent commentary upon the lubricants used.

According to the AAA rules, the tires of all cars running on the speedway had to be replaced for safety reasons at the end of 1,000 miles. However, at the end of the 2,000-mile break-in run, Altas tires showed such little wear that the AAA made an exception and permitted the cars to make the first test run of 1,000 miles at 30 m.p.h. with the same tires. A new set of tires was used on the second thousand miles at 30 miles per hour and through the first two 1,000-mile tests at 55 before they were changed.

After finishing the Indianapolis tests, the cars left Chicago on May 18th on a five-month tour through the thirteen marketing states of Standard to visit dealers, deliver certified results of the tests, and make further road tests. They all traveled the same route, but the tour schedule was so arranged that each one arrived in the towns and cities at widely different times. News stories and posters featuring the Indianapolis speedway tests, the road tests, and the cars were sent to each locality for use in newspapers upon their arrival. The road tour was considered one of the most successful sales efforts that Standard ever made.

The tour was interrupted for a while in order to subject Iso-Vis to the most grueling test ever given a motor oil. The AAA Contest Board again supervised the study. It engaged the cold room of the laboratory of the Bendix Stromberg Corporation and the Studebaker Corporation where a constant zero temperature was maintained. Into it, one by one, the cars were placed and left for 20 to 24 hours. Then, by using stop watches the time was checked between the instant the engine started until Iso-Vis began to flow. Two and three-fifths seconds after the engine started was the average time for all cars. Upon the completion of these tests, the cars resumed their road tour until December when the engines were again torn down and carefully examined. The wear on the bearings was found to be negligible.

On the day the Indianapolis speedway tests were completed, April 9th, Standard announced a drastic and surprising change in its retail marketing policy on gasoline. Recognizing the consumer demand for lower prices and the fact that its sales were in the red, the company introduced Stanolind Blue, a new third-grade gasoline.[29] It was a low-octane "fighting" grade of gasoline to accommodate those who measured gasoline by the price per gallon. It was aimed directly at price cutters. At the same time as the company introduced Stanolind Blue, it reduced the price of its regular and premium-grade gasoline by 1 cent. Stanolind Blue sold at 2 cents a gallon under Red Crown and 5 cents under Red Crown Ethyl. In Chicago it sold for 9 cents per gallon, exclusive of tax. Later, as the color was eliminated, Stanolind Blue became a colorless product called "Stanolind" gasoline.

In putting a third-grade gasoline on the market, Standard had a great advantage over competitors because it had for some time marketed one regular grade and two premium grades at its service stations. By dropping Solite gasoline, it could now handle Stanolind Blue without installing any additional equipment. Many large competitors handled only two grades. If they added a third, in order to compete with Stanolind Blue, they would have to install additional tanks and pumps. Their best alternative seemed to be to lower the price of their regular grade to meet the lowest-priced competition. Adding Stanolind Blue complicated the situation for competitors in still another way. They had contracts with jobbers, and the price was based upon the tank-wagon price of Red Crown, which was not affected by the price of Stanolind Blue.

Not since the famous overnight reduction of 6.6 cents in 1923 had there been such an important development in the market. The oil trade was confused and uncertain as to how to meet the new competition.[30] Pure Oil followed Standard and introduced "Purol Pep," a new blue gasoline. Other companies waited and thought it over. The Sun Oil Company introduced its premium gasoline, Blue Sunoco, just about the time that Stanolind Blue came on the market with the result that people in the Middle West associated Blue Sunoco with cheap third-grade gasoline.[31] Naturally, the situation had an adverse effect upon Sun's sales.

The immediate effect of putting Stanolind Blue on the market

29. C. O. Willson, "Drastic Change in Marketing Policy," *The Oil and Gas Journal* (April 16, 1931), 20.

30. Robert C. Conine, "Introduction of New Grade Gasoline," *The Oil and Gas Journal* (April 23, 1931), 111; *National Petroleum News*, XXIII, No. 17 (April 29, 1931), 31.

31. Interview with Robert E. Wilson, October 5, 1948.

was nullified by two things.[32] First, the Sales Department was instructed by the Board to wait in certain areas, as in St. Louis, before marketing Stanolind Blue to see if major competitors would raise their prices on third-grade gasoline, but they did not. This resulted in a further loss of business for Standard. Secondly, effective April 21, 1931, the authority which the Sales Department had exercised for many years in meeting cut prices in local areas was withdrawn. Thereafter, competitive prices could only be met upon the authority of the President or Board of Directors. For weeks the President and Board refused to approve any recommendations to cut prices on Stanolind Blue in order to meet competitive prices. Consequently, the Sales Department lost much of the immediate benefit expected from Stanolind Blue.

By the end of May, 1931, all major marketers in Standard's territory, except Shell, had put a third-grade gasoline on the market. Shell felt that it was unwise to market a third-grade gasoline, for the increased output of cheap gasoline would have a bad effect upon an already oversupplied market. Furthermore, it would require a heavy capital investment for pumps and tanks, thus adding to an already enormous unproductive investment which the industry could ill afford. Shell, therefore, reduced the price of its regular grade to halfway between Standard's regular grade and Stanolind Blue. Consequently, it made a large gain in sales at Standard's expense.

The marketing of Stanolind Blue permitted Standard to maintain its prices on regular-grade gasoline and Ethyl much nearer the normal level than was possible before, and motor oil sales increased in line with gasoline sales. On August 25, 1931, Standard restored all prices to normal including those on Stanolind Blue, hoping this would induce competitors to do so. When this move failed, Standard's Board commenced freely to approve recommendations of the Sales Department to meet cut prices with Stanolind Blue. "They claim," one Director noted in connection with the Sales Department's efforts to sell Stanolind Blue, "that they are killing off a lot of competitors but they seem to be bleeding to death themselves. They will all be buried in the same grave." [33] During the depths of the depression, Stanolind Blue sales amounted to 13 per cent of Standard's total motor gasoline sales in 1931, 22 per cent in 1932, and 19 per cent in 1939. In poorer local'

32. Marketing Policies Proposed by Allan Jackson on December 1, 1931. Jackson File
33. Diary of Robert E. Humphreys.

ities and in rural areas, where it was used in old cars, tractors, stoves and lamps, the sales ran large.

Acting in accordance with the National Code Practices for Marketing Refined Petroleum Products, adopted in 1931 by the petroleum industry with government approval, Standard took the lead and announced that, effective August 15th, it would discontinue the general practice of leasing and loaning all gasoline-dispensing equipment below or above ground and installing it for resellers.[34] The new policy did not apply, however, to leased outlets under the Authorized Agent's Agreement or private drive-in accounts. On the other hand, all new accounts—garages, tire stores, taxi companies, bus companies, curb pump operators, and others —must pay for their equipment and its installation. The one exception to the new policy was outlets which had pumps of other distributors. These would be replaced in kind or the other supplier's equipment purchased. The company continued to supply lubricating oil equipment but nothing else. Most of the large distributors and jobbers in Standard's marketing area indicated that they would follow the new policy. In fact, for several months previous, Rocky Mountain distributors had been following such a policy, and by the fall of 1931 the loaning and leasing of equipment in that area had been virtually eliminated. Despite these efforts, the policy was not effective because the practice was continued by some competitors, which caused a further loss in business for Standard.

Handicapped by its inability to meet the competition of gasoline tax evaders, Standard was the first oil company to recognize the seriousness of the problem and initiate action. Seubert called a meeting of his Directors in 1931 to discuss the matter and take some drastic action to stop the disruption of legitimate markets.[35] As a result of the discussion, Frank V. Martinek, Assistant Vice-President, was directed to prepare and present a plan for attacking the tax evader. In August the Illinois Gasoline Tax Evasion Committee, headed by Martinek and composed of representatives of the major oil companies and the American Petroleum Institute, was formed to stamp out tax evasion in Illinois and especially in

34. "Indiana Standard Discontinues Lease and Loan of Equipment," *National Petroleum News*, XXIII, No. 28 (July 15, 1931), 22; J. C. Chatfield, "Marketers in the West Revise Their Policy on Loaning Gasoline Equipment," *National Petroleum News*, XIII, No. 29 (July 22, 1931), 34-36.

35. Company Encyclopedia: Marketing, I, Other Competitive Methods—Tax Evasion and Blending, 251-273.

Cook County. Vigilance committees were organized over the state to secure evidence of tax evasion, expose cases, arouse public opinion, and bring prosecution. Numerous investigators were engaged to report on the operations of suspected individuals and companies. As a result of the committee's work, dozens of methods were uncovered by which the state gasoline tax law was being evaded.

Governor Emerson was prevailed upon to appoint a commission to investigate gasoline bootlegging. It went to work and, among other things, recommended that a state-wide audit of gasoline tax reports and collections be made. The audit revealed that the state was being defrauded of gasoline taxes in large amounts. Prosecuting attorneys in the state were supplied with evidence to bring indictments against the tax evaders. The co-operation of the United States district attorney was also enlisted.

In view of the disclosures, Seubert, Chairman of the Marketing Committee of the American Petroleum Institute, urged a sweeping investigation of tax evasion everywhere. Martinek traveled from state to state organizing committees patterned after the Illinois committee until there were twenty-two state committees in the Middle West and Far West. The idea that members of an industry should aid in the enforcement of tax laws applying to their own products was something unique, but it was the only feasible way to remedy a bad situation. The states were not prepared to combat tax evasion because of the lack of personnel and ignorance concerning the operations of the evaders. Furthermore, an ever-changing staff of state employees could not keep abreast of the various methods as could a vigilant state gasoline tax evasion committee. Through the activities of these committees, the extent and character of the evasion and the loss in revenue to the states were revealed to public officials whose duty it was to collect the tax.

Representatives of the state committees met in Chicago on March 15, 1932, and formed the Central Gasoline Tax Evasion Committee with Martinek as Chairman.[36] Acting as a co-ordinating agency for the state committees, its objectives were to arouse public officials to enforce the law, seek the support and co-operation of all states in uncovering gasoline tax evasion, assist state officials in their investigations, protect the public against adultera-

---

36. Factual and Historical Outline of Central and State Gasoline Tax Evasion Committees. An excellent account of the activities of these committees from 1931 to 1947.

tion and other frauds in connection with bootlegging, and bring about a reduction in gasoline taxes. All companies contributed funds to carry on its work, legal counsel was engaged, and investigators were assigned to every state. In each of the states, the investigators reported to Martinek, who supervised their activities and directed their work. Hundreds of civil actions were instituted whereby federal, state, and city governments recovered thousands of dollars in evaded or delinquent motor fuel taxes. In addition, the committee made recommendations regarding a uniform motor fuel tax, many of which were enacted into law. It spurred tax authorities to greater efficiency in making collections. It also prevailed upon state officers to exchange information relative to interstate movements of taxable motor fuel.

Throughout the early part of 1931, Standard's Sales Department recommended the manufacture of a better quality of Red Crown gasoline to meet competition. Price cutters in many instances were selling a better grade of gasoline than Red Crown for the same price. A survey in 1931 of all nonpremium gasoline in eleven states showed that the quality of Red Crown gasoline was inferior to that of many competitors.[37] The average octane number of competitors' regular gasoline was 57.7 to 59.7 while that of Red Crown was 55 to 57. As a matter of fact, the chief concern of every refiner was how to meet competition in the race for motor fuels of higher and higher antiknock qualities since the new octane rating for gasoline, adopted in 1931, had taken the country by storm.

In response to the Sales Department's recommendation for a better-quality gasoline, the company took the offensive and introduced its new "Standard Red Crown" gasoline with an octane number of 62 in the fall of 1931.[38] It was a "seasonally balanced" gasoline, one whose characteristics were not fixed but varied on a prearranged schedule to fit the season and locality. In the winter the amount of long-distance driving diminished and the motorist's problem was to start his engine quickly. Therefore, winter Standard Red Crown gasoline was made with a high percentage of volatile elements. The process developed by Standard's research laboratory provided the light fractions necessary for good winter gasoline entirely from

37. Marketing Policies Proposed by Allan Jackson on December 1, 1931. Jackson File. See letter of Amos Ball to E. S. Seubert, September 15, 1933, and the accompanying report, Gasoline Quality: Standard Oil Company vs. Competitive Brands.
38. Stanolind Record, XII, No. 12 (October, 1931), 13.

crude oil without the use of casing-head gasoline. For summer the high-volatile elements were kept to a minimum to prevent vapor lock. In the fall and spring, with widely varying temperatures, gasoline with characteristics intermediate between summer and winter was manufactured. The budget for newspaper advertising, the spending of which had been previously deferred, was now used to launch the new gasoline.

In the race for higher-octane gasoline, Ethyl announced in November, 1931, that the antiknock standard of the new Ethyl to be placed on the market in the spring of 1932 would be from 74 to 78. Ethyl's action was dictated more by the competition from non-ethylized motor fuels of rising octane number than by a demand of the motor industry for a higher standard. The majority of the cars in 1932 were designed for regular gasoline with a 57–65 octane rating. Ethyl's increase in the octane rating naturally stimulated the race for higher octane numbers and the efforts to get gallonage. Without exception, gasoline manufacturers began increasing the antiknock value of their motor fuels.

To advertise Iso-Vis motor oil in 1932, a novel plan was adopted. Three distinguished writers, Robert J. Casey, veteran news reporter of *The Chicago Daily News*, Miss Margaret Lane, news writer for the London *Express*, and J. Brownlee Davidson, an authority on agricultural engineering at Iowa State College, were sent out over Standard's marketing territory to interview men and women of all walks of life who had used Iso-Vis for thousands of miles. Their short, colorful, human-interest stories about these people, their experiences with Iso-Vis, and photographs of them with their autos, trucks, or tractors provided the copy theme for Standard's advertising campaign. Each week newspaper advertisements featured an interview and picture. To demonstrate to the motoring public the reason a car serviced with the correct lubricant properly applied would run longer and be more economical and safer to drive, Standard produced in 1931 a silent movie on "Automobile Lubrication."

"Syntholube," a new synthetic motor oil, was placed on the market in 1932.[39] It was the first synthetic motor oil ever manufactured in commercial quantities, and it was hailed as superior in many respects to the best natural lubricating oils and as adapt-

39. "For Motorist, One Grade of Lubricant," *Stanolind Record*, XIII, No. 10 (August, 1932), 9-10; "Two Companies to Start Marketing of Synthetic Oil," *The Oil and Gas Journal*, XXXI, No. 13 (August 18, 1932), 27.

able to many special uses. Its development was an innovation in manufacturing, an achievement in the application of science to industry. "Syntholube" combined to an unusual extent the qualities that science and experience showed an ideal motor oil should have. It was not made from any crude but from paraffin wax whose molecules had been broken up and rebuilt to make the particular kind of hydrocarbons which possessed superlative lubricating qualities. Whether summer or winter, the same grade of Syntholube could be used. It was an all-year oil. Featured as a premium motor oil, Syntholube was marketed only in five-gallon cans at $10. At this price the new oil encountered consumer resistance. Since manufacturing costs were inherently high, Syntholube was used principally in certain specialized types of service.

In order to provide better facilities for serving the motoring public, Standard began early in 1932 replacing its old service stations with a new type which provided greasing stalls with pits or mechanical hoists to handle two, three, or four cars, and facilities for automobile accessories. The new structures were of a modified Spanish type with long, low lines and a flat roof. Constructed of glazed brick, ivory in color, with terra cotta trim and tile on a semimansard or hip roof, the stations were both attractive and practical. Attractive waiting rooms and rest rooms were provided. Every station had similar characteristics whether large or small. The first of these new stations, where a motorist could secure everything in one place, was built in Milwaukee. Some thought was given to establishing self-service stations, but nothing came of this.

Since every kind of sales stimulant was used by price cutters to secure business, Standard made an important but short-lived change in marketing policy in August, 1932, with a view to recovering lost business and meeting the practice which many competitiors had been secretly following for some time. Standard's new "Service Station Quantity Discount" plan allowed retail customers who purchased 100 gallons of gasoline a month a discount of 2 cents off the posted price on Red Crown and Red Crown Ethyl and 1 cent off Stanolind Blue.[40] Apparently, the new price policy was based on a reversal of Seubert's principle of maintaining earnings irrespective of gallonage or volume. Now it was to be an increase of sales even if the company lost money. According to the plan, a customer signed a contract and received an identifica-

40. "Discount to Buyers of 100 Gallons a Month Given by S. O. Indiana," *National Petroleum News*, XXIV, No. 34 (August 24, 1932), 15.

tion card entitling him to sales receipts on purchases. At the end of the month he presented these receipts to show 100 gallons had been purchased so that he could secure a refund. The plan applied only to Standard's own service stations or one operated under its AAA. At Authorized Agent's Agreement stations one-half the discount was taken from the dealer's commission at first and later all.

The Service Station Quantity Discount for retail customers resulted in getting more service station business, particularly from larger customers, which Standard was anxious to secure. Competitors made a straight price cut below the discounted prices, and the whole thing resulted in a free-for-all price war. It was an experiment which ended in chaos. Under the circumstances, Standard stopped writing these contracts in September, 1932.[41]

After a lapse of four years in radio advertising, Standard went on the air in November, 1932, on twenty-one stations within its marketing area. The quarter-hour radio program, known as Standard's "Funfest," ran five nights a week for eight weeks. Designed to give the country a "five gallon laugh," the show featured Johnny Murray, stage, screen, and radio performer, as Master of Ceremonies, The King's Men, Ken & Sally, Harrison Greene, Red Corcoran, Aunt Addie, and an orchestra. Electrically transcribed in order that it might be scheduled at convenient listening hours over a large territory, "Funfest" provided the cream of wisecracking, rapid-fire repartee, and current song hits.

Late in the fall of 1932 business was so bad that the sales employees as well as the General Office employees were organized to make a concerted campaign for new customers. It was the first general mobilization of employees ever attempted by the company for a major sales drive. Beginning on December 1, 1932, and continuing for three weeks, employees sold Christmas Coupon Books for $5, $10, and $25 to friends and relatives who did not customarily buy Standard products. The coupons could be used to purchase petroleum products at company service stations.

Driven to distraction by competitors, Seubert proposed in March, 1932, that the company send a number of scouts to different competitive refineries to secure details of their operations. Humphreys, Vice-President in charge of Manufacturing, was horrified

41. "Marketing in Middle West Upset By Retail Discount Policy," *National Petroleum News*, XXIV, No. 35 (August 31, 1932), 15-17; B. B. Stafford, "Marketers Stop Writing Retail QDA Contracts in Indiana Territory," *National Petroleum News*, XXIV, No. 36 (September 7, 1932), 11-12.

at the proposal but he was required to prepare the instructions to be given to the scouts.[42] John F. Cullen and Lawrence Hanna were sent to Kansas, Oklahoma, and Missouri to find out the nature of the equipment in use at refineries, the kind of products made and the amount, the sales outlets, and the source of crude.[43] Inasmuch as only ill will and little information of a beneficial character resulted, the practice was abandoned at the end of about three months.

Although expansion at the refineries was kept to a minimum in order to save money, the competitive situation necessitated a larger production of high-octane gasoline. Replacing obsolete and less efficient equipment was imperative. Standard, therefore, built at Whiting, in 1932, the world's largest combination skimming and cracking plant ever constructed. When completed, it had the capacity to skim and crack in one continuous operation 15,000 barrels of crude daily into 70 per cent gasoline with an octane rating of 70. New units and improvements in units were completed and put into operation at Casper, Wood River, and Sugar Creek.

A further expansion of refining facilities came through the acquisition of a 20,000-barrel refinery at Neodesha and the pipe-line facilities of the Standard Oil Company (Kansas).[44] Standard of Kansas retained its producing properties and certain other assets.[45] After the deal was finally consummated on December 2nd, Dr. Humphreys, Vice-President in charge of Manufacturing, referring to the refinery, remarked: "Now we have that pile of junk on our hands."[46]

For economy reasons and as a part of Standard's general program of bringing together related activities, the Midwest Refining Company's producing properties, undeveloped leaseholds, pipe-lines, gasoline plants, and other properties connected with the producing branch were sold to the Stanolind Oil and Gas Company for more than $13,639,500 in exchange for Stanolind Oil and

42. Diary of Robert E. Humphreys.
43. John F. Cullen to Giddens, August 22, 1951.
44. "Kansas Standard Plans to Provide Retail Marketing," The Oil and Gas Journal, XXX, No. 40 (February 18, 1932), 73.
45. "Indiana Standard Seeks To Limit Use of Standard Name by Kansas Unit," The Oil and Gas Journal, XXXI, No. 5 (June 23, 1932), 28; "Standard of Indiana Offers to Purchase the Refining of Standard of Kansas," The Oil and Gas Journal, XXXI, No. 14 (August 25, 1932), 34.
46. Diary of Robert E. Humphreys.

Gas stock in the fall of 1932.[47] As a result, Stanolind acquired a net daily average production of more than 6,000 barrels and net recoverable reserves amounting to more than 17,778,000 barrels. Stanolind thereby acquired stock in other well-known companies such as the Salt Creek Producers and Mountain Producers and became a major operator in the celebrated Salt Creek field. All other assets and property, including the refineries at Casper, Greybull, and Laramie, were sold to Standard for cash. These had been operated since 1921 by Standard under lease from Midwest. T. A. Dines, Chairman of the Board of Midwest, became a Vice-President of Standard and its representative in the Rocky Mountain region. He retained the presidency of the Utah Oil and Refining Company, which now came under Standard's direct control. These changes were more in name and method of operation than in ownership, for Standard already owned 99.96 per cent of Midwest's stock.

Of the several basic processes in refining developed by Standard's research laboratory, two were developed in 1932. They were both processes related to the manufacture of lubricating oil. One was propane dewaxing and the other chlorex extraction. Owing to the demand for high-quality and thoroughly dewaxed lubricating oils which would not solidify at low temperatures, Standard's research laboratory about 1930 began studying ways to improve the process of separating oil from wax. Intensive experimentation in the research laboratory at Casper resulted in developing a revolutionary process of dewaxing which would enable the company to put a superior oil on the market. The new process, known as propane dewaxing, was first commercially installed at Wood River in 1932.[48] Propane gas under pressure became a light liquid which was a good solvent for oil and a poor solvent for wax. In the process, it was mixed with oil and the pressure released slowly to evaporate a portion of the propane. This chilled the solution to about 40°F. below zero and forced all wax to crystallize, which was then easily removed by filtering under pressure. Propane dewaxing eliminated the heavy expenditure of indirect chilling by

---

47. "Midwest Stockholders Approve Sale of Assets to Stanolind Oil and Gas and Standard of Indiana," *Stanolind Record*, XIV, No. 1 (November, 1932), 18-20. In January, 1933, Ben May, an owner of fifty shares in Midwest, filed suit in the Federal District Court of Maine, Southern District, to have the sale of Midwest's assets set aside and the property recovered. For the facts in the case, see 25 F. Supp. 560 and 121 F. (2d), 431.
48. "Born of the Ceaseless Search for Improvement," *Stanolind Record*, XV, No. 6 (April, 1934), 6-10.

ammonia refrigeration then in general use in the industry. The process was also applicable to a wider variety of oils than the usual commercial dewaxing processes. A somewhat similar process was developed at Whiting for deasphalting residual oils with liquid propane at higher temperatures.

Under the pressure of a commercial need for lubricating oils of high viscosity index, the research laboratories at Whiting and Casper started work on solvent extractions—the separation of oils into fractions by means of a solvent—in 1930 and ultimately proposed the use of dichlorethyl ether, a chemical compound available commercially but never used before in oil refining.[49] Since it appeared to be an excellent solvent, a patent application on the process was filed, and it was given the coined name "chlorex." The solvent extraction process took the place of the old acid-treating process for making lubricating oils and made possible the recovery of material otherwise destroyed by the acid. To insure a supply of chlorex, Standard contracted with the Carbide & Carbon Chemicals Corporation in December, 1931, for its requirements. The first large chlorex extraction plant was placed in operation by Standard at Casper in 1932. Another was built at Wood River in 1933. Subsequently, solvent extraction plants were installed by practically every large refiner in the United States.

After the chlorex extraction plant was installed at Casper, it was found that the Mid-Continent Petroleum Corporation had independently discovered lubricating oil extraction with this same solvent at an earlier date. Standard's principal patent application was declared in interference with it. As a result, Standard negotiated a general agreement with Mid-Continent in 1933, providing that Standard would settle the patent interference, that each company was to have free operating rights and make the process available to licensees, and that they would determine the proportion of royalties to go to each party. A subsequent agreement covered the details. Under it, Carbide & Carbon was to have charge of chlorex licensing, and both Standard and Mid-Continent were to co-operate in supplying information to prospective licensees. Later developed processes, especially The Texas Company's furfural process, the Miller Company's Duosol process, and the JUIK phenol process proved more adaptable to the needs of most re-

49. Company Encyclopedia: Manufacturing, Solvent Extraction, 1-4; "Pioneers in Refining," *Stanolind Record*, XV, No. 5 (March, 1934), 3-7.

finers. The wider use of the process was also limited by the amount of chlorex available.

Standard's patent application for propane dewaxing soon became involved in a six-party interference but Standard was not greatly worried because it felt it could prove priority. When the Union Oil Company became a party to this interference with an allegation of a very early reduction to practice, it seemed as if Standard's Wood River plant might be subjected to heavy royalties unless a settlement were made.[50] Standard proposed in April, 1932, that it and Union exchange operating rights and settle the interference by arbitration. Union insisted that its position was too strong to warrant such a simple settlement, particularly since propane deasphalting and other processes were so closely interwoven with propane dewaxing. It was unwilling to agree unless this exchange could be extended to include propane deasphalting under other patents of Standard. Arrangements were finally made for the two to exchange operating licenses and make the propane processes available under license to the industry under the combined patent rights of both companies. The M. W. Kellogg Company was made the exclusive representative for licensing.

Kellogg, Union, and Standard realized in the fall of 1933 that they would have to have a process to compete with the M. B. Miller Company's Duosol process of combined dewaxing and solvent extraction. Jersey's Stratford patents on phenol extraction were necessary if they were to compete with Duosol. A study of Jersey's patent rights in the field of propane treating revealed that it had done early work on propane dewaxing and had patents covering the use of light diluents with phenol for extraction and propane fractionation of lubricating oils. Anyone using propane deasphalting, propane dewaxing, or propane solvent extraction would also need to have rights under Jersey's patents. Therefore, an agreement, known as the "JUIK Agreement," similar to the one between Standard of Indiana, Union, and Kellogg, was made in October, 1933. By these agreements, litigation was avoided and hundreds of thousands of dollars saved. The greatest benefit to Standard of the "JUIK Agreement" was the avoidance of litigation and freedom of operating rights for its propane dewaxing and propane deasphalting plants as well as the right to use the phenol extraction process. The exchange of information by the "JUIK"

50. Company Encyclopedia: Manufacturing, Propane Dewaxing and Propane Deasphalting Patent Matters and "JUIK," 1-7.

parties and their licensees and their construction of plants added materially to the improvement of the processes and of petroleum refining. These processes were made available to all refiners on a moderate royalty basis.

Beginning in the 1920's, the petroleum industry—and particularly Standard of Indiana, Standard of New Jersey, and Atlantic Refining—started to develop special methods and apparatus for petroleum distillation. Foster-Wheeler installed numerous distillation units embodying these developments, and thus incurred a considerable potential liability for patent infringement. To meet this infringement situation and to resolve the patent conflicts which arose between these three oil companies, Foster-Wheeler, in collaboration with these companies, formed the Petroleum Distillation Corporation in 1932 with a capitalization of $100,000 (30 per cent of the stock being held by each oil company and 10 per cent by Foster-Wheeler).[51] The three oil companies agreed not to sue Foster-Wheeler or its customers. Each company acquired, through PDC, a license under the patents of the stockholder companies, and Foster-Wheeler was appointed PDC's agent to license the patents of the stockholder companies.

Further settlements arising out of the cracking patent litigation were made early in 1933. By this time the licensing agreement between Standard and The Texas Company had become obsolete in several particulars. In the Dubbs settlement of 1931 and other contracts of the same date, patent rights had been extended to 1947 whereas in the agreement of 1921 the date was 1937. A certain disparity had also developed between Standard and Texas over licensing cracking patents abroad. This had become a source of considerable contention. Under the three-party foreign agreement of May 25, 1921, plus the parole agreement with Standard of New Jersey, royalties from cracking patents abroad were split among Jersey, Texas, and Gasoline Products. This situation was incompatible with the fact that Standard of Indiana and Texas had conveyed full licensing rights under their foreign patents to Gasoline Products and were, along with Kellogg, the owners of Gasoline Products. Standard demanded a new deal in foreign royalties and equal participation with Texas in revenues from this source. Texas was unwilling to agree without some consideration. Consequently, the agreement of 1921 was amended in January, 1933, to bring it down to date and include hydrogenation and

51. Company Encyclopedia: Manufacturing, Petroleum Distillation Corporation, 1-3.

catalytic cracking.[52] To secure an equal share with Texas in foreign cracking revenues, Standard agreed that when it had recaptured one-half of the face amount of the A notes acquired in the Dubbs settlement, that is, $1,666,666 plus interest, it would turn over the title to these notes to Texas and let it recapture the remaining half. At the time, Standard felt that the A notes would probably never pay out.

Although Sinclair was involved in many patent interference proceedings with Standard, The Texas Company, Gasoline Products, and Universal Oil Products, none of them had ever sued Sinclair. An infringement suit would probably have been filed by Standard many years before if it had not been for the fact that Standard and Sinclair were partners in the pipeline and crude oil business. Standard's management possibly felt that their close business relations would ultimately enable them to persuade Sinclair to take a license without the necessity of litigation. Standard, The Texas Company, Gasoline Products, and Universal had separate negotiations with Sinclair looking toward the sale of a license covering their cracking operations, but Sinclair took the position that it would not make any piecemeal settlement. If it accepted a license, it would have to include rights under the patents of Universal and Gasoline Products, whose processes Sinclair's subsidiary companies were using. Under the threat of suit, Sinclair finally agreed in March, 1933, to pay $2,000,000 cash to Gasoline Products and Universal for a license.[53] Sinclair also delivered title to certain of its cracking patents to Universal as a further consideration for a grant of immunity. Sinclair also granted Universal and Gasoline Products the right to license its cracking patents. Had not licensing been acquired, many of the licensees of Gasoline Products and Universal would have been in jeopardy of the Bell flue gas recirculation patents as well as other patents covering certain features of the cracking process which Sinclair owned.

In spite of all retrenchments and harder work than ever to hold its business from 1930 to 1933, Standard of Indiana passed through one of the most disastrous periods in its history. After record-breaking net earnings of $78,499,754 in 1929, they dropped to $46,371,438 in 1930. Although the consumption of gasoline in

52. Company Encyclopedia: Manufacturing, Cracking, Revision of the Standard-Texas Contract No. 31, 33-34.
53. Company Encyclopedia: Manufacturing, Cracking, Sinclair Deal, 24-29.

Standard's thirteen-state marketing territory increased from 115,000,000 barrels in 1930 to 121,000,000 in 1931, the company's sales declined 11.2 per cent and its percentage of the business to 24.1 per cent.[54] Net earnings took a terrific nose dive, dropping from $46,371,438 in 1930 to $17,596,396 in 1931 and $16,558,282 in 1932. Sales in 1932 were 76,893,045 barrels as compared with 86,971,621 for 1931. From a financial point of view, the net earnings for 1932 were the lowest since 1918 and the lowest during the 1930's. However, many oil companies were in the red in 1931 and 1932. Standard's cash dividends were gradually reduced from $3.25 per share in 1929 to $1.00 per share in 1932.

54. Company Encyclopedia: Marketing, I, Loss in Business to Competitors, 274-277.

CHAPTER XVII

Standard and Pan American

A CASUALTY OF THE DEPRESSION AND AN OUTSTANDING EVENT IN THE history of Standard was the sale of the foreign properties of Pan American Petroleum & Transport in 1932. The question of selling these properties first arose in July, 1931, when Seubert reported to Standard's Directors that the Standard of New Jersey, which had extensive foreign markets but no cheap sources of gasoline, had indicated an interest in acquiring Pan American's foreign properties.[1] Standard's Directors looked with favor upon the idea for several reasons.[2] Since 1929 Pan American had been spending millions to build up its foreign marketing organization. To firmly establish a place for itself in overseas markets would require an additional outlay of money. It could be done, but it would not be easy. If a tariff or embargo were levied on oil imports to the United States, which was being discussed in Congress, the expenditures would be even greater. Moreover, Pan American's huge investment in Venezuela and Aruba would be seriously jeopardized by reason of its inability to market most of its products in the United States. The prospect of losing Pan American's entire investment in Mexico due to the nationalization of the oil industry also weighed heavily. After considering all factors, Standard's Directors, lacking the fighting spirit of Colonel Stewart and not being experienced foreign oil operators, decided to sell Pan American's foreign properties to some company engaged in foreign trade and one that could fulfill its supply contracts for gasoline with the American Oil Company and for fuel oil with the Petroleum Heat and Power Company. If they could not do this, they would then consider merging these interests with Jersey's for a trial period of five years.

The properties were so extensive that only a large corporation with established foreign markets could handle such a deal. Standard of New Jersey, Shell, and The Texas Company were approached. The Jersey company was the only one which was

1. Diary of Robert E. Humphreys.
2. Interview with Edward G. Seubert, August 25, 1948.

interested and would consider furnishing Pan American's domestic needs. As a result of the negotiations with Jersey, a contract, known as the "Seaview Contract," was made on April 30, 1932, beween Standard of New Jersey and Standard of Indiana.[3] It provided that all of Pan American's foreign properties and ships were to be transferred to the Pan American Foreign Corporation, a new company, in exchange for all of its stock. Pan American, in turn, would distribute Pan American Foreign stock to its stockholders as a dividend on a share-for-share basis, and Standard of Indiana contracted to sell to the Jersey company all of its Pan American Foreign stock. The price of the stock was to be 87.15 per cent of the book value per share of Pan American Foreign's stock and was payable in five yearly installments of cash and Standard of New Jersey stock at its book value as of December 31,

SALE OF FOREIGN PROPERTIES OF PAN AMERICAN PETROLEUM &
TRANSPORT COMPANY—SEAVIEW CONTRACT, APRIL 30, 1932

Basis of the sale:

Net book value of Pan American's foreign property and ships		$161,090,171.92
Additional accounts receivable of the domestic company from foreign companies		1,873,518.97
Total		$162,963,690.89
Deduct cash in hands of foreign companies		1,802,139.42
		$161,161,551.47
87.15 per cent of the above equals		$140,452,292.11
Consideration:		
Cash	$50,000,000	
Standard of New Jersey stock	$90,452,292.11	

3. *Points of Defendant-Respondent Standard Oil Company (Indiana).* Court of Appeals of the State of New York. Jacob Blaustein, Henrietta Blaustein, Fanny B. Thalheimer and Ruth B. Rosenberg, as executors of the Last Will and Testament of Louis Blaustein, Deceased, The Louis and Henrietta Blaustein Foundation, Inc., Jacob Blaustein and American Trading and Production Corporation, suing on behalf of themselves and on behalf of all stockholders of Pan American Petroleum & Transport Company similarly situated, Plaintiffs-Appellants; Fred C. Haas, Plaintiff-Intervenor; Beatrice P. Parry, Plaintiff-Intervenor against Pan American Petroleum & Transport Company, Defendant; and Standard Oil Company (Indiana), Edward G. Seubert, Charles J. Barkdull, Louis L. Stephens, Emmet G. McKeever, James A. Carroll, Jr., and Robert E. Wilson, Defendants-Respondents; and Standard Oil Company (N.J.), Standard Oil Company of New Jersey (Del.), Walter C. Teagle, Allan Jackson, and Edward J. Bullock, Defendants, 30-31. Hereinafter referred to as *Points of Defendant-Respondent Standard Oil Company (Indiana).* See also, Exhibits 18 and 19.

1932. Jersey agreed to offer to buy Pan American Foreign stock issued to others than Standard of Indiana at no less favorable terms.

As essential parts of the transaction, supplemental contracts between the Jersey company and the Mexican Petroleum Corporation (Georgia), a subsidiary of Pan American, provided that the former would supply the latter up to 18,000,000 barrels of gasoline, enough for the needs of the American Oil Company from May 1, 1932, until December 31, 1933, and Bunker C fuel oil up to 16,500,000 barrels per year until April 30, 1937, and thereafter until notice of cancellation. Bunker C fuel oil needs of the Petroleum Heat and Power Company were to be supplied for a period of five years from May 1, 1932, with certain extension provisions. At the expiration of these supply contracts, Pan American would be compelled to make other arrangements.

In the event that the supply contracts were not renewed by the Jersey company and Pan American's marketing properties became useless, two memos were drafted at Seaview and initialed by W. C. Teagle, President of the Standard of New Jersey, and Seubert.[4] The first provided that Standard of New Jersey was to have an option to buy Pan American's domestic retail marketing facilities at their depreciated book value as of the date of the exercise of the option. The option was to run until December 31, 1933, but it was not to be construed to prevent a sale or merger or consolidation with the American Oil Company. In the event that the Jersey company did not exercise the option, it would, at Pan American's request, aid in making a sale to others. The second memo provided that the Jersey company was to have an option extending from May 1, 1932, to May 1, 1937, to buy Pan American's domestic fuel oil facilities, including refineries, at the depreciated book value at the time the option was exercised.

Pan American's Directors approved the sale contract on May 4, 1932, the supplementary one between Jersey and Standard of Indiana, and the contract between Pan American and Pan Ameri-

---

4. *Decision and Opinion of The Court,* Supreme Court, New York County, June 8, 1940. Louis Blaustein, Jacob Blaustein, and American Trading and Production Corporation, Plaintiffs, Fred C. Haas, Plaintiff-Intervenor, Beatrice P. Parry, Plaintiff-Intervenor, against Pan American Petroleum & Transport Company, Standard Oil Company (Indiana), Standard Oil Company (N.J.), Standard Oil Company of New Jersey, Edward G. Seubert, Charles J. Barkdull, Louis L. Stephens, Edward [Emmet] G. McKeever, James A. Carroll, Jr., Robert E. Wilson, Allan Jackson, Edward J. Bullock, and Walter C. Teagle, 21. Hereinafter referred to as *Rosenman's Opinion.* See also, Exhibit 80.

can Foreign providing for the sale of Pan American's foreign
properties for 999,957 shares of Class A common stock and
2,416,125 shares of Class B stock of Pan American Foreign. Standard's Directors approved the sale of its Pan American Foreign
stock to Jersey on May 6, 1932.

When the Blausteins learned of the proposed sale through the
press, they believed that it would break up the contractual relationship between Pan American and the American Oil Company
which had contributed so much to the success of both companies.
They thought that the sale would make American dependent upon
Standard of New Jersey, its biggest competitor. Therefore, the
Blausteins purchased a small quantity of Pan American stock in
April and retained counsel for the purpose of starting an action
to prevent the consummation of the deal.[5] This led to a conference
between the Blausteins, Barkdull, Jackson, Robert G. Stewart,
and the attorneys for both sides, but nothing definite was settled.

At a special meeting of the Pan American Board on May 23rd,
Robert G. Stewart resigned as President to become President of
Pan American Foreign and a Director of Standard of New Jersey.
E. G. McKeever was elected as Stewart's successor. Other personnel
connected with the foreign properties were absorbed for the most
part by Pan American Foreign. At the annual meeting of Pan
American Petroleum & Transport on June 14th the plan for re-
organizing Pan American and the sale of its foreign properties was
presented and ratified by a vote of 975,620 shares to 5,349 against.
On May 27, 1932, Standard's Board affirmed the transfer of 971,897
shares of Class A and 2,301,398 shares of Class B stock of Pan
American Foreign to Standard of New Jersey, for which Standard
of Indiana received $47,910,106.98 in cash and 1,778,973 shares
of Jersey stock.[6] Standard of Indiana thus acquired 7 per cent

5. *Opinion of Appellate Division.* Appellate Division-First Department. Supreme
   Court, May, 1941. Jacob Blaustein, Henrietta Blaustein, Fanny B. Thalheimer
   and Ruth B. Rosenberg, as Executors of the Last Will and Testament of Louis
   Blaustein, Deceased, The Louis and Henrietta Blaustein Foundation, Inc.,
   Jacob Blaustein and American Trading Corporation, suing on behalf of them-
   selves and on behalf of all stockholders of Pan American Petroleum & Trans-
   port Company similarly situated, Plaintiffs-Respondents-Appellants; Fred C.
   Haas, Plaintiff-Intervenor-Respondent Appellant; Beatrice P. Parry, Plaintiff-
   Intervenor-Respondent-Appellant, vs. Pan American Petroleum & Transport
   Company, Defendant Respondent; Standard Oil Company (Indiana), Edward
   G. Seubert, Charles J. Barkdull, Louis L. Stephens, Emmet G. McKeever, James
   A. Carroll, Jr., and Robert E. Wilson, impleaded etc., Defendants-Appellants-
   Respondents, 6. Hereinafter referred to as *Opinion of Appellate Division.*
6. Minutes of the Board of Directors' and Stockholders' Meetings, IV, 2106.

of the outstanding stock of the Jersey company and became its largest stockholder.

Shortly after the consummation of this transaction, Congress passed a tariff, effective in June, 1932, which removed oil from the free list and provided a duty of $1.05 per barrel on gasoline, $1.68 per barrel on lubricating oil, and 21 cents per barrel on crude, fuel oil, and other liquid derivatives. The tariff was effective in stopping gasoline importations entirely and reduced fuel oil importations to a minimum.

By selling off its foreign properties, Pan American was now freed from the problems created by the tariff. It escaped from the nationalization of the Mexican oil properties and the resultant losses. It seemed, therefore, as if Pan American had converted a serious situation, which might have resulted in a considerable loss in assets, into one of comparative security. Pan American still had $36,000,000 in cash and securities and $47,000,000 in net book value of properties in which Standard of Indiana owned about 96 per cent.[7] Standard of Indiana placed itself in a position to profit not only from the foreign properties but on the Jersey company's entire business through its stockholdings. Moreover, it acquired more than $47,000,000 cash with which to build up its domestic production at relatively low prices. As for the Jersey company, it acquired control over the most valuable crude oil properties in the Western Hemisphere.

As a result of the transaction, Pan American lost its foreign properties, all of its tankers, and its entire source of crude. It was left with three small refineries—at Destrehan, Baltimore, and Savannah —which were primarily adapted to asphalt production. It had only a small marketing organization of its own. However, if Pan American's foreign properties had been retained, the company would have been in no better position because of its inability to overcome the tariff barrier to marketing gasoline from the Aruba refinery in the United States.

After lengthy negotiations lasting through 1932, Standard of Indiana, Pan American Petroleum & Transport, the American Oil Company, and Lord Baltimore Filling Stations, Inc., Louis Blaustein, and Jacob Blaustein signed a "Definitive Agreement" for the reorganization of Pan American and the American Oil Company on February 17, 1933, which was predated to January 1,

7. *Annual Report for the Year 1932*, Standard Oil Company (Indiana), 4.

1933.[8] The Board of Directors of each company ratified the agreement before February 21st. According to the agreement, the purpose was to effect a reorganization of Pan American and its subsidiaries, the American Oil Company and the Lord Baltimore Filling Stations, Inc., in order that Pan American might "form a complete cycle and unit in the oil business." Pan American was to acquire the balance of the stock of American from the Blausteins and become the sole owner of American, and American was to acquire all of the stock in the Lord Baltimore Filling Stations, Inc. The Board of Directors and Executive Committee of Pan American was to consist of nine and seven members respectively. The Blausteins were to have the right to name three members of the Board and two members of the Executive Committee so long as they held 50 per cent of the stock in Pan American that they acquired in the deal. They also had the right to proportionate representation upon all committees. Seubert was to be Chairman of the Board and the chief executive, E. G. McKeever Assistant Chairman or Vice-Chairman, Louis Blaustein President, Jacob Blaustein First Vice-President and Executive Vice-President. The Blausteins were to hold these offices as long as the management contract, provided for in the agreement for a four-year period, continued.

Pan American agreed to "provide a refining capacity," including the necessary cracking units, for a throughput of 40,000 barrels of crude per calendar day on or before February 10, 1934. Failure to complete the refining units by the date agreed upon required that Standard indemnify Pan American for the difference, if any, in the price Pan American had to pay for products purchased and the price at which the estimates fixed the cost of products. It was also to indemnify Pan American against any loss if the gasoline contract of April 30, 1932, prevented Pan American from using its own gasoline when the Pan American refinery could supply it. Pan American was to proceed actively to secure a sufficient backlog of its own crude oil production. It was to allocate immediately an initial sum of $3,000,000 to be spent in acquiring crude oil properties. All parties agreed to use their best efforts, resources, and personnel to propose, establish, and carry out the program for the establishment and maintenance of a backlog of crude oil properties sufficient for the operations of Pan American. Until this could be done, Pan American had an option to require Standard to supply, to the extent of its ability and without loss to itself, all or any part

8. *Points of Defendant-Respondent Standard Oil Company (Indiana)*, 35-45.

of the deficiency in crude oil requirements necessary for Pan American at average prevailing field prices.

The American Oil Company was to acquire all marketing subsidiaries of Pan American and Lord Baltimore Filling Stations, Inc. All marketing operations of Pan American for four years were to be directed and managed by the Blausteins "subject to the approval or decision of the Board of Directors of American." Louis Blaustein was to be Chairman and Jacob Blaustein President of American. However, the marketing facilities of the Pan American Petroleum Corporation within Alabama, Louisiana, Tennessee, and Mississippi and the refinery at Destrehan were excluded from the reorganization and transferred to a new company, the Pan American Petroleum Corporation. The latter was entitled to use the trade-marks and the name of Pan American as heretofore and have the benefit of the gasoline supply contract of April 30, 1932. This company became a 100 per cent owned subsidiary of Standard.

On completion of the reorganization, Pan American was to issue to the Blausteins 1,286,876 shares of its stock out of the 3,416,069 shares outstanding for the Class B stock of American and Class B stock of the Lord Baltimore Filling Stations, Inc. Under certain specified conditions, the Blausteins were empowered to demand from Standard at any time within the first six months of the fourth year of the management contract, provided it was still in effect, that it purchase their stock at the book value thereof plus $1 but not less than $13.52 per share. Standard upon the request of Pan American agreed to extend to that company and its subsidiaries all rights under its stock purchase, insurance, pension, or other benefit plans which it was currently extending to other Standard subsidiaries.

The document stated that it contained the entire contract and that there were no oral promises, representations, understandings, or warranties affecting it, except the agreement as to the increase in the Blausteins' salaries and the letter to Standard and Pan American dated February 17, 1933. The latter referred to the Blausteins' efforts to purchase at $1.50 per share 75 per cent of the outstanding capital stock of the Crown Central Petroleum Corporation. They had until February 23, 1933, to secure an option for Pan American and, if they did, this would become a part of the deal if consummated by February 27, 1933. The option was secured and 2,105,586 shares were tendered but Pan American turned down the option.

At a Pan American stockholders' meeting on March 27th, a plan of reorganization and the Reorganization Contract, designed to carry out the "Definitive Agreement," were approved by an overwhelming vote. The next day the exchange of stock was made, and the three Blaustein nominees, Louis Blaustein, Jacob Blaustein, and Alvin Thalheimer, were elected to the Board. Both of the Blausteins were elected to Pan American's executive committee, and Louis Blaustein was elected President and Jacob Blaustein First Vice-President. The other Directors were Seubert, Chairman of the Board, E. G. McKeever, Vice-Chairman, James A. Carroll, Jr., Treasurer, Charles J. Barkdull, and Allan Jackson. Seubert, Barkdull, and Jackson were also Directors of Standard of Indiana.

After the signing of the "Definitive Agreement" on February 17th, the banking situation, which had become serious, came to a climax on March 6th, with the declaration of a nationwide bank holiday. With the banks closed and the wheels of industry at a standstill, the new Pan American Directors held their first meeting with the Blausteins on March 7th. Seubert, Barkdull, and McKeever later testified in court that the Directors discussed the effect of the depression upon future plans. Those representing the Blaustein interests testified to the contrary. In any event, they all knew that Pan American needed about 40,000 barrels of crude per day for its 1934 market and that Jersey's contract with the Mexican Petroleum Corporation (Georgia) provided a supply of gasoline only until December 31, 1933. The basic problem was how to meet Pan American's needs after January 1, 1934.

There was an obligation upon Pan American to provide a refinery with a capacity of 40,000 barrels a day before February 10, 1934, "provided such date of completion is reasonably possible." There was another obligation to begin acquiring crude oil properties. It was inferred in the agreement that Pan American should have its own producing subsidiary. There was no mention as to where crude oil properties might be acquired, but it was generally understood that one of the main sources would be the East Texas field, two hundred miles distant from the site of the contemplated refinery at Texas City. It was also necessary to consider means of transporting the crude to Texas City. In spite of the gloomy economic outlook the Board passed resolutions authorizing the formation of a refining corporation and allocating $3,000,000 for buying crude oil properties.

While Seubert was on a trip to the Southwest in March, he met W. C. Teagle, President of the Standard of New Jersey, in Tulsa. Teagle expressed great concern over the fact that Pan American was going to build a refinery when business, especially the petroleum industry, was in such a demoralized state.[9] Instead of building a refinery, Teagle suggested that Pan American make a processing contract with Humble, a Jersey subsidiary. Seubert told him of the obligation to build a refinery and that he could not make a decision without the Blausteins present. After Pan American's stockholder meeting on the 28th, Seubert discussed the general economic situation with the Directors and raised the question as to whether Pan American's financial condition and the industry outlook warranted the projected construction program. He informed them of his conversation with Teagle and suggested that the Blausteins meet with Teagle, which they agreed to do.

Two days later Teagle, Robert G. Stewart, the Blausteins, and some of Pan American's Directors met.[10] Teagle discussed the economic situation and pointed out the overexpansion and overdevelopment of the petroleum industry. Refineries were operating at only 60 per cent capacity. If the industry did not put its own house in order, Teagle felt sure, from his conference with governmental officials in Washington, that the federal government might take control. Furthermore, if Pan American built a large Gulf Coast refinery, Standard of New Jersey, according to Teagle, would have an excess of 10,000,000 barrels of gasoline produced under the contract with Pan American for fuel oil, and this gasoline would have to be dumped on the market. The Blausteins pointed out the necessity for Pan American to become an integrated company instead of buying or having its gasoline produced by a competitor. They suggested that Pan American might

9. *Brief On The Facts On Behalf Of Standard Of Indiana And The Defendant Directors*, Supreme Court of the State of New York, County of New York. Louis Blaustein, Jacob Blaustein and American Trading and Production Corporation, suing on behalf of themselves and on behalf of all stockholders of Pan American Petroleum & Transport Company similarly situated, Plaintiffs; Fred C. Haas, Plaintiff-Intervenor; Beatrice P. Parry, Plaintiff-Intervenor, against Pan American Petroleum & Transport Company, Standard Oil Company (Indiana), Standard Oil Company (N.J.), Standard Oil Company of New Jersey, Edward G. Seubert, Charles J. Barkdull, Louis L. Stephens, Edward [Emmet] G. McKeever, James A. Carroll, Jr., Robert E. Wilson, Allan Jackson, Edward J. Bullock and Walter C. Teagle, Defendants, 22-23. Hereinafter referred to as *Brief On The Facts On Behalf Of Standard Of Indiana And The Defendant Directors*.
10. *Rosenman's Opinion*, 38-40.

relieve Jersey of its fuel oil commitments in some way. Jersey then offered to process Pan American's crude oil at 25 cents a barrel for the full 40,000 per day, or 28 cents for 20,000 barrels.

After Teagle and Stewart withdrew from the meeting, Seubert said that in view of the economic situation, the earnings of the company, funds available, and the possible disruption of the market resulting from Jersey's dumping gasoline, he was not sure that they should build a complete refinery as agreed upon. He was inclined toward a middle-of-the-road policy. Other "Pan-Am-Indiana" Directors on the Board agreed but nothing definite was concluded.

At the next Pan American Board meeting early in April, it requested A. W. Peake, a Director of Standard and the Stanolind Crude Oil Purchasing Company, to make a study and report on the pipeline and crude oil situation as it affected Pan American. The matter of a processing contract was further discussed. "More has occurred in the last six weeks," Seubert told the Board, "that have expired since the signing of the Indiana-Pan-American-American Oil-Blaustein Contract to cause oilmen to stop and think than has occurred in the last six years." The Board finally voted to build a 24,000-barrel refinery rather than a 48,000-barrel and continue their efforts to make a processing contract for the other 24,000 barrels. The three Blaustein Directors voted against it. In making this decision Pan American's Directors believed that it was better to go slow owing to the complete demoralization of the petroleum industry, the feeling that the government might impose regulations upon the industry, and doubt over the practicability and flexibility of even a 24,000-barrel refining unit which, at that time, was larger than any refining unit in the entire world.

The chief obstacle to pursuing a vigorous policy in acquiring crude oil properties was the disputed question as to whether the Texas antitrust laws would permit Pan American, which was largely owned by Standard, to engage in crude production through a subsidiary, when Standard was already engaged in producing in Texas through the Stanolind Oil and Gas Company.[11] Nothing could be done about organizing a producing subsidiary, although the Blausteins kept on insisting that it be done, until the question was actually settled. There was also the question as to whether or not the Directors of the Stanolind Pipe Line Company and the

11. *Points of Defendant-Respondent Standard Oil Company (Indiana)*, 128-144.

Stanolind Crude Oil Purchasing Company could legally serve under Texas law as Directors of the newly proposed refining and producing companies. Stephens, General Counsel for Standard, advised Seubert and Louis Blaustein on April 27th, that, in his opinion, the Directors of the Stanolind Pipe Line Company, Stanolind Crude Oil Purchasing Company, or Stanolind Oil and Gas Company might serve as Directors of the proposed producing and refining companies without violation of the antitrust laws of Texas.

In his report to Pan American's Board, Peake recommended that the facilities of the Stanolind Crude Oil Purchasing Company be used to supply Pan American's needs since it was already established in the East Texas field.[12] He proposed that for five years Stanolind handle the purchase of crude for Pan American at a flat price of 5 cents per barrel marketing charge until the end of 1933, when the matter was to be reviewed and a future course of action decided upon. Moreover, Peake made several alternative recommendations as to how the crude oil from East Texas might be carried. The cheapest means would be for Pan American to build its own direct line from East Texas to Texas City, the site of the new refinery, yet Pan American did not have any crude connections with the wells in East Texas, it had no gathering system, and no storage facilities to store the oil prior to the completion of the refinery. Under the circumstances, Peake recommended that Pan American use Humble's gathering system in East Texas, its trunk line to Mexia, and the Stanolind Pipe Line Company's line from Mexia to Sinco with Pan American laying two spurs from Sinco to Texas City and from Dawes Station to Baytown. If Pan American entered into a pipeline agreement with Humble, the latter would, in consideration thereof, turn over to Pan American a sufficient number of well connections.

At the May 31st meeting of the Pan American Board, Peake reported that tentative arrangements had been made with Humble, but the Board made no decision. Peake was asked to obtain a definite proposition from Humble and secure data as to the cost of Pan American's putting in a gathering system and building a trunk line from East Texas. Authority was given, however, to organize the Pan American Pipe Line Company and begin the construction of a pipeline for Pan American from Sinco to Texas City and from Sinco to Baytown. Peake urged again that the

12. *Ibid.*, 100-106.

Stanolind Crude Oil Purchasing Company be allowed to handle all of Pan American's buying for three years, but the Blausteins objected because Pan American should have its own crude purchasing department and, besides, the rate was far too high. Finally, it was agreed that for the interim up to the end of 1933 Stanolind would do all the purchasing as suggested and sell to Pan American.

After much negotiation over a processing contract, Standard of New Jersey offered to process Pan American's crude for 22½ cents per barrel. This was lower than the cost in any refinery of Standard of Indiana. Pan American's Board therefore authorized the making of a contract on this basis between Pan American Refining and Humble over the opposition of the Blaustein Directors. Under the contract, which was to expire in December, 1936, unless renewed, Pan American agreed to deliver at the Baytown, Texas, refinery 20,000 to 28,000 barrels of crude daily from January, 1934, to December, 1936, to be processed at 22½ cents per barrel, subject to an increase if the price of labor or materials increased.[13]

At the next meeting of the Pan American Board on June 28, 1933, Peake reported that if Pan American built its own pipeline system, the savings, including depreciation and interest, would be about $1,000,000 per year as compared with using Humble and Stanolind's system.[14] On the basis of Peake's report, the Blausteins agreed in principle to a joint Humble and Stanolind arrangement but insisted on the presentation of formal contracts for approval, which was done on July 28, 1933. At the same time, the contract between the Stanolind Crude Oil Purchasing Company and Pan American Refining, whereby the former would handle the crude buying for three years, was presented. The pipeline agreement with Stanolind Pipe Line and Humble running for five years was approved over the opposition of the Blaustein Directors. The Blausteins strenuously objected to the buying contract because it would do away with the very foundation stone in the integration of Pan American. They claimed that it would keep Pan American from going into crude production for three years; it would make Stanolind not only the purchaser but the seller of the crude with an opportunity to make a profit on the crude it had bought and was buying. The contract was finally withdrawn for revision to

13. *Brief On The Facts On Behalf Of Standard Of Indiana And The Defendant Directors*, 35-48.
14. *Ibid.*, 139-152.

make it possible for Pan American to cancel the contract after 1933, if crude could be purchased more cheaply elsewhere than from Stanolind.

Stephens informed Seubert in August that the Texas antitrust laws prohibited Pan American from entering the producing business in Texas because of Standard's ownership and control of both Pan American and Stanolind Oil and Gas.[15] He stated that his letter of April 27, 1933, related solely to an interlocking directorate and not to the question of restraint of competition under the Texas antitrust laws. When the Pan American Directors met on August 24, 1933, Barkdull presented Stephens' letter to Seubert and announced that due to legal difficulties, nothing would be done to organize a production company in Texas until the legal difficulties could be cleared up to Stephens' satisfaction.

The purchasing contract with the Stanolind Crude Oil Purchasing Company was approved in September over the Blaustein opposition. The Blaustein Directors again insisted on having a producing company. After much controversy between the Blausteins and Standard over going into production in Texas, it was finally decided to submit the question of legality to two well-known Texas lawyers, one to be selected by each side.[16] Their opinion was submitted on November 6, 1934, and they definitely said that it would be legal for Pan American to organize a subsidiary for production in Texas.[17]

Acting under the "Definitive Agreement" of January 1, 1933, the Blausteins exercised their option in 1934 to sell 346,062 shares in Pan American to Standard, which increased the latter's ownership of shares to 78.44 per cent. As the controversy between Standard and the Blausteins deepened, McKeever, who was not getting along very well with the Blausteins, was elected Vice-President and Assistant to the Chairman. In December, 1934, Robert E. Wilson, a Standard Director and Vice-President in charge of Research and a Director and member of the Executive Committee of Pan American since November, 1934, resigned his positions with Standard and was elected a member and Vice-Chairman of Pan American's Board.

The first thermal cracking unit with a 24,000-barrel capacity, the world's largest unit, went into operation at Texas City in

15. *Points of Defendant-Respondent Standard Oil Company (Indiana)*, 148-151.
16. *Ibid.*, 153.
17. *Ibid.*, 54, 153-163.

April, 1934, and achieved full capacity two months later.[18] In spite of its novel features it more than lived up to expectations, having a higher capacity than expected and hence somewhat lower unit costs.

After Wilson had reviewed the Pan American situation early in 1935, he urged that the company go ahead aggressively in the direction of fuller integration. Since the right of the company to enter production had finally been cleared up, he started on a search for a man to head up a producing subsidiary and, after numerous interviews, finally hired E. R. Turner, who was then with the Continental Oil Company. Meanwhile, in January, he urged on Jacob Blaustein that if he wanted to get into production in a hurry, Pan Am might try to buy a $3,000,000 share in the Yount-Lee purchase, a very attractive $40,000,000 deal which Stanolind had recently made. Blaustein, however, was not interested in any such minority interest but insisted on an independent producing company. The Pan American Production Company was incorporated in 1935 and, after building up a small staff, made its first purchase in September.

Wilson also urged that the company start building a new tanker fleet in view of current low building costs and that a start be made on the design of a No. 2 cracking unit to take up the load when the Humble processing contract expired in December, 1936. It soon appeared that the No. 2 unit should be designed to handle Gulf Coast crudes, such as Hastings and South Houston, both of which had been discovered by Stanolind since 1933 and were available to Pan American. These crudes had less gasoline and much more gas oil than East Texas crude but produced a much higher antiknock gasoline. The cracking unit had to have more than double the cracking capacity of No. 1 unit, even though its crude-running capacity was only slightly larger. It also included other new technological developments. This new unit went into operation in February, 1937.

With the increase in demand, a third cracking unit was authorized in 1936 and completed in 1938. In addition, the company built a catalytic polymerization unit, which was for many years the world's largest, to make very high octane gasoline, a pipe still to make high-quality furnace oil, and later another to handle heavy Cayuga crude for Pan American's asphalt refineries. Four

18. *Rosenman's Opinion*, 41-43.

new tanker ships were commissioned in 1936 to transport refined products from Texas City to the Atlantic Coast.

Owing to the lack of sufficient crude oil, Pan American renewed the purchasing contract with the Stanolind Crude Oil Purchasing Company in 1936 and again in 1938 over the objection of the Blausteins. The $3,000,000 set aside as the initial sum to be allocated by Pan American for immediate use in buying crude property was not expended until after April 27, 1935. By January 1, 1937, Pan American was producing from its own properties about 1,850 net barrels per day.

After nearly four years of disagreement and friction over policies relating to Pan American, Louis Blaustein, President of Pan American Petroleum & Transport Company, Jacob Blaustein, Executive Vice-President, and the American Trading and Production Corporation, a Blaustein operating company, commenced action by the service of a summons and complaint on January 26, 1937, and in subsequent months in the Supreme Court, New York County, against Pan American Petroleum & Transport Company, Standard of Indiana, Standard Oil Company (New Jersey), Standard Oil Company of New Jersey, Edward G. Seubert, Charles J. Barkdull, L. L. Stephens, E. G. McKeever, James A. Carroll, Jr., Robert E. Wilson, Allan Jackson, E. J. Bullock, all Directors of Pan American, and W. C. Teagle, President of the Standard Oil Company (New Jersey).[19] Fred C. Haas and Beatrice P. Barry intervened in the suit as plaintiffs in June, 1938.

The suit was a derivative action brought as minority shareholders and Directors. The complaint charged that Standard, through some of its Directors, who were also Directors of Pan American, had failed in its fiduciary duty to Pan American stockholders. The defendants were charged with frustrating the integration of Pan American and preventing its development into a self-sufficient oil company. It was alleged that Standard of Indiana and the Pan American Directors, under the domination of Standard, had exploited Pan American for the benefit of Standard, and that Standard of Indiana and the Standard Oil Company (New Jersey) had participated in and benefited from the breach of duty. It was further alleged that the defendants had conspired with Standard of Indiana and the Pan American Directors in a general scheme to insure benefits from transactions involving Pan Amer-

19. *The New York Times,* March 20, 1937; "From Jobbership to Integration," *National Petroleum News,* August 25, 1954, 34-35.

ican which belonged in justice and equity to Pan American itself. Fraud, conspiracy, waste, negligence, and breach of trust were also charged. The plaintiffs sought an accounting, a restitution of property, damages for Pan American, and an injunction to restrain Standard interests from influencing Pan American policies.

In view of the suit and the fact that the management contract with the Blausteins by the original terms thereof expired on March 28, 1937, Louis Blaustein, President of Pan American and Chairman of the American Oil Company, Jacob Blaustein, Executive Vice-President of Pan American and President of the American Oil Company, and Alvin Thalheimer, President of Lord Baltimore Filling Stations, Inc., and Executive Vice-President of American Oil, resigned as officers of these companies but continued as Directors and members of the executive committees of the three companies. Robert E. Wilson, Vice-Chairman of Pan American, was elected to the presidency of all three companies, and E. G. Mc-Keever was made Executive Vice-President of Pan American. Louis Blaustein died on July 27, 1937, and his executors were substituted as plaintiffs in the suit.

Before the case came to trial the Directors of Standard, believing that Seubert, Barkdull, Bullock, Stephens, Wilson, Jackson, McKeever, and Carroll—Directors and officers of Pan American —had served with entire fidelity to the company's stockholders and the best interests of Pan American, agreed to indemnify and hold harmless these defendants from all loss, expense, and liability in connection with the litigation, and if any money damages were involved, Standard would pay.

The Blaustein suit came to trial on December 4, 1939, before Justice Samuel I. Rosenman with Henry L. Stimson representing the plaintiffs, Ralph S. Harris representing Standard of Indiana, John W. Davis Standard of New Jersey, and David Paine the individual defendants.

The evidence presented by the plaintiffs involved to some extent the interpretation of the "Definitive Agreement" of January 1, 1933.[20] The Blausteins claimed that it was the guide for Pan American's future actions in becoming a well-integrated company; and that it expressed the then existing best business judgment of all signatories and their Boards as to what constituted a sound policy for advancing Pan American's well-being. However, the plaintiffs alleged that Standard of Indiana had broken the letter

20. For the claims of the plaintiffs, see *Rosenman's Opinion.*

and spirit of that agreement in four respects: in regard to building a refinery, the acquisition of crude oil properties, the purchasing of crude oil, and the building of pipelines. Moreover, what had been done was not in the furtherance of Pan American's interest but for the benefit of Standard and its subsidiaries.

Upon the conclusion of the presentation of the plaintiffs' evidence in January, 1941, motions were made by the defendants to dismiss the complaint, but they were denied. The defendants then began the presentation of their case.[21] On the fulfillment of the terms of the "Definitive Agreement," the defendants' defense was that they had adhered to the basic principles but due to unfavorable economic, legal, and other factual conditions at the time, it was impossible for them to carry out the exact terms. Moreover, all measures had been taken by a majority vote of Pan American's Directors, who had used their best business judgment in the furtherance of Pan American's interests. They were honest in their actions and had acted in good faith.

After exhaustive testimony lasting more than three months, the trial came to an end on May 15th. Twenty-nine hundred pages of printed briefs, 1,048 exhibits, and 10,631 pages of stenographic notes were involved.

On June 8, 1940, in a 182-page decision, Judge Rosenman ruled in favor of the plaintiffs on most of the issues and held that Standard had violated its fiduciary duty as a majority stockholder.[22] In upholding the plaintiffs' charges, the court emphasized that none of the individual defendants profited personally in any way in the transactions. They were held liable on the ground that they had appropriated for Standard the transactions and profits of Pan American. On the charges relating to building the refinery and the processing contract, the considerations here were different from the contracts with Standard subsidiaries, for Standard made no profit whatever. On the refinery issue, Judge Rosenman found that no cause of action had been made out against the defendants. The court said that the Directors were entitled to the presumption that their acts and judgments were honest, that they were motivated by good faith, and it found no cause for action for misfeasance, neglect of duty, or waste of corporate assets in doing what they did. Furthermore, the court found no cause for action

21. *Brief On The Facts On Behalf Of Standard Of Indiana And The Defendant Directors.*
22. *Rosenman's Opinion.*

against the Standard Oil Company (New Jersey), the Standard Oil Company of New Jersey, or W. C. Teagle.

Owing to the fact that Judge Rosenman had expanded the scope of fiduciary obligations beyond known precedent and questioned the ordinary, necessary, and long-accepted business practices of Standard and other large corporations, Standard appealed the decision. The Blausteins also appealed because more drastic injunctive relief had been denied.

On December 19, 1941, the Appellate Division of the New York State Supreme Court by a 3 to 2 vote reversed Rosenman's decision, sustained the defendants' appeal, and ordered the complaint dismissed.[23] In regard to holding Robert E. Wilson liable on the refinery, pipeline, and purchasing issues from November 24, 1934, the court held the judgment erroneous because this date was two days before he became a Director. Furthermore, the policies attacked had been made long before Wilson became a Director. There was no evidence that he was guilty of any negligence or fraud.

The Blaustein interests appealed the decision. After seven years of litigation, the suit came to an end when the New York Court of Appeals on July 19, 1944, by a 4 to 2 vote affirmed the decision of the Appellate Division which had ruled in favor of the defendants.[24]

In 1945 Jacob Blaustein, the Executors of the Estate of Louis Blaustein, and the American Trading and Production Company each commenced an action against Standard of Indiana in the Superior Court of Delaware alleging a breach of the "Definitive Agreement." The plaintiffs sought damages aggregating $50,000,-000. Jurisdiction over Standard of Indiana was obtained by means of foreign attachments levied against the stock owned by Standard in Pan American. Standard made several motions in the Superior Court to quash the attachments, from the determination of which appeals were taken to the Supreme Court of Delaware. From the last determination of the Supreme Court, adverse to Standard, an appeal was filed with the Supreme Court of the United States. In March, 1949, the Supreme Court dismissed the appeal for lack of any substantial federal question. The three suits in the Superior Court of Delaware, now consolidated, were still pending in 1951

23. *Opinion of the Appellate Division.*
24. "Indiana Standard Upheld in Blaustein Suit," *National Petroleum News,* XXXVI, No. 30 (July 26, 1944), 44.

and had not come to trial. The issues involved were substantially the same as those raised in the litigation in New York.

The controversy has since been amicably resolved. On August 17, 1954, pursuant to agreement between the Blaustein interests and Standard, Pan American was merged into Standard and the litigation was dismissed. The Blausteins exchanged their stock in Pan American for stock in Standard, becoming one of the large stockholders of Standard. American Oil became a directly and wholly owned subsidiary of Standard and the parent company of the former Pan American subsidiaries. The Blausteins were elected to two directorships and two Executive Committee memberships in American Oil and in its subsidiaries. Jacob Blaustein became a Director of Standard.

CHAPTER XVIII

Under the NIRA

EVEN THOUGH WALLOWING IN A SLOUGH OF DEPRESSION BY 1933,
Standard continued its aggressive efforts to hold its business and
reduce costs. To increase sales to farmers especially, the company
introduced the Farmer Accumulative Remittance Plan, better
known as the FARM plan. Its adoption was due to substantial
losses suffered by the company in extending credit to farm customers. Under the FARM plan a farmer signed a contract with
Standard in the late summer or early fall to supply his motor oil
and greases during the next spring and summer season. Through
the accumulation of sales tickets, he obtained a lower price if his
total purchases during the year reached certain stated amounts.
An added discount was given for early delivery and other discounts for early payment on delivery. An inducement to sign a
FARM agreement was that it protected the farmer against a price
advance for the entire year. Moreover, the plan eliminated the
necessity for farm customers' overstocking and tying up too much
cash in such supplies. While some of the details of the FARM plan
were changed in subsequent years, the basic principles continued
to be followed by the company to the present. The FARM consumers purchased in 1940 something like 9,500,000 gallons of the
company's total sales of 26,500,000 gallons of motor oils.

During the depression the idea of merchandising motor oil in
cans was born. Prior to 1932 dealers had purchased oil in bulk,
poured it into their own highboys, then pumped one, two, or five
quarts into a measuring can and poured it into a customer's car.
Various can manufacturers, needing additional business, developed an aggressive campaign to convince oil companies that
they should can their oil and the public that it should purchase
oil only in sealed cans. About 1932 motor oil in one- and five-quart
cans and in one- and two-gallon cans began to appear. Mail order
houses, auto supply stores, and general stores were soon offering
motor oil in one- and two-gallon cans. Pennzoil and Quaker State
were two of the first oil companies to market oil in sealed cans.

The premium price for Pennsylvania oils allowed sufficient margins to cover the cost. The practice of unscrupulous dealers of increasing revenues by substituting lower-priced oils in bulk for higher-priced oil ordered by a customer aided can manufacturers in selling the public on buying oil in refinery-sealed cans. About 1933 Sinclair started canning its oil and waged a vigorous campaign to warn the public to "Beware the Oil Bootlegger."

Standard's survey of the situation revealed that while there was some substitution of lower-priced oil for higher-priced oil, it was not practiced to such an extent as to justify its paying the cost of canning to eliminate it. Standard had been selling its motor oil in bulk and to some extent in labeled glass bottles at its service stations. To counteract any possible loss in sales to canned oil and to offset the rapid decline in the sale of motor oils, Standard reduced the price of its new Iso-Vis D motor oil in 1933 from 30 to 25 cents a quart and the price of Polarine to 20 cents a quart in bulk. With about 50 per cent of Standard's dealers carrying competitive brands of canned oil, the company improved its glass containers and promoted them aggressively at its service stations and among dealers. It made a number of substitution checks, and whenever substitution was found, a special call was made upon the dealer to show him the error of his way. As a concession, Standard furnished its dealers with unlabeled cans into which they could put their own bulk oil. It also put out a two-gallon can labeled "Dealer Special Motor Oil," later called "Standard Motor Oil." The two-gallon can sold for 98 cents, compared to $1.36 which the same quantity of oil cost if purchased in quarts.

The remarkable success of the Christmas Coupon Book campaign led the company to launch an Atlas Tire Contest Drive beginning on June 1, 1933, and running until July 15th. This was the second major all-employee sales campaign. Every employee in the Sales Department was eligible, except service-station men, salesmen, and A station agents. The campaign was confined to the nonprofessionals. Teams were formed within the various departments and offices to compete for prizes, commissions, and the honors offered. Keen competition early developed when employees discovered what substantial commissions their sales would bring.

For advertising purposes during the Century of Progress Exposition in Chicago in 1933, Standard erected the largest electric sign ever built in the Middle West. Atop the Western Cold Storage

Building on Wacker Drive Extension and facing Michigan Avenue at an angle and height so all pedestrians and motorists could see it, the sign, 136' x 200' and 231' above the ground, flashed consecutively seven changes of copy, all advertising Standard and its products.

For visitors to the Exposition, Standard had more than an exhibit of products. It had a great "auditory spectacle" housed in the circular structure known as the Transportation Dome of the Travel and Transportation Building. Color and lighting were synchronized with music. From a black central pillar supporting a huge jeweled Red Crown, a startlingly beautiful color composition was played on the white canvas walls of the dome, which was in diameter greater than the length of a city block. Simultaneously, there was music—a roll of drums, a great fanfare of trumpets, and a martial composition—then a movie showing the American epic of oil in transportation from the beginning to modern times and how Standard was a leader in the industry. The movie was presented for fourteen minutes on four screens simultaneously. These screens were placed on a contrasting cyclorama below the white canvas. After seeing the movie, visitors could look about and reflect upon the wonders and decorative plan of the great dome, which reached to the height of a twelve-story building. Quotations from the great industrial poet, Joseph Auslander, appeared in luminous letters on a black cyclorama. The roof of the dome was suspended from the sky by cables hung from twelve huge towers arranged in a circle. "The roof that breathes" moved up and outward with the contraction and expansion caused by the heat and cold. At night the dramatic illumination from within made the exterior of the dome and the main building a fascinating spectacle. Standard also provided a personal service bureau and rest room for visitors on the ground floor of its General Office at 910 S. Michigan, where they might check packages and suitcases, get maps, buy transportation tickets, meet friends, and rest.

While Standard was making various efforts to hold its business, the competition furnished by the price policies of a small but powerful minority of producers brought the oil industry close to disaster early in 1933. Despite all efforts to limit production, 150,000 to 200,000 barrels of "hot oil" were daily produced in excess of state allowables during 1933 and 1934. Crude continued to sell for 10 cents a barrel in East Texas and 25 cents in the Mid-Continent field. Finished products were thrown upon the market at ruinous prices. The flood of crude was so great that many in the industry advocated abandoning all attempts at curtailment in order to let East Texas and other flush fields run out in the hope that things would cure themselves in time. The industry was thoroughly disorganized, demoralized, and in a state of despair.

On the same day that President Roosevelt was inaugurated in 1933, Standard's Sales Research Department submitted to the Directors a searching and critical analysis of the effect of the company's price policies since 1920. This was known as the Babb report.[1] So far as was known, it was the first time that any oil company or any competitive marketer of manufactured goods for mass consumption had for its guidance a scientific analysis of the relationship between price and volume. It came at a crucial time because Standard's sales had fallen much more rapidly than those of the industry as a whole.

For years, according to the report, Standard had operated on a policy of attempting to secure a high margin of gross profit per sales outlet wherever and whenever possible. During a period of rapidly expanding consumption in the 1920's this policy had returned extraordinary profits to the company. "The heavy profits of the Standard Oil Company in the 20's," declared the report, "were earned partially at the expense of profits in the early 30's." At the same time, the policy had paved the way for distributors with low selling costs to come into the business, cut prices, and take away both volume and profits. Since it was necessary to find a market for the crude produced, competition could not have been eliminated but, according to the report, economically sound margins could have kept it under control; they would have slowed up the influx of new types of distributors; and Standard could have met them in its stride. If margins and profits had been built on the basis of more modest returns, there would also have been a greater tendency to keep distribution costs free from unprofitable investments and expenditures.

As the market seemed to reach a saturation point about 1930, existing conditions brought about a reduction in available gallonage for each outlet, and marketing expenses continued high. The situation had left Standard in the impossible situation of trying to maintain uneconomic margins to cover an ever-mounting distribution cost. The low-cost marketer was establishing the price at which Standard must sell its products and, as a result, Standard

1. "Price of Gasoline, Part I, Supplement to Part I, and Part II, 1933."

was suffering an enormous loss in volume. Any attempt to maintain the current price structure would endanger future profits. More recently, the situation had been aggravated by the narrowing and even elimination of differences in the quality of products. The cut-price marketer was gradually becoming a first-quality outlet selling at a lower price made possible by a large volume per outlet. If the company were to maintain its dominant position in marketing, which was essential if sufficient volume was to be maintained to pay fixed charges, an immediate acceptance of a policy of selling at a reduced margin of profit per unit was imperative. This Standard could do profitably only if costs and expenses were reduced in proportion and if it adopted, as a permanent policy, the practice of selling at the lowest possible margin of profit per unit rather than at the highest. The problem was not how to maintain volume on present prices or margins but to determine a fair price for products in terms of what competitors could profitably sell goods for, accept that price and its resulting margin, and then bring the company's marketing policy "by finesse or brute force" into line with the margin.

The report made four recommendations. The normal service-station and tank-wagon price of Red Crown should be reduced 2.5 cents to bring the average margin between tank-car and retail prices to approximately 3.65 cents. The normal service-station and tank-wagon price of Stanolind gasoline should be made one cent below Standard Red Crown. The tank-wagon and service-station price of Red Crown Ethyl should be 2.5 cents above Standard Red Crown. All prices should be raised or lowered $3/10$ of a cent with each subsequent change in the spot tank-car price of Group 3, a district which included Tulsa and nearby points from which freight rates on gasoline to the Middle West were identical. Thus the margins between tank-car and retail prices would be narrowed to eliminate practically all cut prices, special discounting, rebates, premiums, rentals, commissions, and excessive guaranteed margins. This, along with the curtailment of marketing expense and increased volume, would provide a sufficient margin of profit to allow a fair return for a long time on the investment.

The second part of Babb's report dealt with the reasoning behind the recommendations. With each $1/4$ cent decrease in the competitive spread, it was found that Standard's sales increased slightly more than 2 per cent. With each increase, there was a corresponding decrease. When the average competitive spread on

Standard Red Crown became 6.5 cents or greater, the company's losses in gasoline sales increased much more rapidly than 2 per cent for each $\frac{1}{4}$ cent increase in the spread. Where possible, price reductions by Standard, according to the report, should be allowed to remain in effect for at least five months. Price cuts of shorter duration showed little or no direct response in sales volume. Since lower margins on gasoline were inevitable, the company should take the lead in the maintenance of retail prices that would result in a lower competitive spread throughout its territory and bring marketing costs within the gross profit such prices would allow. Otherwise, competition would continue to make heavy inroads into the company's volume by cutting prices, and net operating losses would result. The company's retail prices should be related to Group 3 prices and changed with each $\frac{1}{4}$ cent variation.

Allan Jackson, Vice-President in charge of Sales, concurred in the report and considered it the most important and valuable analysis ever made.[2] "It seems to me," he wrote, "our situation is like that of a patient with a cancer in a vital spot, which can be cured by an immediate operation but, if neglected, is sure to be fatal. Shall we have the operation now and take a large loss which may be necessary before we get our volume back, or shall we take a gradually increased loss from year to year and the consequent exhaustion of capital?" The situation was serious.

With cheap gasoline flooding the market, prices in a chaotic condition at hundreds of points, and gasoline selling far below cost, Standard's Directors, after considering the Babb report, decided that the existing margin between the tank-car and the service-station price was too large. By a general adjustment of the basing price at the respective refineries, they hoped to place the prices of the company on a more competitive level.[3] In accordance with this principle, Standard on May 8th made a drastic reduction in its normal tank-wagon and service-station prices on Standard Red Crown all over its territory, except the Rocky Mountain Division, by an amount that would allow an average spread of approximately 3.65 cents per gallon. However, the new policy did not have a chance to operate very long because the passage of

2. *Ibid.*
3. Company Encyclopedia: Marketing, I, Normal Price; R. C. Conine, "Standard of Indiana Makes Drastic Reductions in Gasoline Prices Inaugurating New Policy," *The Oil and Gas Journal* (May 11, 1933), 35; Allan Jackson, "Indiana Standard Explains New Policies Covering Marketing Practices in Middle West Area," *The Oil and Gas Journal* (May 25, 1933), 10.

the National Industrial Recovery Act and the adoption of the oil code of fair competition affected the price of crude and gasoline.

While industry and business fought the depression, the National Industrial Recovery Act became a law in June, 1933. It provided for the self-regulation of business and industry through the formulation of codes of fair competition for the purpose of eliminating unfair competitive practices, reducing unemployment, increasing purchasing power, improving the standards of labor, conserving the natural resources, and accomplishing other objectives.

When it became evident that the National Industry Recovery Act was going to be adopted, the American Petroleum Institute asked representatives of various branches of the petroleum industry to meet in Chicago in June for the purpose of considering a national code of fair competition for the industry. As a result of this and subsequent meetings with NIRA officials, a code for the petroleum industry was written by General Hugh S. Johnson and accepted by the industry. It became effective on September 1st.

The Secretary of the Interior, Harold L. Ickes, was appointed Petroleum Administrator for the oil code. Ickes, in turn, created the Petroleum Administrative Board to perform such administrative functions as he might refer to it. Ickes also appointed a planning and co-ordination committee composed of oilmen to co-operate in administering the code. Under it a marketing committee, headed by Charles E. Arnott, Vice-President of Socony-Vacuum, was created with an extensive organization of regional, state, and local committees representative of the various marketing elements. In addressing the first meeting of the Planning and Co-ordination Committee in September, 1933, Ickes said: "Gentlemen, we have a solemn duty to perform. Our task is to stabilize the oil industry upon a profitable basis. This is the keen desire of the Administration and we will work with you constantly to that end." [4]

Standard co-operated wholeheartedly in the administration of the code. It contributed not only about $65,000 in 1934 and 1935 toward the expenses of administration but the services of its employees, who devoted much of their time to its committee work. [5] Seubert served as a member of the Planning and Co-ordination Committee and the Labor Subcommittee, H. F. Glair on the

4. 105 F. (2d) 809.
5. Company Encyclopedia: Marketing, II, NRA Code.

Refinery Subcommittee and as Vice-Chairman of the Labor Sub-committee, Allan Jackson on the Marketing Subcommittee, R. D. Rexwinkle on the Labor Subcommittee, L. L. Stephens on the Legal Subcommittee, A. W. Peake on the Transportation Sub-committee. Edward J. Bullock served as Chairman of the Com-mittee for Region No. 3 and, at the same time, as Chairman of its Natural Gasoline Committee. Other employees served on state marketing committees and in other capacities.

Despite its relatively advanced labor relations program, Stand-ard was obliged under the oil code to make some adjustments in its working schedules and wages. Service men in 3,600 stations owned and operated by Standard began working a forty-eight-hour week. Twenty-five hundred new attendants were employed in order to comply with the shortened work week.[6] In the offices, a forty-hour week went into effect. Part-time work in the refineries was abandoned, and all workers were placed on the code schedule of thirty-six and forty hours per week, which was a disappointment to some of the men because they had been working longer hours. In providing full work for part-time employees, the company found that it had too many men at Wood River, Sugar Creek, and Casper, but not enough at Whiting, Neodesha, and Greybull. Where there was a surplus of labor, employees were offered jobs at other plants, but it was difficult for most of them to move. Altogether the Manufacturing and Sales Departments employed about 3,400 additional men, which increased the company payroll by about $5,000,000 per year. The Stanolind Pipe Line Company and Stanolind Oil and Gas added about 500 men and increased the payroll by about $700,000 per year. Including all subsidiaries, Standard made jobs for about 5,300 men and paid $6,900,000 more per year in wages.

Under Section 7a of the National Industrial Recovery Act all employees had the right to organize and bargain collectively through representatives of their own choosing. They were to be free from the interference, restraint, or coercion of employers in the designation of such representatives. Furthermore, no employee and no one seeking employment was required as a condition of employment to join any company union. On the other hand, employees might join or organize a labor organization of their own choosing.

6. "Under the Banner of the National Industrial Recovery Act," *Stanolind Record,* XIV, No. 11 (September, 1933), 1.

Under the Industrial Relations Plan established at Standard's refineries in 1919, its employees already had a method by which they could negotiate with management through representatives of their own choosing. However, at the annual spring conferences with the Directors, the Joint General Committees entered into an earnest discussion of Section 7a. Speaking with enthusiasm and unanimity, employee representatives reaffirmed their faith in the Industrial Relations Plan.[7] It was considered the best means available to enable employees and management to carry on negotiations peacefully, intelligently, and understandingly. So far as they were concerned, there was no desire to make any change. They wanted to continue as they had been under the Industrial Relations Plan.

While the employees in the refineries had been under the Industrial Relations Plan for years, nothing had been done by the company toward extending the plan or its principles to employees in other departments. With the adoption of the oil code, Standard's Directors authorized the inauguration of the Employees Representation Plan on November 1st for certain classes of employees in the Sales Department, the Stanolind Oil and Gas Company, the Stanolind Pipe Line Company, and the Stanolind Crude Oil Purchasing Company.[8] By this action approximately 9,000 additional employees were brought into a system of representation similar to the Industrial Relations Plan. On November 1st the plan was extended to "B" station agents and service-station helpers.

In an industrial world seething with strife, strikes, and violence the relations between the employees of Standard and management seemed like an island of peace. The Industrial Relations Plan continued to function as well in time of storm as in fair weather. However, the Joint General Committees had to deal with many more questions than in any two or three years previous. Three times as many appeals came to the President as usual and required no small amount of time and attention. The spirit of the times encouraged employees to be aggressive in demanding concessions in regard to their working conditions. A discussion of some of these questions developed that the employees were right, and in fairness and in furtherance of good relations the company made the changes requested. On the other hand, the company did not hesi-

7. "Let Us Maintain Principles of Co-operation and Confidence," *Stanolind Record,* XV, No. 8 (June, 1934), 1.
8. "Employees Representation Plan," *Stanolind Record,* XIV, No. 12 (October, 1933), 1-4.

tate to resist demands which it believed were unjustified under the existing conditions.

Due to the enforcement of the oil code, the prorationing laws, and a slight increase in consumption, conditions in the oil industry improved toward the close of 1933. The price of crude, which had been materially reduced for a few months, rose from 18 cents to $1.00 a barrel at Tulsa in September. Surface conditions in marketing showed some improvement. However, the oil code and other measures designed to improve conditions came too late to repair the damage done in the early part of the year. Progress was actually more in prospects than in profits. Combined sales of Standard and its subsidiaries dropped from 76,893,045 barrels in 1932 to 71,150,895 in 1933.[9] In 1933 the total consumption of gasoline in Standard's territory was 91,000,000 barrels while Standard's sales amounted to 20,000,000 barrels, or about 22 per cent.[10] Even though Standard had lost in the percentage of its total gasoline business, its net earnings for 1933 increased $1,116,069.35 over 1932. The company after two very disastrous years had turned a corner from a financial point of view.

Adjustments in keeping with conditions and the oil code continued to be made during 1934. As an experiment, the company put into effect on April 1, 1934, a five-day, forty-hour week at the General Office, the refineries, and main stations in the sales fields for a period of six months. The continuation of the plan depended upon conditions and results. After several extensions on a six-months basis, the experiment became permanent in December, 1935. The oil code was amended in April, 1934, in an attempt to balance the supply of gasoline with the demand by allocating the amount of crude which refineries could process. All of Standard's refineries curtailed their operations and were not allowed to produce the amount of gasoline which the company was currently selling. By early 1935 its inventories were very low.[11]

In a spectacular drive for business, Standard's 1934 summer advertising campaign for Red Crown "Superfuel" broke upon the

9. *Annual Report for the Year 1933.*
10. "Motor Oil Merchandising, 1937."
11. *Brief in Support of the Motion for a New Trial, Motions to Set Aside the Verdict and to Dismiss the Indictment and Motions for Arrest of Judgment of Defendants Standard Oil Company (Indiana), Edward G. Seubert, Allan Jackson and Edward J. Bullock.* United States of America vs. Standard Oil Company (Indiana) et al. In the District Court of the United States for the Western District of Wisconsin, 16. Hereinafter referred to as *Brief for New Trial at Madison.*

Middle West in April with all the force of a pack of animals. "More live power per gallon," the theme of an impressive series of large advertisements, carried conviction with action drawings of familiar and strange beasts typifying how nature provided them with reserve power for swift flight or dogged stamina. Radio announcements throughout the Middle West focused attention upon the newspaper advertisements.

On the opening day of the Century of Progress Exposition for the second summer in May, 1934, Standard had a huge "Live Power" parade in Chicago, like a Mardi Gras, led by a forty-piece band and Allen King, the famous animal trainer. The parade, composed of twenty-seven floats on which rode scores of pretty girls and gaily colored and animated replicas of wild animals possessing "Live Power" like Standard's Red Crown "Super-fuel," lasting about two and a half hours, moved from downtown Chicago to the Exposition grounds. The next day the floats were divided into the Red, Blue, and Green "Live Power" parade units and started on a spectacular three-months tour over different routes through Standard's marketing area.

To show the parallel between "Live Power" in the molecules of Standard's motor fuel and "Live Power" in the flesh, Standard provided visitors to the second summer of the Century of Progress with an unusual animal show. In the Red Crown out-of-door amphitheater seating 2,500, Standard presented two "Live Power" free animal acts three times daily featuring Allen King, who worked with twenty-three lions and tigers in a cage, and Estrella Nelson, who put the elephants through their tricks. When not performing, the animals were on exhibit in their cages. It was one of of the most talked-about free performances at the Exposition. By the end of the summer, an estimated 7,000,000 people had seen the free performances and the exhibit.

In Midget City at the Century of Progress, Standard erected a replica of one of its service stations at a strategic intersection. Three midget pumps on the driveway were the last word in design and complete in every detail. Midget cans of Standard products, Atlas tires, and a host of accessories were on display. Two midget attendants serviced the automotive equipment of the little metropolis in a simulated but intensely realistic fashion. Another feature of the 1934 Exposition was the trans-Atlantic flight of twenty-four planes of the Italian Military Squadron from Rome to Chicago. For the co-operation given in refueling these ships in Chicago, the

Italian government presented John Porter, head of Standard's Aviation Department, with a silver medal.

In the fall of 1934, Standard's employees were once again marshaled for a sales drive. In a letter to employees captioned "A Heart to Heart Talk," Seubert urged the 28,000 employees to intensify their efforts to carry out the slogan "Every Employee a Salesman." Along with his appeal, plans and materials were placed in the hands of employees for use in the concerted sales effort. Refinery workers, general office clerks, stenographers, office boys, and executives, apart from the Sales Department, visited neighbors and friends and left an invitation to drive into Standard service stations and purchase "Live Power" gasoline and other petroleum products.

A significant innovation in automotive lubrication was the introduction of the Standix Cartridge Lubrication Kit. Prior to the development of cartridge lubrication, six lubricants needed for the average automobile had to be applied by a pressure gun in order to reach the bearing surface they were intended to protect. The old type of grease gun was filled laboriously and messily from cans and drums. It could not be quickly drained and flushed to make it available for another greasing, and the formation of air pockets and the inclusion of dirt were almost unavoidable. On account of the cost of a complete set of specialized grease guns, a garage owner or the operator of a service station was forced to forego lubrication work, one of the most profitable of all automobile services, or apply lubrication by inefficient means with danger to car parts, or operate with fewer lubricants than called for in the manufacturer's specifications, which was also dangerous.

In the late 1920's the Bendix Aviation Corporation was rapidly expanding its business and acquired options on certain patents covering new types of lubricating equipment. After considering how to proceed with this development, Bendix officials decided that, although they were experienced in manufacturing equipment, they needed the assistance of someone experienced in lubrication. Standard, therefore, was approached about a joint development program. After a thorough survey of the possibilities by Standard, the two companies proceeded to organize the Lubrication Corporation in 1931.[12] The new corporation took over the

12. "Bendix Aviation Corporation and Standard Oil Company (Indiana) Form Lubrication Corporation," *Stanolind Record*, XII, No. 11 (September, 1931), 11; "Design and Sale of Lubricating Equipment," *Stanolind Record*, XVII, No. 10

patent options and set up an experimental laboratory at the Bendix plant in South Bend. The staff worked day after day and far into the night developing guns, fittings, nozzles, adapters, and other essentials of lubrication, each embodying distinct improvements over existing equipment. They made greasing easier and promoted a more thorough greasing by facilitating the use of pressures higher than any previously used.

The idea of packaging lubrication in cartridges was not new, but until the engineers of the Lubrication Corporation perfected various phases, it had never reached a commercially practical stage. The new Standix Cartridge Lubrication Kit consisted of six cartridges filled with different lubricants and a new type of gun packed in an attractive steel case. To fill the grease gun, the operator merely slipped in a factory-loaded cartridge of the desired lubrication. The gun with adapters could service all fittings. After using the required amount of grease, the cartridge could be removed and another inserted. In this way a single gun served for a complete greasing operation involving several lubricants.

Standard started marketing Standix Lubrication Kits about 1933 but soon had to discontinue their sale. Under the code of fair competition, oil companies could not sell any type of equipment for handling oil products. When the code was amended, Standard resumed their sale in 1934. Garage owners, operators of truck and bus fleets, those who serviced their own vehicles, and dealer stations could now buy equipment and lubricate cars without excessive cost and with cleanliness.

Of great significance to the oil industry in the 1930's was the marked increase in the use of oil for heating homes and as fuel for diesel engines. It indicated a new trend which had vast potentialities for the petroleum industry. Domestic oil heating had come into being about 1917 when engineers met the problem of a wartime coal shortage with a practical, mechanically controlled, oil-burning appliance. By 1928 there were over 400,000 homes heated with oil.[13] Oil-burner sales totaled close to 120,000 in 1929, and they continued to be installed at a growing rate. In 1934 the fuel oil demand rose nearly 5 per cent over 1933. No special

---

(August, 1936), 1-4. "Standard Oil Company of Indiana Adopts New Method for Dispensing Grease," *The Oil and Gas Journal* (November 1, 1934), 28; Company Encyclopedia: Manufacturing, The Lubrication Corporation, 1-4.

13. G. Harvey Porter, "Million Oil Burning Homes Consume Over 50,000,000 Bbls. Annually," *The Oil and Gas Journal* (December 26, 1935), 57.

petroleum products had been required for domestic heating; the consumer simply selected his fuel from whatever was available. This resulted in an unsatisfactory operation of heating systems and created a demand for fuels of high quality. Consequently oil refiners began to manufacture fuels in accordance with strict specifications for heating purposes.

Diesel locomotives had been used to some extent for switching purposes prior to 1934, but they were heavy and slow. By 1933 two high-speed diesel-electric locomotives had been developed, and they were on display at the Century of Progress in Chicago. In the spring of 1934 the Burlington "Zephyr," a new diesel-powered, streamlined passenger train, made its initial trip through the East for advertising purposes and to test out public reaction to this new type of railway transportation. In June it made a record run from Denver to the Century of Progress exhibition in Chicago, averaging 78 miles per hour. The fuel bill for the 1,000 miles was only $14.88 as against $255 for coal for a steam locomotive.[14] The placing of this train in regular passenger service marked the beginning of a revolution in railway transportation. The growth in the use of diesel locomotives thereafter was amazing. With the introduction of high-speed diesel engines, the oil industry began studying diesel requirements and improving oil products. In 1934 Standard's laboratory started working on the development of improved fuel and lubricants, and the company created a special organization to handle diesel fuel oil sales.

Price wars continued to sweep the retail markets in 1934 and adversely affected business. One particularly thorny problem was caused by a group of marketers who insisted upon having a differential because their products were unbranded and did not have the public acceptance of Standard's, or else they were located on tracksides and claimed certain economies in marketing. Standard's traditional policy was that no one was entitled to undersell it on a similar quality product. To combat these marketers, Standard's Directors restored to the Sales Department in June full authority to meet competitive prices. However, Ickes, who was interested in stabilizing the market, did not want Standard to press meeting competitive prices from sellers of unbranded gasoline.[15] Seubert, therefore, announced in July that in certain localized areas where

14. "Zephyr Fuel Bill Only 1.5 Cents per Mile," *National Petroleum News*, XXVI, No. 25 (June 20, 1934), 67.
15. Memorandum from Allan Jackson to Edward G. Seubert, August 8, 1938.

special conditions prevailed, Standard would tolerate on an experimental basis a differential of 1 cent between Red Crown gasoline and certain regular grades offered by trackside operators and ½ cent between Stanolind and their third-grade gasoline. In making this concession, Standard reserved the right to determine when, where, and how long it would tolerate the differential.

By the summer of 1934 it was apparent that Standard's price structure was again outmoded and inadequate to meet the competition.[16] In determining the normal tank-wagon price, Standard had used a base price, f.o.b., each refinery. These prices were arbitrarily adjusted so that the tank-wagon price in adjacent areas served by different refineries would not be in material variance. Freight rates from the refineries to the ultimate destination were more or less the controlling factor in the adjustment, but it was also necessary to avoid conflicts with one-price laws and certain federal laws. Consequently, the basing prices at the refineries frequently varied to a considerable degree on any given product. Generally speaking, however, the normal price was the same at all points except for the variation in transportation costs.

The continued wide margins of profit offered by competitors had had a demoralizing effect upon Standard's sales organization, especially the "B" station agents, who were easy targets for competitors wishing to establish jobber connections on a tank-car basis. With a small investment in a bulk plant and buying in tank-car lots, they could easily increase their income. Numerous Standard agents had, therefore, during the previous two years left the company's service for this reason. When they did, Standard's business in the community was completely demoralized. Furthermore, in order to benefit from wider margins, individual dealers or groups of dealers solicited Standard to permit them to buy in tank-car lots. Standard constantly refused to convert resellers on a tank-wagon basis to a tank-car basis. As the pressure increased, it was difficult to hold dealers, particularly when some competitors were seeking outlets of this kind. Another effect of Standard's price policy was that its normal prices were being undercut by competitors in so many localities and to such a degree that the existing normal price structure could no longer be applied to competitive conditions. Standard was selling at subnormal prices

16. For an analysis of Standard's gasoline price policies from 1925 to 1937 and their effects, see Gasoline Price Policy, September 1, 1937. Also, memorandum from Allan Jackson to Edward G. Seubert, August 8, 1938.

in as many places as it was selling at so-called normal prices. Tabulations showed literally hundreds of price cuts. One could not be considered a market leader when competitors refused to follow.

As a result of these conditions, the number of strictly trackside stations in Standard's territory increased from 691 on January 1, 1931, to 1,341 on July 1, 1934, a gain of 94 per cent. These represented only a small percentage of the total low-priced outlets. Moreover, many of the low-price marketers had provided themselves with facilities, service, and products of a kind and quality which were comparable with or superior to Standard's. Standard's owned and operated service stations increased from 2,856 in 1925 to 3,888 plus 7,172 AAA's in 1933, yet competing stations including AAA's had increased from 12,601 to 44,928. Moreover, since 1929 the average yearly sales of gasoline for Standard service stations had steadily declined from 114,778 gallons per service station to 81,694 in 1933. This decline increased marketing costs to a point where many stations could not operate profitably. The over-all picture was that Standard's percentage of the total gasoline consumption in ten states had declined from 33.9 per cent in 1927 to 21.6 per cent during the first four months of 1934.

As petroleum products from Group 3—Tulsa and vicinity—had increased in volume and become more competitive, it seemed logical and reasonable that the normal price structure should be based on the published quotation of the Group 3 spot market. Therefore, in order to put the company in a better competitive position, Standard's Marketing Committee, after an extensive study, recommended in July, 1934, that the established normal service-station price of Standard Red Crown, except in the Rocky Mountain area, be 5.5 cents per gallon above the average Group 3 spot tank-car price plus freight from Tulsa to its destination and taxes.[17] The 5.5 cent spread was arrived at after a careful study of thousands of sales tickets of competitors' prices, which showed that the actual average retail price was 5.5 cents above the tank-car spot market. This was what the company must do to bring its prices into line with competitors and be competitive. As for changes in the tank-car spot market, it was impractical for a company like Standard with thousands of bulk stations to follow each fluctuation of the market. The Marketing Committee, therefore, recommended that changes should be authorized only if necessary or desirable when the spot market had gone up or down at least

17. Gasoline Price Policy, September 1, 1937, 18-19.

$\frac{3}{10}$ of a cent and stayed that way for a period of seven days or more.

The Directors authorized the adoption of the price policy as outlined by the Sales Department and made it effective September 11, 1934, with several additional features. The company would continue meeting local price cuts on comparable grades as advertised and sold by competitors or as determined by octane rating. As a principle, it would not recognize any differential for any type of marketer, but in practice it would handle this type of competition as authorized by the Board. On the basis of proper evidence, local management might reduce the price of gasoline not more than 1 cent below the normal price and then submit such evidence to Chicago for approval. This was in order to reduce the time advantage that competitors had in reducing their prices.

Although the exchange of gasoline between oil companies during the depression saved on transportation costs, Standard of Indiana did not begin the practice until September, 1934. Exchanges generally involved two companies with refineries or terminals located at widely separated points. Rather than ship gasoline a long distance to its marketing outlets, a company would arrange with another near those outlets to supply them with gasoline of similar quality. In return, the former would supply the marketing outlets of the latter from its refinery. Standard's practice of exchanging gasoline was discontinued early in 1935 because of the resistance from the sales representatives.[18] They contended that it was difficult to market products under the company's brand name when employees and a large portion of the public knew they did not originate at Standard refineries.

In spite of increased operating costs and the general depression, conditions within the industry improved during 1934. Standard's net earnings amounted to $18,949,680.41, a gain of $1,275,000 over 1933. Several factors were responsible for the larger volume and dollar sales. An aggressive sales effort and careful management aided in increasing the margin between income and expenses. The consumption of petroleum products increased 6 per cent over 1933 and was within 6 per cent of the 1929 record. A great majority of the marketers had co-operated under the NIRA oil code to bring about more stable conditions and eliminate unsound practices. The control of crude oil was sufficient to hold the output to

18. Company Encyclopedia: Marketing, II, H. G. Naylor to Allan Jackson, March 14, 1939.

"PLAYING" COLOR WITH MUSIC, STANDARD'S EXHIBIT, CENTURY OF
PROGRESS, CHICAGO, 1933

STANDARD'S "LIVE POWER" PARADE, CENTURY OF PROGRESS, CHICAGO, 1934

MASS DEMONSTRATION OF OIL COMPANY EMPLOYEES AGAINST IOWA CHAIN
STORE TAX, APRIL 30, 1935

SOUND AND LIGHTING CREWS IN HOLLYWOOD SHOOTING A SCENE IN
STANDARD'S FIRST FULL-LENGTH MOVIE, *STAN*

E. P. Galbreath (center foreground), formerly Standard's manager at Indianapolis, and
Conger Reynolds (left foreground) Standard's Director, Department of Public Relations,
serve in advisory capacities

less than 1 per cent more than in 1933. At the same time, crude stocks had declined.

During 1934 Standard's Directors departed from tradition and listed the company's stock on the New York Stock Exchange. For years it had been an inviolable rule of the old Standard Oil organization to have nothing to do officially with any security market. The theory was that the Directors and officers owned their stocks as investments and they had no interest whatever in the passing movements of the speculative markets. After the dissolution in 1911, the Atlantic Refining Company was the first of the old Standard units to depart from the tradition. It listed its stock on the New York Stock Exchange in 1920. Between 1920 and 1930 the stock of the Standard Oil Company (New Jersey), Standard Oil Company (California), Standard Oil Company of New York, the Prairie Oil & Gas Company, the Standard Oil Company (Kansas), and the Ohio Oil Company was listed.[19]

In order to add to the prestige of the company after the Stewart affair of 1929 and all the disturbances over the Pan American Petroleum & Transport Company, it seemed advisable in 1934 to have the stock of Standard of Indiana investigated, listed, and the company become a member of the Exchange.[20] Therefore, Standard's stock was listed on the big board on August 30, 1934. Trading in the company's 15,375,175 shares began the following day. This was the largest single issue to be listed on the New York Stock Exchange since 1930 and the first listing since May, 1933. It became the ninth largest issue on the Exchange and the third largest oil company listed. In assets Standard of Indiana was then exceeded by only two oil companies, Standard of New Jersey and Socony-Vacuum.

While Standard of Indiana was attempting to cope with chaotic marketing conditions, the Petroleum Administrator, Ickes, was taking steps to stabilize the market. When the oil code was amended in April, 1934, it authorized the Planning and Co-ordination Committee with the President's approval to arrange for buying gasoline from nonintegrated refineries in order to get rid of the surplus, which was depressing prices. The first of several buying programs, in which the major companies contracted to relieve distressed refiners of their surplus gasoline, began in June.

19. John E. Gray, Assistant Director, Department of Stock List, New York Stock Exchange, to Giddens, August 10, 1951.
20. Interview with Edward G. Seubert, August 31, 1948.

In less than a month after the buying program started, Ickes requested Charles E. Arnott, Chairman of the Marketing Committee under the oil code, to take whatever action he deemed necessary to restore markets to their normal condition in areas where wasteful competition had caused them to be depressed.[21] Ickes not only requested but authorized Arnott to designate committees for each locality, when and as price wars developed, with authority to confer and negotiate, hold public hearings with a view to ascertaining the elements of conflict, and stabilize the price level to conform to that normally prevailing in contiguous areas. Any activities of Arnott's committee must, of course, be consistent with the requirements of Clause 2 of Subsection (a) of Section III of the NIRA. According to this, agreements which might be in conflict with the antitrust laws required specific approval if the companies involved were to receive protection as provided by the Act. If, in any situation, it should appear that this section was not being complied with, the matter should be referred to the Petroleum Administrative Board. "I trust," Ickes wrote in closing, "that I can count on your co-operation." After receiving the letter and agreeing to Ickes' request, Arnott appointed a general stabilization committee with headquarters in Washington and regional, state, and local committees.

The fourth gasoline-buying program, which had been inaugurated early in November, was suspended on the 10th largely because the Department of Justice questioned its legality. With the stoppage of the program, there was an immediate break in prices. Many refiners, owing to the low price of gasoline, were desperate and began to shut down. Spot tank-car prices were ruinously low, and if prompt and immediate steps were not taken to alleviate the condition, refiners would go bankrupt and the industry be deprived of competition. Even the majors were suffering tremendous losses as a result of ruinous prices.

At a meeting of the General Stabilization Committee in Chicago early in January the critical situation was discussed. It was generally agreed that the gains made in stabilizing the retail market could not be kept unless action were taken regarding "distress" gasoline and a firm tank-car market were established. Accordingly, Arnott appointed a tank car stabilization committee consisting of Robert W. McDowell, Vice-President of the Mid-Continent

21. "Arguments to Jury Climax 111 Day Madison Oil Trial," *National Petroleum News,* XXX, No. 4 (January 26, 1938), 32.

Petroleum Corporation, H. T. Ashton, Manager of the Lubrite Division of Socony-Vacuum, Edward J. Bullock, Vice-President in charge of Purchasing for Standard of Indiana, Arthur V. Bourque, Secretary of the Western Refiners Association, and others to make a survey and report recommendations.

The first meeting of the Tank Car Stabilization Committee was held on February 5th in Bullock's office.[22] After discussing the problem, Ashton proposed a gasoline-buying program for the Mid-Continent field. Bourque read a list of sixteen or seventeen Mid-Continent refiners without sufficient regular outlets who would have 600 to 700 cars of "distress" gasoline per month to sell. Bullock and Edward S. Karstedt of the Continental Oil Company both opposed the suggestion. With "hot" gasoline coming out of East Texas, any buying program for the Mid-Continent field would be like trying to dry up the ocean. In view of their experiences with the gasoline-buying program in 1934, when "hot" oil was uncontrolled, neither wanted anything more to do with allocations or commitments or anybody telling them how much to pay for gasoline as in 1934. They felt the only thing to do was cut the price of crude oil. It was finally agreed, however, that the most efficient method of handling the situation was for different major purchasers to arrange with individual small refiners to buy their surplus. The proposed plan was considered much superior to the haphazard purchasing done in 1934. The question of allocating individual refiners to major purchasers was left to a committee of Bullock, McDowell, and Bourque, who were to present a plan to prospective buyers in Chicago on the 11th, together with estimates from Bourque of the surplus involved for the next ninety days for each of the refineries usually having "distress" material. It was generally assumed that all companies would come into the picture since a stable retail market required a higher tank-car market.

On March 1st, Arnott and Ashton explained the buying program to the Mid-Continent refiners at Kansas City, who agreed to co-operate, and they appointed a committee to attend a meeting of the Tank Car Stabilization Committee in St. Louis on March 5th. At the St. Louis meeting, which Bullock did not attend, the final details of the buying program were agreed upon.[23] Each

22. *Brief for New Trial at Madison*, Appendix 2, Exhibit 177; "Defense Version of Buying Given in Madison Case," *National Petroleum News*, XXIX, No. 50 (December 15, 1937), 9.
23. 105 F. (2d) 809; 310 U. S. 179.

major selected one or more of the independent refiners as a "dancing partner" and assumed the responsibility for buying its "distress" gasoline. There were no formal contractual commitments. The arrangements were on the basis of a gentleman's agreement. Bourque was designated to make monthly surveys and furnish information to the major companies on the amount of surplus gasoline available. A mechanical subcommittee, composed of McDowell, Walter P. Jacobi and O. J. Tuttle, was appointed to assist in disposing of the surplus not anticipated by the monthly surveys, maintain fair prices, and handle details between meetings.

On March 6th Arnott telephoned Ashton that the buying program should begin operating as soon as possible since the Federal Tender Board seemed to be cleaning up the "hot" oil quickly. The next day the Mechanical Subcommittee went into action.[24] The three men divided up the major companies. Each man telephoned those on his list, informed them that the buying program had been launched, and suggested that they get in touch with their "dancing partners." Once the buying program got under way, between five and six hundred cars per month were purchased.

As soon as the buying program was started, McDowell telephoned Bullock and informed him of the fact. Bullock thanked him for the information but did not say anything definite about what Standard would do. During the summer and fall McDowell kept in touch with Bullock principally by telephone. Since McDowell got so little satisfaction out of Bullock in some of his conversations, he finally quit telephoning him to save expense.[25] The reason for Bullock's complete indifference was that Standard had been buying third-grade gasoline from the Waggoner Oil and Refining Company of Electra, Texas, since 1931, and there was no reason for Standard or Waggoner to participate in the program.[26] After Waggoner secured a license from Ethyl early in 1934, it did not have any "distress" gasoline to sell. However, Standard purchased 69–70 octane leaded gasoline regularly in 1934, 1935, and 1936.

If the Mid-Continent buying program were to be effective in the Middle West, it was recognized that the "distress" gasoline of East Texas would have to be purchased. Arnott, therefore, called

24. 310 U. S. 179.
25. *Brief for New Trial at Madison*, 48.
26. *Ibid.*, 6-17; "Madison Trial Nears Close; Arnott Completes Testimony," *National Petroleum News*, XXX, No. 2 (January 12, 1938), 17.

several meetings in the East to discuss the problems of the East Texas Refiners Marketing Association. Standard of Indiana was not represented at the meeting because the company did not want to participate in any East Texas buying program. Shortly thereafter, some of the other major companies began a buying program in East Texas.

Arnott saw Ickes on March 12th and, among other things, discussed the buying programs, but he did not ask for approval or disapproval.[27] Ickes asked if the buying programs violated the antitrust laws. Arnott did not believe so. In authorizing the stabilization program, Ickes wrote to Arnott on April 2nd about the necessity of complying with the requirements of the basic law. Where these understandings were made the basis of resolving price wars and were intended to operate over a definite period of time or involved substantial changes in policy of the supplying companies, it was necessary that the procedure set forth by the NIRA be followed in order for the arrangement to be legal. If any such arrangements had been made, Ickes wanted Arnott to report them. If they required approval, Ickes would give consideration to them under the provisions of the Act.

The United States Supreme Court declared the NIRA unconstitutional on May 27, 1935, and the National Recovery Administration came to an end with a crash. Shortly thereafter the Tank Car Stabilization Committee held a meeting to discuss the situation, and it decided to continue the buying program for two reasons. First, it was considered to be a proper and legitimate thing to do, justified by the condition of the industry, code or no code. Secondly, the objects and purposes of the NIRA were just as desirable after the invalidation as before, with Roosevelt, Ickes, and NIRA officials pointing out to the industry its moral responsibility to maintain the gains made under the code. The Tank Car Stabilization Committee, therefore, continued to operate and meet monthly through February, 1936, and continued to buy through April, 1936.

As a result of the two buying programs, it was hoped and intended that both the tank-car and the retail markets would improve. The ultimate purpose was to raise the price of gasoline in the Middle West. Almost all jobber contracts contained price formulas allowing them a 5.5 cent margin under the service-station price posted by Standard. Hence, as the spot tank-car market rose,

27. 310 U. S. 202.

prices to jobbers increased and affected retail prices. From March 8, 1935, to June 14, 1935, the spot tank-car price rose on successive occasions from 3½ cents per gallon to 4¾. From June until the end of 1935, the price remained firm with only slight deviations.[28] Retail prices followed closely the tank-car spot market although there were short lags between the spot market advance and the retail advance. The rise in spot tank-car and retail prices was not only comparable but strikingly similar. Through buying 5 to 7½ per cent of the total gasoline available for distribution and sold by independent refiners, the major companies received prices and profits from the sale of their own products which constituted a very high percentage of the total distribution to jobbers and consumers in Standard's territory.

From the moment that the National Industrial Recovery Act was declared invalid, the Department of Justice began receiving hundreds of complaints from jobbers in the Middle West asserting the existence of a conspiracy among refiners to fix jobber margins and the price of gasoline. The main jobber complaint was based upon Standard's cut of the gross jobber-retailer margin from 6 and 6.5 cents to an average of 5.5 cents in September, 1934, which had been protested loud and long. Although the complaints were isolated and independent from each other, "they seemed to form a pattern." When the Department endeavored to find out about conditions from Arnott and other oilmen, it ran into a stone wall. Therefore, the Anti-trust Division asked the Federal Bureau of Investigation to inquire into the complaints. Moreover, it decided to call a federal grand jury to probe the matter.

From the point of view of the Department of Justice, a grand jury investigation could be inaugurated in any one of ten states. After examining the court dockets, the Department found that the Western Judicial District of Wisconsin was the least crowded.[29] Furthermore, the fact that Wisconsin had a liberal political background and was an agricultural state not connected with oil, except as a consuming area, made Madison seem to the Department of Justice an ideal spot to launch an investigation. Therefore a federal grand jury was convened at Madison on May 4, 1936. To assist the federal district attorney, John J. Boyle, four special

<hr/>

28. 310 U. S. 195.
29. "Cummings Dodges Question on Pool Buying Under Ickes' Direction," *National Petroleum News*, XXVIII, No. 34 (August 19, 1936), 12.

assistants to the Attorney General, Hammond E. Chaffetz, John Henry Lewin, B. Watson Snyder, and Grant W. Kelleher, were assigned.

After hearing many witnesses and examining documents, the grand jury brought in a criminal indictment on July 28th against eighteen major oil companies, five subsidiaries, fifty-four officers and employees of oil companies, two officers of the Western Petroleum Refiners Association, three oil trade journals, and two editors of oil journals. The indictment included Standard of Indiana and four officials—Edward G. Seubert, President, Allan Jackson, Vice-President in charge of Sales, Edward J. Bullock, Vice-President in charge of Purchasing, and Ira H. Smith, Bullock's buyer in Tulsa. A criminal indictment was made instead of a civil charge because the government was convinced that the defendants had deliberately conspired to violate the law and they deserved severe personal punishment.

According to the indictment, the defendants had unlawfully combined and conspired beginning in February, 1935, for the purpose of artificially raising and fixing tank-car prices of gasoline in spot markets, had intentionally increased and fixed the price of gasoline sold in the Middle West, had arbitrarily extracted large sums of money from thousands of jobbers with whom they had contracts, and had intentionally raised the general level of retail prices in the Middle West in violation of the Sherman Anti-Trust Act. This had been done through the defendant companies' engaging in two concerted gasoline-buying programs, one in the East Texas field and the other in the Mid-Continent field. Standard of Indiana, however, was not charged with engaging in the buying program in East Texas.

Beginning about March 1, 1935, the *Chicago Journal of Commerce* and its oil editor, Keith Fanshier, *Platt's Oilgram,* the *National Petroleum News,* and W. C. Platt, the editor, were alleged to have intentionally and wrongfully engaged and participated in the conspiracy. It was charged that they had materially aided the other defendants by knowingly publishing the wrongfully and artificially raised fixed prices for gasoline paid by defendant major companies in the two buying programs.

On November 6th, 1936, the grand jury at Madison indicted some of the same defendants as named in the first indictment and several additional oil companies and individuals on criminal charges for fixing margins in jobber contracts.[30] Standard of Indiana, Allan Jackson, Vice-President in charge of Sales, Amos Ball, General Manager of Sales, and H. A. Lewis, Assistant General Manager of Sales, were included in the new indictment. Beginning in 1931, the indictment charged, the defendants had been engaged in an unlawful and wrongful conspiracy to regulate, fix, and make uniform the guaranteed margin to jobbers by concerted action in violation of the Sherman Anti-Trust Act. In so doing they had unlawfully eliminated, restricted, and suppressed competition among themselves in the solicitation of jobber accounts and they had regulated and restricted the ability of the jobbers to compete with them and each other. The conspiracy had been effected, beginning in 1934, according to the indictment, through various meetings usually held at the Blackstone Hotel in Chicago by representatives of the defendant companies in which they discussed and arrived at an agreement to arbitrarily fix uniform jobber margins, terms, and provisions of jobber contracts, and not to compete for jobber contracts. The meetings were usually presided over by Arnott. About December, 1934, an agreement was made by the defendants to fix the jobber margin at 5.5 cents, which was renewed in 1935 and 1936.

More than a year passed before the defendants were brought to trial. Several challenged the jurisdiction of the court on the ground that the alleged conspiracy had not been charged as having been made in Wisconsin. Others contested their removal to Madison for trial. Defendants had to be arraigned and enter pleas. Pleas of abatement were entered, claiming irregularities in the selection of the grand jury which had made the indictments. A new grand jury finally had to be selected, and new indictments, similar to the old ones, made.

Government attorneys informed the court on April 20, 1937, that they would try first the indictment relating to the buying program. The court finally set October 4th as the date for the trial to begin. With a definite trial date set, defense attorneys formed a committee to arrange for housing the defendants, for most of the important officials of the oil industry and their assistants would be coming to Madison for a lengthy stay. Hotels were booked to capacity, and private homes were leased to various companies to house their officials. William J. Donovan, chief de-

30. "Four New Companies Appear in Second Indictment," *National Petroleum News*, XXVIII, No. 46 (November 11, 1936), 17.

fense counsel, and his staff of twenty opened offices in the defunct Bank of Wisconsin Building. Many of the defendant companies also opened offices in downtown buildings. Dozens of stenographers and clerks were imported. Telephone and telegraph companies augmented their force and facilities. Extra benches were installed in the small courtroom in the Federal Building.

The long-anticipated trial opened at 10 A.M. on October 4th before Judge Patrick T. Stone. Of the fifty-six individuals indicted, forty-six, including Seubert, Jackson, Bullock, and Ira H. Smith of Standard of Indiana, were present. Six defendants were to be tried later. Four Gulf officials were still fighting removal to Madison for trial. There were eighteen major and semimajor companies, among which was Standard of Indiana, five subsidiaries, and three oil trade publications to be tried. A jury, including a gasoline retailer and two with some oil background, was quickly selected. In order that the jurors might not be prejudiced by what they read or heard, Judge Stone announced that the jurors would be locked up for the duration.

So far as Standard of Indiana was concerned, the government's evidence against it was slight. It might not have been indicted at all, except for the fact that it would have looked strange for the government to indict others and not the largest marketer in the Middle West. All of the evidence against Standard was based upon the testimony of W. J. Miller, an agent of the Federal Bureau of Investigation, Walter P. Jacobi, Charles E. Arnott, Charles J. Barkdull, Executive Vice-President of Standard of Indiana, three letters, and a memorandum.[31]

Miller testified that a survey of 1,729 jobber contracts written in 1935 by many different companies in Standard's territory showed 1,461 based on the same margin. However, it was shown that Standard from 1931 to 1936 had written only two jobber contracts, one of which was subsequently canceled, and that neither of them made any reference to trade journal prices.

As for the March 5th meeting of the Tank Car Stabilization Committee in St. Louis and the subsequent ones, Jacobi gave the names of those companies represented but did not include Standard.[32] In regard to the Mid-Continent buying program Jacobi

31. See *Transcript of Record,* United States of America vs. Standard Oil Company (Indiana) et al.

32. "East Texas (Program) Told at Madison," *National Petroleum News,* XXIX, No. 43 (October 27, 1937), 17; *Brief for New Trial at Madison,* 19-20; Madison *Capital Times,* October 22, 1937.

listed Standard of Indiana as one of the twelve companies involved, and that its "dancing partner" was the Waggoner Oil and
Refining Company. When McDowell and Tuttle were out of
town, Jacobi said he kept Barnsdall, Skelly, Pure, Standard of
Indiana, and others "posted" on the price recommendation. While
Jacobi testified that Standard was a member of the buying group,
he did not know if Standard actually bought any gasoline. He
never made any purchases for Standard or directed any purchases
that Standard made. He had not contacted Standard concerning
any purchases. The only information he had concerning Standard's
participation was that McDowell told him of talking with Ira H.
Smith, Bullock's representative in Tulsa, and Smith said that he
would have to take up the matter with his superiors. Jacobi said
that Smith attended only one meeting and had little to say. Jacobi
talked with Smith about the plan several times apart from the
meetings, but he could not remember what was said. He was sure,
however, that Smith knew all about the plan.

Chaffetz, one of the government's counsels, had difficulty in
getting Arnott to name the companies participating in the buying
programs. Arnott could not recall.[33] He was not sure. However,
he named Standard of Indiana as being in the Mid-Continent program but not in the East Texas one. As a matter of fact, Arnott
was not in a position to know from personal knowledge. He had
never attended any meetings of the Tank Car Stabilization Committee at which the program was discussed or the March 5th
meeting in St. Louis or any of the meetings at which the alleged
agreement was made regarding a buying program in the Mid-
Continent field. He did not know from a personal knowledge who
had actually agreed, if anyone, to enter the program.

From Charles J. Barkdull, Standard's Executive Vice-President,
government counsel endeavored to secure information about the
relationship of Seubert, Jackson, Bullock, and Smith to the determination of price policies and the purchase of gasoline.[34] The
particular object of these questions was to bring out that Seubert,
as President, must have been in touch with Jackson and Bullock,
and knew about these buying programs. Barkdull did not know if
Seubert had any knowledge of the company's participation in the
buying program. Furthermore, as Executive Vice-President, Bark-

33. *Brief for New Trial at Madison,* 18-19.
34. *Transcript of Record,* 4899-4965.

dull did not know of any conference in 1935 where the major company representatives sat down and conferred about prices.

There was no evidence, direct or otherwise, that Seubert ever knew of the buying program or authorized any of the acts complained of.[35] He had been a member of the Planning and Coordination Committee but was present at only one meeting—early in January, 1935—when Arnott announced that the Tank Car Stabilization Committee had been appointed. During February, Seubert was away on vacation. Arnott's testimony showed that he had had no conversation with Seubert on the subject or with any individual in the company. No one else spoke to Seubert about the buying program, and there were no letters or documents that mentioned his name or were written by him, to him, or received by him. It was apparent that the government was trying to hold him liable solely because of his position.

The government introduced three letters which implicated Standard indirectly. The first was from Neil Buckley, a representative of the East Texas Refiners Marketing Association, to H. E. Brandli of the Cities Service Export Company on January 12, 1935, in regard to the East Texas situation.[36] In one sentence Buckley referred to companies that would purchase additional gasoline and reported that Continental, Shell, and Standard of Indiana expressed a desire to wait a few days before making purchase commitments. He also spoke of a committee of Mid-Continent buyers, including Bullock, who were to meet with refiners in St. Louis. A second letter from David Gray, manager of Waggoner Oil and Refining, to Bourque dated July 10, 1935, mentioned Barnsdall, Pure, Continental, and Standard of Indiana and referred to selling to the "group." [37] Gray explained that "group" referred only to those refiners mentioned in the letter and no others. The third letter was from a man named Moore, a Chicago broker, of October 2, 1935, saying "the group informed Moore that Waggoner needed no further help."

The most damaging evidence introduced against Standard, Bullock, and Jackson was a memorandum written by A. P. Reuther of the Shell Petroleum Corporation on February 6, 1935, to the executive officials of his company in which he reported upon the

35. *Brief for New Trial at Madison,* 28-34.
36. *Ibid.,* 53.
37. "Madison Trial Nears Close: Arnott Completes Testimony," *National Petroleum News,* XXX, No. 2 (January 12, 1938), 17.

February 5th meeting in Bullock's office.[38] This memorandum showed that Bullock knew that a plan for buying was being formulated. There was no evidence, however, that having this knowledge, Bullock and the company had actually participated. The government contended that because Bullock was Vice-President in charge of Purchasing, such purchases of gasoline as the company made from Waggoner constituted participation in the program.

In regard to Jackson, there was no evidence against him other than that he was Vice-President in charge of Sales and that he was mentioned in Reuther's memorandum about being present at the February 5th meeting. In regard to Jackson's presence at the meeting, the government and defense counsel entered a stipulation to the effect that Reuther had no independent recollection of persons present at the meeting in Bullock's office; that while he did not remember the facts in the memorandum, he believed they were correct at the time he wrote them; and that since Jackson said he was not present, this raised some doubt in Reuther's mind on this point.[39] McDowell testified, however, that Jackson was not present.

Chaffetz in the closing argument for the government referred to the fact that there were no letters or documents written by or received by Standard from others concerning the conspiracy.[40] His remarks were apparently made to arouse some sort of suspicion and have the jury believe that Standard's letters and documents had been destroyed. While it was true that there were no documents or letters in Standard's file, it was also true that there were no questionable letters or documents written by or to the company in the files of any of the other defendants. In answer to the government's subpoena, the company had sent some ninety-eight large boxes of documents and letters to Madison for the grand jury investigation. Even after examining these, the government could not find any incriminating evidence.

The government rested its case against the defendants on November 11, 1937. Motions by the government to dismiss the indictments against the *National Petroleum News*, *Platt's Oilgram*, the *Chicago Journal of Commerce*, W. C. Platt, Keith Fanshier, and four oil companies were granted. Between November 12th and 16th arguments were heard on defense motions to direct a

38. *Brief for New Trial at Madison*, Appendix 2, Exhibit 177.
39. *Ibid.*, 35-40, Appendix 3-18.
40. *Ibid.*, 21-22.

verdict of dismissal for all defendants. Judge Stone granted the
motions to dismiss the charges against the Gulf Oil Corporation,
Gulf Refining, The Texas Company, four Texas officials, Ira H.
Smith of Standard, and several officials of the Tidewater Associated
Oil, but motions for all the rest were denied.

Attorneys for the defense began their presentation on November 29th.[41] While many of the defendants admitted their participation in the Mid-Continent buying program, Standard refused
to admit this fact. In his testimony regarding the February 5th
meeting of the Tank Car Stabilization Committee, McDowell
testified about the decided opposition of Bullock and Karstedt to
the adoption of any buying program.[42] With such an attitude
on the part of Bullock and with no testimony to the contrary, the
defense position was that it was doubtful if he agreed to any buying
program.[43] The government claimed that the agreement complained of was made on March 5, 1935, but Bullock was not even
at the meeting. He did not attend any meetings of the committee
after February 11th and there were twelve of them between
March 5, 1935, and February 27, 1936. While Bullock knew on
February 5th about the plan for buying, there was no evidence
that having this knowledge, Bullock and the company participated.

Although the government contended that the Waggoner Oil and
Refining Company was Standard's "dancing partner" in the Mid-
Continent buying program, Standard offered the testimony of
David G. Gray, manager of Waggoner's, to show that it had purchased gasoline in November, 1934, and in January and February,
1935, when no buying program of any kind was in progress.[44]
After the calling of the federal grand jury in Madison, many of
the companies ceased buying. However, Standard continued to buy
from Waggoner as usual and was still buying at the time of the
trial. Gray testified that he never attended any meeting in 1935;
that he had never seen McDowell, Jacobi, or Tuttle; and that no
one told him that any company or companies would buy his gasoline or for what prices he should sell his gasoline. Gray knew that
the majors were purchasing "distress" gasoline from independent
refiners, but he never considered that his company was a part of
the program because it did not have any "distress" gasoline to
sell. Standard contended that it purchased alone and for reasons

41. See *Transcript of Record.*
42. *Ibid.,* 8218-20.
43. *Brief for New Trial at Madison,* 42-48.
44. *Ibid.,* 10339-10341.

of its own. It was not connected with any concerted buying program, and Waggoner was not its "dancing partner."

Lengthy testimony was given by John C. Marshall, assistant to the General Manager of Sales for Standard, principally upon the background and factors leading to Standard's change in price policy on September 11, 1934.[45] Marshall brought out the fact that the company's new price policy was not something new or sudden or the result of concerted action, because the Sales Department had agitated the idea as far back as 1925. It had been adopted months before the alleged conspiracy, and hence it had nothing to do with the buying program. Furthermore, Standard had no jobber contracts so it had nothing to gain by rigging the market.

After offering 1,000 exhibits and the testimony of sixty witnesses, both the defense and prosecution rested their case on January 14, 1938. Motions were made to dismiss the indictment against Standard, Seubert, Jackson, Bullock, and other defendants. Since the trial had lasted nearly four months, Judge Stone felt that it was unfair to keep the jury sequestered while each of these motions secured a full and fair consideration. Hence, he decided to let the case go to the jury and after the verdict exercise, if necessary, the discretion of the court to prevent any miscarriage of justice.

After the closing arguments on the 21st Judge Stone charged the jury, and it filed out at 1:33 P.M. for its deliberation. At 9:30 A.M. the next morning, the jury informed the bailiff that it had reached a verdict. Court officials, defendants, lawyers, and others quickly gathered. At 10:25 the jury filed in. Judge Stone was handed a sheaf of slips, one for each defendant. As he read the name of each defendant from the slip, he announced: "Guilty as charged." [46] Defense counsel immediately asked to enter motions to set aside the verdict, for a retrial, and for an arrest of judgment, all of which was granted. By 10:45 one of the most famous trials was over and within a few hours Madison, which had been the temporary oil capital of the world for 111 days, was practically empty of oilmen.

Shortly after the end of the trial, the government made preparations to try the case arising out of the second indictment for fixing margins in jobber contracts. However, negotiations for a

45. *Transcript of Record*, 8457-8567.
46. *The Chicago Daily News*, January 22, 1938; Chicago *Herald and Examiner*, January 22, 1938; *The Chicago Tribune*, January 23, 1938.

settlement got under way in New York on April 24, 1938, at a conference between Judge Stone, Donovan, Chaffetz, Lewin, and a committee of the defendants.[47] The government indicated that it was willing that the first case should proceed on its own merits, including an appeal to the United States Supreme Court. Furthermore, it was willing to settle the second case provided that all defendant companies and each head of their marketing divisions would plead *nolo contendere* and each company and each individual pay a fine of $5,000 on each of the three counts. This would not include The Texas Company or Gulf, for the government was determined to prosecute them individually.

Standard officials were advised of the offer early on the 25th by Weymouth Kirkland, their attorney, who was in New York. Kirkland wanted to know by 11:30 A.M. the company's position and the name of the official who would enter the plea. At 9:30 the Directors met, and Stephens presented the situation.[48] At the conclusion of his statement and a discussion of the matter, Amos Ball, General Manager of Sales, stated that after conferring with his three sons, who were lawyers, he would make the plea if necessary. Jackson expressed a desire to consult at least one individual in the city before making a decision. He said that he had gone through a great deal to make his name as good as his bond; that to make a plea of *nolo contendere* would be a tacit admission of guilt to violating the antitrust laws of the United States, which he had not done; and that, if necessary, he would rather go to jail upon conviction than plead guilty. At 11:00 A.M. Stephens pointed out the necessity for action before 12 o'clock noon. Jackson agreed to let him know within forty-five minutes. After conferring with a friend and being advised to follow the position taken by Ball, Jackson reported his willingness to make the plea. About 2 P.M. Stephens called Jackson, Ball, and B. T. Thompson to his office and said that word from Kirkland in New York indicated that Chaffetz and Lewin insisted that Ball make the plea for Standard, which was something of a shock to Ball. Before the plea was entered, the Directors voted to indemnify any of the individual defendants for any sums paid by them as fines, costs, or other expense, direct or indirect, which might be incurred in connection with both indictments.[49]

47. "25 at Madison To Plead Nolo In Second Case," *National Petroleum News*, XXX, No. 22 (June 1, 1938), 17.
48. Memorandum written by Allan Jackson, April 25, 1938.
49. Minutes of the Board of Directors' and Stockholders' Meetings, V, 2792.

On June 2, 1938, Judge Stone accepted *nolo contendere* pleas on the "jobber contract" indictment from eleven individuals and thirteen companies.[50] Eight individuals and eight companies refused to plead *nolo contendere*. Charges against Jackson and H. A. Lewis of Standard and twenty-five other individuals who were officials of the thirteen companies were dismissed. Fines totaling $360,000 plus $25,000 in costs were levied. It was believed to be the largest fine ever levied under the Sherman Anti-Trust Act. Standard paid $15,000 for the company and $15,000 for Ball.

After studying 12,000 pages of testimony and 1,000 exhibits, Judge Stone ruled on July 19, 1938, on the motions for a new trial for the defendants convicted on January 22, 1938, on the buying program indictment.[51] According to Judge Stone, the convincing force of much of the testimony related in varying degrees to different defendants. Since there was no substantial evidence to sustain the guilty verdict in the case of ten defendants, including Seubert and Jackson, Judge Stone set it aside and dismissed the indictment. Since direct evidence of participation was lacking or slight and the circumstantial evidence viewed as a whole possibly obscured other facts and circumstances shown, in some cases, to be highly suggestive of innocence, Judge Stone set aside the verdict and ordered new trials for fifteen individuals including Bullock and three companies, including Standard of Indiana. All motions were denied in the case of twelve companies and five individuals, and sentences were imposed. These companies and individuals appealed the decision.[52] The government also took exception to Stone's dismissal of the indictment against eleven of the defendants.[53]

Shortly after the Supreme Court in 1939 and 1940 upheld Judge Stone in the two cases on appeal, the government indicated that it was willing to accept *nolo contendere* pleas from Standard, Bullock, and the other sixteen defendants who had been granted new trials. All things considered, it seemed advisable for Standard and Bullock to enter such a plea.[54] If they stood trial and were convicted, jobbers, who had already filed triple damage suits against Standard and the twelve companies found guilty in the

50. "Brief Hearing Wipes Slate for 54 Madison Defendants," *National Petroleum News*, XXX, No. 23 (June 8, 1938), 5.
51. 23 F. Supp. 938.
52. 105 F. (2d) 809; 310 U. S. 150-267.
53. 101 F. (2d) 870; 84 Law. Ed. 441.
54. Memorandum from Buell F. Jones to Edward G. Seubert, May 9, 1940.

buying program, could under the Sherman Anti-Trust Act introduce the judgment as conclusive proof of violation of the Act and might collect damages running into thousands of dollars. If there was no trial and conviction, the jobbers would be compelled to prove conspiracy, which would not be easy to do.

The last chapter in the Madison case was written on June 2, 1941, when seven of the remaining defendants scheduled to stand retrial pleaded *nolo contendere*.[55] Standard paid a $5,000 fine, the same amount as Judge Stone fined the companies originally convicted. Bullock paid a fine of $2,500. After five years of litigation and an expenditure of more than $500,000 in attorney fees and fines, to say nothing of the time consumed on the part of executive officers and others, the Madison case so far as Standard was concerned came to an end, with no convictions but two *nolo contendere* pleas.

55. "Last Chapter Finally Written in Madison's Anti Trust Case," *National Petroleum News*, XXXIII, No. 23 (June 4, 1941), 5.

CHAPTER XIX

A Revival of Business

FROM 1935 UNTIL THE LAST QUARTER OF 1937, CONDITIONS WITHIN the petroleum industry steadily improved and there was evidence of more prosperous times. The NIRA, the Oil Code, the Connally Act, and the Interstate Oil Compact were of definite assistance in bringing about a sound and constructive restriction of production at the wells, which resulted in a better price structure and financial returns. Voluntary efforts to stabilize the industry continued to be effective even after the NIRA was declared unconstitutional. The East Texas field declined as a market factor and "hot" oil from there grew less and less important. Crude oil prices held steadier than they had for a number of years. With few new pools yielding high-gravity crude, more and more refiners turned to cracking and producing 63–67 octane gasoline. By the spring of 1937 third-grade gasoline seemed to be on the way out.

Equally important as a factor in the recovery of the petroleum industry was the increase in consumption. The demand for petroleum products increased 7 per cent in 1935, 11 per cent in 1936, and 9.5 per cent in 1937. With automobile traffic increasing, a larger market for gasoline developed; the demand increased 6 per cent in 1935, about 11 per cent in 1936, and 8 per cent in 1937. The growth in the use of fuel oil for diesel engines and heating had become an item of first importance to the petroleum industry. The largest single use of fuel oil was for heating.[1] In 1935 over 150,000 oil burners for domestic heating were sold, a new high record. Oil heat for homes had received wide public acceptance, the market loomed large, and brought into active play competition for fuel oil business. In 1937 over 100,000,000 barrels of fuel oil were consumed. Its manufacture had become a major item in refinery operation. All this tended to utilize the big excess in refining capacity which prevailed during the depression.

The general improvement in business conditions reflected itself

1. G. Harvey Porter, "Million Oil Burning Homes Consume Over 50,000,000 Bbls. Annually," *The Oil and Gas Journal* (December 26, 1935), 57.

in the scramble among oil companies in the Middle West for a share in the new prosperity. One of the significant developments was the further extension of gasoline pipelines into the heart of Standard's marketing territory. In 1936 Socony-Vacuum constructed a line from its refinery at Augusta, Kansas, to Kansas City. The Champlin Refining Company built a line from Enid, Oklahoma, to Superior, Nebraska, which was later extended to Rock Rapids, Iowa. The Shell Pipe Line Company built a line in 1938 from its refinery at Roxana (St. Louis) to Terre Haute, Indianapolis, and Lima, Ohio, where it connected with that of the Standard of Ohio to Toledo.

Another striking development in cutting transportation costs was the beginning of oil shipments on the upper Mississippi River. The Western Oil and Fuel Company of Minneapolis, organized in 1926, was one of the first to use the waters of the upper Mississippi.[2] By 1935 Shell was doing considerable shipping from Wood River to Minneapolis over the Federal Barge Line. The next year Socony-Vacuum completed water terminals at Kansas City and St. Paul. It was the first oil company to make Kansas City a focal point for the distribution of its products with its own equipment on the Missouri River.[3] In September, 1937, its first towboat and barges left Kansas City via the Missouri and Mississippi Rivers for St. Paul. At Minneapolis, Western had storage facilities for 2,750,000 gallons. Shell's terminal, eleven miles below St. Paul, had a capacity of 610,000 barrels and was the largest river terminal in the country for shallow-draft vessels. Socony's terminal had a capacity for 167,000 barrels. It completed water terminals at Bettendorf, Iowa, on the Mississippi in April, 1938, and at Omaha in June, 1939. Deep Rock also had a marine terminal location at Bettendorf. The Stang Engineering Company located one at Burlington, Iowa, in 1938 and the Petroleum Distributors, Inc., one at Fulton, Illinois, in 1939.

As marine terminals and gasoline pipelines increased, truck transportation supplemented the development of low-cost transportation. Trucks hauled gasoline direct from the refineries to service stations in many places and hauled more and more gasoline direct from marine and products pipeline terminals to service stations. With the growth in the exchange of products between

2. M. G. Van Voorhis, "Oil Movement Expanding On Inland Waterways," *National Petroleum News*, XXX, No. 45 (November 9, 1938), 63, 66-67, 70.
3. "Barging Gasoline on Missouri," *National Petroleum News*, XXIX, No. 40 (October 6, 1937), 36, 38, 40.

companies, long rail hauls were reduced and short hauls by trucks became more important. Speed, low-cost operation, and flexibility made trucking a highly desirable mode of transportation.

One of the greatest threats to its business that Standard met head on was the attempt by Standard of New Jersey to gain the benefit of the Standard Oil name and reputation for its marketing operations in the Middle West. Aroused by the nationwide distribution which Shell, The Texas Company, Sinclair, and others had developed, Standard of New Jersey made plans for the use of a single trade-mark and trade name for marketing on a national scale. As early as 1928, unknown to Standard of Indiana, the Jersey company registered the trade-mark "Esso," meaning "S O," in Missouri. Later, it registered "Esso" in all states of the union where it was not already marketing. As early as 1931 Standard of Indiana informed Standard of New Jersey that it would object to any use of the word "Esso" in any of the marketing territory of Standard of Indiana because in the states comprising that territory the latter owned the right to the exclusive use not only of the Standard Oil name but any words connoting that name.[4] Any use of "Esso" would be a violation of those rights and would not be tolerated. In 1932 Esso, Inc., a marketing subsidiary, was organized by Standard of New Jersey. More and more prominence was given to the word "Esso" in the operations of its service stations and in the identification of its products in its old marketing territory. Its principal grade of gasoline, for example, was "Essoline," and "Essolube" was one of its grades of motor oil.

Through Esso, Inc., Standard of New Jersey opened in St. Louis on April 16, 1935, three "Esso" service stations, the first to be opened in the marketing territory of Standard of Indiana. This invasion was interpreted by some in the trade to be in retaliation for the invasion of Jersey's territory by Pan American, a subsidiary of Standard of Indiana. Although Standard of Indiana had not been backward about its subsidiaries' invading Jersey's territory, it had used company and brand names in no way indicative of any connection with Standard Oil. The spearhead of the thrust had been the American Oil Company with its "Amoco" products.

Newspapers in St. Louis carried large advertisements in bold type announcing the opening of the Esso stations and explaining that the products were not from the refineries of Standard of Indiana, although some of the products sold included several of

4. *Transcript of Record*, I, 53.

the same trade names that it used.[5] Very prominently printed at the top of the advertisement were the words: "Not connected with the Standard Oil Company (Indiana)." In large type at the bottom were the words: "Please note that the Standard Oil Co. (Indiana) has no connection with Esso Stations or Esso, Inc." However, red, white, and blue were used on the stations, equipment, and merchandise, the same colors used by Standard of Indiana for identification.

Standard of Indiana promptly objected to the action of Esso, Inc., but the protests were unheeded. Consequently, it filed suit in May, 1935, against the Standard Oil Company (New Jersey), the Standard Oil Company of New Jersey, Esso, Inc., and Esso employees, Hugh Scott and Francis Sheevran, in the Eastern Judicial District of Missouri at St. Louis.[6] The complaint in the suit charged trade-mark infringement and unfair competition, and asked for an injunction to restrain the companies from using the "Esso" name or any other name meaning "Standard" not only in Missouri but in all of the marketing territory of Standard of Indiana. The complaint, bristling with ugly words like "fraud," stated that for about forty years prior to the appearance of Esso in St. Louis, Standard of Indiana had sold its products in the Middle West under the names and abbreviations "Standard Oil Company," "Standard Oil," "Standard," "S O," and others. Millions of dollars had been spent on advertising these products to identify them as products of Standard of Indiana. It pointed out that the term "Esso" was merely the spelled-out form of S O; that the letters S O whether spelled out "Esso" or written as the letters "S O" were identical in sound and meaning; and that they were the initials of the plaintiff's trade-mark, "Standard Oil." Standard of Indiana claimed that Esso's trade-mark registration had been fraudulently obtained and demanded cancellation. It also asked that Esso be enjoined from using the colors red and white or red, white, and blue on service stations in its territory. Subsequent pleadings brought the action to a case between Standard of Indiana and Esso, Inc.

With the filing of this suit, the gong sounded for the opening round in what was considered to be one of the most interesting industrial scraps between two of the biggest Standard companies.

5. *Ibid.*
6. "Standard Companies on Suit Over Use of 'Esso,'" *The Oil and Gas Journal* (May 23, 1935), 29.

The suit was without precedent among Standard units. The case for Standard of Indiana rested chiefly upon the fact that since 1911 in the territory where it marketed under the name Standard Oil Company, the various Standard Oil companies had had the exclusive use of one or more of the Standard trade-marks or abbreviations or variations thereof. Each of the Standard companies had acquired in its own territory the common-law rights in the trade-marks used by it in these states. Each had recognized the rights of the others to use the trade-marks exclusively in their own respective areas. Each competed with others outside these areas but under names and trade-marks which did not include or mean "Standard" or similar words. Standard of Indiana asserted that in using "Esso" the Standard of New Jersey was deceiving the public and profiting from the long-established reputation and good will of Standard of Indiana.

In July, 1937, Judge George H. Moore rendered an opinion in which he held that Standard of Indiana was entitled to the exclusive use of the Standard trade-marks and names in its marketing territory.[7] The use of "Esso" infringed its rights in the states where it operated and constituted unfair competition. He issued a sweeping injunction against Esso, Inc., perpetually restraining it from using in Indiana Standard's marketing territory of fourteen states the term "Esso" alone or in combination with other names, terms, letters, marks, symbols and syllables, from using any of Indiana Standard's trade-marks or names or any symbol, similar in sound, appearance and meaning, from selling and advertising any product of a nature similar to the products of Indiana Standard under any name or mark indicating that it was the product of the Standard Oil Company, and from committing any act calculated to cause confusion or to infringe or injure the rights of Standard of Indiana, its trade-marks and good will, and from otherwise competing unfairly. The court decreed that Standard of Indiana might recover from Esso all profits and gains which Esso had derived from its acts as well as all damages suffered by Standard. For this purpose the court appointed a special master to ascertain the amount due and report.

Esso appealed the decision. However, in 1938 the U.S. Circuit Court of Appeals at St. Paul upheld the decision in favor of Standard of Indiana.[8] There was an abundance of evidence, according

7. *Transcript of Record,* I, 39-69.
8. 98 F. (2d) 1.

to the higher court, to sustain the trial court decision. The long three-year fight finally ended on September 6th when Esso withdrew its intention of appeal to the United States Supreme Court, and the decree was made final. After Indiana Standard's victory, it waived any claim to profits and damages, and the case came to an end.

Moving vigorously, Standard took steps with the return of better times to increase the volume of its business in different ways. In competing with nationwide marketers, like The Texas Company, Sinclair, Socony-Vacuum, and Shell, Standard had been at a disadvantage because its marketing area was limited to the states of the Middle West. Numerous industrial firms, like Ford, Coca Cola, and others, having plants in different parts of the country, preferred to make contracts, centralize their purchase of petroleum products in their general office, secure volume prices, and facilitate the handling of accounts. Those oil companies with national distribution could and did offer contracts allowing a buyer to aggregate all gallonage purchased for the purpose of securing a maximum discount. In December, 1934, Standard of New Jersey advised Standard of Indiana that it was interested in making connections with certain oil companies whereby it might be in a position to offer contracts covering a large area. As a result of a further exploration of the subject with the Jersey company and others, Standard of Indiana entered into an agreement with Standard of New Jersey, Pennsylvania, Louisiana, Ohio, and the Colonial Beacon Oil Company whereby each might solicit contracts on tank-wagon deliveries of premium and regular gasoline over the entire area covered by the contracting companies, and offer discounts upon the aggregate gallonage. As a result, Standard secured fifteen or twenty contracts but business did not develop to the extent anticipated, for many national accounts still allowed branch offices to make their own contracts. Consequently, it was never successful so far as Standard of Indiana was concerned.

In the summer of 1935 Standard opened at the General Office in Chicago a completely organized and equipped service unit known as the Standard Oil Touring Bureau to assist patrons planning trips of any length anywhere. That fall Standard started a new series of radio programs featuring Jack Hylton and "The Band that Jack Built" each Sunday evening over a Midwest network of nineteen stations of CBS. When Standard decided to bring Hylton and his English musical troupe to the United States, they were unknown to the general public. After the first broadcast, the fan mail was enormous. Alec Templeton, noted blind pianist with the troupe, made an instant hit with the American public.

To meet competition, reduce marketing costs, and increase sales, the company made a radical change in its marketing policy in 1935. It began leasing out its company-owned and operated service stations. The change was dictated by two important considerations. First, for some time the growth in the number of service stations and the declining sales per station had been apparent. In 1929 there were 123,513 service stations and 195,719 secondary outlets—garages, repair shops, auto dealers, general stores—making a total of 317,252 outlets in the United States. In 1935 there were 377,000. The growth in these years was not so much in the number of secondary outlets as in drive-in service stations, which numbered 226,000 in 1936. As a result of overexpansion, the sales per station had appreciably declined. The decrease was made considerably more painful by the fact that, in order to meet competition, the physical facilities and the service rendered by service stations had been remarkably improved through the years. Secondly, the change was primarily due to the growth of anti-chain store tax laws during the depression. The oil companies were not affected at first, but some of the leading marketers anxiously watched developments because the gasoline service-station chain system was the fastest-growing organization among chains in the United States.[9] Indiana was the first state to pass a chain-store tax that included oil company service stations. It enacted a graduated chain-store tax in 1929. In 1933 the fee was increased to $150 per station for chains with twenty or more units, effective in 1934.

Owing to changes in the character of neighborhoods, highway rerouting, and other factors, many of Standard's service stations had become unprofitable by 1930. Although unprofitable for the company to operate, a profit could still be made by lessee dealers who were not handicapped by compliance with union regulations on wages and hours. In 1930 Standard leased 128 stations, all but nine of which were in the Rocky Mountain division.[10] By the end of 1931 the company had leased out 322, of which 123 were in the Rocky Mountain region. With the passage of the chain-store tax by the State of Indiana, Standard announced in January,

9. "Service Station Chains Make Greatest Growth," *The Oil and Gas Journal* (January 1, 1931), 122.
10. Company Encyclopedia: Marketing, I, Leasing Out Service Stations, 90-91.

1934, that it would discontinue the operation of 800 low-gallonage service stations.[11] The stations chiefly affected were those leased from individuals and operated by the company's agents. Some of the company's own stations were also closed, and it prepared to close others as soon as arrangements could be made to dispose of the properties. This drastic action meant a serious loss in wages, employment, and business, for the company was doing 20 to 25 per cent of the total gasoline gallonage in Indiana. When Colorado passed a graduated chain-store tax in November, 1934, the Continental Oil Company, The Texas Company, Standard of Indiana, and others began leasing out their stations in that area.

The most punitive anti-chain store tax was introduced in the Iowa legislature in January, 1935. Backed by the Independent Retailers Association of Iowa, two thousand merchants from all over the state packed the House chamber at the hearings on the Harrington-Burington chain-store tax bill in March and applauded their spokesmen as speaker after speaker attacked the giant monopolies.[12] Only one representative appeared to defend the chain stores. The major oil companies apparently made little or no effort to have their service stations exempted in the bill. "It seemed to me," declared one member of the state legislature, "that the majors knew what was going on but didn't give a damn."[13] At a subsequent hearing, a spokesman for the Iowa Independent Oil Dealers appeared and urged that oil company service stations be exempted. All through April, during the debate on the bill, the galleries of both the Senate and House were packed with supporters. As passed on April 25th, the bill provided a graduated tax up to $155 per store per year for over fifty units. Firms with more than one store were to pay a tax on total gross receipts which amounted to $25 on the first $50,000 with a graduated levy up to 10 per cent on annual receipts of $1,000,000 and over. It was the most drastic and highest chain-store tax in the nation. The governor signed the bill on April 29th, and the law became effective July 1st.

Immediately after the passage of the law, hundreds of oil and gas company employees from all over the state, fearing the loss of their jobs, moved on Des Moines by special trains, buses, and

---

11. *The Oil and Gas Journal* (January 25, 1934), 32.
12. *The Des Moines Register,* March 19, 20, 1935; Harry E. Wormhandt, "How The Iowa Plan Started," *National Petroleum News,* XXVIII, No. 44 (October 28, 1936), 36-40.
13. *National Petroleum News,* XXVIII (November 18, 1936), 28.

cars to urge that oil stations be exempted.[14] The crowd, estimated at 6,000, was the largest ever to descend upon an Iowa legislature. Only a relatively small number gained admittance to the legislature chambers while the rest milled about the State House. Despite the pressure brought to bear, both legislative houses refused to suspend their rules and permit a consideration of a bill to exempt oil service stations.

Owing to a highly competitive marketing situation, many service stations in Iowa had not been earning more than their operating expenses for several years. In a number of cases, large companies had kept these stations open simply to serve customers, much as the railroads had done with their branch lines. With the passage of the chain-store tax, it was impossible for Standard or others to operate these stations and be assured of even a small profit. Confronted by this situation, Standard announced that it would withdraw completely from direct retail distribution in Iowa and lease out about three hundred company-owned and controlled service stations.[15] Bulk stations doing a wholesale business would continue to operate as usual. The decision represented a particularly revolutionary change in marketing policy, for Standard more than any other company had been for years the leading exponent of company-owned and controlled service stations.

The effect of such a policy meant dropping about eight hundred men from the company station payroll and a proportionate number of administrative employees by July 1st.[16] So far as possible the managers of company stations were given the first opportunity to lease and operate the stations as dealers, and efforts were made to get them to retain their assistants. These were experienced men who had learned the value of company policies on cleanliness, courtesy and good service. Of the servicemen laid off, about 40 per cent became dealers operating on a lease basis, about 30 per cent got jobs with the dealers, and the rest were out. An unfortunate aspect of the situation was the fact that all employees dropped lost the benefit of the company annuity plan, death benefits plan, and the stock purchase plan.

Rentals of the stations were based upon the previous gallonage of gasoline and motor oil, investment, taxes, maintenance and depreciation, equipment, and the value of other business done,

14. *The Des Moines Register*, May 1, 1935.
15. *The Oil and Gas Journal* (May 30, 1935), 38.
16. "Iowa Tax Forces 800 Standard Oil Employees Out of Jobs," *Stanolind Record*, XVI, No. 9 (July, 1935), 1-3.

such as the sale of tires, lubrication, and car washing.[17] With rentals to be set, lessees to be found, and leases signed for approximately three hundred stations within sixty days, some mistakes in rental values occurred but rectifications were subsequently made. Many lessees were not financially able to pay for the stock in a station, so Standard made loans which were generally secured by mortgages, notes guaranteed by others, Standard stock, or some other good security.

STANDARD'S LOANS TO DEALERS AND DISTRIBUTORS
1931–1938

	Number of Loans	Amount
1931	1	$ 10,000.00
1932	1	13,000.00
1933	2	24,000.00
1934	1	11,000.00
1935	3	29,826.31
1936	1190	842,963.14
1937	293	397,316.61
1938	262	427,982.81

Every effort was made to eliminate everything that might be used against the company to indicate control or supervision over the leased stations. Signs reading "Standard Oil Company" were replaced with those reading "Standard Service" or "Standard Oil Products" to indicate that the company's products were being sold by the dealer. In most instances, lessees put up a sign with their names as the operators. The real estate leases contained no requirement that a lessee should stock and sell Standard products. They specifically stated that none of the provisions should be construed as reserving to the lessor any right to exercise any control or supervision over the lessee's business. The lessee was specifically told that he was an independent merchant operating his own business. He was free to set his own prices, charge whatever he wished for wash and grease jobs, handle any brand of products, set his own hours, fix wages for his help, set his own standards of service, and make whatever profit he could.

The growth of workmen's compensation taxes, the adoption of the Social Security Act, the passage of minimum pay and maximum hour laws, unionization activities, increased cost of annuities, the moderate success of the Iowa experiment, the continued losses

17. Company Encyclopedia: Marketing, I, Distribution Through Service Stations, Leasing Out, 92-93.

in sales due to cut prices and high guaranteed dealers' margins, and the threat of chain-store taxes in other states led Standard to extend in January, 1936, the Iowa plan to every state within its marketing territory.[18] By September 95 per cent of its stations had been leased, and Standard had discontinued posting the service-station price in seven states. Only the company's price to dealers was posted. The dealer fixed his own selling price and margin of profit in competition with other retailers. On March 1, 1937, no service stations remained under company control. Many other large integrated companies, in the meantime, had adopted the Iowa plan.[19]

Standard's original leases were for six months with a provision for renewal on a six-month basis, except in Iowa, St. Paul, and Minneapolis, where they were for one year.[20] The extension of the usual lease period to one year came later. Leases might be canceled by either party on ten days' notice prior to the expira-tion of the original term or six-month renewal period. As in the Iowa leases, rentals were based upon the business value of the location and the ability of the station to pay. Except for Iowa and Colorado, where there was a straight cash rental basis, a cash and gallonage rental basis was used, which seemed fairer. In contrast with many companies, Standard had nothing in its contracts, in-side or outside of Iowa, requiring the lessee to handle its products or establishing any control over retail prices.

Although the Directors of Standard did not adopt a resolution thanking the Iowa legislature for showing the company the way to better management of its stations and profits, Seubert was heard to comment that the Iowa experiment had proved to be a decided blessing. It enabled the company to save money on low-gallonage outlets, increase volume through a more flexible price policy, escape the responsibility for setting dealer margins, and avoid criticism for subsidizing unprofitable marketing operations. In brief, the Iowa plan meant the substitution of a method of market-ing less expensive, burdensome, and vulnerable than through

18. "Who Will Operate the Filling Stations," The Oil and Gas Journal (April 23, 1936), 11.

19. T. F. Smiley, "Iowa Plan of Leasing Filling Stations Is Spreading to Many Other Areas," The Oil and Gas Journal (June 25, 1936), 33; T. F. Smiley, "Sta-tions Going Into Dealers' Hands Fast," The Oil and Gas Journal (July 23, 1936), 21; T. F. Smiley, "Company-Controlled Station Is Vanishing Under Iowa Plan," The Oil and Gas Journal (January 14, 1937), 26.

20. Company Encyclopedia: Marketing, I, Distribution Through Service Stations, Leasing Out, 95-98.

company-owned and operated service stations. In theory, the plan stimulated the interest of the dealer in building up sales, for it was his own business. It permitted him to be more competitive since he set his own price. One of the immediate results was a marked increase in the sale of gasoline because station operators made an effort to hold old customers and gain new ones.[21] On the other hand, there was a reduction in the sales of motor oils, tires, and accessories. Formerly, station operators had been given a sales quota on these products, and they were under constant pressure from company supervisors to sell. Freed from this influence, operators tended to neglect the sale of these products and concentrate upon gasoline. In general, however, the company's sales did not suffer, and the quantity of products distributed to the same stations appreciably increased.

Several problems arose in operating service stations under the Iowa plan.[22] First, there was a gradual deterioration in station appearance and cleanliness. Cars were parked in the driveways. Equipment was not kept in good order. Tourists began to complain. This aspect was particularly disturbing to the company because over a long period of years it had established a tradition for service and a high standard in service-station maintenance. Consequently, the company began holding regular educational meetings for dealers and issuing manuals to assist in improving the service, the appearance of the stations, and increasing sales. In the second place, there was at the outset a great deal of speculation over whether operators would handle competitive products, for the company had no control, written or understood, over the station, and the lessee was free to operate as he chose. However, the company hoped that the lessee would sell its products. In some cases, the lessee did not sell Standard products, and in these instances the company removed all signs and evidence of its identification.

Probably the most serious problem arose from the fact that under the Iowa plan dealers were free to set their own retail prices, determine their margin of profit, and meet competition in whatever way they could. If an operator decided to cut his margin of profit or sell at a loss in an attempt to meet competition, it was money out of his pocket not the company's. There was evidence of

21. "Iowa Leased Service Stations, 1936."
22. Company Encyclopedia: Marketing, I, Distribution Through Service Stations, Leasing Out, 95-100.

a considerable secret discounting, especially to truckers. Some offered free wash jobs, free lunches, and other inducements to increase gallonage. At many points dealers, not being able to hold their own, cut prices hoping to make up the difference in volume. Such practices were a threat to price stability and continued profits. To act as a stabilizing influence upon the retail market and to maintain uniform service station practices, many dealers' associations were organized at the local level.

To teach dealers the fine points of salesmanship, Standard decided to disregard past methods, borrow Hollywood's techniques, and use a brand-new approach—a commercial movie that would combine showmanship and Standard service. Written by Charles A. Logue and filmed in RKO's studios in Hollywood, the movie entitled *It's Up To You* was a mixture of love, melodrama, comedy, and common sense. Centering around "Pop" Kane's service station, the five-reel sound film with Edgar Kennedy in the stellar role of a serviceman, told the story of a home-town boy who wanted to win first prize in Standard's sales contest. To do so, "Pop" Kane had to teach his "slightly dumb" serviceman driveway selling. Beginning in the spring of 1936, the film was sent on tour, shown to 13,000 salesmen and employees and 31,000 dealers and station attendants within thirty days. Salesmen and servicemen were quick to detect "boners" in selling, and they gained a new conception of the character and importance of their jobs. The movie was definitely a pioneering effort of a successful character in the sales fields. It was the forerunner of a new type of sales training. The film attracted nationwide attention and made not only Big Business but movie critics sit up and take notice.

Standard launched an extensive and unusual gasoline advertising campaign in the spring of 1936. Seven hundred prizes, ranging from $10 to $1,000 in cash and five hundred articles of merchandise, were offered to motorists in return for data presented in the "World's Greatest Road Test." The purpose was to debunk, once and for all, fables regarding miles per gallon and secure information about average driving under average conditions. Each contestant who entered was required to drive at least five hundred miles between May 1st and September 18th and keep a record of the amount of gasoline used. Contestants were not required to use Standard's products, but they were required to make a record of the brand used in the test period. At the end of the contest they were to submit their records together with a seventy-five-word statement on "What I Have Discovered About Gasoline Mileage." Newspaper advertisements kept the story before the public all summer. One feature was the publication of "goofy testimonials" by fictitious persons poking fun at long-mileage claims often made for gasolines. This was a part of the debunking process. When the contest closed on September 18th, 1,200,000 motorists had entered it. While the contest was worth while from an advertising point of view, the recording of mileage data in record books involved more time than the average motorist cared to take and, as a result, the return of the completed record books did not meet the company's expectations.

By 1936 practically every oil company was offering one or more grades of motor oil in one- and five-quart cans either at the same price as in bulk or at a higher price. Owing to pressure from Standard's sales organization, its dealers, and the general public, the company started offering Iso-Vis in 1936 in refinery-sealed cans at 30 cents a quart, which was 5 cents higher than in bulk.[23] At first there was a considerable rush of business on canned oil. Sales representatives promoted it aggressively. After the first enthusiasm had worn off, there was no great demand and no great volume of sales. Up to the beginning of 1939, the annual sales of canned Iso-Vis did not exceed 4 per cent of the total reseller motor sales. The company added two-gallon cans of Stanolind in 1939 and ten-quart cans of Polarine in 1940 because of competitive practices.

Many new and improved products were also responsible for the increase of the company's business. To capitalize upon the growth in the number of diesel engines, Stanolind High Speed diesel fuel was introduced in 1935. Shipments from Whiting increased from 23,000 gallons a month late in 1935 to approximately 282,000 gallons per month in 1938.[24] After high-speed diesels began to appear, research work showed that a paraffin-base type of lubricant was unsatisfactory, for it tended to accelerate ring sticking and produce increased amounts of carbon. Oils made from coastal or naphthenic types of crude were better. It was also found that fatty acids or similar additive agents had to be eliminated from lubricating oils because "hard metal" bearings easily corroded. This led to a study of some two hundred and fifty different chemical compounds in an attempt to find a noncorrosive additive

23. Company Encyclopedia: Marketing, I, Method of Distribution, Packaging of Motor Oil, 52-54.
24. Company Encyclopedia: Manufacturing, I, Diesel Fuel and Lubricants, 1-6.

agent. Tributylphosphite was found to be satisfactory, so diesel oils with this agent were manufactured by Standard.

Stanoils, a line of high-grade lubricating oils with a wide range of viscosities suitable for almost any general lubricating application where high-grade mineral oil was needed, were introduced in 1936. Further improvements were made in the killing power of Superla Insect Spray and Bovinol. For use as a tree spray, Superla Summer Spray Oil and Standard Dormant Emulsion were introduced in 1935, Standard Dormant Spray Oil in 1936, Standard Aphid Spray Oil in 1937, and Nicosol Summer Spray Oil in 1938. Nonpareil White Mineral Oil was changed to Superla White Mineral Oil in 1937 and several grades varying in viscosity were put on the market.

Hand-dipped tapers of various colors and lengths were produced in 1930, but in subsequent years a number of new novelty-style candles were introduced—candelabra candles, candles in special shapes such as the Conifers and Santa Clauses, decorative hand dips with applied decorations for Christmas and Halloween, the Pinmade and Tower Candles, red, white and blue dipped.

Owing to the rapid growth of oil co-operatives, which were doing about 4 per cent of the total business in Standard's marketing area, Standard decided to make a full-length institutional sound movie to bring the company's activities closer to the hundreds of towns and cities it served.[25] It was a novel public relations feature. Homer Croy, the well-known novelist and humorist, was engaged to write the story. In order to have it historically accurate, Croy traveled over the sales territory and talked with agents, tank-wagon drivers, and dealers, whose spirit of service inspired him to make the leading character a composite of their qualities. Houston Branch, Hollywood playwright, then adapted the story for the screen. A carload of "props," including uniforms for servicemen, posters, decalcomanias for service stations and trucks, and other items, was shipped from Chicago to Hollywood.

Packed full of fun, excitement and romance, the full-length historical and educational sound movie called *Stan* portrayed the marketing practices and the services rendered by a Standard agent in a small town. The role of Stan Wright, a typical, virile, Middle West Standard Oil agent, whose reputation for service was well established, was played by Robert Armstrong. Beginning with its première on April 9, 1937, *Stan* was first shown at the annual sales

25. Company Encyclopedia: Marketing, I, Other Competition, Co-ops, 211-212.

RED CROWN, FLAGSHIP OF THE TANKER FLEET

Launched in 1937, it had a crew of thirty men and could carry 64,000 barrels of gasoline

DISTRIBUTION TERMINAL NEAR COUNCIL BLUFFS, IOWA

ROTARY DRILLER GUID-
ING A FISHTAIL BIT AND
DRILL STEM INTO A BORE
HOLE

A fishtail bit is used in a soft
formation. When the driller
hits hard rock the whole
string of pipe will have to
be hauled up and disjointed
to put a rock bit on its end

LAYING AN EIGHT-INCH PIPE NEAR EVANSTON, WYOMING

This line, the first major pipeline to cross the Continental Divide, was
built in the summer of 1939 from Ft. Laramie, Wyoming, to Salt Lake
City, Utah

meetings, the annual spring dealer conferences, and at special assemblies of company employees. In May the company began showing the picture in communities throughout the Middle West in football fields, ball parks, civic auditoriums, parks, public squares, and on Main Street. It was shown, together with four other institutional movies, at the annual spring meeting of the U.S. Chamber of Commerce in Washington, D.C., which regarded it as the nation's best. It was considered by many the most entertaining commercial film that had ever been made. By September, 1938, nearly 3,000,000 people had seen *Stan*. This popular film was undoubtedly of great benefit to the company not only as an indirect and subtle defense against the co-operatives but in holding the friendship of hundreds and thousands of loyal farm customers.

Standard's principal problem in competing with co-operatives was with its own agents, but through various rural training programs the company was able to convince them that they could sell products to most of the co-operatives' customers. Standard's tractor fuels, sold on a very close margin, were something the co-operatives could not equal. Moreover, Standard's service and its wide variety of products were generally superior to what the co-ops could offer. The company had a large distributing organization and *esprit de corps* which the co-ops did not have. It also had the advantage of research laboratories, product testing, and engineering service. The co-ops' products generally were variable in character.

As competitors increased their use of water transportation on the Mississippi, established distribution facilities, and cut prices, Allan Jackson, Vice-President in charge of Sales, suggested in 1936 an immediate and thorough survey of all water transportation possibilities. Striking was the fact that 70 per cent of the population of Standard's marketing area lived within fifty miles of navigable waterways.[26] He believed that marine terminals should be established at Davenport, La Crosse, and Minneapolis.[27] Seubert appointed a special committee composed of Robert H. McElroy, Vice-President in charge of Traffic, W. H. Tell, assistant to the General Manager of Sales, and M. A. McNulty, Assistant Treasurer, to study the situation. One tangible result was the building in 1936 of a water terminal at Evansville, Indiana, to

26. W. C. Platt, "Railroads Force Oil Industry to Still Greater Use of Waterways," *National Petroleum News*, XXX, No. 1 (January 5, 1938), 10-11.
27. Allan Jackson to Edward G. Seubert, August 5, 1936. Jackson File.

supply southern Indiana. Another was the addition of a new tanker to Standard's Great Lakes fleet, the *Red Crown,* capable of carrying 2,700,000 gallons.

With the coming of the depression and the need to reduce transportation costs, there had been an amazing growth in the number of marine terminals established by competitors in Wisconsin and Michigan which affected Standard's market. This factor plus water shipments from the eastern seaboard, shipments via the Great Lakes Pipe Line, and competition from refineries in Michigan and at Toledo, Ohio, had created subnormal prices everywhere within the Detroit area. Since supplies from the Group 3 area were no longer predominant in Michigan, the question was: What should Standard do in order to meet the price competition? Amos Ball, General Manager of Sales, J. C. Marshall, and H. A. Lewis, assistants to the General Manager, recommended to Jackson that the Group 3 base be abandoned for the Lower Peninsula of Michigan, and that a new base price be made at River Rouge.[28] This plus 5.4 cents per gallon to cover the cost of handling, profit, and freight from River Rouge to the destination should be the tank wagon price. Jackson doubted that the proposal would solve Standard's difficulties when so many companies had water transportation and terminals in Michigan. McNulty was not optimistic about maintaining the proposed price structure unless it received favorable acceptance on the part of a large number of Standard's competitors. Buell F. Jones, General Counsel for Standard, advised the Sales Department that legal justification could be found for this exceptional move in view of the chaotic marketing conditions in the area and the kind of competition Standard was obliged to meet. It was a different type of competition from that Standard had to meet in any other state in its territory. On December 7, 1936, the situation finally came before the Directors, who approved the recommendation of the Sales Department. The new price policy was to go into effect on December 9th. Although lower prices were established, cut prices continued, and Standard's volume and profit decreased.

Another particularly troublesome spot for Standard was Kansas. In that state its percentage of the total consumption of gasoline had declined from 23.6 per cent in 1927 to 13.9 per cent in 1936.[29]

28. An Analysis of Standard's Position in the Gasoline Market—Michigan, February 16, 1940.
29. An Analysis of Standard's Position in the Gasoline Market—Kansas, June 27, 1941.

With twenty-six small refineries and an excessive production of crude oil at certain times, there had been a great abundance of "distress" gasoline and a rapid growth in the number of marketers operating on cut prices. Probably the most important cause for the decline in Standard's business was the fact that most refineries in central and eastern Kansas had lower transportation costs to most of the state than did Standard's refineries at Neodesha and Sugar Creek.[30] In 1935 the Vickers Petroleum Company was making 73.1 per cent of its deliveries in Kansas by truck, Eldorado 74.7 per cent, Kanotex 73.7 per cent, and Derby 77 per cent. By 1937 the trucking of gasoline had grown into a big business. In that year there were 180 transport companies operating in Kansas with 581 vehicles in service. Truck rates were about 8 per cent lower than those of the railroads. With higher transportation costs, Standard was at a great disadvantage.

After a detailed study of the Kansas situation in 1932, Jackson reported that if a refinery were built at Wichita or refined products were purchased from one of the existing companies in that area, a freight saving of $93,700 per year might be made plus an additional saving in the cost of transporting crude and trucking refined products.[31] No action was taken, but the Sales Department continued to call attention to sales losses in Kansas. The Sales Research Department made a study during the summer of 1936 on building another refinery in one of four Kansas towns.[32] It reported that the location of a refinery at Hutchinson would result in a saving of $230,000 per year but less at the other three points. Ball submitted a study in December, 1936, on building a gasoline pipeline from Neodesha to various locations in Kansas. By having a line from Neodesha to Hutchinson, a saving in transportation costs of $190,879 might be made but less at three other points. These reports of the Sales Department were referred to the Co-ordinating Department for further study. The Department finally submitted its findings on April 19, 1938, showing the annual savings in transportation and production costs from locating a new refinery in Kansas and building a gasoline pipeline from Neodesha to Hastings and Omaha or from Sugar Creek to Council Bluffs and Sioux City.

30. Company Encyclopedia: Marketing, I, Competition.
31. An Analysis of Standard's Position in the Gasoline Market—Kansas, June 27, 1941.
32. Report on Proposed Kansas Refinery by M. H. Hassold, November 19, 1936.

Standard planned to build a gasoline pipeline in 1937 from Superior, Wisconsin, to the Twin Cities but the railroads, threatened with the loss of business, received permission from the Interstate Commerce Commission to slash the rates from 17.5 cents per hundred pounds to 9 cents, effective June, 1937.[33] Shell opposed the cut in rates because it did not want Standard to become more competitive. There was a general 10 per cent increase in freight rates in March, 1938, which raised the rates between the two points to 10 cents. When Standard threatened to construct the pipeline, the Commission restored the old rate in June.[34]

Through exploration and discovery of new fields, Stanolind Oil and Gas greatly strengthened Standard's crude supply. In 1935 Standard was producing about 25 per cent of its crude oil requirements. The goal was to produce at least 50 per cent. In 1933 Stanolind Oil and Gas performed extensive seismographic work on the Texas Gulf Coast, and early the same year it began exploration with the torsion balance. As a result of this exploration, one if its most important fields was discovered, the Hastings field in Brazoria County, Texas, in which Stanolind was able, by fast work, to lease more than 70 per cent of both the proven and prospective acreage. Active development began in 1935. By seismographic exploration Stanolind also discovered in 1935 the South Houston and Turtle Bay fields on the Gulf Coast near Houston.

Stanolind also greatly augmented its reserves through the purchase of producing properties.[35] In 1934, Stanolind acquired from the Devonian Oil Company in East Texas about 225 net producing acres with a net daily average production of 699 barrels. Two years later it acquired a 5 per cent interest in Federal unit acreage held by the Continental in New Mexico. Through this deal Stanolind Oil and Gas acquired 1,489 barrels a day and 35,768 net acres of undeveloped areas. In 1937, Stanolind purchased the Texas properties of the South Gulf Oil Corporation which had a net daily average production of 221 barrels.

The most significant addition was made during the summer of 1935 when Stanolind Oil and Gas bought the properties of the Yount-Lee Oil Company of Beaumont, Texas, one of the largest

33. "Pipe Line Threat Brings Rate Cut to Minnesota Points," National Petroleum News, XXIX, No. 25 (June 23, 1937), 20.
34. National Petroleum News, XXX, No. 24 (June 15, 1938), 24.
35. Company Encyclopedia: Production, Purchase and Transportation by Pipe Line of Crude, 184.

independent companies on the Gulf Coast, for a cash consideration of nearly $42,000,000.[36] Through the purchase, Stanolind acquired producing properties in ten fields scattered over the Gulf Coast consisting of about 680 producing wells with a net daily average production of 18,942 barrels plus net recoverable reserves amounting to more than 71,797,000 barrels, a tank farm at Spindletop, a terminal on the Neches River at the tank farm, a third interest with the Sun Pipe Line Company in a pipeline from the East Texas oil field to the Beaumont terminal, and other property. As a result of this purchase, Stanolind increased its production by about 9 per cent, making its total daily production about 72,000 barrels. Stanolind Oil and Gas now assumed fourth place among the producing companies on the Gulf Coast.

Owing to the rising demand for oil products and the attempt of Wyoming tax officials to evaluate the crude stored in that state far above current prices, Standard decided to move the oil which had been stored at Clayton since 1923.[37] There were approximately 12,000,000 barrels in storage at Clayton and another 8,000,000 at Casper. Under these circumstances Standard served notice on the Northern Utilities Company and the Kansas Pipe Line & Gas Company, which had leased the pipeline from Clayton to Freeman, Missouri, for gas transportation, that it desired to use the line. The line was reconditioned and began carrying the oil eastward to Standard's refineries in 1936.

By the end of 1937, the net production of Standard and its subsidiaries amounted to 88,654 barrels per day, which was 36.7 per cent of Standard's crude requirements.[38] Net crude reserves were in excess of 481,000,000 barrels. Stanolind Oil and Gas accounted for 94.5 per cent of the 1937 net production and 99.5 per cent of the net reserves. The Utah Oil Refining Company, which was primarily a refining and marketing company and not very active in production, had a total net production of 139,278 barrels, or a daily average of 382 barrels. The recently formed Pan American Production Company had a total net production of 1,304,537 barrels, or a daily average of 3,574 barrels.

36. *Ibid.*, 216; Neil Williams, "Stanolind Oil and Gas Company Purchases Properties of Yount Lee Oil Company," *The Oil and Gas Journal* (March 7, 1935), 20; *The Oil and Gas Journal* (August 8, 1935), 18.
37. "S. O. Indiana to Pump Wyoming Crude East," *National Petroleum News,* XXVII, No. 20 (May 15, 1935), 24.
38. Company Encyclopedia: Production, Purchase and Transportation by Pipe Line of Crude, 190-191.

As prosperity returned and the demand for oil products increased, a program of new refinery construction and modernization was undertaken. At Whiting a new propane deasphalting plant, the first commercial plant to be constructed and operated in America and using a new process developed in the Whiting

NET CRUDE PRODUCTION OF STANDARD AND SUBSIDIARIES 1929–1944

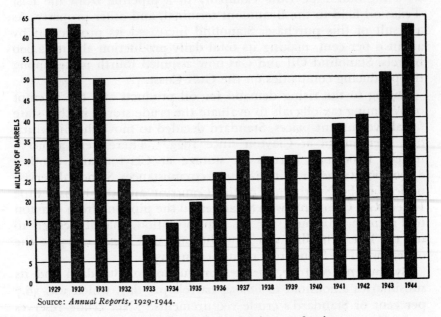

Source: *Annual Reports, 1929-1944.*

The year 1933 includes foreign production.

laboratory, was built in 1936. It made possible the manufacture of heavy lubricating oils and asphalt at lower costs. In 1937 a new combination crude-running, coking, and cracking unit of approximately 18,000 barrels crude capacity per day was being constructed at Whiting. A sludge coker, making possible the economical recovery of acid from sludge and the conversion of the remainder into coke, was built. At Wood River the capacity for making Iso-Vis motor oils was increased. A modern pipe still for making asphalt was built at Sugar Creek. At Neodesha old units were combined into a modern cracking unit of high efficiency. The storage capacity for oil products was increased at several of the Great Lakes terminals.

Crude oil runs to all Standard refineries increased from 66,520,212 barrels in 1935 to 87,207,189 in 1937. In addition, Standard purchased more than a million barrels of gasoline per year from 1935 to 1938.

CRUDE OIL RUN TO REFINERIES BY STANDARD AND SUBSIDIARIES 1929–1944

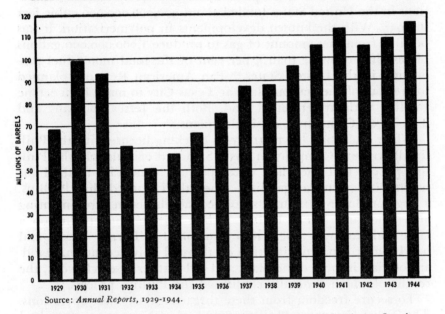

Source: *Annual Reports*, 1929-1944.

The years 1929, 1931, and 1932 include crude oil run to foreign refineries.

To clear the way for greater freedom in the development of various refining processes, several patent conflicts in which Standard was either directly or indirectly involved were settled. The first related to polymerization. In the earlier days refinery and natural gases were burned under the stills or often in the open air. Little attention was paid to using this raw material. As the margin of profit narrowed and competition became more savage, refiners concerned themselves with utilizing every bit of raw materials. Several companies began research on converting these refinery gases into motor fuel of high octane rating.

Since The Texas Company, Standard of New Jersey, and Standard of Indiana were carrying on co-operative research on the cracking process through the M. W. Kellogg Company and since the cracking process made considerable gas, the group included a study of polymerization in its research program. Polymerization involved joining small olefinic hydrocarbons, which were gaseous, into larger hydrocarbons having the boiling points in the gasoline range. By 1935 the group had gone a long way toward developing a commercial process. The significance of such a process could be seen from the fact that the production of gas from cracking operations in the United States totaled about 300,000,000,000 cubic feet in 1935. With the known developments in polymerization, it was possible from that amount of gas to produce 1,000,000,000 gallons of gasoline, or more than 5 per cent of the total motor fuel production in the United States.[39] Pan American Refining planned to erect a polymerization plant at Texas City to make high-octane gasoline without tetraethyl lead. Both the Jersey company and The Texas Company had similar plans.

While discussing the matter of a cracking license with the Phillips Petroleum Company in 1932, Standard officials told the Phillips people that they had developed a commercial method for polymerizing natural gasoline. They then learned that Phillips, a large producer of natural gasoline, had also been experimenting along the same line.[40] In fact, it had been manufacturing on a large scale for over a year in a pilot plant at Borger, Texas, and had built up a patent situation on thermal polymerization. Standard officials inspected the plant and did further research work, the results of which generally confirmed the Phillips process.

To secure freedom from these threats against their operations, The Texas Company, Phillips, Standard of New Jersey, Standard of Indiana, and Kellogg agreed to exchange licenses for thermal polymerization and to make the developments available to the industry through vesting the nonexclusive licensing rights in a jointly owned corporation. Each retained the right to license its own patents alone. At the same time, Phillips agreed to pay $1,300,000 for an unlimited paid-up cracking license from Gasoline Products and Universal, all of which was used by Gasoline Products to purchase an immunity from Universal for Phillips. In accordance with the agreement, the Polymerization Process Corporation, commonly referred to as Polyco, was organized in 1935 by the four companies and Kellogg. Each agreed to purchase one hundred shares of the new company at $100 per share. Fur-

39. "Stanolind Extends Purchases," *The Oil and Gas Journal* (September 5, 1935), 26.
40. Company Encyclopedia: Manufacturing, Cracking, Polymerization, 1-5; Manufacturing, Cracking, Polyco Deal, 38-42.

thermore, they agreed that the company should pay Phillips in perpetuity an overriding 10 per cent of the gross royalty receipts and, in addition, all the net earnings otherwise available for dividends until Phillips should receive $1,300,000. The licensing revenues were small, however, because Pure Oil had a competitive process which gave lower yields but required less of an investment and because Universal Oil Products had a catalytic polymerization process which proved to be better. In fact, after the Polymerization Corporation was formed, both Standard of Indiana and Texas constructed plants using the Universal Oil Products process.

The second conflict related to the Donnelly cracking process, which Joseph F. Donnelly had developed in the 1920's. In the "coil-only" process no large heated or unheated drum or chamber was used. Standard officials inspected the experimental plant at Lemont, Illinois, and had for a brief period in 1926 an option on the process.[41] The Donnelly patent situation at the time seemed uncertain and Standard's engineers felt that, on the whole, it was preferable to crack in a heating coil followed by a "soaking drum" rather than in a "coil-only" apparatus. Consequently, Standard did not exercise its option. Donnelly's patent was acquired by a group which owned the Jenkins process. The Donnelly Process Corporation was formed, and in the early thirties it started licensing on a fairly active scale. By 1936 the Donnelly process patent had been issued, and on its face it dominated "coil-only" cracking. The corporation had eight licensees, but since the process infringed upon various basic patents owned by Gasoline Products and The Texas Company, most of the licensees were under suit for infringement.

From the point of view of Gasoline Products, The Texas Company, and Standard of Indiana, the situation had changed by 1936 because of the development in alloys for the fabrication of oil-heating tubes, and these changes made coil-only cracking much more attractive. Various licensees of Gasoline Products were using or preparing to use the process. Pan American Refining, Standard's subsidiary, was operating a large cracking unit embodying the coil-only principle. Also, at Whiting, Standard had a large cracking unit where part of the oil was cracked by the coil-only process.

By the spring of 1936 it was obvious to both Gasoline Products and Donnelly that some settlement was necessary. After extensive

41. Company Encyclopedia: Manufacturing, Cracking, Donnelly—Gasoline Products Settlement, 43-46.

negotiations a cross-licensing agreement was concluded in July, whereby the licensees of each could be granted rights under both patent structures, and each company could license refiners under the patents of both companies. For the use of the Donnelly process by present and future licensees, Donnelly agreed to turn over to Gasoline Products a percentage of the royalties collected, the percentage to depend upon the particular type of license agreement enjoyed by the licensee. In consideration of the share of royalties received from Donnelly, Gasoline Products agreed to reimburse Donnelly for the cost of defending any infringement suits then pending or filed in future against licensees of Donnelly who were also licensed under the patents of Gasoline Products. The eleven pending suits for infringement were dismissed, and arrangements were made to settle others.

The third patent conflict primarily involved the Universal Oil Products Company and Gasoline Products. The settlement of 1931 only provided immunity for the licensees of Universal and Gasoline Products as of that date. No provision was made for the extension of immunities under the patents of either party to future licensees. Between 1931 and 1997 competition between the two companies continued though Universal got the lion's share due to being a larger organization, having better facilities for providing service, and meeting the engineering requirements of smaller licensees. Each had acquired a number of licensees, and they were either under suit or in jeopardy.

The Behimer "clean circulation" patent, owned by The Texas Company, was the greatest single threat against the new and prospective licensees of Universal. The Behimer patents had never been tested in court although The Texas Company had several infringement suits pending in 1937 against licensees of Universal Oil Products. If the Behimer patents were adjudged valid over the Dubbs "clean circulation" patent, Universal's licensees would be liable for heavy damages for infringement.

With the long and costly record of litigation over the cracking process still fresh in everyone's mind, the principals did the sensible thing. The Texas Company took the lead in negotiating a settlement. Cracking patent history was made in December, 1937, when an agreement was signed by Universal and The Texas Company whereby Universal purchased licensing rights from Texas under the patents of The Texas Company, Standard of Indiana, and Gasoline Products for the benefit of its licensees since 1931 and future licensees for about $1,000,000 in cash and $2,500,000 in D notes.[42] In accordance with Standard's contract with The Texas Company, Universal turned over one-half the cash and notes to Standard. Gasoline Products received full immunity for its past and future licensees.

Not since the "Peace of 1931" had any agreement been made with such far-reaching consequences to the petroleum industry. In recognizing the value and importance of the Behimer "clean circulation" patents, the agreement closed a chapter in the history of cracking by eliminating most of the patent conflicts. Refiners could now choose the type of license they wished with the knowledge that suits were practically eliminated from the realm of possibility. Furthermore, the energy and time of oil company executives was saved for more constructive work, and licensing organizations were free to expand their research.

With the passage of the National Labor Relations Act on July 5, 1935, a change began to take place in Standard's management-labor relationships. Before its passage, the provisions of the proposed bill were carefully examined and studied by company officials. On July 1, 1935, Seubert issued a statement indicating that after the law was passed and regulations issued, it was possible that certain phases of the Industrial Relations Plan would have to be modified, although he was hopeful that the plan would not conflict with the law. However, further study of the law led to the conclusion that the annual Industrial Relations Conference, as conducted in the Manufacturing Department, should be discontinued. However, the Joint General Committees in the Manufacturing Department were continued.

When the Supreme Court declared the National Labor Relations Act valid in April, 1937, Seubert regretfully announced that the company had no alternative but to discontinue the Industrial Relations Plan and its Employee Representation Plan. The fact that the company had originally proposed the plans, appointed one-half the representatives, and paid all of the administrative expenses made the plans illegal. Thus one of the oldest and strongest employee-employer organizations in industry came to a sudden end. The Industrial Relations Department now became the Labor Relations Department. Persons heading the work in

42. Company Encyclopedia: Manufacturing, Cracking, Universal Texas Settlement, 46-49.

each refinery now became supervisors of labor relations, and in the Sales Department they were called personnel supervisors.

Of the entire number of subjects presented to the Joint General Committees in the Manufacturing Department and the General Office during the eighteen-year history of the Industrial Relations Plan, about 64 per cent related to hours, wages, working conditions, and safety.[43] Of the 2,752 proposals presented, 69.8 per cent were approved in whole or in part by the Joint General Committees. Of the 2,541 recommendations submitted by the committees to management, 82.6 per cent were approved. Of the 184 proposals appealed to the President of the company, 25.5 per cent were approved in whole or in part. Of the 41 appeals to the Secretary of Labor, 30 per cent were approved either in full or in part.

In a letter to the employees on April 24th, Seubert pointed out that any employee or group of employees was at liberty to "select representatives to propose and discuss with management any method or plan for collective bargaining." At the same time, he expressed the hope that the company and its employees might continue to consider future problems in the same harmonious spirit as in the past. Management made no effort to dictate or influence the employees in determining the means by which they would be represented in collective bargaining. In fact, it leaned over backwards to conform with the law and remain free of any violation.[44] Although the American Federation of Labor and the International Oil Field, Gas Well, and Refinery Workers of America, CIO, launched plans to organize the workers in the petroleum industry, these efforts were more or less futile in so far as Standard's employees were concerned. Most of the employees of the parent company and its subsidiaries voluntarily organized independent and unaffiliated unions.[45] In general, the employees who had been active in the Industrial Relations Plan and in the Employees Representation Plan assumed the leadership in organizing new independent unions.

Within a few days after Seubert's letter was issued, the non-supervisory employees of the General Office in Chicago had a meeting and appointed a committee to represent them in all collective bargaining with management even before a permanent organization had been effected. Negotiations with management

43. Company Encyclopedia: Manufacturing—Personnel, Labor Relations.
44. Interview with J. W. Curry, May 25, 1949.
45. For details on the organization of these unions, see Company Encyclopedia: Manufacturing—Personnel, Labor Relations Unions, 72-92, 94-133.

resulted in a temporary agreement in May, recognizing the committee as the exclusive bargaining agency and setting forth the procedure for collective bargaining. Within a short time the Standard Oil Employees Association for the General Office, an independent union, came into being and negotiated an agreement for collective bargaining. Except for a few, such as the truck drivers in Chicago, East St. Louis, St. Louis, Kenosha, and Racine, who were organized by the International Brotherhood of Teamsters, Chauffeurs, Stablemen, and Helpers of America and recognized as the exclusive bargaining agent, the employees in some divisions of the Sales Department organized independent unions under various names: Standard Oil Employees Association, Central States Petroleum Council, Tri-State Petroleum Union, Employees Collective Bargaining and Benefit Association, Federated Employees Bargaining Agency, Western Michigan Petroleum Association, Petroleum Employees Union, and others. Some sales divisions, such as the one at St. Joseph, Missouri, were not organized at all. Representing a majority of the employees of a division and in some instances a very high percentage, each independent union approached management and asked to be recognized as the exclusive bargaining agency.

Independent and unaffiliated unions were organized under different names during the spring and summer by the employees at each of the six refineries. Once organized, they asked the company to be recognized as the exclusive bargaining agency and indicated a desire to discuss with management a working agreement.

Throughout the summer of 1937, all through 1938 and into 1939, company officials kept busy conferring with officers of these unions and negotiating agreements. The negotiation of a contract took only a reasonable length of time. The meetings were friendly and, in the main, there was no trouble in arriving at an agreement. Instead of being like a general labor union contract, they were procedural agreements which provided a method of bargaining with respect to wages, hours, and working conditions.[46] If there was a grievance, it was to be taken up with the foreman and then, if necessary, with the department head and a conference of management and union officials. On failure to secure a redress, an appeal could be taken to the President of the company. As a final step, arbitration was provided for, with the exception of certain items. While there was a different contract with every union, the

46. Interview with J. W. Curry, May 25, 1949.

pattern was similar. It was not until about 1944 that complete definitive contracts began to emerge.

In time, the number of leaders who had been active under the old Industrial Relations Plan declined and new leaders, less devoted to the old system and more independent and outspoken, appeared. Gradually, the employee associations became more aggressive and vigorous in asserting claims for their constituents.[47] There was not much difference between these independent unions and others. The employees represented by the independent unions had all the usual advantages afforded by a union but without heavy dues or any outside interference. For these reasons and the fact that Standard continued to follow a liberal policy in providing various benefits for its employees, the company remained relatively free of strikes and labor disturbances.

During the spring of 1939, in order to provide sufficient strength to withstand raids by other unions and unify the group, some of the independent employees' unions in the refining and marketing branches of Standard banded together to form a federation, the Central States Petroleum Union. Gradually other independent locals representing company employees joined the CSPU. It was not until 1945, however, that the Whiting Standard Oil Employees Association, which had the largest number of employees in any one location, joined the CSPU. By 1951 all of the independent locals, except the Research Engineering and Professional Employees Association at Whiting, were a part of CSPU. Each local union continued to bargain collectively for its members but the parent organization advised and co-ordinated the work of the individual unions. While the company dealt with the independent unions locally, it did not bargain with the national organization of the Central States Petroleum Union, although problems of mutual interest were occasionally discussed on an informal basis.

Recognizing the increased cost of living, Standard made two general increases in pay to its employees in 1936.[48] The average wage for all employees amounted to $1,950 per year as of December, 1936. This was 20 per cent higher than the average reported by the American Petroleum Institute for oil field workers. The earnings of workers in all manufacturing industries of the United States averaged $25.14 per week in 1937.[49] The average wage for

47. *Ibid.*
48. *Annual Report To Stockholders For The Year 1936.*
49. *Annual Report Standard Oil Company (Indiana) And Subsidiaries For The Year Ended December 31, 1937.*

Standard and its subsidiaries was approximately $40 per week, which was higher than the average for the petroleum industry and far above the average for industries in general.

In the spring of 1937 three important advances were made in providing for the welfare of the employees and annuitants.[50] To give employees a greater feeling of security during periods of sickness and disability, management adopted in May an employees sickness and disability benefit plan. It applied to all private payroll employees in all departments and salaried employees in the Sales Department and to any illness or disability, unless specifically excluded by the plan, which prevented an employee from performing his duties.

The second measure liberalized the Employees Vacation Plan. Effective January 1, 1937, that section of the plan in regard to "Other Salaried Employees and Wage Earners" was amended so that employees previous to December 24th who had two or more but less than three years of service got one week's vacation. Employees previous to December 17th who had three years or more of service received two weeks. The third measure provided that the reduction of annuities made on March 18, 1932, would not apply to those granted after April 1, 1937.

As a result of the business recovery, Standard and its subsidiaries increased their dollar sales from $290,788,018.88 in 1935 to $358,227,298 in 1937 and their volume from 80,259,234 barrels to 99,216,205. Net earnings after deductions for taxes and other items increased from $30,179,895.21 in 1935 to $55,950,784 in 1937. A cash dividend of $1.00 per share was paid in 1935, $2.40 in 1936, and $2.30 in 1937.

In January, 1937, Standard listed 150,000 additional shares of stock on the New York Stock Exchange. Twenty thousand shares were listed in July in order to buy Pan American Southern Corporation at the rate of one share of Standard for four of Pan American Southern, making the total number of authorized shares listed 15,545,175.[51]

50. Minutes of the Board of Directors' and Stockholders' Meetings, IV, 2619-2624.
51. On June 30, 1937, Standard held 3,336,248 shares out of 3,416,069 shares outstanding of Pan American Southern.

CHAPTER XX

The Recession

AFTER A STEADY IMPROVEMENT IN BUSINESS CONDITIONS AFTER 1934, a sharp recession hit the country late in 1937 which was reflected in the oil industry. In addition to the general economic factors which brought about the recession, the oil industry was adversely affected by a decline in the consumption of all petroleum products, a falling off of exports, the production of too much crude, the manufacture of too much gasoline, and the accumulation of excessive stocks. Consequently, much gasoline and crude oil was sold in 1938 at distress prices which demoralized the market. Late in 1938 national consumption took an upward swing and conditions within the industry improved throughout 1939 and 1940.

The recession placed a heavy strain upon the Iowa plan of merchandising, which had worked only moderately well even in more prosperous times. Dealers, in their zeal to increase profits soon after becoming lessees, began to think that the usual margin of 3.5 cents per gallon was not enough. Local dealers' associations were organized in some areas, and retail prices went up to a margin as high as 5 cents above the price paid by the dealer. The public did little grumbling, for gasoline was still comparatively cheap. Then the trackside or low-price station operator increased his activities. As business fell off and the recession came, regular operators could no longer raise prices or even maintain posted prices. The result was a fight among dealers for business, chaos, and serious losses.[1] Unworried about depreciation and other hidden costs, they began quietly offering rebates and discounts at less than posted retail prices, and price wars became prevalent.

As regular dealers lost business, the suppliers were drawn in. Rather than lose gallonage, they cut the price by reducing or forgoing the rent, dropping the tank-wagon price, giving the weaker dealers a 3.5 cent margin above any price set and guaran-

1. T. F. Smiley, "Iowa Plan Blamed for Crazy Market," *The Oil and Gas Journal,* XXXVII, No. 24 (October 27, 1938), 41, 42.

teeing large dealers substantial payments at the end of the quarter to bring the books from red to black. Oil company credit men worked hard to keep down losses without slaughtering dealer organizations. Owing to dealers' losses, suppliers had to replace equipment on credit. If they did not, they lost the outlet. The trackside operator, finding competition stiffer, looked for cheaper sources of supply. Thus the tank-car market became involved. As the fight grew wilder, suppliers started to lose and plants closed. Thus, the expectation that jobbers and refiners could sit on the side lines and watch while service-station operators fought over retail prices had not turned out as anticipated. The fight had involved the rest of the industry, too. "After three and a half years of experience and press agentry," *Business Week* observed in January, 1939, "the Iowa plan is far from being the keystone of a perfect marketing structure."

Recognizing that its salesmen were spending far too much time in soliciting orders from individual dealers and not enough time teaching dealers how to be better merchandisers, Standard's Sales Department devised "The Season's the Reason Plan" in 1938 to get dealers to concentrate their buying in four major orders—spring, summer, fall, and winter. Reviewing his previous year's sales, a dealer with a salesman's help could make up an order in the spring for all summer and have much of it delivered in three monthly deliveries. The same could be done for each of the other seasons. While it was not possible to accomplish this with all dealers or completely with any dealer, it was a step toward getting the same or a greater amount of business in less time. The procedure eliminated many small orders and gave salesmen more time to assist dealers in driveway solicitation, training helps, improving the appearance of the service station, and soliciting new business.

Even without a recession, Standard was faced with the problem of doing something drastic about its motor oil sales. Following the introduction of Iso-Vis D in 1933 and a reduction in price on it and Polarine, sales showed an increase, but they were not marked. A survey revealed that less than half of Standard's dealers handled its motor oils exclusively.[2] Better than 40 per cent of its service stations handled competitive brands, especially Pennsylvania oils. Of Standard's dealers, 28.6 per cent handled Quaker State, 17.2

2. "Motor Oil Merchandising, 1937."

per cent Pennzoil, and 9.2 per cent Kendall. The percentages were substantially higher in large metropolitan areas. Standard's proportion of the total dealer volume was greatest at outlets where the demand was for medium- and low-priced motor oils and the lowest where the demand was for motor oils of high quality selling at regular retail prices. Furthermore, Standard was securing the motor oil business of only 57.8 per cent of its gasoline customers in 1933 and 60.5 per cent in 1934.

Each subsequent consumer survey showed that nationally advertised Pennsylvania oils ranked higher than Iso-Vis in quality in the consumer's opinion and that low consumption in their view was the most important characteristic of a good motor oil, the one point where Standard suffered slightly by comparison with Pennsylvania oils.[3] From the "World's Greatest Road Test" in 1933 Standard learned that motorists had more frequent additions between drains with Iso-Vis than with any other oils. Of Standard dealers, 67.2 per cent gave "low consumption" as the qualification a premium motor oil must have to be a good seller. Only 21.6 per cent mentioned "easy starting," which was the chief advantage of Iso-Vis.

As a result of further study and a continued decline in motor oil sales, Standard decided that, instead of fighting Pennsylvania oils any longer, it would handle the oil of its leading competitor. More dealers handled Quaker State and more customers used it than any other brand. It was considered by Standard dealers to be the best-advertised oil on the market. Bowing to a definite preference on the part of its customers, Standard negotiated an agreement with the Quaker State Oil Refining Corporation in 1937 whereby Standard became the exclusive distributor of Quaker State motor oil and greases in its thirteen-state marketing area beginning February 18, 1938. Mid-Continent base motor oils and greases continued to be handled at Standard's dealer stations as previously. Thus, in one act Standard solved most of the motor oil problems that had been bothering its sales organization and dealers for years.

Standard's handling of Quaker State meant motor oil and gasoline customers and profit. A survey made in 1939 showed that of Standard's total Quaker State customers, 66.6 per cent were using

3. Company Encyclopedia: Marketing, I, Other Competition, National Brands, 235.

Quaker State oils when it started distribution, 16.8 per cent were diverted to it from Standard's motor oils, and 18.6 per cent had been diverted from using competitive oils.[4] The proportion of Standard's regular gasoline customers using Quaker State motor oil had almost doubled within eighteen months; 23.1 per cent of its Quaker State customers had started using Standard's gasoline since February, 1938, and about one-half of them had done so because of Quaker State. Moreover, there had been a steady decline in the proportion of Standard customers buying major competitive motor oils and other Pennsylvania oils.

One of the knottiest problems confronting the company was price cutting in the Detroit metropolitan area. For years Detroit had been a highly competitive market and cut-price center due to its density of population, large automobile market, the nearness of the Michigan crude production and refineries, and the availability of cheap water transportation. In the fight for gallonage, more distribution facilities had been built in the 1920's than the volume justified. All service stations fought in some way to stay alive.

For years it had been contrary to Standard's marketing policy to sell through jobbers. There was more profit in selling at tank-wagon prices than tank-car prices. In a survey made of the competitive situation in the Chicago area in 1938 Standard was next to the lowest of six major companies in the percentage of gasoline delivered through jobbers.[5] Of its total business, Standard delivered 90.5 per cent directly. Gasoline sales to all jobbers in Standard's territory in 1938 amounted to only 8.85 per cent.[6] The second reason for Standard's not using jobbers was that through the years it had built up a vast marketing organization of its own, and it did not need jobbers. Owing to the fact that Standard distributed a larger percentage of its total trade directly than most major companies in its area, the company was particularly vulnerable to competition from jobbers of other companies, who could pass price cuts on to their dealers and force Standard to cut prices and margins.

Despite its general policy against selling through jobbers, Standard began selling gasoline on a tank-car basis to jobbers in the

4. "1939 Winter Consumer Survey, Part II."
5. "Retail Competitive Conditions in Eight Leading Cities, 1938."
6. Company Encyclopedia: Marketing, I, Methods of Distribution, 26.

Detroit metropolitan area.[7] About 1928 it commenced selling to the Citron-Kolb Oil Company which marketed through a few stations of its own. In 1932 Standard began selling on the same basis to the Stikeman Oil Company. The same policy was followed in 1935 with respect to the Wayne Oil Company of Detroit. Wayne did not have any service stations of its own until after September, 1939.

In 1936 and afterwards Standard supplied about 16 or 17 per cent of the gasoline sold in the Detroit area. It regularly supplied about 385 retail service stations of which it owned about two hundred and leased eight. The remaining one hundred and fifty were independent operators who had contracts to buy their gasoline from Standard.

Owing to the fierce competition in 1936 in the Detroit area, Standard was in danger of losing its jobber customers because other suppliers were offering gasoline at lower prices. Therefore, after June, 1936, Standard met this competition by selling to its three jobbers at 1½ cents per gallon less than the dealer tank-wagon price. Rather than lose another large customer, Ned's Auto Supply Company, Standard began in September selling it gasoline at ½ cent per gallon less than it charged other retailers. Ned's sold to the public through its own retail stations in 1937 for about 2 cents per gallon less than the prevailing service-station price. After January 1, 1938, Citron-Kolb commenced selling to retail stations at ½ cent and 1 cent off the tank-wagon price. Retailers claimed that the price differentials granted to these firms by Standard gave them a substantial competitive advantage over other retailers and caused substantial damage to other service stations selling Red Crown gasoline.

On July 29, 1938, Standard was charged by the Wayne County prosecutor with violating the Michigan Fair Trade Law by selling gasoline at tank-car prices to Ned's Auto Supply Company, which enabled him to undersell competitors.[8] The complaint asked that Standard be restrained from supplying gasoline to Ned's at a price lower than it supplied hundreds of Detroit retailers. In a preliminary hearing held in August, 1938, the prosecution contended that Standard by offering gasoline to one cheaper than to another was discriminating and that it was done with the purpose of in-

7. *Findings As To The Facts and Conclusion. In the Matter of Standard Oil Company, a Corporation. United States of America Before the Federal Trade Commission,* October 9, 1945.

8. *The New York Times,* February 20, 1938.

juring or destroying the business of competitors.[9] Many past and present Standard dealers testified that they had asked the company for a similar consideration as that given to Ned's, but they had been refused.

Standard's attorney argued that the company was justified in selling to Ned's at tank-car prices because Ned's received gasoline in tank-car lots at its own bulk plant and hauled it from there to its own stations in its own trucks. These factors relieved Standard from the cost of storing and hauling. Furthermore, Standard sold to Ned's in tank-car lots at tank-car prices not to destroy the business of competitors but in order to meet a competitive offer made by two other companies. While competitors might have lost gallonage, it was maintained that this was not necessarily due to Ned's price advantage. It was pointed out that during the first half of 1938 gallonage at Detroit had steadily fallen because of unemployment and fewer cars being driven, competition from cheap unbranded gasoline, and improvement in the quality of Michigan-refined gasoline. P. A. Raupagh, Standard's Detroit manager, brought out the fact that his company did not differentiate between a jobber who sold at wholesale only and a jobber who sold at both wholesale and retail in determining an operator's eligibility to receive gasoline at tank-car prices. In order to buy at tank-car prices, Standard required that an operator purchase about one to two million gallons per year, that he have ample credit responsibility, and that he have the physical equipment to handle tank-car shipments. Tank-car shipments had been refused other dealers for one or all of these reasons.

At the conclusion of the hearing the state prosecutor asked that the case be held for trial but Judge Arthur E. Gordon of the Recorder's Court asked for briefs from both sides. On September 1, 1938, Judge Gordon rendered an opinion which dismissed the charge of price discrimination against Standard.

During the depths of the recession in 1938 Shell made a futile effort to raise prices. In defiance of the popular concept that Standard was the leader and "what it said went" on prices, Shell announced on August 1st that on the 3rd it would advance its tank-wagon price in the Middle West by $\frac{3}{10}$ of a cent, which more nearly reflected the current advance in the cost of crude and trans-

9. "Indiana Standard Price Policy Aired at Detroit," *National Petroleum News*, XXX, No. 34 (August 24, 1938), 11-12.

portation and marketing charges. If ever a raise seemed warranted, this was. Other companies announced on the 2nd that they would follow.[10] Companies doing about 70 to 80 per cent of the gallonage went along with the raise. While these companies, which distributed about 50 per cent of their gasoline through jobbers, raised the tank-wagon price at their own bulk stations, they had no control over their jobbers' prices. Many of the jobbers made the advance but the others waited for Standard of Indiana to make a move. Standard, which did only a little over 20 per cent of the gallonage, issued a statement to the effect that, in view of the price cutting and competitive conditions, no advance was warranted.[11] It did not intend to advance its prices. When Standard declined to advance, company officials were thinking of an army of retailers who were selling Ethyl at 5 cents under Standard's price. On August 6th, three days after the raise became effective, Shell rescinded its advance "due to competitive conditions," and many of the majors rescinded their advance in certain areas where they found competitive conditions hard to withstand. By August 17th, the experiment had flopped.[12] Tank-wagon prices were back where they began. As tank-wagon prices fell to the old level, Standard announced that its earnings for the second quarter of 1938 were off 40 per cent over the previous year.

The whole affair raised some interesting questions.[13] Could not the companies doing 70 to 80 per cent of the gallonage make the advance stick? Was Standard of Indiana a "market maker" even though it did only a little over 20 per cent of the business? Was Standard right when it said there was too much competitive chaos to warrant an advance? The result of the attempt to raise prices pointed strongly to the helplessness of a large number of competitive units which marketed at retail as well as a large number of units which distributed at wholesale.

With the hope of stabilizing the market and aiming directly at price cutters, Standard took the trade by surprise on December 8, 1938, and announced the introduction of a new leaded third-

10. "Tank Wagon Price Advance In 8 States Led By Shell," *National Petroleum News*, XXX, No. 31 (August 3, 1938), 9.
11. "Advance in Tank Wagon Price In Middle West Fails to Hold," *National Petroleum News*, XXX, No. 32 (August 10, 1938), 5.
12. "Tank Wagon Price Advance Collapses in Middle West," *National Petroleum News*, XXX, No. 33 (August 17, 1938), 9.
13. "Cannot Change Habit of Years and Follow New Market Leaders," *National Petroleum News*, XXX, No. 33 (August 17, 1938), 14.

grade, green-colored gasoline with an octane of 67.[14] It sold at no advance in price over the old unleaded third-grade Stanolind. It was a revolutionary action, an outgrowth of the new competitive conditions. For many months various oil companies had been faced with competition from unbranded leaded gasoline sold by price cutters at prices as low as 5 cents below the price on house brands of the major companies. In many places it was higher in octane than the majors' third grade, which was in the 62-octane-and-below bracket.[15] Some marketers thought the time had arrived to save the reputation of the house brands with the motorists by improving the third-grade quality. They reasoned that the house brands lost cast when subjected to price cutting. Another factor in influencing Standard to bring out its new leaded third-grade gasoline was Ethyl's announcement on December 5th that all of its refiner licensees, who had been restricted to leading only their premium and next-best grade of gasoline, could now lead any grade of gasoline.

The new green-colored Stanolind gasoline received a few coldly courteous nods and many suspicious looks. There was no warm welcome. It was a disturber. The newcomer caused a spirited and somewhat worried discussion over its effect upon the market, the price structure, and the fortunes of some refiners.[16] Many refiners believed that the introduction of leaded third-grade gasoline was unnecessary. Refiners without cracking facilities and not equipped to manufacture any other grade, except white unleaded gasoline, faced a particularly perplexing problem. Bringing ordinary third-grade gasoline with an octane of 50–52 up to 67 octane involved a huge manufacturing expense. It added a 1/2 to 3/4 cent to the cost of every gallon and cut into profits greatly. In the case of gasoline that did not react readily to leading, the expenses would be even greater. Unless other refiners could compete, farmers would now buy 67-octane gasoline and use it not only in tractors but in their autos as well. Regardless of the difficulties in the path of the new fuel, there was a grudging admission that leaded third-grade gasoline had come to stay. It was in keeping

14. E. L. Barringer, "Hiking Third Grade Octane Is Move Against Unbranded," *National Petroleum News*, XXX, No. 49 (December 7, 1938), 6-7.
15. "Third Grade Gasoline Climbs Octane Ladder," *National Petroleum News*, XXX, No. 49 (December 7, 1938), 5.
16. T. F. Smiley, "War of Octanes May Be Near," *The Oil and Gas Journal* (December 15, 1938), 13; T. F. Smiley, "67-Octane Doesn't Feel at Home Yet," *The Oil and Gas Journal* (February 23, 1939), 42.

with a trend of lifting the octane rating along the whole front. Furthermore, it foreshadowed the end of the skimming plant era, which had seen hurriedly constructed and cheap refineries spring up in all flush oil fields.

Another move looking toward the increase of business was Standard's adoption of the National Credit Identification Card plan in the fall of 1939. The cards, issued quarterly, could be used in most of the United States and Canada through an arrangement whereby thirteen oil companies outside Standard's marketing area honored them at their service stations.

As the recession deepened in 1938, Standard's executives probed more deeply than ever before the reasons for its declining sales not only at the moment but over the past decade. It marked the beginning of a soul-searching experience which brought belated results. Seubert requested Jackson, Vice-President in charge of Sales, to report on some of the marketing policies recommended in the past which, if followed, would have placed Standard in a different competitive situation than it was in 1938.

In August, 1938, Jackson submitted to the Directors a very detailed and voluminous account of past price policies and the recommendations which had been made between 1923 and 1938.[17] In his report, Jackson pointed out that there was bound to be a continued growth of service stations unless the company maintained a policy of smaller margins. In order to do this, the first thing to be considered was greater economies in transportation. Ever since 1929, Jackson reported, he had persistently emphasized that Standard was not in the most favorable competitive position owing to transportation costs, and he had made numerous recommendations to overcome this handicap. Furthermore, Jackson said: "If the policy I recommended in 1922 had been adopted, we would not now be in competition with 57,819 service stations when at that time there were only 2,114 competitive service stations in existence."

As an outcome of the thinking upon the subject and not unmindful of the effect of the Great Lakes Pipe Line upon its business, Standard started investigating the building of a 180-mile, eight-inch gasoline pipeline with a capacity of 20,000 barrels from Standard's refinery at Sugar Creek to Council Bluffs, Iowa, to be used for distributing products in western Iowa and eastern Nebraska.

17. An Analysis of Marketing Recommendations 1923–1938 dated August 8, 1938.

During the fall of 1938 Jackson brought up the matter of lower transportation costs many times in the discussions of the Directors. He was finally asked to prove his statements.[18] Consequently, Jackson went to work gathering his data and preparing a series of maps covering each of the fourteen states to show the competition from trucking and marine terminals on the Great Lakes and on the inland waterways. On October 21, 1938, Seubert sent for Jackson and asked for his views on the cause of the decline in gasoline sales and what could be done about it. Again, Jackson emphasized that the first thing to be considered was transportation economies.[19] Seubert told Jackson that he need not concern himself about transportation as that was being handled by a committee, but Jackson expressed his belief that the committee would not take into consideration everything it should, such as the relationship of trucking to cut prices. Jackson also raised the question as to whether the rental on the company's leased-out service stations was too high.

By May, 1939, Jackson was ready to make an oral report to the Directors of his findings upon the effect of trucking, water transportation, and products pipeline shipments upon Standard's business. Jackson's findings were quite revealing as to the decline of Standard's business in various states of its marketing territory. According to his analysis, from 1930 to 1939 motor fuel consumption had increased from 108,000,000 to 150,000,000 barrels, or 38.3 per cent, in ten states of Standard's marketing area.[20] At the same time, Standard's sales had decreased from 32,000,000 barrels to 29,000,000, or 9.1 per cent, and the company's percentage of the total consumption had declined from 28.8 per cent to 19.6 per cent. In 1940 the percentage dropped to 18.6 per cent in its thirteen-state marketing area of the Middle West.

Between January 1, 1933, and December 31, 1939, 238 Standard bulk stations, representing an investment of more than $700,000, had been closed due to competitive price conditions, low volume, and high marketing costs without the knowledge of the Vice-President in charge of Sales.[21] The discontinuance of service on

18. Memorandum written by Allan Jackson, May 1, 1939. Co-ordinating Department, Transportation Division, Progress Memorandums.
19. Memorandum written by Allan Jackson, October 21, 1938. Co-ordinating Department, Transportation Division, Progress Memorandums.
20. An Analysis of Closing Bulk Stations, January 1, 1933, to December 31, 1939, Particularly in Iowa and South Dakota.
21. *Ibid.*

STANDARD'S PERCENTAGE OF THE TOTAL SALES OF GASOLINE TO
TOTAL CONSUMPTION 1924–1940

	1924	1925	1926	1930	1937	1938	1940
Colorado					9.5	9.3	10.0
Illinois					23.6	21.6	20.2
Indiana	46.6	38.9	39	32.1	22.2	23.2	20.9
Iowa	No record	No record	38.9	31.4	21.4	21.0	20.8
Kansas	30.4	25.1	23.9	17.7	12.6	11.5	10.9
Michigan					20.2	18.8	18.1
Minnesota	34.7	31.9	29.3	25.3	20.0	19.2	19.5
Missouri	31.4	32.5	28.5	24.4	15.8	16.1	15.5
Montana					9.6	10.0	9.6
Nebraska							9.0
North Dakota	69.4	63.3	57.4	41.2	29.9	29.0	29.8
Oklahoma					1.3	1.3	
South Dakota	49.3	45.8	47.2	34.8	24.2	23.1	24.3
Wisconsin	No record	No record	34.5	30.5	21.5	21.3	20.3
Wyoming					14.3	14.3	14.0
Standard's percentage of the total gasoline consumption, excluding Oklahoma					20.0	19.3	18.6

Source: Company Encyclopedia: Marketing, I, 170.

some railroad branch lines, the abandonment of towns due to the area being converted into lakes by the government, and the construction of new roads were reasons for closing some stations but only relatively few. The fundamental reason in most instances, according to Jackson's study, was not the lack of potential volume but cheaper transportation costs of competitors which enabled them to undersell Standard.

In Iowa, which was served by the Great Lakes Pipe Line and competitive marine terminals, Jackson's study showed that while the total gasoline consumed in Iowa between 1927 and 1938 inclusive had increased by 5,214,119 barrels, Standard's sales had increased only 238,236 barrels.[22] Its percentage of the total business had declined from 32.6 per cent to 21. Between 1932 and 1939 Standard had closed forty-seven of its bulk stations because of low volume and high marketing costs. However, in twenty of these towns where competitors had stations the volume in 1938 had increased over 1937 in all instances except six. Standard had not used motor transportation from its refineries, yet considerable quantities of gasoline had been trucked into the twenty-two west-

22. An Analysis of the Competitive Situation in Iowa, September 21, 1939.

ern and southwestern Iowa counties from Kansas and Missouri refineries. Some refiners gave the haulers an f.o.b. refinery price and permitted them to have the benefit of any transportation saving they could make. As a result, these markets had been badly affected by cut prices, and the fact that Standard did not meet their prices meant a loss of business.

GALLONS OF GASOLINE ON WHICH TAX WAS PAID IN IOWA 1937–1938

	Year 1937	Year 1938	Increase or Decr.	Percentage Inc. or Decr.
Standard Oil Company	98,921,189	104,279,448	5,358,259	5.42
Great Lakes Pipe Line				
Mid-Continent	35,226,851	39,829,731	4,602,880	13.07
Phillips	36,734,309	37,984,174	1,249,865	3.40
Sinclair	21,297,315	23,376,399	2,079,084	9.76
Skelly	19,384,103	20,941,531	1,557,428	8.04
Cities Service	12,069,924	12,245,775	175,851	1.46
Continental	10,074,900	10,975,729	900,829	8.95
Texas Company	9,762,684	10,287,374	524,690	5.37
Pure Oil	282,876	1,652,076	1,369,200	483.98
Total	144,832,962	157,292,789	12,459,827	8.60
Other Integrated Companies				
Shell	22,638,718	18,353,395	4,285,323	18.93
Socony-Vacuum	6,595,470	6,745,957	150,487	2.28
Deep Rock	3,924,302	4,536,466	612,164	15.60
National	3,262,547	3,717,868	455,321	13.95
Barnsdall	3,158,749	3,096,902	61,847	1.96
Champlin	4,953,082	2,297,757	2,655,325	53.61
Total	44,532,868	38,748,345	5,784,523	12.99
Grand Total of Above:				
15 Integrated Companies	288,287,019	300,320,582	12,033,563	4.17
Balance Other Companies	202,391,467	227,425,954	25,144,487	12.35
Grand Total— All Companies	490,678,486	527,746,536	37,068,050	7.55

Source: Analysis of the Competitive Situation in Iowa, September 31, 1939.

So far as the effect of the Great Lakes Pipe Line was concerned, the study showed that since its beginning in 1931, its users had a freight advantage that averaged .7282 cents per gallon. In Des Moines, Standard was the largest seller, but it had only 15.3 per cent of the total gasoline sales. To ship gasoline from Standard's Sugar Creek refinery to Des Moines cost 1.782 cents per gallon while over the Great Lakes Pipe Line it cost .116 cents per gallon. Five of the companies using the Great Lakes Pipe Line had increased their percentage of the business in Iowa more than Standard in 1938. In view of the growth of trucking into Iowa, the establishment of marine terminals on the Mississippi, and the effect of the Great Lakes Pipe Line, Jackson recommended that Standard's contemplated pipeline from Sugar Creek to Council Bluffs be extended to Des Moines and that marine terminals be located at Burlington, Dubuque, and McGregor.

Jackson's study gave an unusual picture of the special conditions which had resulted in Standard's declining sales in Michigan from 1927 to 1938.[23] Crude production in the state had increased from 10,603,000 barrels in 1934 to 19,143,000 in 1938. The number of refineries located in the state had increased from one in 1929 to twenty-nine in 1939 with a capacity of 93,300 barrels per day. Products from the Michigan refineries came into competition in the Detroit area with gasoline refined at Toledo and transported by the Pure-Sun pipeline from Toledo not only for themselves but for Gulf and the Standard of Ohio. Since 1928 thirty-three marine terminals had been established from which by rental or exchange agreement eighteen companies received supplies. Against these, Standard had only three marine terminals: at Muskegon, Bay City, and River Rouge. Competitors had marine terminals in eight locations where Standard had none. No city or town in the Lower Peninsula was more than seventy-five miles from a refinery or a marine terminal. Under the price formula of December 9, 1936, Standard's gasoline was being hauled theoretically by tanker past its marine terminals at Muskegon and Bay City to River Rouge, thence by rail to every bulk plant in the Lower Peninsula. Competitors, on the other hand, did not adhere to the River Rouge price base but shipped by water direct to Benton Harbor, Muskegon, Traverse City, Alpena, Bay City, and Port Huron, then trucked at less than rail rates to their bulk plants. All of these factors had helped to develop a low-price area in Detroit and cause a decline in Standard's percentage of the total gasoline consumption in Michigan from 23 per cent in 1934 to 18.8 in 1938.

Inasmuch as the crude produced in Michigan would be refined by someone in Michigan and sold in Michigan, Jackson advocated that Standard should purchase crude in Michigan and refine it at

23. An Analysis of the Competitive Situation in Michigan, February 16, 1940.

Whiting. Standard's position could also be strengthened by installing more marine terminals at Hancock, Marquette, Sault Ste. Marie, Benton Harbor, Traverse City, Cheboygan, Alpena, and Port Huron.

Finally, Jackson recommended that the primary basing price for the Lower Peninsula and possibly the Upper Peninsula, too, should be on the basis of Whiting refinery costs, cost of transportation by tanker to the marine terminals, operating costs of the terminals, plus a profit which would establish a marine terminal basing price. To this should be added rail or motor transportation costs to the bulk plants to make the market price. If applied to the Detroit area, Jackson believed that it would normally meet competitive prices there. Later, on August 12, 1940, the Directors authorized a new method of basing prices for the Lower Peninsula in Michigan which followed the general principles suggested by Jackson.

There was already plenty of evidence by 1939 as to the trend in oil transportation.[24] Oil shipments on the Mississippi River showed increasing gains in 1938. The next year water transportation of petroleum products from Kansas City to Omaha commenced. The Ohio River had about ninety terminals located along its course. From Cairo, Illinois, to Minnesota, there was an average of one every sixty miles. By 1940 water transportation was cutting heavily into pipeline deliveries. The Illana Pipe Line Company (Phillips) was being built from East St. Louis to Chicago, and the Cimarron Valley Pipe Line Company was extending its line from Superior, Nebraska, to Rock Rapids and Sioux City, Iowa. Moreover, Shell was converting its crude pipeline from Wood River to Chicago into a gasoline line. Much of Kansas, Missouri, Iowa, Colorado, and Nebraska was being served by trucks which hauled from water and pipeline terminals to bulk stations and retail outlets.[25] With the growth of gasoline pipelines, trucking, and the tendency to establish lower delivered prices, the practice of selling on a Group 3 basis continued although its importance steadily declined.

Standard's Directors in June, 1939, approved the building of

24. M. G. Van Voorhis, "Oil Movement Expanding on Island Waterways," *National Petroleum News*, XXX, No. 45 (November 9, 1938), 63, 66-67, 70; "Oil Barges Push Farther Up Mississippi Waterway," *National Petroleum News*, XXXI, No. 50 (December 13, 1939), 34-40.

25. E. L. Barringer, "80% of Nebraska's Marketers Use Long Distance Trucking," *National Petroleum News*, XXIX, No. 26 (June 30, 1937), 34-36.

a gasoline pipeline from Sugar Creek to Council Bluffs, Iowa. About the same time approval was given to building a water terminal at Bettendorf, Iowa, to receive large shipments from Wood River, and another on Jones Island at Milwaukee to receive shipments from Whiting. Standard's new gasoline pipeline to Council Bluffs would serve not only western Iowa but eastern Nebraska because in August, 1939, Standard of Indiana purchased the Standard Oil Company (Nebraska). The latter had been organized in 1906 as a marketing company, but it had always been supplied with most of its petroleum products by Standard of Indiana. From 1906 until 1931 the company had operated successfully. Its business was good, and its cash and stock dividends were exceptionally good. Beginning in 1932 and extending through 1938, except for 1936, the company operated at a loss owing to depressed farm prices, grasshoppers, drought, and competition with companies using trucks and products pipelines. Failure to build or adequately maintain good service stations and a number of other management policies also contributed to the decline in revenue.

Continued losses caused considerable restlessness on the part of the stockholders of the Nebraska company and created a desire to sell the company assets or merge with some integrated company. In July, 1938, officials of the Standard of Nebraska approached Seubert and Barkdull of Standard of Indiana, told them the situation, and suggested that they purchase the company or arrange for a merger.[26] In August several Standard officials were sent to Nebraska to make a survey. The result was that Standard of Indiana told officials of the Standard of Nebraska that it was not interested in a purchase or merger. Standard of Indiana was willing, however, to have its Sales Research Department make an efficiency survey and report in order that economies might be instituted. This offer was accepted, and the survey was completed about June 30, 1939. The suggestions made for possible economies were put into effect at once.

After the annual statement was sent out on March 17, 1939, showing a net loss of $111,731.25 as of December 31, 1938, Standard of Nebraska officials asked Standard of Indiana on two subsequent occasions about a purchase or merger, but the latter showed no interest.[27] Legal objections were made by Standard's General Counsel. Henry W. Pierpont, the President of Standard of

26. 15 N. W. (2d), 402.
27. Ibid., 403.

Nebraska, finally sent a communication to Standard of Indiana reviewing the operations of the company, the various offers from other companies to buy the stock, and pointed out that anyone who acquired the Standard of Nebraska would have exclusive use of the name "Standard Oil Company" and the trade-mark brands it owned. Standard of Indiana immediately became interested, and several conferences were held. On July 6th Standard of Indiana tentatively agreed to buy the 161,403 outstanding shares for $17.50 per share and to pay $44,406.44 in unpaid accrued taxes.[28]

The Directors of the Nebraska company approved the offer and recommended it to the stockholders for consideration on August 29th. Standard of Indiana prepared articles of incorporation for a new Standard Oil Company of Nebraska and, as soon as the sale was approved, Standard of Indiana filed the articles of incorporation in order to avoid any lapse and prevent any possible loss of the use of the name "Standard Oil Company." [29] The assets of the old Standard of Nebraska were then transferred to the new company, and all of the stockholders of the old company were paid off as rapidly as possible. Shortly after the purchase, Standard of Indiana evaluated the property, other than current assets, in order to establish a basis for income tax returns. It was evaluated at $1,876,645.60. The assets, as of May 31, 1939, had a book value of $4,629,433.20, but this amount did not include good will or the use of trade-marks.

The purchase of the Standard of Nebraska added one more state to the marketing territory of Standard of Indiana, making thirty-nine states and the District of Columbia in which it and its subsidiaries marketed. It meant adding 213 bulk stations, 193 company-owned service stations, and 101 service stations under lease to Standard's chain of outlets. The purchase did not mean any immediate increase in the volume of its business because Standard had been supplying the Nebraska company with most of its petroleum products.

Clarence E. Winter of Omaha, owner of ten shares of stock in the old Standard Oil Company of Nebraska, filed suit against the new Standard of Nebraska and Standard of Indiana in November, 1939, in the Nebraska District Court of Douglas County at Omaha. His petition charged that the sale of the old company to Standard of Indiana was "wrongful, unlawful and fraudulent" to the minor-

28. *Ibid.*, 404.
29. *Ibid.*, 407-408.

ity stockholders.[30] He asked the court to declare the sale invalid, set a reasonable and just evaluation on the stock, and award him that amount in damages. Winter alleged that the old Nebraska company bought its supplies from Standard of Indiana at excessive prices for the purpose of preventing the profitable operation of the Nebraska company in order to depreciate the value of its stock, that the officers paid themselves excessive salaries resulting in unnecessary losses to the company, that the two companies agreed to operate the new Standard of Nebraska at a loss over a period of time to make the sale seem more advisable, that at the time of sale the assets of the company were worth at least $29.26 per share, and that its sale for $17.50 was unlawful and fraudulent. Winter agreed to a dismissal of the suit in October, 1940, because he had further investigated and was satisfied with the sale.[31]

A similar suit was filed at about the same time by Edgar H. Rettinger, who headed a group of stockholders, against Pierpont and others. The Nebraska District Court of Douglas County found for the plaintiffs. The defendants appealed to the Supreme Court of Nebraska, which reversed the decision in July, 1944, and dismissed the suit.[32]

To meet low-cost transportation and competition in the Rocky Mountain area, the Utah Oil Refining Company built a crude oil pipeline in 1939 from Fort Laramie, Wyoming, to Salt Lake City which had the distinction of being the first pipeline to cross the Continental Divide.[33] Before the building of the line, Wyoming producers were confronted with the problem of finding markets outside of Wyoming or shutting down their wells and stopping all development work.[34] Shipments were being made by truck, rail, and pipeline to refineries in Nebraska, Colorado, Idaho, Utah, and Washington, with approximately 7,000 barrels per day being taken by Standard for shipment through its trunk line to its refineries at Sugar Creek, Wood River, and Whiting. The market, however, was highly competitive owing to the situation in Kansas

30. Petition filed in the Nebraska District Court, Winter File.
31. Alfred G. Ellick to Buell F. Jones, October 10, 1940, November 27, 1940. Winter File.
32. 15 N. W. (2d), 393.
33. "Comin' 'Round the Mountain," Stanolind Record, XXI, No. 7 (May, 1940), 11-12.
34. "President E. G. Seubert Replies to Senator O'Mahoney's Protest," The Oil and Gas Journal (August 3, 1939), 27.

STANOLIND "A" IN THE LOCK AT ALTON, ILLINOIS

This sturdy towboat is capable of pushing six barges, loaded with 2,400,000 gallons of petroleum products, against strong river currents

NEW COMBINATION THERMAL CRACKING UNIT COMPLETED AT THE
WHITING REFINERY IN 1938

This unit processed crude oil directly to gasoline, kerosene, tractor fuel, fuel oil, gas
and coke

and the new fields in Illinois. Standard had curtailed its refining operations at the Casper plant on July 1, 1938, and eliminated the shipment of products to areas which could be served more economically by other refineries. The light oil output was cut to 50 per cent capacity and the manufacture of Iso-Vis oils and greases discontinued.

Owing to the competition from truck transportation and the pronounced and growing tendency of California operators to extend their markets into its territory, the Utah Oil Refining Company was faced with either closing its refinery or building a crude oil pipeline. It had a refinery at Salt Lake City with a distillation capacity of 8,500 barrels and a cracking capacity of 5,400 barrels. Since there was no crude oil production in Utah, the plant's requirements had come for the most part from Wyoming by rail for twenty-five years and from the Iles field in northwestern Colorado. Rather than close the refinery, the Utah Oil Refining Company decided to build a crude oil pipeline from Salt Lake City to Fort Laramie, Wyoming, to carry crude from the Rock River, Big Medicine Bow, and La Barge fields in Wyoming. In addition, a connection was to be made with the Lance Creek field, one of the largest oil reserves in the northern Rocky Mountains, through the pipeline of the Ohio Oil Company.

No sooner was the pipline project made known in July, 1939, than pressure was brought to bear on Governor Nels H. Smith of Wyoming by the State Federation of Labor, the United Mine Workers, and various railroad brotherhoods to call a special session of the legislature to prevent its construction.[35] Senator J. C. O'Mahoney and Representative Frank O. Horton protested in Congress the building of the line. O'Mahoney pointed out to Standard officials the desirability of using all of the facilities for refining and transportation available in Wyoming before any crude oil line was built. In reply, Seubert assured him that the company was deeply interested in maintaining employment and a market in the territory where the company and its subsidiaries operated. In fact, he pointed out, this was why the Utah Oil Refining Company had decided to make a substantial investment in pipeline facilities. This was the only way it could keep alive the business of the company. The proposed line would in no way affect Standard's operations in Wyoming. By building the line, Seubert

35. "Contractors Move In For Construction of Utah Oil Refining Line," *The Oil and Gas Journal* (August 17, 1939), 42.

declared, it would provide a market for Wyoming crude oil, give employment to Wyoming producers, and give temporary employment for more than 1,000 men, who would build the line, and permanent employment to a substantial number who would operate it. Even the railroads would benefit in the end, for they would transport a considerable tonnage of refined products out of Salt Lake City.

Despite the protests, the construction of the 442-mile pipeline was started in August, 1939, and went ahead rapidly under the direction of the Stanolind Pipe Line Company.[36] Digging trenches through sagebrush, rough rocky soil, solid rock, over mountains, and through canyons was by no means easy. Its construction presented some of the most difficult engineering problems. Moreover, the laying of the pipeline at such high altitudes in a cold climate was something that few oil companies had ever attempted. The elevation at both ends was approximately the same, about 4,224 feet, yet the pipeline rose to about 7,660 feet above sea level as it crossed the Bear River divide in southwestern Wyoming. At ten other points the line was laid at a level well above 7,000 feet. The crews met varying weather. In one canyon the temperature ranged from below freezing at night to 90° above in the day. The line crossed seven rivers and several smaller streams. Weber River was crossed and recrossed fourteen times. At numerous places in Weber Canyon the line was laid in the course of the river bed. In a thousand-foot stretch, workmen were limited to a working space of only twelve to fifteen feet in width. Telegraph and telephone lines were built, necessitating the setting of two hundred miles of poles. In spite of all obstacles, the line was surveyed and constructed in record time. By November 25, 1939, the first oil was received in Salt Lake City. The line operated smoothly even with temperatures sometimes 36° below zero along the route. Built for the most part with eight-inch pipe, the line had a capacity of 6,000 to 8,000 barrels per day. It was the largest pipeline project built by the industry in 1939 and cost about $4,500,000.

While Standard was busy with the problem of reducing transportation costs, an event of considerable significance for the future took place in western Kansas. Foreseeing a big increase in the use of tractors, trucks, and autos by farmers and believing that the cost of fuel and lubricants was too high, the first co-operative oil

36. William G. Heltzel, "Building Oil Pipe Line Across Continental Divide," *The Oil and Gas Journal* (May 16, 1940), 144; (May 23, 1940), 81; (May 30, 1940), 44.

refinery in the country was built at Phillipsburg. From its beginning in 1929, the Consumers Co-operative Association had compounded its own lubricating oil, manufactured greases and paints, and bought its refined products from various refiners. The Association was able to capitalize itself quickly as a petroleum wholesaler. More and more local co-ops joined the Association, but it had increasing difficulty in supplying the demand. In 1938 it had 427 co-ops using 54,000,000 gallons of refined fuel.[37] The Association soon found itself, like other oil companies, unable to compete without becoming integrated. It had to follow suit or die. Its own oil-compounding and grease plant had paid for itself quickly, which showed what could be done in other lines. Consequently, the Association decided to go into the refinery business. It formed the Co-operative Refinery Association which built a $551,000 refinery at Phillipsburg and organized a $350,000 pipeline unit and a producing unit. Of the total outlay of some $900,000, the farmers invested $365,000 for preferred shares and the banks for co-operatives the rest.

The refinery at Phillipsburg began operating on January 1, 1940, with a capacity of 3,500 barrels per day. Until its pipeline was completed and sufficient well connections made, Standard of Indiana made available to it about 1,200 barrels of crude oil per day through lease connections.[38] Standard also co-operated in securing for it other connections in the field.

In 1939 the Indiana Farm Bureau Co-operative Association, Inc., began building a $250,000 refinery on the Ohio River near Mt. Vernon, Indiana.

Although a sharp curtailment in drilling in 1938 resulted in a decrease of 1,639,169 barrels in Standard's crude oil production over 1937, crude runs to stills increased from 87,207,189 to 87,756,076. To simplify and consolidate its crude oil buying, Standard on July 1, 1938, acquired the assets and business, except in Texas, of the Stanolind Crude Oil Purchasing Company, and the company was liquidated.[39] All employees were transferred to Standard's payroll and credited with the service they had given to Stanolind in calculating their rights under the various employee benefit plans. A new department, the Crude Oil Purchasing

37. *National Petroleum News*, XXXVIII, No. 35 (August 28, 1936), 30, 32, 34.
38. "Indiana Standard Furnishes Crude to Co-operative," *The Oil and Gas Journal* (July 18, 1940), 29.
39. *The New York Times*, June 29, 1938.

Department under the direction of A. W. Peake of Chicago but with headquarters in Tulsa, was established to handle crude oil buying. Since Standard was not domesticated in Texas, a newly organized subsidiary, the Stanolind Oil Purchasing Company (Delaware), was organized to take over the property in that state.

A new 18,000-barrel combination cracking unit went into operation at Whiting and a third unit was completed at Texas City in 1938. The demand for higher-octane aviation gasoline during the thirties led to the construction at Whiting in 1938 of a plant to manufacture iso-octane upon a large scale. By using iso-octane, 100-octane aviation gasoline could be produced. The bulk of aviation fuel used commercially in 1938 and particularly that furnished by Standard was 87-octane straight run, seven-pound Reid vapor pressure, which complied with the old Army "Fighting" grade specifications.[40] Mid-Continent straight-run gasoline was no longer sufficient for this purpose, so in most instances the use of other stocks was required in order that 87 octane could be obtained without the use of excessive quantities of lead. Stanavo Ethyl 87 contained approximately 3 c.c. of tetraethyl lead per gallon.

In 1937 Standard of New Jersey withdrew from the Stanavo Board. A failure to secure another participant to replace the Jersey company left the Stanavo Board not only without world-wide distribution but even without coverage in the eastern part of the United States. In addition, the unfavorable price situation on aviation products from 1935 to 1938 made this phase of the oil business relatively unattractive. Under the circumstances, officials of Standard of Indiana were reluctant to assume the expense necessary for advertising and development of the Stanavo name. Consequently, the company withdrew from the Stanavo Board in June, 1938. Despite the breakup of the Stanavo organization, Standard of Indiana retained the right to manufacture and market aviation fuels and lubricants under the Stanavo trademarks in the fifteen states of its marketing area.

In the octane race during the late 1930's to improve the quality of gasoline, refiners had resorted to a greater and greater concentration of tetraethyl lead in meeting competition, until by 1939 the maximum of 3 c.c. of lead had been reached. Owing to competition, refiners were making better gasoline than even the newest cars could properly utilize, and the fuel cost was climbing

40. Company Encyclopedia: Manufacturing, Gasoline, Motor and Aviation, 12.

to a point above the price at which manufacturers could produce it and make a reasonable profit. Even so, the octane race continued.

For some time research men had been working with catalysts as a supplement to heat and pressure for cracking purposes. Catalysts were materials which, when introduced into a reaction chamber, aided in bringing about the desired results in ways which were known and could be controlled, although the reason for their effects often remained a mystery. Catalysts greatly increased the range of possibilities in making crude oil yield the kind and quality of petroleum products most needed. The introduction of the Houdry process in 1938, which operated on lower temperatures than in thermal cracking, used a catalyst of a clay type and produced from gas oil intermediate an 80 per cent yield of gasoline of a very high octane. It marked the beginning of catalytic cracking and served as a stimulus to research in finding new methods of getting more and better gasoline from crude oil. Standard investigated the Houdry process but concluded that the royalty was too high.[41]

In 1938 Standard of Indiana, Standard of New Jersey, I. G. Farbenindustrie, and the M. W. Kellogg Company were working co-operatively on a catalytic refining process.[42] The technical staff of Standard made numerous contributions to the rapid and efficient development of the fluid process and supplied a significant portion of the basic thinking leading to an understanding of the principles of handling the finely powdered catalyst by air or vapor lift. The result of the combined effort was the development of a "fluid" catalyst process for use in producing raw materials for synthetic rubber and aviation gasoline. The company built a fluid catalyst pilot plant at Whiting in 1939 and secured fundamental data which was used by the group in further research on the process.

On account of the growing importance of oil for heating, Standard established about 1938 a laboratory with the necessary testing equipment to study fuel oils under controlled conditions. While the laboratory could not test all of the oil burners made by 350 or more manufacturers, it selected the principal types used in the area where its oil was sold and tested various kinds of oil in them.

While the recession was in progress, consideration was given to advancing the welfare of the employees, especially in the matter

41. *Business Week* (May 13, 1939), 38.
42. *Ibid.*

of putting the pension system on a safe and firm foundation. As the end of the Fifth Employee Stock Purchase Plan approached in 1938, employee groups made representations to the management that such plans did not confer benefits upon all employees equally. Either through inability or disinclination, a considerable number had not participated in the plan. Consequently, they did not receive their proportionate share of the company's contribution. While there was considerable to be said for the practice of rewarding thrifty employees, the Directors decided that when the

ANNUITIES PAID BY STANDARD OIL COMPANY (INDIANA) 1903–1938

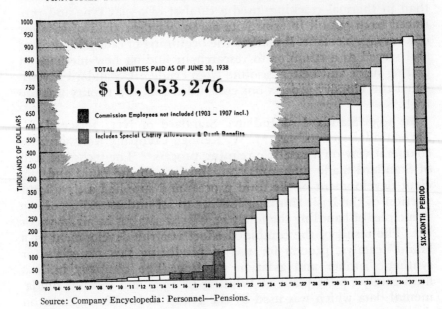

TOTAL ANNUITIES PAID AS OF JUNE 30, 1938

$ 10,053,276

Commission Employees not included (1903 – 1907 incl.)

Includes Special Charity Allowances & Death Benefits

Source: Company Encyclopedia: Personnel—Pensions.

Fifth Employee Stock Purchasing Plan was liquidated in August, 1938, they would not propose another plan to the stockholders. During the seventeen years in which the plan had been in effect, 1,548,823 shares of stock had been distributed. At one time or another 19,916 employees had participated.[43]

The discontinuance of the plan facilitated the adoption of a new annuity plan for employees. As a larger and larger number of employees reached retirement age and the cost of paying

43. "301,509 Shares Distributed to 12,977 in 5th Stock Plan," *Stanolind Record*, XIX, No. 11 (September, 1938), 3.

annuities out of current earnings mounted, it had long been apparent that some plan providing for greater security would have to be devised. The number of annuitants had grown until in 1937 there were 737. A further financial burden was placed upon the company when the Social Security Act became effective on January 1, 1937.

After a thorough study of the problem, an entirely new retirement plan was formulated, approved at a special meeting of the stockholders on December 22, 1938, and made effective on January 1, 1939.[44] Under the plan, equal contributions were to be made by the company and the employee to purchase an annuity from the Equitable Life Assurance Society covering future service after 1938. Employees were to contribute 2 per cent of their monthly pay up to $250 a month and 5 per cent of all pay above that amount with the company matching it dollar for dollar. An employee having ten years' service would acquire a vested right in the company's payments to the insurance carrier on his behalf. If he withdrew from the plan or died before retirement, the employee or his estate would receive his own contribution with interest compounded at 2½ per cent. Those employed on December 31, 1938, who had completed one year of service and were not more than sixty-five years old were eligible to participate. Others employed on that date and those hired thereafter would be eligible after completing one year's service. The retirement age was set at sixty-five for males and sixty for females. Each employee was to have a month in which to decide whether he or she wished to participate in the new plan.

ROSTER OF EMPLOYEE SERVICE ENDING DECEMBER 31, 1936
STANDARD OIL COMPANY (INDIANA)

Less than 5 years of service	5,576
More than 5 and less than 10	3,600
More than 10 and less than 20	7,190
More than 20 and less than 30	1,895
More than 30 and less than 40	330
More than 40 years of service	68

In the final group are four Directors.

Source: *Annual Report to Stockholders for the Year 1936.*

So long as the financial needs and the condition of the company warranted it, annuities for service prior to January 1, 1939, would

44. "New Retirement Plan, Approved by Stockholders, Effective January 1," *Stanolind Record*, XX, No. 3 (January, 1939), 1.

be paid out of current earnings. To insure these annuity payments, the company set up an irrevocable trust fund which was to be increased out of profits as rapidly as possible until an amount sufficient to cover all future payments on account of past service had accumulated.[45] This amount was estimated at $38,700,000. For this purpose the stockholders authorized an initial payment of $2,180,000 into the fund on January 1, 1939. By the end of 1945 the fund had assets with a value of $36,023,732, of which $30,744,950 represented cash contributed by the company.

After the inauguration of the new retirement plan two adjustments were made in 1939. In computing annuities for employees placed on pension subsequent to January 1, 1939, it was found that the amount in some cases would be less than $300 annually. Therefore, in those instances the Board of Directors authorized a special allowance sufficient to bring the payments up to at least $300. In the second place, provision was made to permit employees in a real emergency to temporarily suspend or cease payments to the new plan altogether with certain restrictions.

From a financial point of view, the recession had a most adverse effect upon the company's business. The combined net sales for 1938 decreased in dollar value from $358,227,298 in 1937 to $327,910,574, a decrease of $30,316,724, or about 8 per cent. The volume decreased from 118,114,315 to 110,404,268 barrels. Net earnings after deductions dropped from $55,950,785 in 1937 to $27,771,976, a loss of $28,178,809. Cash dividends dropped from $2.30 in 1937 to $1.00 per share. However, with an upturn in the national demand for petroleum products late in 1938 and the gathering of the war clouds in Europe, business steadily improved. The combined net sales increased from 110,404,268 barrels in 1938 to 121,293,649 in 1939 and the net earnings from $27,771,976 to $34,142,643. The cash dividend was increased to $1.25 per share in 1939. The volume of business in 1939 was the largest in the history of the company, and the percentage gain was in excess of that for the industry as a whole.

In September, 1938, Standard accepted the invitation of the Chicago Stock Exchange to list its 15,280,826 shares of capital stock. It was the nineteenth company to accept an invitation to list its stock under a special listing plan for certain corporations having securities listed on the New York Stock Exchange.

45. *Stanolind Record*, XXI, No. 6 (April, 1940), 2.

CHAPTER XXI

World War II Years

WITH THE OUTBREAK OF WORLD WAR II IN SEPTEMBER, 1939, THE United States began strengthening its national defense system. The oil industry was geared to the national defense program in June, 1940, when Robert E. Wilson, President of Pan American Petroleum & Transport Company and one of the industry's top scientists and oil executives, was placed in charge of the Natural Gas and Petroleum Section of the Raw Materials Division of the new National Defense Advisory Commission. Wilson was the first oilman to be taken directly into the national defense setup. Working as a dollar a year man, he spent three days a week in Washington eliminating bottlenecks in the petroleum industry, serving as technical advisor on various problems, and being general consultant for different government departments on matters pertaining to the petroleum industry. He made strenuous efforts to get the government to do something to stimulate the manufacture of 100-octane gasoline and synthetic rubber, but met with comparatively little success. When this agency gave way to the new Office of Production Management with William S. Knudsen as Director, Wilson continued serving in the same capacity.

The outbreak of war and preparations for national defense had a quickening effect upon Standard and created a sense of urgency to get things done. Standard's officials reviewed all of the company's manufacturing, construction, and research projects and gave priority to those which might aid in meeting the anticipated needs of the government. All others were either dropped or modified.

Standard and its subsidiaries immediately embarked upon an extensive program of expanding and modernizing their facilities. As a result of previous study and planning, three river terminals were built in 1940 at Bettendorf, Iowa, Winona, Minnesota, and Cape Girardeau, Missouri. At the same time, a new streamlined, diesel-propelled towboat named the Stanolind "A" began pushing barges of gasoline and other petroleum products up the Mississippi from Wood River to the new terminals, up the Ohio to

Evansville, and to other places. It was capable of pushing six loaded barges with 2,400,000 gallons of oil products.

After much delay the company's Co-ordinating Department completed its study of the company's transportation problems in November, 1940, and recommended that the gasoline pipeline from Sugar Creek be extended from Council Bluffs to Sioux Falls, South Dakota, that a lateral line be built from Burlington Junction near St. Joseph, Missouri, to Des Moines, Iowa, that a gasoline line be built from Whiting to Indianapolis, Indiana, and that a marine terminal be established at Benton Harbor, Michigan. Seubert finally backed the recommendations. He urged that Standard go ahead and benefit from lower transportation costs because the company was badly handicapped. Competitors had facilities which Standard did not have.[1] He wished that the company had the Des Moines stub in right now. The recommendations were unanimously approved by the Directors, and the lines to Sioux Falls, Des Moines, and Indianapolis were completed in 1941. Consideration was given in 1941 to building a products line from Whiting to River Rouge, but no action was taken. While these measures were being debated, a further invasion of Standard's marketing territory occurred when the Globe Oil & Refining Company completed a gasoline pipeline in 1941 from its refinery at McPherson, Kansas, to Council Bluffs.

Standard had developed truck transportation from its refineries to bulk stations and dealers to some extent, but it still continued as late as 1939 to use rail tank cars for the greater part of its distribution. With the completion of its new products pipelines and water terminals, the company added twenty-four trucks to its fleet in 1940 and had thirty-seven on order. Lacking an adequate trucking fleet of its own, Standard employed contract carriers more extensively.

Recognizing that low-cost transportation was vital not only in meeting competition on finished products but on crude, the Stanolind Pipe Line Company built a crude pipeline from the main trunk line at La Plata, Missouri, to the Wood River refinery in 1940. To provide another outlet for the heavy production of western Kansas crude, a 134-mile pipeline was built from the Bemis pool in Ellis County to Washington, Kansas, where it connected with the line running from Wyoming to Freeman, Missouri.

1. Memorandum by Allan Jackson, November 20, 1940. Co-ordinating Department, Transportation Division, Progress Memorandums.

The Pan American Pipe Line Company constructed a 196-mile crude line to connect with the East Texas field. It also built several towboats and barges to carry Texas coastal crude to Texas City.

The modernization and expansion program not only involved the building of new products lines and river terminals but improvements in manufacturing, production, and marketing as well. Old manufacturing equipment was rehabilitated and new refinery units were constructed to improve the quality of products. Improvement in the reduction of heavy residual oils was made possible through the building of a 12,000-barrel unit at Whiting in 1940. With the completion of the new engine research laboratory at Whiting, technical men studying automotive transportation had unsurpassed facilities for determining facts of value to Standard's customers and its business. A new topping plant, used to take gasoline and other light products from asphaltic base crudes, began operations at Texas City in 1939. The residual stock was shipped to Pan American refineries at Baltimore and Savannah for producing asphalt.

One of the most urgent defense needs was for toluene, a clear, aromatic liquid which was a basic element in the manufacture of TNT. Most of it had been obtained from the steel companies and the Koppers Company as a by-product of coke making, being distilled from coal tar. When Hitler invaded Poland in 1939, Standard was already doing considerable research on new processes for manufacturing high-octane components from crude oil to meet the steadily growing demand for aviation gasoline and other high-octane products. In the course of this research, the laboratory found that in hydroforming naphtha to improve the octane number a substantial amount of toluene was formed.

Designed and constructed on the basis of laboratory experience and the operation of a small pilot plant, the world's first commercial hydroforming process was placed in operation at the Texas City refinery in the fall of 1940 to make high-quality motor fuel.[2] The unit was capable of reforming about 7,500 barrels per day of 40 to 50 octane heavy naphtha produced from two of the largest combination crude-running and cracking units in the world plus small amounts of heavy naphtha produced from miscellaneous crude-topping operations.

The new process was so flexible that it could produce high yields of selected aromatics and high-quality aviation base stock.

2. *Standard Oil Company (Indiana) in the War*, 3.

This feature was particularly important from a military point of view since it afforded a means of substantially increasing the supply of aviation gasoline and toluene. With the assistance of the data secured in operating Pan American's hydroforming unit at Texas City and the findings of the research staff at Whiting, new plants were designed for construction by Standard at Whiting, by the government at its ordnance works at Baytown, Texas, and at several other points.

The effects of newer refining processes, particularly catalytic cracking, alkylation, polymerization, catalytic reforming, and hydrogenation were beginning to appear in the fall of 1939. New "super" motor fuels with higher antiknock qualities were introduced, accompanied by big advertising campaigns. Sun Oil announced its Nu-Blue Sunoco made by the Houdry process. Proclaimed as a "new miracle of gasoline chemistry," Nu-Blue Sunoco was said to have a high knockless power, be quick-starting, and provide economical mileage. Socony-Vacuum, Standard of New Jersey, Shell, and others also introduced new "super" fuels with higher antiknock rating. American Oil and Gulf retaliated with advertisements, not introducing new fuels but emphasizing the fact that their fuels were continually improved. The "octane race" spread rapidly to the Pacific Coast and other sections of the country.[3]

Late in January, 1940, Standard interrupted its regularly scheduled newspaper advertising program to run a special campaign to restate its policy of improving motor fuels and answer competitive claims for new "super" antiknock gasoline.[4] To the millions of car owners using Standard products the company said: "It is our unwavering policy that Standard Oil products will not be excelled in all around quality, for their purpose, at their price." Standard Red Crown was balanced to satisfy most economically all the needs of most of the cars. From time to time its antiknock qualities had been increased so that the majority of the cars could use it economically. It had recently been given higher antiknock quality at no increase in price and no sacrifice in other qualities. It was the intent of the company to keep Red Crown unexcelled among regular grades in all-around performance. If the motorist needed low fuel cost at a reasonable sacrifice in performance,

3. H. Stanley Norman, "Octane Race Spreads," *The Oil and Gas Journal* (February 1. 1940), 10.
4. *The Chicago Tribune,* January 28, 1940.

economical Stanolind gasoline was satisfactory. If the ultimate in performance was desired or if the engine was of unusually high compression, Solite was a perfect answer. Standard's advertisements stressed the importance of all fundamental gasoline qualities —quick starting, good mileage, power, and antiknock—not just one quality.

Further revolutionary changes in refining operations were foreshadowed in 1940 when Standard of New Jersey announced the fluid catalytic cracking process and demonstrated the new method for newspapermen in February, 1941. A number of companies contributed to this development, which had been under wide study. Among the leaders in the development, in addition to Standard of New Jersey, were M. W. Kellogg and Standard of Indiana. Under the old method of catalytic cracking, oil vapors were passed through a chamber containing a catalyst in the form of lumps or pellets. In the course of twenty or thirty minutes coke deposits accumulated on the catalyst and impaired its effectiveness. Operations had to be stopped to burn off this coke in a stream of air. To maintain continuous operation it was necessary to have several chambers. In the fluid process the catalyst was in the form of a powder and was maintained in a turbulent bed by oil vapors passing up through it. The turbulence permitted the catalyst to flow like a liquid. Spent catalyst could therefore be continuously withdrawn to a separate zone where it was regenerated. The fluid process possessed marked advantages over the old fixed-bed method of catalytic cracking in time, efficiency, and yield, and in the quality of the gasoline produced.

In the Sales Department several hundred outmoded service stations were rehabilitated and modernized. When the program was about 60 per cent completed, the outbreak of war brought it to a halt.

One of the very few strikes ever called against Standard up to this time in its history occurred in August, 1940, when its commission agents in the Milwaukee division went on strike.[5] It affected about 100 agents. The strike was the culmination of a series of disputes between the company and the union dating back to February, 1939, when the Cartage and Commission Em-

5. "Wisconsin Commission Agents Walk Out On Indiana Standard," *National Petroleum News,* XXXII, No. 33 (August 14, 1940), 18; "Indiana Standard Seeking Status of Commission Agents," *National Petroleum News,* XXXII, No. 41 (October 9, 1940), 26.

ployees Union had asked for a new schedule of commissions calling for 1 cent per gallon on gasoline and kerosene delivered to
stations within a town and 2 cents on deliveries outside. If the proposed change did not give the agents a 10 per cent increase in
income, the union asked Standard to guarantee the difference.
Standard claimed that the demands would mean a 33 per cent
increase.

The dispute came to a head in May, 1940, when the company
cut the commissions 10 per cent. At a conference in July, the
union asked that the rate of pay be based on the demands made
in February, 1939. The company refused but made counter-
proposals. In the meantime, the union filed charges with the
National Labor Relations Board at Milwaukee claiming that the
company refused to bargain collectively, used intimidation, and
coerced union members. Furthermore, the union went on strike.
During the stalemate the union affiliated with the American
Federation of Labor and attempted to organize all Standard employees in Wisconsin. Within a short time all of the strikers,
except for about sixteen, went back to work. As a result of negotiations, reinstatement and financial settlements were offered to
the sixteen. Three accepted reinstatement and the other thirteen
accepted the financial settlement. The question as to whether the
strike had been an unfair labor practice was dropped. Owing to
the situation which had developed, Standard requested the
National Labor Relations Board to hold an election among the
commission employees of the division to determine the qualified
bargaining agency. The election was won by the AF of L local.

While Standard was modernizing its facilities and aiding in the
national defense program, it became involved in litigation with
the federal government in three cases. The first was an outgrowth
of the competitive marketing situation in the Detroit area. When
the Michigan state court dismissed the charges against Standard
in 1938 for violating the Fair Trade Law, the Michigan Retail
Gasoline Dealers Association made efforts to get the U.S. Department of Justice to investigate, but it reportedly turned down the
case. The Association then turned to the Federal Trade Commission. On November 29, 1940, the Commission issued a complaint
against Standard of Indiana for violation of Section 2a of the
Clayton Act as amended by the Robinson-Patman Act.[6] The law

---

6. *Complaint. In the Matter of Standard Oil Company. United States of America
Before the Federal Trade Commission,* November 29, 1940.

required that every seller market the same article to competing customers at exactly the same price unless there was no effect upon competition. It made no provision for a difference in price between jobbers and retailers. Quantity discounts were prohibited, except where the seller could show that such discounts reflected only savings in manufacturing costs or methods of delivery or were made to meet competition as had formerly been permitted in the Clayton Act. The Commission charged that Standard's practice of selling Red Crown gasoline in tank-car quantities to Citron-Kolb, Stikeman, Wayne Oil, and Ned's at 1½ cents per gallon less than it sold to its retail dealer customers in the Detroit area injured, destroyed, and prevented competition.

The complaint raised a very important issue: Could Standard or any other company, acting in good faith and in order to meet competition, sell on a tank-car basis to jobbers or wholesalers who maintained their own bulk plants but who also retailed at lower prices than to other retailers?

The Commission's hearing on the complaint began in March, 1941. Standard denied that it had violated the Robinson-Patman Act and based its defense upon two considerations. First, price differentials were justified by savings in distributing costs. It was pointed out that, with one exception, Standard had not sold gasoline at tank-car prices to the four companies until they had installed bulk storage. The one exception was Ned's, which had received from September, 1936, to February, 1938, gasoline at ½ cent per gallon less than tank-car prices because competitors had offered such a price to Ned's. When the four installed their own bulk storage, used their own trucks for delivering, and assumed a part of the distributing costs which Standard normally bore in selling to retailers, the company began selling to all four at tank-car prices, which was 1½ cents per gallon less than to other retailers. Standard's general policy in classifying firms as jobbers was that the jobber had to have adequate bulk storage and be able to receive deliveries by tank car or transport truck, have adequate distribution and delivery facilities, be able to buy substantial tank-car volume and do a continuous volume of business, have a satisfactory credit rating, maintain facilities and personnel to operate as a wholesaler or jobber, and be able to assume the hazards and expenses of fully operating his own business. Standard contended that the four companies involved met these requirements.

Secondly, Standard contended that the prices were cut in good faith for the sole purpose of meeting equally low or lower prices of competitors and retaining its customers. At the time, the company had already lost three of its jobber customers in Detroit, and it stood to lose others. The evidence showed that on at least twelve different occasions competitors had offered to supply the four jobbers in question at lower prices than Standard. If Standard had not met the competitive prices, it would have lost the jobbers.

After the conclusion of the hearing, a decision in the case was postponed on account of the war.

The second case involving Standard was unprecedented in scope. Under the direction of Assistant Attorney General Thurman Arnold, the federal government filed a single suit against 367 oil companies, including Standard of Indiana, and the American Petroleum Institute in September, 1940, in the United States District Court for the District of Columbia.[7] Called "the Mother Hubbard" suit because it included virtually the entire industry, the government made sixty-nine charges in the complaint, covering practically every activity of the industry from the oil well to the service station. The suit charged the defendants with working in collaboration with and through the American Petroleum Institute to fix crude oil prices, restrict crude production, compel independent producers to sell to majors instead of to independent refiners, prevent independents from using their pipelines, maintain excessive transportation rates, control wholesale distributors, fix retail prices, suppress technological improvements and deny the benefits to the public, establish exorbitant price differentials, and fix jobber margins.

The government asked for the dissolution of the American Petroleum Institute, an injunction against the alleged practices on the part of the companies involved, and general relief with respect to the organization, functioning, and operation of the defendants. The relief sought was drastic. If the case had come to trial and if the charges had been sustained, far-reaching changes in the corporate and economic situation of the entire oil industry would have resulted. The case, however, was never to come to trial.

On the same day as "the Mother Hubbard" suit was filed, the Department of Justice filed suits against Standard of Indiana and

7. Henry D. Ralph, "Jackson Files Anti-Trust Suit Against Major Companies," *The Oil and Gas Journal* (October 3, 1940), 13.

Phillips Petroleum, as owners of pipeline subsidiaries, and the Great Lakes Pipe Line Company for violating the Elkins Act. In the proceedings against Standard in the Federal District Court at Hammond, Indiana, the Department charged that dividends received by Standard from the Stanolind Pipe Line Company, one of its subsidiaries, constituted rebates under the law. The complaint listed rebates—dividends—of $6,459,412 for the years 1931 through 1939 and demanded an accounting of the receipts for 1940, an injunction, and triple damages for the receipts since January 1, 1939.[8] Such receipts or dividends were alleged in the complaint to be "rebates and offsets." The case involved the question of whether payments of dividends by a subsidiary to its parent company constituted a rebate of the sort forbidden by the Elkins Act. The question had never been raised before, and there was considerable difference of opinion among the experts as to whether the Elkins Act could be applied. If the pipeline were merely a division of Standard, there would be no question of a rebate for there would be no dividends. If such dividends were found to be a rebate, it would be a new and revolutionary construction of the act, and many similar companies would be liable to prosecution.

Standard filed its answer to the suit in January, 1941, and denied that dividends paid by the Stanolind Pipe Line Company constituted illegal rebates under the Elkins Act.[9] It claimed that the Elkins Act provided penalties only when money was knowingly received by the shipper as a rebate or offset. On the other hand, it asserted that it had a legal right to transport its own crude over a wholly owned subsidiary pipeline and receive dividends from that subsidiary. Congress had not included pipelines in the "commodities clause" of the Hepburn Act of 1906 forbidding railroads from owning commodities transported by them. Moreover, it had not enacted any pipeline divorcement legislation. Although the National Industrial Recovery Act had authorized the President to bring about divorcement of pipelines where rates or practices tended to create a monopoly, nothing had been done. In further support of its case, the company cited the fact that the Interstate Commerce Commission had recognized and approved proprietary

8. "Department of Justice Explains Basis for Pipe Line Suits," *The Oil and Gas Journal* (October 3, 1940), 21; "Indiana Standard Hits Back at Pipeline 'Rebate' Charges," *National Petroleum News*, XXXII, No. 41 (October 9, 1940), 24.

9. "Standard of Indiana Replies to Pipeline 'Rebate' Charges," *National Petroleum News*, XXXIII, No. 4 (January 22, 1941), 9.

ownership in terminal and industrial railroads and the payment of dividends to the owner-shippers. Moreover, Standard insisted that enjoining the payment of dividends, as the government asked, would be a deprivation of property without due process of law. For these reasons, Standard believed it was justified in thinking that its dividends from the Stanolind Pipe Line Company were lawful.

The case never came to trial, because in December, 1941, a gigantic omnibus suit, involving millions of dollars in treble damages under the Elkins Act, was filed in the Federal District Court in Washington, D.C., by the government against twenty major oil companies, including Standard of Indiana, and fifty-two common carrier pipelines. The charges were the same as in the previous suits against Standard of Indiana, Phillips, and the Great Lakes Pipe Line Company. After extended negotiations, a consent judgment was entered under which virtually all of the pipeline carriers in the United States were restricted in the amount of dividends which they could pay to their shipper-owners.[10] Under the decree, effective January 1, 1942, each common carrier concerned was forbidden to pay any shipper-owner in any calendar year any dividend derived from transportation or other common carrier services which exceeded 7 per cent of the valuation of the common carrier's property, if the common carrier transported during the year any crude oil or petroleum products for the shipper-owner. Earnings of each common carrier derived from common carrier services in excess of the permitted dividend were to be transferred to the surplus account as a separate item usable for the extension of common carrier facilities, for maintaining normal working capital requirements, and for the retirement of debts originally incurred in the construction or acquisition of common carrier property. The judgment made no provision for the payment of damages unless the companies violated the 7 per cent return limitation. Inasmuch as Standard and Stanolind Pipe Line were involved in the blanket suit and judgment had been entered, the government agreed to a dismissal of the previous suit against Standard for violating the Elkins Act.

As the danger of war came closer in 1941, President Roosevelt took steps toward welding the petroleum industry into a unified organization for supplying the armed forces, industry, and

10. "Pipeline Suit Ends; 7% Return Specified," *National Petroleum News,* XXXIII, No. 52 (December 24, 1941), 3.

civilians. He created in May the Office of Petroleum Co-ordinator for National Defense and appointed Secretary of the Interior Harold L. Ickes to head the agency.[11] When this office was established, Robert E. Wilson resigned his position in the Office of Production Management, and the organization headed by Knudsen was dissolved. Bruce K. Brown, a Director of Standard of Indiana and General Manager of Research and Development, was the first of Standard's men to be called into service in the Office of Petroleum Co-ordinator. Given a leave of absence by the company, Brown was named special consultant on aviation gasoline. His main task was to expedite the building of new refining units and develop measures for the most efficient utilization of existing facilities until new production could be started. In July, 1942, Brown became an assistant deputy petroleum co-ordinator in the Office of Petroleum Administration for War.

To advise and counsel with the Petroleum Co-ordinator, a Petroleum Industry War Council, composed of seventy-eight oil company executives, representing large and small companies and trade associations, was created. Through this body the government channeled its dealings with the industry. It, in turn, had a series of national committees to consider various functional aspects of the oil problems. Seubert and Wilson of Standard of Indiana were appointed members of the Council and, together with A. W. Peake, they served on several standing committees. District committees were established through which the Petroleum Co-ordinator worked on matters relating to the five different districts. To these committees and subcommittees many of Standard's executive personnel were appointed.

Preparations for war meant not only a terrific demand for oil but the extension of governmental control over the petroleum industry to an unprecedented degree. Under the Price Control Act, Leon Henderson, the Administrator, froze prices of crude and most of its products. Also, control of production quotas, normally a function of the several states, was brought under the direction of Harold L. Ickes in his capacity as Petroleum Co-ordinator.

The impact of the preparations for war in 1941 was felt by

11. After the beginning of hostilities the name of the agency was changed to the Office of Petroleum Co-ordinator for War, and after December, 1942, to Petroleum Administration for War.

Standard in many ways. With the passage of the Selective Service Act in September, 1940, and the calling out of the reservists and National Guard units, Standard formulated and announced in January, 1941, its policy regarding military leaves of absence for employees.[12] It divided employees into two categories. In the first group were those who served in any recognized military organization other than the regular Army, Navy, or Marine Corps for a period less than thirty days. They would receive in pay the difference between what the employee would have earned had he been at work and any lesser amount he actually received from the government for the first three weeks of service. Commission employees were paid the difference between gross earnings and any lesser amount received from the government for three weeks. In the second group were those who served in any reserve unit of the regular Army, Navy, or Marine Corps for thirty days or more and those called under the Selective Training and Service Act of 1940. If they had more than one year's continuous service with the company, they would receive one month's pay. If they had served the company for one year or more, the company would pay an additional month's pay. If an employee had been with the company less than one continuous year, he received one month's pay upon the completion of one month's military service. For thirty days' or more military service, commission employees received one month's pay, which would be equal to what they would have earned net during the last full calendar month worked immediately before being checked out, as computed by the company.

Leaves of absence were to be granted upon request for either type of service. With respect to the first group, leaves would be granted for such time as the employee was required to serve but not to exceed twenty-nine days. Leave would be granted for those in the second group for such time as the employee was engaged in active service. Any employee who was required to be away from his work for thirty days or more on military service was entitled to restoration of employment and benefits in accordance with Public Resolution No. 96, 76th Congress, and the Selective Training and Service Act of 1940.

Since the policy announced in January, 1941, did not apply to those who volunteered for military service, the company in December, 1941, made provision for these employees, effective as of

12. "Military Service," *Stanolind Record*, XXII, No. 3 (January, 1941), 1-2.

September 16, 1941.[13] If they had been with the company for one
year, they received a month's pay after thirty days of military
service and another month's pay after their discharge. Those with
the company less than a year got one month's pay upon being discharged from the service. A new provision applicable to all employees who had entered any branch of the military service after
September 16, 1940, or who entered in the future gave them credit
for company service during the time they were in the armed
forces.

As German submarines took a heavy toll of the shipping of
Great Britain and her allies in the summer of 1941, Standard, in
common with others of the petroleum industry, began playing a
part in what became the Battle of the Atlantic. This involved the
delivery of millions of barrels of petroleum products to the East
Coast for use by the Navy for shipment overseas and for military
and domestic supply in that area. These deliveries, made by tank
car, pipelines, tankers on the Great Lakes, and river barges, helped
to supply the extra needs created by the war and replace losses due
to submarine attacks. From May until the end of 1941 Pan
American Petroleum & Transport was called upon to contribute
about 20 per cent of its own and chartered fleet toward carrying
military oil products from the Gulf to Atlantic coastal ports. The
only way that Standard could come near keeping up with the
demand was to have its personnel work with all possible speed in
loading and unloading tank cars.

Standard's refineries were taxed to capacity in 1941 to meet the
demand for oil products. All previous records for crude runs were
broken as 112,562,112 barrels were processed. The company made
every drop of aviation gasoline that could be secured from existing units, and plans were made for additional units.

At a time when all facilities were needed for production, fire
broke out at 5:45 A.M. on September 24, 1941, in the No. 1 Treating Plant at Whiting and set off a series of terrific explosions.[14]
Three long blasts of the plant siren summoned employees to help
fight the inferno. Flames spread to other buildings and storage
tanks. The fire soon covered an area equal to several city blocks.
Black pillars of smoke were visible forty miles east of Whiting. As
tanks exploded, pipe and sections of steel plate were hurled out of

13. "Employees Who Enlist To Receive Same Benefits Granted Others in Army,
    Navy," *Stanolind Record*, XXIII, No. 3 (January, 1942), 14.
14. *Chicago Daily Tribune*, September 25, 26, 1941.

the plant and fell on the railroad tracks, causing several trains to be rerouted into Chicago. By noon all fires were under control, but it was not until late afternoon that the fire was out. One man was killed, three suffered lost-time accidents, and approximately one hundred received minor burns and injuries. It was estimated that 315,000 gallons of naphtha and fuel oil, about thirty treating tanks and six storage tanks, and several buildings were destroyed at an estimated loss of approximately $500,000.

CRUDE OIL PRODUCTION AND REFINERY RUNS 1940–1951
STANDARD OIL COMPANY (INDIANA) AND SUBSIDIARIES

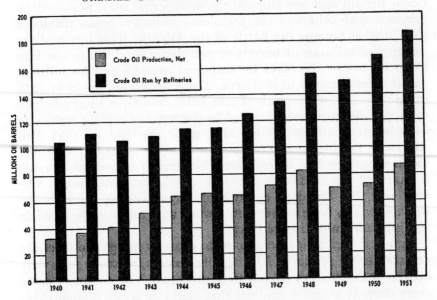

In addition to continuing its aggressive search to discover new sources of crude and obtain oil lands for immediate and long-term development, Stanolind Oil and Gas purchased several important properties and producing concerns in 1941. Approximately $1,100,000 was paid to the Bond Oil Company and Awoeb Oil Corporation for eighteen producing wells and seven thousand acres in the Slaughter field of West Texas. The discovery well and 3,000 acres in the Abell field of the Northern Pecos Company and an additional acreage north of the area in Crane County were acquired. In addition, Stanolind bought a half interest in the M. J. Delaney properties in Ector County and the L. C. Harrison properties in Hockley County. The oil and gas leases and producing properties of the Barnsdall Oil Company in the Permian Basin of West Texas were purchased for $5,000,000 in cash.[15] It was one of the biggest outright sales of oil properties ever made up to that time in West Texas. The deal involved 3,000 acres of leases, 102 wells, and a daily average gross production of about 2,500 barrels. All of the capital stock of the Coronado Corporation of Dallas, Texas, with oil properties in Texas, Louisiana, and Alabama was purchased for a price in excess of $1,500,000. Its principal producing lands were in southwest Texas and in Louisiana along the Gulf Coast.[16]

Even with these additions, the production of Stanolind Oil and Gas was far less than the crude requirements of Standard and Pan American. Pan American's own production in 1941 amounted to only 5,354 barrels per day, which was less than 10 per cent of its refinery needs, and Stanolind had to supplement its crude production in 1941 by purchasing 108,333,285 barrels of crude outside.

The Stanolind Oil Purchasing Company began buying in March, 1941, some six to seven thousand barrels daily of Gulf Coast crude in the Houston, Texas, area and shipping it northward via Stanolind Pipe Line to Wood River and Whiting.[17] This was the first time in the history of Standard that the flow of oil south of Mexia had been diverted northward. To augment this supply, Standard began about the same time to pipe northward ten to fifteen thousand barrels a day of East Texas crude.

The approach of war placed an unusually heavy responsibility upon the research laboratory to find new and more efficient ways of meeting the demand and providing higher-quality products. About 65 per cent of Standard's research expenditures in 1941 were applied to projects directly or indirectly connected with national defense. As the result of research started in 1936, Standard announced on December 3, 1941, four days prior to the Japanese attack on Pearl Harbor, that it had developed a new process for the manufacture of aviation gasoline called "naphtha isomerization," or what was more popularly known as the isomate method.[18] It was an important step forward in producing aviation

15. *Ibid.*, July 21, 1941.
16. "Stanolind Expands Holdings in Texas Oil Properties," *The Oil and Gas Journal*, XL, No. 28 (November 20, 1941), 19.
17. "Stanolind to Pipe Gulf Coast Crudes Into the Middle West," *National Petroleum News*, XXXIII, No. 7 (February 12, 1941), 11, 23.
18. *The New York Times*, December 4, 1941.

gasoline. Prior to the development of this process, it had taken about 65 per cent iso-octane or equivalent and 35 per cent base blending stocks plus tetraethyl lead to make 100-octane gasoline. Under the new process, the Whiting laboratory had converted ordinary naphthas by a catalytic process into a high-quality aviation base stock for blending with synthetics to make 100-octane gasoline. By increasing the octane of the base stock, it was now possible to make 100-octane aviation gasoline and use only 40 per cent iso-octane and 60 per cent base stock. The process not only saved on synthetics used, but the amount of 100-octane fuel which could be produced from this new blending was increased 50 per cent.

Even though immersed in problems relating to national defense, Standard did not overlook civilian needs and many things were done to increase sales. For the 1941 annual sales conference, the company made a short movie entitled *Work To Be Done*, which featured President Seubert sitting at his desk explaining, with the aid of scenes at the refineries and in the sales fields, the accomplishments of the past year and the work ahead. In June, 1941, Standard launched its "Pride of the Community" campaign. Fifty thousand dollars in prizes were offered to dealers who did the best job of improving the appearance of their stations during the summer. Besides, each winning dealer was to be given a special plaque bearing the word "Ace." A new Auction Quiz Radio program was sponsored over the Blue Network of NBC each Friday evening at 7 P.M. during the summer. In order to have a "family" of gasolines, the name of the premium gasoline, "Solite with Ethyl," was changed to Standard White Crown, and the lowest-priced gasoline, "Stanolind," became Standard Blue Crown. As a consequence, the company now had a "family" of Red, White, and Blue Crown gasoline, and all pumps had glass crowns of the proper color surmounting them.

For greater efficiency and economy in management, Pan American Southern Corporation, a holding company, was merged in October, 1941, with Standard of Indiana, the minority stockholders of Pan American Southern receiving Standard stock in exchange for their holdings. Pan American Southern ceased to exist and its subsidiary, the Pan American Petroleum Corporation, a marketing company in Alabama, Louisiana, Mississippi, and Tennessee, became a direct subsidiary of Standard. The familiar Pan American symbol continued, however, to remain on the highways of the mid-South.

As the company headed into the war, Seubert became eligible for retirement in June, 1941, but at the request of the Directors on three different occasions he continued in active service until the end of 1944. Amos Ball, Vice-President in charge of Sales, reached retirement age in May, 1942, but he was also continued in service until the end of 1944. Buell F. Jones succeeded Stephens in 1940 as General Counsel, but Stephens continued in an advisory capacity until April, 1942, on account of the Blaustein suit. Jones became a Director early in 1942. Bruce K. Brown, General Manager of Research and Development, was elected to the Board in 1940 but resigned in the summer of 1942 due to his full-time position with the Office of Petroleum Co-ordinator. Allan Jackson resigned and retired in 1941. H. E. Hanson and Leon C. Welch, Assistant General Managers of Sales, were elected to the Board in 1944.

When the Japanese attacked Pearl Harbor on December 7, 1941, and war came to the United States, Standard and its subsidiaries had already been playing an important role in the national mobilization effort. Now that the nation was at war, a part of Standard's facilities, as well as those of other oil companies, were quickly converted to manufacturing petroleum products for the armed forces. These facilities were closely co-ordinated under government direction to keep the flow of products synchronized with demand and transportation. In the transition from peace to war, many adjustments had to be made, some of which were by no means profitable and required considerable sacrifice for the common cause.

Two days after Pearl Harbor the Petroleum Co-ordinator called the manufacturers of high-octane aviation fuels to Washington to see what each company could do in the emergency and to recommend a course of action. At this conference, Standard's representative revealed that since 1939 it had been producing hydrocodimer, a high-octane ingredient suitable for aviation gasoline at Whiting and had recently reached a capacity of 35,000 gallons per day.[19] Used with a high-quality base stock, this blending agent would provide approximately 88,000 gallons a day of 100-octane aviation fuel. There was at Whiting an inventory of over 5,000,000 gallons of hydrocodimer which represented the results of about five months' operation of the plant. This production was immediately made available to the government. A committee, which included

19. *Standard Oil Company (Indiana) in the War*, 5.

Standard's representative, was charged with securing the maximum volume of aviation fuel from existing facilities. Standard was asked to continue the production of hydrocodimer and to ship the production together with its inventory to a Gulf Coast refinery where high-grade base stock was available for blending near the sources of demand for the finished product. The result was an immediate and substantial increase in the production of aviation fuels.

There were many other ways in which Standard and its affiliates were of immediate assistance in the national emergency. A few days after the Japanese attack upon Pearl Harbor the Army Air Force, believing that the large storage of aviation fuel on the Pacific Coast was very vulnerable to bombing attacks, requested that a tank for storage be made available at Salt Lake City. The Utah Oil Refining Company took a tank out of service, cleaned it, and began unloading the first shipment on December 27th. Early in 1942 government officials met with representatives of the petroleum industry to arrange for storing and servicing 100-octane gasoline. As a result, the Stanolind Oil Purchasing Company leased bulk storage to the Air Force at eleven different points in the Middle West.[20] To meet wartime conditions without using critical materials for building new tanks, Standard leased ten 80,000-barrel steel storage tanks to other oil companies and eleven to a subsidiary. The Stanolind Oil Purchasing Company sold or leased eighty-six of its 55,000-barrel tanks to other companies in addition to three 55,000-barrel and two 80,000-barrel tanks leased to other subsidiaries of Standard. Fifty per cent of Standard's automobile tire reserve stock was sold to the Rubber Reserve Company in 1942. The antiknock rating of its regular gasoline was reduced and better blending stocks and tetraethyl lead were diverted to making aviation gasoline. Many usable pumps and tanks held in reserve stock were released and sold to farmers, contractors, and to the armed services. In order to provide land for Army maneuvers, Coast Guard barracks, aircraft detector stations, training fields, artillery and rifle ranges, Stanolind Oil and Gas turned over to the government about 63,000 acres of land under emergency agreements and without compensation for much of it.

In order to meet the transportation crisis and the shortage of gasoline in the East, Standard released more than 6,000 tank cars between July, 1941, and May, 1944, and made greater use of pipelines, tankers, river barges, and trucks. The tugboat *Outagamie*

20. *Ibid.*, 19.

was sold to the government under requisition in 1942. In the same year seven big ocean-going tankers owned by Pan American and seven other tankers under charter were turned over to the government under requisition. These were operated to move millions of barrels of oil from Gulf Coast ports to the East. In 1943, in addition to moving 11,139,000 barrels of products to its own terminals and those of its competitors, three of Standard's tankers moved 1,446,000 barrels to Lake Erie terminals for use in the East.[21] To have moved this tonnage by tank cars would have required a train fifty miles long with 7,500 cars. These shipments to Lake Erie ports continued throughout the war.

Despite shortages of materials and manpower, the Stanolind Pipe Line Company pumped the largest amount of crude and finished products in its history. Standard's product lines stepped up their operations about 22 per cent in 1943. The Pan American Pipe Line Company reversed the flow of its East Texas-Texas City line and fed crude into the "Big Inch." The Texas City stations pumped finished products into the "Little Big Inch." The Sun-Yount-Lee pipeline, partly owned by Stanolind Oil and Gas, reversed its flow and also fed oil into the "Big Inch."

It was evident from the beginning of the war that to meet the government's need for aviation gasoline, toluene, and lubricants, many new plants would have to be built. The existing facilities were far from adequate although they were producing to capacity. With a desire to speed the winning of the war as its main motive force, Standard embarked upon a $90,000,000 program to convert old refining units and construct new ones. The new fluid catalytic cracking unit already under construction at Wood River in 1942 for producing high-grade motor fuel was quickly modified so that it could produce base stock for 100-octane gasoline. At Texas City the fluid catalytic cracking plant under construction was modified to operate at high temperature instead of low in order to produce additional butylene for making synthetic rubber and aviation gasoline components. Owing to the dwindling supply of low-sulphur crude oil, West Texas crude with a high sulphur content had to be used at Whiting to supplement the sweet. Since the sulphur content resulted in the corrosion of equipment, substantial revisions in the processing methods and equipment had to be made. To provide the necessary alterations and new facilities to run 40,000 barrels a day of this crude, Standard spent about

21. *Ibid.*, 16.

$6,545,000. Plans were made to increase the runs of West Texas crude to 50,000 barrels by the middle of 1945. For increasing the production of critically needed toluene and components of aviation gasoline, ten or a dozen new alkylation, isomerization, catalytic cracking, and related units were immediately started at Whiting, Wood River, Salt Lake City, and Texas City. To increase the supply of additives used in making heavy-duty motor oil, a plant capable of producing 5,000 barrels of finished oil per day was constructed at Wood River.

The addition of so many manufacturing units required the enlargement of facilities for steam production, generation of power, water pumping, chemical preparation, hydrogen manufacture, sewage disposal, blending, and storage had to be constructed at all refineries. In order to have room for expansion at Whiting, 260 acres of land to the south of the refinery were purchased.

With the outbreak of war, practically all of the time and effort of Standard's research staff was devoted to war projects.

RESEARCH EXPENDITURES 1940–1945
STANDARD OIL COMPANY (INDIANA) AND SUBSIDIARIES

1940	$1,330,381.21
1941	1,754,656.12
1942	2,102,016.02
1943	2,782,543.67
1944	3,191,341.86
1945	3,676,068.04

Source: M. A. McNulty, Comptroller, Standard Oil Company (Indiana), to Giddens, August 29, 1952.

The isomerization plants, pioneered by Standard, had the usual starting troubles and cures for their ills, particularly those arising from corrosion, had to be found in study and experimentation. Due to the efforts of the research men and the operating personnel, all of the new units were functioning at capacity within a reasonable time. The rapid expansion of the Air Force created a special need for more high-grade antiknock components for making more 100-octane fuel. By further development of the isomate process, Standard's research men found a way to provide those which used less critical materials. In this process, announced in January, 1943, the hexane fraction of the isomate product was separated from the others and reprocessed through the plant to increase the conversion to neohexane.[22] The product

22. "Indiana Standard Develops New Neohexane Process," *National Petroleum News,* XXXV, No. 4 (January 27, 1943), 15.

had an extremely high antiknock quality and was especially desirable for aviation blending because of its vaporization characteristics. Research in the field of isomerization also led to the isopentane process, by which low-quality pentane from naphtha stocks was isomerized into the high-octane component isopentane. The first isopentane unit was erected at the Texas City plant of Pan American, and it increased the supply of critically needed aviation gasoline toward the end of the war.

In what was considered as a milestone in the progress of aviation, the Research and Manufacturing Departments late in 1944 produced at Whiting a 75,000-barrel batch of a new superaviation fuel with performance ratings of 115–145 as compared with 100–130 ratings for 100-octane gasoline. It was used in the development of still higher-compression aviation engines. Though not in commercial production by the end of the war, the new fuel put American military aviation still further out in front in the efficient application of petroleum power.

Many new and special lubricants were developed for the Army and Navy. Shortly after the United States entered the war a pressing need developed for a heavy-duty lubricant for use in small naval vessels, trucks, tanks, and half-tracks. A few months before, after many years of research, Standard had started to produce an improved motor oil for use in passenger cars. It was made by adding cleansing and stabilizing components to the basic lubricating oils. To aid the armed forces, the general marketing of this oil was stopped and all of the research facilities of the company were devoted to adapting this oil to military needs. By the use of a greater concentration of the additive in the base oil, a heavy-duty product of exceptional quality called Stanolube HD was produced.[23] The improved formula for heavy-duty lubricants proved so successful that Standard's entire output of heavy-duty oil was reserved for use in war, essential transportation, and industrial equipment. The new product was particularly important to the war effort because it could be manufactured without the use of petroleum sulphonates, ingredients in great demand for other heavy-duty lubricants and for other needed war supplies.

In addition to these major research projects, there were dozens of special problems that were solved by Standard's staff. In conjunction with other scientists, the staff played a vital part in the development of the atomic bomb. New methods for treating West

23. *Standard Oil Company (Indiana) in the War*, 11.

Texas high-sulphur crude and new corrosion-resistant materials for the interior surfaces of cracking units had to be found.

When the American forces were sent overseas, servicemen found that gasoline in the tanks of trucks, tanks, and jeeps had a tendency to form gum during storage or long shipments. An intensive peacetime study of motor fuel deterioration during storage by Standard's research men showed that it was due to the catalytic action of the large metal surface in the gasoline tanks of vehicles. They were able to offer a definite solution of the problem in a special chemical compound which, when added to ordinary gasoline, "deactivated" the metal surfaces and kept the fuel fresh and free from gum.[24]

In 1943 the company contracted with the National Defense Research Committee to develop a new type of flame thrower.[25] Technical workers were taken from other assignments to expedite this work. All realized the hazardous character of the project, but they were willing to run the risk. In the course of this experimental work on May 29, 1944, an explosion occurred that instantly killed three members of the Research Department, fatally injured a fourth, seriously injured two executives, and slightly injured six others.

With the unprecedented demand for crude oil, research was started on methods of future production of motor fuels and other products from substitute sources. By 1944 substantial progress had been made in the production of liquid fuels from natural gas by the adaptation of American techniques to the Fischer-Tropsch process, which was used by the Germans in making both synthetic gasoline and chemicals from coal.

Much of Standard's research and development was co-ordinated with similar activities of governmental agencies and other companies. Furthermore, many of its technical men worked in positions of responsibility and importance on national committees engaged in co-ordinating technological developments in the interest of winning the war. To review and co-ordinate the research work in progress within its own organization, Standard inaugurated in 1943 a policy of bringing together annually all of the key technical men of the parent company and subsidiaries for a conference. As the responsibilities of the research staff increased and more room and equipment were needed, top management of-

24. *Ibid.,* 9.
25. *Ibid.,* 13.

ficials began discussing the need for expanding the company's research staff and the construction of new laboratory buildings. In December, 1943, a definite plan was submitted and approval was given to a five-year program of expanding the staff and constructing a new research center at Whiting.

Although handicapped by a shortage of materials and a lack of manpower, Standard made notable progress in the expansion of its refineries. By the end of 1943 much of the $90,000,000 construction program had been completed, and the new facilities were sending forth a continuous stream of essential petroleum products. Production quotas were consistently broken and new records set. Early in the field, the toluene extraction unit at Texas City, with a capacity for producing 42,000 gallons of toluene per day from the hydroformer product, filled the first contract in ten months when it was expected to take twenty. It went on producing while the company was negotiating a new contract. After setting a record in 1943, its production increased 12 per cent in 1944. The cracking units at the Texas City plants enabled Pan American Refining to provide a synthetic rubber plant at Houston, Texas, with 760 barrels daily of normal butylenes.

In October, 1943, the huge toluene plant at Whiting was completed, and the first tank car shipped. To the eye, the plant looked like a little town stretching out over nearly a city block. It had the capacity to produce more than 58,000 gallons of toluene per day. During World War II it produced more toluene than the entire country produced during World War I.[26] Furthermore, it was the largest plant constructed by private capital in the Ordnance Department's aromatics program. By June, 1945, Whiting had produced 29,500,000 gallons of toluene, enough to provide almost a half-million tons of bombs.[27] It was making enough daily for 2,700 thousand-pound bombs.

With its new facilities, Standard had in 1944 a daily capacity for manufacturing approximately 1,150,800 gallons of 100-octane aviation gasoline, and it was a large factor in supplying the nation's needs. This amount of 100-octane aviation gasoline was more than was produced daily by the entire petroleum industry before Pearl Harbor. In addition, large quantities of constituents for aviation gasoline and synthetic rubber were shipped to other

26. *Ibid.*, 8.
27. "Indiana Standard Wins Army's Praise for Toluene Output," *National Petro-leum News*, XXXVII, No. 24 (June 13, 1945), 34.

plants for further processing. When the war ended, Standard's refineries were shipping enough aviation gasoline every day to fuel more than one million miles of flight by B-29's. These supplies, combined with those furnished by other members of the petroleum industry, made possible the tremendous expansion of aerial warfare and victory.

In the synthetic rubber program the company took an active and productive part. On February 9, 1942, the Rubber Reserve Company asked Standard to take the lead in determining the possibility of forming a group of Chicago district refiners to construct, supply, and operate a butadiene plant. Shortly thereafter Rubber Reserve formally requested that such a plant be constructed at Gary, Indiana. A new company, Rubber Synthetics, Inc., was jointly formed by Standard, Sinclair, and Cities Service to build and operate it. The plant was to include steam, power, and other facilities for styrene and polymerization plants, which were to be built at the same location by chemical and rubber companies.

It was early decided that the plant should be identical in design with similar projects authorized for construction at Port Neches and Houston, Texas, by other oil companies. Standard took an active part in the joint technical committee set up to develop this design. In August, 1942, the Gary rubber-plant project was canceled by Rubber Reserve because of a decision to expand the program for producing butadiene from alcohol and correspondingly reduce production from petroleum. The other two plants were completed and produced large quantities of butadiene.

During 1942 Standard also conducted an experimental program on the high-temperature cracking of petroleum fractions for the production of butadiene and aromatics, looking toward the possibility of producing these materials in plants that could be improvised quickly from available salvaged equipment. While some possibilities developed, plans for the construction of a plant at Wood River were canceled when a catalytic butane-butylene dehydrogenation process under development by Houdry appeared to offer greater promise. Research and engineering personnel sent to the Marcus Hook refinery of the Sun Oil Company made substantial contributions to the development of this latter process. Meanwhile engineering designs for the high-temperature cracking process were carried forward. Although the need for the Wood River plant had not materialized, a successful plant was built and

ISOMATE UNIT, WHITING REFINERY

This unit converted naphthas into high-quality base stocks used in
making 100-octane aviation gasoline

ALKYLATION AND BUTANE ISOMERIZATION PLANTS,
WHITING REFINERY

RESEARCH WORK ON DEFENSE PROJECTS,
WORLD WAR II

TOLUENE PLANT AT WHITING

WOMEN WORKERS, KNOWN AS "CHAPMAN EXCAVATORS," AT WHITING REFINERY
DURING WORLD WAR II

STANDARD AGENTS COLLECT SCRAP RUBBER

COLLECTING AND SHIPPING SCRAP METAL

GENERAL OFFICE RAISES MINUTE MAN FLAG,
JULY 28, 1942

Treasury Department officials present certificate in recognition of 96.61 per cent participation of the General Office employees in the payroll savings plan for buying War Bonds. Presented on the day that the 1,000th employee entered the armed services. Employee groups at thirty-seven Standard locations had also won the right to fly the Minute Man Flag

THE BEGINNING OF STANDARD'S 4-H CLUB PROGRAM

The members of Standard's Rural Youth Committee—Wesley I. Nunn, Conger Reynolds, and H. L. Porter—look on as R. F. McConnell, Vice-President in charge of Sales (right), and G. L. Noble (left), Director of the National Committee on Boys and Girls Club Work, Inc., sign first memorandum of agreement in the fall of 1944

DR. ROBERT E. WILSON, CHAIRMAN 1945–

operated by another oil company in California. Another plant was built in Ohio, but it was not operated.

Besides supplying huge quantities of toluene, 100-octane aviation gasoline, 91-octane aviation gasoline for transports and trainers, and 80-octane, an all-purpose gasoline for tanks, trucks, jeeps, half-tracks, and boats, Standard shipped large quantities of Navy diesel fuel; Navy special fuel; lubricating oil for the Navy; heavy-duty motor oil; special hydraulic oil for delicate instruments; white oil for medicinal use; petrolatum for salves and ointments for the Medical Corps; a new lubricant to protect metal against swift corrosion in the tropics; special greases for airplane equipment which would function at 60° below zero or at equatorial heat; a preservative which kept "drive away" gasoline in new trucks, tanks, and jeeps from gumming en route to the front; candles for temporary light, to warm emergency rations, and to stop tent leaks when melted; and a host of other essential products. On the industrial front Standard's cutting oils, heavy fuel oils, petroleum coke, gasoline, and lubricants speeded the output of implements of war. Fuels and lubricants helped to keep railway trains and trucks operating under war pressure. A new type tractor fuel, "Standard Power Fuel," introduced in April, 1943, met the growing demand for a volatile tractor fuel and aided farmers to meet food-production quotas.

Construction of new facilities continued throughout 1944 and 1945 but not on such a large scale as previously. Expenditures for new manufacturing facilities in 1944 ran $17,500,000 and in 1945 $17,200,000. All of the expenditures for war plant facilities were

WAR INDUSTRIAL FACILITIES AUTHORIZED JUNE, 1940, TO JULY, 1945

Companies	Authorizations	Government Financed
Standard Oil Company, New Jersey	$235,866,000	$134,198,000
Gulf	131,334,000	69,284,000
Cities Service	125,030,000	109,470,000
Sinclair	117,159,000	67,690,000
Shell	111,372,000	42,560,000
Standard Oil Company (Indiana)	110,222,000	27,814,000
The Texas Company	102,150,000	29,103,000
Phillips	97,418,000	52,090,000
Sun	90,460,000	71,413,000
Standard Oil Company, California	82,942,000	34,217,000
Socony-Vacuum	72,525,000	18,638,000

Source: *National Petroleum News*, XXXVIII, No. 44 (October 30, 1946), 16.

financed by the company, except for $27,814,000 which the government provided for a catalytic cracking unit, two related units at Salt Lake City, and a pentane isomerization unit at Texas City.

Despite the urgent need of petroleum products at home and abroad, Standard was not able to operate all of its refineries at capacity either in 1942 or 1943 due mainly to the lack of transportation facilities. In the Middle West, government directives imposed to synchronize the flow of products with crude supply, product demand, and transportation restricted the production of motor gasoline from May, 1942, until well toward the end of 1943, when most of the plants were able to run at prewar capacity or better. On the other hand, in keeping with the government's request, Standard during this period produced a maximum of distillate fuel, residual fuel, and coke. Pan American Petroleum & Transport was handicapped by the lack of transportation for crude to its eastern refineries and for products going from its southern refineries to its eastern markets. Not until the summer of 1943 had the transportation situation so improved that the big Texas City plant could operate at full capacity. All of the larger refineries operated close to capacity in 1944, and more crude was processed than ever before in Standard's history, averaging 315,562 barrels a day, which was 6 per cent more than in 1943.

CRUDE OIL PRODUCTION, PURCHASES, AND REFINERY RUNS 1940–1945
STANDARD OIL COMPANY (INDIANA) AND SUBSIDIARIES

	Net Production— Barrels	Crude Run to Refineries Barrels	% of Gross Production to Crude Runs to Refineries	% of Net Production to Crude Runs to Refineries	Crude Oil Purchased Outside Barrels	Refining Capacity Barrels Per Day Year-end
1940	31,872,906	105,715,300	36.1	30.1	97,434,711	319,400
1941	38,165,109	112,562,151	40	33.9	106,333,285	318,889
1942	40,480,720	105,148,290	45	38.49	102,060,593	323,700
1943	50,954,002	108,626,084	54	46.9	110,214,931	323,962
1944	62,682,503	115,458,954	63	54	126,457,781	345,000
1945	64,685,408	114,558,119	64	56.5	129,949,147	351,500

Source: M. A. McNulty, Comptroller, Standard Oil Company (Indiana), to Giddens, August 29, 1952.

Called upon to furnish a greater and greater volume of crude, Standard's producing subsidiaries aggressively carried on their search for new sources of oil. They broke all of their previous records for exploratory drilling. During this period, the most important discovery made by Stanolind Oil and Gas was the Midland Farms field in Andrews County in West Texas. Other important discoveries made during this period were the Winkleman Dome field in Fremont County, Wyoming, and deep production in the Elk Basin field of Park County, Wyoming. Wildcat activities of individuals and other companies, supported in part by Standard's subsidiaries, resulted in finding a number of new major oil fields. In this list, the most important from Standard's point of view were the Anton Irish, Fullerton, and Levelland fields of West Texas and Little Buffalo Basin in Wyoming.

Extensive buying of producing properties began in 1941, and substantial additions were made to the crude reserves especially in East and West Texas. The major additions involved the purchase by Stanolind Oil and Gas of the properties of the Barnsdall Oil Company for more than $4,625,000 in cash, the capital stock of the Coronado Corporation for $7,000,000 in cash, the properties of the Landreth Production Corporation for more than $4,158,438 in cash, the properties of Clifford Mooers for more than $4,213,537 in cash, the properties of H. R. and W. C. Stroube for more than $3,985,100 in cash, the stock of the Permian Oil Corporation for more than $6,395,235 in cash, the stock of the Dickey Oil Company for $6,410,000 in cash, and the properties of Wheelock and Collins for more than $5,115,930 in cash.[28]

Government regulation of well spacing, shortages of materials, and the loss of manpower greatly restricted drilling and production. However, the producing subsidiaries succeeded in producing more crude oil than ever before. Net production jumped from 31,872,906 barrels in 1940 to 64,685,408 barrels in 1945. In 1944 Standard produced 54 per cent of its refinery runs, which was the first time in its history that its net production exceeded the 50 per cent mark. In 1945 it reached 56.5 per cent. As much as Stanolind Oil and Gas did to increase production, it was by no means enough. The heavy demand in 1943 necessitated drawing upon stored oil to the extent of 5,775,000 barrels, which practically exhausted its tank-farm stock in Kansas and Oklahoma. Until 1944 more than half the crude used by Standard's refineries had to be purchased from outside sources. In the last two years of the war only about 43 to 46 per cent was purchased outside.

Co-operation in supplying crude oil to other companies which were without crude, so that they might continue manufacturing either for the military forces or domestic use, was another wartime

28. *The New York Times,* October 7, 1944; *The Oil and Gas Journal,* November 4, 1944.

service rendered by Standard and its subsidiaries. More than 2,500,000 barrels of crude were sold to other companies at a sacrifice of the company's own stock of sweet or low-sulphur crude.[29]

To overcome transportation difficulties and get the increased production to the refineries, five major crude pipeline projects were completed in 1944 by the Stanolind Pipe Line Company and the Pan American Pipe Line Company. Stanolind built a new 385-mile sixteen-inch line with a capacity of 65,000 barrels from the Slaughter pool in West Texas to Drumright, where it connected with Stanolind's trunk line to Chicago. The capacity of Stanolind's line from Mexia, Texas, to Healdton, Oklahoma, was increased by equipping the stations to pump at higher pressure. The Pan American Pipe Line built a short line from Willamar field to Port Isabel, Texas, to make crude economically available at Texas City. A new 231-mile twelve-inch line was constructed from Elk Basin to Casper, Wyoming. The twelve-inch line was later extended from Casper to Welch to give the oil of the Big Horn Basin an outlet to midwestern as well as Rocky Mountain refineries. To enable the Utah Oil Refining Company to dispense with using 100 tank cars, a 107-mile line from the Iles pool in Colorado via Craig was built to connect with the Utah line at Wamsutter, Wyoming. Further construction was undertaken in 1945 in the Rocky Mountain region when the Stanolind Pipe Line, acting as agent for Utah Oil Refining Company, designed and constructed a gathering system in the new Rangely field and built a ten-inch line running out of the field through some very rough terrain to the main line at Wamsutter. From there the oil could be moved west to Salt Lake or east to the Stanolind Pipe Line terminal and on to refineries in the Rocky Mountain area and the Middle West.

Wartime conditions made it difficult to obtain materials to extend the pipelines, but Stanolind's engineers met the challenge. Four hundred and twenty miles of pipe from feeder lines were salvaged. This, combined with the stocks on hand and new pipe allocated by the government, enabled the company to build 670 miles of new lines. Stanolind's total mileage jumped from 9,317 miles in 1940 to 12,478 in 1945.

All through the war Stanolind operated its pipelines at maximum capacity in moving crude oil northward from the Gulf Coast, Texas, and Oklahoma and eastward from Wyoming and Kansas

29. *Standard Oil Company (Indiana) in the War,* 19.

to Standard's refineries and those of other companies. In 1940 its lines transported crude at the rate of 44,110,000,000 barrel-miles per year. At the end of the war it was transporting at the rate of 74,783,000,000 barrel-miles per year.

PIPELINE TRAFFIC 1939–1951
STANDARD OIL COMPANY (INDIANA) AND SUBSIDIARIES

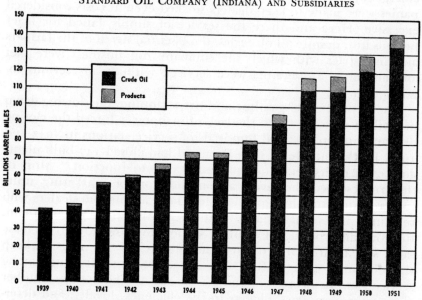

Although supplying the armed forces received first consideration, Standard made every effort to maintain normal sales service and meet essential civilian needs, but it was done under the greatest of difficulties. In accordance with government directives, Standard resorted to trucking in the distribution of its products on hauls less than two hundred miles. Because trucks were not subject to the ordinary rail delays, it was estimated that on short hauls one transport truck released from five to fifteen tank cars for emergency war service.[30] At the start of war the company employed seven trucking companies to handle 19 per cent of its shipments. By the end of June, 1944, seventy-four trucking companies and the company's own trucks were being employed to carry approximately 75 per cent of its shipments. At the end of the war the company was using eighty-two of its own transports and sixty-one of other carriers.

30. *Ibid.*, 15.

Trucks shuttled back and forth over the highways day and night to keep oil flowing to customers. As the war progressed truck transportation was increasingly handicapped due to the lack of new trucks to replace outworn equipment, breakdowns, shortage of tires and parts, and the lack of drivers and mechanics. Many emergency deliveries and exchanges of gasoline with other companies were made to keep dealers stocked even at costs considered excessive. Here and there the service of supply failed for brief periods but, despite all obstacles, the essential needs of the farmers and industries with which the company did business were met and automobile operators were serviced without any serious interruption.

The imposition of gasoline and tire rationing, the slowing down of civilian motoring, and the lack of manpower forced the closing of many bulk plants and hundreds of service stations in 1942 and 1943. By the middle of 1943 Standard had closed 147 bulk plants and 4,754 of its retail outlets had ceased to function.[31] Most of this represented, however, a consolidation of marketing units rather than actual loss in coverage. Many agents and dealers who remained in business stayed with great difficulty. To aid them, the company conducted training schools to show how to increase sales, sell additional products, and obtain new earnings to keep their business going. After May, 1943, the mortality rate among service stations decreased, and by the spring of 1944 the number closing was very few. Thanks to the efficiency, loyalty, and determination of the marketing organization and thousands of dealers, a good job was done in meeting essential civilian needs.

To simplify the corporate organization and obtain the benefits of direct participation in the larger organization's activities, the properties of the Standard of Nebraska and its personnel were combined with those of the parent company on December 1, 1944. Most of the Nebraska organization then became a sales division of Standard.

When the war began to curtail the supply of petroleum products, automobiles, trucks, tractors and tires, the general public faced many new and strange problems. The personnel of the company's dealer service-station organization was taught through driveway training, literature, house organs, and meetings how to render special conservation service for automobiles. Through its sales staff, dealer service stations, and advertising, Standard con-

31. *Annual Report Standard Oil Company (Indiana) and Subsidiaries,* 1943, 12.

centrated upon showing customers how to adjust to wartime conditions. In addition, Standard's advertising was built around the slogan "Care for your car for your country." It featured the dealer's station as car conservation headquarters. It taught consumers how to use petroleum products wisely, save rubber, and lengthen the life of their cars. Motorists were influenced in the right direction. For the operators of trucks, buses, and road construction equipment, Standard inaugurated in March, 1942, the "Fleet Conservation Service" whereby salesmen and automotive engineers gave expert counsel on lubrication and maintenance of equipment. When the Office of Defense Transportation announced its Truck Transportation Corps in 1942, the company co-operated in the operation of its own equipment, in sponsoring the program through its sales organization and fleet advertising, and in urging dealers to become ODT stations for distributing material promoting the idea of the Corps. With new problems arising in industry owing to wartime conditions, Standard called upon the knowledge and experience of its technical, engineering, and research staffs and began an advertising program of spreading useful information. In addition, its lubrication engineers, cutting-oil specialists, and industrial service representatives went into factories and gave skilled counsel on a multitude of problems.

The company's program, showing the farmer how to conserve his tractors and farm machinery by the use of proper fuels and lubricants, was intensified. Conservation became the spearhead of Standard's rural sales and advertising program. Tractor clinics were conducted with the assistance of the company's rural agents, salesmen, and automotive engineers. Slide films, advertising, and booklets gave practical suggestions on tractor care and operation. While fuel oil rationing did not begin until the fall of 1942, Standard started early in the year to assist consumers in conserving this product. Thousands of copies of a booklet entitled "Twenty-Five Ways to Save Fuel Oil," which gave practical suggestions on insulation, storm-window installation, and draft and burner adjustments, were printed and distributed.

Although advertising continued in sufficient volume to keep Standard's products and the company's war service before the public, most of it was of an educational character designed to promote conservation of motor vehicles, tractors, farm machinery, and tires, the scrap drive, rubber drive, Victory Gardens, war bond sales, and various other wartime campaigns. During the war bond drives the company ran advertisements urging the purchase of bonds. The company's radio program featured the daily award of a war bond to a man, woman, boy, or girl for outstanding agricultural achievement. The production drive of the War Production Board in 1942 and the Tool Conservation Program of 1943 were wholeheartedly supported by the company both in its practices and in its advertising. Owing to the general confusion and misunderstanding over the reasons for gasoline rationing which had developed by 1943, the company prepared an advertisement entitled "The Low-Down on Gasoline Rationing" which appeared in 103 leading newspapers at the expense of sixty-six oil companies, with Standard paying more than the next two largest contributors combined.[32] During 1944 the company supported a $140,000 advertising campaign to explain the reasons for and the reality of the gasoline shortage.

Conscious of the desirability of applying its efforts in the furtherance of broad social objectives and, at the same time, promote conservation, Standard in October, 1944, became one of a group of business organizations, such as the Firestone Tire and Rubber Company, the Kraft Cheese Company, International Harvester, Westinghouse Electric & Manufacturing Company, Wilson & Company, Montgomery Ward & Company, American Viscose Corporation, Sears Roebuck & Company, and others in sponsoring various activities carried on by the 4-H Clubs.[33] Standard's part of the program was to sponsor a 4-H project in power machinery operation and maintenance, known as the "Live Power" program, in thirteen central and western states where it marketed. The purpose was to increase among farm boys and girls a knowledge of how to maintain and operate petroleum-powered equipment. This was especially important in view of the manpower shortage and the need for greater food production. The program was one of social service, not a sales promotion plan. Through the program Standard hoped "in some measure to express tangibly to the farmers of tomorrow appreciation of the friendly relationships the company had enjoyed throughout the Middle West with their parents, grandparents, and even great grandparents—during the last 55 years."

As the first step in the development of the farm youth project,

32. *Standard Oil Company (Indiana) in the War,* 23.
33. "Company to Sponsor 4-H Club Project," *Stanolind Record,* XXV, No. 12 (October, 1944), 1-2.

leadership training short courses for volunteer 4-H Club leaders throughout the territory began in the fall of 1944 in the operation and maintenance of petroleum-powered farm equipment and especially the tractor. Standard financed the expenses of the training conferences and made available technological consultants. However, the responsibility and authority for handling the conferences and directing the program were in the hands of 4-H Club officials. By April, 1945, hundreds of 4-H Club leaders had participated in these short courses, and the program was so successful that Standard's subsidiaries, the American Oil Company in the East, Pan American in the South, the Utah Oil Refining in Utah and Idaho, and Stanolind Oil and Gas, inaugurated it.

To produce oil, man the pipelines, operate refineries, and maintain the marketing organization was a tremendous job in view of the diminishing supply of manpower. By the end of the war 7,713 employees of Standard and its subsidiaries had been granted military leaves to enter the armed services. Furthermore, several dozen key executives were loaned to the government on a full-time basis as civilian experts. To offset the shortage of labor, more and more women were employed. Over a hundred women were employed and trained for routine laboratory testing and technical work formerly done by men. At Whiting the success of women in taking over what had always been regarded as a man's job under ordinary circumstances, like handling lumber and maintaining roads and railways, made it possible to move more and more men into critical posts. In 1943 Stanolind Oil and Gas more than doubled its employment of women. They worked in thirty-eight different classifications of which fifteen were formerly filled by men only. By the end of 1944, 5,055 women were employed by Standard and its subsidiaries, and they constituted 15 per cent of the total working force. Another factor in helping to offset the manpower shortage was the higher efficiency of individuals and the extra effort made through overtime work. Employees in many departments worked as never before. With some exceptions, most of those in the refineries and offices exceeded the normal 40-hour week. The return of 596 veterans to their jobs by the end of 1944 was also important in relieving the manpower shortage.

In spite of hiring a large number of new employees and many new operations, Standard set some of the best safety records in the Sales and Manufacturing Departments in its history and in the industry. The Wood River refinery made a new world's safety record for the petroleum industry in 1942 with 6,850,000 man-hours worked without a loss-of-time or disabling injury. The establishment of twenty-two records in 1944 by the Manufacturing and Sales Departments attracted national attention. In setting these records the employees worked 43,000,000 man-hours without a disabling injury. In recognition of the records made by the employees of the Whiting refinery in producing 100-octane gasoline, toluene, and other commodities for the armed forces, the American Petroleum Institute in July, 1945, made sixteen safety awards to different departments for having 1,000,000 or more man-hours of work without any loss-of-time or disabling injury. Of the sixteen awards, the one for the most man-hours worked without a disabling injury went to the employees of the Pressure Stills Department with a record of 5,476,776 man-hours covering eleven years and six months. The award for the longest period of time went to the Engineering Department, whose employees had worked twenty-five years and three months in accumulating a safety record of 3,245,000 man-hours. The frequency rate of accidents per million man-hours for Standard of Indiana alone during the war was consistently less than the average for the entire petroleum industry.

Due to government regulations no general pay increases were made after the wage increases in September, 1942. Adjustments were made, however, in individual cases, and bonus payments were made to a very large group for overtime work.

Absenteeism, a wartime affliction of many other industries, was not a problem among Standard's workers. Management and employees worked together in the traditional spirit of harmony. There were no work stoppages of any consequence. All disputes were settled by the orderly procedure prescribed in the labor agreements. A special effort was made to train supervisors in good methods of developing and maintaining conditions and relationships to keep employees working harmoniously with management and with each other.

Several advances were made during the war in improving the employee vacation plan and the sickness and benefit plan. On July 1, 1943, the Employee Sickness and Disability Benefit Plan was revised to eliminate all distinction between the private payroll employees and other salaried employees. All eligible employees in continuous service for a year or more were allowed two weeks at full pay and four weeks at half pay during the second year of service. This was increased by one week at full pay and two weeks at half pay each succeeding year of service up to and including the tenth year of service. Sick benefits for twelve weeks at full pay and twenty-four weeks at half pay were provided for the eleventh year of service and each year thereafter. The plan included sickness or disability due to pregnancy. Persons employed on a commission or part-time basis or on boats other than masters or chief engineers were not eligible under the plan. The provisions of the vacation plan were further liberalized in January, 1944, and again in September, 1945.

Enviable records were established by Standard's group of companies in the drive for scrap material. To provide urgently needed scrap iron, there was the greatest house cleaning at refineries, supply dumps, distribution plants, and production centers ever seen. In the 1942 drive 19,500 tons of scrap were collected, which was enough to make a battleship, 1,300 medium tanks, 6,500 anti-aircraft guns, or 65,000 one-ton bombs.[34] Standard led all other members of the industry in the National Scrap Rubber Drive in June and July, 1942. A large portion of the time of the personnel in the Sales Department was devoted to directing and handling the collection of the rubber. Commission agents, drivers, and independent dealers were organized and gave generously of their time. The company furnished trucks and equipment and thousands of man-hours for collecting, weighing, and loading scrap rubber in cars and trucks. Newspaper and radio advertising were used to stimulate the collection. The drive resulted in Standard's marketers bringing in 15 per cent of the nationwide collection, or a total of 91,875,000 pounds.[35] The difference between the purchase price and sales price, which amounted to $252,920.66, was turned over to the Petroleum Industry War Council to be distributed to the Navy Relief Society, the Army Emergency Relief, the United Service Organization, and the American Red Cross. By the end of 1943 the parent company had turned in 48,652,000 pounds of scrap iron and steel, 1,260,000 pounds of brass, copper, and lead, 1,700,000 pounds of paper, 91,875,000 pounds of rubber, and 125,000 pounds of scrap canvas.[36] In the six months' scrap drive ending March 31, 1945, Standard shipped

34. *Annual Report Standard Oil Company (Indiana) and Subsidiaries,* 1942, 6.
35. *Standard Oil Company (Indiana) in the War,* 23.
36. *Annual Report Standard Oil Company (Indiana) and Subsidiaries,* 1943, 18.

from Whiting and Wood River almost 2,700 tons of heavy melting iron and steel scrap.

Although the company probably could have secured a priority for steel for making barrels, Standard developed as a conservation measure the "Victory Barrel" for handling greases, heavy lubricants, petroleum, and semiliquid products. It resembled a steel drum in appearance but was made of wooden sheets laminated together. The only metal used was for fasteners to hold the ends of the sheets together and a ring for use in lifting the removal lid. The inner surface was coated with a chemical to prevent seepage through the wood pores. Though its use caused considerable expense and created delivery problems, the "Victory Barrel" saved about 2,000 tons of steel per year. It was given wide publicity to stimulate others to take similar action. More metal was conserved beginning in September, 1942, by substituting glass bottles for tin cans in packaging some petroleum specialty products and lubricants. This resulted in a saving of about 225 tons of tin plate per year.

The company and its employees made an outstanding record in the purchase of war bonds and in the support of the American Red Cross, various relief agencies, and community fund drives. Between April, 1942, and February, 1946, the parent company through the Payroll Allotment Plan issued to its employees 918,754 War Savings Bonds, Series E, with an issue value of $24,540,393.75.[37] Between 1942 and 1945 Standard itself purchased a total of $95,685,000 in war bonds of the United States.[38] For the same period the company contributed over $400,000 to the American Red Cross and over $400,000 to community fund campaigns.[39] Besides making financial contributions, thousands of employees enthusiastically and freely worked on their own time in war bond, Red Cross, Community Chest, and salvage drives, in Civilian Defense activities, and in other wartime projects. Many executives and technical men of the companies served on government and industry committees and played a part in directing and aiding the co-operative wartime program of the petroleum industry.

In recognition of the war service rendered by the company and its employees, many certificates, citations, letters, and telegrams of

37. Walter A. Culin, Treasurer, Standard Oil Company (Indiana), to Giddens, January 8, 1952.
38. *Ibid.*
39. S. K. Botsford, Assistant Secretary, Standard Oil Company (Indiana), to Giddens, September 25, 1951.

commendation were received from various governmental agencies and from other organizations. Among the most significant awards were two for chemical engineering achievement made by the publication, *Chemical and Metallurgical Engineering*. One was for significant contributions to the synthetic rubber program; the other was for participation in the atomic bomb program. A number of companies contributed to these developments, but only two oil companies were on both of the award lists, Standard of Indiana and Standard of New Jersey. Considering the magnitude of the job done, the obstacles encountered, and how well the various tasks had been performed, a distinguished record had been made. Standard and its subsidiaries were proud of the part they played in bringing about the ultimate victory.

The unprecedented demand for war products and the enlarged plant facilities resulted in record-breaking increases in the volume of Standard's sales during the war years. The volume increased from 125,296,080 barrels in 1940 to 215,424,653 in 1945 and the value increased from $349,618,051 to $601,538,202.

SALES BY STANDARD AND ITS SUBSIDIARIES, 1940–1945

	Volume in Barrels	Value
1940	125,298,080	$349,618,051
1941	144,333,778	416,607,572
1942	152,874,310	449,039,660
1943	177,225,798	498,077,237
1944	215,797,159	586,756,144
1945	215,424,653	601,538,202

Source: *Annual Reports,* 1940–1945.

Despite the record-breaking increases in volume, Standard's percentage of the gasoline business in the Middle West dropped to a new low of 17.6 per cent in 1941.[40] Trackside stations did 14.9 per cent of the business, Socony-Vacuum 7.7, The Texas Company 6.5, Phillips 6.1, Sinclair 5.8, Shell 5.7, and oil co-operatives 5.1. In their marketing activities the growth of oil co-operatives had been steady. At the end of 1938 there were 1,268 in Standard's territory with 1,493 outlets.[41] In Minnesota in 1940 Standard did 25 per cent of the rural gasoline business and the co-ops 11.1 per cent, on distillate Standard sold 33.7 per cent and the co-ops 25.8 per cent, on heating oil Standard sold 14 per cent and the co-ops 30.7 per cent, and on motor oil and kero-

40. Company Encyclopedia: Marketing, I, Loss in Business to Competitors, 277.
41. Company Encyclopedia: Marketing, I, Co-operative Oil Companies, 214.

sene Standard was slightly ahead.[42] In Illinois the co-ops had an advantage on four out of five products. The co-ops outsold Standard on heating oil more than anything else in Iowa, Kansas, Minnesota, and Illinois, while Standard led the co-ops constantly on distillate in eight states, except Illinois.

The wartime demand reflected itself in higher net earnings. They increased each year from 1940 to 1944, except for 1942, when rationing and a shortage of crude oil adversely affected sales and earnings. With the sudden ending of the war in 1945 and the slackening off of the demand, earnings fell below those of 1944, the high point of the war. Net earnings per share were the largest since 1930. However, the percentage of net earnings paid out during the war was smaller than in previous years because of the heavy capital demands and the necessity to meet whatever uncertainties might arise out of the war.

STANDARD'S CAPITAL EXPENDITURES 1943–1945

1943	—	$97,000,000
1944	—	90,000,000
1945	—	77,000,000

Source: *Annual Reports*, 1943–1945.

There were three transactions which took place during the war years, although unrelated to the war, which had a bearing upon the finances of the company.

The first pertained to the Carlinville coal mines. In view of the fact that the economic situation did not warrant further retention of the company's coal mines in southern Illinois, which had been acquired in 1917 for the purpose of assuring an adequate supply of coal, these were sold in 1941, resulting in a loss of $2,356,999.[43]

The second arose out of the Universal Oil Products Company settlement in 1931. At that time, Standard of Indiana paid a substantial amount of cash and obtained certain senior and junior income notes from Universal. As a result of the 1937 settlement, Standard also received additional senior and junior income notes of Universal. By 1944, when the retirement of the senior notes was completed, Standard had more than recovered its original investment. Owing to the fact that there was considerable criticism and the possibility of an antitrust action on the ground that the large oil companies which owned Universal were getting a share of

42. "Rural Consumer Survey, Part I, 1940."
43. *Annual Report Standard Oil Company (Indiana) and Subsidiaries*, 1941, 14.

the royalties paid by the smaller ones to Universal, various security holders agreed in October, 1944, to donate their securities to the Petroleum Research Fund, a tax-exempt and nonprofit organization. Therefore Standard gave one $1,156,250 C note and one $953,906.25 D note of Universal to the Petroleum Research Fund.[44] According to the arrangement, the income derived by the Fund from these securities went to the American Chemical Society to advance scientific education and fundamental research in the petroleum field. The results of the research were to be made available at least once a year to the public at large and the donors of the securities.

In the third transaction, Standard in December, 1944, charged off its books a claim against the United States government plus accrued interest, amounting to $6,553,905.81.[45] This claim had arisen out of the Pan American Petroleum & Transport Company's contracts in 1922 with the United States government for materials and construction work done at Pearl Harbor in connection with the leasing of the Elk Hills naval oil reserves. The original claim had amounted to $9,336,956.58, but Edward L. Doheny paid Pan American $3,984,194.10 in 1927 and 1930 with the understanding that Pan American would file a claim with Congress for the entire claim and reimburse him if any money was collected.[46] About January 1, 1933, Pan American assigned to Pan American Southern the right to receive certain net proceeds of the claim which, upon Pan American Southern's liquidation in 1941, was vested in Standard. The U.S. Court of Claims on February 7, 1944, denied the claim because of fraud in the original contracts between Pan American and the government in 1922. Since the efforts to secure approval by Congress had not been successful, Standard, though it believed in the justness of the claim, decided to charge it off against earned surplus as of December 31, 1944.

44. Memorandum from Pike H. Sullivan, Manager of the Development and Patent Department, to Giddens, August 12, 1952.
45. *Annual Report Standard Oil Company (Indiana) and Subsidiaries,* 1944, 3-4.
46. Minutes of the Board of Directors' and Stockholders' Meetings, VI, 3729.

CHAPTER XXII

The New Standard and Its Postwar Expansion

LATE IN WORLD WAR II THERE WAS A COMPLETE REORGANIZATION IN the top management of Standard and younger but experienced men, up from the ranks, were elevated to positions of leadership. In November, 1944, the announcement was made that Edward G. Seubert would retire as President and chief executive officer on January 1, 1945, after fifty-two years of service with Standard of which fifteen were as President, the longest period any man had ever served the company in this capacity.

Under Seubert the company had a remarkable growth and development in many respects despite the lean and chaotic years of the depression. In these fifteen years, the assets of the company had been increased from $697,034,463.95 in 1929 to $945,525,120.15 in 1944. In addition, Seubert's administration had been high-lighted by the acquisition of complete ownership of the Sinclair Crude Oil Purchasing Company, the Sinclair Pipe Line Company, and majority ownership of the Pan American Petroleum & Transport Company, the absorption of the Midwest Refining Company, the purchase of the refining facilities and pipelines of the Standard Oil Company (Kansas) and the Standard Oil Company (Nebraska), the extension of crude pipelines and the building of gasoline pipelines and water terminals. Although the sale of the foreign properties of Pan American resulted in a terrific loss in crude oil production, the loss was partly offset by the use of the cash thus acquired in more aggressive action in exploring for new sources of oil and in significant purchases of crude-oil producing properties. As a result, in 1944 the company for the first time in its history produced more than 50 per cent of its crude runs to refineries. The introduction of the sale of tires, batteries, and automobile accessories, the leasing out of service stations, and the extension of Standard's marketing activities to thirty-nine states and the District of Columbia were significant developments in marketing. The successful conclusion of the Universal Oil Products Company suit and the "Patent Club" suit were of utmost importance. Under Seubert the company had been mobilized to play a vital part in World War II. Through all the vicissitudes of the depression and war the company had emerged in a sound financial condition.

Of equal importance with the material growth was the continued harmonious relations with employees in a period of great industrial disturbances, the placing of the annuity plan on a secure foundation, the extension of the vacation plan to a greater number of employees, the adoption of the Employee Sickness and Disability Plan, and the continued revision and liberalization of all benefit plans. Continued emphasis upon the greater distribution of stock ownership resulted in increasing the number of stockholders from 81,022 in 1929 to 96,237 in 1944.

Effective at the same time as Seubert's retirement was that of Charles J. Barkdull, Executive Vice-President since 1933, and Amos Ball, a Director and Vice-President in charge of Sales. Barkdull had served the company for more than twenty-eight years, more than sixteen of which had been as a Director and eleven as Executive Vice-President.[1] Ball had joined the company in 1897 as a clerk in its Marshalltown, Iowa, office and during the next forty-seven years had advanced through the Sales Department to the top executive position.

The retirement of Seubert, Barkdull, and Ball opened the way for a complete reorganization of the top executive personnel. Robert E. Wilson, President of Pan American Petroleum & Transport Company, became Chairman of the Board and the chief executive officer of the company.[2] After graduating from Wooster College and the Massachusetts Institute of Technology, Wilson had served as a major in the Chemical Warfare Service in World War I, Director of Research in Applied Chemistry and Associate Professor of Chemical Engineering at the Massachusetts Institute of Technology. In 1922 he joined Standard of Indiana as assistant director of research. His ability as a scientist and business executive was recognized, and Wilson advanced to become assistant to the Vice-President in charge of Manufacturing and head of the Development, Patent, and Trade Mark Department in 1929, director of research for all laboratories, a member of the Board of Directors in 1931, and Vice-President in Charge of Research

1. Minutes of the Board of Directors' and Stockholders' Meetings, VI, 3799.
2. "Major Changes in Top Management Announced," *Stanolind Record*, XXVI, No. 1 (November, 1944), 1; *Chicago Daily Tribune*, October 6, 1951; "How Two Top Men Work as Team," *Business Week*, March 5, 1955, 75-79.

and Development in 1933. Active in the affairs of the American Chemical Society, the American Institute of Chemical Engineers, and the American Petroleum Institute and with some seventy technical papers and over ninety patents bearing his name, Wilson was not only one of the most widely known Standard Oilers but one of the industry's leading authorities on cracking, motor fuels, and lubricants, and an expert technical witness in patent litigation. Transferred to Pan American as Vice-Chairman in 1935, Wilson was elected President in 1937. Under his guidance, Pan American had an amazing record of growth between 1935 and 1944.

In the preparations to strengthen the national defense Wilson was placed in charge of the Petroleum & Natural Gas Section of the Raw Materials Division of the National Defense Advisory Commission in 1940. During World War II he served as a member of the Petroleum Industry War Council and on four of its main committees. In addition, he served, at the request of the U.S. Treasury Department, as one of the four managing directors of the General Aniline and Film Corporation, a seized German property. On account of his distinguished work in the field of applied chemistry, Wilson was awarded the Chemical Industry Medal in 1938, cited by the National Association of Manufacturers as a "modern pioneer" in 1940 for his work in cracking and the conservation of hydrocarbon vapors, and awarded the Perkin Medal in 1943. With a reputation as an outstanding scientist, an able and experienced business executive, an excellent public speaker, and a dynamic leader, Wilson and his unbounded energy became a powerful force in molding a "new" Standard.

To share the heavy executive responsibilities and duties of management and leadership, A. W. Peake was advanced from Vice-President in charge of Production to the office of President.[3] Graduating from Stanford University in 1912, Peake started his career as a roustabout on an oil lease in California at $60 per month, then moved up the ladder to pumper, tool dresser, lease foreman, and assistant field representative. In 1916 he moved to Wyoming as field superintendent for the Midwest Refining Company. For twelve years he was busy in the Rocky Mountain area getting out crude oil, piping it to refineries, building casing-head gasoline plants, constructing an electric power plant, and other things. After 1923 Peake was in charge of all field operations of

3. "Disciple of Isaak Walton—New Standard Oil President," *Stanolind Record*, XXVI, No. 4 (February, 1945), 3-4.

the Midwest Refining Company, extending from Montana to the South and Southwest. To head up the Dixie Oil Company, a producing subsidiary, Standard made Peake President in 1928 and sent him to Shreveport, Louisiana. Recognizing his executive ability, long experience, and practical knowledge of producing operations, Standard elected Peake a Director and Vice-President in charge of Production in 1930. From that day forward Peake was the leader responsible for Standard's tremendous drive to increase its crude oil supply and extend its pipeline system. His executive ability and aggressiveness made him an essential member of the new management team.

In filling the other major executive positions on the new team, Frank O. Prior was elected a Director and Vice-President in charge of Production to succeed Peake. He also had general supervision over pipeline and crude oil purchasing matters. Prior had started his career with the Midwest Refining Company in 1919. Since 1930 he had been President of the Stanolind Oil and Gas Company and had been closely associated with Peake in Standard's producing operations. Bruce K. Brown, having returned from government service, was elected a Director and made Vice-President in charge of Development. Roy F. McConnell, who had started with the company as a clerk in the sales office at Detroit in 1907, stepped into Ball's position as Vice-President in charge of Sales. Buell F. Jones, General Counsel and a Director, became a Vice-President, R. J. Lindquist, formerly Vice-President, Treasurer, Comptroller, and a Director of the Curtis-Wright Corporation, became Financial Vice-President in August, 1945. L. E. Harmon succeeded Felix T. Graham as Secretary.

Younger executives were added during the next seven years as death, resignations, and retirements necessitated replacements. When Mr. Seubert retired as a Director in 1946, Lindquist, the Financial Vice-President, succeeded him on the Board. The death of Buell F. Jones and the retirement of L. C. Welch and H. E. Hanson in 1947 led to the elevation of R. F. Baity, General Manager of Sales, and J. K. Roberts, General Manager of Research, to membership on the Board. Mr. Baity, whose service record dated back to 1920, was the first Director to have started his career as a service-station attendant. When Roy F. McConnell retired as Vice-President in charge of Sales in 1949 after forty-three years of service, Baity succeeded him, and Dwight F. Benton, President of the Root Petroleum Company since 1948, became General

Manager of Sales and a Director. Bruce K. Brown resigned in 1949 to become President of Pan Am Southern, a new company representing a merger of the Root Petroleum Company and the Pan American Petroleum Corporation. Thomas E. Sunderland, General Counsel since July, 1948, and Bentley G. McCloud, retired President of the First National Bank of Chicago, were elected Directors in 1949. Upon Baity's death in 1951, Benton became Vice-President in charge of Sales.

A further important change took place in June, 1951, when Frank O. Prior was elected Executive Vice-President. Subsequently, A. C. Sailstad, formerly President of the Stanolind Oil Purchasing Company, was elected to the Board and made General Manager of Sales. S. A. Montgomery, Assistant General Manager of Manufacturing, was also elected a Director. Harry F. Glair, General Manager of Manufacturing since 1933, was appointed Director of Purchases, and Montgomery succeeded him as General Manager of Manufacturing. The last and newest members of the Board are David Graham, Financial Vice-President, who replaced R. J. Lindquist upon his death, and John E. Swearingen, General Manager of Production.

Recognizing the necessity and the importance of streamlining a large organization in order to cut down its reaction time in meeting new situations, the Chairman and President at the outset made a division of executive responsibilities.[4] The "staff" departments—accounting, tax, legal, industrial relations, public relations, research, development and patent activities, and the Pan American subsidiaries—reported directly to Wilson. The Secretary and outside auditors also reported to him. The "line" or operating departments—production, pipeline, refining, sales, the Stanolind and Utah subsidiaries, advertising, traffic, lake and river transportation, and purchasing—reported directly to Peake. To discuss, formulate, and present recommendations relating to over-all operations of the company and subsidiaries and to handle minor matters between the meetings of the Board, an executive committee was created. Because of his intimate knowledge of company affairs, Seubert continued as a Director and served as chairman of the committee until June, 1946. Thereafter, it was composed of Wilson, Peake, Prior, and the Financial Vice-President.

When the management of the company was turned over to the

---

4. "New Executives Divide 'Staff' and 'Line' Duties to Meet Problems of Bigness," *Stanolind Record*, XXVI, No. 4 (February, 1945), 1-2.

new team in January, 1945, World War II was still in progress. Naturally the new executives gave their primary attention and effort to the continued production of petroleum products for the armed services until the war ended. Simultaneously, they made extensive plans for reconversion and peacetime operations.

The coming of V-J Day in August, 1945, brought to an abrupt end all of Standard's war business, which had amounted to approximately $14,000,000 monthly during the four months immediately preceding the end of the war.[5] Reconversion of all facilities to a peacetime basis and the filling of service-station tanks for civilians, who were rejoicing over the end of rationing, now became the main job. Within forty-eight hours after hostilities ended, Standard's refineries had rescheduled their operations in accordance with previously prepared plans so as to manufacture motor gasoline with improved octane and volatility ratings in sufficient quantities for an eager motoring public. The quality and quantity of other civilian products were also increased. A substantial but variable proportion of the major war-plant facilities constructed for aviation gasoline and toluene continued in operation to make motor gasoline as well as new specialty products. Other units were shut down or used intermittently as needed or put to other uses.

The Sales Department immediately went into action with carefully planned programs for doing business on a competitive peacetime basis. Closed bulk plants were opened as rapidly as possible. Increased travel and manpower led to the opening and rehabilitation of retail outlets which had been closed during the war. New training procedures were put into effect and intensified to equip men back from the armed services for the resumption of sales work and to refresh established salesmen, agents, and dealers. With manpower available, it was possible to resume the service and courtesies on which the company's reputation had always been based.

Veterans from the military forces quickly returned to civilian life and resumed their jobs. By the end of 1945, 89 per cent of the 7,713 employees on military leave had resumed their jobs and an additional 2,356 veterans, not previously with the company, had been employed. With the return of veterans the proportion of women employees gradually declined.

5. *Annual Report Standard Oil Company (Indiana) and Subsidiaries For Year Ending December 31, 1945,* 4.

The transition from war to peacetime production necessitated no layoffs, but there was a reduction in the amount of overtime work. With the resumption of the forty-hour week in the industry, many oil companies voluntarily offered to raise wages 15 per cent. The 15 per cent pattern was set by the Standard Oil Company (New Jersey), which had an independent union. The Oil Workers International Union, CIO, apparently felt that it could not afford to let industry carry the ball for a wage boost, especially when the first move was made by a company and an independent union. Perhaps it was a case of being "too quick with too much." Consequently, the OWIU demanded fifty-two hours' pay for a forty-hour week or a 30 per cent increase, a nationwide closed shop, work shift differentials, industry-wide bargaining, and double time on Sunday.

On September 13, 1945, Standard of Indiana announced a new wage and hour plan whereby a 15 per cent general pay increase was offered to all unorganized and union workers not earning over $600 per month and adjustments for those working on a commission basis.[6] The increase was to become effective with the reduction of the work week to forty hours, effective October 1st, in the Sales Department and in all other departments as manpower became available. It was expected that by early in 1946 all workers would be on the forty-hour week. The Standard Oil Employees Association at Whiting rejected the offer and asked for the same terms that the OWIU was demanding.

Ignoring and violating contracts with a "no strike pledge," the OWIU workers walked out at other refineries while negotiations were in progress and shortly after the Truman Administration had decided on a policy of wage increases. The first walkout occurred at Socony-Vacuum's Trenton, Michigan, plant on September 16, 1945. The next day the OWIU went on strike at Socony-Vacuum's plant in the Calumet area and on the following day at the Cities Service refinery. Union workers at the plants of Shell, Texas, Sinclair, and Sun struck on the 19th. The strike quickly spread through the Middle West, and it appeared as if a nationwide shutdown would occur.[7] It was estimated that there was only a fifty-two-day supply of gasoline on hand inside refinery grounds, bulk plants, and service stations; twenty-three days of this supply

6. *Chicago Daily Tribune*, September 14, 1945.
7. "Essential Transportation Threatened as C.I.O. Unions Refinery Strikes Spread," *National Petroleum News*, XXXVII, No. 38 (September 19, 1945), 3.

was for the military. One bright spot in the troubled picture was that Standard's General Office workers accepted the 15 per cent general pay increase and the forty-hour week, but there were rumors that workers at other plants on strike would soon picket those of Standard. Officers of the Standard Oil Employees Association at Whiting indicated, however, that their men would break through any picket line in case one was thrown around the plant by the OWIU.

As the oil strike spread, more than 30,000 men were out by September 20th. In the Calumet area 4,100 men were out in five plants; only the men at Standard's Whiting refinery, the Stanolind Pipe Line, and at Phillips' terminal were still working. In Michigan five hundred men in three plants were out. Twenty-five hundred men affecting nine plants were out in West Virginia and Ohio. In Texas 22,000 men were out of thirteen plants, including 1,500 of Pan American Refining. Charges and countercharges were hurled back and forth.[8] Management charged that the strikes were breaches of faith and contract. The unions maintained that they had sought wage adjustments as long ago as the past spring without getting any satisfaction. About September 26th the OWIU "alerted" all of its members and threatened a nationwide strike.

Although it was estimated there were about six hundred members of the OWIU in the Whiting refinery, Standard had no contract with that union. Members of the Standard Oil Employees Association refused to strike because their contract provided for arbitrating differences and abstaining from walkouts.

Early on Saturday morning, September 29th, an OWIU picket line made up of workers from other refineries was thrown around the Whiting refinery.[9] Within a short time a shoulder-to-shoulder and fender-to-fender picket line surrounded the plant. There were over a thousand pickets and hundreds of autos. Inside the plant about seven hundred men, caught by the picketing, continued at work, and Stanolind Pipe Line, despite the fact that its workers were represented by an OWIU local, continued to supply crude oil. Several clashes occurred during which a few employees were hurt in trying to pass through the picket line to work. The mayor of Whiting and the sheriff of Lake County advised Governor Ralph F. Gates of Indiana that the situation was out of their

8. "Strike Swells to 30,000 Workers, Management Claims Walkout Flagrant Breach of Contract," *National Petroleum News*, XXXVII, No. 39 (September 26, 1945), 4-5.
9. *Chicago Daily Tribune*, September 30, 1945.

control. Four companies of the Indiana National Guard were alerted by the governor to "stand by." At the same time the governor telegraphed officials of OWIU, Local 210, requesting that the pickets be withdrawn. Peake telegraphed Secretary of Labor Schwellenbach to use his influence to secure the removal of the pickets. Schwellenbach telegraphed officials of OWIU requesting that the picket line be withdrawn because a conference in Washington to adjust the dispute was being made "difficult" by the picket line. About 10 P.M. rumors became rife that the governor had ordered state troopers and militiamen to Whiting. The mass picket line was thereupon withdrawn. Following this action, independent union members entered the refinery without further molestation, and normal operations were resumed on Sunday. However, the strike against the other Calumet area refineries continued.

Secretary of Labor Schwellenbach offered a four-point program for settling the nationwide strike which, among other things, involved the appointment of an impartial arbitrator whose decision would be handed down not later than December 1, 1945, and would be binding. By early October the strike had spread so as to involve more than 36,000 men and tied up a refining capacity of 1,491,600 barrels daily. However, no employee of Standard was then engaged in the strike and striking employees in its subsidiaries constituted only 4.5 per cent of the total employee group.

Although the unions accepted Schwellenbach's proposal for a settlement, the companies made so many qualifications that the Secretary of Labor considered this a rejection. After a week or more of attempts to settle the strike, Schwellenbach certified to the President that the work stoppage threatened to injure other industries and the general public. Consequently, President Truman authorized the Navy early in October to seize the strike-bound plants of twenty-six oil companies, involving approximately one-third of the nation's refining capacity. The plants of the Pan American Refining Corporation and the pumping stations of the Pan American Pipe Line Company were among those seized. O. A. Knight, head of the Oil Workers International Union, sent out telegrams ordering all workers to go back to work, and before naval officers arrived at the different plants some 43,000 men were returning to work. Under the terms of seizure, wages and working conditions remained as they were before the strike until a new settlement could be made.

By October 21st a majority of the 108 unions with whom Standard had contracts had accepted the 15 per cent increase. Unable to agree with the refinery workers on the 15 per cent pay increase, the matter was submitted in accordance with the contracts to an arbitrator elected from a panel appointed by the U.S. Department of Labor, which awarded an 18 per cent raise. In keeping with this decision, the company automatically granted the 18 per cent to the employees at Whiting and made the increase generally applicable to all others.[10] Thus, without a strike or the loss of a single day's pay or the use of violence, Standard employees peacefully settled their differences with management under the procedure prescribed in their contracts. The company's action was the general pattern for the final industry settlement.

Long before the war ended, breath-taking plans for peacetime operations, based upon free competition with other companies in the petroleum industry, had been formulated by Standard's new management. They were far-reaching and affected every department and every operation of the company. Based upon the heritage, reputation, and strong foundations laid by their predecessors, the plans of the new executives were designed to infuse new life and power into the organization. In the formulation of these plans, the new team had several fundamental objectives.[11] All facilities were to be enlarged and modernized and new facilities added. More emphasis was to be given than ever before to research so that new and more efficient refining processes might be used to produce new and better products. Crude production was to be increased so that the company might be less dependent. The public relations program was to be greatly expanded in order that there might be a better understanding of the company's acts, plans, and policies by its employees and the general public. Unusual efforts were to be made to make Standard a better citizen. Although the relations of management and employees had been harmonious in the past, every effort was to be made to maintain and improve this relationship. Finally, there was a determination that the long-continued slippage in the company's percentage of the total oil business in its marketing territory must come to an end. Through reducing the cost of its marketing operations, the production of new and better products, and improved service at its stations, Standard intended to make a new drive for business.

10. *Ibid.*, January 19, 1946.
11. Interview with Robert E. Wilson, October 5, 1948.

Basic to the expansion and modernization of the manufacturing facilities was the research program. Before new and better products could be made, improved refining processes used, and new plants built, research and experimentation were essential. Behind the new emphasis upon research was the idea that all efforts in research in the years ahead should be on the basis that "there is a better way to do everything than the way now used." Research had expanded to almost undreamed-of proportions during the war. Postwar research was to continue on an even greater scale. Altogether, it was estimated that over $500,000,000 would be spent by the petroleum industry for research and development and new facilities for them in 1946. The expansion of laboratories and the building of new research centers were either planned by or were under way in many oil companies. Research on nuclear physics, electronic devices, the use of petroleum in plastics, rubber, and medicine, gas turbines, airplanes, auto, diesel, and marine engines, insecticides, herbicides, fungicides, fuels, lubricants, asphalts, detergents, polymerization, cracking, and a host of other subjects indicated the wide character of the work under way.

Having pioneered in research among oil companies, the new Standard executives were determined that their company should stay in the forefront of technological progress.[12] Shortly after they assumed office the research and development staff at Whiting was regrouped and reorganized under Bruce K. Brown, Vice-President, and Joseph K. Roberts, General Manager of Research, and several staff members were moved from the Whiting laboratory to the General Office in Chicago. In view of the contemplated plant expansion, an engineering research department was established, and all engineering activities were reorganized and expanded.

To provide more room, bring together most of the scattered research staff in one building, and provide the finest and most modern facilities, Dr. Wilson, operating a tractor, broke ground for the first group of buildings of a $10,000,000 research center at Hammond, Indiana, on September 7, 1945, just a month after V-J Day. Dedicated on April 16, 1948, the first group of buildings included space for the administration offices, the main research laboratory, a building for research on grease and specialties, process laboratories for work on chemicals, catalysts, and distillation, a cafeteria, and a warehouse. In the Whiting research center 350 technical men, 450 technicians, and some 200 clerks, stenographers,

12. *Research At The Standard Oil Company (Indiana).*

and others were employed. A new Administration and Engineering Building at Whiting was occupied in the fall of 1949. Although Stanolind Oil and Gas had one of the largest and most complete research organizations in the producing branch of the industry, a new research center devoted to the study of problems of exploring for and producing oil and manufacturing liquid fuels and chemicals by synthetic means, as well as separating and refining them, was projected at Tulsa in 1948.[13] It was designed to be one of the most modern and complete research centers in this field. The Pan American Refining Corporation completed a new automotive research laboratory at Baltimore in 1948.

RESEARCH EXPENDITURES 1945–1951
STANDARD OIL COMPANY (INDIANA) AND SUBSIDIARIES

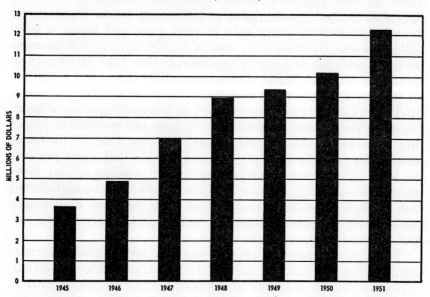

    Indicative of the new stress upon research activities is the fact that expenditures increased from $3,191,000 in 1944 to $12,-291,665.43 in 1951.

    The postwar demand for oil products and the decrease in the supply of desirable crudes required further research in refining methods. Having been one of the pioneers in developing fluid catalytic cracking, Standard continued to study new catalytic proc-

13. *The Oil and Gas Journal* (August 5, 1948), 41.

esses and their operations. Work on jet-propulsion fuels became increasingly important. Standard had been one of the first to improve lubricating oil by adding certain chemicals called additives. It steadily increased its lead in producing heavy-duty motor oil by the discovery of new additives and the development of a large number of new formulas for using them. A new turbine oil, a special nonleaking grease, and a superior airplane grease were developed. The outbreak of the Korean War in June, 1950, furnished an additional stimulus to seeking better ways of making high-octane components for aviation and motor fuels and for developing new additives for heavy-duty motor oils. The phenomenal increase in the use of fuel oil for diesels and home heating intensified research on these products. Outstanding work was done on new products for the farm and household, including sprays to control grasshoppers and the corn borer, insect sprays harmless to delicate crops such as corn, peas, and beans, a weed killer for use on crab grass, and a highly efficient low-pressure aerosol bomb for dispensing new insecticides. The laboratory of Stanolind Oil and Gas at Tulsa successfully developed a method of making synthetic fuels and chemicals from natural gas. Stanolind's large laboratory concentrated on discovering more efficient means of finding and producing oil and gas and methods of pumping deep wells with efficiency and economy. One of its major discoveries was the Hydrafrac process which uses great pressure to fracture oil-bearing formations deep in the earth and holds them open so that the oil can flow more easily into the well. By the end of 1951 Hydrafrac had proved itself in more than 10,000 wells as the best method found in recent years to increase the output of certain types of wells.

Through the newly developed synthetic and catalytic processes used during the war, scientists had discovered that crude oil was a rich and cheap source of all sorts of organic chemicals, and all major oil companies began producing chemicals on a large scale. Reports of the new discoveries during the war frightened the chemical industry because the petroleum industry had become a larger volume manufacturer of synthetic organic chemicals than the chemical industry itself.[14] Synthetic products made from petroleum totaled five times the prewar volume. In the case of butadiene, for example, the petroleum industry was producing twenty-seven times the prewar volume. Many common chemicals

14. *Barron's,* XXVI (September 16, 1946), 23.

like formaldehyde, methanol, and acetic acid could be made from petroleum. Thiophene was invaluable for use in dyestuffs, medicine, and synthetic rubber. Ethylene was used for drugs, dyes, ripening fruit, rubber, and cosmetics, and propylene for chemicals used in synthetic leather, upholstery, and shoes. Petroleum chemicals were used as softeners for rubber compounds, for many synthetic resins and plastics used in coating materials and molded products, for emulsifiers for various materials, as substitutes for linseed and other natural oils in paints, components for potent new insecticides, and in making synthetic household and industrial washing compounds. In view of the enormous potentialities, considerable emphasis was given by Standard's research staff to discovering new methods for making chemical products from petroleum.

Owing to the business depression of the 1930's and then the war, Standard's manufacturing, transportation, and marketing facilities had not kept pace with the demand. If the company were to meet competition and the anticipated peacetime demands for more petroleum products, all facilities would have to be expanded. With confidence in the future and a determination to stop the decline in the percentage of its business, the new management embarked upon the greatest program of expansion and modernization of facilities in the company's history. The gigantic character of the program indicated something of the vision and drive of the new executives. Major emphasis was given first to production, second to refining, and third to transportation facilities. Much of the construction work proceeded under great difficulties owing to all kinds of shortages of materials, but it was completed as fast as labor and materials would permit.

In an effort to produce more oil, Standard's capital expenditures for this purpose increased from $46,300,000 in 1945 to $98,401,194 in 1950. More emphasis was given to exploration and finding new sources of oil rather than buying crude oil properties. The vigorous exploratory and drilling program of Stanolind Oil and Gas in Oklahoma, West Texas, southeastern New Mexico, Wyoming, Utah, and Colorado resulted in a substantial increase both in reserves and production.[15] In the Williston Basin of North Dakota

15. "The Story of Stanolind Oil and Gas," *Standard Torch*, III, No. 3 (March, 1950), 3-21; J. E. Swearingen, "Standard Oil and the Williston Basin," an address before the Twin Cities Society of Security Analysts, St. Paul, Minnesota, July 1, 1952.

and Montana, Stanolind acquired leases on more than four million acres and started wildcat drilling late in 1951. Stanolind's percentage record in completing productive wildcat wells in the postwar period ran well above the average for the entire petroleum industry. Costs of drilling increased sharply from an average of $30,200 per well in 1940 to $69,900 in 1951. In 1951 Stanolind set a record for its production of crude oil and gas. Its total crude oil production topped the 1948 record by 10.6 per cent.

Among the producing properties purchased by Stanolind was that of the Ramsey Petroleum Corporation of Oklahoma City, acquired in 1946, which was mostly in the Cement field of Caddo County, Oklahoma, with some sixty-five net producing wells. The rest consisted of holdings in Pauls Valley, East Pauls Valley, and Hoover pools of Garvin County and about 5,000 net acres of nonproducing leaseholds in West Central Oklahoma. Stanolind also acquired the producing properties of J. C. Hawkins, L. M. Glasco, and J. A. Humphrey in the Slaughter pool, consisting of approximately 5,000 net producing acres and 121 wells. The total monthly allowable oil from the combined properties was approximately 2,000 barrels per day.[16] The purchase boosted Stanolind's number of wells to more than four hundred in the field.

In a further effort to increase production Stanolind turned to the exploration of the tidelands in the Gulf of Mexico and large areas in Canada. Stanolind was one of the first and most active companies to engage in offshore drilling.[17] In 1946 and early in 1947 it had four geophysical crews operating in the coastal waters in the Gulf of Mexico. In November, 1947, Phillips, Stanolind, and Kerr-McGee, which had eleven leases off Louisiana totaling 35,000 acres, drilled a good commercial oil producer ten miles off Terrebonne Parish, Louisiana.[18] It opened the first oil field in the world out of the sight of land. Between 1948 and early in January, 1950, Stanolind drilled four offshore wells of its own and thirteen others in which it had an interest. By 1950 Stanolind had leases on about 250,000 underwater acres off Louisiana and Texas, all acquired after careful geophysical surveys. The Pan American Production Company completed seismic exploration off the coast of Louisiana in 1948 and bought sizable leasehold

16. "Stanolind Buys 121 Slaughter Field Wells," *The Oil and Gas Journal* (March 8, 1947), 36.
17. "The Story of Stanolind Oil and Gas," *Standard Torch*, III, No. 3 (March, 1950), 13-15.
18. *The Oil and Gas Journal*, XLVIII, No. 2 (May 19, 1949), 189, 212-213.

WELLS DRILLED 1945–1951
STANDARD OIL COMPANY (INDIANA) AND SUBSIDIARIES

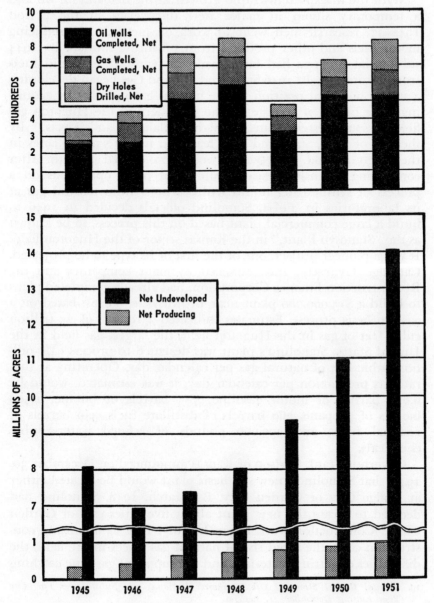

interests. It and Seaboard Oil had about 63,000 acres off Louisiana in 1948.

With the unexpectedly rapid growth in the demand for oil and a temporary slump in major new discoveries in the period 1942–47, research men went to work on methods of producing motor fuels and other products from substitute sources. By 1944 substantial progress had been made in synthesizing liquid fuels from natural gas. In 1946 Stanolind Oil and Gas began developing a strong potential position in the natural gas industry by acquiring large blocks of acreage on the periphery of the Hugoton gas field in southwestern Kansas and in Oklahoma and Texas.[19] By the end of 1946, Stanolind held leases on nearly 750,000 acres in the Hugoton field. Ninety-nine wells were drilled in 1946. After conducting extensive research and pilot plant operations on a process of synthesizing liquid hydrocarbons from natural gas at its laboratories in Tulsa, Stanolind officials decided in 1946 to build a large commercial plant based on this process, to be known as the "Stanosyn Plant," in the Kansas sector of the Hugoton field. It was a pioneer project, one of the first of its type to be projected. Carthage Hydrocol, Inc., financed by eight companies and the Reconstruction Finance Corporation, had already completed plans to build a $15,000,000 plant near Brownsville, Texas, based on a gas synthesis process. Estimates indicated a reserve of 23 trillion cubic feet of gas in the Hugoton field, the largest gas field in the United States. Stanolind's plant was designed to process 94.4 million cubic feet of natural gas per calendar day. Operating at that rate, its production per calendar day, it was estimated, would be 6,080 barrels of motor gasoline, 745 barrels of butane, 1,500 barrels of propane, 360 barrels of distillate fuels, 340 barrels of residual fuels, and 399,000 pounds of refined water-soluble chemicals.

Governor Frank Carlson of Kansas announced on December 30, 1947, that Stanolind's new synthesis plant would be located either at Dodge City or Garden City. By March, 1948, Stanolind had decided to locate the new plant about five miles east of Garden City.[20] Construction work began in July. Due to mounting construction costs, the rapid rise of natural gas prices in the field, the difficulties of getting materials, and the supply of gasoline catching

19. *Annual Report Standard Oil Company (Indiana) and Subsidiaries For The Year Ending December 31, 1946*, 9.
20. *The Oil and Gas Journal* (March 11, 1948), 125; (March 25, 1948), 150.

A. W. PEAKE, PRESIDENT 1945–1955

FRANK O. PRIOR, EXECUTIVE VICE-PRESIDENT 1951–1955;
PRESIDENT 1955–

THE NEW WHITING RESEARCH LABORATORY

GIVING NEW LIFE TO SICK WELLS

A shallow well drilled to test the hydraulic fracturing process developed by the Stanolind Oil and Gas Company to add new life to old wells. Well in foreground has been excavated to show fractures around well bore

A TYPICAL SEISMOGRAPH EXPLORING PARTY

The party consists of fifteen men and eleven vehicles. It cost $100,000 to equip the party and as much as $20,000 per month to operate

AERIAL VIEW OF STANOLIND OIL AND GAS COMPANY WELL BEING DRILLED
OFF THE COAST OF CAMERON PARISH, LOUISIANA

The well is being drilled in thirty-six feet of water

NATURAL GASOLINE PLANT OF THE STANOLIND OIL AND GAS COMPANY,
HASTINGS FIELD IN TEXAS, 1947

up with the demand, Stanolind stopped all construction work in August and abandoned the project.[21]

Despite its withdrawal from the Stanosyn project, Stanolind went ahead with the development of the Hugoton field. In 1948 it began the construction of a natural gasoline plant near Ulysses to process Hugoton gas and recover liquefied petroleum gases and natural gasoline. The processed, or "dry," gas was sold to a gas pipeline company.

The abandonment of the Garden City project, however, did not affect Stanolind's plans made in 1947 to construct a chemical separation plant at Brownsville, Texas, for separating and refining water-soluble chemicals produced by the Carthage Hydrocol synthesis plant then under construction.[22] It was the only one of its kind anywhere. Under a contract with Stanolind, Carthage Hydrocol, Inc., agreed to sell Stanolind the "water stream," containing large amounts of ethyl alcohol, acetic acid, and other industrial chemicals produced as by-products of the gasoline synthesis process. This plant was completed early in 1950 but never operated successfully, owing to many operating difficulties in the synthetic plant.

Backed by the aggressive managerial support of the parent company, Stanolind Oil and Gas rapidly expanded into the business of producing natural, or casing-head, gasoline—the liquid material present in some natural gas.[23] In April, 1947, Stanolind completed one of the outstanding, ultramodern natural gasoline plants in the coastal area in the heart of the Hastings oil field, twenty-two miles south of Houston. The Hastings field had 5,500 productive acres, of which Stanolind had 74 per cent. Casing-head gas coming from over six hundred flowing wells was processed in the new plant, which produced approximately 45,400 gallons of gasoline and other liquefied hydrocarbon products per day. Ten more plants were authorized or under construction in 1948 and represented a capital investment of more than $27,000,000 net.

The new natural gasoline plant in the Slaughter pool, thirteen miles southwest of Levelland, Texas, was completed in the spring of 1949. It was jointly owned by The Texas Company, the Hono-

21. "Stanolind Pigeonholes Plans for Synthesis Plant; High Costs Cited," *The Oil and Gas Journal* (August 26, 1948), 77.
22. "Stanolind Planning Brownsville Plant," *The Oil and Gas Journal* (August 2, 1947), 38.
23. "The Story of Stanolind Oil and Gas," *Standard Torch*, III, No. 3 (March, 1950), 16-17.

lulu Oil Corporation, Magnolia, Devonian Oil, Atlantic Refining, Mid-Continent, Saltmount, and Stanolind. Stanolind operated the plant. With a capacity to process 90,000,000 cubic feet of casing-head gas per day, it was designed to recover about 100,000 gallons of gasoline, 100,000 gallons of butane, and 50,000 gallons of propane per day.

By the end of 1951 Stanolind was operating one refinery and thirteen natural gas and cycling plants, and it owned an interest in ten additional natural gasoline and cycling plants operated by others. With the completion of its three-year expansion program, Stanolind was one of the dominant operators in the natural gasoline industry, and natural gasoline had become important to Standard's operations.

Early in 1948 Stanolind Oil and Gas formed a foreign exploration department to conduct explorations in Canada and Colombia, South America. Offices were opened at Bogotá and in Calgary. Concessions on four tracts in Colombia totaling about 500,000 acres had been acquired.[24] Three of the tracts were concessions from the Colombian government. The fourth concession was on university lands. Two were located on the Caribbean near Barranquilla and the other two on the Pacific Coast near Buenaventura. All tracts were "wildcat" territory. Exploration activities in Colombia, however, were suspended early in 1949 and the crews returned to the United States pending "a more favorable industry situation." The concession rights were retained. Stanolind struck oil in its first Alberta wildcat well at Barrhead in February, 1949, about fifty-five miles northwest of Edmonton, Canada. In 1949 exploratory work increased, and Stanolind acquired leases on more than 2,500,000 acres in Canada.

As a part of its long-range refining program, Standard announced in May, 1946, that it would close permanently its small refineries at Neodesha, Kansas, and Greybull, Wyoming, in 1948 and consolidate their operations with nearby refineries.[25] The installation of catalytic cracking equipment during the war had developed a competitive situation which required such equipment to be installed at Sugar Creek and Casper as well as at other Standard refineries. Engineering studies indicated that the duplication of

24. "Stanolind Acquires Four Concessions in Colombia," *The Oil and Gas Journal* (February 26, 1948), 95.
25. "Indiana Standard To Close Greybull, Neodesha Plants," *The Oil and Gas Journal* (May 25, 1946), 151.

CRUDE OIL AND NATURAL GAS LIQUIDS PRODUCED 1945–1951
STANDARD OIL COMPANY (INDIANA) AND SUBSIDIARIES

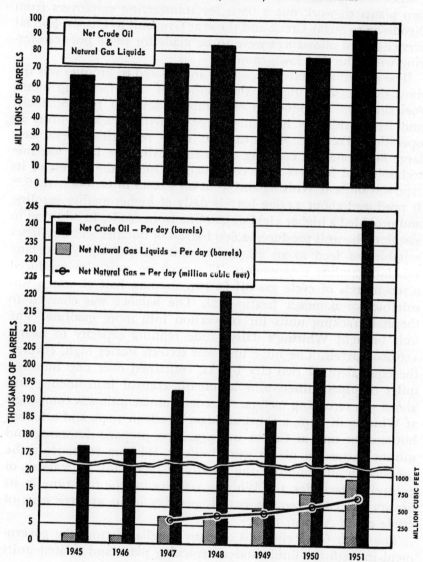

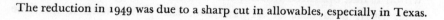

The reduction in 1949 was due to a sharp cut in allowables, especially in Texas.

these facilities at Neodesha and Greybull would be uneconomical. Consequently, negotiations were started with the unions at the two plants to work out a basis for transferring employees from Neodesha to Sugar Creek and those at Greybull to Casper. Special service-record allowances were to be made for those not transferring when the shutdown came.

The advent of catalytic cracking and related techniques was the most significant change in the method of manufacturing motor fuel since the introduction of tetraethyl lead. In 1945 Standard and its subsidiaries had only three catalytic cracking units in operation. To increase the capacity of its refineries, several new large fluid catalytic cracking units embodying the latest wartime technological features were constructed. One of the largest of its type was built at Whiting and went on stream in October, 1946.[26] It produced about 11,600 barrels daily of higher-quality gasoline and provided a higher yield of gasoline from crude. In addition to gasoline, the unit produced 2,600 barrels of butanes and butylenes suitable for feed to an alkylation unit for making high-octane aviation gasoline components. The cracking unit also produced 9,700 barrels of cycle gas oil in two streams, half of which was suitable for domestic heating oil. The balance was charged to thermal cracking units for conversion into more gasoline. The unit brought Whiting's daily crude refining capacity to nearly 150,000 barrels. The huge unit was sixteen stories high, covered the equivalent of two city blocks, contained over one hundred miles of pipes, ninety-nine automatic control instruments, and about 300 recording meters. A second similar unit was completed at Whiting in 1948, a third at Sugar Creek in 1948, and a fourth but smaller unit at Casper in 1949. New propane dewaxing and solvent extraction plants were built at Whiting to increase the production and improve the quality of motor oil. As a result of expanding facilities, the Whiting refinery for the first time in its history exceeded 200,000 barrels per day in its average runs of crude oil in August, 1950.

The Utah Oil Refining Company purchased from the government in 1946 the fluid catalytic cracking plant and related units which it had operated during the war for making 100-octane gasoline. Built at a cost of $15,221,000, the plant, with a wartime

26. "New Indiana Standard Catalytic Unit Goes on Stream in Whiting," *The Oil and Gas Journal* (October 19, 1946), 92.

capacity of 7,000 barrels per day, was bought for $4,148,300.[27] Other improvements resulted in increasing the company's refining capacity from 22,000 to 24,500 barrels in 1949. A propane de-asphalting unit was constructed in 1949 in order to expand asphalt sales.

Late in 1947 the Pan American Petroleum Corporation, "Papco," which marketed in the mid-South, bought the majority stock of the Root Petroleum Company, which had a refinery at El Dorado, Arkansas, with a capacity of 20,000 barrels.[28] The Root plant was the thirteenth refinery in the Standard group. To step up the refinery's output of gasoline and home heating oils and provide high-grade petroleum coke, the company completed a coking unit in 1950 and started the construction of a fluid catalytic cracking unit with a capacity of 9,500 barrels.

The government aviation gasoline plant, built at the Pan American Refining Corporation's refinery at Texas City during the war to produce isopentane by the catalytic isomerization process at a cost of $2,832,000, was sold to Pan American in 1947 for $412,000 and converted to producing petroleum chemicals.[29] In the same year Pan American purchased the refinery of the Stone Oil Company adjacent to its property at Texas City. In 1949 Pan American purchased from General Motors its triptane plant at Detroit, a semicommercial demonstration unit built to produce high-octane trimethylbutane, and moved it to Texas City.[30] Triptane was not produced at Texas City but the precise fractionating equipment from the plant augmented Pan American's facilities for manufacturing solvents for plastics, paint, varnish, ink, and other products. The Baltimore and Savannah plants of Pan American increased their facilities for asphalt production.

With a continued high demand for petroleum products and the outbreak of the Korean War in June, 1950, Standard reviewed and revised its plans for plant expansion. Instead of closing the Neodesha refinery, it made plans to modernize the plant and increase its crude running capacity from 10,400 to 19,700 barrels per day. In 1951 the construction of a catalytic cracking unit and an alkylation unit were started at Neodesha. Plans were also made

27. "100-Octane Plant Is Sold to Utah Oil Refining Company," *National Petroleum News*, XXXVIII, No. 21 (May 22, 1946), 46.
28. *Annual Report for 1947 Standard Oil Company (Indiana)*, 15.
29. "Pan American Is Only Bidder On WAA Avgas Equipment," *National Petroleum News*, XXXIX, No. 12 (March 19, 1947), 40.
30. *The Oil and Gas Journal*, XLVIII, No. 2 (May 19, 1949), 368.

to increase the refining capacity for processing crude at Sugar Creek from 38,000 to 68,000 barrels per day.

As a result of the national defense program, a serious shortage of sulphur, benzene, and other chemicals developed. To relieve the shortage of benzene, Pan American began producing benzene from petroleum in 1950. In 1951 Standard adapted certain facilities at Whiting for the production of benzene at a rate of about 11,000,000 gallons per year.

The company also began constructing a plant at Whiting to extract hydrogen sulphide from by-product fuel gases produced in the refinery and convert it into elemental sulphur. When placed in operation, the plant was expected to produce fifty-five tons per day. Stanolind Oil and Gas also built several desulphurization plants at the same time. Plans were also made for the construction of a complete plant to produce iso-octyl alcohol at the Wood River refinery. The principal use of this chemical is in the manufacture of plasticizers for use in plastics.

Owing to the rapid developments in the Williston Basin, which promised to become one of the major sources of crude oil in the future, Standard announced early in 1952 that it would build a new refinery with a capacity of 15,000 barrels at Mandan, North Dakota. Later the design capacity was increased to 30,000 barrels per day.

Postwar plans called for increasing the capacity of the company's trunk pipelines, the extension of facilities to new fields, the construction of gasoline lines for affiliated companies, and additions to the tanker fleet and river barges. The expansion program was planned to meet the traffic demand in 1950. However, since the postwar demand far exceeded expectations and the twenty-five or more refineries served by the Stanolind Pipe Line, directly and indirectly, required a greater volume of crude, the construction was rushed to completion in 1949, a year earlier than planned.[31]

In addition to building miles of gathering lines in new fields, the Stanolind Pipe Line began looping its main trunk line from Drumright to Sugar Creek, Wood River, and Whiting to supplement the two lines already in use. The new construction increased the capacity of the line by 40,000 barrels per day, raising the total capacity of the line to 240,000 barrels a day. Early in 1947 Stanolind began expanding its line from Drumright southwest to West Texas, to increase the line's capacity from 68,000 to 85,000

31. "Service Pipe Line Company," *Standard Torch*, III, No. 6 (June, 1950), 3-12.

CRUDE OIL AND NATURAL GASOLINE REFINED 1945–1951
STANDARD OIL COMPANY (INDIANA) AND SUBSIDIARIES

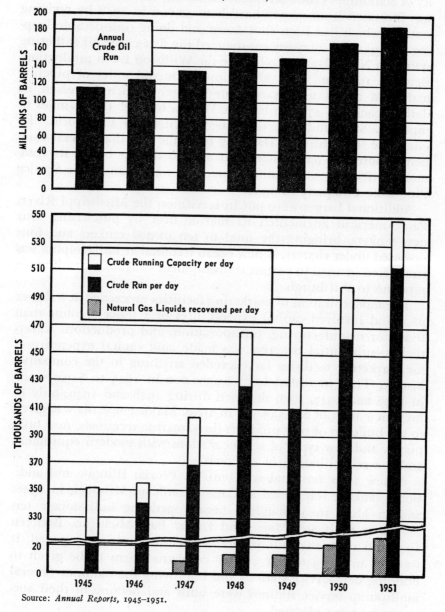

Source: *Annual Reports*, 1945–1951.

barrels daily. As pipe became available the capacity of the West Texas-Drumright line was increased to 126,000 barrels. The capacity of Stanolind's crude oil line from Casper to Freeman, Missouri, was increased from 30,000 barrels to 52,000 in 1948 by reviving stations which had been shut down and doing considerable looping. In 1951 the company constructed the first crude oil gathering system in North Dakota to handle the Williston Basin production. Between 1945 and 1951 about four thousand miles of pipeline had been added to the company's system which increased its daily capacity to 475,000 barrels. With a total of 11,274 miles of pipeline, Stanolind had the longest system in the world. To eliminate the confusion resulting from the fact that several companies bore the name Stanolind and to denote better its common carrier status, Stanolind Pipe Line was renamed the Service Pipe Line Company in 1950.

Additional barges were put in service on the Mississippi River. Pan American augmented its marine fleet by purchasing four new tankers, bringing the total to ten owned tankers and four operated under charter. A new ocean terminal at Philadelphia was completed in 1946 to permit transshipment of Amoco gasoline via pipeline to Pittsburgh.

The modernization of marketing facilities proceeded at a slower pace and involved capital expenditures of a lesser amount than those for manufacturing, transportation, and production. Nevertheless, substantial progress was made, and capital expenditures for marketing facilities far exceeded anything in the company's history. They increased from $5,500,000 in 1945 to $19,000,000 in 1946 and 1947, then declined during 1948 and 1949, only to hit a new high of $23,353,306 in 1950. Major emphasis was given to the building of new products lines, marine terminals, new bulk plants, and new types of service stations with modern equipment and the rehabilitation of old ones.

A new river terminal was built at Peoria, Illinois, and additional tankage was added at Cape Girardeau, Missouri, in 1948; and in May, 1949, Standard began operating bulk-storage terminals at Sault Ste. Marie and Dollar Bay, Michigan. Between 1945 and 1950, 184 bulk plants were either built or reopened. It was not until 1949 that greater emphasis began to be given to building new service stations and improving the old ones. Several multipump service stations were built and because of their success more were planned.

PIPELINE AND WATER BORNE TRAFFIC 1945–1951
STANDARD OIL COMPANY (INDIANA) AND SUBSIDIARIES

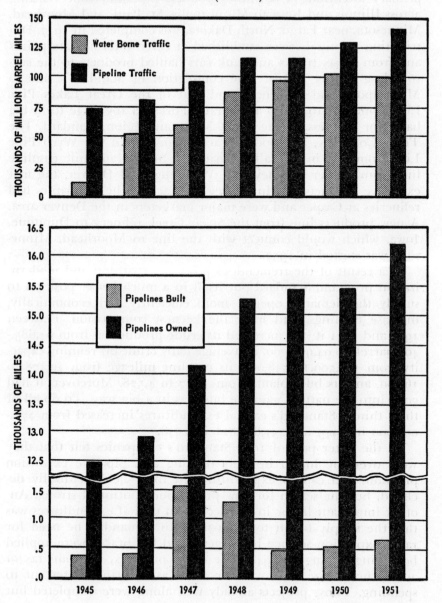

Owing to the need for supplying the demand and the competitive situations, the construction of gasoline pipelines received primary attention. A 662-mile products pipeline from Whiting across Illinois and Iowa to Minneapolis, St. Paul, and Moorhead, Minnesota, near Fargo, North Dakota, was completed in 1947. Distributing terminals were established at three intermediate points and from these, trucks and tank cars hauled products to the surrounding supply points. The completion of Standard's line to Minneapolis and Moorhead and that of the Great Lakes Pipe Line Company to Fargo and Grand Forks set the stage for a big battle for business. In the Rocky Mountain region, Standard, The Texas Company, and Socony-Vacuum organized the Wyco Pipe Line Company in the fall of 1946 and built a 267-mile gasoline line from Casper to Cheyenne, Wyoming, and Denver, the first extensive products line in the region. Each of the companies had refineries at Casper and were major marketers in the Denver area. A new products line from the Sugar Creek refinery to Dubuque, Iowa, which would connect with the line to Moorhead, Minnesota, was started in 1952.

As a result of the tremendous postwar expansion and modernization program, Standard put itself in a much better position to supply the demand, operate more efficiently and economically, increase earnings, and meet the keenest competition. Between 1945 and 1951 it had increased its crude production from 64,685,-408 barrels to 94,990,000, its average daily crude oil refining capacity from 351,500 to 548,000, its pipeline mileage from 12,478 to 16,180, and its bulk plants from 4,437 to 4,528. Moreover, it had gone into the natural gasoline business in a big way. To do all of these things, Standard's capital expenditures increased from $77,-000,000 in 1945 to $251,831,821 in 1948.[32]

By the latter part of 1948 Standard's companies felt that they were over the hump in their refining and pipeline expansion program, and capital expenditures in these fields naturally declined, but the search for new production continued strong. Another important factor in the decline in capital expenditures was that the supply began to catch up with demand. The need for rapid expansion seemed less urgent, and the brakes were applied beginning in August, 1948. The threat of an excess-profits tax of an unknown size in November acted as a further deterrent to spending. Those projects already well along were completed but

32. *Annual Reports,* 1945, 1951.

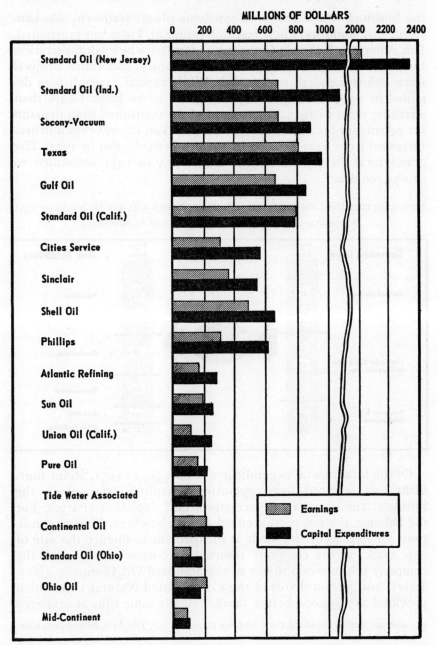

MILLIONS OF DOLLARS

0   200   400   600   800   1000 2000 2200 2400

Standard Oil (New Jersey)

Standard Oil (Ind.)

Socony-Vacuum

Texas

Gulf Oil

Standard Oil (Calif.)

Cities Service

Sinclair

Shell Oil

Phillips

Atlantic Refining

Sun Oil

Union Oil (Calif.)

Pure Oil

Tide Water Associated

Continental Oil

Standard Oil (Ohio)

Ohio Oil

Mid-Continent

Earnings

Capital Expenditures

Source: *Annual Reports*.

Prepared under the direction of S. K. Botsford, Assistant Secretary, Standard Oil Company (Indiana), by the Comptroller's Statistical and Questionnaire Department.

the building of the Hugoton synthesis plant (Stanosyn) was canceled, and Stanolind's new research center at Tulsa was postponed. Pan American Refining Company's plans for a new administration building, an engineering research laboratory, and other projects were also suspended or canceled. While capital expenditures declined in 1949 and 1950, they continued to be large, larger than anything prior to 1945. On account of the continued high demand for petroleum products and the Korean War, capital expenditures increased from $127,439,000 in 1950 to $183,064,000 in 1951. The grand total for capital outlays from 1945 to 1951 amounted to $1,075,700,000.[33]

How a Billion Dollars for Capital Expenditures Came and Went, 1945–1951
Standard Oil Company (Indiana) and Subsidiaries

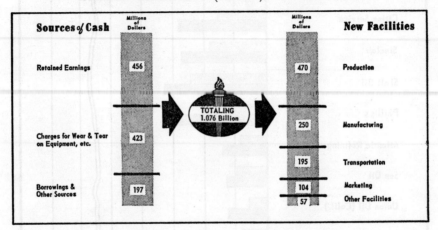

Of the total capital expenditures from 1945 to 1951, about four-fifths was financed from operations—earnings retained in the business, amortization, depreciation, and depletion charges. For the balance, the company secured funds elsewhere. Market conditions for new securities made it inexpedient to finance the sale of new stock, so the company resorted to borrowing. In 1946 the company sold 200,000 shares of the Standard Oil Company (New Jersey) and 52,000 shares of the Consolidated Natural Gas, which provided $17,634,000 before taxes.[34] At the same time it arranged

33. *Annual Report Standard Oil Company (Indiana) For The Year Ended December 31, 1951, 7.*
34. *Annual Report Standard Oil Company (Indiana) and Subsidiaries For The Year Ended December 31, 1946, 5.*

with the First National Bank of Chicago and eleven other banks for loans totaling $50,000,000. In 1947 long-term credits aggregating $123,000,000 were secured.[35] In 1948 the company sold to The Equitable Life Assurance Society of the United States $50,-000,000 of 2¾ per cent Sinking Fund Debentures and, in addition,

CAPITAL EXPENDITURES AND PROVISION FOR DEPRECIATION 1939–1951
STANDARD OIL COMPANY (INDIANA) AND SUBSIDIARIES

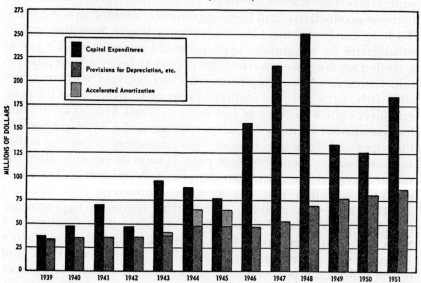

it borrowed $46,000,000 on long-term notes.[36] The operations of the business were sufficient to take care of all capital expenditures in 1949 but in order to restore funds to working capital, funds which had been borrowed, $50,000,000 of 2.9 per cent promissory notes were sold to a group of insurance companies.[37] Repayments for capital expenditures were met in 1950 without any new financing, and an additional $24,884,000 was repaid on loans. By the end of 1950 the long-term debt amounted to $261,620,025.[38] In 1951 it was reduced to $250,351,000.

The expansion program and the re-establishment of peacetime operations necessitated a large increase in employment. Between 1945 and 1951 the number of employees of Standard and its sub-

35. *Annual Report For 1947*, 7.
36. *Annual Report For 1948*, 6-7.
37. *Annual Report For 1949*, 8.
38. *Annual Report For 1950*, 8-9.

sidiaries increased from 36,332 to 49,740. On the other hand, since the start of the Korean War, the armed forces had taken more than 1,600 employees. With many new and less experienced employees and labor unrest prevalent as a result of postwar adjustments, much time and attention were given by management to employee relationships and personnel administration. In the parent company a long-range training program for foremen and supervisors was started to improve the quality of supervision, increase productivity, and keep employees contented in their work. To help employees meet the high cost of living, Standard and its subsidiaries in November, 1946, provided an extra week's pay as a temporary increase covering the period from mid-November to mid-January.[39] A few employees who had received wage increases since July, 1946, were not included in the offer. In applying the plan, employees got a week's pay but not to exceed $100. The amount for commission agents was paid in relation to the number of trucks they operated. Payments to nonunion employees began November 15th and union members were paid as soon as possible after the union accepted the offer. Pan American Petroleum & Transport provided a similar plan for its 6,400 employees. Stanolind Oil and Gas employees received a cost-of-living bonus for 1946 amounting to 10 per cent of their monthly earnings with a maximum of $100. Other oil companies, Continental, Phillips, Carter, Warren Petroleum Corporation, Ohio Oil, Shell, Deep Rock, Gulf, and others followed a policy similar to Standard's. By late November at least twenty oil companies had granted bonuses.

Careful supervision and training enabled the parent company to maintain a top-notch safety record in all departments despite the vast construction program and the employment of many new and less experienced workers. The accident frequency rate was low, much lower than the average for the petroleum industry. As evidence of the effectiveness of the company's program, Standard and its subsidiaries won twenty-four of the thirty-four safety awards made by the American Petroleum Institute in 1947, thirty-four out of fifty-nine in 1948, forty-eight out of ninety-eight in 1949, fifty-four out of 176 in 1950, and forty-one out of 156 in 1951. A change in the system of making awards in 1950 accounts for the decline in the proportion of the company's awards after 1949.

39. *The New York Times*, November 3, 1946.

CHAPTER XXIII

The New Drive for Good Will and Business

THE NEW MANAGEMENT RECOGNIZED FROM THE OUTSET THAT THE interpretation of corporate ideas, plans, and acts to the public and the taking of public opinion into account in the formulation of policies and planning activities would prove a strong element in building good will essential to the growth and security of the company. "It is our desire," declared Wilson, "to get closer to our own organization, the people with whom we do business and others, and tell them of the wartime changes and the new things that they may expect from Standard of Indiana and from the petroleum industry generally." One of the main objectives, therefore, was the development of a long-range public relations program.

No sooner had the new executives assumed their duties than they undertook, as a definite part of their responsibilities, a share of the job in presenting Standard to stockholders, employees, the oil industry, and the general public. Within the first six months Wilson and Peake separately or together visited four refineries, twelve sales fields, and every department of the General Office to get acquainted with employees. As time permitted, they visited the remaining refineries and sales fields. Wilson and Peake, either together or separately, also spoke at dozens of meetings of Chambers of Commerce, service clubs, technical societies, and oilmen's groups all over the Middle West and the country. Other officers, Directors, and members of the executive group likewise appeared in increasing numbers before scientific, professional, and civic groups. Not since the time of Colonel Stewart had Standard of Indiana been so frequently and ably represented before the public.

Of special interest was the appearance of Standard's executives on the programs of state jobbers' and marketers' organizations. To associate with competitors was a striking departure from past policy. More amazing was the straightforward and frank manner with which Standard's executives "laid it on the line" and talked about the company's plans and operations and problems of the industry. No punches were pulled, no issues dodged. It was a simple but effective means of creating better relations and a better understanding within the industry. Commenting upon the effect of the new approach by Standard's executives, the *National Petroleum News* said: "Perhaps one of the greatest influences in erasing skepticism regarding the future type of competition and keeping it above board, is the frank and friendly attitude toward the industry as a whole of officials and personnel of the Standard Oil Company of Indiana in their new and invigorating public-industry relations program." [1] Believing that living right and a frank discussion of the company's acts, policies, and plans would pay off in creating better understanding and good will, Standard's executives steadily increased their public appearances in subsequent years. They formed an essential and permanent part of the new public relations program.

The primary responsibility for building good will for the company fell upon the Public Relations Department, whose size and functions were greatly broadened. [2] In addition to naming a press representative and an assistant director, a public relations representative was appointed in every sales field and at each refinery to assist the General Office and serve as the eyes and ears of the company in regard to all matters affecting it. To supervise the work of the men in the field, aid them, and train them for special activities, a field representative was added to the staff. He also aided with the civic welfare work in which the company was engaged. Surveys of public opinion toward Standard, its products, and activities were inaugurated. Special attention was given to points on which the survey showed the public to be uninformed or misinformed.

In order that the employees might speak for the company with more factual knowledge, the flow of information to them was increased. One of the instruments used to impart this information was the employee magazine. Surveys of hundreds of Standard employees about the type of magazine they liked revealed that they were mostly interested in facts about the company, its people, and its operations. Consequently, the old *Stanolind Record* was replaced by a new magazine, the *Standard Torch,* in January, 1948. Garbed in a new typographical "dress" and with many illustra-

1. *National Petroleum News,* XXXVIII, No. 28 (July 10, 1946), 10.
2. "Expanding Public Relations Dep't. Assists in Creation of Good Will," *Stanolind Record,* XXVI, No. 12 (October–November, 1945), 8-10.

tions, the *Torch* placed less emphasis upon personal news items and more upon lively and interesting articles about how the company carried on its business, how it made and sold products, what the various refineries and sales fields were like, the work of unfamiliar departments, finances of the company, sports activities of employees, hobbies and personalities, and a wide range of subjects.

New emphasis was given to making the annual reports attractive in appearance and understandable to stockholders, employees, and the general public. The use of color, pictures of company operations, graphs and charts, a large-size page, and a better quality of paper were significant new features. For its general excellence, the 1946 annual report was selected by the *Financial World* as the best in the petroleum industry.

Radio was used on a much larger scale than ever before, mostly in the sponsorship of news commentators, news reports, and sports events.[3] As a step in the development of a five-year radio advertising program, the company launched the first of a series of radio news and sports broadcasts over different stations in the Middle West in February, 1945. Eric Sevareid, Everett Holles, Ed Murrow, and Larry LeSeur, all CBS news commentators, Martin Agronsky, E. L. "Ty" Tyson, NBC sports analyst, and many other prominent newscasters were featured. The ultimate objective of the new management was for the company to become the most prominent and popular sponsor of news and sports broadcasts over the leading stations of the Middle West and Rocky Mountain area.

An unusual feature was the extension of Standard's safety program to promoting safe driving to and from football games. On Thursdays and Fridays during the fall season it broadcast safe-driving appeals, and in "time-out" periods during the broadcast of football games similar appeals were made. In addition, Dr. Wilson mailed safety appeals to the presidents of colleges and universities and principals of high schools throughout its fifteen-state area. In recognition of its service, Standard was one of five advertisers to receive the National Safety Council's "Public Interest Awards for Exceptional Service in Accident Prevention During 1948."

Two sound motion pictures were completed in 1948 for showing to the public, employees, and dealer groups. One, *Oil and*

3. "Radio To Carry Standard Oil Advertising Over Leading Stations: Plan Approved for 5-Year Minimum Period," *Stanolind Record*, XXVI, No. 5 (March, 1945), 1-2.

Men, made by the March of Time, portrayed the operations of Standard from the oil well and stockholder investment to service stations and the dividend check. The other, *The Inside Story of Modern Gasoline,* a sound and color film, made novel and entertaining use of atoms and molecules to tell the story of gasoline manufacture.

In the fall of 1947 Standard inaugurated a campaign of institutional advertising in middle western newspapers in support of the Oil Industry Information Committee's efforts to foster wider knowledge and recognition of the industry's accomplishments and progressive character. Illustrated advertisements in laymen's language stressed three main points: competition among the 34,000 oil companies in the United States, the importance of research and development in providing new and improved products to the public promptly, and that prices were not fixed but made by individual oil companies in competition with one another. In other ways, too, the company co-operated with the oil industry's new public relations program. Standard also resumed in 1948 its institutional newspaper advertising campaign for the purpose of informing the public about earnings, profits, employee relations, stock ownership, size of the company, its scope in servicing the public efficiently and well, and other matters of interest.

The company engaged in many activities that were simply a part of being a good citizen. The 4-H Club work in tractor maintenance, started in 1944, continued to grow and spread to forty-two states. In 1947 forty-two state winners in the project were guests of Standard and its subsidiaries at the annual 4-H Congress in Chicago. Six farm boys were selected as national tractor maintenance winners from among the state winners in 1948 and given $200 scholarships to further their education. Between 1944 and 1947 approximately 55,000 rural youths were enrolled in the program. In 1949 more than 3,000 leaders and 35,000 farm boys and girls were enrolled. Other farm youth were aided by the company through contributions to the Future Farmers of America Foundation, Inc. Financial assistance was also given to the promising program of the Junior Achievement movement for urban youth. Contributions to Community Chest funds and other welfare agencies were increased. There was a greater participation in the activities of the American Petroleum Institute. Employees were actively encouraged to engage in local community activities and welfare work.

To stimulate research and the training of new scientists, the new management, departing from past policy, began in April, 1946, establishing graduate fellowships in chemistry, chemical engineering, mechanical engineering, civil engineering, marketing, and management at leading educational institutions of the country to provide "seed corn" for future research workers. The recipients were under no obligation to Standard in regard to future employment nor was the company to receive any patent rights resulting from the work. Stanolind Oil and Gas also established graduate fellowships in geology, chemistry, geophysics, electronics, accounting, and petroleum engineering at various educational institutions. Stanolind Oil and Gas also gave $125,000 in 1948 toward the building of a petroleum science building at the University of Tulsa. Pan American provided graduate fellowships in chemical engineering at the Massachusetts Institute of Technology, University of Illinois, and Rice Institute, and in chemistry at the University of Texas, Ohio State, and the University of Oklahoma. Standard also participated along with other oil companies and industrial concerns in the basic nuclear research program of the University of Chicago, which included an institute for nuclear studies, for metals, and for radiobiology.

Between 1945 and 1951 several new or improved employee benefit plans were adopted. Two were announced in November, 1946. The first was a group life insurance plan insured by the Metropolitan Life Insurance Company and financed through contributions by both the company and the employees.[4] Second was an annuitants' death benefit plan financed and administered entirely by the company. By December 1, 1947, 96.79 per cent of all eligible employees had voluntarily enrolled in the group insurance plan. In 1947 the annuity plan for the employees of the parent company and participating subsidiaries was revised to provide an annuity retirement income, including Social Security, amounting to approximately 2 per cent of an employee's average annual earnings multiplied by the number of years of employment.[5] Inaugurated by the parent company in 1948, a new contributory hospitalization and surgical benefits plan provided low-cost protection for employees and their families. Greater benefits

4. "Low-Cost Group Life Insurance and Death Benefits for Annuitants," *Stanolind Record*, XXVIII, No. 1 (January, 1947), 4.
5. "Revised Retirement Plan Approved By Stockholders at Annual Meeting," *Stanolind Record*, XXVIII, No. 6 (June, 1947), 1-2.

at only slightly more cost were added in 1949, making the plan one of the best of its type.

In May, 1950, the Savings and Stock Bonus Plan for the employees of Standard and ten subsidiaries was adopted.[6] Those participating in the Retirement Plan could have the company deduct from their pay as much as 4 per cent or as little as 2 per cent of what they made the previous year for investment in United States Savings Bonds. The employees received the bonds as they paid for them. At the end of each plan year the company agreed to give one share of Standard Oil stock for each "bonus unit" of payroll deductions credited to them. The "bonus unit" for each plan year was equal to 1½ times the book value of a share of Standard stock at the close of the preceding calendar year. Since the book value of a share at the end of 1949 was $70.88, the bonus unit for the first plan year was $106. The plan was a means of encouraging employees to be thriftier and, at the same time, enable them to share in the ownership of the business. At the end of the first year of the plan, the company distributed nearly $2,000,000 worth of stock to more than 25,000 employees of the parent company and subsidiaries.

Under a new military leave policy adopted in 1947, employees who were in the armed forces reserves would receive a leave of absence up to three weeks per year and pay equal to the difference between their military pay and their regular salary or wage. As a result of the outbreak of war in Korea in 1950, Standard adopted a military leave and job restoration plan.[7] If any employee had been with the company one year or more and entered the armed forces after June 25th, he was entitled to certain benefits. Each received one month's pay after the first thirty days of duty and an additional month's pay upon returning to the company's employment from military service of one year or more. If there was any vacation time coming, he received pay for this. The time spent in the service counted as time worked for the company in figuring service records. The company would keep up the payments toward all annuities at no cost to the employee. If an employee participated in the Savings and Stock Bonus Plan, the company would give monthly credit toward a stock bonus equal to what the

6. "Employee Savings and Stock Bonus Plan Proposed," *Standard Torch*, III, No. 5 (May, 1950), 3-4.
7. "Standard's Policy For Servicemen," *Standard Torch*, III, No. 11 (November, 1950), 10-11.

NUMBER OF EMPLOYEES AND WAGES AND EMPLOYEE BENEFITS 1942–1951
STANDARD OIL COMPANY (INDIANA) AND SUBSIDIARIES

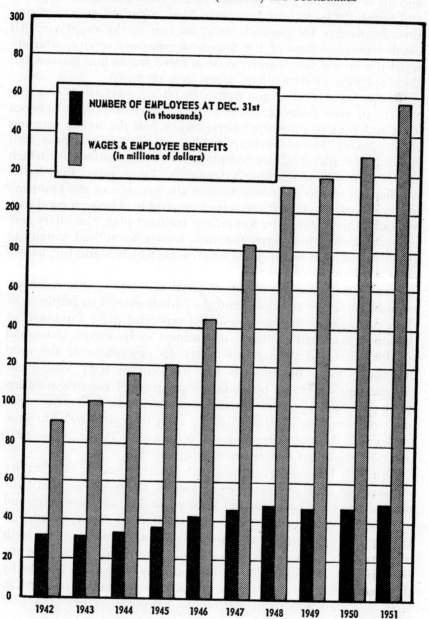

employee would have received for bond purchases. If an employee and his dependents were enrolled in the Group Hospital Expense and Surgical Operations Insurance Plan, Standard provided continued coverage for dependents at no cost to the employee. All employees, regardless of the length of company service, who entered the armed forces were to be granted leaves and guaranteed their old jobs, or equivalent, when they returned.

Except for several minor strikes involving a relatively few employees in each instance, there were no work stoppages between 1945 and 1951 to interrupt operations or halt the steady earnings of employees. Harmony keynoted the company's relations with its 49,740 loyal and efficient employees and 155 unions with which it had collective bargaining agreements. There was a firm belief on the part of top management that the progress of the company and good employee relations were inseparable. Through good pay, various benefit plans, the long-range training plan, the safety program, and in other ways, the new management had sought to promote the well-being of its employees, which made for an efficient working force.

Parallel with the expansion of physical facilities, the improvement of employee relations, and the broadening of its public relations program, there was a new and powerful drive for business. Although Standard's volume of business in its fifteen states had steadily increased through the years, its percentage of the total gasoline business declined to 17.7 per cent in 1944. Under the circumstances, a major plank in the program of the new management was that aggressive efforts would be made to increase sales and stop competitors from chipping away the company's business. Under the vigorous direction of Wilson and Peake, steps were immediately taken to implement the policy.

Although the modernization and construction of new service stations and bulk plants were delayed for the most part until the basic parts of the business had been expanded, between 1945 and 1948, 1,847 retail outlets were either reopened, built, or added.[8] During the same period fifty-three bulk plants were either built or reopened. A special drive was made to rehabilitate service stations in the Dakotas, where the company's business had badly slumped. With the purchase of the Root Petroleum Company in 1947, the Pan American Petroleum Corporation added a fifth

8. *Annual Reports,* 1945–1948.

state to its marketing area and began installing bulk plants in Arkansas.

A study of possible new service station identification signs resulted in the adoption in 1945 of an oval emblem in red, white, and blue colors surmounted by a torch with the single word "Standard" across the face. The Pan American Petroleum Corporation and the Utah Oil Refining Company used the same emblem with either "Pan-Am" or "Utoco" across the face. The sign was particularly suitable for use by Standard's marketing subsidiaries as an identifying symbol for all retail outlets. As soon as metal was available, thousands of these signs were installed at the service stations of the three companies. The new oval emblem began appearing in 1946 on packages and containers of these companies for a great variety of petroleum products. However, American Oil was not willing to change its well-known existing oval.

Out of the research laboratories and new manufacturing facilities constructed by various oil companies in the postwar period, came new and improved products for the motoring public and industrial users. As a result, the American motoring public was able to enjoy the best premium and regular-grade motor fuels with respect to octane ratings ever sold in service stations. During the closing months of the war, octane ratings had reached their lowest levels, the average for premium grade being 74.9 and for the regular grade 69.7. However, during the winter of 1945–46 the average octane number of premium-grade motor fuels sold was 80.9 compared with a 1935–36 winter average of 76.7 and a prewar average of 80.4 in the summer of 1941.[9] The average octane number of regular gasoline sold during 1945–46 was 75.9 compared with 69.5 a decade earlier and a prewar high average of 74.7 in the summer of 1941. However, owing to a shortage of lead and government restrictions, the octane rating of premium gasoline declined in 1946 to 78.5.

Wartime research on heavy-duty motor oils by Standard's research laboratory enabled the company in September, 1946, to introduce Permalube, a new "premium plus" motor oil made from Mid-Continent crude.[10] Developed for and utilized by the armed

9. "Survey Shows Octane Peak Last Winter," *The Oil and Gas Journal* (August 10, 1946), 118.
10. "Standard of Indiana Markets New Motor Oil Next Month," *National Petroleum News*, XXXVIII, No. 35 (August 28, 1946), 36.

forces during the war, Permalube was a highly refined product, unexcelled for passenger-car service. It contained new and patented ingredients that permitted military equipment to operate many millions of miles without a failure caused by faulty lubrication. A special feature was its capacity to protect against varnish deposits on pistons, cylinders, and other engine parts, against sludge deposits and the sticking of rings, and against deterioration or breakdown of the oil itself. Additional properties were maximum engine cleanliness, superior break-in ability, exceptional cold weather performance, and low oil consumption. Permalube was made in six weights and sold for 35 cents a quart at retail. It was the first product which Standard and its subsidiary marketing companies sold under a common name on practically a nationwide basis.

SALES OF PERMALUBE, ISO-VIS, AND QUAKER STATE MOTOR OILS 1937–1951
STANDARD OIL COMPANY (INDIANA) AND SUBSIDIARIES

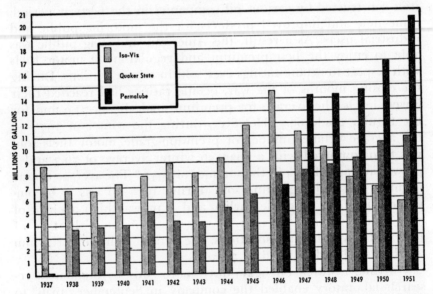

Other new oils and lubricants introduced in 1946 included Indolube HD for commercial vehicles, containing additives, and Standard HD, a lubricant for diesel railway equipment. Since August, 1936, Standard had purchased from the Standard Oil Company of California and distributed RPM Delo lubricating and motor oils. In 1941 a purchase and manufacturing agreement was negotiated and continued until June, 1946, when the entire program was terminated. Standard of Indiana chose to promote the sale of its own products.

With aviation gasoline freed for civilian use, Standard established an aviation department and prepared to take advantage of the postwar demand and increase sales to commercial air lines, airport gasoline dealers, and others. Recognizing the growing importance of the manufacture of chemical products from petroleum, Standard also organized a chemical products department with W. B. Plummer as its head, working under the general direction of Bruce K. Brown, Vice-President in charge of Development. The immediate duties of the department were to explore the market for petroleum chemicals, work with the research and manufacturing departments in developing marketable derivatives, and manage sales and distribution.

A new development in the marketing policy of the American Oil Company was the expansion of its business to include automobile accessories and other items. Beginning in 1942, it was the first oil company to market automobile tires under its regular trade name, Amoco. In 1945 it added Amoco oil burners, batteries, and other accessories, and it prepared to carry a full line of floor waxes, auto and furniture polishes, cattle sprays, and other specialties. With the decline in the demand for 100-octane aviation gasoline, the Pan American refinery at Texas City and American were able to resume the manufacture and sale of premium Amoco gasoline.

Of special importance was the new emphasis given to training all sales personnel through conferences, refresher courses, merchandising clinics, and on-the-job training for bulk-station agents and service-station dealers. To train the men who actually constituted the most important link between the company and the public, Standard decided in the spring of 1946 to operate one hundred of its service stations as training schools for dealers and their employees and, at the same time, provide model service for customers. The first five were opened in Chicago, Kansas City, St. Paul, Detroit, and Milwaukee.[11] Twenty-six others were opened in 1946 in other places within the fifteen-state area. Locations

11. "Indiana Standard Nearly Ready With First Five of 100 Stations Planned to Train Operators." *National Petroleum News*, XXXVIII, No. 20 (May 15, 1946), 20.

were selected which had a substantial patronage so that the trainees would have plenty of opportunity to observe the servicing of all kinds of cars. The training course involved not only practical experience but the use of films and discussion. Every two weeks 250 dealers or their employees entered these short courses. Any operator or his attendant might sign up for the course. Upon its completion they were awarded "service specialist" plaques for display at their stations. Besides training personnel, pilot stations served as laboratories for the introduction of products proposed for sale, the development of improved accounting methods, and for perfecting new services to motorists. By May, 1948, more than 5,000 dealers and their employees had received on-the-job training.

Owing to the rapid mechanization of farms during World War II and the increased use of petroleum products, a richer oil market than ever before had developed in the Middle West. To increase their share of this business, various oil companies, especially jobbers and co-ops, were furnishing all kinds and types of storage units, either mounted or skid tanks, to farmers. In some instances, this equipment was quite elaborate, even to the extent of furnishing electric pumps. As a result of these competitive practices, Standard lost many of its best farm accounts, which not only affected the company's earnings but also its agents' earnings. In order to stop the loss of its better farm customers and regain larger volume accounts previously lost, Standard inaugurated a new marketing feature in the spring of 1946. It offered farmers three-hundred-gallon tanks on platforms high enough to service tractors and other farm equipment at a rental of $3.60 per year.[12] By using these tanks, Standard's agents could reduce the number of trips to a farm, a very important factor in the rush season, and also reduce marketing costs. Other competitive refiners reluctantly went along but deplored the policy. It was looked upon as an effort to recover the farmers' business, which had been partly lost to independent jobbers during the war when Standard was making available its output to the government. Some competitors termed the farm tank program a vicious, unnecessary, and unsound business practice. In the expanding markets of the 1920's the industry had gone wild installing pumps and tanks, regardless of cost and profit. In 1946 the industry seemed to be headed in the same

12. "Indiana Standard Aims at Farm Market Sales," *National Petroleum News,* XXXVIII, No. 5 (January 30, 1946), 12; XXXVIII, No. 45 (November 6, 1946), 18-19; XXXIX, No. 9 (February 26, 1947), 19.

direction. "Why, oh why," asked the editor of the *National Petroleum News,* "do they persist in thus inviting trouble, not only for themselves but for the whole industry?" [13] The 1946 farmers were not so poor financially that they could not afford to pay for the tanks.

The practice of leasing tanks spread slowly all over the Middle West and manufacturers of tanks were flooded with orders which could not be filled owing to material shortages. How to stop the practice seemed to be the principal problem of the industry. The Nebraska Petroleum Marketers' Association, the Kansas Oil Men's Association, and the Iowa Independent Oil Jobbers' Association passed strongly worded resolutions condemning the practice as fraught with evil for the industry and urged that it be discontinued.

Fewer complaints were heard about leasing farm tanks in 1947. Competitors found a means of meeting the practice by selling tanks on a five-year payment plan, and more tanks became available.[14] Standard purchased thousands of tanks but could not meet the demand without making a heavy investment in its rural marketing branch. On the other hand, many farmers wanted to own their storage unit in order to have greater freedom in purchasing their petroleum products. Furthermore, the competition and antagonism aroused did not seem to justify the end. Consequently, Standard stopped renting farm tanks in May and began selling them.[15] A three-hundred-gallon single-compartment tank was offered for $80 and a double-compartment for $90 with a 5 per cent discount for cash. The oil trade welcomed the change. Officials of different national and state marketing associations commended Standard's action, called upon their members to cease the practice of leasing tanks, and urged them to follow Standard's new policy. "It's what marketers everywhere wanted," declared the editor of the *National Petroleum News.*

With the cessation of hostilities in World War II, oilmen had anticipated a temporary but substantial decrease in the demand for petroleum products from wartime peak levels. However, the demand in 1946 slightly exceeded that of any prior year although

13. "Major Companies Invite Trouble for Industry By Giving Small Tanks to Farm Customers," *National Petroleum News,* XXXVIII, No. 44 (October 30, 1946), 19.
14. "Two Jobbers Meet Major Competition By Selling Underground Farm Tanks," *National Petroleum News,* XXXVIII, No. 52 (December 25, 1946), 27.
15. "Indiana Standard To Halt Farm Tank Leasing May 15," *National Petroleum News,* XXXIX, No. 17 (April 23, 1947), 11.

there were over 2,000,000 fewer automobiles in service than in 1941.[16] Refineries operated at or near capacity. Crude runs to stills set a new high record. Standard's gasoline sales rose to unprecedented heights. There was an even greater gain in the sale of motor oils despite the continued shortage of base stocks and the lack of containers. Premium-grade gasoline and motor oil sales reached new high ratios to total sales. The sale of diesel fuel made phenomenal gains. Sales of asphalt showed a marked increase. Sales of automobile tires and accessories more than doubled over 1945 and were the largest in the company's history.

Freed of government controls in July, 1946, crude oil prices, which had been frozen for six years in spite of rising costs, rose sharply in almost all fields east of the Rocky Mountains because of the demand. Humble, the largest buyer in Texas, led off with a 25 cent raise, effective July 25th, which represented a 20 to 25 per cent increase. Other companies followed Humble and made their price retroactive to July 25th. A second raise of 10 cents per barrel came on November 15th. The new crude prices were generally at once reflected in the advance of prices on refined products. Effective August 29th, Standard led the way by increasing its gasoline tank-wagon price a ½ cent in eleven states without increasing refinery prices.[17] This was done for two reasons: One was the increased cost of bulk plant operations; the second was to bring jobber margins in the Middle West into line with slightly higher margins in areas adjoining Standard's marketing territory. Increasing the margin on gasoline was hailed by jobbers as a means of offsetting mounting operating costs. Some competing refiners changed their contracts with jobbers to allow for a 2.5 cent margin, others waited to see what might happen.

The public demand for oil products in 1947 exceeded the ability of the petroleum industry to deliver, especially in the Middle West. It far exceeded anything in the history of the petroleum industry. Although more crude was being produced than ever before, pipelines were running to capacity, and crude runs to refineries were at an all-time high, supplies of refined products were tight all over the country by March, 1947.[18] Some refiners were out of fuel oil, others were one to five weeks behind on fuel oil shipments. Gasoline was hard to get. Some refiners filled

16. *Annual Report Standard Oil Company (Indiana) and Subsidiaries For the Year Ended December 31, 1946,* 2-3.
17. *National Petroleum News,* XXXVIII, No. 36 (September 4, 1946), 9, 11-12.
18. *National Petroleum News,* XXXIX, No. 13 (March 26, 1947), 9.

only regular orders and were refusing new business. Others were rationing their supplies. There was much talk about the United States running out of oil. Complaints were made to the Department of Justice and the Federal Trade Commission. Jobbers called the shortage a squeeze play by the majors.

Stanolind Oil Purchasing Company posted a 25 cent advance in crude in March, 1947. This was the third raise made by Stanolind since the OPA restrictions went off in July, 1946. Other companies immediately posted similar prices. Kansas and Oklahoma crude sold for $2.57 per barrel, which was 60 cents above the 1946 price and the highest price since 1920. Premiums and bonuses of all kinds were being offered for crude in spite of three general price raises.

In searching for causes of the shortages, little thought or attention was given to the fact that much of the tremendous expansion of the petroleum refining industry in the Middle West during the war was for the production of synthetic rubber, toluene, and aviation gasoline. Moreover, governmental restrictions on steel and other materials made it difficult to construct new refineries, build tank cars, and expand the pipeline systems for civilian use.[19] The lack of adequate water and rail transportation facilities to get crude from the field and refined products to consuming centers helped to create a scarcity. The sale of 30,000 tons of seamless and welded pipe to Russia in 1946 made the shortage even more acute. Strikes at various refineries in 1947 reduced crude runs to stills by approximately 12,000,000 barrels. Though the physical damage was not excessive, a rather serious fire at Whiting in 1947 caused the loss of about 28,000 barrels of daily crude-running capacity for a critical three months' period. In the same year Pan American's Texas City refinery suffered minor damage and a loss of six days' operating time owing to the disastrous explosion of two ships loaded with ammonium nitrate on the water front.

Another important reason for the shortage was the unexpectedly rapid growth in the civilian demand for oil products during and after the war. The mechanization of farms since 1941 had been astounding. Farmers appeared to be literally soaking up oil products. Tractors in the Middle West alone were using 100 per cent

19. "Today's Oil Shortage Talk Dangerous, Wilson Declares," *The Oil and Gas Journal* (April 19, 1947), 64; "Shortage Threat Most Critical in Middle West, Wilson Says," *The Oil and Gas Journal* (June 7, 1947), 37.

more fuel than in 1941. Motorists were doing more driving. More airplanes were flying than ever before. Railroads had four times as many diesel locomotives in use in 1947 as in 1941. Hundreds of thousands of homes had switched to fuel oil for heating due to troubles in the coal industry. During 1946 alone over a million and one-half oil burners and space heaters were installed in the country. The demand for heating oils and diesel oil was expanding more rapidly than the demand for gasoline, which had for years been the principal revenue product of refiners. Distillate fuels now ranked as major derivatives of petroleum. Homeowners and the railroads were competing with users of gasoline for their share of the crude oil processed into products. While important and favorable to the petroleum industry, it created new supply problems. Standard's building of stocks of heating oil for the next season, which normally began about the end of March, did not get under way until mid-May and cut into the gasoline supply.

With the oil shortage acute in the Middle West, Standard's executives hated to tell the public that they did not have enough petroleum products, but they did, rather than try to cover up the fact. Taking the public into his confidence, Wilson brought the Middle West supply and demand sharply to public attention in a radio address in June, 1947, when he predicted a real shortage in the country and particularly in the Middle West over the next ten months. He urged gasoline and fuel-oil consumers to moderate their uses for a few months. Effective June 25th, Standard began allocating gasoline to its agents and dealers, except in Wyoming, Colorado, and Montana, on the basis of their 1946 gallonage.[20] With the demand running ahead of supply, such a plan was in the interest of fair treatment for all customers. The company asked that all unnecessary driving be curtailed and that driving at high speeds be eliminated. Large newspaper advertisements appeared in 1,700 dailies and weeklies all through the territory explaining the cause for the shortage, the steps being taken to increase the supply, why the Middle West was pinched, and how the company was handling the situation. Everything possible was being done to meet the full demand regardless of cost. By July 8th other oil companies in the Middle West had adopted an allocation system similar to Standard's.[21]

20. *The New York Times*, June 25, 1947.
21. "Midwest Allocation Plans Announced," *The Oil and Gas Journal* (July 5, 1947), 67.

Standard announced on August 22nd that it would continue its allocation to dealers through September and October. However, the allocations were to be higher than for the previous three months. The long-term outlook was brighter since the second catalytic cracker at Whiting would be completed in December and the one at Sugar Creek early in 1948. Then, too, steel was becoming more plentiful and the new pipeline construction program was well under way.

While endeavoring to cope with the serious shortage of gasoline, Standard's big summer newspaper, radio, and outdoor advertising compaign, which had been set weeks prior to the unexpected shortage, began featuring scenic travel areas within its marketing area, such as Yellowstone Park, Glacier National Park, and Turkey Run Park, urging motorists to visit these places and use Standard's personalized travel service.

Straining to do its full share in alleviating the shortage, Standard set new records in the production of crude, crude runs to refineries, and in moving oil by pipelines. To keep customers supplied, Standard purchased record-breaking quantities of crude oil and products during the last six months of 1947 and shipped them into the Middle West. Because its crude oil pipelines were already working at capacity, it diverted 1,600 tank cars from carrying refined products to haul about 21,500 barrels of crude per day from West Texas and Wyoming to its refineries. These tank-car movements were $2,900,000 more expensive than transportation by pipeline.[22]

Press comments and letters indicated that some customers believed the shortage of gasoline was due to Standard's shipping oil to Russia. To correct this misconception, Standard distributed a memorandum to employees and dealers within its organization in July, 1947, pointing out that the current shortages in the Middle West were not the result of oil shipments to Russia and that Standard of Indiana was not an exporter to Russia.[23] It had not shipped a single gallon of oil products to Russia and was not as a company involved in any way in such shipments. In fairness to whatever companies had made shipments, the memorandum pointed out that such shipments, as shown by government records, had been at the rate of less than 1,500 barrels a day in 1947 as com-

22. *Annual Report For 1947*, 17.
23. "Indiana Standard Memo Provides Facts on Russian Oil Shipments," *The Oil and Gas Journal* (July 26, 1947), 157.

pared with an average rate of 6,889 barrels daily for 1946. Furthermore, whatever shipments were made to Russia had been made with the full knowledge of the government, which had the responsibility to decide whether or not it was a good policy.

Through the co-operation of oil companies, the press, the general public, and the improved public relations of the oil companies, the general public accepted the temporary emergency with calmness and the gasoline supply problem was pretty well solved by October 1st. The shortage did not cause any public hardship, except in a few places like Detroit, Minneapolis, and St. Paul. Some oil companies, however, lost customers because they could not supply all the gasoline a customer wanted. The shortage might have been much greater had it not been for the heavy import of oil, which helped take up the slack in meeting the record-breaking demand.

When the fuel oil shortage became acute again early in 1948, Standard announced its policy in March in a special newspaper advertising campaign all over its territory.[24] Although company officials had previously said that the industry should not choose its customers but the customers should choose the product, Standard now limited those it could supply with heating oil. It stated that government requirements for the military must and would be met. Standard had reached the limit on the number of homeowners it could supply for the season. The limit for farms, churches, and schools had also been reached. Farmers would get the first call in order to operate machinery. Industry, transportation, schools, and hospitals would also get a fair share. The balance of supply would be divided among dealers and agents. Beginning in February, Standard again diverted 1,680 tank cars from hauling gasoline to bring crude to its refineries to alleviate the fuel oil shortage.[25]

Late in May the company began a special advertising campaign urging motorists to conserve gasoline during the summer. The company suggested the elimination of unnecessary driving, using car pools, moderate speeds, avoidance of "jack rabbit" starts, proper tire inflation, and the good maintenance of autos. By August the supply situation had considerably improved. A mild winter in 1948–49 resulted in a surplus of heating oil stocks and the daily rate of crude production fell off 9 per cent for the entire industry in 1949.

24. *National Petroleum News*, XL, No. 12 (March 14, 1948), 16.
25. *National Petroleum News*, XL, No. 6 (February 11, 1948), 16.

NEW CATALYTIC CRACKING UNIT, WHITING REFINERY

The first fluid catalytic cracking unit at Whiting Refinery went on stream in October, 1946, with a daily capacity for making 1,500,000 gallons of gasoline, fuel oil, and other petroleum products

A PUMPING-STATION MANIFOLD HOUSE AT PAYTON STATION, OKLAHOMA

Chief Engineer Frank Ludlum of the Service Pipe Line Company shows how complex
it is to handle oil. A manifold house is much like a railroad switch yard

MEMBERS OF THE BOILERMAKER DEPARTMENT, WOOD RIVER REFINERY

These men are shown with their award from the American Petroleum Institute in
recognition of one million man-hours worked without a lost-time accident

MISSOURI 4-H CLUB LEADERS LEARN ABOUT THE PROPER CARE
OF FARM TRACTORS

DR. ROBERT E. WILSON PRESENTS COMPANY CHECK TO LEADERS
OF FUTURE FARMERS OF AMERICA

A KANSAS CITY SERVICE STATION USED TO GIVE DEALERS ON-THE-JOB TRAINING

SALES MANAGERS ATTENDING SCHOOL

A major factor in relieving the 1947–48 shortage of gasoline and fuel oil was competition. There had never been such intense competition by each and every company in trying to take care of its customers, regardless of cost, retain their good will, and hold their business for the future. Far more expense had been incurred in the Middle West in abnormal transportation costs than in any comparable period during World War II, when the government was ordering such movements and paying for their extra costs.[26] "Seldom has there been a better example," Dr. Wilson declared, "of what individual enterprise can accomplish if left to work out its own problems." By the end of 1948, when the abnormal shipments of crude by tank car were discontinued, Standard had hauled 9,474,000 barrels of crude at an additional cost over pipeline transportation of $7,300,000.[27] "Can you imagine," asked Wilson, "major companies hauling train loads of crude and products thousands of miles every day from remote points to refineries and customers for any reason except to show their ability to take care of their customers' needs?"

One of the least publicized but highly important factors in alleviating the shortage of petroleum products in 1948 was the tractor fuel conservation program conducted through the 4-H Clubs by the extension services of the state agricultural colleges in co-operation with the U.S. Department of Agriculture and Standard. The amount saved was undeterminable but with 75,000 youths in the program, learning in clinics about methods of saving fuel, putting them into practice, and spreading the facts to neighbors, it was considerable. One authority estimated that about 2,000,000 gallons of fuel had been saved by the proper care and treatment of tractors.[28]

After the easing of the short supply in the fall of 1948 Standard resumed its sales efforts. By the end of 1949 almost 9,000 dealers and dealer employees had been trained in good service-station selling and operating methods. In addition, more than 17,000 dealers had been given special sales training on products and services. On-the-job training for bulk-station agents, salesmen, and supervisory employees continued. All-out selling to meet the strongest competition in more than a decade featured the activities

26. "Industry Doing Good Job, Should Confide in Public, Wilson Says," *The Oil and Gas Journal* (October 4, 1947), 38.
27. *Annual Report For 1948*, 19.
28. *National Petroleum News*, XL, No. 47 (December 1, 1948), 9.

of the sales force. During the summer of 1951 Standard conducted a contest among its 18,000 dealers for the cleanest and best-kept service stations and for the operators with the best personal appearance. A $25 defense bond was awarded monthly to dealer winners in each sales field. In September, the grand champion dealers in each field, twenty-nine in all, were awarded all-expense trips to Chicago for three days.

Of the capital expenditures for marketing in 1949, a large share was devoted to building new service stations and rebuilding old ones. Multipump service stations were tested with good results and more were planned. In 1950 Standard added 253 new service stations, American added more than a hundred, Utah Oil Refining twenty-one, and Pan-Am Southern sixty.

To place itself in a better competitive position, Standard abandoned in September, 1949, the so-called Group 3 method of pricing its products which had been used since 1934. It began posting prices at each bulk plant and other supply points based upon local economic and competitive conditions. With the increased competition from newly developed crude-producing areas, from newly erected refineries, and from products lines and river barges, the policy of basing prices on Tulsa had become completely outmoded. At the same time as it abandoned Group 3 pricing, Standard discontinued the practice of making public announcement of its price changes. Although Standard's changes in prices for petroleum products had been for years a matter of public interest, the trend in court decisions had been to sustain government agencies in claiming that a public announcement of a price change could be construed legally as the equivalent of an invitation to competitors to follow the price change. If a competitor followed, it was then possible for the government to claim that this completed a price conspiracy in violation of the antitrust laws.

For the purpose of corporate simplification and operating economies, the Pan American Petroleum Corporation, primarily a marketer of petroleum products, was merged in August, 1949, into its subsidiary, the Root Petroleum Company, chiefly a refiner of crude, under the name of the Pan-Am Southern Corporation. In 1951 Pan-Am Southern marketed in six southern states and operated refineries at Destrehan and El Dorado.

In advertising, Standard began using television in 1949. Its telecasts featured the colorful Wayne King show over ten middle west stations, and important sports events. As a replacement for the Wayne King show during the summer of 1951, the company sponsored a new television show called "The Standard Oil Short Story Playhouse" over a midwest NBC network. It dramatized stories by well-known authors. Extensive use of newspaper, radio, and billboard advertising continued. In addition, the company sponsored the broadcast of the Chicago Golden Gloves finals, the International Golden Gloves boxing bouts, both the Indiana and Iowa State high-school basketball tournaments, and various professional football games. The advertising program was designed not only to sell products but to increase the public acceptance of the company and to create a better understanding of America's successful business system.

Of utmost importance to all oil marketers and business in general was the action of the Federal Trade Commission in the Detroit case in October, 1945. The Commission ordered Standard to cease and desist from violating the Robinson-Patman Act in selling like grade and quality gasoline to competing purchasers at different prices.[29] It applied a novel interpretation of the good-faith-meeting-of-competition provision of the Robinson-Patman amendment to the Clayton Anti-Trust Act, which made price discrimination illegal unless the price difference could be justified by proof of cost savings or as made in good faith to meet competition. The Commission ruled that the good faith defense was not available to the seller where the price discriminations complained of were said to injure competition. However, this order did not prevent price differences of less than ½ cent a gallon. According to the order, Standard's tank-car sales to the four Detroit jobbers involved gave these customers a material advantage over other retailers, including Standard's own retail customers, who paid regular tank-wagon prices. The advantage was capable of being used, and had been used by Ned's and to some extent by Citron-Kolb, to divert business from other retailers and injure them. In issuing the order, the Commission overruled Standard's defense that prices had been cut in good faith for the sole purpose of meeting equally low or lower prices. The Commission said that public interest in the maintenance of free competition was superior to that of an individual or firm who discriminated even in good faith.

29. *Findings As To The Facts and Conclusion. In The Matter of Standard Oil Company, a Corporation. United States of America Before Federal Trade Commission,* October 9, 1945.

Under the order Standard could sell to jobbers only if the jobbers sold through their own service stations at the prevailing market price and sold to independent service stations at Standard's tank-wagon price. The size of the jobber's operations, the number of bulk plants he had, and the amount of his wholesale business could have no effect on the price Standard set for the jobber. Standard was obligated to cut off their supply if it knew or had reason to know that jobber-retailers intended to resell Standard products at less than the prevailing price.

Since Standard had only a few jobbers, the order would not affect it too seriously if it had to discontinue sales to them altogether. However, some jobbers had relationships with Standard extending back over many years. They had built up good will on the basis of Standard's brand names and trade-marks, and they did not relish being eliminated as Standard's customers. The only alternative for the jobber was to get rid of his retail outlets, but to force jobbers to give up direct ownership and operation of retail outlets was to take from them one of their strongest and most important advantages. Much more serious from Standard's point of view was the fact that the order compelled it to discontinue selling to certain jobber-retailers who cut prices, although it was perfectly clear that other suppliers could take over the business and sell in exactly the same manner and at exactly the same price or lower prices and with exactly the same effect on business at the retail level.

Among oil marketers in general the order created a most confusing situation and raised many questions.[30] Was the Commission trying to force the adoption of a new philosophy of marketing? Was it attempting to formulate and impose its own definition of a jobber? Did the order apply only to branded products? Could a jobber still offer unbranded products in any market at any price? Could a supplier restrict persons to whom it sold from reselling at cut prices and avoid trouble with the Department of Justice? In the opinion of one writer, "The Federal Trade Commission had made a notable contribution—not to the law but to lawyers." The only thing that seemed clear was that refiners who sold to bulk-plant operators and charged the same price to all would have no difficulty under the ruling.

30. E. E. Hadlick, "When Is a Jobber Not a Jobber? How High Is Up? FTC Has Industry Running in Puzzled Circle," *National Petroleum News*, XXXVII, No. 45 (November 7, 1945), 5-6, 66-67.

The Michigan Petroleum Association and the Michigan Retail Gasoline Dealers Association approved the order. Officials of both organizations believed that it would prevent destructive and unfair competition and thereby maintain the existence of the small petroleum operator. The National Oil Marketers' Association and the Iowa Independent Oil Jobbers' Association also approved the order. The National Council of Independent Petroleum Associations asked the Commission to reopen the case, for the implications of the order were not clear. Many felt like one lawyer who said: "I think we should have some sympathy with the Federal Trade Commission for it is dealing with a cockeyed, unreasoned and completely vague law. The basic fault lies with Congress. It enacts legislation for the ostensible purpose of correcting a specific evil but with no apparent thought or consideration to the effect of such legislation on all other business."

Leaders of the National Council of Independent Petroleum Associations held several meetings and prepared a brief outlining its objections to the order, which was submitted to the Commission in January, 1946. While the Council did not countenance any illegal or unethical practices of any kind, it found implications in the order which threatened to destroy the jobber who performed a legitimate marketing function.[31] Furthermore, while the order applied to only one company in one area, there were fears that the order would set a national pattern. In fact, the Council asserted that large, integrated oil companies well fortified with local distribution facilities were likely to benefit in the long run by the decision. In support of 12,000 jobbers, many of whom competed with their suppliers' retailers, it pointed out that if they were allowed a maximum gross operating margin of not more than ½ cent, thousands of jobbers were destined to insolvency, voluntary liquidation, or forced sale to large integrated companies. For the cost of distribution and services rendered by jobbers, small businessmen, they needed an average of 1.5 to 2.5 cents per gallon. The order appeared to ignore both the jobbers' costs and the value of the services rendered.

The Council took exception to the Commission's findings that seemed to imply that marketers of petroleum products were not entitled to be designated as jobbers and to purchase at tank-car prices unless they sold only at wholesale. This ran directly contrary to the definition of a jobber in the National Code of Practices for Mar-

31. *National Petroleum News,* XXXVIII, No. 4 (January 24, 1946), 12, 16, 18, 20-21.

keting Refined Petroleum Products approved and authorized by the Commission on June 12, 1931. Furthermore, the debates in Congress on the Robinson-Patman amendment indicated clearly that there was no intent to prohibit price differentials based upon differences in the functional character of services performed by different classes of purchasers. Functional price differences had always been recognized as lawful, justified, and compelled by economic considerations.

Another disturbing implication, according to the Council, was that if a supplier sold gasoline to a jobber at the tank-car price in an area where the supplier had retail outlets or sold to retail dealers, then the jobber in reselling any portion at his own retail outlets must maintain the current dealer price to the consumer. If the supplier sold to a dealer, the firm or company must impose upon that dealer an obligation to resell to the consumer at the retail price current in the area. If these implications were true, the supplier, jobber, and retailer would be violating federal anti-trust laws as well as similar legislation upon the statute books in many of the states. Price maintenance contracts of this kind were not legal in the absence of fair-trade legislation and had been condemned time and again under the antitrust laws.

Standard filed a sixty-five-page brief in January, 1946, dealing with the far-reaching effects of the order and asked the Commission to vacate the order and dismiss the complaint because it was not in the public interest.[32] While the order might temporarily bolster retail prices of certain gasolines in Detroit, Standard contended that it would eliminate competition, seriously disturb jobber operations, cause many jobbers to go out of business, and result in higher prices to the public. From the suppliers' point of view, according to Standard, the findings and order were vague and indefinite. Did the order apply to all sales of gasoline to jobbers or only to deliveries to jobbers across state lines? Did it apply only to Standard's Detroit marketing area or to all of it? Did it establish a pattern for the whole industry? Did it apply only to the sale of branded gasoline or to all grades and types, branded or unbranded? Did the order permit the granting of price differentials without limitation in the case of sales to jobbers who did not engage in retail operations and who did not sell to resellers at less than Standard's tank-wagon price? Standard requested clarification of these and other points so that it and others might under-

32. Motion, For Rehearing and For Reconsideration Of Order To Cease and Desist.

stand the meaning of the order. In the event that the order was not modified, Standard requested a change to exclude those performing the jobber function. If the order was not vacated or amended, Standard asked that the case be opened for further testimony and evidence.

Prior to the filing of Standard's brief the Federal Commission proposed a modification of its order and gave Standard until February 11th to show cause why it should not be allowed.[33]

Even though the Commission proposed modifications, some of which covered Standard's objections, they did not meet all objections. Standard was given time to file an answer and argue the case orally. Prior to the hearing, the National Council of Independent Petroleum Associations, aware of the harmful effects of an adverse decision, petitioned the Commission for permission to intervene in the Detroit case and reopen the proceedings for further hearings.

On August 9th the Commission denied Standard's motion for a rehearing and the petition of the National Council. At the same time the Commission issued a modified order reflecting all changes proposed by it. The principal modification was the elimination of any reference to price differences of less than $\frac{1}{2}$ cent. The modified order, besides prohibiting sales of gasoline to competing purchasers at different prices "in the manner . . . stated in the findings," banned sales at a lower price to any jobber or wholesaler, on gasoline resold by them at retail, than the price charged competing retailers by Standard. Further, the order prohibited Standard from selling to any wholesaler at less than Standard's tank-wagon price (to retail dealers) where a wholesaler resold to its retailers at less than such price. This modified order was the basis of subsequent litigation.

In a vigorous and lengthy dissenting opinion, Commissioner Lowell B. Mason ridiculed the majority action on several counts and declared the Commission's interpretation of the Robinson-Patman Act impractical.[34] He declared that the majority doctrine would mean that a refiner would have to base his price on the uses to which a purchaser put his gasoline, charging one price for that retailed and another for that wholesaled. Mason accused the

33. "FTC Files Motion To Change Order in Detroit Area Case," *National Petroleum News,* XXXVIII, No. 5 (January 30, 1946), 3.
34. *Dissenting Opinion of Commissioner Lowell B. Mason To Modified Order To Cease and Desist.*

Commission of going beyond the language of the law in attempting to regulate competition in the sale of a single brand of product. There was plenty of gasoline of like grade and quality available to Detroit dealers, so that competition was not suppressed by any practices which might have curtailed the distribution of Standard's brand. Mason summarized his dissent in the following words: "The Commission has cut off the facts of the case that do not fit in with the order, and it has stretched out the statute until it is no longer the law Congress passed but becomes the law that the Commission would like to enforce. It requires private policing of one man's business by another. It eliminates profit for one type of distributor and guarantees profit to another. It subjects branded goods to restrictions not applied to unbranded goods. It attempts to settle a private struggle between enterprisers by opening a Pandora's box of governmental directives on a minutiae of accounting and distributing practices that bear scant relation to what Congress sought to inhibit."

Since the order formed the basis of an entirely new and strange concept of competition, the interests of industry in general and the petroleum industry in particular dictated the advisability of having the courts review the order. Standard therefore filed a petition with the United States Court of Appeals, Seventh Circuit, Chicago, to set aside the Commission's revised order. The petition challenged the Commission's jurisdiction. It asserted that compliance would prevent Standard from meeting competitors' prices. It claimed that the order would compel Standard to regulate, police, and control prices at which its customers resold. It contended that the order was vague, indefinite, and impossible for the company and others similarly situated to comply with.

The briefs submitted agreed upon three issues to be decided by the court.[35] First, were any of the products involved in the alleged discrimination in interstate commerce? If not, then the Federal Trade Commission did not have jurisdiction. Second, was it an absolute defense for Standard to prove "by uncontroverted evidence" that its lower price was made in good faith to meet competitors' prices? Third, could Standard be compelled to require its wholesale customers to resell to their dealers at the same price at which Standard sold to its dealers?

As a result of the oral arguments heard on February 16, 1949, observers felt that the odds were better than even that the court

35. *National Petroleum News*, XLI, No. 7 (February 16, 1949), 17.

would invalidate the order because of the searching and persistent questions directed by the three judges at the Federal Trade Commission attorney.[36] All showed deep concern over the Commission's claim that "good faith" made no difference if, by lowering the prices, injury to a large number of other service stations resulted. Their questions indicated that this was a revolutionary premise. Especially significant was the fact that many of the questions came from Judge Sherman Minton, who had been a member of Congress when the Robinson-Patman Act was debated and adopted in 1936.

In view of these observations it was something of a shock when the Circuit Court in a unanimous decision in March upheld the order of the Federal Trade Commission.[37] Judge Minton wrote the opinion. The court rejected Standard's contention that the products were not interstate commerce and held that its "good faith" defense was irrelevant. Even though the court found substantial evidence to make it conclusive that Standard made its low price to the four jobbers in good faith, it was not the controlling factor. The controlling factor, according to the court, was that the differentials Standard made in favor of the four jobbers gave them a substantial competitive advantage which was used by them to work havoc on the retail level. They had the effect of injuring, destroying, and preventing competition, which was the very evil that the Robinson-Patman Act and the Commission were trying to stop. As for the policing angle, the court said that Standard could avoid this by either discontinuing its sales to wholesalers at a price different from that made to retailers as Sun, Socony-Vacuum, and Sinclair had done in Detroit or it could refuse to sell to wholesalers who sold to retailers below the price Standard made to its own retailers. The court ordered the Commission to modify its order so that the company would not be required to police its wholesalers and sell to them at its peril. The company should be liable only when it sold to a wholesaler it knew or ought to have known was engaging in or intended to engage in competitive practices condemned by the law.

The implications of the decision affected all business, for the principle of "good faith" in meeting competitors' prices was held to be immaterial. The decision was particularly harmful to oil jobbers because the court was careful to point out that Standard

36. *National Petroleum News*, XLI, No. 8 (February 23, 1949), 9.
37. 173 F. (2d) 210.

could comply with the order by cutting off its jobber customers rather than police jobber sales. If the Supreme Court did not reverse the order or Congress did not change the law, suppliers who sold to both jobbers and retailers in the same area faced the choice of eliminating one or the other. The court decision created substantial concern in the minds of oil company executives and jobbers with respect to the future conduct of their business.

Standard appealed the Circuit Court's decision to the United States Supreme Court. When the case was argued in January, 1950, contrary to tradition and protocol, attorneys for the Federal Trade Commission had to defend the case because the Solicitor General declined to handle it. The principal issue was whether it was a complete defense to a charge of price discrimination to show that the lower price was made in good faith to meet equally low prices of competitors. After the reargument of the case in October, the court's decision was eagerly awaited for months not only by the petroleum industry but by businessmen in general.

Standard won a signal victory on January 8, 1951, when the Supreme Court by a 5 to 3 vote upheld the company's position.[38] According to the opinion written by Justice Burton, "There has been widespread understanding that, under the Robinson-Patman Act, it is a complete defense to a charge of price discrimination for the seller to show that its price differential has been made in good faith to meet a lawful and equally low price of a competitor. The understanding is reflected in actions and statements of members and counsel of the Federal Trade Commission. Representatives of the Department of Justice have testified to the effectiveness and value of the defense under the Robinson-Patman Act. We see no reason to depart from that interpretation. . . . It is enough to say that Congress did not seek by the Robinson-Patman Act either to abolish competition or so radically to curtail it that a seller would have no substantial right of self-defense against a price raid by a large competitor. . . . In a case where a seller sustains the burden of proof placed upon it to establish its defense under Sec. 2 (b), we find no reason to destroy that defense indirectly, merely because it also appears that the beneficiaries of the seller's price reductions may derive a competitive advantage from them or may, in a natural course of events, reduce their own resale prices to their customers. . . . We may, therefore, conclude that Congress meant to permit the natural consequences to follow

38. 340 U. S. 231.

the seller's action in meeting in good faith a lawful and equally low price of its competitor." The majority opinion, according to the dissenting justices, "leaves what the seller can do almost as wide open as before" the Robinson-Patman Act was passed. "It seems clear to us," the minority said, "that the interpretation put upon the clause of the Robinson-Patman Act by the court means that no real change has been brought about by the amendment." Since the question of "good faith" had not been determined specifically by the Federal Trade Commission, the judgment of the Circuit Court was reversed, and the case was remanded to the Commission to determine if Standard had, in fact, actually lowered its Detroit prices "in good faith" to meet competitive prices.

In commenting upon the decision of the Supreme Court the *National Petroleum News* summed up the feeling of many by saying: "The Indiana company might have dropped the fight some place along the line, as sort of a compromise with the FTC hoping that the FTC would not try to enforce its order beyond the Detroit area. Instead it chose to fight the case all the way, though it was undoubtedly aware that ordinarily the cards are stacked against business, especially big business in today's federal courts. In taking the fight to the finish, Standard of Indiana was serving all industry." [39] By making the long and costly fight, Standard secured an affirmation of something that was basic to the American idea of a free economy, namely, the right of any seller to meet in good faith the prices of his competitor.

In March, 1952, the Federal Trade Commission, without taking any more testimony, ruled that Standard had not acted in "good faith" in reducing prices to its four Detroit jobbers to meet the price of competitors because competition was said to be injured and because Standard was said to know or had reason to believe that competition would be injured. At the present writing Standard is continuing its fight for a principle.

On June 6, 1951, the United States Attorney General, J. Howard McGrath, announced the dismissal of the "Mother Hubbard" suit which had been filed in September, 1940.[40] No steps had ever been taken to bring the case to trial. The difficulties involved in obtaining evidence about the defendants during the past six years was one reason given for dropping the suit. A second was that the basic objectives sought by the government could be obtained more

39. January 17, 1951.
40. *The New York Times*, June 7, 1951.

quickly and with greater assurance of success by preparing and filing separate actions involving fewer defendants and more limited issues.

Despite Standard's modernization program and the new and aggressive efforts made to increase sales, it met with the keenest competition. Established competitors in the Middle West also stepped up their operations, and new competitors came into the area to secure a share in the richest oil market in the country. Especially signficant was the further invasion of parts of Standard's marketing area by Gulf, Standard of New Jersey, and Standard of California. Gulf entered into direct competition with Standard of Indiana for the first time in 1946 in parts of Illinois, Iowa, Wisconsin, and Missouri. In 1946 Penola, Inc., a subsidiary of the Standard of New Jersey, moved its headquarters from Pittsburgh to Chicago and began selling "Oval E" lubricating oils and un-branded gasoline to large wholesale accounts in the Middle West.

In the Rocky Mountain region a real battle for business be-tween Standard of Indiana and three former Standard units began. Although the Carter Oil Company, a subsidiary of the Standard of New Jersey, had held nonoperating interests in certain Wyoming properties for several years, the first producing and refining properties in the Rocky Mountain area were acquired by Standard of New Jersey in the fall of 1942, when it gained control of the Northwest Refining Company of Montana. As a result of the deal, the Jersey company acquired producing properties, pipe-lines, ninety-seven bulk plants and retail outlets, and a refinery at Cut Bank. In 1946 Standard of New Jersey invaded the Black Hills region, when Carter took over the Yale Corporation, which had a refinery at Billings, and the Consumers Oil Company, which had one at New Castle. With the construction of a modern catalytic cracking plant at Billings in 1948, designed to produce aviation gasoline, lubricants, greases and asphalt, Carter loomed up as a strong contender for the business of the region.

Postwar long-range plans of the Standard Oil Company (California) included the expansion of its marketing activities along the eastern seaboard and in the Rocky Mountain area. Through a new subsidiary, the California Oil Company, Standard of California invaded the East and began marketing gasoline either under the brand name "Calso" or the name of its jobbers in five eastern states. Tankers carried gasoline from the West Coast to the East. In 1947 Standard of California started to build a crude pipeline with a capacity of 25,000 barrels from the Rangely field in northwestern Colorado to Salt Lake City. At the same time, plans were made to build a 25,000-barrel refinery at Salt Lake City so that it would no longer have to buy its products from the Utah Oil Refining Company.

The Continental Oil Company, another old Standard unit and the chief marketer in the Rocky Mountain area, determined to hold and increase its business. It planned in 1947 to double the capacity of its Denver refinery, construct a modern refinery near Billings, Montana, and increase the capacity of its Ponca City, Oklahoma, refinery.

An old competitor but a new one in the Rocky Mountain region was the Phillips Petroleum Company. It began constructing a products line in 1947 from its Borger, Texas, refinery to Denver, where the company planned a terminal and product distribution. In addition, Phillips secured options to acquire the stock of the Wasatch Oil Refining Company at Salt Lake City and the Idaho Refining Company at Pocatello.

A striking competitive development in Standard's marketing area was the fast-growing oil co-operatives. As more oil co-operatives joined the Consumers Co-operative Association, the Phillipsburg refinery was insufficient to supply its needs, so the National Co-operative Refinery Association purchased in 1941 a second refinery at Scotts Bluff, Nebraska.[41] The processing capacity of the co-operatively owned refineries in the country was increased by 15,000 barrels in July, 1943, when the Association acquired the Globe Oil & Refining Company refinery at McPherson, Kansas. In addition, it acquired Globe's 229-mile gasoline pipeline extending from McPherson to Council Bluffs, an oil compounding plant, storage tanks, and other facilities. This was one of the largest cash transactions in the history of the co-operative movement in the United States, requiring a capital outlay of close to $5,000,000.

Early in 1944 the Association purchased the refinery of the National Refining Company at Coffeyville, Kansas, together with some producing wells, pipelines, and undeveloped oil lands. Under a contract with the Defense Plant Corporation, facilities for making aviation gasoline were installed at Coffeyville, bring-

41. "Cowden Tells Co-op Plans to Expand Operations in the Petroleum Industry," *National Petroleum News,* XXXVIII, No. 35 (August 28, 1946), 30, 32, 34; Kenneth S. Davis, "A Bigger Role for Farm Co-ops," *The New York Times,* January 4, 1953, Section 6.

ing its capacity to 13,500 barrels. With the acquisition of the Coffeyville plant, the Consumers Co-operative Association not only had a sufficient supply for its members but enough to begin exporting. By 1946 the Association had six full-time geologists at work, and its own producing wells were supplying 31 per cent of its refinery needs. There were altogether nine co-operative refineries in Kansas, Nebraska, Montana, Indiana, Oklahoma, and Louisiana with a combined capacity of 52,000 barrels. The four co-operatively owned refineries in Kansas had a combined capacity of 33,000 barrels. With their volume of business steadily increasing, the oil co-operatives, in advance of any major oil company, took the first steps looking toward the development of the continental shelf. In April, 1946, fifteen applications were filed with the U.S. Department of the Interior for permits to drill for oil in a 1,500-square-mile area of ocean bottom in the Gulf off the coast of Louisiana.

Products pipeline construction during the postwar period was the most extensive in the history of the petroleum industry. The greatest activity centered chiefly in Iowa, Minnesota, and the Dakotas. Beginning after V-J Day, the Great Lakes Pipe Line started a $30,000,000 expansion and modernization program.[42] A major project was the extension of its line 300 miles to Grand Forks, North Dakota, which was completed in December, 1946. When the entire program was completed in 1948, the new lines increased the capacity of the system by 50 per cent, giving it an operating capacity of 104,600 barrels daily and a total length of more than 3,000 miles. It was the largest and longest products line in the country. It crossed nine states and served seven terminals and nineteen refineries in Oklahoma and Kansas and two in Texas.

The experience gained during the war in using tankers on the Great Lakes proved so successful that extensive plans were made in 1945 for the development of new competitive terminals. Cities Service put up new storage tanks at Green Bay and Milwaukee, Shell planned new facilities at Milwaukee, and Phillips Petroleum had already constructed new terminals at Green Bay and Gladstone. The Texas Company had also completed a dock and storage tanks at Green Bay and planned terminals at Marquette and Muskegon.

Although competition was keener than ever before, Standard made an impressive and outstanding record between 1945 and

42. *National Petroleum News*, XL, No. 4 (January 8, 1948), 45.

1951 under the dynamic leadership of the new executives. The expenditure of millions of dollars in expanding and modernizing its facilities had placed the company in a strong position. The new emphasis upon research had resulted in many new and improved processes and products. Refineries were backed by a greater crude supply. Natural gasoline and natural gas products had been developed on a large scale. New crude pipelines, products lines, and water terminals aided in cutting the cost of distribution. Through the modernization of service stations, greater emphasis upon personnel training to render improved services, and the introduction of new sales techniques, new life and power had been infused into the marketing organization. The long and rather steady decline in the percentage of business done by Standard in its marketing area came to an end. The new and determined effort to develop a better public understanding of the company's ideas, purposes, and acts and make the company a better citizen brought tangible results. More attention to improving employee relations and the revision and liberalization of all benefit plans had strengthened morale.

From a financial point of view, the new executive team had also made a remarkable record in seven years.[43] Assets had increased from $946,135,787 at the end of 1945 to $1,800,540,013 in 1951. For the first time in the history of the company, its consolidated assets exceeded a billion dollars in 1946. On the basis of total assets Standard became the second-largest oil company in the United States in 1947. The sale of crude oil and products had increased from 215,424,653 barrels in 1945 to 336,100,000 in 1951 and the dollar value of sales soared from $601,538,202 to $1,499,-000,000. Net earnings after deductions increased from $50,340,475 in 1945 to $140,079,286 in 1948, the largest in the company's history, only to be topped in 1951 when they amounted to $148,-700,000. The dividend paid was increased from $1.00 in 1944 to $1.50 in 1945, $1.75 in 1946, $2.00 in 1947, $2.878 in 1948, $2.687 in 1949, $3.135 in 1950, and $3.954 in 1951. In order to conserve the company's cash, the cash dividends between 1948 and 1951 included payment in stock of the Standard Oil Company (New Jersey), which was part of the stock acquired in 1932 in connection with the sale of Pan American's foreign properties. One share of stock of the Standard Oil Company (New Jersey) for each hundred shares of Standard of Indiana was paid in 1948 and 1949, except

43. *Annual Reports,* 1945–1951.

that no fractional shares were issued. A cash payment was made to odd-lot holders in lieu of the issuance of fractional shares. In 1950 one share of Jersey stock for each seventy-five shares of Standard of Indiana stock and in 1951 one share for each forty shares was paid.[44] The ratio of cash dividends to net earnings remained at a rather low level due mainly to the large amount of capital required for expansion purposes. Nearly two-thirds of the net earnings from 1945 to 1951 were retained in the business.

44. In 1948, 127,583 shares of Jersey stock were issued; in 1949, 127,249; in 1950, 165,325; and in 1951, 339,160 shares.

CHAPTER XXIV

Standard of Indiana Today

ORGANIZED AS A REFINING COMPANY AND AS A PART OF THE STANDARD Oil Trust in 1889, Standard of Indiana was to manufacture and furnish petroleum products to the various marketing companies of the Standard Oil Trust in the West. In 1892 it began to acquire the marketing properties of other Standard companies and develop a marketing organization of its own. With the rapid growth of the West and the demand for kerosene, greases, and lubricants, the company had a remarkable growth. When the Supreme Court of the United States ordered the dissolution of the parent company, the Standard Oil Company (New Jersey), in 1911, Standard of Indiana had three large refineries, a vast marketing organization scattered over ten states of the Middle West, a capitalization of $1,000,000, assets of $28,146,422.26, and undivided profits of $24,217,404.96. Although the company attained its independence in 1911, it was without any crude production or pipeline facilities of its own. During the forty years since 1911 Standard of Indiana has grown and developed until today it is one of the great integrated oil companies of the world with seven principal subsidiaries—the Stanolind Oil and Gas Company, Service Pipe Line Company, Stanolind Oil Purchasing Company, Pan Am Southern Corporation, Utah Oil Refining Company, Pan American Petroleum & Transport Company, and the Indoil Chemical Company.[1] It is engaged in every phase of the oil business from drilling wildcat wells to selling gasoline.

In 1911 Standard did not own any production. At the end of 1951 its subsidiaries owned 1,106 gas wells and 9,043 oil wells located in eleven states which produced 669,000,000 cubic feet of gas and 94,990,000 barrels of crude oil and natural gas liquids per year, more than 963,000 producing acres of gas and oil lands, and more than 14,000,000 acres of undeveloped lands. From these

---

1. Standard of Indiana owns 75.20 per cent of the stock in the Utah Oil Refining Company and 78.63 per cent of the stock in Pan American Petroleum & Transport Company.

resources Standard draws nearly 50 per cent of its crude requirements. In 1951 its subsidiaries drilled 1,103 gross wells. Of these, 152 were "wildcats" which cost on an average about $125,000 apiece. Only fifty were successfully completed. Even though only one out of three was productive, the average for the petroleum industry was only one in nine.

The chief producing subsidiary, Stanolind Oil and Gas, one of the leading crude oil and gas producers of the country, operates through eleven states stretching from Montana to Mississippi. No company in twenty years of its history ever grew so fast or matured so rapidly. Through the growth of Stanolind in the years since 1930, Standard won the battle to restore its crude oil supply, which had been upset by the sale of its Venezuelan properties in 1932. Nothing has contributed so much to Standard's rise to industrial power or to keeping it alive as the growth of Stanolind Oil and Gas. Between the time of its organization on January 1, 1931, and December 31, 1952, Stanolind spent more than $163,892,699 in acquiring producing properties. Of this amount more than $103,772,132 was allocated as the cost of the 376,686,599 barrels of net recoverable reserves purchased. Stanolind's production increased from about 20,000 barrels a day in 1931 to more than 235,000 in 1951. In 1951 Stanolind produced 3.5 per cent of the nation's total supply of crude oil. In addition, it has become one of the leaders in the natural gasoline industry. Stanolind Oil and Gas is the largest profit earner among Standard's group of companies. Moreover, its assets in 1951 were even larger than than those of several integrated oil companies, including Union, Tidewater, Continental, and Sun. The Stanolind Oil Purchasing Company, the chief crude buyer, purchases more than 150,000,000 barrels per year.

Standard of Indiana did not own any pipelines in 1911. In 1951 it had 16,180 miles of pipelines, of which the Service Pipe Line Company (formerly Stanolind), the main transporting subsidiary and operator of the longest pipeline system in the world, owned 11,724 miles of pipelines. The Service Pipe Line operates in or through eleven Middle West and Rocky Mountain states, and delivers oil directly to eleven refineries and to twenty-seven refineries through other carriers about 400,000 barrels of crude oil daily. The longest haul is from the Elk Basin oil field in Wyoming to Chicago, a distance of 1,400 miles, requiring about forty-two days for delivery. The parent company has approximately 1,300 miles

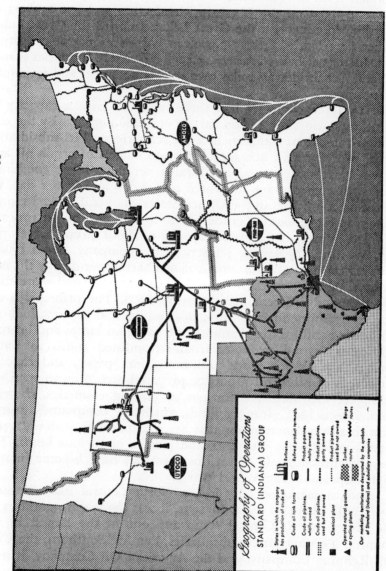

MAP OF OPERATIONS, STANDARD (INDIANA) GROUP, 1951

of private products pipelines which are used to carry finished products from the refineries to its own distributing points. It also uses a towboat on the Mississippi and Ohio and five tankers to distribute products on the Great Lakes. In 1918 the Great Lakes tanker fleet hauled nearly 3,500,000 barrels of petroleum products. In 1951 it hauled nearly 15,500,000 barrels. Together Standard and its subsidiaries today own thirty-one barges and seventeen tankers.

In 1911 the company had three refineries with a capacity to refine approximately 55,000 barrels of crude per day. By the end of 1951 the parent company had five refineries and its subsidiaries eight, processing an average of 514,000 barrels of crude oil and 27,930 barrels of natural gas liquids per day. Their combined crude-running capacity amounted to 548,000 barrels per day. Of all the oil companies in the United States, Standard ranked second in 1951 in the amount of crude oil run to stills per day. In 1911 the Whiting refinery had a crude capacity of about 30,000 barrels per day. Whiting, the largest refinery of the company, had a crude-running capacity of more than 200,000 barrels per day by the end of 1951. At these modern refineries are manufactured more than two thousand different petroleum products. The principal products are: gasoline for airplanes, automobiles and tractors, fuel oils for heating and for diesel engines, kerosene for lamps and heaters, lubricants for all purposes from streamlined trains to watch springs, asphalt for roads and roofs, wax paper, and candles. Hundreds of other oil products, prepared according to specifications, are manufactured for use in making cosmetics, chewing gum, insecticides, cleaning fluids, antifreeze compounds, paints, varnishes, impregnators for matches, rust-proofing materials, preservatives for wood and eggs, and plastics of various kinds. The manufacture and sale of various chemicals have become increasingly important since World War II.

Standard marketed only in ten North Central states through 1,331 bulk plants in 1911. In 1951, it was the largest marketer in the fifteen North Central states and one of the largest in the country. Through three subsidiaries, Pan-Am Southern, the Utah Oil Refining Company, and the American Oil Company, it markets in 26 additional states and the District of Columbia. Standard's marketing activities are almost nationwide in scope. Its products are delivered all the way from the Rocky Mountains to the Atlantic Coast through 4,528 bulk plants and 31,130 retail outlets. Its total sales in dollars and the volume of petroleum products sold in 1951 amounted to $1,499,000,000 and 207,800,000 barrels.

SALES OF PRODUCTS 1939–1951
STANDARD OIL COMPANY (INDIANA) AND SUBSIDIARIES

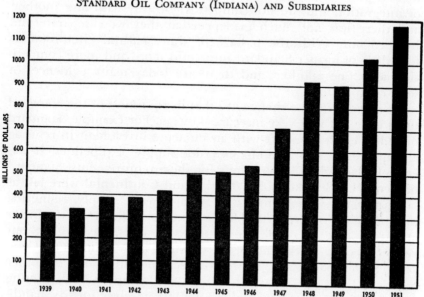

In 1911 Standard had about 85 to 90 per cent of the total business in its marketing territory. By 1940 that percentage had declined to less than 20 per cent and has remained at about that point since that time. The history of oil marketing in the area since 1911 proves that there has been no lack of opportunity for small companies to be organized and grow into strong competitors, like The Texas Company, Sinclair, Shell, Phillips, Pure, Cities Service, Mid-Continent, Skelly, Barnsdall, and hundreds of small companies. Year after year they have helped to beat down the percentage of business enjoyed by Standard. If one looked only at Standard's percentage of the total business today, it would seem as if the once-powerful monopoly was about bankrupt, and this would be a tragic story of the decay of a big business. However, the important thing to note is that in spite of keen competition, Standard's volume of business has steadily increased since 1911 and few oil companies, if any, have equaled its record of growth.

Under the old Standard Oil organization prior to 1911, each marketing company operated within a carefully defined geographical area. Competition among these units as a rule was not tolerated. After the holding company was dissolved in 1911, each of the thirty-four units became independent, separate, and free to do as it pleased. For a period of time, however, they had problems of integration and did not compete vigorously with one another, and there was not much evidence that they were separate and independent. With the passage of time, natural circumstances forced these former Standard units into more and more competition with one another, and there are today many evidences of such competition.

One reason for the change was that in 1911 most of the Standard units were left in a very insecure position. For example, Standard of Indiana had been left with an immense investment in refining and marketing facilities but no crude supply or pipelines. It was entirely dependent upon others for these requirements. Standard of Kentucky, Standard of Nebraska, and Continental were left as large marketing companies without any crude supply, refineries, or pipelines. The Prairie Oil & Gas Company, which was the buyer and transporter of crude for all the companies, was left without refineries or a marketing organization. The Vacuum Oil Company, which had manufactured greases and lubricants for other Standard units, was left without any crude supply or marketing organization. Other companies found themselves greatly handicapped in one way or another. If these companies were to survive and the investment in them was to be made secure, they had to acquire facilities which they did not have and, in so doing, they soon came into conflict with one another.

A reduction in the par value of the stock of several companies, including Standard of Indiana, in the 1920's, so that persons of small or moderate means might invest, was another reason for the growth of competition. These changes meant a wider dispersal of stock among thousands of people who were primarily interested in getting a good return on their investment. They looked to top management for results. These stockholders knew little, and cared less, about old Standard relationships. Consequently, the executives of these companies were put on their mettle. They were obliged to compete wherever and whenever it was necessary to increase the business.

As the old Rockefeller men retired from the active management of these companies, a new group of executives took their places. With the broadening base of stock ownership, they were naturally desirous of making a reputation for themselves and money for the stockholders. Jobs and promotions depended upon their performance. It was, therefore, the case of a king arising who "knew not Joseph."

Finally, with an abundance of crude oil and increased refining capacity, these companies soon found that they could adequately supply their original territory and more too. Hence, they began to break out of the old marketing areas and invade those of other Standard units.

The history of Standard of Indiana affords many examples of conflicts and active competition between it and other Standard units.[2] Standard of Indiana was probably the first company to invade the marketing area of another Standard unit when it began marketing operations in 1913 in southern Missouri, the territory of the Waters-Pierce Oil Company. The negotiations between Standard of New Jersey and Standard of Indiana in 1914 over the desire of the former to use the Burton process revealed sharp differences, unexpected rivalry, and plenty of haggling. When Standard of Indiana acquired a 50 per cent interest in 1921, and later a 100 per cent interest, in the Sinclair Pipe Line and the Sinclair Crude Oil Purchasing Company, it became so much of a competitor of the Prairie Oil & Gas Company that it was ultimately a factor in forcing the sale and reorganization of Prairie. In 1923 Prairie acquired a controlling interest in the Producers and Refiners Corporation, which had about 650 service stations in the West. By 1926 it was selling 1 per cent of all the gasoline in the territory of Standard of Indiana. One of the most unexpected and sharpest differences between old Standard units occurred in 1923 when Standard of New Jersey led the movement to beat down crude prices while Standard of Indiana and Prairie fiercely resisted. By purchasing the Lincoln Oil Refining Company of Illinois in 1924, the Ohio Oil Company began nibbling away at the retail business of Standard of Indiana. The Continental Oil Company, the original and dominant marketer in the Rocky Mountain region, merged with Marland and invaded the Middle West in 1925 and began marketing.

When Standard of Indiana acquired an interest, and later majority control, in Pan American Petroleum & Transport Company, it became a major competitor in the East of at least six former Standard units through the extensive marketing activities of the

2. "Standard Is Strong In Disunion," *Business Week* (June 22, 1946), 71-78.

American Oil Company. Three years later, in 1928, Standard began retail marketing through Midwest Refining in five states of the Rocky Mountain region, where the Continental Oil Company was the dominant marketer. The Vacuum Oil Company acquired in 1929 an interest in the Lubrite Refining Corporation of St. Louis, which had a refinery and marketing organization in the Middle West, and became a direct competitor of Standard of Indiana. The next year Vacuum bought the White Star Refining Company of Detroit and the Wadhams Oil Corporation of Milwaukee, whose stations were scattered all over the Middle West. In 1931 Standard of New York and Vacuum merged into Socony-Vacuum and became one of the strongest competitors in the Middle West. When the Standard of New Jersey opened its Esso stations in St. Louis in 1935, Standard of Indiana quickly swung into action, filed suit, and secured an injunction restraining Jersey from marketing in its territory under the name Esso, Standard, Standard Oil Company, or any similar name. However, this decree did not prevent Jersey from marketing in the area under the name of Penola or Carter, its subsidiaries. Since World War II, Standard of California has been active both in the East and the Rocky Mountain region, building a refinery at Salt Lake City and developing a market. As a consequence of these and other developments, Standard of Indiana today is in active and keen competition in producing, refining, transporting, and marketing with every surviving member of the old Standard group.

In 1911 Standard of Indiana had about 7,400 employees. To search for oil, drill, transport, refine, and sell its products, Standard and its subsidiaries employed in 1951 an army of 49,740 men and women. In addition, there are thousands of independent businessmen—jobbers and retail dealers—who make a living by selling Standard products.

In 1889 the 5,000 shares of stock of Standard of Indiana were owned by the Standard Oil Trust, except for one share held by each of the five Directors. By 1912 the capitalization had been increased to $1,000,000 and 10,000 shares, and the properties were owned by 5,075 stockholders, most of whom lived in the East. In 1951 the company had a capitalization of $500,000,000 with 20,-000,000 authorized shares. The 15,320,249 shares outstanding are owned by 116,800 stockholders representing every state of the union. Widows, professional men, farmers, merchants, youngsters, colleges and universities, libraries and museums, charitable organ-

The Number of Stockholders of the Standard Oil Company (Indiana) and Their Geographical Distribution, 1951

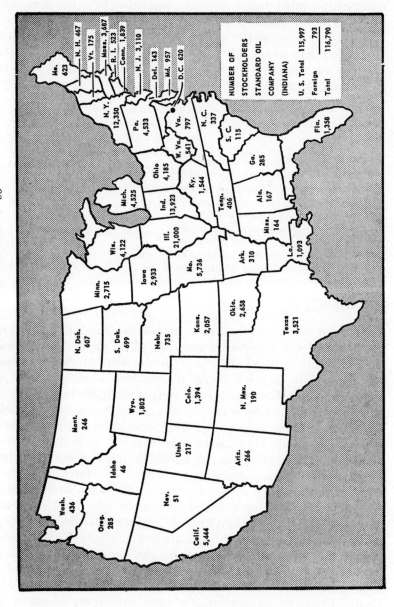

Me. 623
N. H. 467
Vt. 175
Mass. 3,687
R. I. 523
Conn. 1,339
N. J. 3,110
Del. 143
Md. 957
D. C. 620
N. Y. 12,350
Pa. 4,533
W. Va. 541
Va. 797
N. C. 337
S. C. 115
Fla. 1,358
Ga. 285
Ohio 4,185
Ky. 1,544
Tenn. 406
Ala. 167
Miss. 164
La. 1,093
Mich. 4,525
Ind. 13,923
Ill. 21,000
Wis. 4,122
Iowa 2,933
Mo. 5,736
Ark. 310
Minn. 2,715
Nebr. 735
Kans. 2,057
Okla. 2,658
Texas 3,521
N. Dak. 607
S. Dak. 699
Mont. 246
Wyo. 1,802
Colo. 1,394
N. Mex. 190
Utah 217
Ariz. 266
Idaho 46
Nev. 51
Calif. 5,444
Oreg. 285
Wash. 436

NUMBER OF STOCKHOLDERS STANDARD OIL COMPANY (INDIANA)

U. S. Total	115,997
Foreign	793
Total	116,790

izations, civic and fraternal groups, corporations, partnerships, trusteeships, insurance companies, and other fiduciaries are among those who share in the prosperity of the company and its dividends. For the first time in the company's history, in 1946 the number of stockholders in the Middle West exceeded the number in the East. In 1951 more than half of Standard's stockholders lived in the fifteen states in which the parent company operates.

U. S. MANUFACTURING CORPORATIONS
WITH THE LARGEST NUMBER OF STOCKHOLDERS IN 1951

	Number of Shareholders
General Motors Corporation	478,924
United States Steel Corporation	268,226
Standard Oil Company (New Jersey)	254,000
General Electric Company	252,993
Cities Service Company	203,402
Radio Corporation of America	186,592
Socony-Vacuum Oil Company	158,000
E. I. du Pont de Nemours and Company	138,168
Anaconda Copper Mining Company	118,616
Standard Oil Company (Indiana)	116,800

Source: *Monthly Letter on Economic Conditions and Government Finance*, June, 1952, The National City Bank of New York.

Much of the general public is still inclined to believe that today all Standard Oil companies are controlled through stock owner-ship by John D. Rockefeller, Jr., or by a small group of eastern capitalists. But the truth is that no one individual owned as much as 1 per cent of the stock in Standard of Indiana in 1951. It is true, however, that especially in the earlier years Mr. Rockefeller was influential as one of the large stockholders in such matters as sending W. L. MacKenzie King in 1918 to make a survey of Standard's labor relations, in adopting the Industrial Relations Plan, in selecting Colonel Stewart and Dr. Burton as the top executive officers in 1918, in adopting the Employee Stock Pur-chase Plan, in ousting Colonel Stewart in 1929, and in cleansing Pan American in 1929. When Mr. Rockefeller led a movement in 1928–29 to oust Colonel Stewart as Chairman of the Board, his personal holdings amounted to 4½ per cent. Counting the stock held by him, his relatives, and several Rockefeller boards, the most he could actually control was slightly under 15 per cent. Granted that this constituted a most important block of stock, it took weeks of labor on the part of many people and a large personal expenditure by Mr. Rockefeller to insure complete con-

trol of the 1929 annual meeting of stockholders through the solicitation of proxies from other stockholders.

The main purpose of Standard of Indiana, or of any business,
large or small, is to make money for its investors. In 1911 its net
earnings amounted to $6,132,142. Net earnings after taxes and
deductions in 1951 amounted to $148,700,000. Despite severe
business depressions and two World Wars, Standard has made
money every year since 1894. It has also paid a cash dividend every
year since 1894. In addition, investors have been the beneficiaries
of four stock dividends since 1911. If a person had owned one $100
share of stock of Standard of Indiana on January 1, 1912, and
held that stock to the present time, he would have 900 shares worth
$71,550 on the market as of September 13, 1952, and he would
have received in cash dividends $58,040 by the end of 1951.

GROWTH IN ASSETS AND SALES 1922–1951
STANDARD OIL COMPANY (INDIANA) AND SUBSIDIARIES

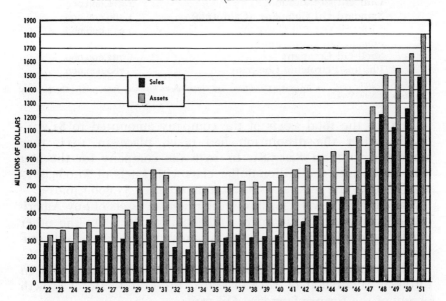

The company has carefully observed throughout its history one
of John D. Rockefeller's precepts: "Always keep your cash box
in good condition." Indicative of this is the fact that in 1930
Standard of Indiana paid $72,500,000 in cash for the remaining
50 per cent interest in the Sinclair Pipe Line Company and the

Sinclair Crude Oil Purchasing Company. In 1935 it paid $42,500,-
000 in cash for the Yount-Lee producing properties. Further evidence of the earning power and soundness of its financial position
is the fact that until 1946 funds for all capital expenditures of the
parent company, and substantially all of the subsidiaries after a
controlling ownership was acquired, came from the operations of
the business. Moreover, between 1946 and 1951 the company's
capital expenditures exceeded a billion dollars, about four-fifths
of which came from the operations of the business and the remainder from loans.

THE TEN LARGEST OIL COMPANIES IN THE UNITED STATES IN 1951

	Assets
Standard Oil Company (New Jersey)	$4,707,000,000
Standard Oil Company (Indiana)	1,801,000,000
Socony-Vacuum Oil Company	1,792,000,000
The Texas Company	1,549,000,000
Gulf Oil Corporation	1,512,000,000
Standard Oil Company (California)	1,366,000,000
Cities Service Oil Company	973,000,000
Sinclair Oil Corporation	889,000,000
Shell Oil Company	792,000,000
Phillips Petroleum Company	780,000,000

Source: *Monthly Letter on Economic Conditions and Government Finance*, June, 1952. The National
City Bank of New York.

In 1890 the total assets of the company amounted to $1,271,-
654.62. After the dissolution had taken place in 1911, they
amounted to $28,118,275.84. In 1946 the company for the first
time broke into the billion-dollar class with assets of $1,065,901,-
190. In 1951 the company's assets amounted to $1,800,540,013.

Standard of New Jersey has by far the most assets of any American oil company. Standard of Indiana is second. On the other
hand, Standard of Indiana is the largest purely domestic oil company.

The company's rate of growth on the basis of assets has been
forty-one times that of 1912, which is the fastest rate of growth
of any of the former Standard Oil units.

Compared with other manufacturing concerns, Standard of
Indiana is the fourth largest in the United States as measured by
total assets.

The history of Standard during the past sixty-five years is more
than one of physical growth. Equally significant has been the

GROWTH IN ASSETS OF FORMER UNITS OF THE
OLD STANDARD OIL ORGANIZATION

FIGURES IN MILLIONS OF DOLLARS
JANUARY 1ST

	1912	1952	Ratio 1952 to 1912
Standard Oil (New Jersey)	$370.0	$4,707.0	12.7
Standard Oil (Indiana)	43.9	1,800.5	41.0
Socony-Vacuum	124.2 *	1,792.5	14.4
Standard Oil (California)	67.3	1,365.5	20.3
Atlantic Refining	28.6	481.5	16.8
Standard Oil (Ohio)	12.9 **	277.6	21.5
Ohio Oil Company	65.6	265.0	4.0
Standard Oil (Kentucky)	5.1	92.1	18.1
South Penn	17.6	64.1	3.6

* Socony-Vacuum was formed in 1931 through the merger of two old Standard Oil subsidiaries: Standard of New York (1912 assets: $92,200,000), and Vacuum Oil Company (1912 assets: $32,000,000).

** Asset figure is for the end of 1915, first available.

Source: S. K. Botsford, Assistant Secretary, Standard Oil Company (Indiana), to Giddens, August 15, 1952.

progress made in other areas. The adoption at an early date of a pension system, the eight-hour day, the five-day work week, vacations with pay, the Employee Stock Purchase Plan, the Sickness and Disability Plan, and many other employee welfare benefits, with the steady improvement in working conditions, are a part of the story of the growth. As a result of the inauguration of a safety program in 1918, the record made in reducing the number of accidents is outstanding. The establishment of the Industrial Relations Plan in 1919 and the maintenance of harmonious rela-

THE TEN LARGEST MANUFACTURING CORPORATIONS
IN THE UNITED STATES IN 1951

	Assets
Standard Oil Company (New Jersey)	$4,707,000,000
General Motors Corporation	3,672,000,000
U. S. Steel Corporation	3,141,000,000
Standard Oil Company (Indiana)	1,801,000,000
Socony-Vacuum Oil Company	1,792,000,000
E. I. du Pont de Nemours	1,599,000,000
Ford Motor Company	1,584,000,000
The Texas Company	1,549,000,000
Bethlehem Steel Corporation	1,542,000,000
Gulf Oil Corporation	1,512,000,000

Source: *Monthly Letter on Economic Conditions and Government Finance*, June, 1952 and July, 1953. The National City Bank of New York.

tions with employees constitute still another major chapter in the story of growth. Striking has been the progress made by the company since 1918, especially under the leadership of Colonel Robert W. Stewart and more recently under the team consisting of Dr. Robert E. Wilson and A. W. Peake, in developing closer and friendlier relationships with those in the petroleum industry and the general public.

While the growth of Standard of Indiana has been most impressive, one of the remarkable things about it has been the fact that the company achieved its present position in the petroleum industry and the business world without crushing or stifling the competition. On the contrary, competition became keener as Standard grew. With the opening of Spindletop in 1901 and other fields in the Southwest and the Mid-Continent area in subsequent years, hundreds of oil companies were organized, and many of them began to market petroleum products in the Middle West. Of the twenty largest integrated petroleum companies in existence today, eight of them—The Texas Company, Sinclair, Cities Service, Shell, Phillips, Skelly, Mid-Continent, and Pure—got their initial start in marketing to a large extent in the territory of Standard of Indiana. Moreover, nine of them—Standard of New Jersey, Standard of California, Standard of Ohio, Socony-Vacuum, Continental, Gulf, Ohio Oil, Sun, and Tidewater Associated Oil —either directly or through subsidiaries greatly expanded their business by invading the marketing territory of Standard of Indiana. As a result of the growth of these petroleum companies and hundreds of smaller companies, the marketing territory of Standard of Indiana in the Middle West became one of the most highly competitive oil markets in the world.

In retrospect, the phenomenal growth of Standard of Indiana was due to a large extent to the development of the nation and especially the Middle West. In turn, Standard contributed directly and immeasurably in many significant respects to the development of the Middle West and the nation.

When Standard of Indiana was organized in 1889, the Middle West was a new and growing country. Ten of the present states west of the Mississippi River had not yet come into existence. Montana, North and South Dakota, and Washington were admitted to the Union in the fall of 1889. Idaho and Oklahoma were admitted in 1890, Utah in 1896, Oklahoma in 1907, and Arizona and New Mexico in 1912. The population of the fifteen states of the Middle West in which Standard of Indiana markets today amounted to 19,266,769 in 1890. By 1950 the population of these states had increased to 40,954,128, which was more than one-third of the total population of the United States.

In 1889 the Indian warfare on the Great Plains and in other places in the West, which had been so widespread during and after the Civil War, had come to an end, peace had been established with the various Indian tribes, and great areas of land had been opened to settlement. The relatively cheap lands in the West had attracted countless settlers with the result that the number of farms and farm families and the area under cultivation had rapidly increased. Four transcontinental railroads, the Union Pacific, Northern Pacific, the Santa Fe, and Southern Pacific, connecting the Mississippi River and the Pacific Coast, accelerated westward immigration and the creation of a market for both manufactured commodities and agricultural products. Although wheat and corn were grown in other states, their production centered in the North Central states. This region also produced large amounts of the nation's oats, barley, rye, hay, potatoes, and other agricultural commodities. The cattle, hog, and sheep-raising industries were likewise concentrated in the region west of the Mississippi River. Moreover, farmers in the North Central states were turning in increasing numbers to the production of milk, butter, and cheese.

As new sources of raw materials were opened in the West, industry moved westward. Although Chicago was the chief center of the livestock and meat-packing industry, St. Louis and Kansas City were developing as important centers since they were nearer to the cattle ranges. Chicago, St. Louis, and Minneapolis were the principal seats of the milling industry but Minneapolis was the main center because of its water power, nearness to the wheat fields, and the use of improved mechanical milling processes. The great Mesabi iron range at the head of Lake Superior was making ore commercially available in large quantities with the result that the steel industry was spreading to eastern Ohio and the Chicago area. Strategically located between the Great Lakes and the West, Chicago was the great gateway of commerce flowing to and from the West because of the vast railroad and water transportation systems that converged upon it.

In 1889, at the time Standard of Indiana was organized, there were no automobiles, trucks, tractors, airplanes, diesel engines, or oil-burning furnaces in homes in the Middle West. Horses and mules were used exclusively for farm work. Coal, wood, and cobs were used for heating and cooking. Kerosene was the principal petroleum product marketed, and it was chiefly used for illuminating purposes. Gasoline was a drug on the market.

As the Middle West grew to economic maturity after 1889, the expanding use of petroleum products was a major factor in its development. There was an increasing demand for greases and lubricants of all kinds in factories, by the railroads, and on the farms. With the development of the internal combustion engine and the introduction of the automobile, the demand for gasoline, greases, lubricants, and other petroleum products was unprecedented. As farms became mechanized especially after World War I, oil-heating units were installed in homes and factories, and diesel engines began to be used, the Middle West became the greatest market in the world for petroleum products. In 1950, 31 per cent of the passenger automobiles and 32 per cent of the motor trucks registered in the United States, 35 per cent of the civilian aircraft, 28 per cent of the homes using oil fuel for heat, 24 per cent of the crawler tractors on farms, 41 per cent of the garden tractors on farms, 50 per cent of the wheel tractors on farms, 50 per cent of the hay balers, 58 per cent of the farms having milking machines, 68 per cent of the grain combines, and 85 per cent of the corn pickers used in the United States were within Standard's fifteen-state marketing area. The total dollar value of all petroleum products sold by Standard in this area in 1951 amounted to $701,000,000.

In expanding the use of petroleum products and revolutionizing the economy of the Middle West, Standard led the way. It was a pioneer. When the company was organized in 1889 and the Whiting refinery was built, there was no large petroleum refinery west of Cleveland, Ohio. Practically all petroleum products for the Middle West had to be shipped from Cleveland. With the building of the Whiting refinery and later the refineries at Sugar Creek, Wood River, Casper, and Greybull, the Middle West could be more easily and adequately supplied. The construction of these refineries not only increased the supply of petroleum products but decreased transportation costs and brought the finished products nearer to consumers. From these refineries flowed all kinds of petroleum products which silently and gradually helped to transform industry, transportation, and farming methods in the Middle West and make living more pleasant.

STANDARD AGENT GIVING FRIENDLY AND DEPENDABLE SERVICE

TANK-CAR TRAIN HAULING CRUDE FOR STANDARD INTO THE MIDWEST IN 1947

AERIAL VIEW OF THE WHITING REFINERY

Through Standard's establishment of direct marketing facilities —main stations, bulk plants, and tank-wagon deliveries—all over the Middle West after 1892, kerosene, gasoline, greases, lubricants, and other petroleum products were made easily available for consumers. In order that the people of the Middle West might benefit from the use of gasoline and kerosene, Standard had specially designed lanterns, cookstoves, lamps, and heaters manufactured which the company sold for a nominal sum. The company's pioneer move in extending tank-wagon deliveries to the farmers of the Upper Mississippi Valley brought petroleum products still closer to the consumers. By making high-quality petroleum products readily available at low cost to every farm and hamlet, Standard played a leading role in the mechanization of agriculture. And when automobiles came into use, Standard, foreseeing the great need for petroleum products, started building service stations everywhere throughout the Middle West in advance of the actual demand and helped to put all the population, rural and urban, on the road. In 1927 Standard began stocking aviation gasoline and lubricating oil at its bulk plants. Even the most remote station carried a limited quantity of aviation gasoline and motor oil in case an airplane had to make an emergency landing. Thus Standard helped to put the population of the Middle West in the air.

Simultaneously with the expansion of its direct marketing system in the Middle West, Standard, through a vast army of tank-wagon drivers and service-station attendants, developed an enviable reputation for giving prompt, courteous, efficient, and dependable service. No day was too cold or hot or wet to interfere with tank-wagon deliveries of oil. Over the many years people in the Middle West have been passing on to posterity stories of how Standard tank-wagon drivers, traveling through rain, sand, mud, and blizzards, met some emergency and delivered the oil. When service stations came into being, Standard's attendants were trained to give friendly and reliable service. They set a high standard for service station maintenance and operation.

Through the purchase of its first airplane, the *Stanolind*, in 1927 and then others, to carry company executives on business trips and to take local celebrities in scores of cities on their first airplane ride, Standard not only aroused public interest in aviation but stimulated the building of many airports throughout the Midwest. At the same time, Standard gave further assistance to the development of aviation by painting on the roofs of its bulk plants on established air routes the name of the towns, arrows indicating north and south, and a direction sign to the nearest airport. Since this was long before radio directional beams, what Standard did in airway identification was of utmost importance to early aviators.

The use of petroleum products and the expansion of the economy of the Middle West as well as the nation was greatly facilitated by Standard's development of the Burton process. Foreseeing a possible shortage of gasoline and the halting of the progress of the automobile unless something was done to increase the gasoline supply, Standard's scientists went to work on the problem in 1909. After extensive research and an expenditure of thousands of dollars, they developed the first practical process for producing gasoline by cracking heavy hydrocarbons through the application of high temperature and pressure into gasoline. Through the Burton process, as this new process was known, twice as much gasoline could be extracted from a barrel of crude as before. The discovery of this thermal cracking process proved to be one of the great inventions of modern times. It resulted in an increase in the supply of gasoline, helped to alleviate the threatened gasoline shortage, insured the future of the automobile, kept the price of gasoline from becoming prohibitive, and aided in the conservation of the crude oil resources of the country.

The development of the Burton process awakened the petroleum industry to the commercial possibilities in bringing about chemical changes in crude oil and created greater interest in research in the industry than ever before. With the advantage it had in developing the Burton process, Standard became a leader—a pioneer—in research. The company gave increased emphasis in subsequent years to improving the quality and yield of all important petroleum products and developing new products for its consumers.

By virtue of its own development, Standard of Indiana helped to industrialize the Middle West. The initial step was taken in constructing the great Whiting refinery in 1889. As the demand for petroleum products increased, Standard built additional refineries at Sugar Creek in Missouri, Wood River in Illinois, and at Casper and Greybull in Wyoming. Parallel with these developments, the company developed a vast marketing organization, investing millions of dollars in bulk plants, service stations, and river terminals. Moreover, it built through the years the longest pipeline system in the world. In Michigan, Illinois, Wyoming, Oklahoma, Kansas, and the Southwest, Standard played an outstanding role in developing their crude oil resources. Since 1951 the company has been a major factor in opening and developing the Williston Basin area in North Dakota, building pipelines and constructing a 30,000-barrel refinery at Mandan. By the end of 1951 Standard's investment in properties—production, manufacturing, transportation, marketing, and natural gasoline plants—represented an investment of $1,137,879,551, and its total assets amounted to $1,800,540,013.

As the scope and size of Standard's operations expanded, the company employed more and more people in the Middle West and enabled them to earn a good livelihood. And in almost all worth-while community efforts—Community Chests, Chambers of Commerce, American Red Cross, and local civic activities—these employees and the company played the role of good citizens.

In various educational programs designed to aid the youth of the Middle West and the nation, Standard of Indiana was also a pioneer. It has actively supported the work of the 4-H Club, Future Farmers of America, and Junior Achievement. To aid in the training of well-qualified college students, the company established scholarships for undergraduates in chemistry and graduate fellowships in science at many leading institutions of higher learning. Recognizing the value and contribution of the private liberal arts colleges to our free democratic society, the Standard Oil Foundation, Inc., made a contribution of $150,000 in 1953 and again in 1954 to be distributed among the college fund associations in the company's fifteen-state marketing area for use in meeting the current expenses of the member colleges.

These are some of the many significant contributions Standard has made to the economic and social growth of the Middle West and the nation. It is, indeed, an impressive record.

Bibliographical Note

INSTEAD OF MAKING AN EXHAUSTIVE LIST OF MATERIALS USED IN THE preparation of this book, the author has elected to indicate only some of the principal sources upon which he has drawn.

The minutes of the Board of Directors' and stockholders' meetings from 1889 to the present made an excellent starting point in gathering data about the history of the company. They provided information about major events. With the minutes as a basis, the author then began drawing freely upon the records in each department and office of the company to secure supplementary material and other data. The *Annual Reports,* especially those since 1927, are important as a source because of their description of developments and operations. The author has also had access to letters, documents, reports, narrative accounts, charts, and tables that officials of the company have written or prepared from time to time.

Of the manuscript material consulted, the following have been helpful: "Autobiographical Sketches of Various Men Connected with the Manufacturing and Research Departments at Whiting" (Collected by Robert E. Humphreys); "Brief History of Standard Oil Co., Indiana, And Its Predecessors from the Experience and Observations of John L. Carter," 1926; "Development of the Utah Oil Refining Company During Four Distinct Periods of Ownership or Control as Related By John C. Howard, Organizer," February 28, 1918; J. W. Foreman, "My Trip to the Refinery of the Utah Oil Refining Company"; Allan Jackson, "Standard Oil Company of Indiana: Pioneer in Aviation Development," May 8, 1939; W. L. MacKenzie King, "Report on the Labor Relations of Standard Oil Company (Indiana)," February 14, 1919; "Milton Storer's Story of Standard Oil Company (Indiana)," February 24, 1926; N. H. Reed, "History of the Standard Oil Company (Indiana)"; "Report on Industrial Relations in the Standard Oil Company (Indiana)," 1923. Prepared by the Industrial Relations Staff—Curtis, Fosdick & Belknap, 4 Vols.; Harold D. Roberts,

721

"History of the Salt Creek Fields," May 15, 1919; Oliver H. Shoup, "When Salt Creek Roared," 1937; "The History of the Salt Creek Fields, Natrona County, Wyoming, As Personally Known and Operated by H. E. Stock"; and the "Questionnaire of the Department of Justice, Bureau of Investigation," December 17, 1923. Some of the personal papers and records of Allan Jackson, Amos Ball, Robert E. Humphreys, retired Directors and officers, Albert L. Hopkins, and John D. Rockefeller, Jr., have been especially helpful on certain events and episodes.

Invaluable on all phases of the company's operations are the files of the company magazine, the *Stanolind Record,* and its successor the *Standard Torch.* The *Midwest Review* provides excellent material on the history of the Midwest Refining Company. *The First Fifty* by F. Lawrence Babcock, published in 1939 by the company, is a very brief history of its operations. *Danger! Keep Out* (Houghton Mifflin Company, Boston, 1943) by Edward J. Nickols is a novel, the setting for which is the Whiting refinery.

Among the pamphlets published by the company bearing upon its history are the following: *Meet Pan Am Southern Corporation; Our Company,* 1947; *Research At The Standard Oil Company (Indiana),* 1948; *Standard Oil Company (Indiana) in the War,* 1944; *Ten Years of Accomplishment 1918–1928; The Story of Petroleum; What Is Good Gasoline?; Welcome to Standard Oil; A Trip Through Sugar Creek Refinery;* and *Opportunities For You With Standard Oil.*

Addresses or articles by company executives upon special problems or phases of the company's history have been illuminating. Some of the more significant are the following: Dwight F. Benton, "Marketing Problems," an address before the Indiana Independent Petroleum Association, Incorporated, Indianapolis, October 8, 1952; A. W. Peake, "Standard Oil Company (Indiana) Outlook," an address before the New York Society of Security Analysts, March 13, 1952; Robert W. Stewart, "It Pays Us To Tell Our 'Business Secrets,'" *System,* XL, No. 5 (November, 1921), 568–570; J. E. Swearingen, "Standard Oil and the Williston Basin," an address before the Twin Cities Society of Security Analysts, St. Paul, July 1, 1952; Thomas E. Sunderland, "Is It Illegal to Meet Competition in Good Faith—Under the Robinson-Patman Law?" an address before the National Petroleum Association, Atlantic City, September 15, 1945; Thomas E. Sunderland, "Save the Sherman Act From Its 'Friends,'" an address before the Dallas

Bar Association, Dallas, March 25, 1950; Robert E. Wilson, "Fifteen Years of the Burton Process," *Journal of Industrial and Engineering Chemistry,* XX, No. 10 (October, 1928), 1099–1101; Robert E. Wilson, *Pioneers in Oil Cracking,* Newcomen Society Address, Chicago, October 29, 1946; Robert E. Wilson, "Research on a Single Reaction and Its Social Effects," the Third Annual Arthur Dehon Little Memorial Lecture at the Massachusetts Institute of Technology, November 23, 1948; Robert E. Wilson, "What Research on Cracking Has Meant to the Industry and to the Public," an address before the Texas Mid-Continent Oil and Gas Association, Houston, October 13, 1949; Robert E. Wilson, *Oil Competition in the Midwest,* an address before the National Petroleum Association, Cleveland, April 13, 1950; Robert E. Wilson, "Competitive and Co-operative Research in the American Petroleum Industry," *Journal of the Institute of Petroleum,* XXXVII, No. 37 (August, 1951), The Cadman Memorial Lecture; Robert E. Wilson, "Is Big Business Bad?—Fact v. Fiction," an address before the Chicago and Illinois Bar Associations, January 18, 1952; and Robert E. Wilson, "We, The Accused," *The Saturday Evening Post,* January 24, 1953.

Much historical data is to be found in the briefs, special court reports, and court decisions in suits in which the company has been involved. Attention is called particularly to the hearings in two important cases. Especially valuable on the history of the company and the entire Standard organization prior to 1908 is the *Transcript of Record, United States v. Standard Oil Company of New Jersey, et al.,* United States District Court, Eastern District, Missouri. This consists of twenty-one volumes of exhibits and testimony published by the Government Printing Office, Washington, 1908. On the history of cracking and the company's relationship thereto, the fourteen volumes of the *Stenographer's Transcript of Hearing Before the Honorable Charles Martindale, Master in Chancery, United States of America, Petitioner v. Standard Oil Company (Indiana) et al., Defendants* in the District Court of the United States for the Northern District of Illinois, Eastern Division, constitute an excellent source.

Of immense value as sources of information on all aspects of the company's history are the following government publications: *Eighteenth Biennial Report of the Attorney General of Kansas 1911–1912* (State Printing Office, Topeka, 1912), containing the Keplinger report; Federal Trade Commission, *Report on the*

Price of Gasoline in 1915 (Government Printing Office, Washington, 1917); Federal Trade Commission, *Report on Pipe-Line Transportation*, February 28, 1916 (Government Printing Office, Washington, 1916); Federal Trade Commission, *The Advance in Price of Petroleum Products*, June 1, 1920, House of Representatives Document No. 801, 66th Cong., 2nd Sess. (Government Printing Office, Washington, 1920); Federal Trade Commission, "Letter of Transmittal and Summary of Report on Gasoline Prices in 1924," June 4, 1924 (Mimeographed); Federal Trade Commission, *A List of 1,000 Large Manufacturing Companies, Their Subsidiaries and Affiliates, 1948,* June, 1951; *High Cost of Gasoline and Other Petroleum Products,* Hearings before a subcommittee of the Committee on Manufactures, United States Senate, 67th Cong., 2nd and 4th Sess., pursuant to S. Resol. 295 (Government Printing Office, Washington, 1923), 2 Vols.; *Immigrants in Industries,* Report of the Immigration Commission, Senate Document No. 633, 61st Cong., 2nd Sess., Vol. 16, Part 20 (Government Printing Office, Washington, 1911); *Investigation of Concentration of Economic Power,* Hearings before the Temporary National Economic Committee, 76th Cong., 2nd Sess., pursuant to Public Resolution No. 113 (Government Printing Office, Washington, 1940), Part 14, 14A, 15, 15A, 16, 17; *Petroleum Investigation,* Hearings before a Subcommittee of the Committee on Interstate and Foreign Commerce, House of Representatives, 73rd Cong., on H. Res. 441 (Government Printing Office, Washington, 1934), 5 Vols.; *Petroleum Requirements—Postwar,* Hearings before a special committee investigating petroleum resources, United States Senate, 79th Cong., 1st Sess., pursuant to S. Res. 36 (Government Printing Office, Washington, 1946); *Prices, Profits, and Competition,* Senate Document No. 61, 70th Cong., 1st Sess. (Government Printing Office, Washington, 1928); *Leases Upon Naval Oil Reserves,* Hearings before the Committee on Public Lands and Surveys, United States Senate, on S. Res. 282 and S. Res. 294 (Government Printing Office, Washington, 1924); *Leases Upon Naval Oil Reserves* (Continental Trading Company, Ltd., of Canada), Hearings before the Committee on Public Lands and Surveys, United States Senate, 70th Cong., 1st Sess., pursuant to S. Res. 101 (Government Printing Office, Washington, 1929); *Regulating Importation of Petroleum and Related Products,* Hearings before the Committee on Commerce, United States Senate, 71st Cong., 3rd Sess., on S. J. Res. 238 and S. Res. 5818 (Government Printing Office, Washington, 1931); *Report of the Commissioner of Corporations on the Transportation of Petroleum* (Government Printing Office, Washington, 1906); *Report of the Commissioner of Corporations on the Petroleum Industry* (Government Printing Office, Washington, 1907), 2 Vols.; *Report of the Federal Trade Commission on the Petroleum Industry of Wyoming*, January 3, 1921 (Government Printing Office, Washington, 1921); *Report of the Federal Trade Commission on the Petroleum Trade in Wyoming and Montana*, July 13, 1922 (Government Printing Office, Washington, 1922); *Report on Gasoline Prices by the Federal Trade Commission*, Senate Document No. 178, 73rd Cong. (Government Printing Office, Washington, 1934); *Report of the Federal Trade Commission on Distribution Methods and Costs*, Part IV, March 2, 1944 (Government Printing Office, Washington, 1944); *Report of the Federal Trade Commission on Interlocking Directorates* (Government Printing Office, Washington, 1951); *Report of the Joint Investigation Committee to Examine the Highway Department of South Dakota to March 3, 1925, Proceedings of the House of Representatives 19th Legislative Session, State of South Dakota, January 6, 1925–March 6, 1925* (Hipple Printing Company, Pierre); *Trusts*, House Report No. 3112, 50th Cong., 1st Sess. (Government Printing Office, Washington, 1888).

Several books containing information about certain aspects of the company's history have been most useful. They are: *William Meriam Burton: A Pioneer In Modern Petroleum Technology* (University Press, Cambridge, 1952); John T. Flynn, *God's Gold* (Harcourt, Brace and Company, New York, 1932); *Industrial Pensions in the United States* (National Industrial Conference Board, Inc., New York, 1925); David McKnight, Jr., *A Study of Patents on Petroleum Cracking With Special Reference to Their Present Status* (The University of Texas Publications, No. 3831, Austin, August 15, 1938); Alfred James Mokler, *History of Natrona County, Wyoming, 1888–1922* (R. R. Donnelley & Sons Company, Chicago, 1923); Allan Nevins, *John D. Rockefeller* (Charles Scribner's Sons, New York, 1940, 2 Vols.); and Ida M. Tarbell, *The History of the Standard Oil Company* (The Macmillan Company, New York, 1904, 2 Vols.).

For general background material on the history of the petroleum industry, the following have been helpful: Leonard M. Fanning, *The Rise of American Oil* (Harper & Brothers, New

York, 1948); Gerald Forbes, *Flush Production* (University of Oklahoma Press, Norman, 1942); and Carl Coke Rister, *Oil! Titan of the Southwest* (University of Oklahoma Press, Norman, 1949).

Many articles about the company are to be found in newspapers and periodicals. The files of the *National Petroleum News* and *The Oil and Gas Journal* are especially important not only for the information they contain about Standard but for the industry's reactions to its policies and the activities of its competitors. The files of *The Chicago Tribune* were thoroughly searched and yielded considerable data. Other newspapers consulted include the *Bradford Era*, *Lima Daily Times*, *Whiting Democrat*, *The Whiting Times*, *Whiting Sun*, *The Whiting Call*, Topeka *Daily Capital*, Topeka *State Journal*, *The New York Times*, *The Des Moines Register*, Pierre *Daily Capital Journal*, *Alton Evening Telegraph*, Madison *Capital Times*, *The Chicago Daily News*, Chicago *Herald and Examiner*, *Chicago Daily Journal*, *Chicago Journal of Commerce*, and *The Pittsburgh Press*. Five special historical editions of oil journals and newspapers have been most helpful: *National Petroleum News*, XXVIII, No. 6 (February 5, 1936); "North American Oil and Gas," *The Oil and Gas Journal*, May 30, 1919; *The Oil and Gas Journal*, XXXIII, No. 14 (August 23, 1914), Diamond Jubilee of Petroleum Industry Edition; *The Oil and Gas Journal*, May, 1951, Golden Anniversary Number; and *The Whiting Times*, August 4, 1939, Historical Edition.

To supplement the records and narrative accounts on different subjects, the author has personally interviewed and corresponded with dozens of persons, most of whom have been or are presently employed by the company or its subsidiaries. Many of these are mentioned in the Preface. The author was particularly fortunate in being able to have extensive interviews with six men whose service record with the company goes back almost to its beginning. William M. Burton started with the company in 1890, Edward G. Seubert in 1891, Allan Jackson in 1896, E. J. Bullock in 1892, Amos Ball in 1897, and Robert E. Humphreys in 1900.

Index

727